The Episcopate and the Parting of the Ways

Dissertationes Theologicae Holmienses
Dissertations from University College Stockholm
www.ehs.se/dth

Main editor:
Thomas Kazen

Editors:
Petra Carlsson Redell
Joel Halldorf
Jonas Ideström
Rikard Roitto
Susanne Wigorts Yngvesson

No. 11

Martin Landgren

The Episcopate and the Parting of the Ways

A Social Identity Perspective on the Emergence of Christian Identity

Enskilda Högskolan Stockholm
2025

The Episcopate and the Parting of the Ways: A Social Identity Perspective on the Emergence of Christian Identity

Dissertation presented at University College Stockholm to be publicly examined in Room 219–220 at Åkeshovsvägen 29, Bromma, November 6, 2025, at 13:00, for the degree of Doctor of Philosophy in Theology (Biblical Studies: New Testament). The examination will be held in English.

Faculty examiner: Paul Foster, Professor in New Testament Language, Literature and Theology, University of Edinburgh
Supervisor: Thomas Kazen, Professor of Biblical Studies, University College Stockholm.
Assistant supervisor: Rikard Roitto, Professor of Biblical Studies, New Testament, University College Stockholm.

Abstract

In this dissertation, the use of the term ἐπίσκοπος and its cognates in Christ-group literature between 60 and 180 CE is analysed. Categories from Social Identity theory relating to leadership – such as prototypicality, identity entrepreneurship, identity impresarioship, and identity advancement – indicate that the emerging episcopal office in the Christ groups played a significant role in the development of a distinct Christian identity. Important Christ-group texts from the New Testament (Philippians, Acts, 1 Peter, and the Pastoral Epistles) and non-canonical writings (Didache, The Shepherd of Hermas, 1 Clement, the Ignatian letters, and Irenaeus's *Against Heresies*, book three) are examined. All these texts highlight the need for prototypical leadership, meaning leadership that exemplifies ingroup norms. The ἐπίσκοπος embodies a developing specific Christian identity. The texts also develop the ingroup prototype as an act of entrepreneurship, in ways that exclude certain traits, such as halakah adherence (except for the Didache). Additionally, the ἐπίσκοπος is viewed as a continuation of the mission of Jesus and the apostles from Acts to Irenaeus, and as a representation of the heavenly realm (Ignatius), so that Christian identity is embedded within the episcopal structure (an example of impresarioship). This suggests that the emerging episcopal office widened the gap between Christ groups and synagogues, with only the rare exception of the episcopal role in the composite text of Didache.

Episkopatet och skilsmässan mellan kyrka och synagoga: Social identitet och framväxande kristen identitet

Akademisk avhandling presenterad vid Enskilda Högskolan Stockholm för disputation i sal 219–220, Åkeshovsvägen 29, Bromma, 6 november 2025 kl. 13.00, för teologie doktorsexamen i bibelvetenskap med inriktning mot Nya testamentet. Disputationen kommer att äga rum på engelska.

Opponent: Paul Foster, Professor in New Testament Language, Literature and Theology, University of Edinburgh.
Handledare: Thomas Kazen, Professor i bibelvetenskap, Enskilda Högskolan Stockholm.
Bitr. handledare: Rikard Roitto, Professor i bibelvetenskap, Nya testamentet, Enskilda Högskolan Stockholm.

Sammanfattning

I denna avhandling analyseras användningen av termen ἐπίσκοπος och besläktade termer i kristna texter mellan 60 och 180 e.v.t. Kategorier från social identitetsteori relaterade till ledarskap – såsom prototypikalitet, identitetsentreprenörskap, identitetsproduktion och identitetsfrämjande – indikerar att det framväxande biskopsämbetet inom de kristna grupperna spelade en betydande roll i utvecklingen av en specifikt kristen identitet. Viktiga texter från Nya testamentet (Filipperbrevet, Apostlagärningarna, 1 Petrusbrevet och Pastoralbreven) och icke-kanoniska skrifter (Didache, Hermas Herden, 1 Klemensbrevet, Ignatiusbreven och Irenaeus *Mot Heresierna*, bok tre) undersöks. Alla dessa texter framhäver behovet av prototypiskt ledarskap, vilket betyder ledarskap som förkroppsligar gruppens normer. Texterna utvecklar också gruppens ideal som ett exempel på entreprenörskap: Vissa drag, såsom efterlevnad av halakha (förutom Didache), utesluts som uttryck för kristet liv. Dessutom ses det framväxande episkopatet, från Apostlagärningarna till Irenaeus, som en fortsättning på Jesus och apostlarnas uppdrag, och som en representation av det himmelska riket (Ignatius), så att kristen identitet är inbäddad i den episkopala strukturen (ett exempel på identitetsproduktion). Detta tyder på att det framväxande biskopsämbetet vidgade klyftan mellan kristna grupper och synagogor, med endast det enskilda undantaget i Didache.

Enskilda Högskolan Stockholm

Enskilda Högskolan Stockholm erbjuder utbildningsprogram i mänskliga rättigheter och demokrati, samt i teologi/religionsvetenskap. Högskolan grundades 1993 genom en sammanslagning av utbildningsinstitutioner med rötter från 1866, hette tidigare Teologiska högskolan Stockholm, och har tre avdelningar: Avdelningen för mänskliga rättigheter och demokrati, Avdelningen för religionsvetenskap och teologi, samt Avdelningen för östkyrkliga studier. Forskarutbildningen i Bibelvetenskap bedrivs inom inriktningarna Gamla testamentets/Hebreiska bibelns exegetik respektive Nya testamentets exegetik. Utbildningen är både bred och djup, och innefattar bland annat filologiska, historiska, litterära, teologiska, socialvetenskapliga, ideologiska och hermeneutiska perspektiv.

University College Stockholm

University College Stockholm offers programmes in Human Rights and Democracy and in Theology/Religious Studies. The university college was founded in 1993 through a merger of educational institutions with roots dating back to 1866, is also known as Stockholm School of Theology, and has three departments: the Department of Human Rights and Democracy, the Department of Religious Studies and Theology, and the Department of Eastern Christian Studies. The doctoral programme in Biblical Studies provides specialisations in Old Testament/Hebrew Bible exegesis and New Testament exegesis. The programme offers both breadth and depth, and includes among other things philological, historical, literary, theological, and hermeneutical perspectives, as well as perspectives from social science and ideological criticism.

Wipf and Stock Publishers
199 W 8th Ave, Suite 3
Eugene, OR 97401

The Episcopate and the Parting of the Ways
A Social Identity Perspective on the Emergence of Christian Identity
By Landgren, Martin
Copyright © 2025 by Landgren, Martin All rights reserved.
Softcover ISBN-13: 979-8-3852-6530-5
Hardcover ISBN-13: 979-8-3852-6531-2
eBook ISBN-13: 979-8-3852-6532-9
Publication date 10/6/2025
Previously published by Enskilda Högskolan Stockholm, 2025

This edition is a scanned facsimile of the original edition published in 2025.

For Maria, Benjamin, Josef, Ester, and Miriam
– my most significant ingroup

Preface

This book could not have been written without the substantial help and inspiration from several people. I am most grateful to the Swedish Methodist Fund FTU (the Fund for Theological Education), which provided the financial means for making this research possible. I am also much grateful to my supervisors, Professor Thomas Kazen and Professor Rikard Roitto. Thomas has, with great patience, guided me through the process. He has also, with a great sense of humour, provided much inspiration and been tremendously generous with his time and knowledge – far more than anyone could have expected. Rikard has not only helped me understand social identity theory and been very generous with his knowledge but has also significantly helped me increase my speed on the Swedish mile, thanks to our Friday morning runs.

I am also very grateful to the seminar in Biblical Studies at EHS and all the skilled scholars there. EHS is a very inspiring place for academic work. Thanks to several other scholars in the Nordic countries who have offered thoughtful critiques of my work during the writing process. Special thanks to Professor James Kelhoffer at Uppsala University for a thorough review of my work in the final stages. I also wish to thank Professor Robert Miller at Juniata College for reviewing my sometimes somewhat confused English. On the same note, I am grateful to Sofie Elebo for helping improve my language.

I want to thank several friends and colleagues in Ulricehamn parish in the Church of Sweden. Thank you for your patience and for several inspiring conversations about the relationship between organisation and theology – social identity and theology are still most often intertwined. Additionally, my mother, father, and siblings Johan and Karin with their families have been generous with their love, inspiration, and support, not least in omnipresent conversations about theology. Lastly, I must thank Maria for all her love, support, and patience. This would have been impossible without you! Thanks also to

Benjamin, Josef, Ester, and Miriam – you have been most patient when I discuss the episcopal office at the dinner table, poor children. Romans 8:38–39.

Ulricehamn, Sweden, August 13, 2025
Martin Landgren

Contents

Preface 9
Contents 11
Abbreviations 17

Part I Introduction: Theory, Method, Research Background 21

1. Introduction 23
1.1 Christian Self-Definition and the Episcopal Office 26
1.2 The Parting of the Ways and Social Structures 29
1.3 The Purpose of This Study 30
1.4 Research Questions 31
1.5 Sources 31
1.6 Theory and Method 32
1.7 Distinctions of Words and Concepts 32
1.8 Outline 35

2. Social Identity Theory 39
2.1 Becoming a Member of a Group 40
2.2 SIT Cornerstones 42
2.3 Critique of the Use of SIT in Biblical Studies 46
2.4 Group Leaders 48
    2.4.1 Prototypicality 50
    2.4.2 Identity Entrepreneurship 54
    2.4.3 Identity Impresarioship 57
    2.4.4 Identity Advancement 60
    2.4.5 Summary 61

3. Did the Ways Even Part? A Recapitulation of the Parting of the Ways Debate 65
3.1 The Ways That Parted – Or Did They? 67
    3.1.1 The First Concern: Theology 68
    3.1.2 The Second Concern: Social Perspectives 73
    3.1.3 The Third Concern: Labels and Vocabulary 76
    3.1.4 The Fourth Concern: Methodology 80
3.2 The Institutional Perspective 83
    3.2.1 Voluntary Associations 83
    3.2.2 Synagogues and Jewish Associations in the First Century CE 87
    3.2.3 Members of Diaspora Synagogues 94
    3.2.4 The Leadership Structure 97
    3.2.5 The ἀρχισυνάγωγος 100
3.3 Conclusion 105

4. The Standard View of the Emergence of the Episcopal Office 107
4.1 Sources and Early Development of the Episcopal Office 108
4.2 Research History and a Consensus 113
4.3 Two Significant Questions in the Debate 119
    4.3.1 A Jewish or a Greco-Roman Template? 120
    4.3.2 The Synonymous ἐπίσκοπος and πρεσβύτερος? 127
4.4 Conclusion 137

Part II Christian Second-Century Texts from an SIT Perspective .. 143

Introduction to part II 145

5. Brief Mentions in the New Testament and the Apostolic Fathers 147
5.1 Philippians 148
    5.1.1 Date, Authorship 148
    5.1.2 The Role of the ἐπίσκοπος in Philippians 150
    5.1.3 An SIT Analysis of Christ-Group Prototypicality in Philippians .. 154
5.2 First Peter and Prototypical ἐπίσκοποι 156
    5.2.1 Authorship, Date, and Text Witnesses 156
    5.2.2 First Peter 2:25 160

5.2.3 First Peter 5:2 161
5.3 Acts of the Apostles 164
  5.3.1 Date and Author 166
  5.3.2 Comments from an SIT Perspective 170
5.4 The Shepherd of Hermas 175
  5.4.1 Date, Authorship 176
  5.4.2 An SIT Comment on Herm. Vis. 3.5.1 (13.1) 178
  5.4.3 Comment on Herm. Sim. 9.27.2 (104.2) 180
  5.4.4 Conclusion about the ἐπίσκοπος in the Shepherd 182
5.5 Summary and Conclusion 183

6. The Local Leaders in the Didache 187
6.1 Date, Place, the Didachist, and *Sitz im Leben* 188
6.2 Charismatic Leadership, Early Catholicisation, and a Trajectory from Max Weber 193
6.3 The Two Ways Tractate and Its *Sitz im Leben* 199
  6.3.1 Prototypical Content in the Two Ways Tractate 203
  6.3.2 The Remainder of the Two Ways Tractate 206
  6.3.3 Summary and Concluding Remarks on Prototypical Behaviour in the Didache 215
6.4 The Leadership Structure of Didache 15 from an SIT Perspective 216
  6.4.1 The ἐπίσκοπος and διάκονος and Their Role in the Community . 217
  6.4.2 The ἐπίσκοπος and διάκονος – Prototypical Leaders or Identity Advancers? 218
  6.4.3 The Testing and Appointing of Local Leaders 224
6.5 The Identity Entrepreneurs and Impresarios of the Didache 226
6.6 Summary and Conclusion 231

7. An SIT Perspective on the ἐπίσκοπος in First Clement 235
7.1 Concerning Date and Authorship 236
  7.1.1 Date 236
  7.1.2 Authorship 241
7.2 Prototypicality 244
  7.2.1 A Prototypical Member Knows His or Her Place and Does Not Create Schisms 244

  7.2.2 Scriptural Examples of the Prototypes in Chapters 1–2 249
  7.2.3 The Prototypical Behaviour of ἐπίσκοποι καὶ πρεσβύτεροι 258
7.3 Identity Entrepreneurship and Impresarioship 261
  7.3.1 Identity Entrepreneurship 262
  7.3.2 Identity Impresarioship 263
7.4 Conclusion 267
  7.4.1 Prototypical Leaders in First Clement 267
  7.4.2 The Episcopal Office, Entrepreneurship, and Impresarioship ... 268
  7.4.3 The Episcopal Office and the Parting of the Ways Debate in First Clement 269

8. The ἐπίσκοπος in the Pastoral Letters from an SIT Perspective 271
8.1 Authorship and Date of the Pastoral Epistles 272
8.2 Identity Impresarioship and Entrepreneurship in the Congregational Order 280
  8.2.1 The Mission of Timothy and Titus – Identity Impresarioship ... 280
  8.2.2 The Teaching ἐπίσκοπος – Identity Entrepreneurship 281
8.3 Prototypicality in the Pastorals 283
  8.3.1 Stoic Versions of Hellenistic Cardinal Virtue and the Pastorals ...287
  8.3.2 Onosander 291
  8.3.3 Wisdom of Solomon and 4 Maccabees 293
  8.3.4 The Community Rule and Ideals in the Qumran Community ..297
8.4 Conclusion: The ἐπίσκοπος in the Pastorals 301
  8.4.1 Prototypical Behaviour in the Texts Compared 301
  8.4.2 The ἐπίσκοπος in the Pastoral Epistles and the Parting of the Ways 303

9. The ἐπίσκοπος as Prototypical Christ Believer in Ignatius of Antioch 305
9.1 On The Provenance and Date of the Ignatian Letters 305
  9.1.1 The Debate 305
  9.1.2 The Dating of Eusebius 309
  9.1.3 Chapter 9 and 13 in the Letter of Polycarp 310
  9.1.4 The Second Sophists and Ignatius 312
  9.1.5 A Fully Developed Mono-Episcopate in Early Second Century? .. 315

  9.1.6 The Ignatian Corpus in the Present Work 317
  Excursus: The Martyrdom of Polycarp and the Episcopate 328
 9.2 An SIT Analysis of the Ignatian Letters 332
  9.2.1 Christian Prototypicality in Ignatius of Antioch 332
  9.2.2 Identity Impresarioship in the Ignatian Letters 341
 9.3 Conclusion: The ἐπίσκοπος in Ignatius, Christian Identity, and the
 Parting of the Ways 351

10. The ἐπίσκοπος and Christian Identity in Irenaeus's *Against Heresies*, Book Three 355

 10.1 Date and Authorship of *Against Heresies* 356
 10.2 The Content 358
 10.3 *Against Heresies* and the Jews 361
 10.4 An SIT Perspective on the ἐπίσκοπος in Irenaeus 362
  10.4.1 Prototypicality 363
  10.4.2 Identity Embedment 364
  10.4.3 Identity Entrepreneurship 368
 10.5 Conclusion 369

Part III Conclusions 373

11. The Emerging Episcopal Office and the Parting of the Ways 375

 11.1 Summary 377
  11.1.1 Prototypicality 380
  11.1.2 Identity Impresarioship 392
  11.1.3 Identity Entrepreneurship 399
 11.2 Conclusions 401

Bibliography **405**
Ancient Sources 405
Modern Sources 406
Literature... 406

Index of Ancient Literature **425**

Index of Modern Authors **437**

Index of Subjects **443**

Abbreviations

Abbreviations follow the SBL Handbook of Style (2nd ed. 2014) when available.

AB	Anchor Bible
AGJU	Arbeiten zur Geschichte des antiken Judentums und des Urchristentums
ANRW	*Aufstieg und Niedergang der römischen Welt: Geschichte und Kultur Roms im Spiegel der neueren Forschung*
AJBT	*American Journal of Biblical Theology*
ASEs	*Annali di Storia dell'Esegesi*
BECNT	Baker Exegetical Commentary on the New Testament
Behav.Sci.	*Behavioral Science*
Bib	*Biblica*
BR	*Biblical Research*
BTB	*Biblical Theology Bulletin*
BZNW	*Beihefte zur Zeitschrift für die neutestamentliche Wissenschaft*
CBQ	*Catholic Biblical Quarterly*
CH	*Church History*
CIJ	Corpus inscriptionum Iudaicarum
ConBNT	Coniectanea Neotestamentica or Coniectanea Biblica: New Testament Series
CSt	*Church Studies*
CTR	*Criswell Theological Review*
CBR	*Currents in Biblical Research*
DCLS	Deuterocanonical and Cognate Literature Studies
DNTB	*Dictionary of New Testament Background*.
EC	*Early Christianity*
ETL	*Ephemerides Theologicae Lovanienses*
EJSP	*European Journal of Social Psychology*
ERSP	*European Review of Social Psychology*
EvQ	*Evangelical Quarterly*
ExpTim	*Expository Times*
Evol. Hum. Behav.	*Evolution and Human Behavior*

FRLANT	Forschungen zur Religion und Literatur des Alten und Neuen Testaments
GLAJ	Greek and Latin authors on Jews and Judaism
HALOT	*Hebrew and Aramaic Lexicon of the Old Testament*
HNT	Handbuch zum Neuen Testament
HTR	*Harvard Theological Review*
HUT	Hermeneutische Untersuchungen zur Theologie
ID	*Inscritiones de Délos*
IG	*Inscriptiones Graecae*
JAJ	*Journal of Ancient Judaism*
JASPs	*Journal of Abnormal and Social Psychology*
JBL	*Journal of Biblical Literature*
JBT	*Journal of Biblical Theology*
JETS	*Journal of the Evangelical Theological Society*
JIWE	Jewish Inscriptions of Western Europe
JJMJS	*Journal of the Jesus Movement in Its Jewish Setting*
JP	*Journal of Philology*
JRS	*Journal of Roman Studies*
JSJ	*Journal for the Study of Judaism*
JSNT	*Journal for the Study of the New Testament*
JSNTSup	Supplements to Journal for the Study of the New Testament
JTS	*Journal of Theological Studies*
KNT	Kommentar till Nya Testamentet
Leadersh. Q	*The Leadership Quarterly*
LBD	Lexham Bible Dictionary.
LCL	Loeb Classical Library
Lit(E)	*Liturgy: Bulletin of Liturgical Conference*
MethH	*Methodist History*
NCBiC	New Cambridge Bible Commentary
NCBC	New Century Bible Commentary
NIB	*The New Interpreter's Bible*
NIBCNT	New International Biblical Commentary on the New Testament
NICNT	New International Commentary on the New Testament
NIGTC	New International Greek Testament Commentary
NTL	New Testament Library
NTS	*New Testament Studies*
NovTSup	Supplements to Novum Testamentum
PSPB	*Personality and Social Psychology Bulletin*
PSPR	*Personality and Social Psychology Review*
RB	*Revue biblique*
RHR	*Revue de l'histoire des religions*
SacSc	*Sacra Scripta*

SAQ	Sammlung ausgewählter Kirchen- und dogmen-geschichtlicher Quellenschriften
SBS	Stuttgarter Bibelstudium
SEÅ	*Svensk Exegetisk Årsbok*
SHA	Scriptores historiae Augustae
SJT	*Scottish Journal of Theology*
SKGA	Studium zur Geschichte und Kultur des Altertums
Soc. Psych. Q	*Social Psychology Quarterly*
STAC	Studien und Texte zu Antike und Christentum
STDJ	Studies on the Texts of the Desert of Judah
StPatr	Studia Patristica
SupJSJ	Supplements to the Journal for the Study of Judaism
TDNT	*Theological Dictionary of the New Testament.*
TLZ	*Theologische Literaturzeitung*
TNTC	Tyndale New Testament Commentaries
TRE	*Theologische Realenzyklopädie.*
TS	*Theological Studies*
TSAJ	Texte und Studien zum antiken Judentum
TU	Texte und Untersuchungen
TynBul	*Tyndale Bulletin*
VC	*Vigiliae Christianae*
VCSup	Supplements to Vigiliae Christianae
WBC	Word Biblical Commentary
WUNT	Wissenschaftliche Untersuchungen zum Neuen Testament
ZAC	*Zeitschrift für Antikes Christentum*
ZNW	*Zeitschrift für die neutestamentliche Wissenschaft und die Kunde der älteren Kirche*

Part I

Introduction:
Theory, Method, Research Background

1. Introduction

The episcopal office is closely linked to Christian self-definition. This has been the case since early Christian history, when the followers of Jesus formed subgroups within Jewish synagogues. As will be explored in the subsequent chapters, the office has historically been seen as a warrant for apostolic faith (as noted by Irenaeus in *Haer.*3.3.3.) or as an earthly representation of God (for example, Ign. *Magn.* 6:1). Consequently, faith in Christ Jesus was intimately tied to the congregation over which the ἐπίσκοπος presided. The officeholders were also regarded as exemplars to follow (as mentioned in the Pastoral Epistles) or as a locally residing continuation of the itinerant charismatic teacher or prophet (as indicated in the Didache).

The self-definition of Christians has remained linked to the understanding of Church polity: during the Reformation and in modern times, the perception of the episcopal office in the earliest Christian groups and early church has been a significant battleground for differing views on the matter. A congregationalist perspective has generally been the most prominent Protestant understanding of early church polity, while a Catholic and Anglican perspective has understood the episcopal office as original, albeit with differing interpretations concerning the bishop of Rome.[1] Catholic theologians, along with some Anglicans, have "defended an essentially continuous polity from apostolic times in unbroken sequence through to the present."[2] This has remained consistent within the Catholic tradition, through the Reformation and beyond. However, contemporary Catholic theologians have also recognised a complex historical process underlying the evolution of the office.[3] Hans Küng, the Swiss Catholic priest and theologian, is an example of this, while he simultaneously

---

[1] Burtchaell 1991, 2.
[2] Burtchaell 1991, 2.
[3] Küng 1967, 430.

affirms the continuation of the apostolic ministry in the emergent episcopal office in the second century.[4]

Protestant, particularly Lutheran, scholars have underscored every Christian's calling to serve, asserting that it is God and God's word, rather than the episcopal order, that form the foundation of Christian ministry. Furthermore, Protestants have highlighted the necessity of local and congregational authority to appoint ministers, contrasting this with an episcopal or papal system authority.[5] Thus, during the Reformation, the episcopal office came to be perceived as a distinctly Catholic invention, diverging from the intentions of Jesus. Several of the Reformers (Wycliffe, Luther, and Calvin) argued for the concept of an original, apostolic office established by Jesus, from which the Church fell into a spiritless episcopal office.[6] The reformation process came therefore, among other things, to be a debate on ecclesial polity.[7] Luther, for example, separated outward ordination from spiritual disposition. Thus, outward ordination was not equal to a Christ-like character, nor Christian identity. These traits only came from the word of God.[8] Christian identity was a product of God's Spirit's work through the divinely inspired word and essentially given to every believer and managed by the local congregation. The Reformation originally severed Christian identity from outward polity and simultaneously separated Protestants from Catholics through a new understanding of the episcopal order. Furthermore, this led to new forms of leadership polity, which were understood as grounded in the New Testament.[9] Leadership polity was therefore essential for self-definition among the contestants of the Reformation.

The broad spectrum of understandings regarding the polity of leadership within different denominations has often been essential for churches' self-understanding, alongside varying interpretations of baptism and the Eucharist. As we shall see in this book, this has been the case since very early on. The episcopal office played a significant role in defining what it meant to be a Christian, in

---

[4] Küng 1967, 416.
[5] Burtchaell 1991, 2–3.
[6] Burtchaell 1991, 3. See also chapter 4 below.
[7] Burtchaell 1991, 34–35.
[8] Burtchaell 1991, 12–14.
[9] Cf. Burtchaell 1991, 38–40.

contrast to other proposed identities for the Christ groups in the second century.

This observation, that leadership polity conveys self-identity, can be exemplified in the beginning of the formation of the Methodist church. When John Wesley appointed Thomas Coke as "superintendent" for the Methodists independent colonies, he did so believing that the ἐπίσκοπος and the πρεσβύτερος were the same order.[10] Thus, he balanced between an Anglican view, and his understanding of the Bible. To motivate his action, Wesley drew on an investigation from 1691 by Peter King regarding the ἐπίσκοπος and the πρεσβύτερος.[11] Being Anglican, Wesley was cautious not to sever the ties to his mother church. Thus, Methodism in Great Britain was in Wesley's lifetime a movement within the Anglican Church, while the Methodist movement after his death came to be separated from the Anglican Church. However, when Wesley ordained Thomas Coke as superintendent, the gap between the Anglican church and the Methodists widened in the United Kingdom. The path to a full-blown separation between the Methodist movement in the free colonies was a bit more complicated. The process that Wesley had initiated was nevertheless unstoppable. Even if the Methodists in the free colonies originally acknowledged the Anglican "structure, clergy, and episcopacy," the movement's conference in Baltimore in 1784 founded the Methodist Episcopal Church.[12] In this conference, the movement's episcopal theology became palpable in the ordination of Francis Asbury as superintendent, a title later changed into "bishop."[13] This ordination was intrinsically connected to the foundation of the Methodist movement as a church in America; there, it understood itself as an episcopal structure, even if Wesley himself contested the title *bishop*. When he first learned in 1788 that Asbury and Coke had received the title *bishop* in the colonies, he responded very sharply to this in a letter. Thus, the title carried a heavy significance for the identity formation of Methodist movement, in terms of self-

---

[10] Stewart 2014, 1.

[11] King 1691, 1–2.

[12] Thaarup 1999, 3.

[13] Thaarup 1999, 3. See also Stewart 2014, 1. One can note with Thaarup that from 1784–1787, the title of Asbury and Coke was superintendent, but was changed to bishop "without indication of any reason." Thaarup 1999, 3.

definition. Further, the growing mission of the Methodist movement in America called attention to the leadership structure. This process was intertwined with self-designation matters for the Methodist Episcopal Church members.[14] The mere change of the title of the local leader from "Presiding Elder" to "District Superintendent" in 1908 led to a lengthy debate in the General Conference, since it, among other things, touched upon the Methodist self-designation.[15] As of today, the Methodist movement world-wide has branches with and without bishops depending on whether the denomination originated in the UK or the US. The process within the Methodist Episcopal Church shows how the episcopal structure carries significant meaning for self-definition also in a reformed context. As we shall see, the significance of the ἐπίσκοπος for Christian self-definition is prominent in several early Christian sources from the first and second centuries.

1.1 Christian Self-Definition and the Episcopal Office

While research about offices in the early church is plentiful, a deeper understanding of how the episcopal office became a symbol of Christian faith is lacking. Especially during the twenty-first century, New Testament scholarship has received fresh insights from the social sciences, not least from social identity theory (SIT, see below). This theoretical framework provides insights into cognitive aspects of group behaviour, and the identity-shaping effects that the individual's identification with a group produce. In leadership research from an SIT perspective, attention has been paid to how group leadership is interconnected to group identity. Three aspects, all of which will be further explained in the next chapter, are of special interest for this present study. The first aspect pertains to the group leaders' need to personally represent and mirror the group's values, lifestyle, and interests if the leaders wish to enhance their chances of success as leaders. Within SIT, this is denoted as a leader's *prototypicality*. The leader who is seen as suffering for the group's values on behalf of the group becomes especially powerful. Prototypical behaviour is behaviour that can be described as faithfully mirroring the values and worldviews of the

---

[14] Williams 2002, 261.
[15] Williams 2002, 261–62.

ingroup,[16] and that also significantly distinguishes the group from other groups. The definition of the ingroup is closely tied to the definition of the outgroup. Thus, leadership forms that are developed in the Christ movement need to significantly correspond to the prototypical traits of the ingroup (that is, their own group), and significantly contrast outgroups (that is, other groups with other group identities). Simultaneously, moving to discuss the second aspect, a prototypical leader, such as John Wesley, with his focus on personal holiness and preaching about the grace of God through Jesus Christ,[17] is given space to renegotiate the prototypical traits of the group, which within SIT leadership research is called *identity entrepreneurship*. The third aspect, which is closely interconnected and can perhaps be seen as an aspect of identity entrepreneurship, maps how leaders construct meaningful patterns for members to adopt as group members with a certain self-identity. This feature in leadership is called *identity impresarioship*.

The example from the Methodist movement illustrates that the debate over titles also involves self-definition. How should the Methodist movement define itself in relation to New Testament texts? How should it position itself against other churches, particularly the Anglican Church? The title *bishop* reflects an interpretation of the New Testament that shapes the Methodist self-perception. The term *bishop* holds significance in relation to other (Christian) groups, including "non-Methodists," and their historical understanding of church polity. Therefore, titles convey meaning regarding members' perceptions of themselves, as evidenced by Wesley's reactions to episcopal titles in America. In this book, I will demonstrate how the episcopal office functioned from late New Testament times until approximately 180 CE, when Irenaeus identified a basis for proto-orthodox Christian faith within the episcopal structure. During this period, as reflected in the New Testament texts, this office provided a means of defining Christian identity. This identity is articulated both positively in group ideals (such as the expectations for the behaviour of an ἐπίσκοπος in 1 Tim 3 and

---

[16] The concept of ingroups and outgroups is to be seen in the context of the term identification, which will be further explained in chapter 2. In general, however, ingroups are the groups with which an individual identifies. Outgroups are groups of people that we understand to be different from us. See further Rosell Nebreda 2011, 38.

[17] Langford 1983, 20–23.

Titus 1) and negatively in the antithesis of the positive group conduct allegedly displayed by outgroups such as the Docetists or "those who Judaize," as seen in the letters attributed to Ignatius of Antioch. Thus, group identity and the indicators of that identity are crucial components for understanding the divisions between groups. In the Methodist movement, the episcopal structure rendered the previous group identity – where Methodist identity was a sub-identity of Anglican identity – obsolete. The new Methodist identity distanced itself from the old Anglican identity through, among other factors, its episcopal structure. Undoubtedly, the process of separation was more intricate than this, but the aspect of group identity is certainly worth analysing. In Biblical Studies, we often overlook how social identity manifests and is reflected in the texts we study. All New Testament texts are products of processes in which group boundaries are negotiated. We can observe the remnants of various groups within the texts, including Johannine Christ followers, Pauline Jewish Christ followers, and Pauline non-Jewish Christ followers, among others. A proper understanding of group identity can provide new insights into the lives of early Christian groups.

It is especially interesting that New Testament scholarship continues to debate how the Christ movement(s) dissociated from a Jewish identity. However, to my knowledge, the so-called parting of the ways trajectory, in conjunction with related fields, has never been analysed from an SIT leadership perspective. Furthermore, there has not been thorough research into how leadership structures within the Christ groups conveyed group identity. This reveals a significant gap in the research history concerning the early church. SIT leadership studies teach us that self-definition and the structures that encapsulate meaning for self-definition are crucial for understanding inter-group relations. These structures also reflect the anticipated self-understanding and prototypical behaviours of community members, which, under certain conditions, leave less room for other social identities, such as Jewish identity. This book aims to bridge the gap and examine how social identity, early Christian leadership structures, and the parting of the ways trajectory converge.

1.2 The Parting of the Ways and Social Structures

In the lands along the northeastern Mediterranean, the relationship between followers of the Messiah Jesus and other Jewish groups, mainly in the diaspora, became increasingly more complicated. The fact that groups connected to the apostle Paul now also included non-Jews made relationships tense. Questions concerning, for example, halakah (Acts 15, Did. 8), table fellowship including non-Jews (Gal 1–3), and the relationship to Jewish Scriptures and emerging Jesus traditions (Ign. *Phld.* 8.), were questions that needed to be solved for the young Christ movement. The claims of the groups, that the Messiah Jesus had also made foreigners into members in a covenant with God *without circumcision*, were provocative for some other Jewish groups. Apparently, however, the mission to the non-Jews was very successful, so the non-Jews gradually outgrew the Jews in the Christ groups. The increasingly non-Jewish membership of the movement probably spurred the inception of groups with few or no connections to diaspora synagogues, even if Paul's initial mission according to the tradition in Acts first started in diaspora Jewish communities. Thus, the Christ groups began to develop an infrastructure separate from the Jewish communities. Different groups probably had somewhat different systems of organisation during the first years, but during the second century, a consolidation in the northeastern Mediterranean area can be traced. Here, the emergence of the office of the ἐπίσκοπος (which can be translated as "one who has the responsibility of safeguarding or seeing to it that somet[hing] is done in the correct way, *guardian*"[18]) can be found increasingly often as a title, from the New Testament and forward, mingled with other titles of leadership. But the Christ movement needed, in a theologically meaningful and coherent way, to motivate the increasingly weaker relationship to the Jewish communities. The relationship to the people of the covenant needed to be theologically addressed, as well as the self-understanding and self-definition of the Christ groups in this new condition with fewer Jews in their ranks. As far as we can see in our sources, the question becomes increasingly acute from the fifties and forward.[19] In the process of self-definition, SIT helps us recognize that a successful

---

[18] BDAG s.v. ἐπίσκοπος (italics original).
[19] Cf. Rom 11 and the Galatians debate as starting points.

leadership from a group identity perspective constructs meaningful structures to participate in that mirror the self-definition. SIT shows the interconnection between actions, both individual and collective, in a meaningful grid designed by an interplay between prototypical group members and self-definition. How a group of voluntary members gathers needs to reflect the self-understanding of the group in meaningful ways. Thus, in the early Christ movement and every other kind of human group, the design of everything, from leadership structures to communal gatherings, expresses central group beliefs.

From a different angle, the early Christ movement is also coloured by other environmental factors. When the Christ movement emerged, the congregations were *de facto* situated in the Greco-Roman world, in which the predominant institution for small gatherings was the voluntary association. Thus, just as Jewish synagogues can fruitfully be described as religious and ethnic voluntary associations, congregations in the Christ movement can be described from the templates found in other Greco-Roman associations. This is important when we try to understand the emergence of a structure that was significant for the members in the congregation. The emerging episcopal office must have negotiated the Christian identity in relation to other groups in the Greco-Roman world, given the patterns that SIT helps us discern.

1.3 The Purpose of This Study

What does this study aim to achieve? It seeks to better understand how the emerging episcopal office – a clearly designated leadership role – shaped first- and second-century perspectives on what it meant to be a follower of Jesus. This self-defining process becomes clearer when applying SIT leadership studies to ancient sources. Furthermore, the intent is to comprehend how this emerging episcopal office influenced the relationship with alternative identities within the Christ movement, most notably the relationship between the developing Christian identity and an alternative Jewish one. In other words, this book seeks to understand how the emerging episcopal office influenced the parting of the ways.

1.4 Research Questions

These perspectives raise certain questions that require answers. First, how did the emergence of the office (in a broad sense) of the ἐπίσκοπος affect Christian group identity? This pertains to prototypicality. Second, which theological ideas were integrated into social patterns through the theology of the episcopal office during the first and second centuries CE (which pertains to the sub-category identity impresarioship)? Third, and most important, this leads up to the question: how did the emergence of the ἐπίσκοπος alter the relation between Christ groups and the Jewish synagogue in terms of social identity in the first and second centuries? This relates to the sub-category of identity entrepreneurship.

1.5 Sources

In this study, the main interest is to revisit commonly consulted writings of the Christ movement. First, we have the New Testament sources that mention the office of the ἐπίσκοπος. The most prominent are 1 Timothy and Titus, but all New Testament instances where the title is mentioned will be considered. This means that some space will be given to analyse Acts of the Apostles, Philippians, and First Peter, even if the information given there is sparse.

Some of the sources from the text group heuristically labelled the Apostolic Fathers are contemporary, or almost contemporary, with the later parts of the New Testament. I will analyse the Didache, the letters of Ignatius, and First Clement. The Shepherd of Hermas mentions the title but treats it only in passing. This source will, however, also be taken into consideration.[20]

Last, I will also take into account Irenaeus's *Against Heresies,* book three. This will complete the discussions of the term in prominent second-century Christ-movement writings.

---

[20] In addition, I discuss the Martyrdom of Polycarp in a brief excursus in chapter 9. For a long time, this text was dated to the latter part of the second century CE, but this has been challenged, and I understand it as a representative of the early third century, even if some fragments could stem from the latter part of the second century. The text thus falls outside the scope of my time frame.

1.6 Theory and Method

As previously mentioned, this dissertation owes much to SIT, which has been increasingly applied in New Testament research. In the following chapter, I will explore the theory in greater depth and position my research within this theoretical tradition. For now, it is sufficient to say that SIT will be employed as a method. The theoretical frameworks of SIT and the questions derived from them guide this study. As will be further elaborated in chapter 2 below, SIT has proven valuable in providing insights into how groups form, develop, and differentiate themselves from others. While SIT is a theoretical framework without a specific inherent method, the categories of the theory can cast new light on the consulted sources. Thus, SIT examines the function of rhetoric (including the ethos of the implied sender) in these early Christ-group documents. Specifically, the SIT categories are beneficial when analysing how group identity is constructed through rhetoric. Since the categories in SIT investigate certain features of the text, such as how a leader's ethos (the prototypicality of a leader) slightly alters the self-perception of members, the application of this theory will enable us to discern patterns of emerging self-identity in the texts more clearly. This will be demonstrated throughout the course of this dissertation, as will be observed below, which also aligns with the extensive application of the method in New Testament research. Apart from SIT, traditional exegetical tools will be used to some extent, including textual and rhetorical criticism.

1.7 Distinctions of Words and Concepts

The main purpose of this study is to analyse how emerging Christ-group offices, particularly the ἐπίσκοπος, affected the relationship between groups with a prominent Jewish identity and Christ follower groups. A few points need to be noted regarding how ἐπίσκοπος relates to the cognate words ἐπισκοπέω and ἐπισκοπή. As mentioned above, the noun ἐπίσκοπος is used in both the LXX, the Greco-Roman world, and the New Testament. The verb ἐπισκοπέω designates "to give attention to, *look at, take care, see to it*" or "to accept responsibility for the care of someone, *oversee, care for*" and is present in both the New Testament (1 Peter 5:2) and the Apostolic Fathers (Ign. *Rom.* 9:1). It is clearly connected to spiritual oversight and the metaphor of shepherding, which is

1.7 Distinctions of Words and Concepts

intimately linked to spiritual guidance and care. The overlap in meaning between the verb and the noun ἐπίσκοπος is obvious. Throughout this analysis, we will examine the various aspects of these words.

The noun ἐπίσκοπος is linked to another noun, ἐπισκοπή. This is defined as "the act of watching over with special ref[erence] to being present, *visitation*," "position of responsibility, *position, assignment*," or "engagement in oversight, *supervision*."[21] There are a few instances in the New Testament and second-century Christian texts that mention ἐπισκοπή, which will be analysed in the course of these chapters. However, some of these instances clearly discuss ἐπισκοπή as visitation. In Luke 19:44, for example, Jesus mourns over the impending destruction of Jerusalem, and it is said that Jerusalem did not recognise "the time of your visitation from God" (NRSV, οὐκ ἔγνως τὸν καιρὸν τῆς ἐπισκοπῆς σου).[22] The visitation of Jesus as a messenger of God is not seen as a judgment in itself. However, the word can be understood as containing an element of judgment: in 1 Peter 2:12, the author encourages the readers to conduct themselves honourably among the gentiles, so that the gentiles will see their honourable deeds "and glorify God when he comes to judge" (NRSV, δοξάσωσιν τὸν θεὸν ἐν ἡμέρᾳ ἐπισκοπῆς).[23] Here, the meaning is interpreted as a visitation for judgement, although it could also potentially signify visitation in a positive sense. This latter interpretation is the most apt in 1 Clement 50:3, which states, "the visitation of the coming kingdom of Christ," (ἐν τῇ ἐπισκοπῇ τῆς βασιλείας τοῦ Χριστοῦ). In all these instances, however, the meaning pertains to some kind of visitation from God, which may carry connotations of judgement. The focus here is not on oversight or appointment to a position as in an office.

In Acts 1:20 and 1 Tim 3:1, however, the word clearly designates a position or role assigned to someone, indicating that the term has multiple shades of meaning. This dissertation examines the instances in which the word pertains to office or appointment.

---

[21] BDAG, s.v. ἐπισκοπή. Italics original.

[22] For Bible texts, I generally use NRSV translation. Note that when nothing else is stated, the translations are my own

[23] BDAG, s.v. ἐπισκοπή; mentions two possible dimensions of the visitation meaning: a salutary kind, and an unpleasant kind.

Here, a caveat is worth mentioning: the concept of an episcopal office in the first and second centuries is often at risk of becoming somewhat anachronistic. The nature of a distinguished office is largely a modern notion. While, at the outset of the fourth chapter, I provide a rudimentary definition of how I use "office" in this book (an office-holder is appointed, has certain tasks, is given authority, and is part of a more or less hierarchical structure), some notes on the topic may be useful. In this chapter, the ongoing debate regarding the nature of early Christian leadership is depicted as existing along a spectrum, as illustrated in Figure 1:

Honorary position   Formalised office

Figure 1. Early Christian leadership.

The two ends of the spectrum are leadership as an honorary position and leadership as a formalised office. A binary perspective on early Christian leadership stretches the evidence in a problematic way. On the one hand, it is true, as John Elliott writes in his review of Alastair Campbell's book, often referred to in chapter four below, that most (if not all) officials at the time investigated were not "'office-holders' within a bureaucratic organization, but ... agents exercising *traditional* forms of authority."[24] On the other hand, the idea that the different titles necessarily had airtight boundaries is incorrect. Conversely, the various usages of the term πρεσβύτερος in the Pastoral Epistles exemplify this multi-valent usage of terms.[25] Thus, the overlapping structures of both formal and informal kinds of authority and leadership in the first- and second-century Christ groups are hard to dismiss. This is worth remembering during the following chapters.

---

[24] Elliott 2003, 6. Original italics.
[25] Young 1994, 145–46.

1.8 Outline

This dissertation has three parts, divided into eleven chapters. The first part is a general introduction that situates my work in the research currents of New Testament scholarship. The second part is where I apply the SIT theory to ancient Christian texts. The third part is a single, concluding chapter.

After this introductory chapter in which the relevant questions are posed, the second chapter will introduce the SIT theoretical framework, and special focus will be given to leadership qualities, and how prototypicality, identity impresarioship, and identity entrepreneurship (and to some extent, identity advancement) have been defined and developed at both experimental and literary levels.

The third chapter will introduce the state of research in the so-called parting of the ways debate. I will give an outline through a thematic review of four concerns in the debate: the theological, the sociological, the concern of labels and vocabulary, and the methodological concern. After this outline, I discuss at some length a sub-category of the sociological concern: the institutional perspective. Recent research on synagogues and Greco-Roman voluntary associations is crucial for this study, since the development of an episcopal office is interconnected to the emerging institutional development of the Christ groups. The institutional perspective in synagogue research, which deals with Jews and non-Jews and their communal lives, has recently developed within this research field.

Chapter 4 situates this study in the research history of the episcopal office. First, I give a recapitulation of the sources, followed by a recapitulation of their earliest reception. Second, I summarise how the office has been discussed in early modern and modern research up to the twenty-first century. That leads further to the third part of the chapter, where I discuss the contested issue of the emerging episcopal office. Especially prominent questions have been the fading charisma of the early church, the relationship between the ἐπίσκοπος and the πρεσβύτερος, and the origins of the ἐπίσκοπος himself; was the ἐπίσκοπος a product of the Greco-Roman voluntary association template, or of a synagogue template, or even a household template? This last part is tightly interconnected with the last part of chapter 3.

After this, we turn to the main part of the dissertation. Part two is where the SIT framework is applied to ancient texts. In chapter 5, I look at the brief mentions of the ἐπίσκοπος in the New Testament texts and the Shepherd of Hermas. To the extent that these sources allow for an SIT analysis, this will be done with each text in turn: Philippians, Acts, 1 Peter, and Hermas.

In the sixth chapter, I will discuss how SIT categories help us better understand the Didache. We will first look at the very complicated question of date and provenance of the text. Second, I will discuss the schema of early catholicisation that has been an underlying assumption in much of the research history of the Didache. Third, I will analyse how the prototypical identity is constructed in the Two Ways tractate. Fourth, we will turn to Didache chapter 15, where the local leaders are discussed, to define their role and the behaviour they should adhere to. Fifth, we will turn to how the teaching expected by the leaders (of which the role ἐπίσκοπος was one) is constructing the unique Christ-group identity: the ἐπίσκοπος among other teaching leaders is an identity entrepreneur. Sixth and last, we will draw out the long-term consequences of the group-defining role of the ἐπίσκοπος for the separation between the Jesus groups and other Jewish groups.

In the seventh chapter, I turn to First Clement. There, I first situate the letter in its context. Second, I show how the episcopal leaders in First Clement are pictured as *prototypical* leaders in relationship to the provided examples from Scripture. Third, I show how First Clement is *embedding* a Christian identity in the episcopal role (identity impresarioship), suggesting that the new congregation is, in practice, superseding the old identity. Fourth, I will draw out the implications of this pertaining to the separation between the Christ groups and the synagogues.

In chapter 8, the Pastoral Epistles are analysed through my SIT method. After addressing the texts' authorship and dates, I turn to the SIT analysis proper. The author embeds the ingroup identity within the episcopal structure since it is a continuation of the apostolic ministry of Paul. Thus, the author functions as an identity impresario. The prototypical member, the ἐπίσκοπος, defined in 1 Timothy 3 and Titus 1, is compared to the prototypical ideals of other group prototypes in the ancient world since the ingroup prototype, according to SIT, provides the sharpest contrast to outgroups. I engage in a comparison with

Stoic ideals, as well as with Jewish group ideals. The ἐπίσκοπος is more like the Stoic ideals than the Jewish ones.

Ignatius of Antioch is the topic of the extensive ninth chapter. Since there has been a long debate concerning the provenance and date of these letters, the first part of the chapter discusses at some length the date and authenticity question regarding the so-called middle recension (seven letters) from Ignatius. I conclude that part of the chapter by arguing the letters were composed by an anonymous Christian leader around 160 CE, and are thus late and inauthentic, with the exception of Ignatius's letter to the Romans, which could possibly be earlier and authentic. After that, I analyse the norms given in the letter corpus for congregation members from an SIT perspective. Three types of norms are found: individual norms regarding ethical behaviour stemming from the New Testament, group behaviour relating to gatherings and dogma, and norms regarding how the member(s) should interact with the ἐπίσκοπος. These kinds of norms show how the author of the Ignatian letters provides a Christian prototypicality and simultaneously functions as an identity impresario in his stress of the emergent episcopal office. I infer this on the basis of the argumentative power found in the name of Ignatius, a prototypical leader, suffering on behalf of group norms. The sending of the letters in Ignatius's name is thus a kind of identity entrepreneurship.

In the tenth chapter, I apply the SIT perspective to Irenaeus's *Against Heresies*, book three. The development of Christian self-identity is closely linked to the apostolic teachings, which are now more accessible through the stable episcopal office. This episcopal order also provides prototypical patterns, grounded in the lives of the apostles that are important for Christians to adhere to. Irenaeus views the episcopal office as the necessary remedy and safeguard against "gnostic" heresies. Christian self-definition is no longer primarily dependent on the LXX/Hebrew Bible but on apostolic teachings. Therefore, a fully Christian identity is upheld through the episcopal structure.

In the third part of this book, the eleventh and final chapter provides a summary and conclusion of the effects of the emerging episcopal office on the relationship between the Christ groups and the synagogues. As has become abundantly clear, an SIT perspective may help us to see that a prototypical leadership from the officeholders provided incentives and a template for a new self-identity, distinct from other groups, particularly from other Jewish groups. Prototypical leaders in the Christ movement also pursued an identity in which a prominent Jewish identity became untenable. This was achieved by integrating a Christ-group identity within the episcopal structure. This structure articulated significant Christ-group beliefs, such as the unity of the Son and the Father. Furthermore, this became increasingly evident as time progressed.

In this book, I do not suggest *the* conclusive explanation about the separation between Christ groups and synagogues. Other perspectives will flesh out the development further. However, I show how the complex interplay between *group identity* and *institutional realities* widened the rift between self-identified Christ-group members and Jews who did not identify as Jesus followers. This sheds new light on the emergence of the two religions Judaism and Christianity, with their own, identity-carrying institutions, further down the road.

Long after the second century, the episcopal office did not cease to carry identity-shaping qualities. As we saw above, it was tightly interconnected to the issues debated in the Reformation, and the theologians of the Reformation needed to address the Catholic claim of an unbroken apostolic succession. The question of the nature of the episcopal office in the New Testament was at the core of discussion. The episcopal office was a key question in the relationship between the Anglican community and the emerging Methodist church. Thus, by the time of John Wesley, ancient church polity still played such a prominent role in self-definition that it had the power both to be essential for the Anglican community *and* to function as a starting point for the Methodist Episcopal Church. Church polity apparently matter.

2. Social Identity Theory

From the 1970s, the social dimensions behind the texts of the New Testament once again began to engage scholars. While scholarship in the late nineteenth and early twentieth centuries showed significant interest in the *Sitz im Leben* of the New Testament texts, this fell out of fashion in favour of a more individualistic approach to New Testament research after World War II.[1] Bengt Holmberg describes the process as a shift from an interest in the socio-cultural setting of the early Christ movement into "dialectic theology and the existential hermeneutics of biblical texts."[2] From the 1970s onward, this lack of interest in a sociological perspective began to be remedied. This sociological shift has offered new insights into the study of the early Christian movement as a collective process. Simultaneously, the interest in social aspects has made scholars aware of potential methodological pitfalls.[3] Henry Maier, not least, points to the fact that social scientific theories do not provide additional data about a given text. Since sociological research is particularly interested in the typical, common features of specific phenomena, it is an improper use of these theories to suggest that "where evidence is lacking it may be assumed that the typical elements were present."[4] One theory that has increasingly been used during the last thirty years of New Testament research is social identity theory (SIT), which addresses how individual and group identities interact. SIT also addresses intergroup competition and how group processes and identity formation are connected. This is useful since the processes through which the Christ groups and the synagogue separated are *group processes*. The separation process can be

---

[1] Holmberg 1990, 1–3.
[2] Holmberg 1990, 1.
[3] Barclay 2011, 4–9. Cf. Holmberg 1990, 78–80.
[4] Maier 2002, 8.

understood through how groups form, develop, and split, and how group identity and self-identity are intertwined. This chapter describes the cornerstones of SIT and what SIT can teach us about efficient and influential leadership in general. These findings provide new insights into the parting of the ways process. In this chapter, I will describe the ways that SIT is a meaningful model for understanding group process in the early Christ movement. First, I will recapitulate where SIT comes from, then describe the theory's cornerstones. After that, I will briefly address a couple of objections to the use of SIT in New Testament research. Lastly, I will deal at some length with the categories of leadership that SIT suggests as useful in understanding how leadership relates to the development of group identity.

2.1 Becoming a Member of a Group

SIT has been an important theoretical framework within the social sciences for some forty years as a means of understanding how social groups explain individual identity. Groups are not just something that adds personal gain for the individual but are a distinct part of explaining the individual's place in society.[5] Before the works of Henri Tajfel and John Turner at the end of the 1970s,[6] the assumption had been that people joined groups for three reasons: (1) people like the activities of the group, (2) people like the members in the group, (3) group membership is a means of satisfying the needs of the participants, albeit indirectly.[7] The way of understanding groups was through the psychology of the individual. Hence, Floyd Henry Allport could say that "[t]here is no psychology of groups which is not essentially and entirely a psychology of individuals."[8] This conception was a reaction against a quasi-metaphysical view of groups as "possessing a group mind,"[9] in which the processes going on in

---

[5] Haslam, Reicher, and Platow 2011, 50.
[6] Tajfel and Turner 1979; Tajfel 1981.
[7] Haslam, Reciher, and Platow 2011, 47.
[8] Allport 1962, 4.
[9] Brown and Pherson 2020, 3.

groups explained horrific behaviour. With the rise of SIT,[10] an explanation was provided that could account for group processes and leadership efficiency. The SIT perspective provided an understanding of groups without demanding that groups be understood as quasi-metaphysical. On the other hand, it provided a non-reductionistic framework since SIT recognises that some elements of group processes are not reducible to individual psychology.[11] SIT accounted for the perception that groups contained more than just the sum of the individuals in the group.

Another important feature of the new perspective on groups was the definition of who was a member. As will be accounted for below, self-categorisation of the individual into a group was the most important factor. Rather than perceiving groups as either individuals who share a common goal[12] or individuals participating in formal or implicit social structures such as families or work-related groups,[13] the subjective act of self-categorisation functioned as an apt tool for describing identity processes within both large and small groups.[14] The point would be that experiments showed that self-categorisation affected the individual's behaviour towards others. Favouritism towards the ingroup develops very quickly in group formation. Tajfel et al showed in 1971 that even minimal categories for group membership still showed that members chose to favour ingroup members over outgroup members. Even when there was a total absence of any previous group interests or previous hostility, the ingroup members still discriminated against outgroup members when possible.[15] Tajfel and Turner showed in numerous publications how people derive their self-image, and in extension their behaviour, from the groups they define themselves as members of. In different ways, they both applied the insights of self-

---

[10] Not to be confused with "Rise of the Sith," which belongs to another galaxy of meaning far, far away.

[11] Tajfel 1981, 254.

[12] Campbell 1958, 17–18.

[13] Sherif and Sherif 1969.

[14] See also Brown and Pherson 2020, 1–2.

[15] Tajfel et al. 1971, 28, note that the discrimination was not total, since the subjects tried to "achieve a compromise between the two norms which, in their view, pertained to the situation: ingroup solidarity and fairness."

categorisation and an individual's behaviour in a group to a person's social identity. Tajfel thus defines social identity as "that *part* of an individual's self-concept which derives from his knowledge of his membership of [sic] a social group (or groups) together with the value and emotional significance attached to that membership."[16] We will now delve a little bit deeper into the foundations of SIT.

2.2 SIT Cornerstones

So how does SIT describe this cognitive process of how individuals derive parts of their identity from groups? SIT is built upon three general concepts of how humans shape their identity: *categorisation, identification,* and *comparison*.[17] As noted in several surveys, social categorisation, identification, and comparison most often result in an ingroup bias for the group members.[18] In the first instance, *categorisation*, the main idea is that to be able to understand "objects or persons, we categorise them to make sense of their social context."[19] In this categorisation process, two things occur: we (a) tend to enhance the differences between things categorised, and (b) smooth over differences within the groups we categorise.[20]

In this process, a positive affirmation of ingroup values is perceivable, but also a description of how ingroup and outgroups are essentially different according to the member's view.

> Because group identification depersonalises self-conception in terms of the evaluative and prescriptive attributes of the ingroup, in group contexts members are powerfully motivated to learn what the context-specific group attributes are, and thus what the group prototype or norm is. The prototype is configured to capture both ingroup similarities and intergroup differences, in such a way as to maximise the meta-contrast of

---

[16] Tajfel 1981, 255. Italics original.
[17] Cf. Rosell Nebreda 2011, 37.
[18] Brown and Pherson 2020, 280–81, note that "in a meta-analysis of three decades' worth of intergroup relations research, we found that across all the studies where an ingroup evaluation had been compared to an outgroup evaluation, 75 per cent of them revealed a bias in favor of the ingroup."
[19] Rosell Nebreda 2011, 37.
[20] Cf. Brown and Pherson 2020, 7; Rosell Nebreda 2011, 37.

intergroup and intragroup differences. The prototype is that position within the group that has the maximum meta-contrast.[21]

Especially important is the fact that the view of ingroup prototypes, which hereafter will be referred to as prototypicality, maximises the differences between in- and outgroups. Categorisation and identification are closely related since it is a small step from categorisation to self-categorisation. On a side note, the three general concepts of social identity should perhaps best be understood as a totality, a singular process with three functions, and not as three neatly separated processes.

John Turner demonstrated in 1982 that individuals and their self-categorisation as members of a specific group were sufficient for group behaviour.[22] The theory developed from the empirical work of Turner is called Self-Categorizing Theory (SCT). SCT further explains the idea that it was not such things as personal gain or attraction to group members that made a person behave as a member of a group, but rather the categorisation of oneself as a member of a group. This made Turner conclude, "Social identity is the cognitive mechanism which makes group behaviour possible."[23] SCT describes the cognitive process involved in moving from personal identity into social identity and under which circumstances such cognitive moves happen.[24] Self-categorisation is not the end of the process of belonging to a group but rather the beginning. Another important feature is learning the group norms, which leads to stereotyped behaviour. When a member applies group norms, the membership becomes salient for the member.[25] In other words, one has not only to self-categorise as a member, but also to act accordingly.

The next step for the individual who attains a group identity is the step of identification. Identification within an SIT framework thus includes: "A cognitive recognition (of belonging to the group, membership); Evaluative connotations (of value added to such belonging); and Emotional investment."[26] In

---

[21] Hogg, van Knippenberg, and Rast 2012, 262.
[22] Turner 1982, 23.
[23] Turner 1982, 21.
[24] Turner 1982, 31–33.
[25] Turner 1982, 31.
[26] Rosell Nebreda 2011, 38.

this process of identification or self-categorisation, something occurs that Turner refers to as depersonalisation. This is defined as "a process of self-stereotyping through which the self comes to be seen in terms of a category membership that is shared with other ingroup members."[27] Membership in a group affects the cognition of the members, who want to understand themselves as aligned with group norms.[28] Through what is known as the accentuation effect, a member of a group "brings one's own behaviour in line with the norm."[29] Ingroup behaviour and identification are tightly connected.

In the third important part of SIT, *comparison*, group members compare themselves to members of outgroups in order to feel good about themselves. From the ingroup identity, the member can form a positive view of the self.[30] Leo Festinger had already in the 1950s seen that social comparison was an important feature of the individual's self-image.[31] This provides impulses for SIT in general and provides a cornerstone for understanding how identity is formed against outgroups. Sergio Rosell Nebreda concludes, "By extension people perceive themselves positively; since social comparison is done in such a way that they receive positive feedback by comparison and/or contrast."[32]

Comparison is the perspective in SIT that, at length, deals with inter-group behaviour. The comparison any group member engages in is made in such ways so that the ingroup members should be able to understand his/her group identity as positive when contrasted to outgroups. This observation stems from three foundational assumptions onto which the comparison dimension of SIT rests. First, people generally prefer a positive self-view rather to a negative one. Second, because self-perception is linked to group identity, people generally prefer a positive social identity. Third, the value of one's own group is only accessible through comparison with other social groups.[33] This results in the

---

[27] Haslam, Reicher, and Platow 2014, 52.
[28] Manstead and Hewstone 1995, 557.
[29] Manstead and Hewstone 1995, 557.
[30] Rosell Nebreda 2011, 38.
[31] Tajfel 1981, 254.
[32] Rosell Nebreda 2011, 38
[33] Brown and Pherson 2020, 8.

group identity being contrasted with those of other groups.[34] This indicates that the SIT framework can provide insights into inter-group conflicts and competition.

Since ingroup status gives status to the individual member, members will be engaged in the status of the ingroup. SIT suggests three strategies through which members of groups that are perceived and treated as inferior by a dominant group can react to change the situation: *individual mobility*, *social creativity*, and *social competition*.

Individual mobility occurs when members, because of the low social standing of the ingroup, decide to dissociate themselves from the ingroup, while instead attempting to "assimilate into a higher status one."[35] This strategy demands that it is possible for the individual to change groups. An example of this can be a person with a low-status job who pursues education to gain a higher-status one.

If group members perceive the boundaries between groups as impossible to cross, they can instead choose to use *social creativity*. This is usually a collective effort in which members of the group do not change the social standing of the group but redefine the group as socially superior to the outgroup, at least in some dimension.[36] An ingroup rhetoric of "poor but honest" explains to the group why the members are poorer than the dominant group but morally superior. This redeems the ingroup's self-perception while not really changing the inequalities between groups.[37] An alternative to this strategy, but still within social creativity, is the so-called downward social comparison. That simply means to agree that the ingroup is inferior to the dominant group, while still being more valuable than an outgroup perceived to be even worse. For example, in a situation where a football supporter realises that a local competing team will win the gold medal of the season, the supporters can, in order to feel

---

[34] Tajfel 1981, 258. Italics original.
[35] Brown and Pehrson 2020, 236.
[36] Brown and Pherson 2020, 240.
[37] See further Brown and Pherson 2020, 240–43.

good about themselves, start to compare their team's achievement with the team ending up last.[38]

The last method for social change suggested by SIT is *social competition*. Provided that the current social order is perceived as illegitimate and possible to change, the group as a collective can move into social action for social change.[39] Importantly, "[i]n order to take action, people need to believe that things could be different and that they therefore have the power to change them."[40]

2.3 Critique of the Use of SIT in Biblical Studies

SIT has been a successful theory in the sense that it has proved to be a useful tool in several disciplines and that it can function together with several different methods of analysing data. As Philip Esler points out, SIT is a widely used theory and has been found to be able to function in "field studies, case studies, surveys and archival research."[41] Ancient texts, from both the Hebrew Bible and the New Testament, have proved suitable for several studies on identity formation in Jewish as well as early Christian texts. Thus, the SIT framework provides further empirical information on how groups work within human society. In a field so invested in the formation of a given group (or groups) as New Testament exegesis, the framework has new and intriguing perspectives on the texts that are analysed.

However, SIT has also received some critique on a methodological level as a tool for the study of biblical texts. It is precisely the application of the theory to ancient texts and the relationship between experiments in a controlled

---

[38] A perfect example can be the relationship between the competing football teams of BK Häcken, IFK Göteborg, GAIS, and ÖIS, all from Gothenburg, Sweden. The four teams are all related to strong group identities. The formerly most successful team in the last thirty years, IFK Göteborg, found themselves in a rather unsatisfying eighth place in the season of 2022, and even worse from their perspective, BK Häcken won. In this situation, IFK Göteborg supporters could find solid comfort in comparing themselves with supporters of GAIS and ÖIS, whose teams were not even playing in the highest division during 2022.

[39] Brown and Pherson 2020, 243.

[40] Brown and Pherson 2020, 243.

[41] Esler 2022, 26.

environment that has been the focal point of the critique. John Barclay warns that SIT expects social laws to be in play that cannot be tested in the biblical accounts,[42] and that the controlled milieu in a social experiment is nowhere to be found in the Hebrew Bible or the New Testament documents.[43] These objections need some attention. Philip Esler's response in 2022 addresses Barclay's critique, not least about using SIT as a detector of social laws. Esler responds that the SIT framework used in Biblical Studies has a heuristic dimension and that SIT mainly discusses probabilities.[44] SIT is not made for a naïve transition from experimental conditions into other spheres, such as Biblical Studies, nor does it require the postulation of social laws (comparable to natural laws).[45] The biblical data is not used as an illustration of social laws, but rather as a way of asking new questions to the biblical material.[46] Barclay's critique revolves around how experiments and reality are understood within the theory. One can, however, note that the experiments that have been performed by SIT researchers have not been used as confirmation of social laws but rather as events that demand explanation outside of an experimental milieu.[47] The observations from the experiments need to be fitted into an explanatory model. This is the only thing SIT aims to do.

To discuss this last point even further, empirical evidence always needs to be understood in a context, which the SIT framework is indeed trying to provide. The significant results in socio-psychological experiments, such as the famous minimal group experiment by Tajfel and others from 1971, have yielded substantial cultural implications beyond the experimental milieu variation.[48] This has been accounted for by the researchers. John Turner noted the need for social science models in order to explain the reality outside of the experiments. The reason for this is that experiments are not constructed to mimic reality but rather constitute a first step towards predicting natural events (that

---

[42] Barclay 2011, 6–7, n. 10; Esler 2022, 21–22.
[43] Esler 2022, 21–22; Barclay 2011, 6–7, n. 10.
[44] Esler 2022, 25.
[45] Esler 2022, 22–23.
[46] Esler 2022, 22.
[47] Esler 2022, 23.
[48] Esler 2022, 24; Tajfel et al. 1971.

is, a way to perceive under what circumstances X usually occurs and an explanation for the case).⁴⁹ In doing so, one can detect the variables that are necessary to understand. From the amassing of data points, a theory can be formed. Several scholars in the field recognise the need for experimental as well as non-experimental empirical evidence.⁵⁰ Especially, when it comes to constructing identity, it is also important to take an interest in how this is done in extra-experimental groups. Fortunately, there are several examples of how modern leaders manage to capture or craft a sense of "us," and this leadership ability can sometimes be crucial for the leader's survival.⁵¹

Esler's conclusion is, therefore, that since SIT takes cultural variation and cultural norms into account, it has a long-lasting value for our understanding of group behaviour in any cultural context. Furthermore, SIT has both experimental and extra-experimental grounds for its results.⁵² The probabilities that it identifies are significant and have proved useful in many fields. To disregard these probabilities as far as we can perceive them in the biblical accounts would also demand an explanation.⁵³

After this introduction to the general outline of SIT, I now turn to look at the understanding of leaders and leadership in SIT, which will be significant for my study.

2.4 Group Leaders

One of the most prominent ways of using SIT has been in leadership studies.⁵⁴ According to the theory, the importance, salience, and rhetoric of group norms become significant in group leadership. SIT theorists have discussed mainly four aspects of leadership,⁵⁵ *prototypical leadership, identity entrepreneurship,*

---

⁴⁹ Esler 2022, 23.
⁵⁰ Haslam, Reicher, and Platow 2011, 137–38.
⁵¹ Haslam, Reicher, and Platow 2011, 138–40.
⁵² Esler 2022, 26–27.
⁵³ Esler 2022, 25–26.
⁵⁴ See Haslam and Reicher 2007, 125–28. See also for several rhetorical analyses of leadership prototypicality formation Haslam, Reicher, and Platow 2011.
⁵⁵ Steffens et al. 2014, 1003–5.

identity advancement, and *identity impresarioship.* These categories will be discussed below. The aspects all, to some extent, discuss how group identity is at play in efficient leadership and how leadership gains in efficiency if the sense of "us" is taken into account when the leader exercises power.

After considering the more recent developments in identity leadership approach, I use the term identity entrepreneurship in this book, which denotes the leader's ability to redefine ingroup identity.[56] As I will discuss below, there exists a slight confusion in the vocabulary concerning the categories. Haslam, Reicher, and Platow 2011 understand the terms identity artistry and identity impresarioship as sub-categories of identity entrepreneurship. In Steffens et al. (2014), four different leadership categories are used, which I will follow. Theoretical and empirical reasons for the categorisations are given in that context also. Thus, identity entrepreneurship is used to alter ingroup prototypicality and craft a sense of ingroup identity.[57]

Two methodological ways of studying SIT leadership have been dominant, one experimental and one that I, for practical reasons, call rhetorical.[58] While the experimental, because of the nature of this kind of experiments, have tended to focus on followership (why followers invest authority in a leader), the rhetorical studies focus on leaders' ways of constructing group identity.[59]

---

[56] One can note that there is a slight confusion in Katja Kujanpää's otherwise well written and accurate article on 1 Clement. The confusion regards the references to identity entrepreneurship (as she quotes Haslam, Reicher, and Platow 2011) Identity artistry is described as a sub-category of identity entrepreneurship in Haslam, Reicher, and Platow 2011. In Steffens et al. 2014, several prominent SIT scholars provide an inventory of four different leadership categories, which is the grounds for my usage in this book. Here, entrepreneurship is used as a term for altering ingroup prototypicality and crafting a sense of ingroup identity, Steffens et al. 2014, 1004.

[57] Steffens et al. 2014, 1004.

[58] Haslam, Reicher, and Platow 2011 discuss several kinds of speeches but also actions that craft a sense of "us" throughout the latter part of the book. Thus, to call this dimension "rhetorical" is a bit one-dimensional.

[59] Haslam and Reicher 2007, 127.

2.4.1 Prototypicality

Prototypical leadership is the ability of the leader to embody perceived group ideals.[60] As we saw above, when discussing the categorisation process, prototypicality concerns the group attributes of ingroup similarities and intergroup differences. Hogg, Van Knippenberg, and Rast define what happens when someone is designated as a group member:

> When someone, including oneself, is categorised as a group member we depersonalise them – a process causing us to view them as group members rather than autonomous individuals, and to assign them cognitively and perceptually the prototypical attributes of the group. Group prototypes and group norms differ in that a prototype is an individual's cognitive representation of what he or she believes to be the normative properties of the group.[61]

Prototypicality is thus not equal to the *average*, typical group member but rather equal to the *ideal* member of the group.[62] A dissociation from outgroup prototypes also occurs in the context of cognitive identification with a prototype.[63] All this relies on the assumption that the individual member of the group can gain reliable information about group norms. This information is often gathered through observing more experienced group members in their words and actions. By observing how group members relate (verbally and non-verbally) to ingroup members and outgroup members, new members can gain crucial information about belonging to the group.[64] It has been shown that a person in a group who is skilled in perceiving and defining group norms is a reliable source for other group members on group prototypicality. Also, when trying to sort out which norm information is most correct, we tend to draw from members whom we understand as the most prototypical.[65] This means that persons with prototypical behaviour "have disproportionate influence over the identity and behaviour of group members."[66] A leader who gains

---

[60] Esler 2022, 31–38.
[61] Hogg, Van Knippenberg, and Rast 2012, 262.
[62] Steffens et al. 2014, 1002–3.
[63] Hogg, Van Knippenberg, and Rast 2012, 262.
[64] Hogg, Van Knippenberg, and Rast 2012, 263.
[65] Hogg, Van Knippenberg, and Rast 2012, 263.
[66] Hogg, Van Knippenberg, and Rast 2012, 263

followers, then, is the leader who is "manifesting what it means to be a member of the ingroup and in representing it in ways that differentiate it from outgroups."[67]

In early Christian writings, norms for behaviour are presented through numerous exhortations on how a believer is expected to live. But the exhortations are also incarnated in the examples of Christ-group members adhering to these norms in ways commendable to follow for other members. The exigency for good examples to follow is apparent when new members arrive at the group.[68] Simultaneously, the exemplary person who becomes followed is given influence over the group members' actions. In novel or ambiguous situations, the leader who performs good examples of shared group norms is thus most likely to be followed and succeed as a leader, according to several studies.[69] That is to say that leadership is more efficient when leaders adhere to the ingroup norms themselves in a reliable way that is possible for members to mimic.[70] In his study of 2 Corinthians from a SIT perspective, Esler writes,

> One of the major discoveries of [SIT] has been that leaders are more efficient in eliciting followership if the members consider that they are 'prototypical' of the group they lead, that is, in manifesting what it means to be a member of the ingroup and in representing it in ways that differentiate it from outgroups.[71]

Groups can thus be said to strive for a stereotyped way of acting that will help members separate ingroup from outgroup behaviour.[72] Joint behaviour reinforces the boundaries of the ingroup and can also provide ways to enter or exit the group. Rikard Roitto shows, as an example of how this works in one New Testament text, how Ephesians constructs grounds for membership in a group that are collectively applied by the members and thus more efficient. *Knowledge* of Christ leads to *Faith in Christ*, which leads to *Baptism* which leads to *Being*

---

[67] Esler 2022, 32.
[68] Brown and Pherson 2020, 111.
[69] Brown and Pherson 2020, 111.
[70] Brown and Pehrson 2020, 109.
[71] Esler 2022, 32.
[72] "Stereotype" in this context does not carry any negative connotations, but is just a way to signify the joint behaviour of a certain group, Tajfel 1981, 143–46.

in Christ.⁷³ Here we can see that knowledge, faith, baptism and being in Christ all have practical implications in which members engage – the ingroup norms expect a certain behaviour of the ingroup members. It is important that this behaviour is ingroup stereotypical and differs from outgroup behaviours. To be able to hear, then, one needs to be present in group gatherings. To have faith includes commitment to the group, baptism obviously has a practical side, and being in Christ is related to being a part of the group, which includes choices in everyday life.⁷⁴ Esler also points out, as the most obvious example, how the ethical admonitions in the New Testament set an example for the group members: they are supposed to live up to the prototypical ideas of the Sermon of the Mount (Matt 5–7), the fruits of the Spirit (Gal 5:22–23), and so on. This means that the group leader is the individual who can reliably provide a new member with information and guidance on how to adapt to boundary-setting rules.⁷⁵ In this process, the leader's prototypicality plays an important role: does the leader demonstrate how these rules should be followed in practice? Leaders must apply the ingroup norms to themselves at a higher level than average group members.⁷⁶ In this way, prototypicality becomes an embodiment and an assemblage of the group norms.

The leader is thus leading through *exemplarity* according to SIT. Exemplarity is a version of prototypicality: instead of defining the group through a derivation of group ideals into a prototype, one could choose to define the group through an individual *example* of the group.⁷⁷ Paul, Peter, and John, as instances, can provide a pattern of the ideal of the group.

To dig a little deeper into the background of the usefulness of prototypical or exemplary behaviour, one can note how Joseph Henrich shows how behaviour that is costly for the individual, such as rituals of sacrifice, vows of celibacy, and even martyrdom, is evolutionarily beneficial for a group.⁷⁸ This is closely linked to the fact that individuals who advocate for a costly action and

---

[73] Roitto 2020, 222.
[74] Roitto 2020, 222.
[75] Esler 2022, 32.
[76] Esler 2022, 33.
[77] Esler 2022, 33.
[78] Henrich 2009, 245.

undertake these actions themselves are more likely to be committed to group norms and, therefore, to group survival.[79] The actual behaviour pattern of a leader is important for followers to monitor closely, enabling them to discern whether the leader is attempting to deceive them or not. If a group leader *says* that blue mushrooms are tastier and more nutritious than grey ones but is never seen eating anything other than the grey mushrooms, one might suspect the leader of not telling the truth. Thus, monitoring influential group members addresses the obvious danger of manipulative leadership. Henrich suggests that the emergence of so-called CREDs (Credibility-Enhancing Displays), which is the leader's behaviour aligned with his/her words even at a personal cost, plays the evolutionary role of safeguarding against manipulation from influential members. Henrich also recapitulates four experiments regarding food consumption,[80] opinion transmission,[81] cultural transmission of altruism,[82] and counterintuitive concepts.[83] In all these experiments, CREDs from an influential person made a significant positive difference in the adherence to a suggested behaviour, such as trying a new food or altering one's opinion. This suggests that individuals who demonstrate consistency between their words and actions are perceived as more trustworthy influencers compared to those who say one thing and do another. This aligns with the earlier expression regarding prototypicality: the influence exerted by group members who adhere consistently to expressed group norms is more significant for new members than that of those who do not exhibit such behaviour consistency.

In this study, I have a special interest in the prototypical behaviour that is expected from members of the groups for whom the texts I analyse were produced. A methodology for detecting the prototypical behaviour is to ask the text which ideals (ethical and others) are explicitly or implicitly expected by the group member. While we cannot get actual access to a group leader from a second-century Christ group such as Ignatius, we have access to the rhetorical texts describing ingroup norms that are explicit grounds for prototypical

---

[79] Henrich 2009, 247.
[80] Henrich 2009, 248.
[81] Henrich 2009, 248.
[82] Henrich 2009, 248–49.
[83] Henrich 2009, 249.

behaviour. We also get some information on how group leaders are portrayed or portray themselves as the sender of the rhetorical texts. As we shall see, the willingness to suffer for ingroup ideals is ever-present in second-century Christ-group texts. The more norms that are detected and the more descriptions of how leaders relate to these norms we can gain, the better picture we can gain of how the prototypical member acts. It is also interesting to analyse how these group norms set the group apart from outgroups since prototypicality also displays the contrast between the ingroup and outgroups. Thus, comparing ingroup and outgroup ideals will present a prototypicality, highlighting the differences between being part of "us" or "them." The way to convey this from a text is then to make a rudimentary rhetorical analysis: what does the author explicitly (and sometimes implicitly) expect from the reader in terms of behaviour? How does the behaviour of the addressed readers comply with the norms set up for ingroup prototypicality? How are the leaders portrayed in relationship to the group norms? This will be one important part of my analysis.[84]

To summarise, prototypicality is the leader's ability to embody and act out group ideals and norms. The more a person is perceived to be prototypical, the more efficient his/her leadership becomes. SIT leadership assumes that leaders who are prototypical, that is, align with group values, get a higher level of influence on members, who look to prototypical members to gain information on how to live according to group norms. Costly displays, in which a leader commits to the group norms at a high personal cost, are efficient ways to influence followers to a suggested action or norm.

2.4.2 Identity Entrepreneurship

Identity entrepreneurship is the name of the leader's ability to create, develop, and uphold a coherent picture of identity and group norms (thus, prototypicality). The precise group ideal is often in a state of flux; therefore, the individual who successfully defines and embodies it in a trustworthy manner gains

---

[84] It is perhaps useful note that we only have access to written or sometimes inscriptional evidence of group ideals. This means that we can say something useful only about how prototypicality was conveyed in texts. We cannot really say anything about how oral negotiations on prototypical behaviour in group life functioned in the groups these ancient texts portray. Thus, this study discusses how prototypicality is conveyed in ancient Christian texts.

influence within the group. The leader reconstructs the group's identity through a new and slightly altered prototypicality – often through a narrative in which the leaders themselves appear as prototypical as possible.[85] The prototypicality of a given group, then, is probably not the present form of the ingroup (shaped by the group's present social realities), but rather what a leader describes prototypical membership to look like in the future when every member fully acts out their membership.[86] Apt leaders can shape the future vision of group membership in ways that mobilise members into joint action. This is to say that identity entrepreneurship is about redefining ingroup prototypicality in ways that align with the leader's vision of the group. That is not too far from altering the group identity.[87] The redefinition process is, of course, only possible if the group perceives the leader as a valid leader (that is, if he/she is sufficiently perceived as a prototypical member). If not, the leader might apply different strategies, such as drawing new boundaries or putting down other leader candidates as a means for enhancing the view of the leader's own prototypicality.[88] The goal of entrepreneurship can in practice be to evolve existing structures, or perhaps to suggest new ones, in harmony with the ingroup vision of a desired reality.[89] All this can be summarised in the words of Hogg, van Knippenberg and Rast.

> There are many strategies that prototypical leaders can employ to manage their own prototypicality and shape their group's identity. These strategies largely involve rhetoric and strategic communication but also behaviour that supports the rhetoric – consistency between rhetoric and overt behaviour significantly strengthens credibility and legitimacy … and thus, in the case of leaders, their moral credentials … and leadership effectiveness.[90]

As mentioned above, the possibility of changing group norms is built on trust. This creates the apparent paradox that a trusted leader is given the means to

---

[85] Esler 2022, 39–40.
[86] Haslam, Reicher, and Platow 2011, 162.
[87] Hogg, Van Knippenberg, and Rast 2012, 267.
[88] Haslam, Reicher, and Platow 2011, 146.
[89] Haslam and Reicher 2007, 128.
[90] Hogg, Van Knippenberg, and Rast 2012, 268.

modify significant group norms and practices into something new.[91] One can note that this is related to the relatively fluid state of group identity. Social context, joint social action, group prototype, leader prototypicality, and leadership are stages in a cycle in which leaders and groups interact. In this process, leaders can both react to social context and initiate social action towards a new identity.[92] Social identity is inherently fluid, allowing for new interpretations and proposals on how group identity is articulated or performed.[93] When we discuss entrepreneurship, we analyse how the leader is an active part in identity formation: "The core of this activity [the ways leaders construct identities] lies in shaping social identities so that the leader and his or her proposals are seen as the concrete manifestation of group beliefs and values."[94] This is important since people, as we have seen, tend to act in alignment with their social identity and the perceived prototypical behaviour of their own group.[95] Thus, if someone aspiring to leadership succeeds in shaping the perception of group identity, group members are likely to act in accordance with the aspiring leader's suggestions vision.

As we have seen, rhetoric plays a crucial role in entrepreneurship. If one wishes to investigate how leaders try to shape their ingroup, one should examine how their rhetoric shapes a vision of an ingroup prototypicality. Now, what the student of ancient Christian texts has access to is only the rhetoric of Christ groups, primarily testified to by the written sources. Thus, it is indeed possible to gain access to how Christ-group leaders, presumably, tried to shape a new vision for the group identity of its members. In this study, I will show how the early Christian authors constructed an ingroup prototypicality, that is, how they were *entrepreneurs* of Christian identity, sometimes through using the authority, prototypicality, of apostles (as in the Pastoral letters) or martyrs (as in Ignatius's letters). This rhetorical construction of an ingroup ideal also meant that some identities were shut out. A concrete example that will be further investigated in chapter 8 is how the author constructs an ethical ideal through the

---

[91] Hogg, Van Knippenberg, and Rast 2012, 274.
[92] Haslam, Reicher, and Platow 2011, 72–73; 142.
[93] Haslam, Reicher, and Platow 2011, 143–47.
[94] Haslam, Reicher, and Platow 2011, 142.
[95] Haslam, Reicher, and Platow 2011, 143–45; Haslam and Reicher 2007.

lists of the character traits of the ἐπίσκοπος in 1 Timothy 3:1–7 and Titus 1:5–10, with significant similarities with Stoic ideals of the wise man, and a well-situated *paterfamilias* in a Greco-Roman context. In this ethical vision, the absence of even minimal Torah observance (such as the observance suggested in Acts 15) is notable. A salient Jewish identity becomes impossible for any group member, according to the vision of prototypicality in the Pastorals.

A method to detect how these processes of identity entrepreneurship are played out in second-century texts is basically to ask the texts a set of questions. What aspects of the text suggest an altered or new group identity? Who is the person who makes these suggestions? If the person is perceived or described as a prototypical member of the group, like for example Ignatius of Antioch, who showed costly displays to ingroup values (that is, he was martyred for his faith), the authority comes through prototypical behaviour. Thus, the delicate interplay between entrepreneurship and prototypicality will be considered.

To summarise, identity entrepreneurship means that a leader actively constructs an ingroup identity through a (most often rhetorical) redefinition of the ingroup prototypicality. In this process, the redefinition often frames the (aspiring) leader himself/herself as prototypical.

2.4.3 Identity Impresarioship

In this section of *identity impresarioship*, I align myself to the definition of Steffens et al. Impresarioship refers to what a leader engages in when they do any of the following:

> Developing structures, events, and activities that give weight to the group's existence and allow group members to live out their membership. Promoting structures that facilitate and embed shared understanding, coordination, and success (and not structures that divide or undermine the group). Providing a physical reality for the group by creating group-related material and delivering tangible group outcomes. Making the group matter by making it visible not only to group members but also to people outside the group.[96]

The point with impresarioship is that group members are invited to actively participate in joint actions and structures, which embeds the group identity.

---

[96] Steffens et al. 2014, 1005.

When members participate in the structure or engage themselves to make the structure a lived reality, it is not just any structure they engage in or work for. The crucial point for impresarioship is that the structure is closely connected to the member's group identity. The eucharistic meal would be a relevant example. The self-categorising Christian, who participates in the eucharist engages in a ritual that he or she believes connects him or her with Jesus Christ. It connects the believer with several crucial beliefs of the ingroup (the salvific death of Christ). It reinforces the communal aspect of the group, as participating in the eucharist is typically a collective event. Therefore, the form of the eucharist holds significance for every group member, as it reaffirms social identity.

The literature regarding leadership from an SIT perspective can be confusing because different kinds of vocabulary are used concerning impresarioship. Haslam, Reicher, and Platow suggest that identity entrepreneurship comes in three versions, of which impresarioship is one. The three versions all discuss how the leaders gain power through using different kinds of means to construct a shared identity with group members. Leaders try to create a vision (recognising as the leader as an *artist of identity*), structures (the leader as an *impresario of identity*) and, on a grand level, societies (the leader as an *engineer of identity*), all of which are perceived as outcomes of the ingroup identity.[97] The leader's ability to create these features rests on his/her ability to embed a sense of group identity into the visions, structures, or societies: the group member should *want* to be a part of the structure due to his/her sense of belonging to the group.

When Steffen and others 2014 discuss impresarioship, they do not describe it as a sub-category of entrepreneurship.[98] Instead, they discuss it as its own category, which denote the leader's efforts to "establish structures, implementing practices, formalizing rituals, and organizing events" that aim to embed a sense of "us" for the group.[99] They also coined the definition which I use above. The strength of Steffen's and others' definition is the empirical evidence presented

---

[97] Haslam, Reicher, and Platow 2014, 171.
[98] Steffens et al. 2014, 1004–5.
[99] Steffens et al. 2014, 1005.

for the categorisations, as well as the attempt from several leaders to create a unified language for the different terms, which will decrease the level of confusion. [100] Further, while the definitions used by the different authors are similar enough in content, I maintain that impresarioship is not necessarily a sub-category of entrepreneurship. Haslam, Reicher, and Platow are correct when they emphasise how social identity is perhaps re-shaped through the embedment. Still, the main point with impresarioship is how the structure suggested by impresarios of identity conveys group identity in its own right. For example, constructing a leadership structure that encapsulates group identity does not necessarily demand that the structure alter the ingroup prototypicality in any significant way (which is what entrepreneurship is about). Also, I believe that in the discussion of rhetorical texts from the second century, the artistry level and the impresario level overlap significantly, making the distinction unhelpful. The authors in the second-century Christ groups opt for a leadership structure that is infused with group identity. Here, we analyse *the texts* about the structures, and not the structures themselves. Thus, the envisioned structure is basically the only level of the structure to which we have access. Therefore, throughout this book I will use the term *impresarioship* to denote the rhetorical construction of structures or rituals that significantly embed group identity.

To detect impresarioship in the sources, one can ask the following questions: What (new) structures or rituals are described as meaningful embodiments of ingroup identity? How do suggested structures or rituals embody the self-perception of the group?[101] The answer to these questions gives us insight into how social identity was used to create structures that held significance for the members of second-century Christian texts.

To summarise, impresarioship, which will be used as a term also covering identity artistry (and if ever actual, identity engineering), denotes the leader's rhetorical construction of structures or rituals that embed ingroup identity.

---

[100] Steffens et al. 2014, 1006–20.

[101] These questions are adaptions of the statements of leaders developed to detect impresarioship suggested by Steffens et al. 2014, 1021: "This leader devises activities that bring [the group] together ... This leader arranges events that help [the group] function effectively ... This leader creates structures that are useful [for group members]."

Impresarioship also includes calling for active participation in these structures, leading to the mobilisation of group members for joint action.

2.4.4 Identity Advancement

The fourth and final aspect of SIT leadership involves the leader actively championing ingroup norms and group status among outsiders, as the group's status is reflected in the individual's status. When the group achieves honour among outsiders, so does the individual member through association. This is called *identity advancement* and will be important during one specific part of this study. Comparison to outgroups is, of course, a crucial driving force in this aspect of leadership. As we shall see, a debate over the role of the ἐπίσκοπος (primarily) in the Didache has been about whether the ἐπίσκοπος actually functioned rather as a patron of the society, which means he served the financial needs of the ingroup. This will be discussed further in chapter 6, but it is possible that identity advancement had a crucial role in the Didache context, since the discussion concerns whether the episcopal leaders actually bear the financial cost of the Christ group in Didache.

A closer look reveals that identity advancement works as follows:

> This research [laboratory and field experiments] shows that a leader identifying with a group, that is, demonstrating that he or she is working for the group, by standing up for it and by championing collective interests, represents a path to successful leadership in addition to prototypicality (= being representative of the group).[102]

A crucial point is that the identity advancer needs to be understood as someone who advances the interests of the ingroup "rather than their personal interests or those of other outgroups."[103] This does not automatically mean that outgroups are derogated.[104] Leaders who are perceived as only serving their own interests will not gain followership from group members. Rather, the point of the category is that the leader who is perceived as advancing ingroup interests will be followed. Interestingly enough, a leader who advances ingroup interests does not necessarily need to be perceived as prototypical, which means that the

---

[102] Esler 2022, 39.
[103] Steffens et al. 2014, 1004.
[104] Steffens et al. 2014, 1004.

leader can deviate from group norms.[105] Jetten and others refer to several studies in which this is clear. One example is taken from a study of the words and actions of politicians. In this study the findings from other studies was repeated: "[I]f ingroup members perceived that their party was losing support and that it was likely they would lose the next election, they tolerated and even applauded deviating from previously endorsed positions because this was perceived as advantageous to the group."[106] It has also been shown that a deviant member of a group, who "had damaged the reputation of the group" can be punished by the group for identity reasons: "precisely because deviants undermine the integrity of our group, derogating such individuals and excluding them from the ingroup serves the important function of maintaining a positive and distinctive social identity."[107] Social identity may allow for leaders to behave in un-prototypical manners if the group identity is perceived to be enhanced by the leader's actions. Under these circumstances, the leader is not liable to punishment by the ingroup: "the more ingroup members would appraise an act as deviant and harming the interests of the dominant group ... the less likely they would want to punish the transgressor."[108] It is important to note that identity advancement also functions in situations without stress for the group.[109]

This demonstrates that a group leader who advocates for group interests, including caring for the financial needs of the group, can act in non-prototypical ways under certain circumstances without losing followers or authority in the group.

2.4.5 Summary

The categories in SIT leadership have overlapping qualities, as can be seen not least with the relationship between impresarioship and entrepreneurship discussed above. As previously noted, I will follow the terminology found in

---

[105] Esler 2022, 39.
[106] Jetten et al. 2011, 131.
[107] Jetten et al. 2011, 118.
[108] Jetten et al. 2011, 130.
[109] Steffens et al. 2014, 1004.

Steffens and others. To summarise how the terms will be used in this study, Table 4.5 might be helpful.

	Prototypicality	Entrepreneurship	Impresarioship	Advancement
Function	Embodiment of the ideal of the group	Redefinition of the ingroup prototypicality	Embedment of ingroup identity in structures and rituals and so forth	Advancement of ingroup interests, not least among outsiders.
Catch Phrase[110]	"Being one of us"	"Crafting a sense of us"	"Doing it for us"	"Doing it for us"

Table 2.4.5. Summary of SIT leadership categories.

As noted in this chapter, the primary aim of these categories is to illustrate how group leaders typically achieve greater success within human groups when they manage to connect with a group's sense of social identity. This identity motivates and mobilises the members to joint action. In especially impresarioship the mobilisation into action is important, since this category denotes how structures and rituals and so forth become vehicles for members to express their identity, both to themselves and to outgroups.

In this chapter, I have briefly discussed how SIT leadership categories can be applied to the source texts, through a rudimentary rhetorical analysis. This is done in order to discern how Christ-group authors conveyed a distinct, social identity through group leadership and the structures initiated by these leaders. In the following chapters, I will demonstrate how this social identity in practice prevented members from expressing or engaging in any other social identity, such as a salient Jewish identity. This makes the function of leadership in first- and second-century Christ-group texts interesting from the so-called parting of the ways perspective.

Before we turn to this demonstration of social identity processes in first- and second-century texts, we will examine two important research fields within which this study is situated. First, I will review the parting of the ways research

---

[110] The Catch Phrases are all picked up from Steffens et al. 2014.

field, which discusses the separation process that led to the emergence of two distinct religions: Judaism and Christianity. Secondly, I will review the research regarding the emergence of the episcopal office.

3. Did the Ways Even Part? A Recapitulation of the Parting of the Ways Debate

An intrinsically important question for this thesis concerns the power balance in the second century CE between Jesus-followers who observed certain halakic rules and Jesus-followers who did not. The claim I present throughout this book – that the ἐπίσκοπος became a symbol of identity for Christ-alignment among certain Christ groups, as evidenced by the second-century texts I analyse – assumes that there was a tension between, and sometimes within, Christ groups about which role halakic behaviour had for Christian self-identity. I believe that this tension is obvious in and between the sources I use. We can see this as soon as the Christ groups began to formulate what it meant to be a *Christian*, that is, a member of a Christ group. This was portrayed as something fundamentally different from being Jewish, that is, engaging in halakic behaviour. Most explicitly, the letters of Ignatius strongly suggest that it is impossible to be part of ἡ καθολικὴ ἐκκλησία (Ign. *Smyrn.* 8:2) without being subject to the ἐπίσκοπος. This left no room for a salient Jewish identity. At the other end of the spectrum, the Didache community is less indebted to the emerging institution of the ἐπίσκοπος, yet it still regards the ἐπίσκοπος as a continuation of the ministry of Jesus, the apostles, the prophets and the teachers. While there has been a growing interest in the role of institutions in the early Christ movement (see below), no one has yet formulated what the ἐπίσκοπος meant in terms of identity markers and boundary makers for the emerging Christ groups. In this chapter I will situate the present research within the parting of the ways debate. Indeed, the institutional perspective will situate the ἐπίσκοπος as crucial for early Christian identity formation. To do this, we need to recapitulate the parting of the ways debate and the recent synagogue research.

The parting of the ways debate began with an increasing awareness that the language used in the research so far had not always enhanced our understanding of the emergence of Judaism and Christianity. In fact, the research strongly suggests that the terminology had actually blurred our understanding. Before we can discuss the emergence of a Christian identity, we need to answer some of these pressing questions, at least tentatively. How should one properly describe the Jesus movement ("Christianity") and the synagogue fellowship ("Judaism") in antiquity? Several terms have been proposed for these movements, and while each carries certain benefits, they also possess drawbacks. In this chapter, I will recapitulate the modern scholarly trajectory called "the parting of the ways" and responses to it. The main question that lingers is how to understand the separation between what heuristically will be labelled as Christ groups and synagogues. The meaning of these terms will be clarified during the course of the chapter. The evidence we find in the ancient sources, on a general level, are traces from the lives of groups, steles, inscriptions, archaeological findings, and literary evidence. Some of these groups in antiquity were formed around a Jewish identity, with the God of the Jewish Scriptures as patron God and were in the diaspora *generally* called synagogues. Within the range of these groups, there were slightly different perspectives on understanding the Torah, halakah, Jesus as Messiah, ethnicity, and so on. Two examples of such groups could be the addressees of Galatians, and the group(s) addressed by the Didachist.[1] The separation between Christ groups and synagogues is thus, as we shall see, intrinsically interconnected to the relation between labels of ingroups and outgroups and how these labels could or should be understood from both emic and etic perspectives. Thus SIT, as described in chapter 2 above, is a genuinely useful tool in this debate.[2]

This chapter has three basic parts. First, I will briefly recapitulate the parting of the ways debate, which started some forty years ago. In this part, I will discuss the terminology that I will use for different groups. Second, I will

---

[1] Schröter, Edsall, and Verheyden 2021, 5.
[2] See Holmberg 2008, 16–20.

recapitulate the research history of the synagogue and its leadership. Findings from the parting of the ways debate show the importance of socio-cultural and local perspectives, in which leadership questions are situated. This will be analysed under the heading "the institutional perspective." Third, I will draw out the conclusions and situate this book in relation to the parting of the ways debate, and the socio-cultural history of the synagogue in the diaspora.

3.1 The Ways That Parted – Or Did They?

A few basic facts are crucial for a full understanding of this debate on early Jewish/Christian identity. First, there was a distinctive Jesus movement from around 30 CE and onward, forming around Jesus of Nazareth. From its beginning, this movement had an exclusively Jewish leadership and was originally intended for Jews. However, it also had boundaries separating it from other Jews, which is the only reasonable explanation for why Saul/Paul of Tarsus decided to persecute the young movement.[3] This may have been linked to the elevated self-perception associated with the Jesus movement.[4] Furthermore, the Jesus movement could seem quite extreme to many first-century Jews, both in Jesus's time and afterwards, because of its belief about its relation to non-Jews, the Torah, and Christology.[5] Thus, the new movement came to have tense relations with other groups in the ancient society, both Jewish and non-Jewish. These tensions resulted in the Jesus movement ultimately evolving into the religion of Christianity, and few individuals from other Jewish groups became members of either the Jesus movement or the latter religion. But when exactly did the gap between Jesus followers and other Jewish groups become unbridgeable? According to the first version of the parting of the ways-model, it happened early; according to later versions, it is impossible to give one simple answer to that question.

What, then, is the parting of the ways-model? What are the implications of the model, and what has the debate been about? In summary, the concept of the parting of the ways offers frameworks for understanding how the followers

---

[3] Holmberg 2008, 1–3.
[4] Holmberg 2008, 3.
[5] Alexander 1999, 19–21.

of Jesus, who viewed him as the Messiah, initially began as a wholly Jewish group but ultimately developed into a new religion, Christianity, distinct from what would become Judaism. When, where, and how did this happen? Martin Goodman's timeline can illustrate the multiple events that have been suggested: the emergence of Jesus's ministry, Paul's missionary activity and acceptance of non-Jewish members, the destruction of the temple in 70 CE, and the Bar Kochba uprising, have all been understood by biblical scholars to be pivotal events.[6] All these events have been problematized and discarded by several scholars as *the* decisive event when Judaism and Christianity emerged as fully separate religions. However, each of these events, and several more such as the *fiscus judaicus*, a tax levied by Vespasian on Jews in the Roman empire in the early seventies of the first century CE, have been scrutinized during the debate.[7] The beginning of the debate tends to favour an early separation, whereas the trend during the later part of the debate is towards a more complex and prolonged process. In fact, some later participants in the debate perceive key figures like Paul as operating within Judaism and regard the separation process as rather late or consider the question altogether faulty.[8] According to many later participants of the debate, therefore, it is not relevant to talk about separation before the fourth or even fifth century. It is also important to distinguish between group names and people. Thus, even if theological differences and conflicts lingered during the first three or four centuries, it does not mean that individuals could not move in and between groups.[9] The first part of the chapter summarises the debate regarding four central concerns that have been significant for understanding the relationship between early Christians and Jews.

3.1.1 The First Concern: Theology

One concern is the role of the ingroup ideologies, that is, the *theology* of the groups analysed. This theological process was the focus at the very beginning of the debate. Questions regarding Christology, Torah, and worship are central

---

[6] Of course, more events could be added, for examples see Goodman 2003, 122.
[7] Heemstra 2010, 1.
[8] See Nanos and Zetterholm 2015.
[9] Cohen 2018, 307–8, carefully lays out this perspective.

here. These questions were the main subjects discussed by James Dunn and others in their book *Jews and Christians: The Parting of the Ways A. D. 70–135*.[10] In this book, built on the presentations of a symposium in Durham in September 1989, the conclusion was that the period 70–135 CE was crucial for the separation process (hence the subtitle of the book).[11]

> [T]he symposium ... focused on the period between the Jewish revolts (70–132), ... the years between apostolic age and post apostolic age, between second Temple Judaism and rabbinic Judaism, between the Jewish Christianity of James and Jerusalem and the Jewish Christianity of which the Fathers speak, are the hinge on which major issues hung and decisive events turned. It was the urge to shed further light on these obscure but crucial years which was the principal inspiration behind the symposium.[12]

One can see that not only the writings associated with Ignatius of Antioch, but also, for example, Justin Martyr and Melito of Sardis, suggest an awareness of a growing theological tension, where some Christian group(s) (according to the reading of the early participants of the debate) started to claim that their own identity was significantly different from an allegedly pharisaic Jewish identity. Thus at least some groups were separating themselves from their Jewish identity during the second century. This involved conflict, contact, and competition between the two strands of Judaism that eventually can be seen as parted around 135 CE.[13] It is worth noting that the Durham symposium followed Joseph Lightfoot's work on Ignatius of Antioch that placed Ignatius firmly around 110 CE.[14] One can ask if a later dating of Ignatius, which a large part of the German-speaking research area has adopted in recent years (see chapter 9 below) would have changed the perception of the symposium in any significant way? In any case, Dunn posits the question central for the debate at that point regarding different kinds of Jewish and Christian particularism.

> The underlying theological question with which the symposium wrestled was precisely this: how and why the Jewish national particularism and the Christian Christological

---

[10] Dunn 1999. Note that the first version of the book was printed by Mohr Siebeck 1992, where some of the essays were in German.

[11] Dunn 1999, 367–68.

[12] Dunn 1999, ix–x.

[13] For a visual model of this "classic" version of the partings model, see Goodman 2003, 121.

[14] Dunn 1999, ix.

particularism came into ever sharper confrontation until a decisive parting of the ways was unavoidable.[15]

The point of departure was thus already at that early stage a certain kind of essentialism regarding Jewish and Christian identity. The final products of the process carried certain character traits along the lines of these identities until they turned into separate religions that Dunn labelled Christianity and Judaism. An important question then becomes if the development of a separation process was necessary or should be considered a historical accident.[16]

The debate has also been interested in how the rise of rabbinic Judaism influenced the relationship between Jesus followers and (other) Jews.[17] With rabbinic Judaism, a group emerged that provided practical and theological reasoning for the suggested rabbinic ingroup identity. This development, in turn, is perceivable only later than the original early partings idea, which is already noted by Dunn. In a concluding note in *Jews and Christians,* he wrote, "From the perspective of the rabbinic sources, we cannot really talk of a parting of the ways within the Jewish community until the triumph of Rabbinism within the Jewish community."[18] The point being made was that since the rabbis also suggested what a Jewish identity was, in a way that eventually came to define Jewishness for the major part of the Jewish community,[19] the rabbinic understanding of Jewish Jesus followers were that they were *minim* (heretics).[20] This came to define rabbinic Jewishness in ways hard to combine with belief in Jesus as the Messiah. The discussions of m. Quidd. 4:1, m. Sanh. 10:1 and t. Sanh. 13:4 are crucial because they are instances of rabbinic demarcation for the community: who is within the covenant, who is outside of it, and who has a place in the world to come? The rabbinic definitions are, however, not understood to have been normative until Amoraic times.[21] Thus, the *later* rabbinic definitions of in- and outgroups, cannot be taken as normative in the first and second

---

[15] Dunn 1999, viii.
[16] Dunn 1999, ix.
[17] Alexander 1999, 2, 4–19.
[18] Dunn 1999, 364.
[19] Alexander 1999, 4–5.
[20] Alexander 1999, 7–11.
[21] Alexander 1999, 5.

centuries CE. It is possible to assume a greater diversity among Jewish movements in these two hundred years. Therefore, it is "possible to locate the early 'Christians' within that diversity."[22] The neatly drawn *theological* lines were not sufficient for an all-encompassing picture of what had occurred.

On the other hand, demarcation between Jewish groups and followers of Jesus did obviously occur during the first half of the second century.[23] Shaye Cohen understands the second-century Christian texts as clearly distinguishing who is in and who is out. This is especially true regarding Jewish groups, which are described as outgroups in central surviving texts such as Didache, the Ignatian letters, Justin Martyr, Melito of Sardis, and the Martyrdom of Polycarp. Cohen concludes,

> There is no evidence in any of these texts – or anywhere else in Antiquity for that matter – for the existence of a community, whether Jewish or Christian, that included on equal terms gentile believers in Christ, Jewish believers in Christ, and Jewish non-believers in Christ. In other words, these texts assume that Jews and Christians inhabit separate social spaces, each with its own leadership and membership.[24]

These theological demarcations exist at an early stage, and the clear evidence of this cannot be ignored. Theological demarcations are also what make Thomas Robinson emphasise the theological perspective in his reading of Ignatius. Since I analyse Ignatius in chapter 9 at some length, Robinson's contribution needs to be addressed.[25] Robinson advances the view that the labels Judaism

---

[22] Lieu 2016, 21.

[23] Cohen 2018, 308–9, n. 5.

[24] Cohen 2018, 315.

[25] Robinson 2009, 207–27. In his book from 2009, Robinson discusses six perspectives of the parting of the ways-trajectory, that could be understood as a parting of the ways-reception. These perspectives give examples of how to understand the relationship between Jesus-followers and the synagogue and are a summary of the debate as of 2009. The perspectives on the relation between Jesus-followers and Judaism discussed by Robinson are: Siblings (since Jesus followers and Rabbinic Judaism have a common root in a common religious world); Subspecies (since the groups are intertwined until the fourth or fifth century); Christianities and Judaisms (to emphasise the plurality of groups that existed in different traditions); Fluid boundaries and Flexible membership (where different groups such as Christ groups and Rabbinic Judaism were all part of "one religious polysystem"); Narrowing the Labels (which means that labels used by an

and Christianity still have great value despite the severe critique of these labels in the understanding of the parting of the ways trajectory.[26] thus stands for a positive reception of the first, theological partings paradigm. While there are some insights in Robinson's critique, his defence of broad labels leads him to dismiss too quickly the benefits of discussing the complexity of the relationship between the Christ groups and the synagogue during the years leading up to his book (see below). The primary insight in Robinson's critique is the warning against *overly* problematizing the general labels used in the discussion. This is a constant through Robinson's treatment of the perspectives, and consistent with his understanding of an early separation between Judaism and Christianity. In summary, he thinks that the differences have been "muted" and the significance of an early parting of the ways between Judaism and Christianity has been "minimized."[27] The main problem with this critique, however, is that it is primarily focused on the Ignatian correspondence and does not take other texts into consideration. It is true that the author of Ignatius distinguishes the ingroup from other groups ("docetists" and "Judaizers"), but this is particular to this group of texts. Robinson thus misses out on the point made by Judith Lieu, among others, who emphasises the need for a *local* perspective on Christ groups and their relation to the synagogue.[28] The Ignatian correspondence is engaged in providing the readers with information about how to be proper members of the ingroup (to use SIT vocabulary). In this process, the author emphasises (as I will show in chapter 9) the ἐπίσκοπος as not only *a*, but *the*, guarantee for ingroup values (the self-designation as χριστιανισμός being the most essential fountainhead for these values). The author is providing a compelling vision of how to be a Christian (in Ignatius's own terms). From this does not automatically follow that, for example, the Didachist shared the same understanding of the ingroup definition as the author of the Ignatian letters,

---

ancient author such as the author of the Ignatian letters does not necessarily mean the same as scholars today take the label to refer to) and Elite labels ("Judaism" and "Christianity" should be understood as the labels of the elite in the ancient world). These six perspectives are then discussed from the perspective of the Ignatian letters.

[26] Examples of this can be found in Robinson 2009, 220–21.
[27] Robinson 2009, 208.
[28] Lieu 2016, 47.

nor that a Jesus follower could be expected to express his or her convictions in general in this way. Both theory and practice might have been perceived to vary, whether someone looked at it from the inside (emic perspective) or outside (etic perspective). These insights are gained from the discussion that has scrutinised labels, groups, and sociological perspectives of the so-called partings paradigm. Therefore, claiming that χριστιανισμός meant the same for insiders and outsiders based solely on the texts in the Ignatian correspondence does not adequately address all the material and perspectives of the parting of the ways debate. This becomes even clearer when a perspective from the social sciences is applied, such as SIT. Robinson is correct that self-labelling and labelling of outsiders have great significance in the life of a group, but he fails to engage in how group labels function in inter-group relations. As an SIT perspective can help us see, group labels show both a closeness and a distance in relation to neighbouring groups.

To summarise, the theological perspective was prominent at the beginning of the partings debate, and it has throughout the debate continued to be significant. That theological language was used as demarcations during the second century is clear. From that does not follow, however, that Judaism and Christianity as fully developed entities rose during the first and second centuries, only that we have access to texts that demarcate their own group from others.

3.1.2 The Second Concern: Social Perspectives

Another concern has been the *sociological* perspective on the partings paradigm.[29] This perspective has offered a significant critique of the original parting of the ways paradigm that stems from the symposium in Durham. The evidence that was used to support the partings perspective, so the critics claimed, basically consisted of *theological tractates*. The original partings discussion did not sufficiently consider the implications of daily life in an ancient city.[30] Anette Yoshiko Reed and David Becker provide the following critique of the partings paradigm.

---

[29] Yoshiko Reed and Becker 2003, 2.
[30] Fredriksen 2003, 36–38.

Even after the second century, the boundaries between "Jewish" and "Christian" identities often remained less than clear, consistent with the ambiguities in the definition of both "Jew" and "Christian." Likewise, attention to the entire range of our extant evidence suggests that the continued diversity of Judaism and Christianity found expression in the variety of ways in which Jews and Christians interacted in different geographical, cultural, and social contexts.[31]

One important feature of the critique is whether a theological separation ultimately leads to a sociological one. Political events such as the destruction of the temple and the Bar Kochba uprising,[32] the *fiscus judaicus*,[33] and the rise of Constantine have all been discussed as identity-shaping events on a larger scale.[34] The question remains to what extent large-scale events affected the small everyday life of groups. A paradigm that considers other data points than the mere theological ones suggests that the separation *did not* occur in the time span suggested by the early parting of the ways-paradigm, since Jews and Christians obviously had continuing contacts, testified to by both literary and archaeological evidence.[35] The multiple evidence of continuing contacts together with the vitriolic outbursts from ancient Christian authors to secure the borders against outsiders leads Paula Fredriksen to conclude, "When, then, did 'the ways' part? Our answer – and indeed, the question itself – depends upon what evidence we consider."[36] The multiple evidence of continuing, everyday contact between Jesus followers and other Jewish groups defies the neatly drawn lines.[37] Inscriptions as well as literary evidence of both *extra* and *intra muros* suggests

---

[31] Yoshiko Reed and Becker 2003, 2.

[32] Carleton Paget 2018, 303–6.

[33] The role that was played by the *fiscus judaicus* has been debated. The thesis that Vespasian's taxation of Jewish males 20–50 years of age was the incentive for formulating an identity distinct from Jewish groups (Bremmer 2021, 58–59) has been criticized, mainly because it depends on a "precise dating of some New Testament writings" and a postulation of the widespread persecution of Domitian (p. 59). Also, the tax was probably levied upon the upper classes of Rome and Italy. See further Heemstra 2010 and Frey 2013, 339–77.

[34] Goodman 2003, 122.

[35] Yoshiko Reed and Becker 2003, 2–3.

[36] Paula Fredriksen 2003, 61.

[37] Lieu 2016, 46–48. Note also as example of a late close relationships between Jews and Christian in the north-eastern part of the Mediterranean area, Markschies 2021, 25–26.

that the definition of who was in and who was out was not easily made, from either side.[38] Therefore, one question that must be addressed is how theological and sociological concerns intersect in the process of identity construction. This dissertation, which analyses how Christian identity is invested in the emerging episcopal structure, aims to be a part of such a solution.

In the introduction to the second edition of her book *Neither Jew nor Christian? Constructing Early Christianity*, Judith Lieu focuses on the local character of this new perspective on the separation process.[39] Lieu's perspective hesitates to use a grander narrative. She instead looks only to the written, theological evidence, and thus turns the attention to *local* findings and texts, rather than assuming an all-encompassing "Christianity" through the Mediterranean area during the first centuries CE. Ignatius of Antioch, for example, should not, from this perspective, be seen as an example of "proto-orthodox Christianity" but rather a window into the situation in second-century Antioch and Asia Minor. Lieu's thoughtful critique of the *model* parting of the ways is that when we have only local data from varying places and times, it is problematic to construct an all-encompassing structure too easily from these varying points, "What we need is a more nuanced analysis of the local and specific before we seek to develop models, which will set them within a more comprehensive overview."[40] Many scholars, after having considered these factors, understand around 400 CE to be a more reasonable date for the definite partings between what by then had turned into two separate religions.

To summarise, the sociological perspective discusses how Jews and Christians obviously had continuous contact, even if theological tractates of the time suggest that the demarcation lines would already be clear. This perspective often, though not always, considers sources beyond just literary ones and emphasises the local dimension of these sources before adopting an all-encompassing, essentialist grand narrative about Christianity or Judaism.

---

[38] Goodman 2003, 127. See also Fredriksen 2003, 41–42.
[39] Lieu 2016, 2–3.
[40] Lieu 2016, 38.

3.1.3 The Third Concern: Labels and Vocabulary

The third concern relates to vocabulary and definition. What is the correct way of describing the groups under debate? Are the group names and descriptions emic or etic? Several important results from the debate arise from careful attention to the labels attached to different groups. We have already touched upon the third concern above, but a few more things should be noted here. David Frankfurter responds to the debate up to 2003 and notes that the labels we use to describe certain phenomena or groups also suggest to us basic taxonomies, which might blur our understanding of the origins of certain texts.[41] The theological development of later centuries has tended to be read into the sources, and theological reasoning for understanding certain texts as either Jewish or Christian has not always been able to handle overlapping self-identities.[42] Thus, a growing concern for accurate definitions has developed during the partings debate. This has led to some important conclusions.

First and foremost, the idea of "Jewish" and "Christian" as labels for the first century has been criticised by many as anachronistic.[43] The discussion of how to label these two entities (or were they even entities during the second century?) has developed considerably since the 1990s. The book edited by Dunn, mentioned above, is a starting point for the discussion concerning the labelling of the traditions. As Anders Runesson puts it, "scholars perceive of such a 'parting of the ways' as the key to understanding the origin of Christianity as a religion separate from Judaism."[44] Significant questions regarding labels and their connotations have been raised and aired during the debate. Daniel Boyarin notes that one key question is when something can be considered a "religion" at all. In terms of the multi-facetted reality of the first and second centuries, neither Christianity nor Judaism can be understood as existing in a modern sense. Rather, it is by the fourth century that they exist as all-encompassing *religions* (with institutions, consistent rituals and coherent theologies). Boyarin suggests that rabbinic Judaism was in several ways responding to an emerging

---

[41] Frankfurter 2003, 133–34.
[42] Frankfurter 2003, 133.
[43] See for example Esler 2003, 12. See also Schröter, Edsall, and Verheyden 2021, 1.
[44] Runesson 2008, 60.

Christianity. Language and naming are intrinsically connected to social realities and, in fact, shape them as much as the other way around.[45] The debate concerning labels has therefore taken an interest in the names of ancient groups in general. Boyarin is one of several scholars who have discussed the meaning of the term Ἰουδαϊσμός.[46] It can be found both as an emic and an etic description.[47] Together with Steve Mason, he argues that the best term to translate the word Ἰουδαῖοι with is *Judaeans*, not *Jews*. Ἰουδαῖοι often re-occurs in Christ-group texts.[48] The reason for this, according to Mason, is that the emic understanding for first- and second-century inhabitants of the Mediterranean area of the term Ἰουδαῖοι must have been to connect a people with a land.[49] Thus, for a non-Judean to join the Jesus movement poses exigent questions such as whether a person baptised in the name of the messiah Jesus of the Ἰουδαῖοι would from now on would be a part of the ἔθνος labelled Ἰουδαῖοι, associated with a certain land and certain customs?[50] Those questions are according to this perspective at the heart of Acts 15, Gal 2, and several other texts in the New Testament. The term Ἰουδαϊσμός (found in Ign. *Magn.* 9, for example), furthermore, was an abstraction from a very concrete connection between label and people of an area.

> *Ioudaismos* as a belief system and way of life – as a concept abstracted from the realities of Judaea, Jerusalem, temple and priesthood, sacrificial cult, aristocratic governance, political constitution, ancestral laws, and traditions – was the construction of an ascendant *Christianismos* from the third to fifth centuries C.E.[51]

---

[45] Boyarin 2003, 65–68.
[46] Boyarin 2003, 67–68.
[47] In biblical literature one can note for example 2 Macc 2:21 (emic) and John 9:22 (etic).
[48] Boyarin 2003, 67.
[49] Mason 2007, 511. Boyarin also connects this to the context of 2 Macc 2:21–22. In this context, he draws out the comparison to how Athenian citizens understood inhabitants of the city that were "aping Persian manners" as *Medismos*, loyal to Persians rather than the own society. The same pattern can be seen in this first instance of the term Ἰουδαϊσμός – it was pitted against the badge of disloyalty, the *Hellenismos*. In this case the Ἰουδαϊσμός stood firmly against the hostile Hellenismos, "those aping Hellenistic manners," Boyarin 2003, 67–68.
[50] Mason 2007, 512.
[51] Mason 207, 511–12.

One important part of this discussion is how to translate the ancient Greek labels into modern languages in ways that keep the connotations of the original terms. These considerations lead Mason to conclude that the most reasonable label for avoiding anachronisms should be to translate Ἰουδαῖοι with "Judeans."[52] Mason's view can be summarised as follows: "*Ioudaioi* in antiquity refers not to "Judaism" understood as a system of beliefs abstracted from ethnic and cultural customs, but rather indicates an ethnic group, its culture, and its politico-geographical homeland."[53] This indicates that the etic use of *Ioudaioi* in Christ-group texts such as the Ignatian letters, is a construct that stands opposed to *Christianoi*. This would imply that using the term Judaism in translation would necessarily signal an understanding of Judaism primarily as a belief system similar to modern religions.

Runesson, after a thorough discussion with Mason, understands the primary task of translating terms to maintain continuity with the content of the ancient term. Since there is still a focus on Israel and Jerusalem, practice, ethnicity, and culture, in contemporary Judaism, the term Judaism sufficiently covers what was also covered in the second century. The term Judaism can therefore be used as a reasonable translation, and still preserve the emic perspective of a label, whether it refers to modern or first-century Judaism.[54] A similar perspective that takes both emic and non-polemic etic perspectives into consideration could be applied when the term *Ioudaioi* is translated as Jews, and not Judeans.[55] Since "Jew" in English covers the emic perspectives that also are covered by Judaism, the word can be used as a translation.

When turning to Jesus-followers, Runesson suggest that before what became Christianity was conceptualised as Christianity around the fourth century, the term *Christianoi* should be used for group members.[56] The name of the followers of Jesus during the shaping of Christian identity in the so-important second century should thus be *Christianoi*. This would perhaps help

---

[52] Cf. Runesson 2022, 269. This geographical perspective on the term would bring light to the tensions of John 7:1 and similar texts
[53] Runesson 2022, 263.
[54] Runesson 2022, 267–68.
[55] Runesson 2022, 266–68.
[56] Runesson 2022, 270.

settle the ever-lingering danger of anachronistic uses of the term.[57] However, several other scholars, such as Judith Lieu and Shaye Cohen, chose to use the terms "Jews" and "Christians" as names of the groups, even after recognising the heuristic character of the labels.[58] Lieu can simultaneously describe the distinguishing factor in naming a group as Christian while also warning against reading later developments into first-century contexts.[59]

An interesting qualification regarding the terminology is Jan Bremmer's treatment of the term Ἰουδαϊσμός, which adopts a dynamic perspective of the label.[60] Bremmer traces the usage in Greek materials from 2 Maccabees to the late second century. His point, following Mason, is that Ἰουδαϊσμός is used as a definition against something else (even if some static usages exist). This would mean that the word signifies an activity rather than a static notion: to Judaize. In second-century Christ groups, the meaning does not refer to the ethnic group Jews, but rather to a group within the Jesus movement that opted for more thorough Torah- or halakah-observance.[61] In significant second-century texts, both from Ignatius and the reconstruction of Marcion, the term signifies a type of Torah-observant Christ group: "the opposite of this way of life [as *Christianismos*] is *ioudaizein*, presumably propagating a kind of Jewish Christianity."[62] With Origen and Tertullian, the term becomes static: it now describes a Jewish person. In these instances, Jews are outsiders. Bremmer's reasoning builds upon the idea of how a word form usually is made, and it provides a reasonable reading of Paul in Gal 1:13–14 with a highly significant qualification. It is also possible, however, to acknowledge that the word form is used differently in various contexts and time periods. This usage notably influences the understanding of Ignatius, suggesting that the letters in his name pertain even more clearly to ingroup politics in the Asia Minor region.

---

[57] Runesson 2022, 271.

[58] Cohen 2018, 308; Lieu 2016, 239–43. During the second century, self-definition as χριστιανισμός became more common, and a translation of the word into "Christian" seems acceptable, if awareness is shown to the delicacy of the matter of labels.

[59] Lieu 2016, 25–26.

[60] Bremmer 2021, 61.

[61] Bremmer 2021, 65–66.

[62] Bremmer 2021, 66.

For practical reasons I will use the most common terms, which are "Jew" and "Christian," as broad labels and will, when the context so demands, qualify the meaning throughout this book. While this is a bit impractical, the whole matter of definition during the second century is impractical, and this is hopefully the solution that is least bad. Living with the ambiguity of terms that can carry modern and ancient meanings is possible. I will, however, use the terms Judaism or synagogue and Christ groups/Jesus groups as labels on a group level. When I use the term Judaism, it refers to groups that designate themselves that way in terms of a common ancient understanding (both emic and etic) of "*ethnos*, (national) cult, philosophy, familial traditions/domestic worship, (unofficial) associations, and astrology and magic."[63] Thus, it is possible to understand some parts of the Jesus movement as situated within Judaism. As to the use of synagogue, this is a way to indicate that any ancient belief existed primarily in a social setting. The synagogue is a group that exemplifies how the "*ethnos*, (national) cult, philosophy, familial traditions/domestic worship, (unofficial) associations, and astrology and magic" actually played out in local situations. Within this local framework, several of the Jesus followers could also be found.

3.1.4 The Fourth Concern: Methodology

The fourth concern of the debate involves a methodological perspective, potentially influenced by a post-modern understanding of how all research exists within a specific context. The beginning of the project to understand the separation process was a debate between philosophical versus philological methodology. The preface to Dunn and others unfavourably contrasts Baur's method with Lightfoot's. Baur's method of hastily extrapolating a single pattern found in exegetical findings is criticised, while Lightfoot's "unbendingly steadfast ... rigorous historical analysis of language and context" is set as the opposite.[64] The critique against Baur was that he too easily assumed that the whole ancient Jesus movement was mirroring the opposition between Pauline and Petrine congregations. While many more methodological concerns have risen after the original partings paradigm, this concern to carefully avoid extrapolations from

---

[63] Runesson 2022, 264.
[64] Dunn 1999, ix.

earlier paradigms has continued in the whole partings debate, as we shall see. The critiques of the methodological flaws of the early partings debate have had some similarities: the *modernity* of the idea of the separation between two *religions* comes to the fore after the work of Dunn and others.[65] Religion, in the modern sense, is not a suitable category, as it is an abstraction and fails to comprehend the phenomenon in ancient context.[66] This perspective has also been thoroughly laid out by Brent Nongbri.[67] Nongbri notes that the difference between religion as a modern entity and the practical approach detectable in believers of ancient sources has not been properly addressed in scholarly discourse.[68] The modern concept of religion suggests the possibility of a non-religious lifestyle, which misses the mark when aiming to describe the lives of ancient people in the Mediterranean area.[69] Boyarin and other authors extensively discuss how both language[70] and power relations[71] shape our understanding of history. Several insights about hermeneutics and predispositions emerge when attempting to understand the separation between Jesus-followers and other forms of Judaism. In this regard, post-colonial perspectives might be helpful when trying to understand how a given discourse (say, the parting of the ways paradigm) rests on presuppositions (in this case, the nature of Christianity and Judaism in a modern sense).[72] Discourses may rely on simplistic readings. In the case of second-century Christ-group texts, these are rhetorical texts intended to distinguish one's group from outgroups.[73] The actual historical events are inaccessible to us; we only have access to a text or an artefact that describes or perhaps hints at the event. The text as such is a rhetorical device, with certain aims and goals. From this arises an insight into the need to understand the entanglement of texts, history, and our description of history. Thus, there are *future*

---

[65] Cf. Lieu 2016 30–34; Runesson 2022, 260–61. See also Smith 1996.
[66] Runesson 2015, 53–55.
[67] Nongbri 2013.
[68] Nongbri 2013, 1–3.
[69] Nongbri 2013, 4–5.
[70] Boyarin 2003, 65–66.
[71] Ehrman 2003c.
[72] Runesson 2011, 33–39.
[73] Boyarin 2003, 67–70.

implications of historians describing the past; that is how history writing becomes a part in future politics in the relationship between groups and in this case religions.[74] Lieu discusses how the early Jesus follower texts described a past and *constructed* an identity.[75] Rather than describe the past, the texts can, therefore, in fact, obscure it.[76] An analysis of the texts is not really concerning history, but rather concerning the rhetoric of the ancient authors.[77]

> It is not simply that these texts are the sources for accessing the people behind them: often they may be seeking to represent a position that would not have been visible or persuasive to all those concerned; sometimes, as recent study has increasingly emphasized, they may be masking or silencing other voices, which we now may want to recover. Moreover, the texts do not simply reflect a 'history' going on independently of them, they are themselves part of the process by which Judaism or Christianity came into being. For it was through literature that the ideas were formulated, a self-understanding shaped and articulated, and then mediated to and appropriated by others, and through literature that people and ideas were included or excluded.[78]

To summarise: during the partings debate, methodological aspects of what history writing is have come to the fore. When describing rhetorical texts, or interpreting artifacts, the interpreter's context must be factored into the results. The modern debate concerning these questions also shapes our future understanding of groups, identity, and belonging. To write history is not a neutral enterprise, despite rigorous attempts from historians to be neutral. This does not imply that the endeavour of writing accurate history is, by definition, impossible; rather, it suggests that a comprehensive understanding of power relations (both ancient and modern) yields a more accurate picture.

Following this brief overview of the four main concerns in the parting of the ways debate, we now move on to the next section of the chapter, which addresses the institutional perspective.

---

[74] Lieu 2016, 21.
[75] Lieu 2016, 22.
[76] Lieu 2016, 21–22.
[77] Cf. Holmberg's reading of Lieu, Holmberg 2008, 6–11.
[78] Lieu 2016, 21–22.

3.2 The Institutional Perspective

These four concerns (theological, sociological, vocabular, and methodological) have been important when discussing the separation between Jesus followers and other Jewish groups. As of the last ten years, an institutional perspective might be added, which we now turn to discuss in some depth in a second part of the chapter. One is probably correct to say that this is actually a sub-category of the sociological concern mentioned above. However, since this perspective so important in the present investigation, it will be given special treatment. This part will have two divisions; first, a general background on voluntary associations and synagogues in antiquity, and after that, a lengthy discussion of the research history of relevant leadership.

One finding that runs through the critique of the early parting of the ways paradigm, as we have seen, is that the paradigm fails to account for everyday life because it is too busy with theological analysis. We have to remember, as Paula Fredriksen suggests, that the context of the texts provides key insights into how people related to each other, whether or not they saw each other as members of the same group.[79] In the context of the texts, it is most likely that the emerging Christ groups were institutionalised based on an existing Greco-Roman pattern, the voluntary association.[80] The Jewish diaspora synagogue was also moulded from this template. Research concerning Greco-Roman voluntary associations has increased significantly over the last twenty-five years.[81] This makes it reasonable to investigate further how theological and social patterns interacted in institutions, which is part of the main interest of this book.

3.2.1 Voluntary Associations

Research on the associations of the Greco-Roman world has surged in recent years: Richard Ascough notes that before 1998, only about a dozen books and articles were published on voluntary associations. By 2015, the number had increased at least sixfold.[82] Although the source material remains fundamentally

---

[79] Fredriksen 2003, 36.
[80] Runesson 2015b, 43–44.
[81] See for example Kloppenborg 2019; Ascough, Harland, and Kloppenborg 2013.
[82] Ascough 2015, 208.

the same, it has recently become more accessible through collection, translation, and publication by several leading scholars in the field. Notable among them are John Kloppenborg, Philip Harland, and the already mentioned Richard Ascough, who have all made the source material more accessible.[83] The source materials of associations are of several kinds: archaeological remains, inscriptions, literary material, papyri, etc.

How, then, does the associational perspective improve our understanding of ancient society? It provides us, first and foremost, with information about a social grid to which most ancient peoples were connected. One way of understanding the benefits of membership in an association is *connectivity*, which Kloppenborg expresses as follows.

> In antiquity ... identity was largely associated with the group or groups to which one belonged. Social capital flowed from those groups to individuals, and groups profited (or suffered) from the deeds (or misdeeds) of members. The value of connectivity is exemplified in a number of practices, from keeping and displaying lists; to holding common meals; to collecting funds, both for the group's activities and, in some instances, for other groups in an imagined fictive polity; to participating in the burial of members. These should not be treated simply as activities that the association decided to engage; they were instead the activities that constituted the group as a group. Eating together, participating in a subscription, engaging in processions, and attending the funeral of a colleague were ways of materializing connectivity and displaying the group to itself. These activities were not epiphenomenal but constitutive.[84]

Since the existing material from associations provides a glimpse into ordinary life in groups from the ancient Mediterranean region, it suggests the advantages of applying tools from the social sciences to the discourse. Thus, SIT's core objective of comprehending group identity as essential for the members' self-appreciation aligns well with the goals of understanding life in Christ groups.

On a general level, associations tended to mimic already existing structures from civic organisations or imperial structures. Yonder Gillihan wrote an important study, released in 2012, about the Qumran community's similarities to voluntary associations found throughout the Roman Empire.[85] Gillihan's

---

[83] Ascough, Harland, and Kloppenborg 2013, 1–2.
[84] Kloppenborg 2019, 345.
[85] Gillihan 2012.

study takes earlier research on voluntary associations further. It builds upon the general pattern discerned in the ancient world for how associations mimicked the functions and rites of the state.[86] This mimicking involved "terminology for rulers, cultic officials, legislative bodies, courts, deliberative councils, military units, and so forth."[87] The borrowing of terms (and hence authority) was something widely practiced in the first and second centuries CE, since "[s]uch adaptation was practical: state organization and law provided familiar, easily adaptable templates for the formation of new groups."[88] Therefore, in Athens, the names of the officials of an association were more likely ἐπιμελητής, ταμίας, and γραμματεύς, since state officials in Athens bore those titles.[89] This indicates that there is a great diversity in titles that do not always fit with the name of the group, but often fit with the name of the officials in the area or city it was located in.[90] Thus, the title of the main interest of this book, the ἐπίσκοπος, existed in several different kinds of voluntary associations, according to inscriptional evidence. Locally, in places like Thera and Delos, the ἐπίσκοποι "appear to be the officers in charge."[91] The fact that the title is mentioned in a few instances in the New Testament (see below in chapters 5 and 8) is thus not in itself enough to understand it as a coherent and well-defined office. The shift in New Testament studies over the past twenty years has increasingly focused on understanding the emergence of offices in the early church and Christ groups as a process viewed through the lens of social realities. This means the recent understanding of early church history is informed by social-scientific perspectives. This has not always been the case. Even if someone like Rudolph Sohm, who was a church historian who rather read back Christianity as an entity into the first century, was aware of the existence of, for example, voluntary associations, his understanding of the early church is primarily theological, and not local and sociological.[92]

---

[86] Gillihan 2012, 2.
[87] Gillihan 2012, 2.
[88] Gillihan 2012, 3.
[89] Kloppenborg 2015, 74.
[90] Kloppenborg 2015, 74.
[91] Kloppenborg 2015, 74.
[92] Sohm 1958, 4.

One can note that the term "association" is a scholarly term, an etic umbrella term for a wide range of fellowships with emic designations of themselves.[93] A common definition of associations in recent research is phrased as follows: associations in antiquity are groups of men and women "normally organized around a common ethnic identity, deity or cult, trade or profession, or neighbourhood, and are to be distinguished from civic organizations."[94] The question of definition has been an area of debate within the research field. Much effort has been put into the debate over whether synagogues should be defined as associations or considered *sui generis*. This also matters in the question of how to understand Christ groups. Ascough notes (as the first concern in the partings debate above describes) that there has been a tendency among some scholars to make too much out of the self-understanding ("theology") of the Christ groups.[95] The consensus has moved towards, if not yet completely, an understanding of (1) synagogues as a kind of association since this was the way synagogues were understood by outsiders and governors in the Hellenistic era, and simultaneously (2) Christ groups as resembling a synagogue (at least during the first century) and thus treated as such.[96] For these reasons, synagogues and Christ groups will be treated below as kinds of associations. This is the simplest way to understand a cult of divine character with a patron god in the Mediterranean region between 1 and 200 CE, which organised common meals, monetary collections, etc.

It would be intriguing to work from the assumption of a relationship from greater to lesser. The larger pattern of associations that mimic states also operates in the smaller context where a subgroup within a voluntary association (such as a Christ group within an associational synagogue in the diaspora) imitates the mother association. The thought has been discussed to some extent regarding the leadership question concerning the emergence of the ἐπίσκοπος. Since the Christ groups emerged within the first-century CE Jewish milieu, one would assume that the synagogue pattern would have been natural for the

---

[93] Harland 2014, 2
[94] Ascough 2015b, 27.
[95] Ascough 2015b, 47–48.
[96] Ascough 2015b, 37, 43.

Christ groups to adopt or borrow.⁹⁷ It is, however, hard to discern to what extent this occurred. I operate under the assumption that Christ groups first emerged within diaspora synagogues as sub-groups. As tensions grew regarding the membership of non-Jews, these Christ groups established their own organisations. It could be natural for these new groups to mimic the structure of the mother association and thus borrow some of its authority. To take a more modern example, this was what the Methodist movement in North America did when they appointed bishops: they borrowed the structure of the Anglican church to form a church with easily recognisable leadership. On the other hand, it does not necessarily follow that groups that are formed after tension in other groups would always mimic the organisation they left. One could also assume that they would select a system that shows the maximum distance to the former group. It is noteworthy that the leadership in the second-century Christ groups in the northeastern quadrant of the Mediterranean was centred around the ἐπίσκοπος, according to extant texts. The term ἀρχισυνάγωγος, for example, is not used as the name for the leader, which would possibly have signalled closer ties to the synagogue. The meaning of the terminology for leaders in the emerging Christ groups will be further discussed to some extent in chapter 4 below. It is however impossible to know exactly what occurred here, since we only have access to texts, and not the historical situation *per se*. It seems reasonable to assume, from an SIT perspective, that the structure (and therefore also the terminology) carries some meaning for the identity of the ingroup. An anti-Jewish rhetoric is extant in second-century Christ-group texts, which would suggest that large factions within the Christ groups displayed maximum difference from the synagogues rather than intimate closeness.

3.2.2 Synagogues and Jewish Associations in the First Century CE

There is a need for a short recapitulation of the state of the research in the evolution of the synagogue. This is crucial because one can note that recent research has highlighted the emergence of Christ groups as subgroups existing within the framework of synagogues.⁹⁸ A vast number of scholars have

---

⁹⁷ Cf. Burtchaell 1992, 283–84.
⁹⁸ Runesson 2015b, 51–52. Cf. Burtchaell 1991, 227.

researched the field. As well as in the larger field of associations in general, the last years have seen a boom in the field of synagogue research.[99] As noted by Runesson, Binder, and Olsson, by 2008, the field had grown significantly during the 21st century.[100] Even though some scholars since early modern times have researched the field, recent years have brought much clarification. Both new archaeological findings and the application of new methods and perspectives in interpreting known sources have been significant.[101] Overall, the perspective has shifted from an early modern view of the origins of the synagogue, which suggested that the beginnings could be traced back to the Babylonian exile.[102] Now, it is common to place the origins around Persian and Hellenistic times.[103] The end of the Second Temple period is a significant boundary mark in research, as the fall of Jerusalem in 70 CE marked a shift in power hierarchies within the Jewish communities.[104] After this shift, a new era in the lives of synagogue communities emerged. Certainly, the primary focus of this book relates to the post-70 climate in diaspora synagogues.

Also, significant clarification has been brought about in the development of methodology. Donald Binder noted in 1997 that earlier research tended to mingle sources from vast time periods and several places, thus creating an anachronistic and static view of ancient synagogues.[105] This practice has been abandoned for a significantly more diversified and contextualised analysis of synagogue evidence.[106]

Much of the discourse has been regarding definitions: Was the synagogue a public meeting place, or a place of liturgy/worship?[107] The public reading of the Torah allegedly initiated by Ezra and Nehemiah was previously seen as an

---

[99] Levine 2005, 11–17, Catto 2007, 10–14.
[100] Runesson, Binder, and Olsson 2008, 5.
[101] Runesson, Binder, and Olsson 2008, 6.
[102] Runesson 2001, 65. See also Kraus 1922, 65–72.
[103] Runesson 2001, 232–33.
[104] Binder 1997, 1–2.
[105] Binder 1997, 4–7.
[106] Cf. Catto 2007, 199.
[107] Levine 2005, 42–44.

origin of the synagogue ritual.[108] Torah reading has thus been a significant part of the discussion concerning the development of the institution.[109] It appears to be the case that Torah reading was a common denominator in the evidence from both the diaspora and the land in the first century CE.[110] This makes Stephen Catto conclude that even though there were diverse types of synagogues in the diaspora (see below), the common feature of the Torah reading among all synagogues (in the land and in the diaspora) was enough to produce a unified Jewish identity among different Jewish groups in various places.[111] In Judea, the local synagogue developed from the city gate into a building during the first century CE. This building would resemble a town hall in its function. As is well-attested in the sources, a town's official and semi-official businesses would have a prominent place in the synagogue, not only the Torah reading service. The synagogue would have also been a centre for Jewish life in the diaspora. Not only the worship dimension of communal life, but several others pertaining to the community's everyday life. The need for a complex to house the diaspora community became exigent, but the organisational form adopted was similar to some version of a voluntary association.[112]

It is worth remembering that the synagogue is a place for several important events in the New Testament (both in the Gospels and Acts). In the analysis of New Testament texts, the different settings for diaspora synagogues and the synagogues of the land need to be remembered.

> Behind the many terms for "synagogue" we find in the first century two basic kinds of institution: a local public civic institution on the one hand, existing where Jews were in administrative control in the land of Israel, and an association type of institution, i.e., a Jewish association, which could be found both in the Diaspora and in the land, on the other.[113]

---

[108] Runesson 2001, 123–27.
[109] Runesson 2001, 396.
[110] Runesson, Binder, and Olsson 2008, 7 (n. 14). See also Catto 2007, 116–25.
[111] Catto 2007, 200.
[112] Levine 2005, 44.
[113] Runesson 2015b, 49.

Thus, the diaspora setting significantly differs from the synagogues with which Jesus interacted.[114] Jesus seems to interact with the *public synagogues* – that is, the synagogues that had a public, political, as well as a religious function in the local community. Paul, on the other hand, interacted with diaspora synagogues, moulded on Greco-Roman association patterns. This distinction between public synagogues in areas where the majority of people were Jewish and voluntary association synagogues, primarily (though not exclusively) found in the diaspora, has come to be referred to as the "two-types approach" in recent scholarship.[115] The associational synagogue

> could assemble in public or private spaces and were membership-based, being formed primarily around various kinds of social networks, for example, shared occupations, social practices, neighbourhoods, geo-ethnic connections, or shared ideology, such as devotion to a particular cult or philosophy.[116]

The public synagogue of the land had a slightly different function, as a municipality and was a socio-religious centre of the Jewish town or village.

One can note that the second century is generally well-represented among synagogue sources. There are several archaeological remains, as well as literary evidence, for the institution during the time span of this study. While few archaeological pieces of evidence are attested to before 70 CE, the archaeological remains after that year are numerous.[117] Runesson concludes:

> The earliest architectural remains identified by a majority of scholars as synagogue buildings date from the 2nd or 1st century BCE. By the 1st century CE, in addition to the continued and increasing presence of architectural and inscriptional evidence, we find frequent mention of synagogues in literary texts, both Jewish and non-Jewish: Philo, Josephus, the New Testament, and Greco-Roman texts. Geographically, evidence from this time period come from most parts of the Mediterranean world, making a circle with

---

[114] Also note an early example in the research of the distinction, Hatch 1881, 58–59: "In other words, the same community met, probably in the same place, in two capacities and with a double organization."

[115] Cirafesi 2023, 682–87.

[116] Cirafesi 2023, 683.

[117] Levine 2005, 8–9.

Italy in the west, Hungary and the northern shores of the Black Sea in the north, Syria in the east, and Egypt and Libya in the south.[118]

Runesson, Binder, and Olsson mention four aspects of synagogue research that have been of certain interest, namely spatial aspects (archaeological issues, iconography, and art), liturgical aspects (the liturgical research was revolutionized by the discovery of the Cairo Genizah, Qumran texts, and the form-critical study of oral Jewish prayer),[119] social or non-liturgical aspects (the synagogue as a community centre resembling a municipality),[120] and institutional aspects (leadership factors and functions in society).[121]

Several scholars have noted that life in the diaspora synagogue was the centre of the social grid in which Jewish life was expressed.[122] In the definition of the diaspora synagogue, multiple factors are thus essential to cover.[123] It can, however, be argued that the most important point that defined the synagogue is the liturgy of publicly reading the Torah.

> The communal reading of Jewish Scripture was a characteristic feature of synagogue institutions during the Second Temple period. This was true for both public and association synagogues in the Second Temple period, in the Land as well as in the diaspora.[124]

As the evidence originates from both literary and inscriptional sources from different groups and locations, it is reasonable to assume that the reading of the

---

[118] Runesson 2010.

[119] Levine 2005, 11–13.

[120] See also Richardson referred in Ascough 2015a, 38. The community-shaping activities shows a broad resource centre for Jewish communities: "meals, education, and civil law."

[121] Runesson, Binder, and Olsson 2008, 7–9.

[122] Runesson 2001, 190–91.

[123] Runesson 2001, 81–82. Note also the "ironic reversal" during the Byzantine age, Levine 2005, 4: "With regard to the church, an ironic reversal took place between the first and seventh centuries CE. Whereas nascent Christianity drew heavily on religious and liturgical elements derived from contemporary Second Temple Jewish life, this trend was largely reversed after the ascendancy and dominance of the church in the Byzantine period, as Jewish life generally, and the synagogue in particular, began absorbing elements of contemporary Christian practice."

[124] Ryan 2017, 39. Ryan then lists the following instances of literary sources for of communal Torah reading: Acts 15:21; Josephus (*C. Ap.* 2.175; *A.J.* 16.43; *B.J.* 2.292); The Theodotos Inscription (CIJ 2.1404); and Philo (*Prob.* 80–83; *Leg.* 156).

Torah was a prominent feature of synagogues, regardless of where they were situated. While the study of the Torah is important for the synagogue in itself, this book focuses on the social and institutional aspects of the synagogue, with a special interest in leadership models. As we shall see, lately, the tendency has been to understand the diaspora synagogues as much more multi-faceted phenomena than *only* places of study.[125] Levine provides sources for the use of synagogues as meeting places, courts, charity centres, places of study, libraries, residences, and to meet individual needs.[126] While not all of these aspects necessarily existed in the same way everywhere, multiple pieces of literary and archaeological evidence provide insights that the diaspora synagogues contained several of these aspects during the late first and second century CE.

This communal aspect emphasises a development in the research from at least the early 2000s. Earlier, there was an understanding of Jewish synagogues and Christ groups as intrinsically exclusive, or sectarian compared to other groups. The views of, for example, John Elliot and Henry Maier suggest a strict separation by these groups from the rest of society.[127] The communal aspect of the synagogue, which also contextualises the group in terms of occupation and neighbourhood, suggests that the synagogue, as well as Christ groups, would be similar to most ancient associations.[128] Given the complex grid of social life in an ancient association and *polis*, a theological urge for separation from society was not easy to adhere to.[129] Much archaeological evidence suggests that the members of synagogues usually participated in the surrounding society on several levels, not least as members of certain guilds.[130] This is well attested, not least in inscriptional evidence.[131]

While there has been broad agreement on understanding the synagogue as a public institution in Galilee and Judea, and the diaspora synagogue as influenced by Greco-Roman associations, some tensions (or developments) exist in

---

[125] Runesson 2021, 40–42.
[126] Levine 2005, 390–411.
[127] Elliot 1990, 282–88. Maier 2002, 5–11.
[128] Harland 2000, 100. See also Harland 2003, 3.
[129] Harland 2000, 101.
[130] Harland 2000, 110.
[131] Harland 2000, 108.

synagogue research concerning the homogeneity of the institution in the second century CE.¹³² Not only does συναγωγή refer to building and congregation, but to several other features.¹³³ The evidence indicates that the institution, in fact, consisted of multiple different Jewish institutions, sorted under different networks such as occupation, cult, neighbourhood, or household.¹³⁴ Thus, the disparity of the institution was far greater than the single term "synagogue" might suggest. Nevertheless, the research concerning the synagogue shows great awareness of the synagogue as a community centre for Jewish life, both in the diaspora and as a kind of "town hall" in Galilee and Judea. Lee Levine understands the development as primarily communal before the destruction of the temple, while also having a religious dimension. As a result of the destruction of the Jerusalem temple in 70 CE, and under some influence of Greco-Roman associations, the religious dimension became more salient in the synagogue in the second century and onward.¹³⁵

No matter how one understands the emphasis of the religious dimension in the synagogues, the communal dimension is still constantly present, as can be seen in, for example, m. Ned. 5:5, which discusses what belongs to a town and what belongs to a pilgrim.¹³⁶ The synagogue is, in practice, a social meeting point that provides the spatial needs for a social identity. As such, the ethnicity of the members is of course crucial. Not least, Paul's insistence on the inclusion

---

¹³² Neatly summed up in the review article by Hørning Jensen 2019: "Levine argues that the synagogue evolved from the ancient-city gate and not as a substitution for the lost temple. For this reason, it served many functions such as a courtroom, school, hostel, meeting place, place for social gatherings, and more. Runesson accepts that the evidence also points toward a synagogue tradition that evolved under the influence of the Greco-Roman voluntary associations, which would have been more closed and analogous to clubs. However, Ryan argues that the bulk of the evidence of association synagogues stems from the diaspora, whereas the evidence from Galilee points in the direction of an open, public synagogue, as witnessed by the way in which Jesus could freely enter. There is also no indication that any of the known Galilean synagogues belonged to a certain Jewish group."
¹³³ Levine 2005, 1.
¹³⁴ Runesson 2021, 40–44.
¹³⁵ Levine 2005, 4. See also Binder 1999, 2–3.
¹³⁶ Levine 2005, 381.

of non-Jews into the ἐκκλησία was challenging for the Jewish institutions.¹³⁷ We now turn to this pressing point of membership and ethnicity in the synagogues.

3.2.3 Members of Diaspora Synagogues

The institutions in which the theological thinking of the early Jesus-followers developed were fundamentally based on already existing structures, which must be considered when, for example, discussing the boundaries of the groups. The next chapter will deal extensively with the research history of the institutional background of the emergent episcopal office. However, the view on membership in these existing structures must be considered when discussing the development of Christ groups. A crucial question is whether the institutions contained both gentile and Jewish Jesus followers, or just one of those groups. As for a general perspective,

> Jewish Associations were rarely exclusively Jewish in terms of the ethnicity of their membership. Just as non-Egyptians had found Isis a powerful deity and, accordingly, had begun to join her worship, non-Jews, in a similar process that removed ethnic requirements for participation, sought the benefits associated with what they believed to be a powerful deity, the God of Israel. This did not change when the Jesus movement entered the scene. As with other Graeco-Roman associations, then, we should envision associations honouring the God of Israel as their patron deity, with or without a Messiah, as mixed groups: Jews and non-Jews, slaves and free, men and women.¹³⁸

Runesson argues that the best way of understanding the texts in a socio-cultural context is that first- and second-century diaspora synagogues could contain different groups. He suggests that associational synagogues were formed around different common identities, such as occupational identity (for example, weavers), as well as locational identity (Jews living in a neighbourhood of a certain town).¹³⁹ This is reasonable, given our knowledge of voluntary associations in general.¹⁴⁰ In the diaspora, there would likely have existed non-Jewish members of Jewish groups with the God of Israel as patron deity if the group identity was formed around, for example, occupation. There were, however,

---

¹³⁷ Runesson 2022, 213–16.
¹³⁸ Runesson 2021, 43–44.
¹³⁹ Runesson 2021, 42.
¹⁴⁰ Ascough and Kloppenborg 2011, 1–4.

also exclusively non-Jewish Christ-worshipping groups in the early second century, according to Runesson.[141] These non-ethnic followers of Jesus developed an anti-Jewish rhetoric as the so-called Jewish Christ-believing groups became increasingly rare. The declining Jewish groups found themselves trapped between, on the one hand, non-Jewish Jesus-followers, a group growing in numbers, and other Jewish groups that, for different reasons, were hesitant to accept Jesus as the Messiah.[142] An example of such Jewish groups during the second century was the rabbinic movement (while the best sources are later, in the third century CE).[143] While we do not know the exact influence of the rabbinic movement on diaspora synagogues in general in the second century, the institutional separation between non-Jewish and Jewish Jesus followers in the diaspora appears to have already taken place.[144] Non-Jewish Jesus-follower groups and synagogues never belonged together in the first place and can, therefore, not part, according to Runesson's view.[145]

This makes it plausible to assume that an institutional separation occurred "quite early."[146] It is not to say that Jesus followers separated themselves from all synagogues at once in a synchronised action.[147] Rather, it is a question of who belonged to what association; non-Jewish Jesus followers in diaspora contexts seem to have formed their own groups quite early. Within these groups, boundaries against Jewish followers of Jesus observing halakah were drawn.[148]

---

[141] Runesson 2021, 49.

[142] Lightstone 2008, 317–18.

[143] This movement also engaged in the process of Jewish self-definition in which the canon and the authority from Moses played an important part, Cohen and Lapin 2022, 3. Much could be said about the rabbis in terms of SIT. It would be interesting to further investigate the rabbis as, for example, identity impresarios, but that is a topic for another book.

[144] Runesson 2021, 49.

[145] Runesson 2021, 51–52.

[146] Runesson 2022, 256. See also Runesson 2021, 47.

[147] See Cirafesi's well-argued paper that contextualises the process in Public Assemblies ("Synagogues in the land"), in Cirafesi 2023, 693–96.

[148] The classic thesis, that John 9:22 refers to the *birkat haminim* rests on the idea that the rabbis would have had the power over the liturgy in public synagogues at the end of the first century (Runesson 2021, 35–37). There are two problems with this assumption. First, it appears

The institutional separation, in which non-Jewish Christ followers formed their own institutions, while the Jewish synagogue remained an essentially ethnic association, was a process, according to Runesson, in two steps.

> Jesus-oriented Jews established associations in which the cultic component consisted of Christ-focused worship of the God of Israel. As the non-Jewish Christ-followers rose in number in such settings, we find further institutional separation, this time between Jewish and non-Jewish members of the Jesus movement.[149]

First, Jesus-oriented Jews formed groups into which other ethnicities would be welcomed. Second, if and when these groups started to contain more non-Jews than Jews, the tension between the members would make it reasonable to assume the initialising of a separation process. The institutional setting of Christ allegiance as beginning in a Jewish voluntary association does not necessarily mean that the members assumed a new religious identity. Runesson's point is that the separation process was within a religious sphere that can be labelled Judaism (note Runesson's repeated discussion on the matter of the name).[150] However, the literary evidence we have from non-Jewish Christ groups in the second century CE suggests that these groups both became increasingly institutionalised (as the emergence of an episcopal structure testifies to) and that this institutionalisation contained boundary settings against a salient Jewish identity.

---

that the rabbinic movement was too small to exercise that kind of influence at that time. Note the observation made by Levine regarding the reception of rabbinic rulings in Hammat Tiberias, some 150 years after the rulings of Mishna regarding prohibition against images were codified. "[T]he donors or artisans were indeed familiar with this [prohibition against images, in this case the issue regards the Helios depiction in Hammat Tiberias] law but, for whatever reason, chose to ignore it." (Levine 2011, 88). As Levine also notes on the same page, Tiberias is "the site of the most important rabbinic centre in fourth-century Palestine." Also, earlier evidence for one party controlling the public synagogue of the land is missing altogether (Levine 2005, 40–41, Runesson 2021, 36). Second, there have been notorious problems with the exact dating and interpretation of the *birkat haminim* (Runesson 2021, 35–36). Thus, the *public* synagogue of the land is not what was in scope in John 9:22. It is easier to understand an exclusion process from *some kind of associational synagogue,* which observed an exclusive halakah pertaining gentile inclusion.

[149] Runesson 2022, 256.

[150] Runesson 2022, 261–69, cf. Runesson 2008, 62–70.

This institutional discussion can be perceived even more clearly with the help of SIT. The theory can help us understand separation processes better, given the explicit interests of inter-group relations addressed by the framework. Institutionalisation can, in general, be understood as an embedding of the identity of a group that safeguards it from merely being an idea. Identity impresarioship (as we saw in the previous chapter) means that ingroup identity is embedded in an institution. As such, it takes a certain shape consistent with its identity and ideology/theology.[151] Thus, the roles of functionaries (and sometimes names) to some degree mirror the self-categorisation of the group, expressed as exigent in the group's ideology/theology. For example, the need for apostles and prophets in 1 Cor 12:28 is consistent with a theology of the apostles and prophets continuing the mission of Jesus. These functionaries embody the core beliefs of the Pauline Christ groups. The second part of this dissertation will further address the way Christ groups embed their identity in an episcopal structure.

3.2.4 The Leadership Structure

As a final part of the institutional perspective, we now turn to the research on the leadership structures in the synagogue, under two sub-headings. This topic is closely related to the next chapter, which reviews the standard understanding of the emergence of the episcopal office. Even though there might be some overlaps, the topic needs to be addressed in both chapters, since the different perspectives on the topics facilitate a more multifaceted view.

The ἐπίσκοπος, as leader of Christ groups, needs to be situated in relation to the different synagogue institutions. Already Vitringa, at the end of the seventeenth century, discerned a synagogical structure of the early church.[152] Edwin Hatch, on the other hand, understood the early church to be similar to *collegia*, or voluntary associations.[153] Adolf von Harnack, in the wake of the study of the newly rediscovered Didache, suggested the following.

---

[151] Holmberg 2008, 20–21, discusses how institutionalizing beliefs influences a person's cognition (from the perspective of Theissen, 1999). Theissen's semiotic understanding of the early Christ movement has several connections to what SIT would label as identity impresarioship.

[152] Bradshaw 2002, 192.

[153] Bradshaw 2002, 192.

[There were] two forms of leadership alongside one another in early Christianity: itinerant apostles, prophets, and teachers on the one hand; and congregationally elected bishops and deacons with administrative duties on the other, the latter eventually taking over the role of the former when the charismatic ministry disappeared, and a distinction then emerging between bishops and presbyters.[154]

Von Harnack's view, with different forms of leadership alongside one another, in one way still prevails; even though the details may differ, a view argued by later scholars is that the uniformity of the leadership structures was anachronistic. Rather, the idea has been that the leadership structures could be understood as working through different trajectories.[155] Paul Bradshaw states,

Rather than trying to force the New Testament and post-apostolic testimony to fit into one single mould, therefore, the evidence is better served by the presumption of the probable existence of varied patterns of leadership in different early Christian communities, and also of a variety of influencers in bringing those patterns about.[156]

The Jewish leadership structures are of particular interest, because local leaders would be closely connected to how groups lived their lives. They would be among the first to know if some sub-groups were leaving or trying to take over or other behaviours on the same note. The situation with leadership studies on ancient synagogues is that the source material concerning leadership within the synagogue is inconsistent in its terminology. Moreover, the sources consist of emic and etic material from different ancient Jewish groups. The sources on leadership, both literary and epigraphical, generally come from more than a thousand years (early Hellenistic period into Late Antiquity), and from the areas of Babylonia to Spain and Central Europe to North Africa. Many officials bear multiple titles without explanations regarding the terms' exact meanings. It is thus in general a hard task to speak of clear-cut titles in the synagogue.[157] The main interest in this book, however, is an institutional perspective on the parting of the ways debate, and the role of the emerging episcopal leadership in that parting. The source material that we need to deal with thus comes from

---

[154] Bradshaw 2002, 192–93.
[155] Bradshaw 2002, 194.
[156] Bradshaw 2002, 194.
[157] Levine 2005, 412–13.

the late first and second century from the northeastern quadrant of the Mediterranean world.

One title that keeps emerging in both literal and epigraphical evidence in the relevant period and region is the ἀρχισυνάγωγος.[158] In the next section, I will discuss more fully those sources and the research history of the use of the term ἀρχισυνάγωγος. There were, however, also other titles for the synagogue leadership. The ἄρχων is attested in epigraphical evidence from the areas of Rome and Asia Minor.[159] The *Pater Synagoges* is found in epigraphical evidence in Rome nine times.[160] The titles πρεσβύτερος and πρεσβύτερα are found in several places throughout the empire, not least in Asia Minor, though not in Rome.[161] The title γραμματεύς is found prominently in Rome and appears to have referred to some kind of secretary who was tightly connected to the administration or services of the synagogue.[162] Another title, whose exact nature is hard to understand, is the φροντιστής. It appears to be related to oversight of building projects, and appears also in verbal form in some inscriptions.[163] In the Tosefta, the חזן (ὑπηρέτης in Greek)[164] of the synagogue has a prominent role as overseer and distributor of readings, blessings, and prayers in the synagogue service.[165] The חזן is perhaps the most well-defined role in rabbinic literature, and is connected to prayer and reading of the Torah in the liturgical context. The role could also be connected to the teaching of children or other liturgical tasks.[166] The ἀρχισυνάγωγος has been suggested as a pattern from which the episcopal office was modelled and thus will be given extensive treatment. Also, the way that the

---

[158] Levine 2005, 417; Cirafesi 2023, 685: "the functionary mentioned most often both in and outside of the New Testament, the ἀρχισυνάγωγος."

[159] Lifshitz 1967 mentions the ἄρχων in inscriptions nos. 9; 11; 33; 85. Cf. Levine 2005, 427–29. Levine notes that in Lifshitz 33, the ἀρχισυνάγωγος and the ἄρχων are mentioned together.

[160] Noy 1993–1995 II:538.

[161] Levine 2005, 433.

[162] Levine 2005, 434; Noy 1993–1995 II:538.

[163] Levine 2005, 435; Lifshitz 1967, nos. 1; 2; Noy 1993–1995 II: no.540.

[164] Levine 2005, 447–49.

[165] Note that in Luke 4:20 when Jesus has read from Isaiah, he hands the scroll back to the ὑπηρέτης.

[166] M. Shabb. 1:3, The role is also discussing diverse tasks of the חזן in t. Meg. 3:21 and t. Sukkah 4:6. Levine 2005, 442.

ἀρχισυνάγωγος represents the synagogue congregations gives it a prominent place of interest.

3.2.5 The ἀρχισυνάγωγος

Since the ἀρχισυνάγωγος is characterised as a leader, particularly in the diaspora synagogues, and has been understood as the model that the ἐπίσκοπος is emulating, I will treat it at some length.

One significant question in the research on the synagogue leadership, is to what extent the ἀρχισυνάγωγος was a religious/spiritual leader or rather a patron and benefactor of the synagogue.[167] The perception of what the office entailed has evolved over the past forty years or so. Initially, scholarly consensus suggested that the ἀρχισυνάγωγος was a religious title. More recently, however, this perspective has shifted to view the ἀρχισυνάγωγος as an honorific title for a benefactor or the like. The first perspective relied prominently on the New Testament, as well as rabbinic sources. The second perspective relies primarily on epigraphical evidence and was in its first form pronounced by Tessa Rajak and David Noy in 1993.[168] An analysis of that evidence suggests that the ἀρχισυνάγωγος was primarily an honorific title. Even so, the ἀρχισυνάγωγος served as the spokesman for the synagogue. Furthermore, the ἀρχισυνάγωγος had power and money to promote the community's interests.[169] In the rabbinic sources, the ἀρχισυνάγωγος is always subordinated to the rabbi. The ἀρχισυνάγωγος also had few exclusive roles in the liturgy of the synagogue, the Mishnaic texts of Yoma[170] and Sotah[171] being rare exceptions. Thus, even if one takes literary evidence into consideration, not much of the spiritual leadership is prominent.

So what evidence is there for the title ἀρχισυνάγωγος during the first two centuries CE? The rabbinic material compiled in the Mishna (ca. 200 CE) and also the Tosefta[172] (ca 260 CE) is of some interest regarding the ראש הכנסת,

---

[167] Levine 2005, 415–16.
[168] Rajak and Noy 1993.
[169] Cf. the "all-encompassing" view of Levine 2005, 416–17.
[170] M. Yoma 7:1.
[171] M. Sotah 7:8.
[172] T. Meg. 3.

which is the Hebrew equivalent for ἀρχισυνάγωγος. It is likely that the material from the Mishna and Tosefta somehow addresses the situation of the second century or perhaps earlier.[173] The New Testament mentions the title in late first-century texts (gospels and Acts). In the middle of the second century, Justin Martyr briefly comments on the ἀρχισυνάγωγος in *Dial.* 137.2. In this comment, Justin appears to see the role of the ἀρχισυνάγωγος as a teacher, a representative of a synagogue, and as connected with the Pharisees. However, not much more *literary* evidence exists for the period. Other literary sources are too late: both Epiphanius (late fourth century) and Palladius (early fifth century) provide information about how the title is used but are too late to be useful for this investigation.[174] Thus, the evidence for a clearly religious role discernible in the fourth and fifth centuries is too late to take into consideration. After the time period this study discusses, one can find two instances from the Imperial Biographies in which Roman emperors mention the ἀρχισυνάγωγος; both instances concern the understanding from the fourth century of the ἀρχισυνάγωγος as representative of the synagogue, even with a religious role.[175] The Theodosian Code in the fifth century provides an understanding of the ἀρχισυνάγωγος as a religious functionary.[176] So the later general understanding of the ἀρχισυνάγωγος was a Jewish leader and religious functionary. While this appears to be the general direction of the office in more recent times, our period has little evidence for a liturgical role.

There are, apart from the New Testament and the rabbinic literature, also inscriptions regarding the ἀρχισυνάγωγος from the period. However, these sources provide little evidence of the exact nature and function of the ἀρχισυνάγωγος. Rajak and Noy comment on the epigraphs.

---

[173] Levine pushes the date to first century CE, Levine 2005, 420.

[174] Still, it is interesting that the Ebionites are said to have had names associated with Jewish practices: "Ebionites have elders and heads of synagogues, and they call their church a synagogue, not a church; and they take pride in Christ's name only." Epiphanius, *Pan.* 30.18.2. Translation found in Williams 2009, 145.

[175] *Life of Saturninus* 8.1–3 (SHA, III, 398–99); M. Stern, GLAJ, II, 637–38, *Life of Alexander Severus* 28.7 (SHA, II, 234–35); M. Stern, GLAJ, II, 630

[176] *Cod. Theod.* 16.8.4.

Much of the epigraphy consists of names of individuals, figuring in epitaphs or as donors, and those names often go with titles, not only that of archisynagogos, but also archon, gerousiarch, presbyter, father or mother of the synagogue, grammateus, phrontistes, and occasionally others. These evidently represent a spectrum of positions within the community.[177]

As mentioned above, they suggest that given the inscriptions found mentioning the title, the office of the ἀρχισυνάγωγος is by no means a clearly distinguishable liturgical office. Rather, the office is mentioned as an honorific title that did not even require Jewish ancestry to attain.[178] The inscriptions, in general, honour those who had donated money for building or renovation projects.[179] Indeed, Levine's comment on the debate about the office of the ἀρχισυνάγωγος is accurate; what view one holds of the function of the title-bearers is related to which sources one consults.[180]

One factor that increases the complexity of the matter is the already-mentioned confusing terminology. The ἀρχισυνάγωγος, seen through the inscriptions and the literary evidence, seems to be a leading benefactor and wealthy member of the society, with few explicitly liturgical roles. That definition, however, also fits other offices that are found in the sources, both literary and inscriptional. An example is the passage from Josephus, *B.J.* 2.285–92. Here, a conflict in Caesarea has arisen between a Jewish synagogue and an anti-Jewish mob. Proconsul Flores refrains from protecting the Jewish community from the mob that has desecrated the synagogue. Josephus mentions in this context a group of notables, οἱ δυνατοί, led by John the Tax collector (Ἰωάννης ὁ τελώνης, 2.287). These notables were intervening on behalf of the synagogue, complaining against Flores's unwillingness to react, even after having received eight talents of silver (2.292). Thus, even though the title ἀρχισυνάγωγος is absent, John the Tax collector stands up for the community and defends it. Likewise, in December of the year 55 CE, a stele was erected in Berenice, Cyrenaica, in honour of those donating to the repair of the synagogue. Out of eighteen

---

[177] Rajak and Noy 1993, 77.
[178] Noy and Rajak 1993, 88–89.
[179] See for example inscriptions Rome, Via Portuensis: CIJ 336; Ostia: JIWE I. 14; Teos: CIJ 744.
[180] Levine 2005, 416.

legible names, ten carry the title ἄρχων.¹⁸¹ In other words, there is obviously evidence that shows that functionaries with other titles in the synagogue were advancing the community's interests, which as multiple inscriptions show, is also something that the ἀρχισυνάγωγος does.

As mentioned above, one way of understanding the relation between the Christ groups and the synagogue is that the Christ groups mimicked the synagogue patterns when the Christ groups became institutionalized. Of certain interest is Burtchaell's thesis that the Christ assemblies were using Jewish language for their institutions and functionaries, but not the language of the "mainstream" synagogue.¹⁸² Burtchaell notes how the Essene and Therapeutic fellowships tend to do the same: They use terminology within the biblical spectrum but are separated from other synagogues.¹⁸³ Burtchaell also claims that even though the terminology of the leadership differed in, say, the Essene community, the leadership role was basically the same. The מבקר of the Essene community was supposed to teach the congregation from the Law, control recruitment, examine and train novices, control financial transactions, preside in presbyterial meetings, and hear grievances.¹⁸⁴ Burtchaell's reconstruction of a synagogue fellowship equates the roles of the ἀρχισυνάγωγος with those of the מבקר. He then presses the point that in several Jewish sects, one can perceive a pattern: the titles of the notables, the community leader, and the elders are slightly changed, even though the basic assumption of the roles of these title-bearers stayed the same. Even more, the Jewish sects tend to "avoid ... whenever possible ... the official names the other groups had selected as theirs."¹⁸⁵ The pattern of the early church was also that the term ἐπίσκοπος gathered different

---

¹⁸¹ See also closely related examples of someone honoured for services to the community. For example the ἄρχοντες of a Jewish community (πολίτευμα) in Berenice, Macedonia, honoured Decimus Valerius Dionysius for his work with the plastered floor of the communal amphitheatre, Runesson, Binder, and Olsson 2008, 163–64.
¹⁸² Note here Runesson's discussion on how disparate the phenomena of the diaspora synagogue were during the first and second centuries, Runesson 2021, 39–44.
¹⁸³ Burtchaell 1993, 277–84.
¹⁸⁴ Burtchaell 1993, 269.
¹⁸⁵ Burtchaell 1993, 283.

titles as a collective name, such as president, shepherd, or even elder.[186] In Burtchaell's view, the title ἀρχισυνάγωγος was too closely associated with the synagogue. He adds,

> This characteristic process whereby a variety of terms gives way to one; the one is converted from a generic descriptor or title; and the title is selected so as to differentiate the group from rival groups: all this is very traditional in Judaism and betokens continuity more than it does innovation.[187]

The Christ groups, in their choice of titles, are in other words showing their connection to Jewish Scriptures, in the same way the Essenes or the Therapeutes did. Burtchaell, then suggests that the vocabulary of the early church simultaneously signalled continuity and discontinuity with the synagogue. There was continuity in the sense that several Jewish groups chose not to use the terminology of the mainstream synagogue, and thus the Jesus movement (ἐκκλησία) with their ἐπίσκοποι (compared to ἀρχισυνάγωγοι) were choosing to use similar functions that existed in the synagogue, but with other names. There was discontinuity with the synagogue because they did not choose to name the movement "synagogue." A problem with this reconstruction is the conjecture; where no sources are available, Burtchaell fills the gaps with sources from ideologically different groups such as the Essenes. The fact that we have some sources on the מבקר does not mean that these sources can fill the silence from the lack of evidence regarding the role of the ἀρχισυνάγωγος of, say, the second-century diaspora synagogues of Asia Minor. Levine labels the reconstruction as "artificial and speculative."[188]

All this suggests that a simple one-to-one comparison with the clearly liturgical leader/officer ἐπίσκοπος that we can find in Christian literary sources from the second century is not uncomplicated. The comparison between ἐπίσκοποι and ἀρχισυνάγωγοι does not hold, however, since the sources suggest that the offices had different functions in different communities.

---

[186] Burtchaell 1993, 283.
[187] Burtchaell 1993, 283–84.
[188] Levine 2005, 417. While this is undoubtedly the case, some level of conjecture is inevitable in the reconstruction of the second-century Christ groups, for example Runesson 2001, 308–9.

3.3 Conclusion

Throughout this chapter we have seen how the parting of the ways debate has addressed the questions of the relationship between Judaism/synagogues and Christ groups in the second century. The debate has concerned theology, sociology, vocabulary, and methodology. While the literary sources from the second century show a theological turn of demarcation from the Christian and Rabbinic sources, the meaning of this demarcation has been debated, not least because archaeological and literary sources betray an ever-present contact between the groups even after mutual theological demarcation lines are drawn. The power balance between different second-century groups has been of particular interest for historians of the parting of the ways, as well as an insight into how historical enterprises always are contextual.

The institutional perspective, which has drawn on findings from the study of voluntary associations, synagogue research, and investigations of the leadership structures of second-century synagogues, has advanced our understanding of this era as a multi-faceted time in which various groups provided competing visions of what it meant to be a Jew or a Christian. The ἀρχισυνάγωγος is viewed in this context as an honorific promoter of group interests, as well as a boundary setter for his community. However, apart from the dismissed comparison between the ἀρχισυνάγωγος and the ἐπίσκοπος made by Burtchaell, no substantial analysis has been offered regarding how the emerging episcopal office influenced the relationship between the Christ groups and the synagogue. As discussed in this chapter, the institutional perspective provides new insights into how human institutions develop and influence ingroup identity. This viewpoint – that institutions carry identity-defining aspects – needs further development. Aspects of social identity are interlinked with the formation of institutions, as institutions and structures hold significance for and embed group identity. Within the diverse landscape of second-century Christ groups, the meaning-carrying developing structures require special attention, so that we can enhance our understanding of how institutions shaped Christian identity. As noted in this chapter, the ongoing debate thus far lacks this perspective.

After this review of the parting of the ways-debate, research on voluntary associations, and research on the synagogue, we now turn to a review of the standard view of the emergence of the episcopal office, before we turn to this book's actual investigation: how an emerging leadership structure informs Christian self-definition.

4. The Standard View of the Emergence of the Episcopal Office

Before I turn to an extensive review of sources and the development of the episcopal office, I must briefly address the word "office," which is used here and in scholarly discourse. The sociologist Pierre Bourdieu defines the term *office* as the end product of a sociological process in which religious experts monopolise the distribution of religious goods.[1] This definition can be found lingering in the notion of the routinization of charisma, which is prominent in the Protestant perspective on the evolution of the episcopal structure. The term *office* can also be somewhat broad, denoting the appointment, authority, and responsibilities of a specific officer within a more or less hierarchical framework. When *office* is used in this book, I mainly mean the latter, unless otherwise specified. It is important to note, however, that this idea suggests a certain degree of organisation. The institutional perspective that I will discuss in this chapter suggests that the congregations existed within some kind of framework that provided, among other things, an initial pattern of leadership.

This chapter has four aims. First, I present a short recapitulation of the earliest sources of the episcopal office. Second, I delineate an overview of the prevailing consensus regarding the genesis of the episcopacy, as recognised within prominently Protestant and scholarly circles from the 16th century and onward. Third, I probe certain unresolved issues that carry particular relevance to the current study. This includes the interrelation between the terms ἐπίσκοπος and πρεσβύτερος, which has been much contested over the years. It also includes the question of whether the beginnings of the episcopal office can be traced to Judaic or Greco-Roman antecedents. Fourth, after summarising these

---

[1] Cf. Bourdieu 1991. For further discussion, see below.

findings I will situate this present work in the research history. The social identity perspective described in the second chapter above will, in a novel way, show how leadership structures convey meaning for group identity. As we shall see, this is significant for understanding the separation of Christ groups and synagogues.

4.1 Sources and Early Development of the Episcopal Office

Throughout this book, we will primarily delve deeper into the texts of the second century CE. It is important to remember that the texts to which we have access provide a snapshot of the role of the ἐπίσκοπος within a specific group or coalition of groups. Consequently, it is challenging to make broad claims based on singular texts, which often have notably unknown contexts.[2] Recent developments in the research on voluntary associations have provided a backdrop for the reconstruction of the leadership structures of the early church/ Christ movement, which might help scholars gain new insights into early offices. Several inscriptions, as we shall see subsequently, reveal how associations from different parts of the Mediterranean area appointed or mentioned an ἐπίσκοπος for a certain role. The reconstruction must, however, to some extent be based on conjectures since inscriptions and literary evidence are scattered around large areas and over a long period.

The earliest sources relevant for the discussion of the emergence of the Christian episcopal office are found in the New Testament, with Philippians (about 60 CE), followed by 1 Peter (90–100), followed by Acts (about 110), and the Pastoral Epistles (120–135). Contemporary with the later New Testament texts are the ones that stem from the so-called Apostolic Fathers, in which the Ignatian letters are most prominent in regard to the episcopal office (160–175, see chapter 9), because the author provides a theological (that is, ingroup ideological) description of the role of the ἐπίσκοπος. However, Didache (around

---

[2] One can note the pedagogical article by Koch 2010. In this article, Koch presents a reading of the New Testament and Apostolic Fathers based on generation in the Christ groups, and geography. Koch situates every text, such as Acts, the Pastoral Epistles, and Ignatius along these lines, but sometimes relies too heavily on conjecture (for example in his dating of 1 Peter on the basis on a large persecution in Asia Minor in second decade of the second century, 186–88).

110) and 1 Clement (around 120), as well as the Shepherd of Hermas (around 110–140) are also important sources for the different stages of the development of the episcopal office. Around 180, Irenaeus discusses the role of the ἐπίσκοπος as a remedy for what he identifies as heresies. I will provide reasons for my dating of the texts in each respective chapter.

These earliest sources have all been referenced in later discussions about office and order in the early church, and many slightly younger sources, such as the church orders from the third century, utilise these earliest sources as prooftexts. Thus, there appears to be an early reception of texts regarding leadership functions. Already during the second century, several sources suggest that the office of the ἐπίσκοπος was understood as a warrant for apostolic faith. This can be found most prominently in the Ignatian letters or Irenaeus's *Haer.* 3.3.1–3.[3] An author whose texts are lost but have been reconstructed and who appears to have opted for similar ideas is Hegesippus (second century). It is generally understood that his ideas have been preserved and further developed in Epiphanius's *Panarion* (*Pan.* 27.6, late fourth century).[4] The concept of the episcopal office as a foundation for apostolic faith would logically culminate in the synodal practice, where bishops from major cities convened to discern orthodox theology and practice.[5] Closely associated with the development of the episcopal office was the emergence of church orders at the close of the second century and the beginning of the third.[6] These church orders are notoriously difficult to account for in terms of tradition and provenance. One example might suffice: the *Apostolic Tradition* of Hippolytus has been much debated regarding its provenance. The traditional view that Hippolytus wrote the *Apostolic Tradition* in Rome has been challenged since the headings and subtitles of the work appear to be later. Also, incoherencies, doublets, lack of unity, and so

---

[3] Eusebius probably used the collection of names gathered by Hegesippus. For a lengthier treatment, see Eurell 2022, 148–57

[4] McGuckin 2017, 984–85.

[5] McGuckin 2017, 987–88.

[6] The *Did. apost.* uses material from the Shepherd of Hermas and the Ignatian letters in the beginning of the third century. The composite text in turn becomes later, sometime in the fourth century, picked up by and incorporated in the Const. ap. 1–6. See McGuckin 2017, 980–81 for an overview.

forth occur throughout the document. This suggests that the *Apostolic Tradition* cannot be a single-author text.[7] Thus, Bradshaw, Johnson, and Philips conclude that the *Apostolic Tradition* is a composite work representing no actual early church tradition but an ideal perceived by the compilers.[8] This could account for the similarities with the Didache (see chapter 7). Bradshaw and others "judge the work [*Apostolic Tradition*] to be an aggregation of material from different sources."[9] The difficulty of associating a certain text with a certain author from a certain time applies to several of these church orders. However, the compilation process of church orders in the early third century testifies to a concern for a better-defined structure in the circles from which the texts stemmed. In the fourth century, another church order, *The Apostolic Constitutions* opts for an understanding in line with the earlier view in Ign. *Magn.* 7:6 where the ἐπίσκοπος presides as God, and the πρεσβύτεροι gather around him as the apostolic council.[10] Several third- and fourth-century texts testify to the reception and development of the ideas of second-century authors regarding the role of the ἐπίσκοπος. To provide some context for this dissertation, I will briefly glimpse the development up to 500 CE.

By the third century, the roles of the ἐπίσκοπος, πρεσβύτερος, and διάκονος are possible to discern as broadly recognised church offices (appointment in a hierarchical structure, with certain tasks and a given authority), which makes it reasonable to use the titles bishop, priest, and deacon from around then. If and to what extent this is an expression of clerical monopolisation, as Bourdieu understands it, is open for debate.[11] Due to lack of space, this dimension cannot be further explored, but there seems to be a connection between the embedding of Christian group identity into the emerging episcopal structure (impresariship) as found in the second-century texts and Bourdieu's understanding of the clerical order as a systematisation and moralization of religious practices and myths.[12]

---

[7] Bradshaw 2000, 8–9.
[8] Bradshaw, Johnson, and Philips 2002, 13–15.
[9] Bradshaw, Johnson, and Philips 2002, 14.
[10] McGuckin 2017, 981.
[11] Bourdieu 1991, 9; Torjesen 2008, 389.
[12] Bourdieu 1991, 8.

Rank was an important topic to discuss in the third to fifth centuries CE. The Ignatian letters provide a vision (see chapter 9 below) in which the ἐπίσκοπος is superior to πρεσβύτεροι and διάκονοι. Other authors further discuss this in subsequent centuries. A general way to summarise the development is that during the third century, the bishop sent the priests under his supervision from the city into village congregations, where they preached and celebrated the eucharist.[13] The deacons stayed as "special episcopal attendants."[14] This suggests that the bishop became emphasised as a role during the third century, as the bishop remained at the centre while dispatching lower-rank officials out from it. The prestigious great cities with their episcopal sees gave a monarchical flavour to the bishop during the third century and onwards, since great power invested in the leader was helpful in relation to city officials.[15] Cyprian of Carthage connected the episcopal function with the high priest in the Hebrew Bible. Here, a distinction in rank is perceivable: Cyprian understood the bishop as equal to the high priest, while the presbyters/priests were lower in rank.[16] On the other hand, Jerome, in the late fourth or early fifth century, writes that the ἐπίσκοπος and πρεσβύτερος share the same office, while deacons are "mere servers of tables."[17] He uses several New Testament proof texts, such as Acts 6:1–2, Phil 1:1–2, Titus 1:5–7, and 1 Tim 4:14. A similar understanding is also found in Jerome's contemporaries John Chrysostom (while he holds deacons higher than Jerome did),[18] and Theodore of Mopsuestia.[19] While this reading of the New Testament sources was recognised, the emperor Constantine elevated the bishops to magisterial rank in the fourth century, which also improved the bishops' possibilities for higher education. This in turn consolidated the power

---

[13] Concerning the priests as episcopal "envoys," see McGuckin 2017, 982.

[14] McGuckin 2017, 982.

[15] McGuckin 2017, 983–84.

[16] Cyprian of Carthage, *Epist.* 3; *Epist.* 63.14.

[17] Jerome, *Epist.* 146, *nam cum apostolus perspicue doceat eosdem esse presbyteros, quos episcopos, quid patitur mensarum et uiduarum minister, ut super eos se tumidus efferat, ad quorum preces Christi corpus sanguisque conficitur? quaeris auctoritatem?*

[18] John Chrysostom, *Hom. Phil.* 1:1.

[19] Theodore of Mopsuestia, *Commentary on 1 Timothy*, 3. See also further Ambrosiaster, *Commentary on Ephesians*, 4:11; *Commentary on 1 Timothy*, 3:10.

of bishops in society.[20] It is thus reasonable to conclude that during the fourth and fifth centuries, the instances of ἐπίσκοπος and πρεσβύτερος in the New Testament and in the second-century sources were seen as somewhat synonymous.[21]

After the beginning of the fourth century, episcopal synods became increasingly common. Anthony McGuckin holds that the regulations for ordained ministry (bishops, priests, deacons) became more detailed, both pertaining to standards (moral and intellectual) and pertaining to church order.[22] This development went hand in hand with a perceived separateness of the clergy, which reminded of cultic purity. The distinction between the ordained and laymen was emphasised. Simultaneously, this early form of Christian priesthood was not perceived as changing the inherent character of the priest, as distinct from the debate around the Reformation. Rather, the works of Gregory the Theologian, John Chrysostom, and Gregory the Great suggest that the exemplarity of the ministers is of utmost importance. This exemplarity suggests that the ministers have the nature of any Christ follower and that the existence of non-exemplary leadership was a possibility that the sources would prefer to avoid.[23]

To conclude: certain New Testament texts and some texts of the Fathers discuss leadership structures. The emerging episcopacy was understood as a warrant for apostolic faith by several early authors from the second century and onwards. The compilation of church orders from the early third century and onwards are examples of an urge for better-defined structures and can be seen as a reception and development of earlier sources. Also, during the third century the terms ἐπίσκοπος and πρεσβύτερος in the New Testament are treated somewhat synonymously (as part of the same function), with the ἐπίσκοπος sending out πρεσβύτεροι from a central city to surrounding villages. The idea to understand the bishop as a high priest, modelled on a Hebrew Bible template, is found in Cyprian of Carthage. From the fourth century onwards,

---

[20] McGuckin 2017, 990.

[21] So Mounce 2000, 189.

[22] McGuckin 2017, 981.

[23] Gregory of Nazianzus, *Orat.* 2; John Chrysostom, *Sac.*; Gregory the Great, *Pastoral Rule*. (1.10 especially).

episcopal synods became more common and regulated the clergy in greater detail. In this process, the clergy is perceived as separated from the laity.

4.2 Research History and a Consensus

To establish what role the ἐπίσκοπος had in the process of second-century identity formation, it helps to review the research history of the emerging church, since this research also discusses the episcopal office at length. Different views have been advocated regarding the role of the ἐπίσκοπος in the second century. Of course, the material is vast and comes in different colours, depending on matters like church politics and denominational aspects. Additionally, throughout the twentieth century the significance of the episcopal office in contemporary ecclesial debates has played a substantial role.[24] The role of the World Council of Churches and the ecumenical movement spurred great interest in, for example, the second-century view of apostolic succession.[25] However, even though the episcopal office has been debated with regard to its origins (Greco-Roman or Jewish), it has neither been investigated from an SIT

---

[24] Note the comment by Alistair Stewart, that one of the most prominent proponents of the view that that ἐπίσκοπος and πρεσβύτερος were the earliest offices was J. B. Lightfoot: "Lightfoot himself no doubt had some role in establishing the 'fact' in the Anglophone world, not the least in that he was an Anglican and in time would become a bishop himself. In the history of the study of church order one constantly finds explicit or implicit statements of the author's own fundamental convictions and of the direct ecclesial interest motivating the work." Stewart 2014, 12–13. Note also Burtchaell 1991, 101.

[25] Burtchaell 1991, 137. See also p. 101: "It was the new ecumenical movement that was to put the consensus under new challenge. The legitimacy of officers, and in particular of episcopal succession from the apostles, was now to be defended not merely by Catholics who were the traditional and distant (and controlling) adversaries, but by Anglicans who, as also rooted in the sixteenth-century break from Rome, and now amicable partners with the Protestants, Lutheran and Reformed, in the convergence of the ecumenical movement, deserved a more considerate reply to their criticisms. But then they in turn became embroiled in heated debate with their British neighbours, Presbyterian and Congregationalist and Methodist, over the matter of bishops. Although Scripture and the Fathers were quoted and interpreted fastidiously during the early years of this century, the conclusions one drew were very severely governed by one's theological loyalties on the matter of apostolic succession."

perspective nor studied in-depth regarding its relationship to a process of distancing the Christ group from a Jewish identity.

Much of this chapter discusses a consensus that emerged in the nineteenth century, which did not have access to all our current sources. Further, research on synagogue patterns and voluntary associations has developed significantly in the last twenty-five years or so. As a concrete example, shortly after Edwin Hatch, the once-lost Didache was discovered and published by Philotheos Bryennios. The distinct emphasis on itinerant teachers and prophets in the Didache was somewhat confusing for the debate on the organisation of the earliest congregations. In the wake of the study of the newly rediscovered Didache, Adolf von Harnack suggested that there were two parallel forms of leadership: itinerant apostles, prophets, and teachers on the one hand and local bishops and deacons on the other.[26] Von Harnack's view prevailed to some extent: even though the details may differ, later scholars viewed the uniformity of the leadership structures as an anachronism. Leadership structures come in different shapes.[27] This did not stop the scholarly discussion from debating the role of the ἐπίσκοπος, διάκονος, and πρεσβύτερος in relation to each other; suggestions were made that the older ἐπίσκοπος was merely supervising the younger διάκονοι, since the titles seem to be intimately connected, while the evidence is inconclusive regarding which of the officers did what.[28]

The works of Hatch, Lightfoot, and later von Harnack are still important pillars for subsequent works on episcopal structures. As we shall see, however, the question of the role of the officers is intimately connected to the question of the routinization of charisma, which I will discuss at some length in chapter 7 and also below in this chapter. As we shall also see, the routinization schema applied by von Harnack and others presupposes a law-bound chain of events that eventually resulted in the episcopal office. This betrays a certain view of the process of charismatic leadership and episcopal officers as necessarily binary options. I will now briefly summarise the Christian offices' research history, in which the routinization of charisma plays a vital part.

---

[26] Von Harnack 1884:88–151.
[27] Von Harnack 1884, 194.
[28] Burtchaell 1991, 84.

4.2 Research History and a Consensus

The debate regarding the New Testament and Early Christian leadership structures has gone on for several centuries and has been surrounded by Church politics. In 1928, when the debate was already centuries old, Burnett Streeter commented dryly,

> For four hundred years theologians of rival churches have armed themselves to battle on the question of the Primitive Church. However great their reverence for scientific truth and historic fact, they have at least hoped that the result of their investigations would be to vindicate Apostolic authority for the type of Church Order to which they were themselves attached.[29]

The many centuries of debate have resulted in an almost unsurmountable number of investigations regarding the emergence of the episcopal office. Shortly after Streeter, in 1932, Olof Linton wrote that the material concerning early Christian leadership was in fact, so vast that it would suffice to review the works from the prior fifty years.[30] James Burtchaell uses 135 pages to describe the Christian leadership debate until the early twentieth century.[31] It is a very thorough review and well worth the time to gain an overarching perspective of the vast material. However, a consensus came out of that debate among (mainly Protestant) scholars about how the early Christ groups developed an episcopal structure that can be described as follows, in Stewart's words.

> The foundation of the consensus is that *episkopoi* and *presbyteroi* were the earliest offices in the church. The terms, however, according to the consensus, were synonymous and interchangeable because every local church was originally under the direction of a group of persons, a collegial leadership deriving from the synagogue (from which the title "presbyters" derived). From this group ... grew an individual leader. Although frequently manifested in the nineteenth and twentieth centuries, this picture seems to have originated in the seventeenth century and subsequently to have become the fundamental assumption from which further explorations departed.[32]

Below, I will give an overarching outline of the long debate.

In the general consensus, the idea of a mono-episcopate or monarchical episcopate is considered not to be original and apostolic but a rather late

---

[29] Streeter 1928, viii.
[30] Linton 1932, 3.
[31] Burtchaell 1991, 1–136.
[32] Stewart 2014, 6.

development.³³ I follow Stewart's definition of the mono-episcopate ("mone-piscopate" in the terminology of Stewart), defined as "an [ἐπίσκοπος] exercising leadership over several Christian communities with subordinate ministers in those communities."³⁴ This is what by some is called monarchical episcopate. One can compare to Torjesen's views in 2008 in which mono-episcopacy is where a single episcopal officer allegedly controlled the full ministry of the house congregations in a city, from teaching to distribution of financial aid. According to Torjesen, this turned into a monarchical episcopacy in which "house churches were welded into a single socio-political body within a city, under the authority of the bishop who co-ordinated the ministries within the city through a hierarchy of clerical offices."³⁵ The difference lies in the *degree* of authority given to the bishop, and the extent of the hierarchical framework, and not in any important way in the *kind* of authority. These views (Stewart's and Torjesen's) differ from the definition offered by Georg Schöllgen, who understands mono-episcopate as referring to one bishop exercising leadership in one congregation.³⁶ The difference would be that Torjesen and Stewart understand the bishop as leader over several small house congregations, while Schöllgen sees the mono-episcopate as one bishop who leads only one congregation.

The mono-episcopate, as we shall see, is generally understood to have developed during the late second or early third century. This reconstruction by Protestant theologians was accompanied and sometimes driven by a view of an egalitarian ideal in the Jesus movement. The egalitarian ideal can be summarised as charisma being the primary leadership function, gradually becoming replaced by a hierarchical structure, the mono-episcopate, mirroring a proto-Catholicism shunned by Protestants.³⁷ Thus, Burtchaell summarises what he understands to be the view (albeit with some difference in emphasis) of both German-speaking and English-speaking scholars as follows:

---

³³ See Stewart's discussion on the terminology, Stewart 2014, 3–4.
³⁴ Stewart 2014, 3.
³⁵ Torjesen 2008, 398.
³⁶ Schöllgen 1986, 146–51.
³⁷ Burtchaell 1991, 136.

The polity of the primitive church was essentially egalitarian. Though ministers might preside, they had no headship or hierarchy of rank. The power of the keys, to bind and to loose, was given to the community, not to its officers. Thus the rights of governance did not belong to the clergy. The polity was also congregational. No church authority was superior to another. Ultimate authority was vested, not in a primatial see, but in a representative synod. The ancient rite of laying-on of hands was of apostolic origin and hence desirable. Since however it had been an essential component of the corrupt claims of Catholics to ritually transmitted legal status and authority, it might be discontinued, and thus it need not be considered essential.[38]

Reading the early Christian history in the Protestant movements could have local variations on this theme.[39] The ecumenical movement rekindled the debate in the twentieth century because of an emergent interest in apostolic succession. Parts of the Anglican church played a major role in their interest in understanding their own movement as being in communion with the Roman Catholic church.[40]

The main idea, both in early examples of the consensus, such as the so-called first church historian of the Protestants, Gottfried Arnold (1666–1714) and in later versions, such as Max Weber (1864–1920), who was much indebted to von Harnack,[41] was the transfer from charismatic authority into a "hierocratic organization."[42] From his earlier perspective, Arnold understood the episcopal office as one that permitted free preaching, where the highest authority was not located within any papal see, but rather each bishop held the highest authority within his own jurisdiction. This authority was not given by an organisation's

---

[38] Burtchaell 1991, 35.

[39] Two poles were salient in the Protestant discussion; on the one hand inner charisma (opted for by for example the Quakers) and on the other hand the view of for example the Scottish church, that in 1578 understood the word of God as providing a structure, *Second Book of Discipline*, chapters 3–4. See Kirk 1980, 178–84 for text.

[40] Burtchaell 1991, 101. Stewart notes Lightfoot's interesting role here; while Lightfoot understood the term ἐπίσκοπος and πρεσβύτερος as interchangeable (see below), he was also a part of the Anglican church, which claimed catholicity and apostolic succession. Stewart 2006, 12–13.

[41] The influence of von Harnack is also intimately connected to that of Weber, since Weber relied on von Harnack in his sociological analysis of charismatic leadership. Thus, to rely on Weber as proof of von Harnack's theses is a clear example of circular argumentation. See Burtchaell 1991, 138.

[42] Burtchaell 1991, 138; Weber 1968, 3–62; 212–301; 399–634, 1111–66.

central, hierarchical head (in this case, a pope), but rather by an episcopal council of equals.[43] Like many others, Arnold understood the second century as a pivotal time for the episcopal office. During this century, according to Arnold and several others, the church went from a fraternal organisation authorised by the office-holder's zeal and spiritual power, where the interchangeable titles πρεσβύτερος and ἐπίσκοπος spoke of a spiritual brotherhood, to a highly hierarchical mono-episcopate,[44] with a never-ending pursuit of rank and honour.[45] A main concern in the debate at this point was the jurisdiction of the churches. In general, the consensus has favoured a congregational view in contrast to an overarching ecclesial structure (which would have been too similar to a Catholic structure).[46] Several works from Protestant circles at the turn of the twentieth century share these views.[47]

Furthermore, part of the debate has been intimately related to the emerging church's relationship with its Jewish ancestors. The Protestant view understood the Jewish legacy as legalistic, while the congregations championed by Paul came with a theology of grace.[48] The emergence of a growing church structure would, in this Protestant view, signify a fading charismatic leadership, coined as the routinization of charisma, and a legalistic governing by ecclesial leaders (mirroring Protestant views on the Roman Catholic church). Even if this was not the only way Protestant scholars understood the ecclesial development in the first centuries, it was certainly the most prominent view.[49]

On a sociological level, a distinction between laity and clergy, which also is at play in the description of early church history, has gained some interest.[50] Pierre Bourdieu suggests that the emergence of this distinction arises from the

---

[43] Arnold 1731:2, 1–5.
[44] In this process, however, Arnold does not understand a character like Ignatius to be the villain, since he thinks a full-blown power-hungry hierarchy evolved only by the age of Constantine, Burtchaell 1991, 51.
[45] Arnold 1731, 2:6–20.
[46] See for example von Weizsäcker 1895 2:314.
[47] Sanday 1887, 110. Sohm 1909, 27. See also Sabatier 1904.
[48] Burchaell 1992, 100, 102–3.
[49] See for example von Weizsäcker 1894–95.
[50] Bourdieu 1991, cf. Torjesen 2008, 389.

need for systematisation and moralization of religious practices in developing religions.⁵¹ This leads, however, to the monopolisation of religious practices by the clergy.⁵² The process of systematisation leads, in short, to a clearly distinguished leadership that had clearly distinguished roles pertaining to the religious (and at times civic) practices of a certain group. This clerical group came to be the sole distributors of "religious goods" within a community.⁵³ In the research history of early Christianity, there has been an analogous understanding of the process in which, for example, Tertullian, who opted for the similarity between the senate and the Christian clergy, and the plebeians and the Christian laity, seems to dovetail with Bourdieu's views.⁵⁴

The summary of the consensus then, primarily among Protestant scholars at the beginning of the twentieth century, was that the ἐπίσκοπος and πρεσβύτερος were originally used interchangeably in an egalitarian, congregational milieu. Initially, the titles were not clearly distinguished and defined offices. During the second century, a development within the Christ groups led to the ἐπίσκοπος becoming the most prominent leader. This was understood according to Weber's model as a fading of charismatic leadership into a hierarchical structure, the routinization of charisma. Protestant scholars also saw this hierarchical structure as a legalistic development of the Christian faith. The emerging office can also be seen as an example of the monopolisation of religious goods, as found in Bourdieu's work.

4.3 Two Significant Questions in the Debate

This reconstruction of the research history of the episcopal office provides the main features of the consensus. As indicated above, this chapter also encompasses two additional significant questions that have resurfaced time and again over the centuries. These questions are first, whether the episcopal office was moulded from a Jewish or a Greco-Roman template, and second, the alleged synonymity between ἐπίσκοπος and πρεσβύτερος. As can be understood from

---

[51] Bourdieu 1991, 8.
[52] Bourdieu 1991, 9; Torjesen 2008, 389.
[53] Bourdieu 1991, 9
[54] Cf. Torjesen 2008, 398.

the review of the consensus above, these questions also hold significant weight for the consensus view. The latest challenges to how these questions are posed and answered highlight the need to carefully re-evaluate the views held as of the twentieth century.

4.3.1 A Jewish or a Greco-Roman Template?

While a consensus had emerged regarding the charismatic leaders of the earliest congregations and the hierarchical structures of the later congregations, there remained a notable interest in the origins of the episcopal office. A significant part of this interest concerned the origins of the early episcopal terminology. This question was intimately connected to the question of when the Christ groups got their main influence on their organisation. Two major suggestions were made throughout the debate, beginning in the nineteenth century. The first suggestion held that the major influence came from Greco-Roman associations, the second that the major influence came from diaspora synagogues.

At the end of the nineteenth century, Edwin Hatch began using insights from the emerging studies of Greco-Roman inscriptions related to voluntary associations.[55] He discerned a similarity between the early church and some forms of associations[56] and saw explicit connections between the role of the ἐπίσκοπος, διάκονοι, and πρεσβύτεροι on the one hand, and the functionaries and council of elders in the associations on the other.[57] One can note that several subsequent scholars have assumed a *general* view similar to Hatch. While the detailed financial perspective (see below) has not been fully embraced, most scholars acknowledge the relationship between the ἐπίσκοπος and the titulary of some associations.[58]

Based on the evidence of how the title ἐπίσκοπος was used outside of Christian groups, Hatch considered the role of the ἐπίσκοπος to be primarily financial. Many of the inscriptions from the first and second centuries that mention

---

[55] Hatch 1881, 208–9.
[56] Hatch 1881, 27–54, see also Bradshaw 2002, 192.
[57] Hatch 1881, 36–39.
[58] See for example Jeremias 1947, 23; Veit-Engelman 2022, 237–38.

the title refer to the financial role of the officer.⁵⁹ For example, one inscription on a stele (IG I³ 34) mentions how the ἐπίσκοπος is responsible for ensuring that the right tributes are collected and paid to Athens in the aftermath of the Peloponnesian war.⁶⁰ Thus, the role of the διάκονοι in, for example, Acts 7 mirrors this in that they were understood as distributors of financial aid.⁶¹ Hatch also lists early Christian literary evidence in which the ἐπίσκοπος as distributor of financial means to the poor is at the centre.⁶² On the other hand, the use of the title ἐπίσκοπος can also be found in Greco-Roman inscriptions pertaining to cultic roles.⁶³ Stewart takes up Hatch's work more than a century after its publication. In doing so, he continues the reconstruction of the economic origins of the episcopacy and discards many other versions of episcopal origins. For example, Stewart refutes the suggestion by Charles Bobertz from 1992, that the ἐπίσκοπος should be a Christian adaption of the LXX priest (see Numbers 4:16).⁶⁴ Bobertz's general association between the priest and the altar in Numbers 4:16, where the priest Eleazar is referred to as an ἐπίσκοπος in the LXX translation, is instead qualified by Stewart. He recognises that it is in the high priest Eleazar's capacity as responsible for "the material of sacrifice," that is, his economic role, that he is labelled ἐπίσκοπος.⁶⁵ The liturgical role emphasised by Bobertz is thus not what is indicated in the Greek version of Numbers. One key instance in the debate of the tasks of the ἐπίσκοπος is 1 Clem 40:2–5. From this, Bobertz describes the high priest, the priests, and the Levites as depicted in the Torah as templates for an orderly congregation and takes this as a warrant for the liturgical role of the ἐπίσκοπος.⁶⁶ Stewart claims, in alignment with

---

⁵⁹ IG XII.1, 731; IG I³, 34; *Lindos* II.378, line 55. Note the well-researched and thorough article on inscriptional evidence (that lists several instances more pertaining the ἐπίσκοπος) by Zamfir 2012, 202–8.

⁶⁰ Stewart 2022, 58.

⁶¹ Hatch 1881, 65–66, see also Burtchaell 1991, 79.

⁶² Hatch 1881, 41–48, referencing Justin *1 Apol.* 67; Pol. *Phil.* 4; Herm. Sim 9.27 (104); Jerome *Epist.* 52.6.

⁶³ ID 1522; *Lindos* II.378.

⁶⁴ Bobertz 1992, 185–86.

⁶⁵ Stewart 2014, 58–59.

⁶⁶ Bobertz 1992, 187. See also Von Campenhausen 1969, 85.

Hatch's argument, that the essential role of the ἐπίσκοπος rather was to provide for the offerings than perform liturgy.[67] Continuing with additional arguments for the view of the ἐπίσκοπος as primarily an economic functionary, Stewart lists more early Christian texts such as 1 Clement,[68] Ignatius *To Polycarp*,[69] and the Church orders from the second century onwards as evidence for the nature of the episcopal office in the life of early Christian groups.[70] In these texts, there are significant financial components in the way the ἐπίσκοπος is described. A central issue in the view of the ἐπίσκοπος as a financial officer is the understanding of the constantly recurring word λειτουργία. This notion should be understood in terms of providing financial means, at one's own expense. In Didache 15, then, the λειτουργία of the ἐπίσκοπος would carry connotations of providing "financial support for the prophets and teachers and enable them to carry out their ministry."[71] The financial aspect of the word λειτουργία is backed by various instances from papyri and ancient texts literature.[72] Stewart also provides a reading of how this understanding works with Philippians 1:1 and Acts 20.[73]

The elaborated connection between the ἐπίσκοπος and financial responsibilities has also been discussed but criticised elsewhere. Korinna Zamfir notes several instances from both Greco-Roman literature and inscriptions. However, she notes that while there are some examples of financial functions of the ἐπίσκοπος, oversight in general (over building projects or *polis*-matters) is just as common.[74] After a close study of the idea that the ἐπίσκοπος must either stem

---

[67] Stewart 2014, 62–63.

[68] Stewart 2014, 62.

[69] Stewart 2014, 63. Note Ign. *Pol.* 4 which discuss the need for Polycarp to attend to the financial needs of the widows.

[70] Stewart 2014, 64, quotes *Didascalia Apostolorum* 2.27:1–2.

[71] Stewart 2014, 61, compare with Didache 15:1, ὑμῖν γὰρ λειτουργοῦσι καὶ αὐτοὶ τὴν λειτουργίαν τῶν προφητῶν καὶ διδασκάλων.

[72] Stewart lists P.Oxy. 1119; P.Oxy. 1412; P.Oxy. 82. For literature: Dio Chrysostom, *Ven.* 26.2–4; *Sec.* 2.2; *2 Tars.* 1.4; *Tumult.* 6; 14 and also Strabo, *Geogr.* 14.2.5.

[73] Stewart 2014, 63–67.

[74] Zamfir 2012, 205, lists the inscriptions IGL 1990 (financial); IEph 716 (polis-supervision – the exact function is unclear), and supervision of a building project referred to in TDNT, s.v. ἐπίσκοπος.

from (other) Jewish contexts such as the Qumran movement,[75] or from the LXX vocabulary for offices in the Hebrew Bible,[76] Zamfir concludes that it is more reasonable to assume a Greco-Roman voluntary association influence for the emergence of the early Christian offices. The suggestion once made by Barbara Thiering about the resemblance between leadership in early Christian groups and the Qumran movement is discarded.[77] According to Thiering, a surface-level comparison between these offices suggests a close relationship between the Qumran and Jesus movements. The Qumran connection is, however, discarded by Zamfir since מבקר has a different meaning than ἐπίσκοπος: "The MT has seldom בקר where the LXX translates ἐπισκοπέω, and even in such cases it rarely refers to the attribution of an official."[78] The origin of the מבקר office was earlier associated with Ezek 34:11, but Zamfir objects to this view by noting that, in this instance, the term refers to God and not to a human office. Further, the title ἐπίσκοπος is most prominently used in Hellenistic communities, which Zamfir argues would hardly have been influenced by Essene communities.[79] Thus, she finds the most probable origin of the episcopal office in the Greco-Roman context, since she sees the office as a combination of a financial office and an oversight office. When turning to the distinction between πρεσβύτερος and ἐπίσκοπος, Zamfir understands the offices as from different origins:

---

[75] Jeremias 1962, 296–97; Thiering 1981, 59–74; Brown 1980, 333–34.

[76] Zamfir 2012, 208–9 lists Num 31:14; 4 Kgdms 11:15; 2 Chr 24:12, 17; Neh 11:9; 14:22; Isa 60:17; 1 Macc 1:51.

[77] Thiering 1981.

[78] Zamfir 2012, 210.

[79] Zamfir 2012, 211. Note also Stewart 2014, 96–100. While Stewart does not find it principally impossible that the ἐπίσκοπος and the מבקר should hold comparable offices, he doubts that this should be the case in for example Phil 1:1, given the apparent gentile background of the Philippian congregation and given the spatial distance between the groups. Stewart also notes two further problems with the idea of a Jewish background via the מבקר: that the liturgical function of the מבקר is hardly described, while the ἐπίσκοπος is important in the "proceedings of most Christian communities" (p. 99). A further problem is brought by the possibility of a general understanding of Essene fellowships as voluntary associations themselves (p. 99). This last point will be further discussed below.

When *episkopos* and *presbyteros* figure together, as in the Pastoral Epistles, there is no clear distinction between the function of the two. It seems therefore probable that the terms denote offices with similar attributions but different origins. This elasticity of the terms and attributions matches that noticed in the Greco-Roman world.[80]

The origin of the πρεσβύτερος is, however, unclear according to Zamfir.[81] This relationship will be further addressed below.

To summarise: The idea that the ἐπίσκοπος originated from a Greco-Roman template was championed by Hatch at the end of the nineteenth century. According to his reconstruction, the ἐπίσκοπος primarily served as a financial officer. This view was further developed by Stewart, who provided additional evidence unknown to Hatch. Zamfir agrees with Hatch and Stewart regarding the Greco-Roman origins. The perspective that the ἐπίσκοπος primarily was a financial officer, however, is also problematized by Zamfir, who notes that inscriptions show that the ἐπίσκοπος had oversight responsibilities (for example, for building projects), and not only financial responsibilities.

The other late nineteenth-century suggestion for where the Jesus movement got its organisational form is that the offices emerged as primarily mimicking diaspora synagogue patterns. Hatch's understanding of the organisational structure, based on Greco-Roman templates, was opposed by von Harnack. Instead of viewing the ἐπίσκοπος as ultimately becoming the sole leader through a process among the πρεσβύτεροι, as Hatch did, von Harnack regarded ἐπίσκοπος and πρεσβύτερος as representing two entirely different structures, each with its own unique history.[82] While the elders were collegial and responsible for congregational discipline, according to von Harnack, the ἐπίσκοπος had a presiding role at worship gatherings, and a strictly spiritual role, as opposed to a financial role. The meaning of the office titles will be discussed below. It is worth noting how the understandings of Hatch and von Harnack differ substantially regarding the emerging episcopal office. As discussed in the previous chapter, Burtchaell developed the perspective of von Harnack at the end of the twentieth century when he claimed that the terminology

---

[80] Zamfir 2012, 221.
[81] Zamfir 2012, 217.
[82] Harnack 1883, 229–51, see also Burtchaell 1991, 82.

4.3 Two Significant Questions in the Debate

throughout the Christ groups was Jewish, but not the language of the "mainstream" synagogue.[83] Burtchaell saw the same pattern in the Essene and Therapeutic fellowships: they use terminology within the biblical spectrum but separated from the use of other synagogues' terminology.[84] He also claimed that even though the terminology of the leadership differed in the Essene community, the leadership role was basically the same. The מבקר of the Essene community was supposed to teach the congregation from the Law, control recruitment, examine and train novices, control financial transactions, preside at presbyterial meetings and hear grievances. This would then have been basically the same tasks as the ἐπίσκοπος would have performed in the Christ groups.[85] Also, as discussed above, Burtchaell's reconstruction of a synagogue fellowship equates the roles of the ἀρχισυνάγωγος with the role of the מבקר. All Jewish groups had one shape, but with different names for their leaders. Also, Jewish groups "avoid ... whenever possible ... the official names the other groups had selected as theirs."[86] The early church was then in alignment with this pattern so that the title ἐπίσκοπος signalled continuity with other Jewish groups. The leadership term was an assemblage of multiple roles such as president, shepherd, or elder, which would naturally align with the ἀρχισυνάγωγος or the מבקר.[87] Since the title ἀρχισυνάγωγος would resemble too much of the synagogue, it was necessary to change it, in Burtchaell's view.[88] Christian group's titles would still need to display their connection to Jewish Scriptures while simultaneously differing from other Jewish groups. He suggests that the vocabulary of the early church signalled both continuity and discontinuity with other synagogues through their choice of titles in accordance with an alleged Jewish tradition.

As discussed above, the level of conjecture is problematic in Burtchaell's reconstruction. The fact that we have some sources on the מבקר does not mean

---

[83] Note here Runesson's discussion on how disparate the phenomena of the diaspora synagogue were during the first and second centuries, Runesson 2021, 39–44.

[84] Burtchaell 1991, 277–84.

[85] Burtchaell 1991, 269.

[86] Burtchaell 1991, 283.

[87] Burtchaell 1991, 283.

[88] Burtchaell 1991, 283–84.

that these sources can compensate for the silence from the lack of evidence regarding the role of the ἀρχισυνάγωγος in second-century Asia Minor. Another problem was Burtchaell's axiom that only one mainstream synagogue form existed in the diaspora.[89] As has been broadly discussed during the debate, the idea that one single movement defined the synagogues in the diaspora during the first and second centuries CE (often understood as the rabbinic movement) does not hold, simply because the "rabbinization" of the synagogues is not attested at the time when Burtchaell suggested that this process would have unfolded.[90] Also, the hypothesis of the elaborated reconstruction of the role of the ἀρχισυνάγωγος is strained[91] because we lack much evidence for this office.[92] One can, however, observe that although Burtchaell's hypothesis has been dismissed by prominent scholars in synagogue research, it has also been repurposed. For example Vasilije Vranic considers the diaspora synagogue model to be the most probable template for post-Pauline congregations to adopt.[93]

To summarise: The claim by von Harnack that the evidence would suggest that the early church picked up its organisational pattern from the diaspora synagogue is further developed by Burtchaell. His thesis that the shape of the Christian congregation resembled the patterns of the synagogue, and that the ἐπίσκοπος was a Christian variant of the ἀρχισυνάγωγος, also suggests that this pattern offered an important identity for the Christian groups. They showed

---

[89] See for example Runesson 2021, 35.

[90] Alexander 1999, 24.

[91] Burtchaell 1991, 244: "What emerges from the evidence is an enduring perception from within the Jewish people that this officer, the archisynagôgos, was not simply a master of religious ceremonies. He was the executive of the local community, acting under the formal oversight of the elders. [...] He presided over the community, he convened it for its activities, he superintended its staff. It was a position of some permanency, and one in which fathers might hope to see their sons succeed them. The community chief was, if not the most prestigious member of his community socially, the one who worked, often professionally, as the man at the forefront of his people. As broad as were the interest and the programs and services of his community, so broadly reached the breadth of his responsibility. If he presided at worship, it was because he presided at all community functions." This reconstruction is also discussed by Levine 2005, 417.

[92] As noted above, Levine labels the reconstruction of Burtchaell as "artificial and speculative," Levine 2005, 417.

[93] Vranic 2012, 29.

an affinity with the Jewish synagogue and a separate identity. This view, however, has not attracted many followers, as it relies significantly on conjecture.

4.3.2 The Synonymous ἐπίσκοπος and πρεσβύτερος?

As noted above, a major idea in the (Protestant) scholarly consensus was that ἐπίσκοπος and πρεσβύτερος are synonyms in the New Testament writings and second-century texts.[94] This synonymity is a crucial point in the reconstruction of the emerging offices. As we observed from the earliest reception of the New Testament texts and the Apostolic Fathers, third and fourth-century Christian authors regarded these labels as rather synonymous. The modern consensus, however, is built on the works of a few prominent scholars: J. B. Lightfoot and F. C. Baur. These scholars wrote in a context. Linton traced similar ideas in the seventeenth century in Salmasius and Edward Stillingfleet, who both saw the titles as synonyms.[95] Stewart, in 2014, regarded the nineteenth century as a period when a prevailing Protestant view about the synonymity of the offices was consolidated.[96] This view held by Lightfoot and Baur was still prominent at the end of the twentieth century.[97] When we now turn to discuss this significant feature of the debate, three components are necessary to address. First, there is the question of the Gentile or Jewish origins of the presbyterate. This perspective is closely related to the question of the organisational templates of the Christ groups discussed above, although it is not precisely the same question: the presbyterate is a distinct sub-group found in both Greco-Roman and Jewish contexts. Second, there is the question of how the term πρεσβύτερος is related to the household organisation of the Greco-Roman world. Third, there is the most recent turn of events, the suggestion of Stewart that the local Christ group in an ancient city formed a federation that contained every group's

---

[94] Baur 1835, 80. See also Lightfoot 1881, 95–99; Hatch 1881, 39, n. 31. See also Alastair Campell's review article of Benjamin Merkle's book from 2003, *The Elder and the Overseer: One Office in the Early Church*: "Without it [the insights from social history] Merkle is really saying no more than Lightfoot said almost one hundred and fifty years ago," Campell 2005, 283.

[95] Linton 1923, 3–5.

[96] Stewart 2014, 12.

[97] Cf. Knight, 1992, 175–77; Hawthorne 1983, 10; Mounce 2000, 186–92, provides only a short reader on the topic and refer to lengthier discussions by, for example, Kirk 1946.

ἐπίσκοπος and when the ἐπίσκοποι gathered they formed a collective presbyterate.

Hatch, who otherwise perceived the Christian structures as derived from a template of Greco-Roman voluntary associations, recognised a synagogical influence in his interpretation of the early congregation, particularly in his comprehension of the πρεσβύτεροι. He suggested that the Jewish Christ groups simply continued with their organisational form, whereas the entirely gentile Christ groups used a more generic association template for the leadership structure.[98] In this template, the ἐπίσκοποι had, as mentioned above, a specific role in overseeing the financial aspects of the group and serving as officers for financial aid to the poor members.[99] These gentile groups had, however, according to Hatch, simultaneously also kept the presbyterate from a synagogical setting as responsible for disciplinary matters.[100] Lightfoot also viewed the presbyterate as the primary body of the Christian groups that collectively oversaw the liturgical and financial aspects of the congregation life.[101] Certain texts have been used as proof texts for this view.[102] Special emphasis is put on Acts 20:17–18 and Titus 1:5–8, where the use of the terms seems impossible to understand in any other way than as synonymous. This synonymity will be further addressed in chapter 5 below.

In 1994, Alastair Campbell understood it as a consolidated consensus view that the πρεσβύτεροι were a continuation from the synagogue origins.[103] This was a summary of Lightfoot's,[104] Hatch's, and von Harnack's work, which many others had followed. One can note that few studies were done with a specific interest in the presbyterial rank of the Christ groups.[105] During the

---

[98] Hatch 1881, 55–81.
[99] Hatch 1881, 40–41.
[100] Hatch 1881, 64–68.
[101] Lightfoot 1881, 192.
[102] Stewart lists several works that all understand the words as synonyms, among them Rohte 1837 and Ritschl 1847. Also, more recent examples exist: Merkle 2003. See Stewart 2014, 14, n. 16.
[103] Campbell 1994, 2.
[104] Lightfoot 1881, 93–97.
[105] In mid-twentieth century, Wilhelm Michaelis published what has been deemed as an "synthesis" (Campbell 1994, 1, n. 2) of the New Testament teachings, Michaelis 1953.

twentieth century much of the focus was on episcopal offices since the ecumenical movement discussed the role of apostolic succession.[106] Campbell, however, endeavoured to understand the leadership of the πρεσβύτεροι in the Christ groups, which is important given the synonymity of the roles assumed by the scholarly consensus. The exact function and role of the πρεσβύτεροι had already gained some attention, even if few had made such an effort to understand the background of the πρεσβύτεροι as Campbell came to do. Another solution was offered by Joachim Jeremias, who focused on the term πρεσβύτερος as merely a designation of age.[107] This view has been seriously criticised as too simplified; the evidence appears to suggest a broader usage of the term than Jeremias acknowledges. While a designation of age might be possible to argue regarding the usage in 1 Timothy in general, it is harder to imagine such a use in the context of Acts 20.[108] A more generally accepted view can be summarised in Campbell's words as follows:

> Were the elders then necessarily old men? ... [T]he answer is No. Their authority did not rest on age alone, but on the prestige of the families whose heads they were. The society we have been studying can properly be described as an aristocracy. ... Age, of course, was an important factor in a man attaining headship, but hardly a sufficient or necessary cause. In a society prone to disease and death in war, many men must have succeeded their fathers at a comparatively young age. At the same time, we should not neglect the probability that there was an ideal of eldership at work. Eldership connotes age, wisdom and honour, even when not all of those denoted by "the elders" in a particular context possess these qualities.[109]

One can note that the term πρεσβύτεροι appears to be used both of age (aligned to the view of Jeremias) and of an office (superseding the view of Jeremias) in both synagogues and Christian congregations.[110] Günther Bornkamm tried to describe the use of elders in the Hebrew Bible, other Jewish sources and Greco-Roman sources. He perceives the elders as a governing body in ancient Israel. This perspective maintains that the elders, as a governing body, are first

---

[106] World Council of Churches 1982, 26.
[107] Jeremias 1947.
[108] See Stewart 2014, 16.
[109] Campbell 1994, 66, italics original.
[110] Bornkamm 1968, 654.

identified in Numbers 11:16f. Here, the elders receive a portion of the Spirit to assist Moses in his tasks, which Bornkamm interpreted as an aetiology for the genesis of a presbyterate in Jewish circles.[111] In the Pentateuch, the elders are also representative of the people, as *pars pro toto* for the whole people, while they simultaneously are subjected to the leaders Moses and Joshua. The usage in the LXX is a translation of the word זקן in the Pentateuch and the Deuteronomistic History. In texts outside the LXX, the word used to denote elders as authority changes in exilic and post-exilic times into שב (Aramaic).[112] One can note that the original זקן just means "bearded" and speaks of an adult man rather than an old man per se, even if age probably must have factored in.[113] There is an aspect in the Hebrew Bible where the elders function as a council or governing body, suggesting that it was never solely a matter of age. As Bornkamm also notes, in the designation of being an elder (in whatever language the term is used) there was an honorific tone. For example, the use of "elders" for the members of the Sanhedrin or in the designations by the later Mishna suggests that the term designates a person worthy of reverence, such as a Torah scholar.[114]

Bornkamm traces the use of the idea of the elders as a governing body in the Hebrew Bible.[115] According to Bornkamm, the biblical sources suggest increased importance for the council of elders during exilic times, perhaps in the absence of other governing bodies for the exiles. Traces throughout the Hebrew Bible show that elders appear to have been members of village or city councils. Aristocratic tendencies are probably found here so that the members of some families were, in practice, more important than others. The term is also used by Jesus in the New Testament in Mark 7:8 as a reference to an authoritative tradition that he rejects, calling it a human tradition. Of course, the term is also used in Acts 20 and Titus 1. The Christian use in Acts, according to

---

[111] Bornkamm 1968, 655.
[112] Bornkamm 1968, 658.
[113] Bornkamm 1968, 655, n. 20.
[114] Bornkamm 1968, 659-61.
[115] So for example 1 Sam 4:3; 8:4; 15:30; 1 Kings 21:8; Deut 19:11-13; Neh 2:16; 4:8; Ezra 10:7-17, etc.

4.3 Two Significant Questions in the Debate

Bornkamm, signals Luke's view of an authoritative position of the Jerusalemite presbyterate for the early Jesus movement.[116]

Turning to extrabiblical usage, Bornkamm shows through comparison of several inscriptions from different areas that there is a difference between Greek and Egyptian uses of the term πρεσβύτερος. In the Egyptian context, the πρεσβύτερος is not necessarily old but rather a part of an annually elected governing board.[117] Bornkamm thus understands the role as being formalised, even if only one inscription displays this use. In the Greek context, however, the official aspect appears to be missing in the inscriptions, and πρεσβύτερος primarily refers to someone of a certain age and thus worthy of respect. Campbell notes an overlapping or similar use in Greco-Roman and Jewish societies.[118]

When it comes to the πρεσβυτέριον as a governing body, inscriptional evidence reveals an overlap of governing bodies with similar functions but different names. While the terminology varies, the functions appear to be comparable enough. The term γερουσία is found in several places in the eastern parts of the Mediterranean area, prominently in Asia Minor from the third century BCE onwards.[119] The difference between the βουλή and the γερουσία/ πρεσβυτέριον seems to be that the latter had "no administrative functions or executive power."[120] The term γερουσία/ πρεσβυτέριον is rather common in inscriptions from Syria and Asia Minor, but neither Campbell nor Bornkamm understand these instances as referring to a well-defined office.[121] The term's use in Greco-Roman society suggests that this body exercised power through influence, relationships, and the honour associated with its position, similar to what the Jewish usages suggest. Campbell, with his focus on the πρεσβύτερος in the life of the Christ group, takes a special interest in the synagogical use of the term. He suggests similar use in the diaspora context, as Bornkamm does regarding the Greco-Roman use of πρεσβύτερος:[122] the πρεσβύτερος was not an office per

---

[116] Bornkamm 1968, 663.
[117] Bornkamm 1968, 653.
[118] Campbell 1994, 67–68.
[119] Campbell 1994, 73.
[120] Campbell 1994, 74.
[121] Bornkamm 1968, 661.
[122] Campbell 1994, 54.

se, but rather an honorary position of an approved man in the Jewish community. The lines are blurred between this and a formalised office.

> The elders are the senior men of the community, heads of the leading families within it, who as such exercise an authority that is informal, representative and collective. It is a term both flexible and vague. It neither denotes particular office-holders, nor excludes them, but can easily associate with more precise official titles. An author who does not wish to do so is not obliged to use it at all, and can describe the local aristocracy by a range of other titles.[123]

These approved men ran, according to Campbell, the diaspora synagogues through the ὑπηρέτης and the ἀρχισυνάγωγος.[124]

On the other hand, in the scholarly debate regarding the governing presbyterate, it was consistently contrasted with the ideal Protestant view of charisma as the original authority, according to Campbell. This is because the presbyterate was seen as too close to the synagogue by several Protestant scholars.[125] A prominent example that Campbell uses throughout his book is the view of the emerging offices found in Rudolf Sohm's work. The offices are ideally portrayed as stemming from a charismatic authority, as contrasted to a Jewish (perceived legalistic) background.[126] The concept of Christ groups usurping the synagogical presbyterate was viewed negatively, according to this consensus perspective, reflecting the prevailing understanding of Jewish followers of Jesus in the nineteenth century as legalistic, in contrast to the Pauline gentile followers.[127] Sohm understood the gathered ἐκκλησία as the place where charismata were functioning and the ministry of the word was most prominently found.[128] Thus, Sohm is, on the one hand, sceptical regarding the Jewish influence from a presbyterate like that of the synagogues, and on the other hand, sceptical about a too early appearance of an obvious single leadership, a mono-

---

[123] Campbell 1994, 65.

[124] Campbell 1994, 54, 65–66.

[125] One can however note the view of Lightfoot, who recognised the disparity of the Jewish groups in the first century and hence escaped a too binary view at least in this instance, Lightfoot 1881, 191–93.

[126] Sohm 1923, 28.

[127] Campell 1994, 2–3.

[128] Sohm 1923, 137–39; Campell 1994, 9–10.

episcopate.¹²⁹ According to Sohm, it was during local meetings led by gifted and charismatic teachers or at larger gatherings with several groups where the ἐπίσκοπος presided over the eucharistic meal that the theology of the Jesus movement became clear. Here Sohm could keep a charismatic understanding of the group while simultaneously balancing up the perceived risk of an early mono-episcopate. However, the reception of Sohm's reconstruction connected the presbyterate with a proto-catholic development in which the presbyters were the guardians of tradition. Paul, on the other hand, was understood as opting for a spiritual form of the ἐκκλησία, which had never seen its equal either before or since.¹³⁰ This view was taken further by the work of von Campenhausen.¹³¹ However, the perspective was also contested by several scholars from across the Protestant side of the aisle, that is, Roman Catholic scholars.¹³² Campbell also notes a significant difference between German and Anglo-Saxon scholarship, in which the former discusses the difference between charisma and "Amt," while the latter primarily discusses the relationship between ἐπίσκοπος and πρεσβύτερος, with the specific focus on the emergence of the episcopal office as such.¹³³ Campbell drives the thesis that this pattern of fading charisma also reemerges in the important work *In Memory of Her* by Elisabeth Schüssler Fiorenza.¹³⁴ While Schüssler Fiorenza provides a novel reading in her understanding of the earliest Jesus movement as egalitarian, and while she also clearly sees Jesus's and Paul's Jewish context, the tendency is to understand the shift in the early Jesus movement from an ideal past (egalitarian or charismatic) into an institutionalised and clericalized movement.¹³⁵ Thus, the pattern of Rudolf Sohm seems to reiterate itself in different guises.

To summarise: The πρεσβύτερος was early understood as a Jewish heritage of the Christ groups and understood by Lighfoot among others as synonymous with the ἐπίσκοπος. The term πρεσβύτερος is not only (*contra* Jeremias) a

---

[129] Campbell 1994, 10.
[130] Campbell 1994, 11.
[131] Von Campenhausen 1969, 77; Campbell 1994, 13.
[132] Campbell 1994, 13, n. 46.
[133] Campbell, 1994, 14.
[134] Schüssler Fiorenza 1983.
[135] Campbell 1994, 16.

designation of age, but rather a designation of importance in the community. A scepticism towards what was perceived as a legalistic heritage from a Jewish presbyterate made scholars like Sohm suggest a charismatic leadership of the Christ groups, as opposed to a legalistic Jewish or Catholic organised leadership as the presbyterate. The elders in the Hebrew Bible/LXX function as a governing body that resurfaces throughout the texts. Bornkamm notes that in non-Jewish sources, the title πρεσβύτερος is, in one instance in Egypt, an example of a member of a governing board. At the same time, in Asia Minor it rather suggests that someone is perceived as a person of honour. Here age factors in, but it is not everything. Turning to the γερουσία/ πρεσβυτέριον in Asia Minor as a function, it seems to stand in contrast to the βουλή. It seems to have had no administrative functions or executive power but instead exercised power through relational influence. Campbell suggests that this would have been the case for the πρεσβυτέριον in the diaspora synagogue as well.

Apart from the debate whether the origins of the presbyterate as a leadership model stemmed from the synagogue or voluntary associations, a suggestion has been made by Frances Young that it primarily stemmed from the Greco-Roman household organisation. She recognises the many early Christian sources that appear to group together the διάκονος and ἐπίσκοπος, while the πρεσβύτερος seems to stem from a different source.[136] She then suggests that the church offices were modelled on a household template and that the ἐπίσκοποι and διάκονοι thus were the appointed offices, while the πρεσβυτέριον was a council of seniors.[137] The ἐπίσκοπος then functioned as the οἰκονόμος in the house, the "steward," with the διάκονοι functioning as servants (just as Titus 1:7 would imply). An οἰκονόμος would be a trusted slave who was given responsibility for the whole οἶκος. Given the authority that the οἰκονόμος received from the owner, the position was, in practice, very powerful.[138] According to this model, πρεσβύτερος was used in a non-technical way, simply denoting "old" and thus worthy of some reverence due to old age.[139] Simultaneously, the

---

[136] Young 1994, 142.
[137] This is also held by Vranic 2012, 32.
[138] Young 1994, 144.
[139] Young 1994, 144–48.

council of elders functioned as a safeguard of the tradition: the role of the πρεσβύτεροι was, according to Young, to preserve the tradition inherited from the apostles (the memory of the congregation). Even further, the name used was in fact mirroring a tradition in which the apostles were seen as the πρεσβύτεροι.[140] This threefold use of the term πρεσβύτερος (designating age, safeguarding of tradition, and alluding to the apostles), naturally causes confusion in our interpretation of the organisation of the Christ groups in the second century.[141] Here, we can see a compatibility between, on the one hand, the household template and, on the other hand, the honorary position of elders in both Greco-Roman and Jewish contexts. In Young's view, it seems likely that the πρεσβύτεροι made the appointment of the ἐπίσκοπος in the congregation.[142] One can also note that Young suggests that the household template of the Christ group was original and that the synagogical influence only came later because of an emerging self-understanding of the Christ groups as God's household and God's people.[143] In this instance, Young understands the main influence of the presbyterial structure as stemming from Jewish communities, in which the presbyters were appointing officers (the presbyters appointed an ἀρχισυνάγωγος).[144] Later developments in synagogue and voluntary associations research problematize this air-tight distinction between the two kinds of associations (Jewish and Gentile). Young's analysis is also sensitive to a critique that she relies heavily on data conjecture. She admits herself that her reconstruction relies on probabilities based on analogies from the land.[145]

To summarise Young's view, the ἐπίσκοπος functioned as the οἰκονόμος in the house, the "steward," with the διάκονοι functioning as servants, while the πρεσβύτερος was something like a *paterfamilias* – safeguarding the tradition. There is a compatibility between, on the one hand, the household template and, on the other hand, the honorary position of elders in both Greco-Roman

---

[140] Young 1994, 148. See also 1 Tim 4:14; Ign. *Trall.* 3.
[141] Young 1994, 146 quotes the Papias fragments from Eusebius's *Hist. eccl.* 3.39.
[142] Young 1994, 147.
[143] Young 1994, 144–48. See also Bradshaw 2002, 197.
[144] Young 1994, 148.
[145] Cf. Young 1994, 147.

and Jewish contexts. Young suggests the household template to be the most original; other templates, like the synagogical, are secondary.

Last, in this part of the chapter, we turn to the most recent suggestion regarding the synonymity of πρεσβύτερος and ἐπίσκοπος. Alistair Stewart argues that synonymity is not the best way to understand the terms. Instead, he argues that the apparent synonym usage by the authors of Acts and Titus should be interpreted as indications of an early system of Christian federations. The early congregations were aware of each other, and when their leaders (the ἐπίσκοποι of the congregations) gathered, the members of these leadership meetings were referred to as πρεσβύτεροι. The individual leaders from every congregation, however, were referred to in their congregations as ἐπίσκοπος.[146] According to Stewart, there are two reasons for the rise of these federations. First, a need for doctrinal succession arose; the necessity to demonstrate that one's teachings originated with previous teachers became significant in the process of self-definition. Here, similar congregations must have formed alliances early on. Second, Stewart saw persecution as a hotbed for charismatic leadership. In this process, the role of the ἐπίσκοπος changed from an economic office into a teaching one; the presbyterate of ἐπίσκοποι policed boundaries and represented the church.[147] A key issue is the extent to which it is possible to confirm the federal nature of the Christian congregations.[148] Stewart argues from the relatively numerous sources from Rome (Romans 16, Justin, Hermas, 1 Clement, and more). Rome exemplifies an ancient city where it is possible to present a fairly extensive picture of the life of Christian congregations. Both Peter Lampe and Allen Brent conducted broad analyses of various sources in their studies on churches in Rome.[149] Stewart summarises the conclusion of the evidence as follows:

> The hypothesis of federation, and the terming of the federated leaders as *presbyteroi*, clarifies this otherwise confusing usage. In other words, far from Rome being under presbyteral leadership, ... and far from the presbyters being those from whom *episkopoi*

---

[146] Stewart 2014, 15–16.
[147] Stewart 2014, 351–52.
[148] See the review of Stewart's book, Baldovin 2016, 367.
[149] Lampe 1987; Brent 1995.

are recruited, ... the *episkopoi* were the individual congregational leaders from whom came the *presbyteroi*, those leaders who met as a council and so formed the federation.[150]

Now, this appears to be the context of *one* ancient city. Does the Roman pattern necessarily repeat itself in other cities? Stewart is inclined to think so in his reading of evidence for Corinth (1 Corinthians and 1 Clement) and Ephesus (Acts and Titus).[151]

4.4 Conclusion

In this chapter, I have recapitulated the scholarly understanding of the emergence of the episcopal office. In this last part of the chapter, I will summarise the debate so far, discuss the results in relation to the parting of the ways and the synagogue research, and draw out some pivotal conclusions for this study. A consensus has emerged from the debate regarding the limited relevant sources we possess from the first and second centuries. These sources demonstrate a dynamic development of leadership structures, and it is reasonable to assume that the emergence of the offices within the Christ groups varied across different regions of the Roman Empire. In the northeastern part of the Mediterranean region, stretching from Syria through Asia Minor to Rome in the west, the ἐπίσκοπος and πρεσβύτερος are regarded as the oldest offices of the Christian groups. This perspective was already present in the scholarly community of the seventeenth century, but it was solidified during the nineteenth century and continued to prevail into the subsequent century. According to this view, the ἐπίσκοπος and πρεσβύτερος are regarded as interchangeable in relatively "egalitarian" Christian congregations. However, Protestant scholars contend that the routinization of charisma led to the ἐπίσκοπος becoming the most prominent officeholder by the end of the second century. This aligns with the Protestant perspective of a subsequent development in Christian congregations, which resulted in hierarchical structures that were legalistic in nature. The consensus had important parts. The questions of Jewish or Greco-Roman origins for the offices and of synonymity between ἐπίσκοπος and πρεσβύτερος

---

[150] Stewart 2014 22.
[151] Stewart 2014, 27–45.

in New Testament sources had far-reaching implications for the reconstruction. Regarding the first question, the debate concerned whether the office came from the template of Greco-Roman offices in voluntary associations or from the template of diaspora synagogues. There was a tendency among nineteenth-century scholars to associate a perceived Jewish legalism with a proto-Catholic episcopal office. Thus, the Greco-Roman template was favoured for ideological reasons: according to this perspective, the emerging church liberated itself from legalistic Jewish patterns and adopted models from the surrounding Greco-Roman society.

The interpretation of ἐπίσκοπος as a financial officer, rooted in a Greco-Roman framework, was initially proposed by Hatch and later revisited by Stewart. This view clarifies a peculiar aspect of the sources that frequently highlight the relationship between the ἐπίσκοπος, seen as a distributor of communal resources, and the διάκονοι, who acted as the agents of this distribution. A financial dimension of the episcopal role is perceivable both in Greco-Roman inscriptions and in second-century Christian texts. The other suggestion, proposed by von Harnack and followed by Burtchaell, indicated that the diaspora synagogues were the most viable path for reconstructing Christian offices. Von Harnack emphasised the role of the presbyterate in this reconstruction. Here, Burtchaell made intriguing connections between the meaning-carrying names of the offices, which both signalled continuity and separation from the diaspora synagogue. Burtchaell compares, for example, the Essene movement to the early Christian groups. However, he received significant criticism for his far-reaching reconstruction, which relied too heavily on conjecture and on the assumption that the diaspora synagogue was a single mainstream synagogue.

As the reconstructions of the earliest congregations in the recent developments of the parting of the ways debate and synagogue research (addressed in chapter 3 above) suggest, the plurality of diaspora synagogues and voluntary associations reflects a scenario where the notion of a single "early church template" becomes outdated. Rather, as the discussion from the last chapter shows, the best way to understand diaspora synagogues would be as a kind of ethnic voluntary association in which the members worship a patron god. This suggests that the templates from which the offices of the ἐπίσκοπος and πρεσβύτερος were derived had both Jewish (in some respects) and non-Jewish (in others) influences. It may be more accurate to state that both Jewish and non-Jewish associations exemplified voluntary associations in a Hellenistic milieu. The voluntary association and its leadership models played a significant role in forming leadership for the early Christ groups. This is especially so if Runesson is correct in his evaluation of the parting of the ways from an institutional perspective (see chapter 3 above). Runesson's point here, then, is the existence of non-Jewish Christ-worshippers organised in an association, while Jewish Christ-worshippers could be organised in a Jewish synagogue.[152] The different organisational forms, which existed in parallel, would suggest that the leadership models could also exist in parallel.

Regarding the second question, the synonymity of ἐπίσκοπος and πρεσβύτερος, a cornerstone of the consensus described in this chapter, has recently been challenged by Stewart. One can note that Hatch and von Harnack understood the presbyterate leadership as a model prominent in diaspora synagogues that was imported into Christ groups or became the most prominent model in what these scholars understood as Jewish-Christian groups. In the LXX, the πρεσβύτεροι as a collective were a leading group in exilic times. The reconstruction of the function of the πρεσβύτεροι by Campbell suggests that it was a group that exercised its power not through legal rulings or official proceedings but through informal means and influence. Young suggested that the role of the ἐπίσκοπος and πρεσβύτερος should be understood in relation to a household template that would qualify the roles of the two groups as not interchangeable, as the ἐπίσκοπος would be the head of the servants in the house. At the same time, the elders would be the *paterfamilias* who stand for continuity with the tradition. The reading of Stewart, that group leaders of every Christ group in an area, the ἐπίσκοποι of the groups, met together in a federation and then were collectively designated as πρεσβύτεροι, challenges the assumption of a synonymity between the ἐπίσκοπος and the πρεσβύτερος from another perspective. Stewart's interpretation provides new perspectives on the data, not least the instances in Acts and 1 Peter. The reading brings an interesting flavour to the relationship between the ἐπίσκοπος and the πρεσβύτεροι as attested in the sources. Thus, some significant questions have arisen regarding the view that

---

[152] Runesson 2021, 49.

has been the prevailing consensus for a long time. Simultaneously, it is worth noting that most scholars still consider the ἐπίσκοπος and the πρεσβύτερος as rather synonymous at the beginning of the second century. However, the development suggested by Stewart presents a new way to reconstruct the emergent dominance of the mono-episcopate. For the purposes of this book, it suffices to say that the ἐπίσκοπος and πρεσβύτερος often appear as overlapping categories in ways that align with Stewart's reconstruction. However, the findings of this study are by no means reliant on Stewart's thesis. The main focus here is the ἐπίσκοπος and the manner in which this leadership role was intertwined with Christian self-definition. Stewart's view may suggest that the identity-producing features of the ἐπίσκοπος also applied to the πρεσβύτερος, as these two titles referred to essentially the same individuals but in different contexts (convening as ἐπίσκοπος within the local Christ group and meeting as πρεσβύτεροι at the city-wide gathering). My research primarily focuses on how the ἐπίσκοπος conveyed group identity and prototypicality as a leader for a group of Christ followers. Consequently, the city-wide gathering itself holds little interest for me, as it is not explicitly represented in the sources I utilise.

A few concluding remarks can prepare for the next chapter. First, it is notable that institutional critique may cast new light on these matters. As seen in the examples of the critique from other scholars against the suggestions made by Burtchaell, the perception of synagogue institutions, Christ groups, and voluntary associations has everything to do with how we understand the leadership structures and ancient institutions. The conjectures made from other sources play a significant role in understanding the early Christ groups. The recent research on voluntary associations, Christ groups, and synagogues, which will be further discussed in subsequent chapters, shows how the perspective on these institutions has been too simplified thus far in the debate. The designations have sometimes been too bound up with modern perceptions of early Christianity. Thus, in the present work, special attention must be paid to how institutions worked and shaped identity, particularly in the second-century CE Jewish diaspora. Second, while some of the reconstructions described in the emerging offices implicitly discuss matters of group identity (notably Burtchaell), an overall perspective on how leadership carries group identity is missing. Perspectives from social identity theory, such as prototypicality, identity entrepreneurship, and impresarioship, are lacking. Third, the perspectives applied in the research history so far do not fully address how the emerging episcopal office contributes to the separation between Christ groups and (other) Jewish groups. The institutional perspectives that exist in the debate do influence the discussion of the extent to which diaspora synagogue templates and Greco-Roman templates underlie the emerging offices of the Christ groups. Still, no conclusions in terms of emerging Christian group identity are drawn from these findings. Throughout the field in general, far-reaching assumptions of an already fixed Christian identity in the second century are often present. Although such an identity emerged during the second century, it is partly a result of rhetorical texts like those of Ignatius of Antioch, which advocate for a specific Christian identity distinct from a Jewish one. In these texts, which will be examined throughout this book, the leadership structures play a significant role in shaping the emerging identity. Thus, the formation of leadership would probably (given an SIT perspective on group leadership and group identity) be intimately connected to the process of an emerging Christian self-identity.

Part II

Christian Second-Century Texts from an SIT Perspective

Introduction to part II

We now turn to the actual investigation of this book, which analyses how the ἐπίσκοπος provided an exclusive Christ-group identity. Several texts from the second century discuss the ἐπίσκοπος or use the leadership role of the ἐπίσκοπος in ways that make it possible and meaningful to examine the role from an SIT perspective. Moreover, some texts refer to the title so briefly that a thorough SIT analysis of them becomes difficult, even though there are specific identity-shaping elements related to the leadership role that can be identified and extracted. In general, the earlier texts tend to have a shorter treatment of the role, while the later texts tend to give a more comprehensive picture. This second part of the investigation will then, in chronological order, present how the ἐπίσκοπος conveys Christ-group identity throughout the texts of the first and second centuries.

The dating of each text is contested. I will thus use some space for my argumentation for the dates of the different texts. Note, however, that the dates are only approximate. For some texts, providing anything more than a range of dates is impossible, which will also have to suffice in this book. It is, however, clear that the further we go into the second century, the more defined the office of the ἐπίσκοπος becomes. Therefore, the Christian self-definition tied to the emergent office also becomes clearer. By the middle of the second century, much has happened to the concept of the ἐπίσκοπος. By the end of the second century, the ἐπίσκοπος had become the warrant for a correct apostolic tradition and is thus a symbol of Christian faith. The emergence of the ἐπίσκοπος leaves no room for alternate ingroup identities, according to second-century Christ-group authors.

The texts analysed can thus be separated into two groups. First, we have the texts that mention the title ἐπίσκοπος only briefly or in passing. I will provide short comments on these occasions based on what can be said from an SIT perspective. The shorter texts that must be addressed occur in Philippians, Acts of the Apostles, 1 Peter, and the Shepherd of Hermas. Several of these instances are too brief to provide enough material for a full analysis from an SIT perspective, but I will treat them in as much depth as possible. The texts provide snapshots of the lives of early Christian groups and offer insights into their view of the ἐπίσκοπος. Second, we have the more extensive texts of Didache, 1 Clement, the Pastoral Epistles, the Ignatian letters, and Irenaeus's *Against Heresies*. These texts give a more detailed view of an emerging office and will thus be treated extensively. For the sake of clarity, I start this part of the book with an overview of when I place all the texts I analyse.

Approximate date CE	Text
60	Philippians
90–110	1 Peter
100–110	Acts, Didache
100–140	The Shepherd of Hermas
110–120	1 Clement
120–125	The Pastoral Epistles
160–175	The Ignatian Letters
180	Irenaeus, *Against Heresies*

Table II.1. *Approximate date of texts.*

As will become clearer in this second part of the book, the later the text, the more elaborated the view of the ἐπίσκοπος as a warrant for Christian identity becomes. I will start with an analysis of the brief and early mentions of the ἐπίσκοπος, all of which will be accounted for in chapter 5. Didache is the earliest text that will be given extensive treatment and will be analysed in chapter 6. I will treat 1 Clement in chapter 7, the Pastoral Epistles in chapter 8, Ignatius of Antioch in chapter 9, and lastly Irenaeus's *Against Heresies* in chapter 10. The concluding eleventh chapter of the book will summarise the results of how the ἐπίσκοπος affected the parting of the ways.

5. Brief Mentions in the New Testament and the Apostolic Fathers

The present chapter collects the relatively early and brief mentions concerning the role of the ἐπίσκοπος. While these texts are too limited to warrant a more extensive analysis, they deserve some attention because they are among the earliest witnesses to the development of the episcopal office. As we shall see, several features that are crucial for Christian group identity and, in the long run, the separation between Christ groups and other Jewish groups, are already present in these brief texts. When identity impresarioship (the construction and embedding of ingroup identity through the inception of a structure that mirrors the core beliefs of the group) and prototypicality (behaviour aligned with the ingroup ideal) are considered, these features are clearly discernible in these brief descriptions (see chapter 2 for the SIT leadership framework).

Three points can be made from the material, even though not all points are discernible in every text: first, a distinct Christ-group prototypicality is already salient in the descriptions of the emerging office. The leaders are prototypes to be mimicked by the congregants. This prototypicality goes beyond ethical behaviour in general since it also conveys salient Christ-group beliefs. Second, the emerging leadership office is expected to protect the ingroup narrative or theology of the Christ groups against outgroup theology/narrative. Third, the idea of succession from apostles to ἐπίσκοποι can be traced, even though this feature is not yet full-blown. It is safe to say that the earliest sources associate the ἐπίσκοπος with the continuing mission of the apostles.

5.1 Philippians

Notably, Phil 1:1 is the sole instance in the authentic Pauline corpus that uses the noun ἐπίσκοπος, and it does so in the plural: Παῦλος καὶ Τιμόθεος δοῦλοι Χριστοῦ Ἰησοῦ πᾶσιν τοῖς ἁγίοις ἐν Χριστῷ Ἰησοῦ τοῖς οὖσιν ἐν Φιλίπποις σὺν ἐπισκόποις καὶ διακόνοις. "Paul and Timothy, servants of Christ Jesus, to all the saints in Christ Jesus who are in Philippi, with the bishops and deacons" (NRSV).

5.1.1 Date, Authorship

Philippians has traditionally been dated to around 60 CE. A significant debate surrounds whether the letter introductions are genuinely Pauline in origin or a later addition. This issue is intrinsically linked to the broader question of the partition of Philippians, which has been a matter of contention for many years. Paul Holloway offers a concise summary of the ongoing debate questions.[1] He argues that the letter should be regarded as a unity, despite both external and internal evidence. This suggestion considers the thematic parallels present in both contested and uncontested sections of the letter. According to Holloway, the themes found in the various sections affirm the document's cohesiveness. In Holloway's view, the letter remains consistent throughout.[2] The argument for a later addition of the introduction pertains to several issues, concisely summarised by Wolfgang Schenck. These include the peculiar use of σύν in the introduction and a reliance on a later redactional "Umkreis der Pastoralbriefe," a distinct school of thought related to the Pastoral Epistles and their perspective on the offices.[3] Schenk also mentions that the idea of leaders labelled ἐπίσκοποι and διάκονοι does not exist earlier in the Pauline corpus. Its use in the Christ movement is not commonly attested until the early second century. This is contested by Davorin Peterlin and others.[4] Peterlin observes that Paul appears to use a variety of leadership titles in his letters, which somehow reflects the local situation. Moreover, as the leaders had specific roles, it is entirely plausible

---

[1] Holloway 2017, 10–19.
[2] Holloway 2017, 18–19.
[3] Peterlin 1995, 20–21. Cf. Schenk 1984, 78–82.
[4] Peterlin 1995, 21.

that they would receive a direct address, distinguished by the preposition σύν. Its late placement in the sentence might otherwise seem like an unusual use of the preposition. Linda Belleville argues generally against a closeness to the Pastorals, as themes that are prominent in the Pastoral Epistles are absent in Philippians.[5] The textual tradition remains unbroken; no text-critical issues indicate a later addition.[6] Note also that the greeting in 1:1–2 is not the part that is most frequently questioned in the letter.[7]

Even if it only has limited implications for this work, I maintain that the Letter to the Philippians should be considered as (at least) two letters that were merged before the textual tradition we have access to was transmitted. Concerning internal cohesion, the interruption of thought, as seen in 3:1, has been

---

[5] Belleville 2021, 9.

[6] Philippians has an "unbroken textual tradition in which the letter is always known as a complete whole" (Martin 1959, 36). The idea that Philippians should be a composite letter before the extant text has a few components. First, the Syriac Canon mentions the first letter of Paul to the Philippians. Second, Polycarp mentions in his letter to the Philippians in 110–35 CE, that "Paul ... in his absence wrote you letters" (ὃς καὶ ἀπὼν ὑμῖν ἔγραψεν ἐπιστολάς) in the plural form (Peterlin, 1995, 12). Third, the problem of internal cohesion of Philippians has made some scholars doubt the unity of the letter. The passages most prominently mentioned as arbitrarily placed in the letter would be the "thank you-note" of 4:10-20, as well as the section from 3:2 up to 4:9. The usual conclusion of a letter in 3:1 (τὸ λοιπόν), is followed by several discourses, including a polemical section starting in 3:2. Sellew (1994, 20) gives a brief overview and suggests that the pseudepigraphic *To the Laodiceans* was modelled on Philippians, verse by verse. In his dissertation from 1997 Jonas Holmstrand noted that nearly half of the commentaries, articles, and monographs on Philippians he had reviewed were certain that mainly chapter three was an interpolation or a compilation, which is a sign of the different views of the matter within the Pauline research field (Holmstrand 1997, 82–83). Some counterarguments against a partition need to be mentioned: The argument stemming from the Syriac Canon has been explained with a scribal error. The Canon is also relatively late (Holmstrand 1997, 84). The Polycarp argument can also be explained by the fact that Polycarp knew of other letters written to the Philippians, and the plural form could also, in this context, as it does in a passage in Eusebius, mean "letter of importance" (Peterlin 1995, 13; Martin 1959, 37, n. 2). I do not find these counter arguments compelling, and understand, for the reasons described in this chapter, that the letter is initially at least two letters that were merged together.

[7] Holmstrand 1997, 82–83. See also Holloway, who agrees with this view twenty years later, Holloway 2017, 66.

explained differently. Martin explains that the dictation of the letter would have been interrupted, and when taken up again, Paul addresses new information he received. No doubt, certain layers of speculation that are impossible to verify arise with such a solution.[8] The argumentation by Peterlin is better: "The striking verbal and theological parallels between chapter three and previous texts, and especially between 2:5–11 and 3:20, 21, point in the same direction."[9] Philip Sellew has an intricate reading of Philippians related to the apocryphal *Laodiceans*.[10] Sellew suggested that *Laodiceans* might have omitted parts of Philippians that were not original.[11] Holloway challenges this by proposing editorial reasons for these exclusions in *Laodiceans*.[12] Some years later, he suggests that 2:19–24 is best understood if Timothy would be sent to the Philippians as consolation, aligned to several other ancient texts.[13] On the contrary, the unusual change of subject in 3:2 leads me to assume that Philippians consists of correspondence from at least two letters written by Paul, rather than just one. It is reasonable to consider that the letter represents Paul's side of a dialogue, thereby indicating correspondence between different letters, owing to the dramatic shift in tone and subject in Phil 3.

However, the arguments supporting a later redactional addition of titles in 1:1 are insufficient. Even if such an addition were made by an unknown redactor, there are no text-critical issues within the letter, nor variant readings of the introduction that suggest this. Furthermore, there is no substantive evidence that supports positing a later school of thought associated with the author of the Pastorals due to the use of episcopal titles in 1:1.

5.1.2 The Role of the ἐπίσκοπος in Philippians

The way the ἐπίσκοπος is mentioned is important. Most certainly, as most commentators are aware, the title does not need to signify a developed theology of a clearly defined office labelled ἐπίσκοπος. This is important from an SIT

---

[8] Cf. Martin 1959, 38–39.
[9] Peterlin 1995, 14–15.
[10] Sellew 1994.
[11] Sellew 1994, 20.
[12] Holloway 1998, 324–25.
[13] Holloway 2008, 556.

perspective: the data do not support the view of the ἐπίσκοπος as an identity entrepreneur, impresario, or advancer of ingroup interests. Thus, nothing in the brief mention or in Paul's treatment of the leaders suggests the leadership structure embedded Christ-group identity among the recipients. However, since we have no further discussion on the case in the genuine Pauline letters, the data only take us so far. In research history, several suggestions have been made concerning the origin of the titles and the nature of the role of these otherwise un-described officials. For a more extensive review of the topic, see chapter 4 above. Here, various commentators' views on the use of ἐπίσκοπος in Philippians will be noted, sometimes reiterating the findings from the previous chapter. What is crucial for the analysis in the next section is that while lack of data makes it impossible to label the leader as neither an entrepreneur, impresario, or advancer of identity, there are several reasons to consider the ἐπίσκοπος as a prototypical leader. Therefore, there is an expectation that the leader should embody the ideals of the Christ group.

Ralph Martin suggested that the title was borrowed from "contemporary society," but was used in the Philippian context to describe the "responsibility which was assumed by certain Christians in the local church."[14] He connected the ministry of the ἐπίσκοπος with the idea of elders in Acts 20:17, 28 and, as such, they had mainly spiritual responsibilities.[15] Hans von Campenhausen, on the same note, suggested from his understanding of the spiritual power and authority of a leader that the use of titles in Phil 1:1 simply means that Paul does not always address leaders in terms of their gifts but also with common titles found in the general society of the time. The singling out of a leader and labelling him with a title does not imply a general emergence of a hierarchical structure. When Paul uses the term ἐπίσκοπος on a leader, he is just recognising a responsibility invested in an able leader.[16] Markus Bockmuehl also understands the term similarly: "Paul's address here, then, appears at the very least to recognize and respect a group of people who in his own absence exercise a ministry of supervision and care for the Christian polity at Philippi, possibly according

---

[14] Martin 1959, 57.
[15] Martin 1959, 57–58.
[16] Von Campenhausen 1969, 68–70.

to its several 'households'."¹⁷ Bockmuehl suggests that the episcopal office was just beginning when it was mentioned in Philippians, indicating that the absence of a single leader for the congregation was intentional. Instead, Paul permitted various models of leadership to remain flexible under his apostolic supervision.¹⁸ John Reuman and Larsolov Eriksson understand the word to signal Greek background for the usage in Philippi.¹⁹ Ben Witherington emphasizes the civic use of the term ἐπίσκοπος, asserting that it refers to a commissioner of a new colony, including Roman colonies. This implies that the recipients possessed a heavenly citizenship when Paul employs it.²⁰ Peter O'Brien does not decide where the inspiration for the titles originated, but he lists LXX usage alongside other Greek influences and notes the similarities with the מבקר of the Qumran communities.²¹ In 2004, Ralph Martin and Gerald Hawthorne expressed views that had evolved from Martin's views in 1959.²² Martin and Hawthorne now suggest inspiration from Jewish counterparts (especially the Qumran communities' overseer מבקר who could serve as a role model for the inception of the office in the Christ group(s) of Philippi).²³ Hawthorne and Martin see it as "by no means unthinkable" that the usage of the term ἐπίσκοπος was some kind of official and rudimentary defined office:

> [The term] does not refer to functions that just any Christian on any required occasion could be led to fulfil ... but to officials, that is, specific individuals who were appointed by the apostle and his companions (cf. Acts 14:23) and whose duties were fairly well defined. They were in some sense to govern, to administer, to oversee the affairs, both material and spiritual, of the community (cf. Acts 20:28). The idea of "supervision" or "protective care" still lay at the heart of the meaning of ἐπίσκοπος, even after centuries of usage.²⁴

---

[17] Bockmuehl 1997, 55.
[18] Bockmuehl 1997, 54–55.
[19] Eriksson 1982, 19–21 suggest not least financial duties in the oversight mission, given the usage in contemporary Greek. See also Reuman 2008, 62–63.
[20] Witherington 2011, 63.
[21] O'Brien 1991, 47.
[22] Hawthorne and Martin 2004, 8–10.
[23] See chapter 4 above for a review of this perspective in a larger context.
[24] Hawthorne and Martin 2004, 10.

They therefore view the office in Philippians as somewhat more organised, as the ἐπίσκοποι are specifically mentioned and seem to possess some form of official status, even though they are not directly addressed "over the heads of the congregation."[25]

Jeannine Brown agrees with earlier perspectives in the discourse on Philippians, that *"overseers and deacons"* would have been the earliest offices of the Christ groups.[26] She also suggests that the inclusion of the titles indicates a specific interest in status among the recipients in Philippi. The self-designation of Paul and Timothy as slaves or servants of Christ (δοῦλος) would then be a conscious method of addressing this issue among the recipients. The choice of words then resurfaces in 2:5–11.[27] The views of the commentators mainly focus on the heuristic dimension of the title; however, a hierarchical perspective is still lacking. Other commentaries do not explore the background of the title in greater depth.[28] Stewart has more recently argued that the plural suggests that there would have been many congregations in a single city, and every congregation had its own ἐπίσκοπος, a view that previously had not been further developed by any other commentator (see further chapter 4 above).[29]

All this suggests that the insufficient data makes it difficult to draw any conclusions regarding whether the origin of the titles would, at this point, hold a deeply significant meaning for the original readers. It is interesting to note the possible backgrounds for the titles, but the only meaning the text of Philippians can provide is that the leaders had a specific role, which meant, among other things, that they served as prototypes for the group. This will be further analysed below.

---

[25] Hawthorne and Martin 2004, 9. See also Fee 1995, 68–69.
[26] Brown 2022, 1A, italics original. [Kindle version].
[27] Brown 2022, 1A. [Kindle version].
[28] Hendriksen 1962, 48; Bruce 1989, 27–28. Holloway 2017, 66–67, comments that we can only speculate on the nature of the tasks of the titleholders.
[29] Stewart 2014, 4. This aligns with his view that the ἐπίσκοποι in every city gathered for consultations in a presbyterion, a city council in which every congregation was represented through its leader.

5.1.3 An SIT Analysis of Christ-Group Prototypicality in Philippians

The ἐπίσκοποι seem to have been leaders, with what we must assume are fairly well-defined roles, but no theology of the ἐπίσκοπος is explicitly evident in Paul's usage here.[30] Given that the main thrust of the commentators is correct, and that the leaders addressed functioned as a rather general type of leader (pastoral and practical), along with that Paul *the apostle* addresses them in their specific roles, it suggests that it is reasonable to assume a somewhat *prototypical* leadership. At this point in the history of the episcopal office's emergence, no further Pauline sources suggest that Paul ascribes any specific identity-bearing aspect to this leadership role. What Philippians allow us to discuss is that leaders still are expected to adhere to the norms established by Paul. Philippians 1 further implies that Paul presents himself as an example of what it means to be a prototypical member (1:12–26) and underscores his expressed willingness to suffer for these norms, provided that Christ is preached. In 1:27–30, Paul directs his focus to the readers or listeners, emphasizing that they should live in a manner worthy of the gospel of Christ (μόνον ἀξίως τοῦ εὐαγγελίου τοῦ Χριστοῦ πολιτεύεσθε). We remind ourselves that this phrase is also aimed at the leaders and that, according to SIT, effective leadership is only enacted when an individual demonstrates prototypical behaviours in ways that encourage other group members to follow the leader's example. The prototype presented in the letter (for instance, 2:5–11) offers an ideal to emulate that may not have been consistently upheld.[31] In particular, there appears to be "selfishness and strife" among the congregation.[32] The existing ideal, the antidote to these behaviours, is theologically motivated; members are expected to adopt the mindset of Christ Jesus (2:5). Paul's own example from prison, along with his eager call for humility (2:1–11), suggests that he expected the leaders to lead exemplary lives. The ideals presented in Philippians generally align with those found elsewhere in the Pauline corpus, such as Galatians 5:22.

---

[30] Most commentators point out that the officers in 1:1 are mentioned separately, suggesting that roles existed, even though we cannot know about their exact content. See for example Hawthorne and Martin 2015, 9; Peterlin 1995, 22.

[31] Peterlin 1995, 8.

[32] Hawthorne and Martin 2015, lxxii.

In one instance in Philippians, Paul addresses group identity concerning an alternate Jewish identity. In 3:2–11, Paul employs an explicitly sharp tone against a certain group that seems to advocate for a notable observance of the Torah. Witherington, for example, interprets the slur κύνας as an inverted Jewish slur against non-Jews.[33] The harshness of the chapter and its apparent capriciousness have been explained by a rush of emotions resulting from Paul's imprisonment and dire situation.[34] Cristopher Zoccali explores the passage from the perspective of a Jewish group identity. For Paul, the retention of the Philippian readers' non-Jewish status is significant, given his views on salvation history.[35] Further, Zoccali understands the rhetoric as directed against those who undermine the Christ-follower identity of the group for any reason. Thus, just as Paul conceives his own past as a loss (3:7), any boasting among the Philippians, apart from their faith in Christ, is considered a loss.[36] This perspective, which is also touched upon by Witherington, where the Philippians are called upon to take on a new identity in Christ, connected to certain behaviours, is the main focus of the passage.[37] Consequently, the prototypicality in question – that the Philippians (including their leaders) should uphold – refers to the identity obtained "in Christ" as exemplified by the apostle Paul. Pride in alternative identities, such as the prominent Jewish identity that Paul claims to have possessed but now regards as a loss, is categorically deemed unacceptable for members of the ingroup.

Given the SIT framework, Paul expects more from leaders than he does from any member. We do not know the exact circumstances under which Paul wrote, and we cannot even say how many times he wrote with certainty! However, the ideals presented are theologically motivated and exemplified by Paul himself. Therefore, what Philippians can contribute to our understanding of the emerging episcopal office is primarily through the construction of a Christian ideal articulated in the letter. While this is a conjecture, it aligns with what SIT teaches us about leadership: prototypical leadership is the most efficient.

---

[33] Witherington 2011, at Probatio 4 [Kindle version].
[34] Hawthorne and Martin 2004, 171–72.
[35] Zoccali 2017, 85.
[36] Zoccali 2017, 89.
[37] Witherington 2011, at Probatio 4 [Kindle version].

According to this conjecture, the leadership exercised by the anonymous Christ-group leaders in Philippi was expected to be prototypical leadership, in keeping with Paul's example. A prominent Jewish identity, which Paul himself considers a loss, is condemned in the second part of the letter.

We now turn to the view on episcopal leadership presented in 1 Peter, about 30–40 years later.

5.2 First Peter and Prototypical ἐπίσκοποι

As we proceed with our SIT analysis of the ἐπίσκοπος in early Christian texts, we will now focus on 1 Peter. There are two instances where ἐπίσκοπος and the cognate masculine active participle are used: 1 Peter 2:25 and 5:2. In both cases, the word relates to spiritual leadership and the metaphor of shepherding. Before addressing this, we must situate 1 Peter in its historical context.

5.2.1 Authorship, Date, and Text Witnesses

I understand 1 Peter to have been written between 90 and 100 CE, and thus not by Peter the apostle. I will dedicate some space to argue this point before I turn to the SIT analysis of the relevant instances. A strong ecclesial tradition associates 1 Peter with the apostle Peter. Apart from 2 Peter (3:1), which claims Petrine authorship of 1 Peter, Irenaeus understands the letter as written by Peter in *Haer.* 4.9.2, and Eusebius and several later Church fathers allude to or cite the letter and assume Petrine authorship.[38] The letter is well attested on several occasions in Pol *Phil*. First Clement has themes that echo those in 1 Peter, and Ramsey Michaels lists several parallels in 1 Clement but understands them rather as drawing on a common source. Michaels concludes after an extensive list of similarities between 1 Peter and 1 Clement (such as 1 Clem 12:7 and 1 Pet 1:18–21) that "yet none of this qualify as hard evidence for literary dependence."[39]

Karen Jobes advocates for a traditional perspective that Peter authored 1 Peter in Rome. She proposes that pseudonymity could present a challenge for the early church, which regards the text as authentic. Drawing on first- and second-century genre conventions, she contends that this issue would indicate

---

[38] Michaels 1988, xxxii–xxxiii.
[39] Michaels 1988, xxxiii.

genuineness authorship.⁴⁰ Otherwise, why would the early Church have accepted it? The evidence should favour authentic authorship, as the letter is well-documented from an early period and, according to Jobes, distinctly resonates with the teachings of Jesus traditions.⁴¹ However, the silence surrounding the conflict with Paul, as noted in Galatians, is peculiar and remains unaddressed by Jobes.⁴² This, along with several other circumstances that will follow, leads me to assume a non-Petrine authorship. Ok (very briefly) and Holloway argue for a pseudonymous interpretation of the text in the latest research.⁴³

Given that we do not have access to conclusive biographical evidence in the epistle itself, aside from 1:1 and generic titles such as "fellow elder" in 5:1, we are left with conjectures. Commentators agree that the knowledge and influence of Pauline texts are evident in the letter. More significantly, the text of 1 Peter indicates a general awareness of Christian tradition and the use of the LXX, yet it cannot be claimed to depend directly on Pauline sources.⁴⁴ However, if Peter did indeed write the letter, it reveals inconsistencies with the scholarly portrayal of the Petrine mission.⁴⁵ When could Peter have gone to and been in contact with the congregations in Asia Minor? Would this not have been Paul's area of mission? Furthermore, the fine Greek seems difficult to connect with the hardworking fisherman from Galilee whose mother tongue was Aramaic.⁴⁶ While this can be balanced in theory by the use of a secretary or amanuensis (a certain Silvanus is said to be the author of the letter instrumentally, 1 Pet 5:12), other evidence must be weighed.⁴⁷ The author is obviously well-versed in the LXX, understands rhetorical structures, and likely possesses some rhetorical

---

⁴⁰ Jobes 2022, 5–21.
⁴¹ Jobes 2022, 15–19.
⁴² Cf Jobes 2022, 5; Holloway 2009, 15–16.
⁴³ Ok 2021, 1; Holloway 2009, 15–17.
⁴⁴ Achtemeier 1996, 17.
⁴⁵ Davids 1990, 40 [Kindle version].
⁴⁶ Davids 1990, 40 [Kindle version]; Michaels 1988, lxii; Achtemeier 1996, 1.
⁴⁷ Michaels 1988, lxii. See also Olsson 1982, 202–3.

expertise.[48] The allusion to hardships in 1 Peter 4 and the relatively positive view of the Roman state do not align with external evidence regarding local persecution under Nero. Instead, it fits better with the circumstances at the beginning of the second century and similar to the situation addressed in Pliny the Younger's correspondence with the emperor Trajan.[49] Further, no material that would suggest the author's personal knowledge of the mission of Jesus in Galilee and Jerusalem is extant, *contra* Jobes.[50]

The traces of episcopal leadership have been suggested as a counterargument against Petrine's authorship, but this is a problematic argument since we do not know how developed the leadership structure was at the time of Peter.[51] As we have just seen, Paul mentions the ἐπίσκοπος in the plural in Phil 1:1, but neither denies nor confirms the structure apart from that. It is true that the evidence on the structure generally is from the second century, but it is impossible to say anything conclusive on the matter from Paul's single mention roughly contemporary to the historical Peter.

No conclusive evidence is available regarding the actual situation in which 1 Peter was written. It has been suggested that the letter was intended to encourage members of the Christ groups during times of persecution. Persecutions under Trajan are externally attested by the letters of Pliny the Younger and took place in the cities that 1:1 mentions,[52] but the descriptions of coming hardships (1 Pet 4:12, 17) seem too unspecific to be conclusive regarding the situation and time.

The letter mentions Rome, "Babylon" (1 Pet 5:13), as its place of origin. Several commentators agree on that, which also the common themes with 1 Clement would suggest.[53] The letter appears to be written for a non-Jewish

---

[48] Olsson 1982, 203. See also Achtemeier's thorough review of the language and rhetoric in 1 Peter, Achtemeier 1996, 2–9.

[49] Michaels 1988, lxiii–lxvi; Olsson 1982, 203.

[50] Olsson 1982, 204; Achtemeier 1996, 1.

[51] Achtemeier 1996, 2.

[52] Davids 1990, 43. [Kindle version].

[53] Davids 1990 45. [Kindle version]; Michaels 1988, xlvii; Olsson 1982, 202.

audience.[54] The self-understanding of the readers is that the new identity in Christ has provided access to the promises given by God in the Hebrew bible/LXX.[55] The Jewish identity is generally foregone by silence, just as in 1 Clement.

The affinities with 1 Clement, the persecution, which does not seem to fit the situation under Nero, and the general peculiarities that make it hard to associate the letter unproblematically with Peter the apostle lead me to adopt a date of origin between 90 and 110 CE.[56] An unknown leader (1 Pet 5) well-versed in the LXX, living in or writing from Rome, with perhaps some knowledge of the situation in Asia Minor, is as much as we can know about the author. The defence of a genuine Petrine authorship by Steve Matthews (albeit in passing) fails to address these critical issues.[57]

A short comment on the manuscript tradition for 1 Pet 5:2 is in order before we turn to a short SIT analysis. As is well known, the reading in 1 Pet 5:2–3 is uncertain. The apparatus in NA²⁸ deems omission or retention of ἐπισκοποῦντες in the text as a difficult redactional decision.[58] The editors put ἐπισκοποῦντες in brackets because the word is omitted in ℵ* and B, and NA²⁸ reads thus: [59] ποιμάνατε τὸ ἐν ὑμῖν ποίμνιον τοῦ θεοῦ [ἐπισκοποῦντες] μὴ ἀναγκαστῶς ἀλλ' ἑκουσίως κατὰ θεόν, μηδὲ αἰσχροκερδῶς ἀλλὰ προθύμως, μηδ' ὡς κατακυριεύοντες τῶν κλήρων ἀλλὰ τύποι γινόμενοι τοῦ ποιμνίου· ("to tend the flock of God that is in your charge, [exercising the oversight] not under compulsion but willingly, as God would have you do it – not for sordid gain but eagerly. Do not lord it over those in your charge but be examples to the flock," NRSV.) The more difficult reading (where ἐπισκοποῦντες is original since the

---

[54] Michaels 1988, xlix–l. The letter is written for a non-Jewish audience, given the addressees in 1:1; the use of temple language in 2:4–6 where the identity predominantly is pronounced as "through Jesus Christ"; and the peculiar silence on any kind of reference to Torah-observance, even if the tone is not explicitly hostile towards outgroups.

[55] Michaels 1988

[56] See also Eurell 2021, 151–52.

[57] Matthews 2022, 59–61.

[58] The text has been altered from NA²⁷, where the use of ἐπισκοποῦντες was not marked as uncertain, as it now is. Several MSS witness the extant reading.

[59] Other text critical signs from NA²⁸ are left out.

text would run more smoothly without it) has been suggested by Michaels, who takes it as the original.[60] Olsson's explanation that there were theological or hierarchical reasons for removing ἐπισκοποῦντες in some text witnesses seems implausible since πρεσβύτερος/ἐπίσκοπος were used interchangeably in a similar way in the Pastoral Epistles and Acts, the need for a theological redaction only in the relatively contemporary 1 Peter seems arbitrary.[61] Rather, it is more probable that the cumbersome repetition of synonyms would lead some copyists to omit the redundant word ἐπισκοποῦντες. I understand the wording here as original, to the best of our understanding. As Achtemeier points out, the same cluster of words appears in Acts 20:17–36 and may suggest an association among the terms in the emerging leadership tradition in the northeastern part of the Mediterranean area.[62]

After these text-critical comments, we turn to a short SIT analysis of 1 Pet 2:25 and 5:2 and their relevant contexts.

5.2.2 First Peter 2:25

Prototypicality, which, as we remember, is the embodiment of the group's ideal, is at the heart of 1 Peter 2, and Jesus is the optimal example. The chapter as such lays out the implications of the theological idea that Christ suffered undeservingly (2:20–21), and Jesus's actions provides an example (ὑπογραμμόν) to follow. The chapter in general works with the antithetical word couple ἐλεύθερος/ δοῦλος. The exhortation addresses the congregation as ἐλεύθεροι (2:16), but the congregants are to act as God's servants or slaves ὡς θεοῦ δοῦλοι. Christ is then described as the servant of God who undeservingly is abused and eventually dies for the sinners: "When he was abused, he did not return the abuse; when he suffered, he did not threaten; but he entrusted himself to the one who judges justly" (NRSV, 2:23). The servant theme is present both in the quotation and allusions from Isaiah 53 in 2:22, but also through the familiarity with the abuses that slaves often encountered in their lives.[63]

---

[60] Michaels 1988, 276, n. b, so also Achtemeier 1996, 320, n. 4.
[61] Olsson 1982, 172.
[62] Achtemeier 1996, 325–26.
[63] Achtemeier 1996, 193–94, 152.

The work of Christ is a crucial, salvific action, pivotal for ingroup self-identification: the wounds of Christ heal the members. No person could be more prototypical (as God's servant) or important (as executor of salvific actions) than Jesus, according to the author of 1 Peter. Jesus is then described as "the shepherd and overseer of your lives/souls" (τὸν ποιμένα καὶ ἐπίσκοπον τῶν ψυχῶν ὑμῶν). Oversight is intimately connected to Jesus, the prototype and bringer of salvation. As several commentators point out, and as will be evident in the comment on 5:2, the language of shepherding often recurs in the Hebrew Bible.[64] The works by the πρεσβύτεροι in 5:2 are intimately connected to the works of Jesus, on which I will further comment below. This association between Jesus and oversight connects the spiritual leader, the shepherd, with Jesus, and thus the leader becomes closely associated with the ingroup identity stemming from Jesus.

5.2.3 First Peter 5:2

In 1 Peter 5:2, we again encounter some ambiguity regarding the relationship between ἐπίσκοπος and πρεσβύτερος. The terms with cognates are used interchangeably; or rather, the πρεσβύτερος is expected to execute oversight, ἐπισκοπέω. This overlap of use for the words ἐπίσκοπος/πρεσβύτερος is mirrored in the uncertain text tradition (see above and below). The active participle ἐπισκοποῦντες emphasizes and qualifies the aorist imperative ποιμάνατε. Thus, the spiritual leadership of the πρεσβύτερος is associated with oversight.[65] Shepherding and oversight appear to be overlapping but not interchangeable. God as ἐπίσκοπος in the LXX "is the all-seeing observer and judge." The concept of shepherding as a metaphor for spiritual leadership, particularly with God as the subject, frequently appears in the Hebrew Bible/LXX.[66] The theme of shepherding associated with oversight (1 Pet 5:2, ποιμάνατε τὸ ἐν ὑμῖν ποίμνιον),[67] is interconnected to the office of overseeing in both Acts 20 and 1 Peter. It is reasonable to understand the prototypical elder as mirroring Christ,

---

[64] Achtemeier 1996, 204; Davids 1990, 122 [Kindle version]; Michaels 1988, 151.

[65] Michaels 1988, 151, understands the word ἐπίσκοπος as qualifying the shepherding theme in the LXX (Job 20:29; Wisd. Sol 1:6) and Philo (*Leg.* 3.43; *Mut.* 39, 216; *Somn.* 1.91).

[66] Ps 23; 100; Isa 40:11; Jer 13:17; Ezek 34:23–24, and so on.

[67] For the peculiar way of using ἐν ὑμῖν, see Achtemeier 1996, 325.

given that Christ was labelled shepherd in 2:25, so that subjugation under the elders is subjugation under Christ.

As has often been observed, chapter 5 belongs to a portion of 1 Peter that predominantly addresses elders.[68] Leaders are encouraged to act as role models, that is, what SIT labels as prototypical; when they do so, they mirror Jesus's and God's saving actions and thus exemplify identity impresarioship. Shepherding is expressed in the Hebrew Bible as a prototype of good spiritual leadership. In Christian teachings, Jesus is described as a good shepherd (John 10:14, 16). In the later Pauline tradition (Eph 4:11), also, shepherding is a metaphor for leadership. According to ingroup norms, good leadership mirrors God's work and indicates ingroup identity.

Regarding prototypical leadership, four aspects of the passage 5:1–4 require comment. First, pastoral care is described through contrasting word pairs.[69] The antithesis in the exhortation relates to the motivation for spiritual leadership: compulsion (ἀναγκαστῶς) and financial gains (to which 'greedily' or αἰσχροκερδῶς likely refers) are not appropriate motivations for pastoral work. The language emphasises prototypical leadership: practising leadership properly means not doing it for personal gain (μηδὲ αἰσχροκερδῶς) or to exercise lordship (κατακυριεύοντες), but becoming an example for the Christ-group members (τύποι γινόμενοι).[70] This leads to the second theme worth noting about prototypical leadership: the idea that financial compensation for pastoral work seems to have developed by this time (Matt 10:10; 1 Cor 9:3–14; see also 1 Tim 5:17–18). Thus, as 1 Cor 9 shows, full-time pastoral workers are always at risk of being accused of misusing common funds.[71] The warning against greed in v. 2 suggests a knowledge of this exposure to greed in the leadership model. Instead, it is suggested that inner motivation consistent with ingroup ideals is expected from an elder. Chapter 4 spelled out ideal membership, as in 4:16, where suffering as a Christian (Χριστιανός) is considered honourable. The prototypical behaviour in chapter 4 is expressed both in the negative (4:3, 15) and

---

[68] Michaels 1988, xxxiii–xl.

[69] Achtemeier 1996, 326.

[70] Michaels 1988, 278, explicitly connects the passage with the qualifications for the ἐπίσκοπος in the Pastoral Epistles.

[71] Davids 1990, 162 [Kindle version].

in positive sense (4:7–11). Fourth, the connection between the chapters is important when we try to understand the prototypical leadership expressed in the passage. Chapter 5 is connected to the ingroup ideals presented in chapter 4 through the particle οὖν.[72] These four observations show that leadership is, on the one hand, intimately connected to the exercising of good example, according to 1 Peter 5. On the other hand, the shepherd metaphor provides the ingroup with a meaningful structure as a vehicle for believing in Christ. The shepherd metaphor is worth noting as an expression of identity impresarioship when applying SIT terms. Identity impresarioship is, as we recall, the embedding of ingroup identity in structures and rituals. The shepherd language, as noted, positions the discourse within a significant theme in the Hebrew Bible/LXX, that spiritual leadership is like the work of a shepherd. The leadership model in the Christ groups, which is described in shepherd terms, connects the ingroup with God's saving acts. The synonymous use of shepherding and overseeing (ποιμάνατε τὸ ἐν ὑμῖν ποίμνιον τοῦ θεοῦ [ἐπισκοποῦντες]) connects the elders to the shepherd theme. To be shepherding and exercising oversight is connected to the saving and nurturing actions of God, for example, when God saved the Israelites from slavery in Egypt (Ps 78:52). This theme is also explicitly connected to Jesus in v. 4, in which Jesus is labelled "the chief shepherd" (ἀρχιποίμενος). In 5:1, the author describes himself as a συμπρεσβύτερος καὶ μάρτυς τῶν τοῦ Χριστοῦ παθημάτων ("fellow elder and witness to Christ's suffering"). In 2:21–25, the suffering of Christ is both an example to follow (ἵνα ἐπακολουθήσητε τοῖς ἴχνεσιν αὐτοῦ, "so that you should follow in his footsteps") and God's saving action *par excellence* (1 Pet 2:23–25). Thus, to be a prototypical shepherd is to partake in the mission of Jesus, who is the ideal shepherd and the source (ἀρχή) for good shepherding. The oversight and shepherding of Christ are also executed within the Christ group, when the πρεσβύτεροι exercise their leadership properly. The leadership model is closely associated with central themes in Christ-group theology; it is an embedding of Christ-group theology in the leadership structure and is thus an example of identity impresarioship.

---

[72] Michaels 1988, 276 (n. a); Achtemeier 1996, 322.a

In summary, in 1 Peter, Christ serves as the model of behaviour that congregants should emulate. The care of Christ and the archetypal πρεσβύτεροι are closely intertwined. The expected behaviour for πρεσβύτεροι is outlined clearly, indicating that leaders should be motivated by inner conviction rather than greed. Leaders are also anticipated to be prepared to endure suffering for the ideals of their group. While remaining humble (in line with the principle delineated in 1 Pet 4), the πρεσβύτεροι embody Christ-like qualities. Concurrently, the work of the πρεσβύτεροι and the oversight they provide are likened to shepherding, thereby reflecting the prominent shepherd theme in the Hebrew Bible. On numerous occasions, God is described as a shepherd. Consequently, when the πρεσβύτεροι fulfil their leadership responsibilities correctly, they resonate with the salvific acts of God throughout the Hebrew Scriptures. Thus, to submit to the ministry of the πρεσβύτεροι is to submit to the works of God and Christ. The author of 1 Peter illustrates an example of identity impresarioship, wherein the salvific acts of God are linked with the episcopal/presbyterial ministry, which emerges as a significant structure of identity. We now turn to the Acts of the Apostles and two pertinent instances regarding the role of the ἐπίσκοπος.

5.3 Acts of the Apostles

When we turn to Acts, there are two instances where words derived from ἐπίσκοπος are mentioned. In 1:20, there is a quote from Psalm 108:8 in the LXX stating that "may another take his place of leadership" (NRSV; τὴν ἐπισκοπὴν αὐτοῦ λαβέτω ἕτερος). As discussed in chapter 1 above, the instance of the noun here designates a role or perhaps an office associated with oversight. Commentaries do not elaborate significantly on the wording; the main point is the use of citations from the Hebrew Bible, understood as the fulfilment of promise, as well as the context of the Psalms. Of course, from the quote in 1:20, one cannot establish a leadership structure, and not much can be deduced beyond noting the existence of the term. However, it does hint at a theological pattern that began to emerge at the end of the first century. This also exemplifies how Peter, as a prototypical member of the Christ group, is granted authority (according to Luke) to present a slightly altered ingroup prototypicality. This alteration of ingroup prototypes is referred to as identity entrepreneurship in the SIT framework.

In Acts 20:17, Paul sends for a meeting with those designated τοὺς πρεσβυτέρους τῆς ἐκκλησίας in Ephesus. In 20:28 Paul addresses the elders from v. 17 further (τοὺς πρεσβυτέρους) as "appointed as ἐπίσκοποι to shepherd the congregation of God" (ἔθετο ἐπισκόπους ποιμαίνειν τὴν ἐκκλησίαν τοῦ θεοῦ). There is a close connection, if not identification, between πρεσβύτεροι and ἐπίσκοποι.[73] This passage is one of the factors contributing to the understanding of research history (see chapter 4 above), indicating that the πρεσβύτεροι and ἐπίσκοποι were synonymous in the earliest Christian group contexts.

Before we turn to a closer examination of these passages, a few words are needed regarding the research on Acts and its neighbouring Jewish groups. Throughout the 2010s, a trend has been thoroughly tracked by Jason Moraff to interpret Luke-Acts in relation to its contemporary neighbouring Jewish communities.[74] Here, a range of perspectives exists; on the one hand, Shelley Matthews depicts the parting of the ways as a process reflected in Acts's violent depiction of the stoning of Stephen.[75] Conversely, the divergence is illustrated through scriptural appropriation in Luke-Acts and Justin Martyr.[76] While this dissertation is interested in general with this topic, few works have examined the Christ-group structure in Luke-Acts. None have analysed the leadership structure specifically from a SIT perspective.

In the following section, I will clarify what the emerging episcopal structure signifies concerning the formation of a group identity. We shall observe that the two occurrences in Acts are instances of identity impresarioship, where the leadership structure promotes continuity with the mission of Jesus and the apostles, serving as a vital vehicle for Christ-group identity. To be linked with the apostolic Christ groups is, in essence, to be linked with the mission of Jesus, as suggested by the leadership structure. Before I proceed, I will place Acts within the context of early second-century writings.

---

[73] Fitzmyer 1998, 678–80. See also Conzelmann 1987, 175; Witherington 1998, 623 [Kindle version].
[74] Moraff 2020.
[75] Matthews 2010, 4–5.
[76] Wendel 2011, 2–3.

5.3.1 Date and Author

Who was the author of this work, and when was it written? It is well known that the overwhelming majority of scholars consider Luke and Acts to have been written by the same author. Colossians 4:14 refers to λουκᾶς ὁ ἰατρός, which tradition connects to the author of Luke-Acts. Furthermore, the prologue of Acts presumes knowledge of the Gospel of Luke. The *Muratorian Canon* (lines 34–39) connects Luke the evangelist with Acts; lines 2–9 says that Luke was a physician.[77] Irenaeus *Haer.* 3.10.1, and 3.1.1. connects Luke with Paul and claims that he was "a doctor" from Syrian Antioch who died unmarried at the age of eighty-four, full of Holy Spirit."[78] These unverifiable traditions provide us with later and secondary information. Luke 1:2 indicates that the author gathered data from sources beyond his own eyes.[79] From the text of Acts we note that his style is slightly higher than other New Testament texts, apart from Hebrews.[80] The vocabulary "is considerable and exhibits points of contact with Josephus, Plutarch, Lucian, ... and most of all with the LXX."[81] The author shows "technical knowledge," and appears as someone who intends to write "literature," and someone who portrays "Christian witnesses as adept in their appearance before representatives of the political and intellectual world."[82] The author is well-versed in philosophical concepts, depicting the Christ groups as a philosophical school.[83] Luke also has an apologetic perspective on Christians, portraying them as meek, humble, and self-controlled.[84] Here, I will, for practical reasons, name the author Luke and note that he is a skilful author, well-versed in ancient literature and the LXX. Since the author is familiar with Asia

---

[77] See however Clare Rothschild's recent discussion on the date of the Muratorian Fragment, where she argues that the text is a fourth-century forgery claiming to be a second century text, Rothschild 2022, 1–4.
[78] Conzelmann 1987, xxxii.
[79] Mason 2003, 252, note 2.
[80] Conzelmann 1987, xxxv.
[81] Conzelmann 1987, xxxv–vi.
[82] Conzelmann 1987, xl.
[83] Mason 2003, 284.
[84] Mason 2003, 285–88.

Minor, I will tentatively assume that the tradition of connecting the author with Syrian Antioch is plausible.

There has been a long and considerable debate over the date of Luke-Acts.[85] The matters concerning the date (and thus the origins of the text) have not been settled thus far, and recent years have seen a debate between early and late daters.[86] Dates ranging between 60 CE to the middle of the second century have been suggested, and the middle ground of dating in the 80s has come to be seen as a "political compromise."[87] The present work does not provide new insights on the matter, but there are several factors to consider when discussing the age of Acts, particularly regarding the instance that mentions the role of the ἐπίσκοπος.

Several components are important when discussing the date. The scholars suggesting an earlier date tend to emphasise the following points: Luke's relationship to Paul;[88] the literary accounts of the destruction of Jerusalem in Luke 19:43–44 and 21:20–24;[89] the peculiarity that Acts does not explicitly mention the death of Paul,[90] and makes few if any allusions to the letters of Paul (while for example 1 Clement, which many authors assume to have an earlier date in the last decade of the first century than I do, makes clear allusions to Romans and 1 Corinthians) has been arguments for an early dating.[91] However, this is refuted by Ryan Schellenberg, who elegantly presents a thesis widely accepted

---

[85] A pedagogical overview from an early dating-perspective, including the state of research thus far in the twenty-first century is provided by Armstrong 2021, 4–19. An overview which emphasizes the different socio-cultural milieus of Luke-Acts and Justin Martyr is found in Wendel 2011, 7–11, 281. See also Rackham 1899, 76, and von Harnack 1911, 95.

[86] Pervo 2006 as an example of a late dater. Armstrong 2021 is an early dater.

[87] Armstrong 2021, 1–3; Pervo 2009, 29–46. One can note that both the perspectives of an early and a late dating respectively firmly discard Joseph Fitzmyer's perspective that "there is no good reason to oppose that date, even if there is no real proof for it" regarding his dating 80–85 CE, Fitzmyer 1998, 54.

[88] Cf. for example Armstrong 2021, 15.

[89] Baker 2011, 204. See also Witherington 1998, 68 [Kindle version].

[90] Conzelmann 1987, xxxiii.

[91] Witherington 1998, 370–71 [Kindle version] lists the speech themes in Acts 20:17–38, themes found both in the Pauline epistles and Acts. The section is the only time in Acts Paul is given a longer discourse addressed to believers in Jesus Christ.

in recent debate developments.⁹² He vigorously argues for a remarkable resemblance between the itinerary of Paul in the genuine letters (and perhaps 2 Timothy), on the one hand, and Acts on the other.⁹³ It is likely that Acts makes use of the Pauline letters, ruling out a very early dating of Acts. While Karl Armstrong's arguments against the latest dating are compelling (assuming Marcionite teachings emerged too early), his arguments for very early dating lack strength.⁹⁴ When he pushes the date earlier, he argues from silence about the great fire in Rome and believes that Luke 21 should not be interpreted as aware of the fall of Jerusalem in 70 CE. Both arguments fail to convince.

On the other hand, the idea driven by, for example, Steve Mason and Richard Pervo, that Acts is literarily dependent on Josephus (cf. Acts 5:36 and *A.J.* 20:97–98; Acts 12:21–23 and *A.J.* 19:343–50; Acts 21:38 and *B.J.* 2:261–63/*A.J.* 20:169–72) would give an earliest date of composition around 93 CE.⁹⁵ For Pervo, the date would thus end up rather close to the Pastoral Epistles and Polycarp, ca. 115 CE.⁹⁶ An objection against Acts's use of Josephus, which has been debated for a long time, has most recently been raised again by Armstrong.⁹⁷ The similarities between Josephus and Acts would seem to suggest that Acts was written no earlier than the last decade of the first century CE.⁹⁸ Armstrong has contested the cases where Luke may have used Josephus, suggesting that, for instance, Acts 5:36-37 and Josephus *A.J.* 20:97–102 refer to different situations. In this instance, it is impossible to rule out different situations, considering the commonality of the name Theudas and the political turmoil of the time described.⁹⁹ However, what Armstrong fails to address in his book is not the

---

⁹² Schellenberg 2015, 193.

⁹³ Schellenberg 2015, 213.

⁹⁴ Eurell 2025, 158–9, discusses several problematic features of Armstrong's argumentation, notably an apologetic stance in the book.

⁹⁵ Conzelmann 1987, xxxiii.

⁹⁶ Pervo 2009a, 5.

⁹⁷ See for example Conzelmann 1987, xxxiii. See also Mason 2003; Pervo 2009a.

⁹⁸ See Baker 2011, 206.

⁹⁹ Armstrong 2021, 86–92. This view was also held by Bruce 1988. Mason 2003, 252, points out that generic parallels exist between Luke-Acts and Josephus, "for many other works of the

commonalities of Josephus and Luke-Acts that point to a dependence on Josephus; those exist simultaneously in many other ancient works. What is important, and Armstrong fails to refute, is the common themes in Josephus that describe Judaism and Christ groups as philosophical schools.[100] More to the point, the designations of the various groups within Judaism (Essenes, Pharisees, Sadducees) are referred to as different versions of Jewish "sects" (αἱ αἱρέσεις), and both the Lukan Paul and Josephus describe the Pharisees as "the most precise school."[101] These peculiar overlaps between Josephus and Luke-Acts gravitate towards the idea that Luke had access to Josephus when he wrote Acts. This pushes the date to 93 CE the earliest, given that Luke read Josephus's texts on αἱ αἱρέσεις within Judaism immediately after they were written.[102] A more inference from Luke's knowledge of Josephus would be around 100 CE.[103]

Further arguments suggest an even later date: Joseph Tyson's argument that Luke in Acts should address Marcionite heresies requires a widespread understanding of Marcionite ideas in the early to mid-second century.[104] This idea has been defended by Glenn Snyder.[105] However, Armstrong makes a strong case against the Marcionite thesis since we have no data of Marcionite teachings before the 140's.[106] The different socio-cultural milieus described by Wendel sustain this argument.[107] The argument for a later date from ecclesial polity is furthermore double-edged. Acts 7 and 20 seem to know of an ecclesial structure, which Pervo would suggest lies in the second century only. Since there are signs of at least rudimentary developed Christ-group polity structures in the first

---

period shared similar features," but not too much can be concluded from these parallels: "Nor can the commonly reported incidents prove dependence, in the absence of extended verbal agreement."

[100] Mason 2003 283–91.
[101] Mason, 2003, 292.
[102] Cf. Baker 2011, 204.
[103] Baker 2011, 206, also comes to this conclusion.
[104] See Baker 2011, 205; Tyson 2006, 1–23.
[105] Snyder 2013, see also Lieu 2015.
[106] Armstrong 2021, 18–19.
[107] Wendel 2011, 205–6, 281. Note however Matthews 2010, 5–6, who rather pushes Luke-Acts closer in time to Justin Martyr, due to their similarities.

century (for example, Phil 1; Gal 5; 6; 1 Thess 5), Armstrong sees it as an argument best understood for an earlier date.[108] While I do not follow Armstrong regarding an early dating, and given that there seems to be a broad theological consolidation around the ἐπίσκοπος during the first part of the second century (as this work largely discuss), and given the close connections between Luke-Acts and Josephus, a date between 100–130 CE is rather credible. My assumption, when trying to narrow the spectrum, is around 110 CE.

5.3.2 Comments from an SIT Perspective

The book of Acts is as book with a purpose. Joseph Fitzmyer suggests that "[t]he narrative account of Acts ... continues the Jesus-story and spreads abroad 'to the end of the earth' the Word that Jesus 'taught from the beginning'."[109] It is also a book stressing the Jesus movement's continuance with the Hebrew Scriptures and "Judaism, especially the Pharisaic form of it."[110] Fitzmyer depicts Acts as a

> pastoral assurance [that] aims to assure Theophilus and other Gentile-Christian readers like him that the church of his day was ... rooted in the Period of Jesus, in the teachings of Jesus himself, in order to strengthen the fidelity to that teaching and practice, even when that proved unacceptable to many Jews and pagans of Luke's day.[111]

Thus, the ingroup identity as Christ follower is a salient topic in Acts. Christian identity formation is also distinguished through the rite of baptism and the experience of the Holy Spirit.[112] Mitzi Smith evaluates how the ingroup identity is formed against the backdrop of "others." She distinguishes how women, charismatics ("magicians"), and Jews are understood as "others" throughout Acts.[113] The prototypical member, to align Smith's investigation with SIT, proposes thus that Christ-follower identity is different from Jewish identity in

---

[108] Armstrong 2021, 18.
[109] Fitzmyer 1998 59.
[110] Fitzmyer 1998, 58, cf. Conzelmann 1987, xlvi-xlvii, where the continuation from and connection to Judaism also is acknowledged. See also Bruce 1998, 9–10; Witherington 1998, 64–65 [Kindle version]. For a special study on the use of Scripture in Luke-Acts, see Wendel 2010.
[111] Fitzmyer 1998, 59.
[112] Baker 2011, xv–xvi.
[113] Smith 2011.

some respects. In relatively recent Luke-Acts scholarship, the relationship between a salient Jewish identity and a salient Christ-follower identity is at the fore.[114] Moraff's observation is quite to the point when he notes that where "one locates Luke-Acts vis à-vis Judaism profoundly affects interpretation of these narratives."[115] From a perspective close to SIT, Coleman Baker suggests that the purpose of Acts is to present a new kind of identity, where Jewish and non-Jewish Christ followers are merged into one new identity, "a common superordinate Christian identity" as a response to the identity conflicts in the Christ movement during the first century. This new identity is presented through two prototypical leaders, Peter and Paul.[116] Further, this new identity "distinguishes between distinctly Christian belief and practice on the one hand and Judean and Greco-Roman belief and practice on the other."[117] The fact, however, that there are instances present in Acts where a leadership structure connected to the Christ groups is denoted as ἐπίσκοπος, πρεσβύτερος, and διάκονος, is interesting from the perspective of this present book. These titles somehow convey a message to the readers about the ingroup identity. Some version of an organization connected to the separate Christian identity is forming through the inception of an office. In this organization, according to Acts, the ἐπίσκοπος is connected to apostolic authority (chapter 1) and spiritual leadership (chapter 20). Since the aim of this study is to understand how the ἐπίσκοπος conveys a new Christian identity, I will analyse the role of the ἐπίσκοπος and, to a relevant extent, the πρεσβύτερος.

Acts 1

In Acts 1, the use of ἐπισκοπή exemplifies identity impresarioship, as the emerging office embeds identity in structures and rituals, (see chapter 2 above). As found in Acts 1:20, an LXX rendering of Psalms 109(108):8 is provided in response to the defection of Judas Iscariot: τὴν ἐπισκοπὴν αὐτοῦ λαβέτω ἕτερος. ("'Let another take his position of overseer.'"). Originally, in Psalms, the quote

---

[114] Moraff 2020, 64–65.
[115] Moraff 2020, 64.
[116] Baker 2011, xv.
[117] Baker 2011, xv.

was a curse in the optative mood. Luke transforms it into the imperative tense, addressing the appointment of a new apostle following the casting of lots.[118] The aim of casting lots is to select someone who, having been part of the community from the outset (v. 21), ought to be a "witness with us to his resurrection [μάρτυρα τῆς ἀναστάσεως αὐτοῦ σὺν ἡμῖν]" (v. 22). Therefore, the role of the replacer practically involves assuming a teaching or preaching position within the community as a witness of the resurrection.[119] The roles of preaching and teaching are also assumed by Peter and Paul throughout Acts. The number of twelve apostles corresponds with the twelve tribes of Israel and is, therefore, an important figure for the emerging Christ groups, containing identity-shaping information. The twelve suggest that the Christ groups are closely linked to God's chosen people. This tradition appears in the Gospels on multiple occasions.[120] The overseeing office of the apostles is thus linked to the mission of Jesus, and filling the vacant position signifies that the role of the Christ groups remains relevant. The number of twelve apostles and the election of a substitute for Judas are expressions of an identity impresarioship in which the institution of apostles serves as a vehicle for emerging Christian identity. Furthermore, regarding Christ-group identity, the office of oversight vested in a departed apostle (τὴν ἐπικοπὴν αὐτοῦ) can be taken over and succeeded. The method of selecting a successor through the casting of lots has numerous precedents in Scripture (Lev 16:8, Num 26:55, cf. 1 Chron 26:13–14). It is also documented in the Qumran library and the Community rule (1QS V, 3, VI, 16). This implies that at least one other Jewish group, *relatively* close in chronological terms to the Christ groups, employed this method of discerning the divine will.[121] However, there is not any description of how Matthias is consecrated through the laying on of hands (as in Acts 13:3 when Paul and Barnabas are sent out from Antioch), but the text simply states that Matthias "was added to the eleven apostles," (συγκατεψηφίσθη μετὰ τῶν ἕνδεκα ἀποστόλων, 1:26).[122]

---

[118] Conzelmann 1987, 11–12.
[119] Witherington 1998, 106 [E-book].
[120] Conzelmann 1987, 12.
[121] Witherington 1998, 106–7.
[122] BDAG s v. συγκαταψηφίζομαι: "Be chosen (by a vote) together with."

Peter, the central figure in the passage, is further developed throughout Acts as a prototypical Christ-group member.[123] Peter embodies the ideals of the ingroup. Baker highlights how Peter, when discussing the fulfilment of Scripture in Acts 1:16, echoes Jesus's words from Luke 24:44. Peter's identity now serves to remind the readers of Jesus's identity as part of the divine plan unfolds.[124] The prototypical leader Peter is constructed as suggesting that readers may still have access to the works of Christ and the apostles through the succeeding leaders, who are the overseers of the group. When Luke invests this authority in Peter in his portrayal, he functions as an entrepreneur of identity. Entrepreneurship is the ability that prototypical leaders are granted by the group to redefine ingroup prototypicality (see chapter 2 above). Even more to the point, Peter stands as the identity entrepreneur, as he, as a prototypical group member, presents a new vision of what it means to be a member of the group: to subject oneself to the structure that succeeds the apostles. Competing groups suggesting other visions of ingroup prototypicality would then need to disprove Peter's authority if they wish to prevail.

In summary, Peter's prototypicality, combined with the emerging leadership in alignment with the mission of Jesus, suggests that the identity of the emerging Christ groups is closely connected to the apostles' successors. This is an example of impresarioship: embedding ingroup identity in structures. The message conveyed to the readers regarding Christian identity is that partaking in the Christ groups is equivalent to participating in the mission of the apostles and, consequently, the mission of Jesus. Also, this is an example of entrepreneurship. The new vision of ingroup prototypicality that arises from this structure, in which the group member is committed to the continuing mission of the apostles, exemplifies identity entrepreneurship. A prototypical member participates in the Christ groups that originated with the apostles. This suggestion of a new identity is made possible primarily by the prototypicality of Peter, who initiates the apostolic succession. Several of these features are evident in Acts 20, to which we now turn our attention.

---

[123] Baker 2011, 69–70, 72.
[124] Baker 2011, 81.

Acts 20

In the section Acts 20:17–36, Luke embeds ingroup identity in leadership structures. Paul is on his way to Jerusalem, and as he passes by, he sends for the πρεσβυτέρους τῆς ἐκκλησίας from Ephesus. Since J. B. Lightfoot, this passage has been seen as important proof that πρεσβύτερος and ἐπίσκοπος were used interchangeably in the Christ groups at this stage.[125] The passage carries connotations of a spiritual testament, where Paul, apostle and prototypical Christ-group member, sends a powerful message to local representatives ("elders") of a given Christ group.[126] In this particular context, Paul exhorts the elders to be good "shepherds of the flock": προσέχετε ἑαυτοῖς καὶ παντὶ τῷ ποιμνίῳ, ἐν ᾧ ὑμᾶς τὸ πνεῦμα τὸ ἅγιον ἔθετο ἐπισκόπους ποιμαίνειν τὴν ἐκκλησίαν τοῦ θεοῦ, ἣν περιεποιήσατο διὰ τοῦ αἵματος τοῦ ἰδίου, "Keep watch over yourselves and over all the flock, of which the Holy Spirit has made you overseers, to shepherd the church of God that he obtained with the blood of his own Son" (v. 28). This means in practice a teaching responsibility against the "wolves" (λύκοι) who will try to lead the sheep astray (v. 29).[127] The debate regarding whether ἄφιξιν μου means that Paul is discussing his coming death (not explicitly stated in Acts 28), points to the double meaning of "departure," in which Paul, the prototypical apostle leaves the elders with the task *as successors of Paul*, to be warrants for the congregation's resilience against false teachers who lead astray (λαλοῦντες διεστραμμένα). Once again, the prototypical Christ-group leader invests authority in holders of a rudimentary office who will guard the congregation.[128] It can be observed that Paul's primary emphasis in this section is not on the continuation of a mission to unreached groups, but rather on safeguarding against false teachings.

Paul's prototypicality as an embodiment of ingroup ideals is also highlighted in vv. 34–35, in which he becomes an example of hard labour on behalf

---

[125] Lightfoot 1881, 95–99. See chapter 4 above for further discussion.

[126] Witherington 1998, 371 [Kindle version], notes genre similarities with Gen 49, Josh 23–24, 1 Sam 12, and the pseudepigraphal texts As. Mos., T. 12 Patr., but also with John 13–17, and the deutero Pauline 1 Tim 4:1–16 and 2 Tim 3:1–4:8. Conzelmann 1987, 173, notes also 2 Pet.

[127] Conzelmann 1987, 175.

[128] Baker 2011, 181–82, portrays Paul in the light of Christ, on his way to Jerusalem to suffer.

of the ingroup values of the Christ group. In vv. 28–30, the oversight office safeguards the ingroup narrative and values against threats from outsiders. These outsiders also appear to be part of the ingroup but lead the flock astray. Luke warns against a misguided perception of ingroup narratives and values. Thus, the prototypical Paul of Acts presents the office of the πρεσβύτερος/ἐπίσκοπος as an antidote to camouflaged heresies. Ingroup values and narratives are safe as long as the emerging office oversees them. Paul in Acts (as the voice of the author) is an identity impresario, who guards ingroup teachings through the leadership structure. To be safe as a Christ-group member, then, is to stick to the perspective of the πρεσβύτερος/ἐπίσκοπος. This perspective is, to somewhat anticipate the following chapters, visible throughout the later second-century texts, not least Ignatius and Irenaeus. The close relationship between the elders and Paul (vv 36–38) presents an intimate connection between the apostles and the emerging polity of the Christ group in Ephesus. To summarise the SIT findings of Acts, there are examples of entrepreneurship and impresarioship. In the long run, the overseeing office in Acts is associated with Peter and Paul. Peter continues the mission of Jesus and is prototypical in his behaviour. Thus, the leader is expected to work with Peter as a role model. Peter's authorisation of the succession from the apostles serves as an example of identity entrepreneurship, as the leadership structure is essential for alignment with prototypical group members. Further, Luke acts as an identity impresario when he embeds the ingroup identity within a structure. The leaders in chapter 20, for example, are the successors of Paul the Apostle. They are installed to safeguard the congregation against false leaders and teachings that may lead the group astray. To be associated with these leaders is to align oneself with Paul's mission. The antidote for an ingroup member to avoid being misguided is to remain close to the πρεσβύτερος/ἐπίσκοπος. Thus, this leadership structure becomes a safe haven for their faith, provided they restrict themselves to the care of the leadership structure.

5.4 The Shepherd of Hermas

The next text to be analysed is the first non-canonical source among my references. Nevertheless, it appears to have been quite a popular book among the members of the Christ group since its inception. Dan Batovici surveys the reception history of and modern research on the Shepherd and notes that it was counted as *Scripture* (in the senese of being useful for the soul) even if it was not *canonical*.[129] Bart Ehrman notes that Hermas the Shepherd "was copied and read more widely in the second and third centuries than any other non-canonical book," given the number of remains from manuscripts.[130] Peter Lampe suggests that the book partly discusses a conflict between social groups in the Roman congregation(s).[131] The edge against rich members of the congregation (see for example 14:5) would suggest a theme important for the unity of the congregations.

The title ἐπίσκοπος occurs twice in the Shepherd, one in the famous tower metaphor in 13:1 (Herm. Vis. 3.5.1), and one in the parables of the mountains, in 104:2 (Herm. Sim. 9.27.2). We can note that the office of the ἐπίσκοπος is only mentioned in passing and that the leaders' personal examples and ways of life seem to have been more important for the author, than their titles.[132] This will be discussed further from an SIT perspective in due time. I will comment on both instances below. First, however, the text needs to be situated in history.

5.4.1 Date, Authorship

The picture concerning the author that emerges throughout the text comes from autobiographical notes in the Shepherd. If these instances are taken at face value, a freedman from Rome would be the author (see Herm.Vis.1.1). There is a debate, however, about whether it is plausible that there was only a single author, and to what extent the reported autobiographical events actually occurred. Additionally, some information can be inferred from the style: it has been argued that the author was neither the most skilled writer nor necessarily one of the leaders (whom the author discusses in the third person) because of

---

[129] Batovici 2017, 104–5.
[130] Ehrman 2003b, 162.
[131] Lampe 1987, 74–76.
[132] Buie 2022, 21.

5.4 The Shepherd of Hermas

their "superficial theology."[133] The geographical descriptions in the text make Rome the most probable place of origin.[134]

It has been debated when the text should be dated. Since the text carries several peculiarities, such as the relationship between the older women in Vision 1–4 and the Shepherd, who emerges only in chapter 5, suggestions have been made that the book was circulated in parts.[135] Since the manuscript tradition is complex, the fact that different parts have been found in different manuscripts speaks in favour of this.[136] The book is, however, quoted by several church Fathers, such as Origen and Tertullian, who quote from different passages and appear to have understood the work as a single unit.[137] Apart from the manuscript tradition, a few other things are relevant for the dating: Hermas is familiar with Clement from Rome, a "kind of foreign correspondent" for the congregation(s).[138] The Muratorian Canon, often dated between 150–200 CE, wants the Shepherd to be excluded from the New Testament canon and understands it to have been written quite recently.[139] Traces of a high ecclesiology from Ephesians is found in the text, suggesting that the Shepherd was written in the latter part of the time frame 95–150 CE.[140] These somewhat contradictory reports make an exact date difficult to pinpoint, but Ehrman's suggestion between 110 and 140 CE seems plausible, with the Muratorian Canon as the latest possible date.[141]

---

[133] Ehrman 2003b, 167. John Muddiman deems Hermas "an amateur, idiosyncratic visionary," Muddiman 2005, 121.

[134] For discussion, see Grundeken 2015, 9–11.

[135] Buie and and Svigel 2023, Introduction [Kindle version], Ehrman 2003b, 165–66.

[136] Ehrman 2003b, 166.

[137] Grundeken 2015, 11–16, Buie and and Svigel 2023, Introduction [Kindle version].

[138] Ehrman, 2003b, 168. See also Grundeken 2015, 4–5.

[139] Grundeken 2015 5–6, Ehrman 2003b, 168.

[140] Muddiman 2005, 117 assumes that Ephesians is older than Hermas and 2 Clement.

[141] Ehrman 2003b, 169. Lampe (1987, 30) places Hermas in the first half of the second century. Grundeken's view, which is sceptical of most modern attempts to date the text, still ends up with a rather traditional view: "Hermas was probably written somewhere between the end of the first and the middle of the second century. On the basis of the available evidence, an exact date cannot be established" (Grundeken 2015, 9). The sound reasoning regarding *the terminus ante quem* is

5.4.2 An SIT Comment on Herm. Vis. 3.5.1 (13.1)

The first of the two instances that discuss the ἐπίσκοπος requires some context: Hermas has fasted and prayed for guidance on how to interpret his previous visions. Now, an elderly woman (who is a personification of the congregation, Herm. Vis. 3.3.3.(11.3)) reveal herself in a field together with six young men (Herm. Vis. 3.1.6 (9.6)). Hermas is said not to please God enough (3.1.9 (9.9); 3.2.2 (10.2)), nor to have suffered for "the name" sufficiently to be allowed to sit at the right hand of the women (3.1.9 (9.9)). In chapter 10, Hermas is shown a vision of a tower being built by the six men, and stones brought in to build the tower by thousands of men. The tower looks as if it was built by a single stone (3.2.6 (10.6)). Some stones for the building were discarded or even thrown far away. The tower is described as a parable for the ἐκκλησία, the congregation (3.3.3. (11.3)).[142] Then (chapter 3.4. (12)) a dialogue occurs in which Hermas asks the elderly woman about details in the parable, which she answers. In chapter 13, the stones in the building are interpreted. Here, the first instance that discusses the ἐπίσκοπος reads as follows:

> οἱ μὲν οὖν λίθοι οἱ τετράγωνοι καὶ λευκοὶ καὶ συμφωνοῦντες ταῖς ἁρμογαῖς αὐτῶν, οὗτοί εἰσιν οἱ ἀπόστολοι καὶ ἐπίσκοποι καὶ διδάσκαλοι καὶ διάκονοι οἱ πορευθέντες κατὰ τὴν σεμνότητα τοῦ θεοῦ καὶ ἐπισκοπήσαντες καὶ διδάξαντες καὶ διακονήσαντες ἁγνῶς καὶ σεμνῶς τοῖς ἐκλεκτοῖς τοῦ θεοῦ, οἱ μὲν κεκοιμημένοι, οἱ δὲ ἔτι ὄντες (Herm. Vis. 3.5.1. (13.1))
>
> Now, the squared and white stones which fit together through their joints, they are the apostles, ἐπίσκοποι, teachers, and deacons who walk with the proper respect towards God and in a pure and respectable way oversees, teaches, and serves, the chosen ones of God, some of whom have fallen asleep, while others are still living.

In this context, οἱ ἀπόστολοι καὶ ἐπίσκοποι καὶ διδάσκαλοι καὶ διάκονοι are described as prototypical; they embody ingroup ideals in a credible way. Consequently, they are seamlessly integrated into the building as building blocks, unlike those stones in the parable that were being tossed away because they were cracked stones or blocks of unfit shape (3.2.7-9 (10.7-9); 3.5.5 (13.5)). Their

---

helpful: Grundeken (2015, 6) traces citations and mentions of Hermas in Irenaeus, Tertullian, Clement of Alexandria and the Muratorian Fragment "before the late second century."

[142] *Congregation* is a better translation than *church*, due to the somewhat anachronistic connotations church might bring, *contra* Ehrman 2003b, 201, Osiek 1999, 65.

behaviour is exemplary, and their service is pure and respectable (ἁγνῶς καὶ σεμνῶς). They also act in harmony and peace with one another (3.5.5. (13.1)). Evidently, since the chapters before also have discussed prototypical behaviour, the deficient behaviour of Hermas, and exemplary behaviour in suffering on behalf of the faith (3.2 (10)), brings proper conduct to the fore in Hermas's vision. The leaders are expected to behave in this way. This is even more so since the text as a whole is a prophetic vision aiming to be read and followed by the readers. Thus, perhaps the content in the vision is not what Hermas knew to be true in his time, but rather what he wished to be true.[143] There has been a debate whether the vision of the tower is a representation of the congregation in Hermas's own time, or if it is a window into an anticipated future. In any case, the main interest of the passage is to warn against the "dire eschatological consequences for failure to repent."[144] Prototypical behaviour lies at the core of how the congregation is perceived in the vision.

Carolyn Osiek notes that the building of a city or a house is an oft-recurring feature in apocalyptic material, such as in 4 Ezra 10:25–54. Some themes are different in Shepherd, but parallels exist.[145] While οἱ ἀπόστολοι καὶ ἐπίσκοποι καὶ διδάσκαλοι καὶ διάκονοι are mentioned first and with honour in the explanation of the vision, it is not explicitly stated that they are the foundation, such as the apostles and prophets are said to function in Eph 2:20 (ἐποικοδομηθέντες ἐπὶ τῷ θεμελίῳ τῶν ἀποστόλων καὶ προφητῶν). Given the presence of the echo from Ephesians and the concept of high ecclesiology reflected in both texts, it is reasonable to assume that οἱ ἀπόστολοι καὶ ἐπίσκοποι καὶ διδάσκαλοι καὶ διάκονοι are viewed as foundational for the congregation.[146] An interesting feature in the Shepherd, however, is that the leadership is described not so much as a function as an example: it is not the titles that are constitutive for the congregation, but any member's prototypical lifestyle (at least in Herm. Vis. 1.3 (3)). Given an echo from Ephesians, the presence of the leaders in the building block

---

[143] See for example Lampe's reading of the social situation behind the Shepherd, Lampe 1987, 71–74, and Grundeken's (2015, 2) sound comment that "Hermas aims to change the community for the better."

[144] Buie and Svigel 2023, at Comment on Vision 3.5–3.8 [Kindle version].

[145] Osiek 1999, 68.

[146] Cf. the thematic analysis in Muddiman 2005, 110–11.

metaphor suggests that Hermas had some kind of knowledge or at least wished for the foundational character of leadership structure.[147]

All this suggests that while the ἐπίσκοπος is part of the identity-carrying leadership structure (which applies to identity impresarioship), the power of the metaphor lies in the ἐπίσκοπος and other leaders' ability to lead prototypical lives. The ingroup values are to be held in such high esteem that they might even be suffered for (chapter 10). Thus, Hermas's aim with the text relates to prototypicality and is not to be seen as an example of impresarioship. That is to say, the leadership polity is not viewed as identity-carrying in itself, and in itself not necessary for closeness to God. Rather, proper Christ-group behaviour is crucial for a valid ingroup identity.

As we shall see next, prototypical behaviour is at the centre also in the second occasion in which an ἐπίσκοπος is mentioned, in Herm. Sim. 9.27.2 (104.2).

5.4.3 Comment on Herm. Sim. 9.27.2 (104.2)

The context of this chapter is that Hermas has met the Shepherd and seen a vision of twelve mountains. These twelve mountains, according to chapter 94, are all the tribes or nations on the earth. All have been called by God's son's name (Herm. Sim. 9.17.4 (94.4)). The twelve mountains thus represent twelve different kinds of "spiritual receptiveness" of all the people of the nations.[148] The Shepherd goes on to explain the different mountains.[149] Betrayers and apostates inhabit the first mountain, hypocrites and teachers of evil the second.[150] Then follow wealthy believers on the third mountain and the double-minded on the fourth. The fifth mountain is inhabited by slow learners in the

---

[147] Muddiman 2005, 119. Still, as Muddiman points out, the theme of building up the congregation (either as body or temple) is continued in Eph 4:11–16, in which another list of functionaries is brought up (καὶ αὐτὸς ἔδωκεν τοὺς μὲν ἀποστόλους , τοὺς δὲ προφήτας, τοὺς δὲ εὐαγγελιστάς, τοὺς δὲ ποιμένας καὶ διδασκάλους). The shepherding theme (which is connected with ἐπίσκοπος in 1 Peter) is here linked to teaching. It is hard not to assume some "proto-episcopal" figure behind the Ephesians section.

[148] Buie and Svigel 2023, at Comment on Similitude 9 [Kindle version].

[149] For a neat summary, see Buie and Svigel 2023, at Comment on Similitude 9, table 6 [Kindle version].

[150] Ehrman 2003b, 437–39.

faith, and the sixth by believers who hold grudges and slanders. Innocent and simple believers inhabit the seventh mountain. The eighth mountain has dwellers who are apostles and teachers, while the ninth mountain is inhabited by those who wrongfully have gained wealth from ministry in the congregation, and this mountain is described as a barren land. Then, on the tenth mountain, the faithful ἐπίσκοποι are found.

> ἐπίσκοποι καὶ φιλόξενοι, οἵτινες ἡδέως εἰς τοὺς οἴκους ἑαυτῶν πάντοτε ὑπεδέξαντο τοὺς δούλους τοῦ θεοῦ ἄτερ ὑποκρίσεως· οἱ δὲ ἐπίσκοποι πάντοτε τοὺς ὑστερημένους καὶ τὰς χήρας τῇ διακονίᾳ ἑαυτῶν ἀδιαλείπτως ἐσκέπασαν καὶ ἁγνῶς ἀνεστράφησαν πάντοτε. (104:2)
>
> [They are] the ἐπίσκοποι and the hospitable, those who gladly always received the servants[151] of God into their homes without hypocrisy. And the ἐπίσκοποι always and unceasingly provided shelter for those lacking and for the widows through their service, and they always lived in a holy way.

There are a few notable matters worth discussing. First, prototypicality is salient. Hospitability is found as an important feature of the lists of expected behaviour from the ἐπίσκοπος in 1 Tim 3:2 and Titus 1:8. While hospitability is a virtue found in other instances in the NT, such as in 1 Pet 4:9, Heb 13:2, and Rom 12:13, it is here also connected to the ministry of the ἐπίσκοπος. Hospitability should be practiced "without hypocrisy," and for the benefit of the weaker community members. The opposite of this prototypical behaviour has been demonstrated in the previous mountain, where all dwell who "are διάκονοι who minister badly and plunder the livelihood of widows and orphans, and gain property for themselves from the ministry entrusted to them to perform." (Herm. Sim. 9.26.2 (103.2), διάκονοί εἰσι κακῶς διακονήσαντες καὶ διαρπάσαντες χηρῶν καὶ ὀρφανῶν τὴν ζωὴν καὶ ἑαυτοῖς περιποιησάμενοι ἐκ τῆς διακονίας ἧς ἔλαβον διακονῆσαι·) Faithfulness in what had been entrusted to the διάκονοι was of utmost importance in the eyes of the community. A common fund for the congregation is necessary for the passage to make sense.[152] This leads to the second aspect worth noting: the office of the διάκονος clearly had financial dimensions, but the office of the ἐπίσκοπος must also have possessed some as well. The discussion presented in the research background (see chapter 4 above)

---

[151] Compare with Ehrman 2003b, 453, where he reads "slaves" instead of "servants."
[152] Osiek 1999, 249.

concerning the emerging episcopal office as a financial office, as suggested by Hatch and elaborated upon by Stewart, has some foothold in Hermas.[153] Thus, there is a connection between the office of the διάκονος and the ἐπίσκοπος. While this suggests a financial dimension of the office, this function is also tightly interconnected to the prototypical behaviour: to receive travellers or the needy in their homes is to live a holy life. While a failure to live up to such a behaviour as, for example, in Ignatius (Ign. *Smyrn.* 7) is connected with heresy, one could say that the episcopal office is in itself a warrant for a Christian identity in Ignatius, as long as it is properly exercised. The episcopal structure is identity-carrying in Ignatius; thus, the office is an example of identity impresarioship. In Hermas, no such explicit connection exists. The standards expected from the office holders are high, but the office in itself is not constitutive for the community. The group identity is not embedded in the episcopal structure in Hermas. Rather, the identity-carrying structure provided for the congregation appears to be associated with the continuing work of the apostles.[154] The mission of the apostles and the ἐπίσκοπος is not explicitly connected in the Shepherd. Behaviour, not structure, separates the ingroup from the outgroups.

5.4.4 Conclusion about the ἐπίσκοπος in the Shepherd

Since the author appears not to be an officeholder himself but rather a prophetic, charismatic figure of some sort who aims to discuss a social tension within the Christ community in Rome, he does not explicitly address the offices as constitutive for the ἐκκλησία. Rather, the authority of the officeholders comes primarily from the prototypicality of the leaders when they succeed in embodying central Christ-group ideals. Thus, from an SIT perspective, the leader primarily leads through example, not through a given position and perception of the office as inherently holy. Rather, the failure to live up to Christ-group norms as a leader, thereby robbing "widows and orphans" of their livelihood, is held as extremely problematic (so Herm. Sim 9.26 (103)) and would, according to the author, in practice, disqualify the leader for office. The identity as a Christ-group member is only valid if the leader acts accordingly. This

---

[153] Osiek 1999, 249. See Hatch 1881, 27–54; Stewart 2014, 62–63.
[154] Buie and Svigel 2023, at Comment on Similitude 9 [Kindle version].

differs from Christ-group texts later in the second century, which understand the leadership structure as invested with features significant for ingroup identity. In Irenaeus and Ignatius (see below), the structure of the congregation is in itself carrying group identity as an unmistakable sign of valid Christ-group identity. While behaviour is not without interest for these later authors (see Ign. *Smyrn.* 7), the leadership structure in itself is identity-carrying. In SIT terms, this is to say that the author of the Shepherd is more interested in prototypical leaders than in leaders who embed the Christ-group identity in the leadership structure (impresarios). Even though it would be easy, for example, in the parable of the tower, to express the foundational role of the emerging episcopal order in terms of ingroup identity, this is not done. Rather, the focus consistently rests on the appropriate exercise of prototypical behaviour by every member.

A point of further investigation would be whether ancient Christian authors who themselves were members of the episcopal order were more prone to define ingroup identity in terms of identity impresarioship.

5.5 Summary and Conclusion

As we have seen, all the texts analysed from an SIT perspective here have high expectations regarding the behaviour of the ἐπίσκοπος. However, thepassages referring to some form of overseeing office in Acts do not associate the mission of the πρεσβύτεροι with prototypical behaviour *per se*, but rather with an expectation that the leaders should guard the congregations against false teachings. In Acts, the embedding of identity is far more salient than expectations of ethical behaviour according to ingroup norms. The πρεσβύτεροι and the oversight connected to them, is expected to guard against false teachings (Acts 20). The continuing mission of Christ, embedded in the apostolic office, and the connection between the πρεσβύτεροι and a ministry as "shepherds of the flock" suggest that the readers'/ingroup members' self-identification with Jesus and the apostles is mirrored in the leadership structure. This would call on any member who wished to be aligned with the mission of Christ to adhere to the oversight exercised by the πρεσβύτεροι. In 1 Peter, the oversight exercised by the πρεσβύτεροι is also viewed as a continuation of God's saving acts through

Christ and in the Hebrew Bible, embedding core beliefs into the leadership structure. The view of the apostles' ongoing mission, upheld in the episcopal structure, exemplifies identity impresarioship, which is defined as the "embedding of ingroup identity in structures and rituals"; see chapter 2.

In 1 Peter, but also in Philippians (as far as the data allows) and Hermas, the oversight office is connected to a salient ingroup prototypicality, that is, the leader's ability to embody the ideal of the group (see chapter 2 for additional SIT background). The ingroup traits highlighted in the context of the texts indicate that an exemplary leader is humble (Philippians), willing to suffer for ingroup ideals (1 Peter, Hermas), driven by inner motivation (1 Peter), and generous and faithful in the responsibilities expected of them (1 Peter, Hermas). The opposite case is showcased in Hermas, where the unfaithful leaders who have gained financially from their positions inhabit the barren mountain, thus serving as a cautionary example. The perilous possibility of wrongful financial gain is thus prominent in the texts.

Ultimately, the overseeing office in Acts is associated with Peter. According to Acts, Peter continues the mission of Jesus and authorises the succession of Judas's office. Peter is deeply connected with Jesus and is portrayed throughout Acts as prototypical in his behaviour. Thus, the leader is expected to work with Peter as a role model. Peter's authorisation of the succession from the apostles can be seen as an example of identity entrepreneurship. As described in chapter 2, identity entrepreneurship denotes the prototypical leader's ability to redefine ingroup prototypicality. Essentially, what Luke is conveying is that the leadership structure is (a) authorised by Peter and (b) serves as the framework within which it is safe to exercise faith in Christ. This excludes alternative suggestions regarding where ingroup identity should be manifested, thereby altering ingroup prototypicality in that an ideal Christ-group member is subject to the leadership established by Peter.

Considering these brief references to the ἐπίσκοπος and his role, a Christ-group prototypicality is already salient in the descriptions of the emerging office. Also, a mission for the emerging leadership office to protect the ingroup narrative or theology can be discerned. It is also presented as an ideal to live subjected to this structure.

5.5 Summary and Conclusion

Several instances in the texts have been analysed above, although in different immediate contexts than the leadership structure, which critiques neighbouring Jewish groups. In Phil 3:2, Paul warns the Philippians against "the dogs," "the evil workers," and the "those who mutilate the flesh" (NRSV).[155] In Acts 18:1–17, Paul's mission in Corinth distances the Christ group from the Jewish groups. Here, the Christ groups move out of the synagogue and into a neighbouring house. The Paul of Acts also expresses disappointment over the refusal of the Jewish group to accept Jesus as their Messiah, even after his substantial efforts. In 1 Peter and Hermas, Jewish identity is passed over in silence. Thus, in the contexts to which these texts attest, the leadership role is not yet a distinguishing factor for Christ-group identity. However, the beginnings of these distinguishing roles can be discerned through emerging prototypicality, the protection of ingroup theology, and the concept of succession from the apostles found in these texts. These features will, as we shall see, be further developed during the second century. Later, questions of exemplarity and the embedding of Christian identity become clearer, particularly through the expression of prototypical ideals in the Pastoral letters. This will be addressed in due time.

---

[155] βλέπετε τοὺς κύνας, βλέπετε τοὺς κακοὺς ἐργάτας, βλέπετε τὴν κατατομήν.

6. The Local Leaders in the Didache

Didache, or the Teaching of the Twelve Apostles, is a unique case in this book. While it exhibits traces of an episcopal structure, it also encourages group members to a certain degree of Torah observance. The text, to which I will soon return, is quite contemporary with Acts and somewhat earlier than the Pastoral Epistles and Ignatian writings.[1] The term ἐπίσκοπος occurs only once (chapter 15). The Didache primarily discusses how a local group of Jesus followers, likely in Syria, should lead their lives, worship, organise themselves, and manage interactions with numerous itinerant charismatics. Several observers have noted a tension in this practical guidance between local leaders and itinerant charismatics. Also, a primary concern in the text is how followers of Jesus should behave, specifically by leading prototypical lives. Didache 1–6 essentially describes the ideal member, and since prototypicality denotes a member's ability to embody ingroup ideals, these described ideals are essential for understanding the ingroup identity of the community. The ingroup prototype is defined against the backdrop of Gentiles on the one hand and on the other, Jewish groups who do not recognise Jesus as the Messiah. The expectations for the baptised member arise from a tradition established by Jesus and a contemporary Jewish theme that discusses the paths of death and life as parallels to the Decalogue and recurs in several Jewish texts. This theme is represented in the Didache as a subsection and will be discussed below as the Two Ways tractate. Several overlapping leadership functions are evident in the Didache that appear to be the consequence of the composite nature of the text (see below). In various ways, all leaders provide insights into ingroup identity. The ἐπίσκοπος, alongside the διάκονος, ἀπόστολος, προφήτης, and διδάσκαλος, can be analysed,

---

[1] For a thorough discussion of the title of the text, see Niederwimmer 1998, 5–57; Rordorf and Tuilier 1978, 13–17.

through a SIT lens, as an embodiment of a specific identity. Although not much is stated explicitly about the ἐπίσκοπος, one can glean secondary information from the text regarding his function. In Didache, the ἐπίσκοπος is portrayed as a local leader, associated with itinerant prophets and teachers. Nevertheless, while there is an emphasis on the prototypical nature of the ἐπίσκοπος, the role ascribed to him suggests that he could also be described as an identity impresario, that is, as embedding a specific Christ-group identity.

In this chapter, we will first look at the date and provenance of the text for a deeper understanding of the issues discussed. Second, we will discuss the paradigmatic schema of early catholicisation that has been an underlying assumption in much of the research history of the Didache. Third, we will analyse how the prototypical identity is constructed in the Two Ways tractate, and how that is connected to the ἐπίσκοπος. Fourth, we will turn to chapter 15, where the local leaders are discussed. The aim is to define their role and the behaviour expected of them. Fifth, we will turn to how the leaders (such as the ἐπίσκοπος) is constructing and embedding the unique Christ-group identity: the ἐπίσκοπος, among other leaders, is an identity impresario. Last, we will draw out the conclusions regarding the group-defining role of the ἐπίσκοπος in the long-term separation between the Jesus groups and other Jewish groups.

6.1 Date, Place, the Didachist, and *Sitz im Leben*

The Didache was discovered for modern readers relatively late, despite being referenced and discussed by the church fathers. Since its modern discovery in 1873 by Philotheos Bryennios, the significance of an early text from the followers of Jesus, potentially even predating the final writings of the New Testament, has been acknowledged. Understanding the provenance and date of the text is essential. However, its history is intricate because it comprises at least four distinct texts, each with its own particular history.[2] The compiler is generally described as "The Didachist," a term I will use hereafter. A compilation of four different discourses is obvious:[3] the Two Ways tractate (1:1–5:2, but if one includes the epilogue of the tractate, the first section ends at 6:3), the liturgy (7:1–

---

[2] Zangenberg 2008, 48–49.
[3] Following Niederwimmer 1998, 1.

10:7), the church order (11:1–15:4), and finally the apocalyptic discourse (16:1–8). I focus primarily on chapters 1–6 and 15 of the Didache, which will serve as the main material for analysis. The selection of these sections is driven by comprehending the influence of the emerging leadership structure on the identity formation of the early Jesus movement. Therefore, the prototypical ideal found in these sections is crucial for understanding the self-perception of the group behind the Didache.

The precise where and when of the different discourses is hard to discern.[4] The difficulties lie not in the traditional dating of the *compilation* or *redaction* of the text (ca 100–110), which has been broadly accepted for a long time.[5] Instead, the questions primarily discussed are when the various pieces were written and how they were transmitted, since several parts of the text appear in different later contexts. The different sections of the book originate from diverse genres and contexts, *Sitze im Leben*.[6] The original uses of the text's building blocks provide information regarding certain early Christ groups. This original use is of great interest when accounting for the origins of these groups but might be hard to reconstruct. It is also well known that large parts of Didache were used in later Church Orders, such as the *Apostolic Constitutions*, book seven. This suggests that even if the text was initially sent to a particular community, its later use must have extended beyond that initial group setting.[7] In this dissertation, the primary interest is the redaction of the building blocks into one text. Particularly intriguing for my investigation is the insight that the redaction offers into the ideals and leadership structure of the Didachist's

---

[4] Ehrman 2003a, 411–13, is sceptical that it is possible to find conclusive evidence concerning the sources.

[5] Niederwimmer 1998, 53, compare Draper 2010, 7–8, who wants an earlier dating ("not too far into the second century (if at all)." Draper assumes that Matthew draws on Didache, and not the other way around. See also Ehrman 2003a, 410, 412. See also van de Sandt and Flusser 2002, 52.

[6] Niederwimmer 1998, 2.

[7] Draper 2007, 13.

community.⁸ As will be discussed further below, the rather sudden introduction of the leadership categories ἐπίσκοποι and διάκονοι is probably a way for the Didachist to bring together different leadership structures found in the communities addressed. The redactor tries to equate the various leadership roles and in chapter 15 offers a synthesis that makes it possible to include the ministry of the ἐπίσκοποι and διάκονοι in the larger liturgical framework.⁹ The mention of the ἐπίσκοπος in chapter 15 highlights the need to confer authority, akin to the itinerant prophets and teachers, upon the local leaders.

Of secondary interest for this dissertation is the scholarly interest in the *sectio evangelica* in 1:3 b–2:1 (a part of the two-ways tractate that includes material from a gospel source closely related to the Matthean tradition) from the perspective of Q and an oral Jesus tradition. This book's primary interest in the *sectio evangelica* is the identity-shaping effects of the content, as a part of the order of the Didachist's community.

Even if there was once a lack of consensus regarding the place and situation of the Didachist's recipients, scholars are now relatively agreed on Syria (more specifically, Antioch). Earlier suggestions that proposed Egypt as the place of origin no longer hold sway.¹⁰ The use of τὸ κλάσμα in chapter 9 echoes its later usage in Egypt; furthermore, the text has a history of use in the region, for example, a Coptic translation and P. Oxy. 1782. On the other hand, it is also found in several other contexts, where it is perceived as ancient and significant, in some sources understood as "Scripture."¹¹ Most scholars now prefer Syria and Antioch as a reasonable place of origin.¹² The trend has shifted towards

---

⁸ Zangenberg 2008, 50, assumes that the Didachist's purpose was primarily to reassure common ground for the group and points out that the traditions function differently throughout the text.

⁹ Niederwimmer 1998, 200.

¹⁰ Example for the Egypt hypothesis: Kraft 1965, 76–77.

¹¹ Draper 2010, 10.

¹² A selection of views from the commentators: Ehrman 2003a, 411–12, holds it impossible to know, Niederwimmer 1998, 228, holds it unlikely that the setting was Antioch, but sees Syrian borderlands as the most probable place. Draper 2010, 10–11, seems to lean toward the Syrian-Palestinian position. Also, van de Sandt and Flusser 2002, 48–49, also lean towards a position of Antioch, or at least Syria-Palestine. See also Meier 1983, 12–86; Slee 2003; Zetterholm 2003.

Syria for several reasons.¹³ Partly, the reasons are internal (though somewhat inconclusive): the language regarding the wheat grown on the mountain slopes (9:4) aligns much better with Syria than with Egypt. Moreover, the close, well-documented connection between traditional Jewish communities and communities of Jesus followers in Syria could be implicit in the text.¹⁴ Furthermore, the guidance regarding baptism indicates a region where water is scarce, aligning more closely with the Syria hypothesis (7:2–3).¹⁵ Also, the itinerant preachers discussed by the Didachist (for example, in chapter 11) seem to indicate a location closer to Syria, as several other documents relating to itinerant preachers were written in this area.¹⁶ The instructions also suggest a shift from rural to semi-rural areas, as the travelling preachers were to be equipped with provisions for one day's journey (11:4–6), implying an approximate distance to the next village.¹⁷

Partly, the reason for assuming Syria as the place of the original compilation is a conclusion after reading the text in tandem with the gospel of Matthew. The reconstruction of the community that was the original *Sitz im Leben* for Matthew also seems to fit the Didache well.¹⁸ The relationship between Matthew and the Didache has attracted attention over the past thirty-five years.¹⁹ Even if the Gospel citations (see below) likely did not originate from the Gospel of Matthew but rather from a shared tradition between Matthew and the Didachist, the similarity of the texts requires some explanation, which would be provided by their common context and interests. This has recently become the

---

¹³ The trend is not unanimous; Bas ter Haar Romeny 2005, 13–33, suggests Palestine.

¹⁴ Ehrman 2003a, 411–12.

¹⁵ Van de Sandt and Flusser 2002, 51.

¹⁶ Van de Sandt and Flusser 2002, 51, list Gos. Thom.; *Peregr.* by Lucian of Samosata; *Ad Virgines* by Ps.-Clement.

¹⁷ Following Van de Sandt and Flusser 2002, 51–52.

¹⁸ Van de Sandt and Flusser 2002, 51–52.

¹⁹ As of the latest thirty-five years or so, the Didache has been read in close relation to the Matthean community. One can note that Draper and Jeffords as key characters during these years has assumed a rather close relationship between Matthew and the Didache, while Aaron Milavec assumes a more distant relationship between the two contexts. The conclusion must however be that "the Didache's relationship to Matthew, and a more distant affirmation with James, is a top consensus." For summary, see Wilhite 2019, 269, 274, 279, 293 (citation).

most widely accepted interpretation concerning the background and circumstances of the text. I shall, therefore, assume a Syrian location for the compilation of the text.

For a long time, there has been a consensus that the Didache, for want of a better term, should be understood as a *Church Order*.[20] Kurt Niederwimmer notes that there were no literary models upon which to draw when constructing this early work.[21] The cultural, social, and ethnic contexts of the composite are difficult to ascertain, except through internal evidence, which only offers limited insights. As Niederwimmer suggested, the composition's purpose was to provide guidance in times of transition, and "to harmonize ancient and revered traditions of the church with new ecclesial necessities."[22] Jonathan Draper suggests the Didache discusses "initiation into the community and ... socialization at the core."[23] Draper's primary interest in a later version of his research lies in the socialisation of non-Jews into the Didachist community, which has much in common with the Pharisaic tradition of Judaism.[24] Huub van de Sandt and David Flusser provide a slightly different perspective.

> We have concluded that the two major concerns of the Didache at the level of redaction can be found in the attempt to define a new (religious) position distancing itself from Judaism and to equip the community in the face of the influence of potential troublesome visitors.[25]

---

[20] Niederwimmer 1998, 1, 37 (n. 56), 38 (n. 59), and so forth, provides no explicit definition of the *Sitz im Leben* of the final composite text, but discusses thoroughly how different phrases and units originally were set or used. See also Wengst 1984, 18. Closely related to this is Bihlmeyer 1970. Zangenberg 2008, 53–54, argues that Niederwimmer goes too far when he concludes that the Didache is primarily a "handbuch." The *ad hoc* nature of the text (at least after chapter 6) is built on a theological rationale but does not always show the theological reasoning behind the statements in the composite text.

[21] Niederwimmer 1998, 2.

[22] Niederwimmer 1998, 3.

[23] Draper 2010, 11.

[24] Wilhite 2019, 273.

[25] Van de Sandt and Flusser 2002, 51.

Therefore, the establishment of a new group identity is the primary focus of the text.[26] All these perspectives have something in common: constructing a social identity, whether it delineates itself from this group or that. In terms of SIT, the definition of prototypical behaviour and the inception of rituals and structures (impresarioship) that align with the group identity are essential for every kind of group. What differentiates the group from other groups is especially significant.[27] The traces of different systems of leadership in chapters 7–15, and the relatively late introduction of the local leaders, the ἐπίσκοποι and διάκονοι, suggest that the Didachist recognised a need to include local leaders in the framework of the composite text provided. This is especially so because the local leaders are said to share in the ministry of itinerant prophets and teachers (Didache 15).

While we, of course, have no access to the Didachist's mind and ideals, several clarifying points become clear when applying a SIT perspective, which we will do shortly. First, however, we must address the underlying assumption of the early catholicisation in the Didache.

6.2 Charismatic Leadership, Early Catholicisation, and a Trajectory from Max Weber

The debate regarding early Catholicism in the text, as an indicator of the transition from an earlier dynamic phase into a "routinisation of charisma," has cast long shadows over the understanding of chapter 15. Max Weber defines charisma as a quality of personality among specific leaders, a power, often traditionally understood as magical, supernatural, or at least qualitatively extraordinary, and accessible only to a few.[28] These extraordinary, God-given (as it was understood) charismatic leaders were long regarded as representative of an initial phase of the Jesus movement, followed by early catholicisation.[29] In this context, the itinerants of Matthew (see Matthew 10) and the Didache (see chapters 11–13) labelled as apostles in Matthew and prophets and perhaps teachers in

---

[26] See also for example Finlan 2015, 24.
[27] Finlan 2015, 23.
[28] Weber 1976, 140–41.
[29] Draper 2008, 139–40. The term was coined in von Harnack 1902.

Didache, were understood to have settled down and assumed the episcopal office. In this transition, the power went from the God-given leader to the structure itself. This was a result of the fading of charismatic powers among the individual leaders, which called for different power structures. This idea of catholicisation and routinisation of charisma (invested in the episcopal offices) was championed by, among others, Adolf von Harnack (who was the first to address the topic), Heinrich Kraft, and Hermann Stempel.[30] Their perspective was indebted to the understanding of charisma crafted by Weber. Draper suggests that this schema is not necessarily the best way to understand the communities of Didache (and Matthew and James). Instead, a reassessment of the material might sustain a slightly different situation, where the terms "charismatic," "travelling," and "functionary" are at the centre. From the outset, the concept of itinerant charismatic leadership was embedded in a framework where the wandering prophets consistently journeyed, remaining indifferent to familial connections, material concerns, and local contexts and traditions.[31] According to the schema, these itinerants came in a subsequent phase of the Christ movement to settle down; thus, the Didache mirrors a transition phase in the community. However, according to Draper's reconstruction, Didache suggests that the itinerants still seemed to have experienced a heyday during the time of the Didachist but were viewed with ambivalent feelings.[32] This reading takes the text at face value. Prophets and apostles had, in fact, not settled down after their travelling ministry. The practice of regularly receiving and sustaining itinerant charismatics remains an essential question for the communities that the Didachist is addressing. The language of itinerant charismatics, viewed from the perspective of early catholicisation, assumes a situation that does not entirely align with the extant material; it presumes that the routinisation of charisma was a necessary step in community life. This routinisation *par excellence* is the episcopal office, according to the schema, where the itinerant phase had effectively been concluded at the time of the redaction work of the Didachist.

---

[30] Kraft 1975, 93, Stempel 1980, 209–17.

[31] Draper 2008, 140–41.

[32] Draper 2008, 173. Draper wants to place the Didache very early, which plays a role here, cf. p 167, see also Draper 2007, 15.

The concept underlying the schema, that itinerants were perpetually on the move (with no transitional phase), is also unknowable and somewhat unlikely. A significant portion of it is based on assumption, motivated by the thesis of Weber, who himself built his thesis on Von Harnack's work on early catholicisation.[33] According to the schema, but not the existing material, the travellers who settled down necessarily needed to signify the routinisation of charisma. The schema is blind to other models and assumes that the settling down is a natural law in the process of catholicisation. However, the material in the Didache still exhorts the congregation to receive apostles as the Lord (11:4, cf. 12:1), while simultaneously accepting the notion that some itinerant prophets could have settled down (13:1). It does not explicitly claim that the powers of the local leaders had failed and that it therefore would be necessary to invest more authority in the structure.

Draper makes a distinction concerning the differing vocabulary in the Didache and Matthew. "Apostle" is not a title of an office but rather a function:

> [The apostle] is not viewed by Matthew as a separate office, but rather a function of representation. The offices in view are primarily conceived as prophets, since just as the scribes and the Pharisees stand in the line of the murderers of the prophets, so those who are Jesus's apostles stand in the line of the prophets of old.[34]

The prophet is perhaps the most important office in the Matthean community, which is viewed as closely linked to the Didache community. The prophets also share some similar characteristics in both the Didache and Matthew. In Matthew, they are expected to perform miracles, to speak in the spirit when taken before rulers and kings, and to serve as a connection to the prophets of the Hebrew Bible. (Matt 5:11–12, 10:1, 10:18–20). In the Didache (11:7–11), the prophets speak in the spirit and are linked to the prophets of the Hebrew Bible tradition. In both texts, they must be acknowledged as genuine prophets through their

---

[33] One can note that Niederwimmer 1998, 175–76, works from this schema. See also p. 200, commenting on 15:1, where the tension between the itinerants and the settled clergy is the exigent problem that Niederwimmer argues is the key to understanding the situation in the Didachist's community.

[34] Draper 2008, 150.

actions (Matt 7:15–20, Did. 11:10); their behaviour must align with the values of the ingroup.

The notion that leaders should be recognised by their (prototypical) actions also aligns, on a broader level, with the Gospel of Matthew. Jesus warns the congregation in Matthew of wolves dressed up as sheep. It seems to be a warning against leaders who only appear to follow the ingroup values.[35] The view of the prophets in the Didache, in this respect, is somewhat divided. On the one hand, one should not test the prophet's words, as this is closely linked to testing the Holy Spirit.[36] On the other hand, the actions of the prophets require constant evaluation, and the teachings of the prophets must align with the blueprint of chapters 1–10 in the Didache. The prophets who settle down in Didache 13 are held in high esteem and become some kind of local congregation officers.[37] However, the title does not change, which is important to note, given the schema of early catholicisation. The schema suggests that the titles changed as the prophets settled down. In Didache, the lines are not that clear cut.

The office of the prophets is perceived in practice as a continuation of the priestly office in the Hebrew Bible. This stands in clear contrast to the language

---

[35] Draper 2008, 150–52, cf. Deut 18:19; Matt 23:39; Did. 11:7–12.

[36] Draper 2008, 151.

[37] One can note the ambiguous ending of chapter 10, 10:7 τοῖς δὲ προφήταις ἐπιτρέπετε εὐχαριστεῖν ὅσα θέλουσιν – "but you should allow the prophets to celebrate the eucharist as often as they like." The situation regarding exactly who celebrated the thanksgiving meal/eucharist is impossible to conclude from the context. Do the formulations mean that an itinerant prophet suggests the celebration, or is it a settled prophet? First, one can note that chapter 9:5 forbids anyone who is not baptised to eat or drink. This would suggest that the officiating functionary had some kind of knowledge concerning the social context. Second, the proper discussion concerning itinerants does not start until chapter 11. Would it not be more natural to have chapters 11–14 before the discussion on how to perform baptism and thanksgiving meal (eucharist) if the situation was that it always was itinerant prophets (rather than settled) who performed the liturgy? On the other hand, chapter 11 starts with the accepting of itinerants who teach according to the earlier ten chapters; 11:1 reads Ὃς ἂν οὖν ἐλθὼν διδάξῃ ὑμᾶς ταῦτα πάντα τὰ προειρημένα, δέξασθε αὐτόν ("if someone comes and teaches you all what is said above, you should receive him"), which suggests that someone could come and have the proper understanding of both prototypical and liturgical matters, and thus be the one who is implied when discussing the liturgical minutiae in chapters 9–10. I suggest that it is more likely that it should be a settled prophet who is leading the liturgy in chapter 10, while it is impossible to know.

found in both 1 Clement and the Ignatian letters, where these texts view the ἐπίσκοπος as a priestly role. The sustainment of the prophets is explicitly paralleled to the priestly office when it is suggested in chapter 13 that the "first portion" (ἀπαρχή) should be set apart as given to a priest. The wording in 15:1, however, speaks of an overlap between the prophet and the permanent offices (ἐπίσκοποι καὶ διάκονοι, while no explicit succession is mentioned). The description ὑμῖν γὰρ λειτουργοῦσι καὶ αὐτοὶ τὴν λειτουργίαν τῶν προφητῶν καὶ διδασκάλων appears to pronounce the ἐπίσκοποι καὶ διάκονοι as stand-ins for the itinerant prophets and teachers.[38] This will be further discussed below, but regarding the idea of a schema, the material from the Didache does not suggest any clear succession of offices but rather a situation with mixed forms of leadership.

While the exact meaning of the disposition of the material is difficult to ascertain, it can be noted that the most natural way to interpret chapters 10:7–14 is that the prophets preside over the eucharistic table in verse 14.[39] In Draper's reconstruction, alongside Zangenberg's immersive discussion of the Didachist community's milieu, the ἐπίσκοπος would serve as a patron for the group through his financial resources. The ἐπίσκοπος is primarily an honourary position, and perhaps this honour is reflected in the meal of κυριακὴν δὲ κυρίου, particularly in regard to obtaining the finest seats. Simultaneously, prophets and teachers held an equally esteemed role, albeit as religious functionaries, given that they are the only ones described as presiding over a eucharistic meal in 10:7.[40] The tension this presents is evident in the third part of the Didache. Draper suggests that the text reflects a situation where refugees from the

---

[38] See Zangenberg 2008, 64.

[39] Cf. Zangenberg 2008, 52, who means that the meal described in chapters 9–10 and the breaking of bread on the Lord's day (Κατὰ κυριακὴν δὲ κυρίου) are in fact two different meals; the meal in 9–10 appears to be a meal when the congregants can have "enough to eat," Μετὰ δὲ τὸ ἐμπλησθῆναι, while the key words in chapter 14 are κλάσατε ἄρτον and θυσία. Zangenberg does not however properly discuss that εὐχαριστήσατε is a key verb in the sentence. The connotations in chapter 9–10 and chapter 14 should be just as strong in both cases. The "compositional nature" (p 50) of the Didache, where different layers can carry different meanings and "functional contexts" does not mean that the conceptual apparatus necessarily need to change in different layers. Quite to the contrary, since the text had on a very basic level the aim to communicate and provide a common ground of the reader and the Didachist.

[40] Draper 2008, 166–67.

Jerusalem War of 68–70 drove large groups of Jesus followers to places such as Syria. These refugees brought with them teachings (such as the tradition of Q) that significantly impacted the local Jesus groups. The incoming teachers competed with local honourary figures and patrons.[41] While this is an intriguing thought, we have no concrete evidence to support such a detailed reconstruction. Furthermore, Draper does not provide a satisfactory explanation for 15:1b ("for they [ἐπίσκοποι and διάκονοι] also perform [λειτουργοῦσι] the ministry [τὴν λειτουργίαν] of the prophets and teachers for you") with the obvious connotations in τὴν λειτουργίαν of a type of priestly office, comparable to the work of prophets and teachers. While this strongly suggests that Draper is correct in shifting the discussion away from an overused schema of early catholicisation, which is too intertwined with the episcopal structure, he neglects how the liturgical functions of the ἐπίσκοπος and διάκονος in 15:1 reinforce his case. The ἐπίσκοπος and διάκονος are not signs of ritualisation of charisma but rather a part of living communities where prophets and teachers were the functionaries who were travelling far distances, and the ἐπίσκοπος and διάκονος were the functionaries of the local community. The ritualisation of charisma was not necessarily bound to happen. The situation in the Didache cannot be taken as an account of such a process. Rather, we can see that the material in the Didache provides a mix in which different offices work together. There are no evident signs that further ritualisation was necessary in the Didachist communities. An episcopal office emerging in the northeast Mediterranean area need not be understood to have developed according to the schema described by Weber and others. It is not a natural law that settled leaders should be less charismatic than itinerant preachers. Rather, the evidence from the Didache suggests that the emerging episcopal office was a continuation of the wandering prophets. The expectations on every member to follow the explicit ideal in chapters 1–6, and the association between prophets and ἐπίσκοποι and διάκονοι, as outlined in 15:2, would suggest a primarily prototypical authority for the ἐπίσκοποι and διάκονοι. Therefore, understanding the Didache as another stop on a law-bound road from itinerants to the mono-episcopate does not hold. This will

---

[41] Draper 2008, 166–67.

also be discernible when we turn to a SIT analysis of the local offices of the Didache.

6.3 The Two Ways Tractate and Its *Sitz im Leben*

Next, we will examine the concept of prototypicality within the Christ groups, which I have referenced several times earlier. Considering the SIT emphasis on this analysis, the lifestyle advocated in the Two Ways tractate (1:1b–6:3) is critical for the analysis.[42] Prototypicality, as closely described in chapter 2 above, embodies ingroup ideals. Leadership is most effective when the leader exhibits prototypical traits, and the description of the ἐπίσκοποι καὶ διάκονοι characterises them as "worthy of the Lord," "humble," "not greedy," "true, honest," and "tested." Therefore, one must assume that the leaders were expected to display behaviour aligned with ingroup prototypes. Given that the notion that a tree is known by its fruit was addressed concerning the itinerants, and since the itinerants' office overlaps with local offices, it is difficult to envisage an alternative perspective on leadership in the Didache. Now, since a described prototypicality reveals the kind of self-understanding that a group possesses, the first six chapters should offer a clear perspective on the self-understanding of the Didachist group.

When discussing the Two Ways tractate, one must separately address the first section of the text, the *sectio evangelica* (1:3b–2:1), and subsequently, the latter part of the Two Ways tractate 2:1–6:3. The discourse on the two ways has several counterparts in other texts, both from followers of Jesus and other Jewish groups. Most scholars regard a Jewish version of the Two Ways tractate as one of the sources for the Didachist.[43] The introduction of the two ways section is a gospel source known as the *sectio evangelica*, which has been much debated during recent years. It has been labelled an oral sayings source by several scholars.[44] On the other hand, there has also been a relatively steady position regarding the first hypothesis concerning the *sectio evangelica*, which holds

---

[42] Finlan 2015, 18.

[43] See first Audet 1952, 219–38. See also for example Niederwimmer 1998, 44; van de Sandt and Flusser 2002, 57; Draper, 2010, 8–9.

[44] Koester 1957; Audet, 1958, see also Niederwimmer 1998, 75–76; Draper 2010, 10; 11.

that the text in Didache is dependent on Matthew.⁴⁵ Undoubtedly, the relationship between various sources for the Didache is quite complex, and determining which sources rely on which is often difficult.⁴⁶ The most common conclusion, however, is that chapters 2–6 were an adaptation, derived from an original Jewish tractate concerning the paths of life and death.⁴⁷ The Didachist then provided the introduction to the discourse, the *sectio evangelica* (1:3b–2:1).

Significantly enough, apart from the *sectio evangelica* the rest of the tractate (up to 6:1) shows few signs of gospel traditions.⁴⁸ One can, however, note 3:7, ἴσθι δὲ πραΰς, ἐπεὶ οἱ πραεῖς κληρονομήσουσι τὴν γῆν: "but be humble, for the humble shall inherit the land"⁴⁹ that has clear parallels to Matthew 5:5. Niederwimmer interprets these words more as an echo of Psalms 36:11a than as derived from Matthew.⁵⁰ I find the distinction impossible to make and quite unnecessary. Since the Two Ways tractate seems to have had earlier parallels, for example in Qumran, one can note that the *sectio evangelica* in 1:3b–2:1 (which echoes a tradition close to Matt 5–7) is a unique feature of the Didachist version of a Two Ways tractate.⁵¹ The discovery of the Qumran documents in the mid-twentieth century provided a safer ground for assuming that the Two Ways were widely used in both Qumran and other Jewish groups. The followers of Jesus in the Didachist community can be seen as a single group possessing a Jewish identity; however, the specific identity of Jesus followers ultimately came to overshadow the Jewish identity.⁵² The *sectio evangelica* was thus a novelty in this context, communicating a unique characteristic from other Jewish groups.⁵³

---

⁴⁵ See Vokes 1938; Massaux 1950; Wengst 1984.

⁴⁶ For a thorough review, see Niederwimmer 1998, 13–17. See also Ehrman 2003a, 407–11.

⁴⁷ Niederwimmer 1998, 36–40, see especially table 4, on page 40, for a pedagogic overview of the complex issue.

⁴⁸ Van de Sandt and Flusser 2002, 57.

⁴⁹ Translations are my own if nothing else is stated.

⁵⁰ Niederwimmer 1998, 100.

⁵¹ Ehrman 2003a, 408.

⁵² Draper 2007, 14. See also Koester 2007, 7.

⁵³ See Finlan 2015, 21–22, who understands the main thrust of chapter 1–6 as a thorough way of anchoring the group's prototype in Jewish ethics, and not Jewish rituals. Thus, Finlan concludes that "the group had a kind of Jewish identity, while also having a Christian identity," 22.

6.3 The Two Ways Tractate and Its Sitz im Leben

The literary feature of the two ways was, and became increasingly, a popular theme in various contexts: Hesiod,[54] Xenophon,[55] and several biblical and apocryphal texts from different groups use some version of the idea of the road to life or death that the first section of Didache echoes.[56] In the Hellenistic realm, the theme of Roads or Paths often had both moral and aesthetic aspects.[57] Different authors might emphasise various perspectives, particularly Hesiod, who utilised the choice between paths as a metaphor for the journey towards virtue or "badness" (κακός).

The theme of the road or path is firmly rooted in Hebrew Scriptures: both the Deuteronomistic History and Wisdom literature employ the path as a metaphor for a life obedient to the Torah: "The intent of the PATH metaphor is clear: staying straight on the road preserves life, while deviation leads to disaster."[58] The aim for Jewish Two Ways tractates and the Didache is the relationship between God and humans. Since studies of the Two Ways tractate from a metaphorical perspective demonstrate how the metaphor addresses both life choices and destiny, the tractate has a concrete bearing on the moral behaviour of a group member.[59] During the last two decades, it has been argued that the two ways tradition in different Jewish texts functioned as guidance for proselytes.[60] The text has a special edge against non-Jewish behaviour, and was a "Jewish perspective on Pagan society."[61] This is also evident in the Didache, where it serves as a baptismal teaching (that is, intended for converts) and provides guidance on ingroup behaviour for newcomers. The later Christian texts *Doctrina Apostolorum*,[62] the *Apostolic Church Order*,[63] and *Life of Shenute*[64]

---

[54] *Op.* 287–92. For Greek text, see Niederwimmer 1998, 59, n. 5.
[55] *Mem.*, 2.1.21–34. For Greek text, see Niederwimmer 1998, 59–60, n. 6.
[56] Ps 1 (1:6); Prov 2:13; 4:18–19; T. Ash. 1:2–9; 1 En. 94:1–5; 1QS III, 18–4.26, see also Niederwimmer 1998, 59–60.
[57] Kazen and Roitto 2024, 48–49.
[58] Kazen and Roitto 2024, 49–50.
[59] Kazen and Roitto 2024, 52.
[60] Slee 2003, 78–79.
[61] Slee 2008, 79.
[62] Van de Sandt, "Doctrina Apostolorum." Consulted online on 21 February 2024.
[63] See Schermann 1914, 12.
[64] See Leipoldt 1903.

were texts from Jesus followers, which all contained some kind of discourse concerning the Two Ways.⁶⁵ The metaphor served as a living template for teaching morals within Jewish communities and later Christian groups that did not consist entirely of ethnic Jews or proselytes.

As mentioned, there is a broad consensus that the Two Ways tractate in the Didache primarily served as instruction before baptism.⁶⁶ The moral program expected from the baptism candidate was thorough and provided important information concerning prototypical behaviour in the group; see below. It also echoed a familiar sense of morality, influenced somewhat by contemporary Hellenistic thought but more deeply rooted in the Hebrew Bible. The themes in this instruction pertain to the realms of thought, word, and action at the personal level (1–3, and 5). Additionally, there are expectations for the baptismal candidates to conduct themselves appropriately towards other group members and leaders (chapter 4).

All this suggests that the Didache is an adapted version of a popular theme, but featuring a gospel introduction moulded for the use of the Didachist group.⁶⁷ The Two Ways tractate, which was to be taught to the baptismal candidate, ensured that the new group member who was initiated through baptism knew how to behave according to group principles. This indicates that the Didachist utilised existing Jewish traditions, or perhaps reiterated them in a manner suited to the group's needs. Following van de Sandt and Flusser, the group required boundaries against malpractice amongst itinerant charismatic preachers while simultaneously distancing themselves from other types of

---

⁶⁵ Draper 2007, 14–15.

⁶⁶ See Kraft 1965, 1 and Stempel 1980, 215.

⁶⁷ Niederwimmer 1998, 67. There has been an extensive debate concerning the material of 1 3b–2:1, since it has been argued that the Didachist can provide insights to the Q source. Alan Garrow and Jonathan Draper argue that the Didachist redaction is older than Matthew, which has crucial implications for the dating of the text. See Garrow 2004, 244–52, and Draper 2005, 217–41. The suggestion has, however, failed to convince most scholars. See the review by John Kloppenborg for a thorough critique, especially on the lack of sequence from Didache in Matthew. One can, for example, see an extensive use of Mark's sequence of events, and probably Q's, in Luke and Matthew. No such sequencing is found in the alleged Didache material. Kloppenborg 2005, 438–41.

groups, such as non-Jews and various forms of Judaism apart from that of the followers of Jesus. In this context, it is quite sensible to employ well-known and frequently reiterated moral principles, while also incorporating unique in-group features.

6.3.1 Prototypical Content in the Two Ways Tractate

The prototypical ideal for the baptized member is outlined in the two-fold section of chapters 1–6. In the following, I will provide a somewhat lengthy analysis of the ideals presented, reflecting the group's self-identification. Interestingly, this section presents an ideal in which many commonplace Jewish ethical principles are embraced and even regarded as natural (see especially Did. 2 and 5). Simultaneously, the introductory chapter (from 1:3b) presents an ideal drawn from a gospel source, which offers a more refined understanding of the group identity; this identity represents a unique fusion of the ideals of Jesus's group (the *sectio evangelica*) and other Jewish group ideals (the remainder of the Two Ways tractate). This indicates that the group's self-understanding is that of a Jewish community with a specific revelation.[68] Themes found in other Jewish texts are found in the Two Ways tractate. Even if some commonplace Hellenistic ideals are found in the Two Ways section proper from Did. 2 and onwards, the ideals are *primarily* picked up from a Jewish sphere of thought. In this analysis of group prototypes, we first turn to the *sectio evangelica*, followed by the remainder of the Two Ways tractate (1:1–14) .

> Ὁδοὶ δύο εἰσί, μία τῆς ζωῆς καὶ μία τοῦ θανάτου, διαφορὰ δὲ πολλὴ μεταξὺ τῶν δύο ὁδῶν. Ἡ μὲν οὖν ὁδὸς τῆς ζωῆς ἐστιν αὕτη· πρῶτον ἀγαπήσεις τὸν θεὸν τὸν ποιήσαντά σε, δεύτερον τὸν πλησίον σου ὡς σεαυτόν· πάντα δὲ ὅσα ἐὰν θελήσῃς μὴ γίνεσθαί σοι, καὶ σὺ ἄλλῳ μὴ ποίει. Τούτων δὲ τῶν λόγων ἡ διδαχή ἐστιν αὕτη· εὐλογεῖτε τοὺς καταρωμένους ὑμῖν καὶ προσεύχεσθε ὑπὲρ τῶν ἐχθρῶν ὑμῶν, νηστεύετε δὲ ὑπὲρ τῶν διωκόντων ὑμᾶς· ποία γὰρ χάρις, ἐὰν ἀγαπᾶτε τοὺς ἀγαπῶντας ὑμᾶς; οὐχὶ καὶ τὰ ἔθνη τοῦτο ποιοῦσιν; ὑμεῖς δὲ φιλεῖτε τοὺς μισοῦντας ὑμᾶς, καὶ οὐχ ἕξετε ἐχθρόν. ἀπέχου τῶν σαρκικῶν ἐπιθυμιῶν· ἐάν τίς σοι δῷ ῥάπισμα εἰς τὴν δεξιὰν σιαγόνα, στρέψον αὐτῷ καὶ τὴν ἄλλην, καὶ ἔσῃ τέλειος· ἐὰν ἀγγαρεύσῃ σέ τις μίλιον ἕν, ὕπαγε μετ' αὐτοῦ δύο· ἐὰν ἄρῃ τις τὸ ἱμάτιόν σου, δὸς αὐτῷ καὶ τὸν χιτῶνα·

---

[68] Relevant Jewish parallels are the Qumran fellowship (which claimed special revelation in the *raz pesher*-interpretation, compare for example 1QpHab, I, 3), and the later Rabbinic movement, which claimed that the oral tradition came from Moses (m. Avot 1).

ἐὰν λάβῃ τις ἀπὸ σοῦ τὸ σόν, μὴ ἀπαίτει· οὐδὲ γὰρ δύνασαι. παντὶ τῷ αἰτοῦντί σε δίδου καὶ μὴ ἀπαίτει· πᾶσι γὰρ θέλει δίδοσθαι ὁ πατὴρ ἐκ τῶν ἰδίων χαρισμάτων. μακάριος ὁ διδοὺς κατὰ τὴν ἐντολήν· ἀθῷος γάρ ἐστιν. οὐαὶ τῷ λαμβάνοντι· εἰ μὲν γὰρ χρείαν ἔχων λαμβάνει τις, ἀθῷος ἔσται· ὁ δὲ μὴ χρείαν ἔχων δώσει δίκην, ἱνατί ἔλαβε καὶ εἰς τί· ἐν συνοχῇ δὲ γενόμενος ἐξετασθήσεται περὶ ὧν ἔπραξε, καὶ οὐκ ἐξελεύσεται ἐκεῖθεν, μέχρις οὗ ἀποδῷ τὸν ἔσχατον κοδράντην. ἀλλὰ καὶ περὶ τούτου δὲ εἴρηται· Ἱδρωσάτω ἡ ἐλεημοσύνη σου εἰς τὰς χεῖράς σου, μέχρις ἂν γνῷς, τίνι δῷς.

There are two ways, one to life and one to death, and there is a great difference between them. The road that leads to life is this: first, you shall love God who has made you; after this, you shall love your neighbour as yourself. All that which you want not to happen to you, you should not do to another. These are the words of this teaching: Bless those who curse you, and pray for your enemy, fast for those who persecute you. For what credit is it to you if you love those who love you? Do not also the gentiles do this? But love those who hate you, and you will have no enemy. Avoid the desires of the flesh. If someone slap you on the right cheek, turn to him also the other, and you shall be perfect. If someone forces you to [walk] one mile, walk two with him. If someone takes your robe, give him also your tunic. If someone takes something that belongs to you, do not demand it in return, for you will not be able to [get it back]. Give to everyone who asks from you, without demanding anything in return, for the father want to give to everyone from his own gifts. Blessed is the one who gives according to the commandment, for he is innocent. But woe to those who receive. For if someone receives for a need he has, shall he be innocent. But the one who has no need shall give account for what reason and what he received. He will be put in prison and be carefully examined concerning what he did and will not come out from there until he has given back the last cent. For it has been said about this: Let your alms sweat in your hands, until you know to whom you shall give it.

Before analysing the content, two brief comments regarding the redaction may be appropriate. First, this section is well attested in the earliest manuscripts, and all texts that depend on the Didache include 1:3b–6, which makes it plausible to assume that the addition of the gospel section is indeed the work of the group of the Didachist.[69] Secondly, the texts share characteristics with a gospel source. The relationship between the various sources remains a topic of ongoing debate, and this study's aim is not to resolve that issue. However, it is notable that the material appears primarily to stem from Q and from the source

---

[69] Niederwimmer 1998, 68.

used by Matthew that was unique to him (M).⁷⁰ Unfortunately, this cannot be analysed further here.

Turning to the prototypical content, one can note that the *sectio evangelica* provides unique group prototypes, which separate the group from other primarily Jewish groups.⁷¹ The group member is expected to love God first and, second, his or her neighbour *and* his or her enemy. The definition of this practice of love is first explained in terms of a negative form of the Golden Rule. This negative form is not present in the synoptic material but is found in several other Jewish sources.⁷² When defining how to love your enemies, two fields are particularly important that will distinguish group members from "the gentiles," τὰ ἔθνη (1:3). First, it is the love extended towards those who are hostile to you (1:3–4). This encompasses acts of service towards the enemy (bless, pray for, fast for your enemy 1:3).⁷³ The group member must refrain from seeking revenge, and will therefore be perfected (καὶ ἔσῃ τέλειος, v. 4). This nearly grotesque expectation to refrain from revenge and even protection against evil distinguishes the group members from the surrounding society and serves as a tangible means to act in accord with the central principles of the group.⁷⁴ Second,

---

⁷⁰ Draper 2010, 9.

⁷¹ One can of course note similarities in the prototypical patterns with other groups. The point here, from a SIT perspective, is however that the rules were set to give members a pattern to live that separated them from other groups. The group prototype only needed to be unique enough regarding the immediate neighbours, to be successful in separating the group from others. See Finlan 2015, 18–19.

⁷² See a variant in Letter of Aristeas 207; Tobit 4:15, and so forth. For an extensive list, see Niederwimmer 1998, 66, n. 14.

⁷³ εὐλογεῖτε τοὺς καταρωμένους ὑμῖν καὶ προσεύχεσθε ὑπὲρ τῶν ἐχθρῶν ὑμῶν, νηστεύετε δὲ ὑπὲρ τῶν διωκόντων ὑμᾶς reflects the tendency of not sticking exactly to "M," see Niederwimmer, 1998, 74–77.

⁷⁴ One can debate to what degree the Didachist's community knew about a Kingdom of Heaven teaching depending on how familiar they were to the source material of Matthew and Q. Since the text knew of some of this material, it does not automatically mean that they knew everything. The eschatological understanding mirrored in chapter 16 hints that they may have been aware of some kind of version of a teaching of the Kingdom of heaven. Since, to make sense, the ethical teaching in Matthew is quite dependent on an understanding of Jesus as the

we find the principle of giving instead of receiving. This relates to an understanding of the poor, as in their right to receive alms, a concept found in various Jewish texts sources.[75] The wealthy are thus also expected to give alms. Therefore, it is important that the right to receive alms is not exploited, placing a considerable burden on recipients to avoid accepting too much. The saying of unknown provenance urges the giver to discern who is a worthy recipient of alms, likely to prevent the misuse of the right to receive.[76] As will be seen in Didache 2 and 5, a still, quiet, and poor life was the ideal.

The call to loving one's neighbour and enemy (defined according to established principles) was thus regarded as the first and, therefore, most significant aspect in the teaching. The beginning of 1:3, "these are the words of this teaching," defines how to follow the Golden Rule. In 2:1, a follow-up is made, which is the rest of the Two Ways tractate. The Golden Rule, as defined for the given ingroup in chapter 1, represents the most significant expectation of the group member.[77]

6.3.2 The Remainder of the Two Ways Tractate

Turning now to the subsequent chapters that contain the Two Ways tractate, we can summarise this section as follows.

The first section covers the way of life (chapters 1–4), while the second section addresses the way of death (chapter 5). Chapter 6 provides instructions on discerning sound teaching and a halakah for non-Jews in the group. Below is a summary table of the contents of 1–6.

---

eschatological "Son of Man" (God will eventually vindicate the humble), the reason for the expectations in Didache 1:3b–6 should be similar. One can also, on a different note, see that Finlan 2015, 17–18, has a point when he sees perfection as a crucial theme for the Didache community.

[75] Niederwimmer 1998, 82–83. See Lev. Rab. 34.2, on Lev 25:25. See also Prov 19:17.

[76] Niederwimmer 1998, 86.

[77] Finlan 2015, 20, sees the Jesus tradition as the most significant part of the teaching when he writes that "the things [...] commended in the Two Ways section are not Torah-specific but are morality, kindness, fairness, and honesty and echo the Sermon on the Mount more than any other source."

	Prototypicality
1:1	Introduction, "One way to life, and one way to death," followed by the *sectio evangelica*, see above.
[2:1]	Redactional material: "This is the second command of the teaching" – Δευτέρα δὲ ἐντολὴ τῆς διδαχῆς.
2:2–7	Prohibitions closely modelled on the second table of the decalogue. The prohibitions pertain to actions, words, and thoughts: **Actions:** Murder, exposing infants and abortion, sorcery, sexual immorality and pederasty. **Words:** False testimonies, "double tongue and mind," meanness, scheming. **Thoughts:** Greed, rapaciousness, hypocrisy, arrogance, and hate in general.
4:2–14	Exhortations concerning fellowship (4:2, "seek the fellowship of the holy every day") and unity (4:3), giving (4:5–8), child-rearing (4:9), relation between slaves and masters, ("God does not call according to position, but calls those whom the spirit has made ready," 4:8), and lastly to confess "your infringements" "in the congregation" (4:14). The exhortations are closely related to *Haustafeln*-theology, concerning how the relationships within the community were expected to play out.
5:1–2	The road to death is basically a negative repetition of the previous chapters; those who act according to the road to death will perish. The content of the road to death is thus also concerned with the same topics as the road to life but in the negative form; the text warns for those who engage in murder, adultery, desires, sexual immorality, theft, idolatry, magic, witchcraft, violence, false testimonies, hypocrisy, "double-heartedness," deceit, arrogance, evil, stubbornness, greed and so on. Also, the person following the road to death persecutes the good ones, hates the truth, and loves lies. Also, the greed of the person following the road to death makes him/her work together with the oppressor of the poor. The baptismal candidate is warned against any contact with such persons.
6:1–3	Chapter 6 gives concluding admonitions and provides a sign of faithful preachers: To teach true is to teach according to what is previously said, according to the introduction of chapter 6. Here is also an expectation to "carry the full yoke of the lord" (ὅλον τὸν ζυγὸν τοῦ κυρίου), or as much as possible. The minimum expectation pertaining to food is to abstain from what has been offered to idols (ἀπὸ δὲ τοῦ εἰδωλοθύτου λίαν πρόσεχε). Here we can find, as we will return to, traces of a halakah for non-Jews, akin to the sources for Acts 15.

Table 6.3.2. *Content in the Two Ways tractate of Didache.*

As mentioned above, the trope of two ways existed in many different contexts, both Jewish and Hellenistic. It is, however, reasonable to assume that the *Vorlage* for the Two Ways tractate in Didache had a primarily Jewish background.[78] Even if the biblical passages from the LXX/Hebrew Bible did not give a template[79] *per se,* other forms can be seen as crucial impulses for the text in Didache. The work of Audet, followed by van de Sandt and Flusser, provides a reasonable tracking of the tradition from the Community Rule (1QS III, 13–IV.26).[80] The problem with this understanding is that the tracking of a Jewish *Vorlage* requires a lost form of the earliest Jewish Two Ways tractate, that was behind other (for lack of better words) *Christian* forms of the Two Ways tractate.[81] This must be posited since the text in the Community Rule obviously is not the *Vorlage* but rather shows the possibilities of such a text. But since the *Vorlage* idea is the only option that provides some substantial literary affinities to a Two Ways tradition, this solves more problems than it creates and must thus be taken as a heuristic solution for the problem. It accounts for the similarities between the Two Ways found in the Community Rule, the Letter of Barnabas, and Didache.[82] However, this investigation aims not to solve the textual genealogies but to understand group ideals.

When examining the content of the tractate, it is crucial to remember that it served as a manual of conduct for baptismal candidates. Several commentators observe that chapter 2 essentially aims to contemporise the second tablet of the Decalogue.[83] The themes and areas of life covered are fine-tuning the general prohibitions of the second tablet. The regulations adhere to the order of Exodus 20:13–17, though several of the prohibitions are further delineated.

---

[78] van de Sandt and Flusser 2002, 57.

[79] "[T]he topos of the Two Ways frequently occurs in such passages as Deut 11:26–28; 30:15–19 ; Jer 21:8; Pss 1 ...[Pss] 119 (118):29–30 ; 139 (138):24; Prov 2:13; 4:18–19; 11:20; 12:28 (LXX), and so forth," van de Sandt and Flusser 2002, 58.

[80] Audet, 1952, van de Sandt and Flusser 2002, 70.

[81] van de Sandt and Flusser 2002, 70.

[82] van de Sandt and Flusser 2002, 71.

[83] Audet 1952, 283; Niederwimmer 1998, 88; van de Sandt and Flusser 2002, 56. One can as Niederwimmer does follow the order of the Decalogue in the admonitions in chapter 3; Niederwimmer 1998, 88–93.

6.3 The Two Ways Tractate and Its Sitz im Leben

Thus, the prohibition against adultery is clarified through two stipulations: it does not permit pederasty or sexual immorality (οὐ μοιχεύσεις, οὐ παιδοφθορήσεις, οὐ πορνεύσεις). The great exception from the order of Exodus 20 is the strange placement of οὐ μαγεύσεις, which also is further qualified in three ways: not to mix potions, engage in abortion, or kill infants.[84] There appears to be no clear reason for the placement of the prohibition here, and this is not the appropriate context for further speculation on the matter. One can only observe the awkward positioning of the prohibition, considering the Exodus pattern found elsewhere in the text. Moreover, the similarities with, for example, a Jewish physician's oath and the rulings of Didache 2 and 5 have been noted.[85] In this way, the community of the Didachist seems to adhere to a Jewish understanding concerning sexual behaviour, behaviour towards children, blasphemy, and the understanding of omens (see 2:2; 3:4). The list, in general, provides moral guidance for non-Jewish believers to turn from actions that horrified contemporary Jews.[86] The vices listed in the subsequent chapter, which were formulated in chapter 2, were understood as "especially abhorrent when practised by gentiles."[87] The baptismal candidate was thus expected to follow this contemporised decalogue (as well as the gospel teaching) after baptism.[88] As the theme consistently revolves around words, thoughts, and actions throughout the section as a whole, the material reiterates the weight of the Decalogue as moral guide for the believer. Both the road to life and the road to

---

[84] Niederwimmer 1998, 88–90, understands the order as somewhat confused and compares it with the order found in Barnabas. See also van de Sandt and Flusser 2002, 56. One can note that beginning with a prohibition against engaging in magic does not necessarily entail a prohibition against killing infants.

[85] van de Sandt and Flusser 2002, 57, n. 5.

[86] Draper 2007, 17.

[87] Niederwimmer 1998, 89. See especially n. 10 which lists predominantly biblical source texts for a Jewish prohibition against sorcery.

[88] van de Sandt and Flusser 2002, 56: "Although this parenetic catalogue is expanded with specific additional elements, it is in fact a development of the more general themes of the second table of the Decalogue. Thus, the commandment not to commit adultery is extended to include a prohibition on pederasty and fornication. Also, other items expressing a firm stand against the danger of contemporary threats can be explained as modifications of the Decalogue."

death consequently address the same vices: the similarity between chapter 2 and chapter 5 ("not in form but certainly in content") is obvious.[89]

Chapter 3, containing the "my child" sayings (the sixfold repetition of the phrase τέκνον μου calls to mind wisdom traditions, with a personified wisdom; compare Prov 7:24), had the goal of showing that minor vices in fact could lead to dangerous practices and results.[90] Niederwimmer points to themes and methods akin to the *Testament of the Twelve Patriarchs* throughout the chapter.[91] What is presented throughout chapter 3 aligns with the content of both earlier and subsequent chapters: the concerns in the chapter revolve around themes of murder, adultery, idolatry, and theft. The triad of thoughts (3:2), actions (3:4), and words (3:3) is a constant. The theme from the first chapters that the followers should be perfect (τέλειος, 1:4) is visible in the recurring "my child" trope in chapter 3. In 3:7, a new theme is picked up: humility. The sentence ἴσθι δὲ πραΰς, ἐπεὶ οἱ πραεῖς κληρονομήσουσι τὴν γῆν "be humble, for the humble shall inherit the land" reflects a Jewish piety form reflecting humility.[92] The ideal encourages a quiet, still life. Pertaining to both attitudes and actions, followers are urged not to exalt themselves or associate with the powerful in society, but rather with the righteous and humble. Additionally, a certain passivity is expected (3:10). Chapter 3 concludes that humility, passivity, and poverty are linked to the anticipated group behaviour. As will be revealed in the path to death in chapter 5, association with and advocacy for the lofty is viewed as a route to death.

In chapter 4, the focus shifts from the individual to the group. The chapter brings up the relationship between the individual and teachers of the faith (who are to be as revered "as the Lord," ὡς κύριον, v. 1), to others in the group (labelled as "the saints/the holy," τῶν ἁγίων, v. 2), towards the poor and one's possessions ("share everything with your brother and do not label anything to be your own," συγκοινωνήσεις δὲ πάντα τῷ ἀδελφῷ σου καὶ οὐκ ἐρεῖς ἴδια εἶναι, v.

---

[89] Niederwimmer 1998, 88–89.
[90] Niederwimmer 1998, 95.
[91] Niederwimmer 1998, 95.
[92] Audet 1958, 316; Niederwimmer 1998, 100; TDNT s. v. πραΰς. Cf. HALOT s. v. ענו.

5–8), children (v. 9), slaves (v. 10), and masters (v. 11). Verses 12–14 conclude regarding life together in a community.

Verses 9–11 resemble a *Haustafel*, which regulates the lives of every member of the household. Much has been written about the genre, whether it comes from Stoic morals or from an economic realm.[93] In this investigation, it may be sufficient to state that the genre was prevalent in the Hellenistic world and that several Jewish authors sought to demonstrate a connection between Jewish law and Hellenistic moral values.[94] A few points are worth mentioning regarding the group identity conveyed by the Didachist in chapter 4. The emphasis placed on leadership, along with the fact that the leader preaches according to a well-regulated teaching for the community (see 7:1, 11:1), grants the leader a role that uniquely represents the divine in the congregation; "where the authority is preached, there is the Lord" (v. 1). "The Lord" (κύριος), in this instance, probably refers to Jesus.[95] One can also observe a similar concept in Matt. 18:20 (or in a shared source for Matthew and the Didachist). Consequently, the act of teaching, along with the receiving of such teachings, is linked to the mission of Jesus. Thus, the Didachist operates as an identity impresario, as the act of teaching and being taught includes communion with Jesus. As we recall, impresarioship refers to embedding ingroup identity within structures and rituals. We will return to this function of teaching (that must be the result of a teacher from the community). The teaching that should be upheld and imparted is likely the dual content of chapters 1–6. Moreover, the understanding among the group members, or ingroup, as sacred naturally influences how one perceives both membership within the group and those outside of it, a theme further explored in chapter 8. This is particularly intriguing as a significant issue of the Didache concerns how to discern genuine outsiders among travellers (itinerants who merely exploit the community for their own advantage). Membership depends on initiation, prototypical behaviour, and proper behaviour

---

[93] Already Dibelius 1912 understood the Haustafeln in the New Testament as ethical codes from the Stoic thought on duty. Lührmann 1980 suggested a more fruitful comparison in ancient economics.

[94] Keener 2000. As is well known, the genre is used by the authors of, for example, Ephesians and Colossians.

[95] So Niederwimmer 1998, 105.

after mistakes are made. Verse 14 calls upon members to "confess infringements in the congregation" (ἐν ἐκκλησία ἐξομολογήσῃ ἐπὶ τὰ παραπτώματά σου), which makes life in the community possible even after infringements.

In chapter 5, the focus shifts to the road towards death. Verse 4:14c concludes the road to life section with the concluding statement, "This is the road to life," αὕτη ἐστιν ἡ ὁδός τοῦ ζωῆς. As mentioned earlier, however, the dense chapter 5 is essentially a reflection of chapter 2 and thus relates to actions, thoughts, and words. The chapter urges the baptismal candidate to avoid the individuals exhibiting negative behaviours. The introduction is nearly an exact counterpart of 1:2: Ἡ μὲν οὖν ὁδὸς τῆς ζωῆς ἐστιν αὕτη (1:2b), Ἡ δὲ τοῦ θανάτου ὁδός ἐστιν αὕτη (5:1), which provide some balance to the tractate, even though the road to life is more elaborated with not least the *Haustafeln* and τέκνον μου-sayings. The road to death is divided in two parts: actions that follow from being on that road (such as murder and adultery), and a list of personifications of the vices ("persons who persecute the good ones, who hate truth" and so forth).[96] The list of actions and personifications follows roughly the order of the Decalogue.[97] In contrast to the ingroup ideal of humility, those who embody the path to death are said to side with the oppressor (5:2c, "turning away from those in need, mistreating those in difficult circumstances, advocates for the rich" – ἀποστρεφόμενοι τὸν ἐνδεόμενον, καταπονοῦντες τὸν θλιβόμενον, πλουσίων παράκλητοι). This portrayal of outsiders is an antithesis of the humble ideal presented in chapter 3. Therefore, prototypical group members ought to lead lives that assist those in need and those facing difficult circumstances and collaborate with the impoverished.

Chapter 6 offers an intriguing perspective on membership in relation to Jewish food regulations and halakic rulings. The perspective that the recipients, to a high degree, knew of or followed some kind of halakah seems plausible when reading that "if you can pick up the whole yoke of the Lord ὅλον τὸν ζυγὸν τοῦ κυρίου you will be perfect" (6:2). The suggestion that it ought to have been the complete ritual aspect of the law was the initial understanding of this

---

[96] Niederwimmer 1998, 115.
[97] Niederwimmer 1998, 116.

6.3 The Two Ways Tractate and Its Sitz im Leben

verse.[98] However, both in wisdom literature such as Sir 51:26 and in later rabbinic material (m. Avot 3:5, m. Ber. 2:2), the yoke has some technical meaning pertaining to living under the Torah and learning from it and fully accepting it as a guide for life, which in practice means a certain halakah.[99] Niederwimmer discusses the difference between עול מלכות השמים קבל and ζυγὸν βαστάζειν and points to the difference between "taking on" and "enduring."[100] The difference suggests the possibility for the individual to fully engage in the teaching of the chapters, in contrast to the rabbinic technical term of leading a life of Torah observance according to halakah. However, it is difficult to imagine that the use of ζυγόν, with its associations of halakic observance, would play no role at all here. Rather, chapters 1–6 as baptismal teaching seems to be a kind of minimum demand for the members of the community and signs of the individual's willingness to be subject to the group ideal. The halakah of the Didache group thus pertains *primarily* to moral law and not ritual law. But 6:3, which demands certain attention to avoidance of food offered to idols, suggests that the ideals were *not only* moral but also had some ritual concerns for non-Jews.

Not all have followed this view. For example, there have been suggestions by von Harnack and Knopf that the verse discusses an unspoken denunciation of marriage.[101] This suggestion, however, cannot point to any concrete evidence in the texts supporting the claim, and no traces can be found in later texts stemming from the Didache tradition.[102] Since the immediate context (6:3) discusses the need to abstain from food offered to idols, the connection to a tradition akin to the tradition behind Acts 15 is much more likely than to an unknown rule of sexual denunciation of unclear origins and content. Suppose one were to suggest documents that have some bearing on the subject discussed in Didache 6. In that case, one can note that Acts 15:20 (see also 15:29) discusses a halakah for non-Jews and concludes that the non-Jews in the Jesus groups are to abstain from food offered to idols, from sexual immorality, and choked animals and their blood: ἀλλ' ἐπιστεῖλαι αὐτοῖς τοῦ ἀπέχεσθαι τῶν ἀλισγημάτων τῶν

---

[98] This was suggested already by Schaff 1886, 182.
[99] See Levina and Brettler 2017, 32 (note to Matt. 11:29).
[100] Niederwimmer 1998, 121.
[101] Von Harnack 1886, 19–21; Knopf 1920, 21.
[102] See Niederwimmer 1998, 122; see alsoKnopf 1920, 21.

εἰδώλων καὶ τῆς πορνείας καὶ τοῦ πνικτοῦ καὶ τοῦ αἵματος ("but we should write to them to abstain only from things polluted by idols and from sexual immorality and from whatever has been strangled and from blood"; NRSV).[103] Of course, we cannot have conclusive evidence regarding the extent to which a halakic ruling like the one from Acts 15 was known, but at least Acts 15 is a roughly contemporary tradition that echoes a discussion on the same topics.[104] Also, given the closeness to Matthew, the Didachist would have addressed the text in this context, where matters of ethnicity and faith were exigent. Non-Jews in the congregation were encouraged to live by basic halakic rules (possibly similar to Acts 15), in which abstaining from food offered to idols is regarded as the most significant aspect for non-Jewish believers (6:3).[105] Since the question of sexual immorality already had been covered several times in the previous chapters, the need now was to finish the section with the concrete question about food regulations and, in the long run, table fellowship.[106] This then would be a "yoke" for non-Jews covering both food regulations (6:3) and sexual immorality (chapters 2 and 5). The suggestion by Rordorf and Tuilier, picked up by Niederwimmer, that the *sectio evangelica* in the beginning of the tractate should be the yoke in question is missing out on the connotations of ζυγόν in a Jewish milieu that is intimately connected to some kind of halakah. The ritual minutiae of everyday life are missing.[107] The chapter, therefore, adds food regulations to the ethical guidelines for non-Jews in the congregation, should they be unable to take on the full yoke (a whole halakah).

---

[103] One can in this context note Paul's use of ζυγὸν in Gal 5:1; Τῇ ἐλευθερίᾳ ἡμᾶς Χριστὸς ἠλευθέρωσεν· στήκετε οὖν καὶ μὴ πάλιν ζυγῷ δουλείας ἐνέχεσθε ("For freedom Christ has set us free. Stand firm, therefore, and do not submit again to a yoke of slavery" NRSV). This seems to suggest a view of halakha for non-Jews as totally different from the view of the group that received the Didache, see Draper 2007, 16. See also Acts 15:10: νῦν οὖν τί πειράζετε τὸν θεὸν ἐπιθεῖναι ζυγὸν ἐπὶ τὸν τράχηλον τῶν μαθητῶν ὃν οὔτε οἱ πατέρες ἡμῶν οὔτε ἡμεῖς ἰσχύσαμεν βαστάσαι; ("Now, therefore, why are you putting God to the test by placing on the neck of the disciples a yoke that neither our ancestors nor we have been able to bear?" NRSV).

[104] Note Smee 2003, 88, citing Jefford 1989.

[105] When Rordorf and Tuilier wrote, the affinity to the decree in Acts 15 was already noted by several commentators, see Rordorf and Tuilier 1978, 33 (n. 5).

[106] Draper 2007, 16.

[107] Rordorf and Tuilier 1978, 32–33; Niederwimmer 1998, 122.

6.3.3 Summary and Concluding Remarks on Prototypical Behaviour in the Didache

To summarise this section, the ethical behaviour outlined in chapters 1 to 6 is expected of all members of the group, as it lays the foundation for baptism (7:1). The ethical behaviour partly stems from a section of the gospel that emphasises the necessity for group members to love their neighbours and enemies, as a means of distinguishing themselves from outsiders. This section shares a common source primarily with the Gospel of Matthew, but the ethical guidelines also derive from a shared Jewish Two Ways tractate with an unknown origin. The remainder of the Two Ways tractate serves to contemporise the Decalogue, particularly regarding abhorrent gentile practices, providing moral guidelines for members that align with various other Jewish sources. Although Two Ways tropes were prevalent in Hellenistic thought, the close alignment in content with the Decalogue and the admonition against contemporary gentile practices indicate a predominantly Jewish context for the tractate. The moral guidelines conclude with an expectation for members to adhere to some basic food regulations, not significantly different from the halakah for non-Jews outlined in Acts 15, even if no literary dependence can be traced.

The prototypical behaviour is thus a peculiar blend for the group that (through the Jesus tradition) sets it apart from other Jewish groups, and through the remainder of the Two Ways tractate sets the group apart from common non-Jewish practices concerning, for example, divination and certain sexual behaviours that were viewed as abhorrent. We can now note that, since prototypical members typically elicit followership according to SIT theory, the need for leaders to embody these kinds of ideals is essential and crucial.[108] This will be further analysed below, but here it suffices to say that since the ἐπίσκοπος should have been "tested" (δεδοκιμασμένους, 15:1) and otherwise needed to live up to the expected rules, one must assume that he aimed for a prototypical life, which would equal a life in harmony with Didache 1–6. One can note here that the expectation that the leaders should be worthy of the Lord, not be fond of money, and be humble and honest echoes the humility ideals of chapters 2 and 5.

---

[108] Esler 2021, 34.

There is, however, also an expectation that these views should be continuously upheld in the teaching by itinerants. According to the understanding of an overlap between itinerants and local leaders, it is reasonable to assume that the last group also carried out the teaching. The teaching ability of the leaders plays an important role, making both itinerant and local leaders not only prototypes but also impresarios, embedders of identity, according to the SIT framework outlined in chapter 2 above.

6.4 The Leadership Structure of Didache 15 from an SIT Perspective

Given this rather extensive analysis of prototypical behaviour (the ingroup ideals that members should embody), we now turn to the chapter that explicitly addresses the leadership structure. The only passage directly discussing an emerging episcopal leadership structure is 15:1. Although this may not seem substantial, it provides important information. We can observe that while there is no explicit theologising regarding the emerging episcopal office in Didache, there is a contrast with the discussion of the role of the ἐπίσκοπος found in the Ignatian letters and 1 Clement. The ἐπίσκοποι καὶ διάκονοι in Didache (15:1, note the plural) are local leaders who stand for both continuation of the office of itinerant prophets and teachers *and* stability and long-time commitment, as will soon be analysed further.[109] This local role, however, involves teaching and liturgical leadership, as well as the prototypical role modelling performed by the leaders, making it a meaningful role to analyse from SIT leadership categories. Impresarioship (the embedment of ingroup identity in structures and rituals) and prototypicality (the embodiment of ingroup ideals) are visible through the association with the ministry of the itinerants. This, in combination with the presence of itinerant teachers and prophets, seems to suggest a mixed form of leadership in the Didachist's communities, which would have provided an incentive for a presentation of a unified understanding of the leadership.[110] As we have seen above, Didache is a composite text. Several sources have been joined together to form a unified whole. Chapter 15, with its rather

---

[109] This is consistent with the reassuring purpose of the text according to Zangenberg 2008, 50.
[110] So Ehrman 2003a, 409.

6.4 The Leadership Structure of Didache 15 from an SIT Perspective

late introduction of the ἐπίσκοποι and διάκονοι, appears a bit strange. Further, the joining together of the roles with the roles of the prophets and teachers appears to be a way the Didachist combines leadership roles found in different parts of the community.

6.4.1 The ἐπίσκοπος and διάκονος and Their Role in the Community

For a better understanding of the message of this crucial chapter, we start with the text itself.

> Χεριοτονήσατε οὖν ἑαυτοῖς επισκόπους καὶ διακόνους ἀξίους τοῦ κυρίου, ἄνδρας πραεῖς καὶ ἀφιλαργύρους καὶ ἀλεθεῖς καὶ δεδοκιμασμένους· ὑμῖν γὰρ λειτουργοῦσι καὶ αὐτοὶ τὴν λειτουργίαν τῶν προφητῶν καὶ διδασκάλων. Μὴ οὖν ὑπερίδητε αὐτούς· αὐτοὶ γάρ εἰσιν οἱ τετιμημένοι ὑμῶν μετὰ τῶν προφητῶν καὶ διδασκάλων. (15:1–2)
>
> Now choose among you ἐπίσκοποι and διάκονοι worthy of the lord, men who are humble, not fond of money, truthful and who have been tested. For they perform the ministry of the prophets and teachers among you. Do not despise them! For they have been found worthy among you, with the prophets and teachers.

Two things are especially interesting when analysing the local leadership here. First, should the ἐπίσκοποι καὶ διάκονοι be understood as prototypical leaders or identity advancers, based on the expressed expectation that they should be generous? As we remember from chapter 2 above, prototypical leaders are the most successful since they elicit followership based on the authority of their behaviour. The fact that a leader manages to embody ingroup ideals provides him/her with authority in the group. Identity advancers, on the other hand, advance ingroup interests, not least financially and not least among outsiders. The advancer is not necessarily perceived as prototypical in behaviour, but followers recognise him or her as advancing the group's interests rather than their own. This question of what kind of leadership the ἐπίσκοποι καὶ διάκονοι exercised is intimately related to what kind of relationship the local leaders had to the itinerants.

Second, the local leaders should have been "tested." This pertains to the appointment procedure and discernment in the appointment.

6.4.2 The ἐπίσκοπος and διάκονος – Prototypical Leaders or Identity Advancers?

First, we turn to whether leaders behave prototypically or primarily function as identity advancers. As we have seen, leaders are generally found among those who manage to (or at least seem to) adhere to ingroup prototypes. The first section of Didache, as we have noted, focuses on establishing a perceived prototypical pattern of life; while it aligned with some common Hellenistic thoughts, it primarily echoed Christ-group ideals from the M source and Jewish values regarding idolatry, sorcery, and sexual morality. The explicit expectation is that baptised members should live up to these standards, and when they fail, they should confess their sins to be rectified (14:1).

Throughout the third section of Didache (chapters 11–15), commonly labelled as "church order," there is a distinctive emphasis on the behaviour of and towards itinerants. Both teachers and prophets are addressed. Both teaching ("receive now anyone who teaches you all this previously said," 11:1–2) and behaviour ("and every prophet who orders a meal in the spirit does not eat from it but if [he does], he is a false prophet. Every prophet who teaches you the truth but does not do what he teaches is a false prophet" 11:9–10) should be accurate for itinerants. Niederwimmer understand this third section as an ancient tradition picked up in the time of the Didachist, who provided a revision to fit into the pattern of his time.[111] As Niederwimmer understands it, "there is a contrast between the itinerant apostles and prophets on the one hand and the resident groups on the other."[112] However, in 15:2 the resident leaders ἐπίσκοποι and διάκονοι are perceived as just as honourable as the itinerants, and are in practice seen as the residing prophets and teachers; ὑμῖν γὰρ λειτουργοῦσι καὶ αὐτοὶ τὴν λειτουργίαν τῶν προφητῶν καὶ διδασκάλων ... αὐτοὶ γάρ εἰσιν οἱ τετιμημένοι ὑμῶν μετὰ τῶν προφητῶν καὶ διδασκάλων, "For these perform the ministry of the prophets and teachers among you ... For those have been found worthy among you, with the prophets and teachers" (15:2). Thus, what is expected of itinerants in practice and theology, is expected from the residing officers. The rules for baptised members, as well as itinerants, are applicable for

---

[111] Niederwimmer 1998, 169.
[112] Niederwimmer 1998, 169.

an ἐπίσκοπος and a διάκονος, too. Niederwimmer makes a point that the election process mirrored in 15:1 suggests a perceived secondary quality to the offices of the local leaders (contrasted to itinerants who would have a more esteemed role, and thus should be welcomed "as the Lord" ὡς κύριος (11:4).[113] This explains the emphasis placed on the worthiness of the local offices as a means of balancing the roles.[114] Some disdain for the local leaders might lie behind the Didachist's exhortation. It might, of course, be the case that there is a local emphasis on the worthiness of local officers at the expense of the authoritative travelling charismatics. However, from a SIT perspective, the most important aspect is that the local officers are associated with offices possessing prototypical or identity-constructing qualities. Regardless, the local offices share in the glory as well as the expectations placed on the prophets, according to the text. It is also reasonable to assume that the local offices were effective enough in their leadership to avoid falling out of favour. If the local leaders were not prototypical enough in their ministry, their leadership would not have garnered any followership. We can observe that the frequency of the leadership titles διάκονος and ἐπίσκοπος increased during the second century and beyond. In the static snapshot provided by the Didache, we do not yet find any explicit signs of this increase.

Draper's view is that the διάκονος and ἐπίσκοπος are honorary titles for the community's patron figures. Consequently, they are not truly prototypical or liturgical leaders (impresarios in practice), but rather enablers of the ingroup identity:

> They are patrons of the community who have the resources to assist the community and homes large enough to meet in: finance, influence in the wider community which might serve to protect the community and enhance its status in the wider society, education and administrative competence. The possession of their resources depended, of course, on their being settled and influential members of the wider local society.[115]

The διάκονος and ἐπίσκοπος should then be more akin to identity advancers than prototypical leaders. This is because identity advancement, as we have

---

[113] Niederwimmer 1998, 200–201.
[114] Niederwimmer reads οἱ αὐτοί in as emphatic 1998, 201–2. See also the similar translation in Ehrman 2003a, 441.
[115] Draper 2008, 167.

seen, does not require prototypical leadership *per se*: "Indeed, leaders who worked strongly for the interests of the group were able to inspire followership even if they were not particularly prototypical."[116] Group leaders who explicitly have the interest of the group as salient in their actions, and advance the group's standing socially, can gain massive support in the group.[117] This would suggest, that the leaders of the group in the Didachist's community built themselves a leadership platform when they supported the group financially. From a purely theoretical point of view, the signs of an emerging episcopal structure mentioned in chapter 15 would have a somewhat solid ground for their leadership on mere financial grounds if one follows Draper and understands ἀφιλάργυρος as signs of the διάκονοι and ἐπίσκοποι being patrons of the community.

It appears, however, that this is not the case according to Didache 15:1, and as I touched upon above. Rather, 15:1b ("for they [ἐπίσκοπος and διάκονος] also perform [λειτουργοῦσι] the ministry [τὴν λειτουργίαν] of the prophets and teachers for you") in practice equalises the work of prophets, teachers, διάκονοι and ἐπίσκοποι. This is also repeated in 15:2: Μὴ οὖν ὑπερίδητε αὐτούς· αὐτοὶ γάρ εἰσιν οἱ τετιμημένοι ὑμῶν μετὰ τῶν προφητῶν καὶ διδασκάλων ("Do not despise them! For those have been found worthy among you, with the prophets and teachers"). The formulation οἱ τετιμημένοι ὑμῶν suggests that the local leaders, instead of giving financial aid to the community, are receiving financial support as a result of their ministry. The formulation οἱ τετιμημένοι ὑμῶν carries a financial implication.[118] In chapter 13, the prophets and teachers receive priestly dues through the first fruits. The equalisation of honour between itinerant and local leaders in 15:1–2 implies that the dues can now be given to the διάκονος and ἐπίσκοπος also. Hence, the "priestliness" of the office of the prophets is transferred to the settled officers. The local offices also possess financial dimensions that are comparable to the itinerant's charismatic leadership.

Draper's assertion that the demand for leaders to be generous suggests a patron role is indeed important to discuss further. It is true that patron systems

---

[116] Esler 2021, 39.
[117] Esler 2021, 38–39.
[118] Contra Niederwimmer 1998, 202, who understands τιμή or τιμάω as only an honorary title, τιμή and cognates carry a dimension not only of honour but of salary; cf. 1 Tim 5:17, which explicitly connects the work of good πρεσβύτεροι with double pay. s. v. τιμή, τιμάω, BDAG.

functioned through wealthy individuals who provided resources for groups, which elevated their significance as members.[119] To some extent, Draper's perspective holds validity, as patrons within the broader Mediterranean region could offer legitimacy, financial resources, and possibly even venues for a group. Consequently, a wealthier individual was often elected to leadership positions, ensuring the group received financial support.[120] However, there was a slight distinction between how patrons were perceived in Greco-Roman society and in Jewish society. As previously noted, chapter 1:5–6 reflects a Jewish understanding of the divine obligation to assist the poor, as poor.[121] In a Greco-Roman understanding, giving could be linked to, for example, pity, but it was not regarded as a religious duty or a means of expressing piety, except in certain philosophical schools. Supporting the poor was not viewed as a religious obligation as it was in Jewish circles.[122] The incentive to give alms was therefore less in the Greco-Roman society, unless the recipient was a client capable of supporting the patron in significant situations. It is also worth noting that a more prominent idea within Jewish communities was the understanding of ethnicity as a key factor in deciding which poor to assist.[123] There are, however, no real reasons to assume a wholly different system of reciprocity in Jewish life apart from this divine duty towards the poor.[124] Therefore, the patron system likely served as inspiration for wealthy Jewish individuals who were also leaders of

---

[119] On a general level, generous donations were paid back in honour and positions, as can be seen in for example in the contemporary inscription in Trache, " IPerinthos ... A Synagogue of barbers." One can note that it seems to be comparable also with other times and places in the north-east part of the Mediterranean area, as in this earlier example from Athens: IG II2 1252+999 "Honorific decree by the *orgeōnes* of Amynos and Asklepios." Both found in Kloppenborg and Ascough 2011, 43–44.

[120] For an extensive review of theological implications for the patronage system, see Barclay, 2015, 24–32; 35–45. A definition of patronage relationship that is prominent in Barclay is that of Saller 1982, 36: "[A patronage relationship is] a reciprocal exchange of goods and services, which is personal, enduring and asymmetrical (thus involving the exchange of different kinds of service)."

[121] Barclay 2015, 41–43. Cf. Niederwimmer 1998, 82–83.

[122] Barclay 2015, 43.

[123] Barclay 2015, 42.

[124] See the discussion by Barclay 2015, 41–43, which engages with Schwarz 2010, 10–41.

groups, as these leaders would have had a particular duty to provide for the group. But where does this lead us in relation to the Christ groups of the Didache? A key question in this debate is the connotation of the word ἀφιλάργυρος. Does this word necessarily imply patronage? The answer is no. The virtue is not always connected to patronship. Onosander, for example, demands that the military general should be ἀφιλάργυρος, while the rest of the traits of the στρατήγος do not immediately suggest that this means that he should be a patron:

> Φημὶ τοίνυν αἱρεῖσθαι τὸν στρατηγὸν οὐ κατὰ γένη κρίνοντας, ὥσπερ τοὺς ἱερέας, οὐδὲ κατ' οὐσίας, ὡς τοὺς γυμνασιάρχους, ἀλλὰ σώφρονα, ἐγκρατῆ, νήπτην, λιτόν, διάπονον, νοερόν, ἀφιλάργυρον, μήτε νέον μήτε πρεσβύτερον, ἂν τύχῃ καὶ πατέρα παίδων, ἱκανὸν λέγειν, ἔνδοξον.
>
> I believe, then, that we must choose a general, not because of noble birth as priests are chosen, nor because of wealth as the superintendents of the gymnasia, but because he is temperate, self-restrained, vigilant, frugal, hardened to labour, alert, free from avarice, neither too young nor too old, indeed a father of children if possible, a ready speaker, and a man with a good reputation.[125]

Rather, the demands by Onosander suggest a humble standing of the στρατήγος. The list suggests only important traits for the ideal general. There is thus nothing inherent in the word which would demand that ἀφιλάργυρος means to be a patron. While the local leaders in the Didachist's community *could* have been seen as patrons because of the expectation to be ἀφιλάργυρος, they were not necessarily so. There is a temptation to understand the role of the local leaders so, also from a SIT perspective: On a general level, when a wealthy leader invests in the group identity and provides resources for the group, the group's ability to establish structures and symbols meaningful to the group identity is significantly enhanced. If one understands the need for the ἐπίσκοπος not to be fond of money as a paraphrase of a patron of a society, the ἐπίσκοπος would now be understood also as an identity advancer. But how does that relate to the financial support that the local offices, according to 15:2, had the right to receive? Honouring as a sign of gratitude could also, in totally different contexts, come in the form of payment for services to the community, for example,

---

[125] Translation and text: Conzelmann and Dibelius 1972, 158.

when Semnos of Lollia Katylla was honoured after two years of service as a priest for the *mystai* of Dionysos Kallon.[126] The ἐπίσκοπος in Didache also served his community and would thus have been worthy of receiving gratitude, even in financial form, for his service. The context in the Didache suggests that even if it is remotely possible that ἀφιλάργους could have been a marker for the expectation of a local patron, the ἐπίσκοπος, it is more straightforward to understand the expectations on the ἐπίσκοπος and διάκονος from the perspective of prototypical leaders, that is, leaders who embody the ingroup ideal to be generous (aligned to the prototypical behaviour expressed in Didache 1–6). In the Didache's first part, as we have seen, prototypical behaviour and rules for the itinerants are clearly defined. Especially in Didache 1:5–6, it is deemed proper not to cling to property or money. The thrust of the whole text is that every member, the leader included, needs to be aligned with the ingroup values. This speaks louder than a general application of a patron-client relation supposedly hidden in the text. That would be to draw out the implications of a rather common word too far. This word was evidently not used in a patron-client aspect in the example from Onosander either. Thus, the local leaders are primarily leaders due to their example and association with prophetic and apostolic authority rather than their wealth and social standing.

The expectations that the settled leaders should perform the work of the prophets and teachers but also be ἀξίους τοῦ κυρίου, ἄνδρας πραεῖς καὶ ἀφιλαργύρους καὶ ἀλεθεῖς καὶ δεδοκιμασμένους, suggest that the character of the chosen ones is not related to social standing from an outsider's perspective, but to the leaders' ability to lead sufficiently prototypical lives. Particularly interesting is the requirement that the ἐπίσκοποι and διάκονοι should have been tested, δεδοκιμασμένους (v. 1), before being appointed (or chosen). The testing would naturally have been related to spiritual maturity and experience.[127] If, like the prophets and teachers, the appointed local leaders failed to meet the expectations placed upon them, the incentive for the congregation to appoint them

---

[126] See inscription from Thrace, from between 85–96 CE, "IByzantion 31 Dedication by an association of mystai," Kloppenborg and Ascough 2011, 400–401.

[127] Niederwimmer 1998, 201, takes this to mean that the appointed leaders should not be "neophytes," but tried and tested. In other words, they needed to have led recommendable lives for a substantial time.

would likely diminish. Since the ἐπίσκοποι and διάκονοι were settled, however, it was significantly easier to assess the extent to which the leaders succeeded in adhering to ingroup rules, compared to the itinerant prophet, for obvious reasons. Given the Didachist's aim to compile a unified vision of ecclesial life, it is reasonable to expect a consistent prototypical behaviour from both itinerants and local leaders.

In sum, I have argued that the ἐπίσκοποι and διάκονοι should be understood as prototypical leaders rather than identity advancers. Given (1) the different ways ἀφιλάργυρος was used alongside the nature of the Jewish expectation to give to the poor, (2) the financial aspect of how they should be honoured among prophets and teachers (οἱ τετιμημένοι ὑμῶν μετὰ τῶν προφητῶν καὶ διδασκάλων), and (3) that they should have been tested to live up to the ingroup prototypes, δεδοκιμασμένους, we conclude that the patron dimension is not prominent in the selection of leaders.

6.4.3 The Testing and Appointing of Local Leaders

As we have seen, the Didache assigns to the local officers both a continuing ministry of the prophets and teachers, and the right to financial support. This implies that what is significant for itinerant prophets and teachers is also significant for the local officers. Discernment, or testing, is important at a general level before leaders can be given the mandate to lead. This is crucial in the process of appointing local leaders, as well as in determining which itinerants should be welcomed and which ought not to be received.

As indicated in Didache 11, several guidelines are provided for the proper reception of itinerants. First, there is an expectation regarding the right teaching of any travelling charismatic: the section commences with a conditional statement, 11:1; Ὃς ἂν οὖν ἐλθὼν διδάξῃ ὑμᾶς ταῦτα πάντα τὰ προειρημένα, δέξασθε αὐτόν ("Whoever comes and teaches all this that is said before, you should receive"). "What is said before" refers to the teachings about the Two Ways and the practices related to the eucharist, baptism, prayer, and fasting. Therefore, anyone who properly adheres to established group norms is accepted. Several prototypical traits are expected from any baptised member within these group norms, as we have observed.

Second, the proper reception of itinerants should be κατὰ τὸ δόγμα τοῦ εὐαγγελίου (11:4). The gospel, in this case, seems to be some kind of summary of gospel tradition, presumably known to the readers.[128] Some echoes of Matt 10:9–15 (or a preceding tradition) is present, for example, the expectation to travel without money (see Matt 10:9). The reception of itinerants according to the δόγμα τοῦ εὐαγγελίου is defined by the Didachist as (1) to receive the apostle "as the Lord," but (2) to give hospitality for only one or maximum two days. The traveller (3) could be given bread enough for travel to the next lodging, but (4) not money. If asking for money, the itinerant was labelled ψεδοπροφήτης (11:6).

Third, the rules regarding itinerants pertain to how they use their spiritual influence in relation to their lifestyle. As is commonly found in the third section, the church order, the Didachist aims to set rules for a life that, on the one hand, does not stifle charismatic gifts ([κ]αὶ πάντα προφήτην λαλοῦντα ἐν πνεύματι οὐ πειράσετε οὐδὲ διακρινεῖτε, "every prophet who speaks in spirit you shall neither try nor judge" 11:7), but on the other hand prevents any kind of selfish misuse from the itinerants (ὃς δ' ἂν εἴπῃ ἐν πνεύματι· δός μοι ἀργύρια ἢ ἕτερά τινα, οὐκ ἀκούσεσθε αὐτοῦ, "would anyone say in the spirit: Give me money (or something else), do not listen to him," 11:12) The way of life, the prototypical behaviour of the itinerant, is the crucial point for understanding whether or not an unknown prophet is a true prophet or not. The behaviour should be τρόπους κυρίου, according to Jesus's way of life.[129]

If the itinerants are assessed according to these three criteria, it stands to reason that local leaders should similarly undergo evaluation. This would be more likely if the composite nature is considered, for it seems that the Didachist places the same expectations on the local leaders (ἐπίσκοποι and διάκονοι) as he does on itinerant leaders, as a way of merging different systems into a unified whole. Although the Didachist unfortunately does not provide clear examples of how the ἐπίσκοπος and διάκονος ought to be examined, chapter 15 encourages the congregation to elect or appoint (χειροτονήσατε) local leaders who are "worthy of the Lord" (αξίους τοῦ κυρίου), "humble" (πραεῖς), "not greedy"

---

[128] Niederwimmer 1998, 173.
[129] Niederwimmer 1998, 179.

(ἀφιλαργύρους), "true, honest" (ἀληθεῖς) and "tested" (δεδοκιμασμένους). The Two Ways tractate emphasises a humble lifestyle, as well as honesty and financial modesty. The local leadership must align with group prototypes. This is unsurprising from a SIT perspective and within the broader context of the Didache. In fact, it would be surprising if the Didachist communities accepted local leadership that did not reflect group prototypes, given the significant effort to present a prototype that both delineated the group from the Pharisees and simultaneously defined it in relation to the Gentiles.

6.5 The Identity Entrepreneurs and Impresarios of the Didache

As the book's title says, the Didache's content is providing a teaching, allegedly from the twelve apostles. Teaching in the community was carried out by prophets, teachers, and ἐπίσκοποι καὶ διάκονοι. The phrase πᾶς δὲ προφήτης διδάσκων τὴν ἀλήθειαν in 11:10 suggests that prophets were understood to be involved in teaching, while 15:1 links ἐπίσκοποι καὶ διάκονοι to τὴν λειτουργίαν τῶν προφητῶν καὶ διδασκάλων. As we have seen in the SIT paradigm, teaching is an action that can and will construct group identity, as leadership is often connected to rhetorical skills in providing a vision of the group identity. The term identity entrepreneurship, as discussed in chapter 2 above, refers to the construction of a group narrative, particularly in new situations. Identity entrepreneurship encompasses the leader's ability to alter the group narrative and its perception of its own history to accommodate a new set of prototypes, primarily through the use of language.[130] It "involves the use of language in order to create a compelling vision of identity and its implications for action."[131] From this, we can learn that the ἐπίσκοποι, along with prophets and teachers, were identity entrepreneurs. They conveyed the content of the ingroup identity to members and were therefore afforded the flexibility to customise and reactualise the ingroup identity in novel situations. In the Didache, it is stated that the content of the teaching performed must align with the teachings summarised

---

[130] See Kujanpää 2021, 373. See also Cinnirella 1998, 232; 235. See also Haslam and Reicher 2007, 127.

[131] Haslam et al. 2011, 171.

6.5 The Identity Entrepreneurs and Impresarios of the Didache

in chapters 1–6 (7:1, 11:1). Thus, even if we do not know exactly how teaching was conducted in the communities, we understand that it had to operate within a set of boundaries. As we have seen, the teaching concerns prototypical behaviour for baptised members. It would have conveyed a lot to the members regarding boundaries with other groups, even if little flexibility was allowed to alter the written prototype. Therefore, a few more comments on teaching as an identity-shaping activity need to be made.

As noted above, the content of Didache 2–6 discusses words, thoughts, and actions among the baptised, establishing clear expectations for new members. When these expectations are not met, the member requires rectification (4:14, 14:1). An important aspect of this text is that behaviours such as sorcery, sexual immorality, infanticide, and others are linked to non-Jewish, repugnant behaviour.[132] As previously mentioned, it has been argued that Two Ways teachings had a role in Judaism as teaching for proselytes.[133] We can also see how the discussion concerning the ζυγόν in 6:2 aligns with an understanding of some kind of Torah observance.[134] The Didachist seems to advocate for the possibility of non-Jewish members of the community maintaining a somewhat "less stringent regime" regarding the Torah-observation.[135] It is interesting to note that what appears to be the second title of the work, "the Lord's teaching through the twelve apostles to the Gentiles," suggests a teaching intended for non-Jews.[136] This suggests that the community encourages non-Jewish converts to adopt a more Jewish approach to everyday life. Some of these practices may have social implications, such as the call to abstain from food offered to idols, to avoid fortune-telling, and potentially also matters of sexual conduct. Jewish-born members of the community are urged to be perfect, τέλειος, as they bear

---

[132] Weren, 2008, 197. Cf. Niederwimmer, 1998, 89.
[133] Weren 2008, 197; Slee 2003, 79.
[134] Weren 2008, 197–98.
[135] Weren 2008, 198.
[136] Slee 2003, 57, makes a certain connection between title and the composition of situation. While I believe Slee to be too speculative in aguing that the text was composed to resolve the aftermath of Gal 2:11–14, there are several valid points to which I will return about the unresolved matters of Gentile inclusion in the northeastern Mediterranean area.

the entire yoke of the Lord. (6:2).[137] This likely indicates that Jewish-born members are encouraged to maintain some version of a full halakah.[138] In this case, the group managed to contain (or at least aimed to contain) different kinds of ethnicities of Jesus followers within the same group. The community of the Didache thus had ethical standards unique to the group, a prototypical ideal to adhere to, taught by both itinerant and local leaders and functionaries. The constant reactualisation of this ingroup identity performed by different kinds of teachers would be crucial to uphold the joint "we-ness" of the group, which emphasises the need for local functionaries who perform identity maintenance.

Furthermore, the instruction to the members prevalent in chapter 8 is meant to distinguish themselves from those labelled hypocrites, τῶν ὑποκριτῶν (8:1), in the areas of fasting and praying.[139] Here the teachers of the community recommend a ritual and a structure that is identity shaping and setting members apart from outgroups. In SIT terminology, this makes the different kinds of teachers identity impresarios.[140] The ingroup identity was invested in a specific structure and in certain rituals. The expected behaviour involved the individual member's calendar and efforts. Days and hours bear ingroup identity: Monday and Thursday are inappropriate for fasting; instead, the members of the group are to observe fasts on Wednesdays and Fridays.[141] Fasting grounds

---

[137] Finlan 2015, 17–18.

[138] Weren 2008, 197.

[139] Finlan 2015, 24.

[140] Cf. Esler 2021, 40, for a short reminder what this means in practice: "Typical means adopted by leaders to embed identity include erecting physical structures, establishing and/or implementing institutions and practices, formalizing rituals and organizing events that are related to the values of the groups they represent." Also note that the performers of the teaching could be prophets, teachers, διάκονοι or ἐπίσκοποι. Who did what at certain times is impossible to tell, but all the offices were possible performers of the teaching, as it seems.

[141] Niederwimmer 1998, 132, suggests that this refers to the "pious of Israel" in general, and no particular Jewish group. Slee 2003, 92, however, shows later Rabbinic sources (m. Meg, 1:2; 3; 3:6; b. Ta'an 12a; m. Ta'an 2:1; 4:2), for a practice of this kind of fasting, and comments that there is no evidence that Jews from other groups would have fasted on these days. See also Draper's (who understand them as Pharisees) thorough review of the understanding of the hypocrites of Didache 8 in Draper 1996, 233.

members in a well-known practice linked to a particular piety while also distancing them from similar Jewish groups such as the Pharisees.[142]

The prayer that follows in 8:2 resembles a version of the Our Father (cf. Matt 6:9–13), a prayer that summarises the teachings of Jesus. This prayer, said to be recited three times a day (8:3), connects the member with identity reflecting teachings aligned with a gospel tradition (cf. Did. 1) that also distinguishes the group from other Jewish groups. If it was a common practice in the time of the Didachist for Jews to pray the Shemoneh Esreh (or a predecessor) three times a day, the practice of praying the Our Father instead would embed the identity within an already established, meaning-laden practice.[143] The teaching provided by the community leaders was an immediate means for members to not only express their group membership within the realm of morality or during community meetings (services), but also in their everyday lives. Thus, the teaching anchored the identity of Jesus followers in each member.

Before concluding this chapter, one further matter needs to be noted: the SIT meaning of the liturgical actions of the ἐπίσκοπος in the Didache. The performance of a joint ritual, closely associated with the ingroup identity, would serve as a textbook example of identity impresariosiship. But does this even apply here since there are no references to an ἐπίσκοπος performing liturgical actions? Undoubtedly, we are left with some degree of conjecture. However, we can see that the liturgical actions described in Didache 7 and 9–10 instruct in the second person, sometimes plural (βαπτίσατε in 7:1, εὐχαριστήσατε in 9:1), and sometimes singular (ἔχῃς, 7:2, etc.), with no further clue of to whom the instructions are directed. The enigmatic sayings regarding the prophets are the only hint here; that the prophets should be allowed to εὐχαριστεῖν as often as they like (10:7), and that "no prophet who orders a meal in the spirit will eat from it unless he is a false prophet" (11:9). However, as the overlap in tasks has been previously acknowledged, we can reasonably assume that the ἐπίσκοπος was at least present, and most likely presiding over, the communal meals (one

---

[142] Cf. Zangenberg 2008, 58. See also Finlan 2015, 24, for a SIT perspective.

[143] See Slee 2003, 92, who discusses the relation to the later rabbinic teachings on threefold prayers during the day (Shemoneh Esreh). Slee notes Daniel 6:9, 11, and chronologically later b. Ber 26b, regarding the prayer of the Shemoneh Esreh, to be recited three times a day, t. Ber 6:3; m. Ber. 4:1; 7:1.

can be less certain about the role of the ἐπίσκοπος in baptisms).[144] Thus, in these highly identity-shaping rituals, the ἐπίσκοπος was one of the main figures. The actions of baptism and eucharist are practices that concentrate group identity. Baptism, as an initiation rite into the community after the candidate had undergone catechesis from the Two Ways tractate, was performed in the name of the Father, the Son, and the Holy Spirit (7:1), echoing a tradition also found in Matt 28:19.[145] Even if no substantial theological implications are inferred from the Didache, the words of the initiation rite indicate a focus on an ingroup theological understanding. The member participates in a ritual taught by community leaders as a means of bestowing a new identity upon the member. The interest in water in 7:1 (ὕδατι ζῶντι – running water) and the subsequent verses echoes biblical traditions from Leviticus 14 and displays similar concerns as the later rabbis in the Mishna (m. Mik 1:1–8). The rite has thus been understood, not least by Niederwimmer, to be intimately connected with purification in many contexts; in Leviticus 14:5–9, for example, running water is related to purification after leprosy.[146] Some understanding of water as purifying appears to be at play in Did. 7. Connecting baptism with a new, pure state effected by the ritual is thus possible. From a SIT perspective, this new state after baptism signifies an "anticipation of the world to come," serving as an experience for the new member to step into an identity deeply connected to God.[147] Likewise, the participants in the eucharist meal have gained knowledge about "the holy vine of David" through Jesus (9:2). Thus, participants are given a special life and a special knowledge that Jesus brought to the congregation (9:3). Participating in the congregation means engaging with the vine of David, along with the life and knowledge of Jesus. In 10:3, God also provided the congregation with "spiritual food and drink" and "eternal life through your servant [Jesus]." The meal serves as a ritual that allows members to engage in the theological centre of the group and thus affirms the group's self-designation.

---

[144] Note Zangenberg 2008, 64, who takes it as certain that the role of the ἐπίσκοπος primarily focused on the communal meals on "the Lord's day."

[145] Niederwimmer 1998, 126.

[146] Niederwimmer 1998, 127.

[147] Haslam, Reicher, and Platow 2007, 179.

A final short note on the identity-shaping leadership structure is that the local leaders, just like priests, are entitled to tithes through their association with the prophets and teachers. In this way, the Didachist becomes an identity impresario, who embeds the identity of a holy and separate ingroup through temple language in the leadership structure. In 13:3, the settled prophet and teacher should be entitled to the first fruits, since αὐτοὶ γάρ εἰσιν οἱ ἀρχιερεῖς ὑμῶν ("they are your high priests"). A priestly dimension is also discerned through association in local leadership, where the connection to the temple is carried over to the leader. This also happens in the financial realm. Thus, the holiness and dignity of the high priest and the temple are moved into the midst of the community through prophets *and* local leaders. The ingroup identity is, thereby, heightened. The dignity of the Didachist's group is conveyed through association with it to the spiritual high priestly office represented by the leaders.[148]

By now, it is necessary to conclude the findings of this chapter. How did the local leaders, ἐπίσκοποι, participate in the construction of a separate Christian identity in the Didache?

6.6 Summary and Conclusion

This chapter has demonstrated that the Didache, although not extensively discussing the role of the ἐπίσκοπος, provides crucial insights into the significance of the office in the identity formation of the Didachist community.

After situating this analysis in the Didache research history and placing the origins of the Didache in Syria or Antioch ca 100–110 CE, we have seen that the text did not automatically fit in the early catholicisation schema. Instead, we observed a situation characterised by a mixed leadership involving itinerant prophets, teachers, and local leaders. This is also clear at the textual level, as chapter 15 appears to be an attempt in the composite text to harmonise the authority between prophets and teachers (itinerants), and ἐπίσκοποι and διάκονοι (local leaders). As noted, these local leaders were not chiefly patrons (identity advancers) of the communities; rather, the expectations articulated regarding

---

[148] Cf. Finlan 2015, 21.

the leaders throughout the Didache indicate that their authority derived from their prototypicality. They were also seen as carrying out overlapping duties with the itinerants, both in terms of rituals (most likely) and in matters of teaching. In fulfilling these duties, the local leaders were examples of what the SIT framework refers to as identity entrepreneurs (upholding and creating identity through rhetoric) and impresarios (embedding identity within structures and rituals). This means that they were also teachers of the group who needed to teach in accordance with the prototypical pattern suggested primarily by Didache 1–6. These chapters indicate that the Didache endorsed a Jewish moral ideal found in many neighbouring groups, which is evident in the Two Ways tractate. The tractate begins with the second table of the Decalogue and defines ideal behaviour in opposition to non-Jewish, repulsive behaviour. Chapter 6 suggests that non-Jews should adopt some aspects of Torah observance, not too far off from the apostolic decree in Acts 15. Additionally, the tractate expects members to lead humble lives that do not seek earthly riches.

However, the tractate's *sectio evangelica* also echoes a Jesus tradition that set the group apart from other Jewish groups, in their belief in Jesus the Messiah. The prototypicality of the group thus established boundaries not only towards non-Jews, but also against other Jewish groups. The prototypical behaviour that set the group apart from other Jewish groups was further emphasised when the group's teaching instructed that they should pray and fast no longer like the Pharisees, but rather as members of Christ groups. The baptism and eucharist rituals, presumably officiated by the ἐπίσκοπος if no prophet was present, were significant for the group's identity. This again demonstrates an identity modelled on themes familiar from Jewish Scriptures and later rabbis while simultaneously suggesting a new identity that takes several themes for granted yet also delimits itself from rabbinic groups. Baptism, which was both concerned with living water and given a new significance with the initiation in the name of the Father, Son, and Holy Spirit, illustrates this distinction.

The role of the ἐπίσκοπος is not elaborated upon in the text, as mentioned. The composite nature of Didache makes it probable that the redactor attempted to harmonise the local and itinerant leadership roles. Thus, the tendency to emphasise the similarity in ministry and worthiness and thereby the right to communal upkeep is a sign of this harmonising tendency. This makes the ἐπίσκοπος one of four functionaries. However, the description of the local offices as fulfilling the roles of itinerants within the local community (chapter 15:1) suggests that, in practice, the ἐπίσκοπος engaged in teaching and functioned as a teacher (constructing local identity as an identity entrepreneur), performed identity-shaping rituals (identity impresarioship), and served as a role model (demonstrating prototypicality). Moreover, the ἐπίσκοπος was associated with a priestly office (through the prophets and teachers). This identity links the entire community to a new temple and bestows dignity and holiness upon the whole group. This resembles a form of impresarioship exercised by the Didachist, as the ingroup identity is presented as intertwined with the Jerusalem cult and all its holiness.

This suggests that the identity that the local leaders embedded was not entirely the identity of the later Ignatian letters. As we shall see, the Ignatian correspondence leaves little room for a prominent Jewish identity. Instead, Didache assumes that leaders, as well as any baptised member, would engage in halakic behaviour. On the other hand, members of other Jewish groups, presumably groups informed by Pharisaic teachings, are labelled as "hypocrites." Significant behaviours are presented to make members separate themselves from these other Jewish groups.

The ἐπίσκοπος is thus an identity impresario and prototype, even if he was not the *only* impresario and prototype. In the long run, however, prophets seem to have become less common; in 1 Clement and the Ignatian letters, they are absent as a function. The role of the teacher can, however, be found in the office of the ἐπίσκοπος in these texts, but also in other texts. Thus, the ἐπίσκοπος in Didache is not *the* functionary in the emerging Christ group, but *a* functionary, due to the Didachist's need to bring together different systems. On the other hand, the ἐπίσκοπος seems to have basically performed the same tasks as in other important early Jesus-group texts and represented a distinct Christ identity. The construction of a Christian identity, which delineates itself from both Jewish identity and other groups, is detectable but not unique in the role of the ἐπίσκοπος in the Didache.

7. An SIT Perspective on the ἐπίσκοπος in First Clement

First Clement addresses a faction within the Corinthian congregation. From what can be discerned from the text, which aligns with the prevailing understanding of the letter throughout research history, the situation seems to be that a group of possibly younger leaders have attempted to overthrow the established leaders of the congregation (chapters 1, and 42–44, 47, 51, 54, etc.).[1] The introduction of the letter is rather lengthy, featuring extensive quotations from a text similar to our received LXX, and the actual discussion of the faction does not commence until chapter 42. The chapters in the main body of the letter (chapters 3 to 41), however, provide an important backdrop for the reprimand of the factionist.[2] From a SIT perspective, the ingroup prototype, as discussed in chapter 2 above, is illustrated and supported by scriptural examples (see chapters 11, 12, 17, and 18) and examples from the Jesus traditions and the traditions concerning the apostles (chapters 42 and 44). Further, the pattern of leadership that the author of 1 Clement wants the addressees to follow, the emerging episcopal structure, is portrayed as scriptural (chapters 43–44) and aligned to prototypical behaviour. Thus, the author of 1 Clement is an *impresario* of the group identity of the members of the Christ groups. As we remember, impresarioship involves embedding ingroup identity within structures and rituals. The author embeds the ingroup identity within the leadership structure, as we shall see. In this embedding process, the ideal followers of Jesus are subtly presented as the inheritors of Jacob, while the people of Israel are portrayed as rebellious. The ideal presented in the letter ties the identity of the

---

[1] Ehrman 2003a, 18.
[2] For a thorough review on historical examples in Hellenistic thought that dovetail with 1 Clement, see Breytenbach 2013.

group member with both ancient heroes of the Hebrew Bible on one hand and Jesus and the apostles on the other. In 1 Clement, the ideal of ancient heroes of the Hebrew Bible is portrayed as exemplary Christ-group member behaviour through the close connection to Jesus and the apostles, as we shall see.

In this chapter, I will first situate the letter within a context. Second, I will illustrate how the episcopal leaders in 1 Clement are portrayed as prototypical leaders in relation to the examples provided from the Scriptures. Third, I will suggest that the author, as an impresario of identity, embeds a Christian identity within the episcopal role, showing that the new congregation is in practice superseding the old identity.[3] Fourth, I shall explore the implications of this in relation to the separation between the Christ groups and the synagogue.

7.1 Concerning Date and Authorship

Even though the aim of this study is to understand how a Christian identity was formed with the aid of the leadership structure associated with the ἐπίσκοπος, and therefore cannot serve as a complete commentary on 1 Clement, some historical considerations are necessary.

7.1.1 Date

The question of the date is important as it situates a step in the emergence of an episcopal office and facilitates comparisons to other texts. For a long time, there was a consensus that 1 Clement should be dated between 93 and 97 CE, a consensus built on the traditional perspective of not least Eusebius.[4] Eusebius has it in *Eccl. Hist.* 3.15 that the letter was written some years after Clement

---

[3] In this analysis, I am not taking rhetorical structure into account, due to lack of space. It is obvious that rhetorical features are significant in the letter, especially when discussing Identity Entrepreneurship since SIT frequently discusses rhetorical aspects of influence (see Haslam and others 2011, 373). For a proper analysis of 1 Clement as an example of deliberative rhetoric, see Bakke 2001, or for that matter Breytenbach 2013, 23. Lona 1998, 21, comments on the problematic nature of putting a rhetoric genre name on a letter. While this is true, it is obvious that the author of 1 Clement is using deliberative rhetoric when he wants the addressees to take a proper course of action (reinstalling the leaders). For the purpose of this study, the different suggestions by Lindemann 2010, 47–69, and others are a bit too extensive.

[4] Lona 1998, 75, n. 3.

became ἐπίσκοπος of Rome, which would mean around the traditional date.[5] This has also been the hypothesis adopted by Adolf von Harnack,[6] Joseph B. Lightfoot,[7] and Rudolf Knopf,[8] primarily based on ancient tradition and somewhat later texts, such as Irenaeus and Hegesippus.[9] The understanding during the twentieth century has been that the letter was written during the reign of Domitian (81–96 CE), or perhaps during the first year or so of Nerva's short reign (96–98 CE).[10] The relationship between 1:1 and 1 Clement 5–6 and the meaning of these instances have been significant in the discussion. In 1:1, the author states that "because we have been burdened and encountered sudden and repeated trials, we have been slow to attend to and think regarding the matters that are discussed among you" (Διὰ τὰς αἰφνιδίους καὶ ἐπαλλήλους γενομένας ἡμῖν συμφορὰς καὶ περιπτώσεις βράδιον νομίζομεν ἐπιστροφὴν πεποιῆσθαι περὶ τῶν ἐπιζητουμένων παρ' ὑμῖν πραγμάτων). In chapters 5–6, the theme of ζῆλος, which is prominent through the letter, is discussed concerning martyrs in the ranks of Jesus followers. Peter (1 Clement 5:4) and Paul (5:5) are said to have become "contenders in conquest recently" (ἐπὶ τοὺς ἔγγιστα γενομένους ἀθλητάς). However, given the formulations in verse 7, the events of Peter and Paul are not the most recent, as Paul is described as finishing his race "having come to the end of the west" (ἐπὶ τὸ τέρμα τῆς δύσεως). On the other hand, 5:5, claims the life of Peter and Paul to be "within our generation" (τῆς γενεᾶς ἡμῶν).[11] Chapter 6 also asserts that "a multitude of chosen ones" (πολὺ πλῆθος ἐκλεκτῶν) has since joined in martyrdom, including otherwise unknown persons as Dircae and some women compared to the Danaids. During the course of the twentieth century, research into these formulations has led some scholars to suggest an earlier date, specifically during the reign of Nero, alongside the

---

[5] Lona 1998, 75; Knopf 1905, 36.

[6] de Gebhardt and von Harnack 1876, see Lona 1998, 75, n. 2, for a review of different suggestions from von Harnack on the dating of 1 Clement.

[7] Lightfoot 1890, 67.

[8] Knopf 1905, 36.

[9] Lightfoot 1890, 63–67; Knopf 1905, 36.

[10] Lona 1998, 75.

[11] Ehrman 2003a, 24.

persecution that occurred under him.¹² Franklin Young¹³ claims on linguistic grounds that Jas 2:25 is dependent on the version of Rahab in 1 Clem. 12, thus suggesting a date well before James wrote his epistle.¹⁴ The primary reason for re-evaluating the traditional date was, however, the work of Lawrence Welborn,¹⁵ who, partly on rhetorical grounds (what the introductory remarks in 1 Clement 1:1 truly signify), and partly on historical grounds (the limited evidence for a significant Domitian persecution), questioned the date around the year 96. Welborn built his work on among others Elmer Merrill, who investigated the contemporary writings in the time of Domitian and found no evidence for "organised and systematic persecutions [of Jesus followers], legal in form and carried out by public judicial authority."¹⁶ The range and severity of the persecution have been much debated.¹⁷ While there is no doubt that Domitian had a bloody reign against his political opponents, particularly towards the end of his rule, Merrill is sceptical about the extent to which the Book of Revelation can provide well-grounded facts regarding how Domitian's wrath affected Jesus followers.¹⁸ Therefore, the outset of 1 Clement can readily be

---

[12] Powell 1981; Herron 1989

[13] Young 1948.

[14] The date of James has in itself been debated for a long time. List (2024, 576–77), notes similarities between James, 1 Clement, and Clement of Alexandria. He thus argues for an earlier *terminus ante quem.* than otherwise assumed. Before that, a *terminus ante quem* is only in the mid-third century, when Origen quotes the epistle. Several scholars have however an early dating for James, which pushes the date of 1 Clement earlier also, not far from the traditional dating 62 CE. One can among others note that Davies (1982, 49, ePub), claim an early date for the source material (the 40's) with a redactional process taking place between 55 and 85 CE. He also provides a table for the positions on the matter by nineteenth- and twentieth century research, p. 24 (ePub). Martin (1988, lxxvi-vii), suggests a redaction process from Syrian Antioch some time after 48 CE. Luke Timothy Johnson argues on internal evidence (and similarities with Pauline thought and Q) for an early dating in Johnson (1995, 118–21). Most lately, Gabrielson assume that 2 Enoch shows literary dependence on James (Gabrielson 2020, 240), and since 2 Enoch is assumed to date pre-70 CE, so must also James. Due to limited space, I will refrain from delving deeper into the matter.

[15] Welborn 1984. See also Welborn 2020.

[16] Merrill 1924, 158.

[17] Already Merrill 1924.

[18] Merrill 1924, 152–53, 157.

7.1 Concerning Date and Authorship

understood in a context different from that proposed by those advocating for the traditional dating.[19] Welborn's work has generally broadened the perspective on the date of 1 Clement beyond approximately the year 96–97.

> As the years have passed, the verdict has become general that 1 Clement cannot be confidently dated to the end of the reign of Domitian, when a persecution of Christians allegedly took place, and that a wider date range must be considered for the composition of the Roman epistle.[20]

Horatio Lona summarises the argument that the formulations in 1 Clemens 1:1 are too imprecise to serve as conclusive evidence of a context in the aftermath of Domitian persecution.[21]

There have been calls both before and after Welborn for a later date. Henri Delafosse interprets the letter as relating to the theological controversy surrounding Marcion, and thus the most likely date is circa 150.[22] The allusions in the letter to the Marcionite controversy, however, appear to be lacking.[23] Richard Hanson does not specify more than 120 to 130 CE.[24] Bart Ehrman suggests from internal evidence (most notably, the congregation in Corinth is "ancient," and someone appointed by Paul seems to have been a leader in the congregation, well known to the Corinthians, according to 1 Clement 47) that, although the traditional dating had incorrect reasons, the date cannot differ significantly from around 96 CE.[25] Ehrman, along with Merrill, also points out that no evidence from either internal or external sources suggests that 1 Clement 1:1 necessarily needs to discuss the persecution of Jesus followers in Rome during the period of Domitian. While Lona sees no need to presuppose persecution in the formulations of 1 Clement 1:1, he nonetheless regards the traditional dating as largely accurate; the last decade of the first century is his conclusion on the matter after a substantial discussion.[26] A fail-safe perspective is

---

[19] Gregory 2002, 148–49, follows this closely.
[20] Welborn 2020, 100–101.
[21] Lona 1998, 77.
[22] Delafosse 1928, 82.
[23] Lona 1998, 77.
[24] Hanson 1978, 535.
[25] Ehrman 2003a, 25.
[26] Lona 1998, 76–78.

offered by Andrew Gregory, who argues that there are no convincing arguments for any specific date aside from the period between 70 and 140 CE.[27]

But is there truly no significant evidence for a more specific date than between 70 and 140? Gregory believes that the earlier date is suggested by internal evidence, such as how to interpret the "recent examples" in 1 Clement 5, where Peter and Paul have died not long ago.[28] Simultaneously, 1 Clement is not referenced by other early Christian authors until around 150, which establishes a timeframe of roughly eighty years (seventy if we assume a reasonable gap of at least ten years from the writing of the letter to the acknowledgement of Hegesippus in 150).[29] Since the assumption of a Domitian persecution is widely dismissed during the last twenty-five years or so, and since several authors demonstrate 1 Clement 1:1 to have referred to other events or functions,[30] other external references need to be considered for a correct date. Hermas (Herm. Vis. 2.4.3 (8.3)) mentions a "Clement" responsible for writing letters to other Jesus followers. The situations described in Hermas and in 1 Clement appear related, even if they occur in different places.[31] The theme of concord and peace also resonates well with other Hellenistic authors from the early second century, providing a fitting cultural backdrop between 110 and 150.[32] Aside from this, since the first theological analysis of the episcopal office was traditionally attributed to 1 Clement, dated 96 CE, and this dating is no longer considered valid due to the lack of evidence for a persecution, it is more reasonable to position the theology regarding the leadership structure somewhat later. The discussions in the Pastoral letters concerning the prototypical ἐπίσκοπος are usually dated around 110–130 CE. Ignatius's letters were written after 160 CE, even if one can argue for an earlier date of Ign. *Rom* (see chapter 9 below), and the

---

[27] Gregory 2002, 142–66.

[28] Gregory 2002, 144–46.

[29] Gregory 2002, 145.

[30] Welborn 2020, 101, takes the now common view that 1 Clement 1:1 should primarily be understood as a *captatio benevolentiae*, before that also Bakke 2001, 100–105.

[31] So the later view of Welborn 2020, 102. See also Ehrman 2003a, 167–68.

[32] Van Unnik 2004, 151–68. Welborn understands this as a reasonable context for the passage, while admitting that it is somewhat perilous to date texts on the basis of cultural references, Welborn 2020, 102.

letters are not quoted until ca. 180 CE. The thorough discussion on the nature of the ἐπίσκοπος that we find in 1 Clement 10–46, is more likely to appear in the second century than before 100 CE. In this study, I will assume that the letter of 1 Clement forms part of a discourse on the episcopacy that emerges in the first half of the second century. As there are no indications of a discourse concerning Marcion in 1 Clement, I would prefer to place it well before 140 CE. Based on this assessment of the evidence, I propose the timeframe of 110–120 CE.

7.1.2 Authorship

I will discuss below that the disposed leaders of the Corinthian congregation never speak for themselves. Instead, someone from Rome speaks on their behalf and sends a letter to the congregation in Corinth. The group behind the letter seems to have taken an interest in the Corinthian congregation and views it as an obligation to intervene. Why this interest leads to the action of writing a lengthy, expository letter is beyond what can be known. However, assuming that the author represents the leadership of the Roman congregation, an inherent interest in order is natural. It could also stem from deeply held theological convictions or relate to friendship with the deposed leaders in Corinth.[33] As we have neither access to a fixed date nor an attested author (or this author's inner motives!) of the letter, we cannot ascertain the reason for the author producing the letter, aside from the internal evidence within the letter itself.

Several points regarding the author are usually emphasised. The prescript states that it is "the assembly of God that resides in Rome" that sends the letter.[34] The first-person plural is frequently used throughout the letter, and the name of Clement is not mentioned at all. The use of the first-person plural likely indicates that the author represents the Roman congregation, most probably the leadership there.[35] Even though the name Clement is never mentioned

---

[33] Lona 1998, 20, argues that the friendship language of the letter hints pastoral care from the Romans for the Corinthian congregation.

[34] Ἡ ἐκκλησία τοῦ θεοῦ ἡ παροικοῦσα Ῥώμην τῇ ἐκκλησία τοῦ θεοῦ ἡ παροικοῦσα ἐν Κόρινθον. See further Lindemann 2010, 64, "according to its prescript, 1 Clement is a text by the (entire) Roman ἐκκλησία."

[35] Kujanpää 2021, 372.

in the text, the letter was early (for example, by Tertullian) associated with a person named Clement, according to church tradition the third ἐπίσκοπος of Rome.[36] Lona comments that although traceable traditions regarding the author's name (Clement) exist, we do not possess sufficient unambiguous external sources to conclude either that the author must have been called Clement or that the author ought to have been ἐπίσκοπος in Rome. The author's considerable skill suggests that it could not have been merely anyone, but rather someone with access to Jewish education who was well acquainted with Hellenistic letter writing. While this is true, Lona concludes, one cannot impose an idea of the author as a head of a later episcopal structure onto the letter solely because the author is skilled.[37] While we have no explicit confirmation from the letter itself, it is probable that the author was a leader and representative of a Roman congregation. Furthermore, the text seems to have been written by a single person: the style is concise and consistent. The letter is clearly composed by someone well-versed in Jewish Scriptures, though he may not be a Jew himself.[38] One may speculate about traditions suggesting that the third ἐπίσκοπος in Rome was named Clement, ordained by Peter himself according to Tertullian.[39] Origen (ca. 185–ca. 253) understands the passage in Phil 4:3 to refer to Clement, the author of 1 Clement. However, this otherwise unknown Clement is situated in Philippi, and we have no further biographical information about him, leaving us with mere speculation.[40] On the same note, one can remember the previously mentioned tradition regarding a Clement in Rome in Hermas (Herm. Vis. 2.4.2 (8.2)), who is said to have written letters to foreign congregations: "Now write two scrolls and send one to Clement and one to Grapte. Clement will send his to the outer cities, because he has been instructed for that."[41] Nothing is said about the title of Clement in Hermas, however, even

---

[36] Lindemann 2010, 64.

[37] Lona 1998, 72.

[38] Lindemann 2010, 64–65; Kujanpää 2021, 372; Lona 1998, 43–48. Compare to Lampe 1987, 59–60.

[39] Lindemann 2010, 64

[40] Note already Lightfoot 1890, 22.

[41] γράψεις οὖν δύο βιβλαρίδια καὶ πέμψεις ἓν Κλήμεντι καὶ ἓν Γραπτῇ. πέμψει οὖν Κλήμης εἰς τὰς ἔξω πόλεις, ἐκείνῳ γὰρ ἐπιτέτραπται.

though the ἐπίσκοπος has a significant role in, for example, the building of the tower of the elected (Herm. Vis. 3.5.1 (13.1), see above chapter 5). However, this tradition surrounding Clement will once again be limited to speculation alone, as it is presently impossible to ascertain anything beyond the fact that the tradition regarding Clement existed. One can note the valid critique from Welborn concerning the speculations of (in this instance) Lightfoot and Lampe. They both fail to take into account the difference between the claims of the substantially later novels, the Pseudo-Clementines, regarding the identity of Clement,[42] and what can be learned from 1 Clement itself.[43] The advanced reconstruction of Clement's life found in Lightfoot too easily assumes a connection between literary passages, archaeological findings, and deduced knowledge about Clement.[44]

There have been attempts to reconstruct the educational level and social standing of the author of 1 Clement based on internal evidence. For example, there is the suggestion that the author of 1 Clement was employing "Kanzleistil," that is, a style of writing associated with the emperor's secretaries.[45] While this aligns with the perception of Clement as closely associated with the emperor's court, the text is deemed too limited according to Peter Lampe.[46] Instead, Lampe suggests that the only thing we can know for certain is that the author had experience in schools in Rome, some common knowledge of Hellenistic thought, a thorough understanding of Jewish Scripture, perhaps from the synagogue, and not much else is possible to know.[47]

All this leads to the conclusion that it is impossible to ascertain the identity of the author of 1 Clement. While we can find traditions surrounding "Clement" in various instances, these are either late inventions (like the Pseudo-Clementines) or lack an immediate connection to the author of 1 Clement. Therefore, it suffices for the purposes of this chapter to state what can be discerned within 1 Clement: the author at least posed as a leader of the Roman

---

[42] Lim 2015.
[43] Welborn 2020, 98–99, see especially n. 27. Cf. Lightfoot 1890, 16–21; Lampe 2003, 184–85.
[44] Cf. Lightfoot 1890, 19–24.
[45] Lösch 1937, 177.
[46] Lampe 1987, 173.
[47] Lampe 1987, 170–82.

congregation, viewing it as his duty to write to the Corinthians about a faction within their congregation. He likely represents a group of leaders within the Roman congregation. The author demonstrated skill in writing and possessed considerable knowledge of Jewish Scriptures and Hellenistic philosophical ideals. That said, we may for convenience refer to the author as "Clement" in the following sections.

After this introduction regarding the date and authorship of 1 Clement, we turn to the analysis of the letter from an SIT perspective.

7.2 Prototypicality

When examining how prototypicality is described in 1 Clement, the author takes three significant steps to establish what constitutes a prototypical member. First, he points to accepted norms to which he assumes everyone should strive to adhere. Second, he employs scriptural examples to illustrate both a positive instance and a negative counterpart. Third, the deposed leaders are presented as examples to follow. It is important to note that although there appears to be a conflict regarding leadership, the text in 1 Clement shows no evidence of a dispute concerning which sources are regarded as valid for group prototypicality; the scriptural references and Jesus traditions used are treated as accepted authorities by the factionists.

7.2.1 A Prototypical Member Knows His or Her Place and Does Not Create Schisms

To remind ourselves, prototypicality concerns a member's ability to embody ingroup norms (see chapter 2 above). This embodiment is closely related to how membership in a salient group manifests in a social context. In the constructed prototype, the maximum difference from outgroup norms is displayed. A prototypical leader demonstrates salient group traits even at a personal cost. Individuals embodying group values have been shown in multiple experiments to exhibit more effective leadership, illustrating that leadership traits primarily reflect those associated with the group rather than being specific abilities of the leader.

Now turning to the situation in 1 Clement, the group conflict regarding leadership may suggest that something has occurred within the social context of the group. When group boundaries are redefined, for instance, it is possible for new individuals to emerge as leaders (or perhaps attempt to seize leadership), or for other individuals to be included in the group who were previously regarded as part of outgroups.[48] Moreover, it is possible that the factionist, in practice, envisioned a different prototype than that of the congregation's leaders.[49] It is also entirely possible, and perhaps more likely (see below), that some individuals who had no issue with the group identity *per se* within the Corinthian congregation(s) became weary of the old leadership and chose to challenge it. In any case, according to SIT, it is likely that the factionists did not perceive the leaders as embodying a sense of identity for the members, at least not sufficiently, and were therefore dissatisfied with the leadership. We do not have access to exactly what transpired within the congregation that prompted the Roman congregation, of which the author of 1 Clement was a part, to intervene. However, it is important to note that the critique by the author of 1 Clement regarding the factionists' behaviour was that their removal of the old leaders was, in fact, contradicting biblical principles and ideals. Nowhere is it stated, for example, that the factionists should have questioned their collective identity as followers of Jesus,[50] neither that they should have doubted the Scriptures or Jesus tradition as valid sources of valuable information of the identity of the members (see for example 1 Clem. 4–5, 13).[51] The reason for the strife, as described by the author, is that within a wealthy congregation, some young individuals (perhaps not literally young, but rather immature in spirituality) arose due to ζῆλος (envy, chapters 3–6). Therefore, for the letter to serve as an

---

[48] Haslam, Reicher, and Platow 2011, 88–89.

[49] As a comparison, research has demonstrated that job teams led by prototypical leaders, who embody a sense of "this-is-who-we-are," have members who are more satisfied and effective than their counterparts teams, see Haslam. Reicher, and Platow 2011, 90.

[50] See for example the letter prescript: Ἡ ἐκκλησία τοῦ θεοῦ ἡ παροικοῦσα Ῥώμην τῇ ἐκκλησία τοῦ θεοῦ ἡ παροικοῦσα ἐν Κόρινθον, κλητοῖς, ἡγιασμένοις ἐν θελήματι θεοῦ διὰ τοῦ κυρίου ἡμῶν Ἰησοῦ Χριστοῦ ("The congregation of God that resides in Rome, to the congregation of God that resides in Corinth, called and made holy through the will of God through our lord Jesus Christ").

[51] Kujanpää 2021, 372, 375.

effective correction to the factionists, it does not need to delve into the recipients' self-categorised identity (which seems to be a point of agreement between both the sender and the recipients). Rather, the letter needs to show how self-categorising Christ-group members should behave appropriately, that is, to show the prototypical behaviour according to scriptural references, and to show that the deposed leaders display all signs of group ideals that are needed for the congregation to follow them. As Katja Kujanpää demonstrates in her analysis of the use of παρρησία in 1 Clement as identity entrepreneurship, the solution to the crisis in Corinth is for the factionists to adopt a new prototypical behaviour: the humility to leave the congregation.[52]

The first two chapters of the letter narrate a glorified past in which everyone lived in prototypical relationships "in Christ."[53] Chapters 1 and 2 are therefore the best sources for ideals for the group to follow, as the past is commended by the author of 1 Clement. The ideals presented in these two chapters are consistently reflected in the main thrust of the letter. The past and its ideals are significant for the Corinthians to live by once again.[54] In 1:1–3:1, an extensive list of virtues from the congregation's past life, which no longer exists due to the strife, is portrayed. This first part of the letter essentially serves as a blueprint, a set of norms expected of the members of the Christ groups known to the author of 1 Clement. This model later functions as a standard by which the current state of the Corinthians is measured. It is also clearly articulated in the subsequent section (particularly chapters 3–28, but to some extent throughout to chapter 39)[55] through scriptural examples of prototypical behaviour. Furthermore, examples that contradict the expected behaviours are plentiful.[56] The congregation is first lauded for their past behaviour, as they correctly acted as Christ believers, in line with the prototypical behaviour the author expects

---

[52] Kujanpää 2021, 376–77.

[53] Khomych 2015, 51, makes a good case for the ideal time in 1 Clement is being in the past.

[54] Khomych 2015, 56–57.

[55] There is a general agreement that the letter contains two parts: chapters 1–39, and chapters 40–65, where the first part states the problem and provide scriptural proof for the need of concord, while the second part starts to deal with the problem proper, Khomych 2015, 54, Ehrman 2003a, 18

[56] See 1 Clem. 4; 11:2; 23:3; 30:8; 36:6–12; 39, etc.

from them. As previously discussed in chapter 2 above, salient group norms, closely connected to a distinct group identity, produce conformity among individuals to the expressed norms.[57] In the first three chapters of the letter, the author aims to remind the addressees of the norms regarding unity, behaviour, and modesty that are consistent with the salient group identity.[58] The author references numerous exemplary figures from scriptural and gospel traditions for readers to emulate before properly addressing the conduct expected of the leaders. To remind readers of their shared identity, the author begins with a salutation that refreshes their memory. In the subsequent chapters, the author instructs the congregation on how to act in line with that identity. Importantly, the correct manner of embodying prototypical behaviour is primarily depicted as non-schismatic, orderly, and natural in these two chapters. Terms associated with unity, purity, and life in the Spirit (that is, prototypical life) are repeatedly contrasted with the rebellion against leaders that characterises the current state of the congregation. The ideal member of the past, as illustrated in these two chapters, is described as follows (1:2–2:1):

> τίς γὰρ παρεπιδημήσας πρὸς ὑμᾶς τὴν πανάρετον καὶ βεβαίαν ὑμῶν πίστιν οὐκ ἐδοκίμασεν; τήν τε σώφρονα καὶ ἐπιεικῆ ἐν Χριστῷ εὐσέβειαν οὐκ ἐθαύμασεν; καὶ τὸ μεγαλοπρεπὲς τῆς φιλοξενίας ὑμῶν ἦθος οὐκ ἐκήρυξεν; καὶ τὴν τελείαν καὶ ἀσφαλῆ γνῶσιν οὐκ ἐμακάρισεν; ἀπροσωπολήμπτως γὰρ πάντα ἐποιεῖτε καὶ ἐν τοῖς νομίμοις τοῦ θεοῦ ἐπορεύεσθε, ὑποτασσόμενοι τοῖς ἡγουμένοις ὑμῶν καὶ τιμὴν τὴν καθήκουσαν ἀπονέμοντες τοῖς παρ' ὑμῖν πρεσβυτέροις· νέοις τε μέτρια καὶ σεμνὰ νοεῖν ἐπετρέπετε· γυναιξίν τε ἐν ἀμώμῳ καὶ σεμνῇ καὶ ἁγνῇ συνειδήσει πάντα ἐπιτελεῖν παρηγγέλλετε, στεργούσας καθηκόντως τοὺς ἄνδρας ἑαυτῶν· ἔν τε τῷ κανόνι τῆς ὑποταγῆς ὑπαρχούσας τὰ κατὰ τὸν οἶκον σεμνῶς οἰκουργεῖν ἐδιδάσκετε, πάνυ σωφρονούσας. 2:1 Πάντες τε ἐταπεινοφρονεῖτε μηδὲν ἀλαζονευόμενοι ὑποτασσόμενοι μᾶλλον ἢ ὑποτάσσοντες, ἥδιον διδόντες ἢ λαμβάνοντες, τοῖς ἐφοδίοις τοῦ Χριστοῦ ἀρκούμενοι· καὶ προσέχοντες τοὺς λόγους αὐτοῦ ἐπιμελῶς ἐνεστερνισμένοι ἦτε τοῖς σπλάγχνοις, καὶ τὰ παθήματα αὐτοῦ ἦν πρὸ ὀφθαλμῶν ὑμῶν.

For who visiting you could not testify to the all-encompassing virtue and steadfastness in your faith, and who was not amazed by the self-control and gentleness in your piety in Christ? And who did not proclaim your enormously hospitable habits? And who did not bless your perfected and sure knowledge? Impartial, you walked in the laws of God, in subjection under your leadership and while you showed fitting respect for your

---

[57] Hogg, van Knippenberg and Rast 2012, 262.
[58] This section is obviously also a piece of *captatio benevolentiae*, Bakke 2001, 205–7.

presbyters/those who are older among you. You taught your young men to think temperately and honourably. You instructed the women to perform all their duties, while enduring all that is proper for their husbands' sake, with blameless, honourable, and holy conscience. You taught them to rule their houses with good character with very good sense, being under the rule of submission. While everyone was humble in mind and no-one prideful, you submitted yourselves rather than made each other submit, gave rather than received, and were satisfied with the provisions of Christ. And you carefully paid close attention to his words, and they were stored in your hearts, and his suffering was before your eyes.

All the traits portrayed refer to knowing one's place in the group, as well as in society.[59] As shown in the table above, there are different but overlapping ideals for grown men, young people, and women. However, emphasis is placed on what constitutes appropriate behaviour towards other sub-groups within the fellowship and society as a whole. Submission to superiors is highlighted. Particularly significant, as we shall observe, are the scriptural instances that illustrate exemplary figures from the Jewish Scriptures, who are depicted as humble, even though they possessed the ability to be prideful.[60]

Primarily, both men and women are labelled with the verb καθήκω ("what is proper/fitting").[61] The honour due a member is important to respect. That goes for both marital relations and relations to older persons. The meaning of τοῖς παρ' ὑμῖν πρεσβυτέροις ("those older among you") in 1:3 is also possible to understand as analogue to the leadership in the congregation (ὑποτασσόμενοι τοῖς ἡγουμένοις ὑμῶν, "while you submitted to your leaders").[62] Therefore, just as every ancient reader recognised the importance of giving due honour to their elders, they understood that proper conduct towards the congregation's leaders meant offering them the same respect.

---

[59] It is interesting that the traits mentioned in the letter dovetail nicely with the ideal put forward in the Pastoral letters. The lists for proper behaviour for the ἐπίσκοπος, διάκονος, and the χήρα, in 1 Tim 3:1–13; 5:3–16 are worth noting as a close relative to 1 Clement. This is a venue for further research.

[60] See, for example, Jesus, Elijah, Elisha, Ezekiel, and David, all portrayed as humble in chapters 16–18. See also Kujanpää 2021, 372, and her discussion about the portrayal of Moses as both bold and humble for the sake of love and group-prototypical values.

[61] BDAG, s. v. καθήκω "To be appropriate."

[62] Ehrman 2002a, 37, also notices the ambiguous language.

First Clement 2:2 describes the results of these prototypical behaviours. These results primarily concern unity and brotherly love. In other words, the manner in which the congregants acted when they understood their role, as described in chapter 1, fostered unity and vitality in the spirit. The consequences are spelled out from the verbal phrase οὕτως ... ἐδέδοτο (2:2) "this has given/produced." Among the things produced by this prototypical behaviour, the congregation received a "deep and rich peace" (εἰρήνη βαθεῖα καὶ λιπαρὰ), a will to "do good" (ἀγαθοποιΐαν) and an "outpouring of the holy spirit in full" (πλήρης πνεύματος ἁγίου ἔκχυσις). The congregation "was struggling day and night" (ἀγὼν ἦν ὑμῖν ἡμέρας τε καὶ νυκτὸς) for the salvation of the brotherhood. The addressees were pure/sincere (εἰλικρινεῖς), pure/innocent (ἀκέραιοι), and forgetful of wrongdoings against each other (ἀμνησίκακοι). All factions and schisms (πᾶσα στάσις καὶ πᾶν σχίσμα) were detestable (βδελυκτόν) to the congregants. In verses 8 and 9 of chapter 2, the author concludes that the previous way of life that the congregation had led was "virtuous" and "honourable" (παναρέτῳ, σεβασμίῳ). The section of praise for former good actions is concluded with "the commands and righteous actions from the Lord were written on the tablets of your hearts."[63]

In conclusion, the prototypical ideals of the congregation place distinctive emphasis on the importance of knowing one's place and exhibiting non-schismatic behaviour. Following this introduction, the main points are substantiated through scriptural examples, and the author provides suggestions for actions to take. These actions are further reinforced with examples from Scripture.

7.2.2 Scriptural Examples of the Prototypes in Chapters 1–2

The central portion of 1 Clement is a lengthy exposition derived from a text similar to the LXX, offering evidence for the prototype presented in chapters 1

---

[63] Greek text: τὰ προστάγματα καὶ τὰ δικαιώματα τοῦ κυρίου ἐπὶ τὰ πλάτη τῆς καρδίας ὑμῶν ἐγέγραπτο, 2:8.

and 2.⁶⁴ It is significant that the prototypes for the Jesus followers in Corinth are supported by scriptural evidence. In this section, I will discuss three aspects of how the use of Jewish Scriptures assists in constructing the ideal of a Jesus follower.

First, the Scriptures are used solely as support for an identity as a follower of Jesus, while the Jewish identity is largely passed over in silence and thus subtly discarded. This process will be explored in detail in this section. Second, I will also examine how Hellenistic rhetorical ideals provide impulses for a new prototypical identity. This identity is neither rabbinic-Jewish (despite the extensive use of Scriptures) nor Hellenistic (even though it employs Hellenistic ideals and rhetorical dispositions to communicate its message); rather, it represents the identity of the Jesus group. Third, I will provide an overview of how the prototypical traits of Jesus followers described in 1 Clement 1–2 are supported by scriptural evidence. These three topics offer an overview of how the prototypicality of Jesus followers is shaped by scriptural support at the expense of a Jewish identity throughout 1 Clement.

Jewish Scriptures, Jesus Follower Identity, and Mutual Authorization

It is worth pondering how 1 Clement utilises the Jewish Scriptures; specifically, how they offer a significant impetus for self-designation for both the sender and the readers of 1 Clement.⁶⁵ There is no doubt that the Scriptures are regarded as authoritative by both the author and the readers. It is notable that the author of 1 Clement neither acknowledges nor addresses any tension between the Hebrew Bible and the belief in Jesus Christ.⁶⁶ Instead, Scripture serves as authoritative guidance for Christ followers without hesitation. The use of Scripture highlights a fundamental self-understanding expressed by 1 Clement,

---

⁶⁴ Lona 1998, 42: "Die Textgrundlage der alttestamentlichen Zitate und Wendungen in I Clem ist eine griechische Fassung, die der heutigen LXX nahe steht – die Bezugnahme auf eine hebräische Fassung ist an keiner Stelle nachweisbar." Also, it is worth noting that almost 30 percent of the text in the letter is citations, Lona 1998, 31.

⁶⁵ Lona 1998, 42, provides a table of all references to the Scriptures, as well as a list of names from the Scriptures.

⁶⁶ Lona 1998, 47, neatly sums up: "Die Rezeption des AT vollzieht sich in I Clem in der Form einer unreflektierten, problemlosen Vereinnahmung ohne jede Spur von Spannung."

7.2 Prototypicality

which perceives a continuity with the Jewish Scriptures, but with a Jesus-follower identity emerging as a result. An example of this identity shift from Jewish to Jesus follower is the ambiguous designation of "Israel" in the letter, a point to which we will return. One way to understand the extensive use of Scripture is to regard it as an appropriation of Jewish traditions.[67] The use of Scripture suggests that the view of the author of 1 Clement is that the community of Jesus followers had fully taken over the role of God's people since the Jewish identity is foregone with almost complete silence. To be a Jew is not an alternative when 1 Clement refers to Jewish Scriptures. Kujanpää sums up her perspective: "There are no explicit supersessionist arguments in the letter; in fact ... it is as if the Jews did not exist."[68] While it is true that no explicit supersessionist claims are made, the use of Jacob as a portal figure for the priests, kings, princes, and rulers of the Scriptures is closely linked to the followers of Jesus. The portal offices and functions in the Jewish Scriptures are associated with Jacob, in contrast to Israel, which is instead linked to envy and, consequently, destruction. 1 Clement 32:2 highlights Jacob as the source for the priestly office, as well as for the kings and princes.

> ἐξ αὐτοῦ γὰρ ἱερεῖς καὶ λευῖται πάντες οἱ λειτουργοῦντες τῷ θυσιαστηρίῳ τοῦ θεοῦ· ἐξ αὐτοῦ ὁ κύριος Ἰησοῦς τὸ κατὰ σάρκα· ἐξ αὐτοῦ βασιλεῖς καὶ ἄρχοντες καὶ ἡγούμενοι κατὰ τὸν Ἰούδαν·
>
> Because from him [Jacob, see 31:4] [came] all priests and Levites, who minister to God's altar. From him [came] the lord Jesus according to the flesh. From him [came] all kings and princes and rulers over Judah.

In a cautious formulation (compared to for example Irenaeus, *Haer.* 4.21–23, and Ignatius, Ign. *Magn.* 10:3) Jesus followers, designated as Jacob's heirs, are seen as the recipients of Abraham's blessing since chapter 31 discusses the blessings through faith (διὰ πίστεως) (31:2). The designation of Jacob as chosen over Esau (a theme already found in Rom 9:10–13) likely serves as the foundation for this interpretation of Jewish Scriptures. Similarly, Jos Verheyden notes that the history of Israel (which appears to be the term for Jewish identity throughout 1 Clement) is presented negatively to remind the Corinthians of what might

---

[67] Lona 1998, 47. See also Carleton Paget 2017, 224.
[68] Kujanpää 2020, 134.

occur if they persist in their rebellion.[69] Israel is associated with rebellion, while Jacob is linked to order. Indeed, a consensus has recently emerged among scholars that 1 Clement's use of Jewish Scriptures indicates a silent transition regarding the chosen people of God, from Israel to the Jesus followers.[70] Therefore, the quotes from Jewish sources are not creating a Jewish prototype, but a distinct prototype for followers of Jesus. The ideals presented in chapters 1–2, then, are primarily derived from Jewish Scriptures, but consist of principles for the Jesus follower, whether Jew or non-Jew.[71]

When discussing the Scriptures as sources of identity for followers of Jesus in 1 Clement, the term *mutual authorization* enhances the perspective.[72] The authority of an ancient text is primarily a relational concept. When the author of 1 Clement creates the new text (1 Clement), that utilises Jewish Scriptures as a relevant source for Jesus-follower identity, something crucial occurs in how the text is perceived by the receiving community. The base text (Jewish Scriptures, such as Isa 53) authorises the new text by the new text's reference to it (1 Clem. 16), while the new text (1 Clem. 16) also legitimises the old text (Isa 53) as a relevant source for group identity.[73] This is, of course, dependent on whether (or to what degree) the community accepts the text (1 Clem.) as relevant. Scriptures thus simultaneously authorise the parenetic from the author and the letter of 1 Clement as an authority to adhere to itself.[74]

Through the lens of the theoretical framework of oracular authority (coined by G. H. van Kooten),[75] Kujanpää provides a comprehensive perspective on how Jewish scriptures are utilised in 1 Clement. The understanding of the Jewish Scriptures is that Christ (1 Clem 22:1), as well as an active spirit associated with God, denoted as πνεύματος τοῦ ἁγίου (22:1; 45:2), speaks through the

---

[69] Verheyden 2015, 242, see also 1 Cor 10:1–13 for a Pauline example of negative examples from Scripture.
[70] Skarsaune 2018. See also Hagner 1973, and Schreckenberg 1993.
[71] Carleton Paget 2017, 224, points to the argumentation from the portal figure Jacob, the younger brother, who got the inheritance and the blessing, see 1 Clem 32:2.
[72] Kujanpää 2020, 128.
[73] Kujanpää 2020, 128.
[74] Kujanpää 2020, 129.
[75] Kujanpää 2020, 131. See also van Kooten 2010.

Hebrew Bible. Kujanpää also points out that in 13:1 and 16:2, the Spirit is understood as the speaker.[76] In 1 Clem. 16, Christ is equated with God's servant in Isa 53; thus he is practically a key to understanding the Scriptures correctly (see also 1 Clem. 17:1). The ownership and impulses for identity in the Jewish Scriptures are thereby fully transferred to the group(s) of Jesus followers. The use of Jewish Scripture in 1 Clement attests to a process whereby the Scriptures are read entirely from a Christological perspective, linking Jewish identity to rebellion against a God-given order. This becomes even more intriguing in comparison to, for example, Paul in 1 Cor 7:10 and the author of Revelation in Rev 1:1, where the authors claim divine knowledge and revelation that provide supplementary information about God and Christ apart from Jewish Scripture. The author of 1 Clement does not explicitly claim divine revelation separate from the Scriptures and, therefore, draws on the positive examples of faithfulness in Jewish Scripture to reference the Jesus followers exclusively. There is, in practice, not much space left for a Jewish identity without Jesus after the scriptural reading in 1 Clement.[77]

Hellenistic Rhetoric Ideals and Jesus Follower Identity

From a rhetorical perspective, Cilliers Breytenbach provides a key to understanding the pattern in the letter. He illustrates a scheme from Greek rhetoric, where both positive and negative examples of various behaviours are presented. The extensive use of historical examples was frequently employed in ancient deliberative rhetoric and discussed by Aristotle.[78] The power of historic example, as expressed by Aristotle and succinctly summarised by Breytenbach, is the following:

> On the basis of similarity, it is assumed that future things will be like those of the past. The historical example in deliberative rhetoric thus relates things that have happened

---

[76] Kujanpää 2020, 132.

[77] Kujanpää 2020, 132.

[78] Breytenbach 2013, 24. For an extensive analysis of the rhetorical genus, see van Unnik 2004, 115–81.

before, making use of the known individual cases to induce a general principle that can be used to give advice in an analogous case.[79]

Also, according to Aristotle "persuasion is brought about either by the use of example (παράδειγμα) or rhetorical conclusion (ἐνθύμημα)." That is why the use of historical examples was abundant in deliberative rhetoric.[80] Breytenbach illustrates how the common Greek rhetorical practice of using historical examples, as seen in the speeches of Dio Chrysostom, Aelius Aristides, and Plutarch, is adopted by the author of 1 Clement.[81] Just as these ancient authors employed deliberative speech, the author of 1 Clement utilised examples *drawn from the Scriptures*. Whereas Greek authors referenced Homer, the Roman author of 1 Clement employs biblical examples and Jesus traditions.[82] These examples, according to Breytenbach, create a pattern that combines Jewish historical teachings with Greek rhetorical traditions. The result, however, provides a distinctly new identity, separate from both Jewish and Hellenistic ideals, to which the addressees are expected to adhere. Kujanpää comments on the use of Jewish Scriptures in 1 Clement as obviously authoritative, yet distinctly marked as Scripture through explicit formulas. This is important for readers to recognise the authority of what is written by the author.[83] From an SIT perspective, the Hellenistic approach to employing Jewish Scriptures constitutes a significant aspect in the development of a distinctly Christian identity. The author of 1 Clement "systematically emphasises the virtues of humility, submission to divine order, and peace, summoning forth one scriptural hero after another to demonstrate that these virtues are constitutive of who 'we' are."[84] Just as the heroes of the faith in Jewish Scriptures are transferred into heroes of faith in Jesus in the past, the pattern of those heroes is expected from the Corinthians

---

[79] Breytenbach 2013, 24.
[80] Breytenbach 2013, 24.
[81] Breytenbach 2013, 25–28.
[82] Breytenbach 2013, 32.
[83] Kujanpää 2020, 129–30.
[84] Kujanpää 2021, 373.

in a way akin to the use of rhetoric examples in the Hellenistic world.[85] The former heroes are prototypical examples (παράδειγμα) for the readers to follow.

The Authorisation of the Jesus Follower Prototype through Scripture

Following these two theoretical perspectives, we now turn to how the prototypicality in 1 Clem. 1–2 is supported by scriptural evidence in the main part of the letter (primarily 3–39). The section on biblical examples begins in 3:1 with a citation of Deut 32:15, from another tradition than the LXX to which we have access.[86] This passage in Deuteronomy describes an initial apostasy from YHWH by members of the well-off community, who began to sacrifice to other gods. The author of 1 Clement adopts this frame of reference, viewing the people of God as apostates during prosperous times, when discussing the process of the schism in 3:1. Consequently, the depiction of the Corinthian congregation is compared to the apostates of Israel in the Deuteronomistic history. This apostasy leads to "envy and spite, strife and discord, persecution and insurrection, conflict and captivity" (3:2).[87] As a conclusion to the topic, the author accuses the addressees for not living according to what is fitting in Christ (...μηδὲ πολιτεύεσθαι κατὰ τὸ καθῆκον τῷ Χριστῷ, 3:4). As we will see in the next section, the author describes the *ones rising up* against οἱ πρεσβύτεροι as οἱ ἄτιμοι ("the dishonourables"), while the elders are ἔντιμοι. Thus, there are those guilty of strife, displaying non-prototypical behaviour (the factionists), and there are those who are not (the old leaders). Through Jewish scriptural examples, the author then goes on to show the difference between a just, wise, and pious life on the one hand and apostasy on the other in the main section of the letter (4–39).

To provide a brief overview of the prototypical patterns discussed in this section, the following will suffice. In chapters 3–6, the disastrous effects of

---

[85] See for example chapter 17 where Elijiah, Elisha, Ezekiel, and Abraham all are portrayed as witnesses of Jesus Christ.

[86] LXX reads ἔφαγεν Ιακωβ καὶ ἐνεπλήσθη, καὶ ἀπελάκτισεν ὁ ἠγαπημένος ("Jakob ate and enjoyed and my beloved one kicked away") while the tradition in 1 Clement reads ἔφαγεν καὶ ἔπιεν καὶ ἐπλατύνθη καὶ ἐπαχύνθη καὶ ἀπελάκτισεν ὁ ἠγαπημένος ("My beloved one ate and drank and enjoyed and became fat and kicked away").

[87] ζῆλος καὶ φθόνος, ἔρις καὶ στάσις, διωγμὸς καὶ ἀκαταστασία, πόλεμος καὶ αἰχμαλωσία.

ζῆλος καὶ φθόνος, meaning "jealousy and envy," in biblical stories and more recent traditions are articulated. Chapter 4 examines Cain and Abel, and subsequently Jacob and Esau, Joseph and Moses, Aaron and Miriam, Dathan and Abiram, and David and Saul. Chapter 5 addresses the fate of the heroes of faith, Peter and Paul, who were persecuted due to ζῆλος. In chapter 6, first the great multitude of the elect is considered, followed by the mentioning of women "persecuted as Danaids and Dircae", a puzzling reference, perhaps used as a euphemism for public rape and torture that some Christian women might have suffered.[88] Whatever the original reference might have been, the persecuted women are presented as exemplary figures of endurance, having suffered severe αἰκίσματα (torment, mistreatment). Chapter 6 also discusses how ζῆλος alienates men from women and incites nations into war. Breytenbach contends that this phenomenon is also common in other examples of Greek rhetorical tradition; the examples come in groups of seven (Peter, Paul, the multitude of the elect, the Danaids and Dircae, the dynamics between men and women, and the relationships between nations), the last two referring to domestic life and politics.[89] Chapters 7 and 8 start with a short recapitulation and exhort the readers to repentance, and then give numerous examples of repentance in Scripture: Noah, Jonah, and quotes from Isaiah and Ezekiel. Chapters 9 and 10 show the benefits of a righteous life (which one can gain through repentance) in Noah, Enoch, and Abraham.

The prototypical list expected from the congregation in chapters 1 and 2 admonishes the prototypical trait of hospitality. Lot (with Lot's wife serving as an anti-example) in chapter 11, and Rahab in chapter 12, exemplify this trait effectively. Chapters 13 to 18 discuss the antitheses between, on one hand, ταπεινοφροσύνη, meaning "humility" (a prototypical trait for everyone, 2:1) and, on the other, ἀλαζονείαν, καὶ τῦφος καὶ ἀφροσύνην καὶ ὀργάς, translating to "pride and conceit and foolishness and wrath," which can perhaps be summarised as arrogant pride. This antithetical lineup follows extensive quotations from texts regarded as Scripture: the Matthean-Lukan Jesus tradition (13), Proverbs and Psalms (14), Isaiah and Psalms (15–16), Job, Genesis, Exodus, and

---

[88] See Ehrman 2003a, 44–45, n. 16.
[89] Breytenbach 2013, 31.

Numbers, where the prophets, Abraham, and Job, are presented as examples (17). In chapter 18, the books of 1 Samuel and Psalms are quoted concerning David as a humble prototype. David was already portrayed in 4:13 as a positive prototype in contrast to Saul, "king of Israel," who persecuted him out of envy (διὰ ζῆλος). This perspective is taken a step further, as David's positive trait was his humility in repenting when he had sinned ("Have mercy on me, God, according to your great kindness," Ps 51). In 1 Clement 13 and 16, Jesus's exemplary humility is emphasised; "because if the Lord humbled himself in this way, what should we then do, who have come in under the yoke of his grace through him?" (6:17).[90] Thus, to be a member of the congregation is to be humble, like David and Jesus, and not envious like Saul, the "king of Israel."

The author of the letter, then, in 1 Clem. 19–28, engages in a discourse concerning the deeds of God in history. These deeds should make the readers attentive not to live in unworthy manners, but in accord with the prototypical ideals. This section reflects the former behaviour of the addressees in seeking a profound understanding of God (1:2). Once again, the biblical story is referenced to testify to the acts of God (19:1–2), and the Corinthians are urged, along with the author of the letter, to reflect on the wisdom of God: ἴδωμεν αὐτὸν κατὰ διάνοιαν καὶ ἐμβλέψωμεν τοῖς ὄμμασιν τῆς ψυχῆς εἰς τὸ μακρόθυμον αὐτοῦ βούλημα ("we should observe him through understanding and consider through the soul's eyes the patience of his purpose," 19:3). In the following chapters, the author offers a meditation on the harmony of creation and urges the Corinthians to live in accord with this wisdom. To show reverence, ἐντρέπω,[91] for the blood of Jesus (21:6) has a counterpart in respecting (αἰδεσθῶμεν) the leaders, honouring (τιμήσωμεν) the elders (πρεσβύτεροι), disciplining (παιδεύσωμεν) the young ones, and setting wives tona straight path to the good (διορθωσώμεθα). The states of life and the appropriate ways to act in accord with each state have a counterpart in chapter 2, where, as previously mentioned, the key term is καθήκω (to do what is proper). The purpose of this section is to demonstrate that when one contemplates the wisdom of God and His creation, one must live in alignment with this wisdom in an orderly

---

[90] For a detailed list of scriptural and gospel traditions, see Erhman 2003a, 57–65.
[91] The second sense of the word according to BDAG, s. v. ἐντρέπω.

fashion. This is supported by the quotation from Ps 34 in 1 Clem. 22, alongside references to Isaiah and Malachi in chapter 23, the orderliness of the resurrection as observed through natural life in chapter 24, and the example of the Phoenix bird "in the area close to Arabia" (25:1 and following), further evidence for the possibility of resurrection in chapter 26, and a conclusion of the section that summarises the argument. The author of 1 Clement aims to show that a wise way of life, anchored in a thorough knowledge of God's ways in Scripture and the evidence from nature, is to live a life in harmony with God's order. The orderliness of nature and the wisdom of God serve as the framework for a necessary pattern to follow. The letter presents numerous examples of prototypical behaviour aligning with the first two chapters. It is sufficient to say that the prototypical pattern remains consistent throughout the letter. In chapters 40–46, a well-ordered life, free from factions and strife, is situated within a pleasing structure according to Scripture. A worthy life, as defined by ingroup principles, is framed within a scriptural context through the exposition of the antiquity of the episcopal office. Following these chapters, a call to action emerges based on the previous exposition: to reinstate the deposed leaders for the sake of prototypical behaviour.

The composition of prototypical traits alongside examples from biblical and gospel traditions presents a clear depiction of what the group has failed to uphold. The exordium of chapters 1–3 has through scriptural examples (loosely connected to the term rhetorical notion of *narratio*) provided a case for repentance,[92] to which the factionists in the congregation are exhorted.[93] On the other hand, as we shall see, the leaders (ἐπίσκοποι καὶ πρεσβύτεροι) have lived prototypical lives, which we now turn to analyse.

7.2.3 The Prototypical Behaviour of ἐπίσκοποι καὶ πρεσβύτεροι

It is important to remember that when analysing prototypical behaviour, a key aspect of prototypical leadership is that the more prototypical a person is, the

---

[92] This case is in itself described through ample scriptural passages, see for example chapter 18, quoting Ps 51.

[93] This section is also a narrative for the "core values and characteristics that define Christ-followers," Kujanpää 2021, 373.

greater their influence within a group of self-categorised members.[94] While the letter presents a depiction of the congregation in Corinth, where the group members have faltered in their behaviour and are urged to repent, the leaders are depicted quite differently. The leaders are shown as blameless, excelling in their duties, with their offices aligned with Scripture and tradition.[95] Clement attempts to enhance the ethos of the old leaders, thereby increasing the Corinthians' willingness to reinstate them. In 3:3, the difference between the leaders and the factionists are made clear: "in this way, the dishonourables rose up against the honourables, those without reputation against the splendid ones, the foolish against the wise, the young ones against the Presbyters," 4:3.[96] These antitheses are naturally understood against the backdrop of the first and second chapters, with their blueprint of prototypical behaviour; the previously well-regarded prototypical Corinthians (see 1:1) have lost their good reputation, the honour-giving in an appropriate manner has ceased (1:3), just as has the wisdom (1:2). The lessons on envy and strife in the subsequent chapters are thus intended not for the leaders, but for the factionists, who are linked with the deadly envy (ζῆλος, 3:4). It is therefore evident that the leadership should still be viewed as prototypical, while the factionists are called to repentance. In chapter 6, the known victims of envy within the congregation (apostles and Scriptural examples) are presented as models to follow (ὑπόδειγμα, 6:1). The leaders, who are also depicted as victims of envy according to the text, are thereby associated with those suffering for their faith. A significant characteristic of prototypical leaders, namely their willingness to suffer for group ideals, is fulfilled in this fame-by-association.[97] The same type of fame-by-association continues in chapter 42, where the offices ἐπίσκοποι καὶ διάκονοι are first fruits (ἀπαρχὰς, 42:4) of the ministry of the apostles, and properly tested by the spirit (δοκιμάσαντες τῷ πνεύματι). The works of the spirit, thorough testing, and the

---

[94] Haslam, Reicher and Platow 2011, 88, 90.

[95] Even if this is how the author of 1 Clement portrayed the leaders, it is likely that the reason for the deposing of the old leaders was that they were no longer perceived as examples of prototypical behaviour. That would mean that the description of the old leaders was heavily idealised.

[96] Greek text: οὕτως ἐπηγέρθησαν οἱ ἄτιμοι ἐπὶ τοὺς ἐντίμους, οἱ ἄδοξοι ἐπὶ τοὺς ἐνδόξους, οἱ ἄφρονες ἐπὶ τοὺς φρονίμους, οἱ νέοι ἐπὶ τοὺς πρεσβυτέρους.

[97] See Henrich 2009, 244–60.

association with the apostles work together to create a faultless prototypicality in the leadership structure. This is spelled out even more clearly in 44:3; the leaders have performed their duties blamelessly, humbly, peacefully, unselfishly, and even further, all testify to it.[98] The act of deposing the leaders from their offices (44:6) is here compared to the situation in Scripture where the righteous are always persecuted by the ἀνόμον (lawless, 45:4). This places the factionists in the wrong company, alongside the tormentors and persecutors of the holy (45:7–8). Throughout the letter, the group's ideals are clearly associated with the deposed leaders, while the factionists stand in stark contrast to these ideals.

The leadership structure will also be discussed from the framework of identity impresarioship in the next section. Before I turn to that, it is worth noting that the continuity with the priests in the Scriptures not only embeds the identity of the leaders of the Christ groups as aligned with Aaron and Levitical priests, but also functions as a prototypical pattern that borrows its ethos from the Scriptures. The priests symbolise the defence against "disorderliness" in Israel (ἀκαταστασία, 43:6) and are, as chapter 41 aims to illustrate, an example of the intrinsic connection between what is fitting (καθήκω, see chapters 1 and 2) and a properly performed sacrifice. As stated in 41:3, the significance of taking the correct actions in accord with God's plan is a matter of life and death. The ideal and appropriate way is not something undertaken at random, but rather in line with the divine knowledge provided in Scripture and tradition. This indicates that a proper understanding of orderliness is closely linked to the primary aim of the letter.

In conclusion, the old leaders are closely connected to an appropriate and suitable way of life according to ingroup prototypes throughout 1 Clement, which would enhance the willingness among the Corinthians to reinstate them. The letter depicts the leaders as exemplifying this prototypical life, as they embody the scriptural ideals that are constantly encouraged. These ideals are closely linked to both scriptural teachings and the apostles. They are also portrayed as diligently striving to adhere to ingroup ideals, even when this

---

[98] καὶ λειτουγήσαντας ἀμέμπτως τῷ ποιμνίῳ τοῦ Χριστοῦ μετὰ ταπεινοφροσύνης, ἡσύχως καὶ ἀβαναύσως, μεμαρτυρημένους τε πολλοῖς χρόνοις ὑπὸ πάντων.

entails a cost. The leaders, within the God-given structure led by an ἐπίσκοπος, thus serve as carriers of ingroup prototypicality and as assurances for the well-ordered alignment with apostolic and scriptural ideals. The identity in Christ groups that aligns with scriptural concepts, as well as apostolic ideals, is manifested through the offices. The leadership structure, therefore, offers a model to emulate through the prototypical behaviour of the officials. This becomes even clearer when we now turn to the leadership structure as an illustration of identity impresarioship.

7.3 Identity Entrepreneurship and Impresarioship

Having analysed how the prototype of Jesus followers is enforced with evidence from Jewish Scriptures and identified with the behaviour of the deposed leaders, we now turn to how the author employs language that can be meaningfully analysed with categories from SIT. Identity impresarioship is, as we have seen in chapter 2, the embedding of ingroup identity within structures and rituals.[99] Entrepreneurship refers to the leader's ability to alter the group narrative and perception of its own history to align with a new set of prototypes, primarily through the use of language.[100] Identity entrepreneurship "involves the use of language in order to create a compelling vision of identity and its implications for action."[101] When I have analysed how the author of 1 Clement portrays the leadership ideals of the overthrown leaders as embodying the values of the group, and thus effectively opts for a different kind of prototypicality, I will turn to the final section of the chapter: identity impresarioship. I will also analyse how the SIT term *mobilisation* aids our understanding of the recommended leadership structure in 1 Clement.[102] In the context of 1 Clement, the author employs ancient biblical heroes exemplifying humility to inspire readers to transform their social world through radical humility. Kujanpää

---

[99] Haslam, Reicher, and Platow 2011, 177. Steffens et al. 2014, 1004. See also Esler 2021, 40.
[100] See Kujanpää 2021, 373; Cinnirella 1998, 232; 235; See also Haslam et al., 170–77.
[101] Haslam, Reicher, and Platow 2011, 171.
[102] In their book on nationalism and social identity, Steve Reicher and Nick Hopkins discuss different ways for leaders to mobilize followers into support and action for a perceived social identity; Reicher and Hopkins 2001, IX.

examines one such example, Moses, and his bold παρρησία for the sake of salvation, while simultaneously maintaining humility towards God.[103] In the following section, I shall perform a similar operation with regard to the submission under the leadership as mobilisation.

7.3.1 Identity Entrepreneurship

We only have access to the author's perspective of the conflict in Corinth, as the deposed leaders do not speak directly to the factionists. As discussed above, these leaders never voice their own opinions in 1 Clement. For the letter's author, however, it is crucial to portray the deposed leaders as prototypical representations in line with the group's ideals consistently emphasised in the letter. The description of the leaders' prototypicality aligns seamlessly with the exemplary figures of David and Jesus. This supports the goal of an identity entrepreneur, which is to construct a vision of a leader as prototypical through narrative and language. We do not know, however, the impact of the intervention by the congregation in Rome. Perhaps the intervention was perceived positively by the Corinthian congregation, leading the factionists to step down and leave the assembly in Corinth (chapter 54). Alternatively, the author may have addressed an indifferent audience. Nevertheless, the author's rhetoric (the identity entrepreneur) draws upon the scriptural examples provided and anticipates the congregation's mobilisation for the reinstatement of the deposed leaders, thereby shifting the group's ideal from that of the new leadership back to the old ideal. I showed above how the group leaders were generally connected to the prototypical traits of heroes from the past. In this section, I will take one of these instances and show how it provides a mobilisation of social identity applicable to several chapters in 1 Clement.

The most obvious example of how this entrepreneurship operates can be found in chapters 15 and 16. In 16:1, the author states that "Christ is for those humble in mind, not the haughty over his flock" (ταπεινοφρονούντων γάρ ἐστιν ὁ Χριστός, οὐκ ἐπαιρομένων ἐπὶ τὸ ποίμνιον αὐτοῦ). The particle γάρ refers to the quotation of Ps 12 in chapter 15, where the Lord (ὁ κύριος) deals with the boastful and prideful (δόλια, μεγαλορήμονα, 1 Clem. 15:5), but raises up the lowly

---

[103] Kujanpää 2021, 372, n. 15; 376.

(πτωχῶν, πενήτων) from their miseries. Thus, the author goes on in chapter 16 with the portrayal of Jesus Christ as humble-minded (ταπεινοφρονῶν) and states, "he did not come in ostentatious pride or arrogance" (οὐκ ἦλθεν ἐν κόμπῳ ἀλαζονείας οὐδὲ ὑπερηφανίας). The scriptural evidence employed for this is Isaiah 53 (1 Clem. 16:3–14) and Ps 22 (1 Clem. 15–17). The messianic figure is portrayed as severely damaged or crushed in these two instances. The application of this scriptural passage is that if the Messiah endured such humiliating circumstances and embodies such a description (ταπεινοφρονῶν), and if the haughty and prideful are struck down by the Lord (15:7), how vitally important must it be to act in a humble manner, a point also emphasised by the rhetorical question in 16:17? The humble-minded are those who have access to Christ (16:1). The identity of being "under his yoke of grace" for the congregation means living humble lives aligned with the ideals exhorted by the author. Thus, the overall theme of the letter about the sinfulness with the deposing of the old leaders is connected to those who are boastful in chapter 15. The Lord deals with the boastful. Those whose identity is connected to Christ, however, live humble lives for the sake of others (chapter 16), even if they are mocked for it (16:16). This, of course, motivates the readers to rethink their relationship with, on the one hand, the deposed former leaders, and on the other hand, the new leaders. It mobilizes the congregation in Corinth to shape their identity in line with the rhetoric of chapters 15 and 16. Given the description of the situation by the author of 1 Clement, it would be nearly impossible for the situation to linger since that would entail acting in ways contrary to the teachings of Christ. As haughtiness is something that Christ would not be associated with, any actions that support haughty behaviour would be opposed to prototypicality, according to the author. While it is impossible to know the exact reason for the deposal, 1 Clement provides a narrative for the group that makes it impossible to maintain old behaviours; the Corinthians are mobilized towards a pattern of behaviour that aligns with the humble life of Christ. Numerous examples of this type of identity entrepreneurship appear throughout the letter.

7.3.2 Identity Impresarioship

Impresarioship, as we have seen, is about structuring the group's actions to conform to ingroup values. The leadership structure suggested by the author of 1 Clement, specifically the emerging episcopal office (chapter 44), reflects the core values of the group: the understanding of the episcopacy is that it is ancient, scriptural, and instituted by God. Since disorderliness is depicted as a sin deserving severe punishment (41:3), the well-ordered congregation serves as the ideal, prototypical assembly. The author of the letter views the office as a spiritual continuation of the liturgical role of the priests of the Hebrew Bible.[104] The section, which builds on the main theme of the letter (that leaders of factions attempting to undermine or overthrow the leaders of the congregation should repent), provides four important insights into the theology of the emerging episcopacy. It is *exigent, apostolic, scriptural*, and the *antidote against schisms*. These impulses correspond with the ideals that the author expects from the Corinthians congregation.

First, *the exigency* of the scriptural ordinances concerning liturgy in the temple is emphasized in chapters 40–41.[105] In the order established by God (40:1), it is essential for everyone to recognise their rightful place and act accordingly (41:1). The ideal, presented at the outset of the letter, highlights the significance of behaving appropriately according to one's position in society (καθήκω, 1:3) and is elaborated upon in the portrayal of the office assigned by God to the Israelites (40:5). Proper conduct in accord with one's place is consistently depicted as exemplary behaviour and is connected in this section to the liturgical structure, the liturgical rites, and the office of leadership. Now, according to the author, *every detail* needed to be attended to in the Israelite law, and analogically, the rules pertaining to the congregation's leadership must be kept in detail to avoid death (42:3–4). Therefore, the appropriate relationship with the office is essential for the group if its members wish to adhere to the minutiae of God's commands (40:1). It provides a means to carry out the Lord's directives in an organised manner, which is closely linked to the understanding of the desired behaviour.

Second, pertaining to the *apostolic character* of the office, the first fruits of the apostolic ministry are appointed (καθίστανον) and "examined/tested by the

---

[104] This dovetails nicely with the glorious and prototypical past, Khomych 2015, 58.
[105] See Lona 1998, 428–29.

spirit" (δοκιμάσαντες) *by the apostles*.[106] The title these first fruits are given are ἐπισκόπους καὶ διακόνους (42:4). The leaders of the congregation continue to support the work of the apostles and, ultimately, the work of Jesus. This is an important point in the first verse of chapter 42; "The apostles were given the gospel for us by the Lord Jesus Christ, and Jesus Christ was sent from God."[107] The proclamation of the resurrection by the apostles in v. 3 is, therefore, both a continuation of the work of God *and* the reason for the existence of the leadership. From an impresarioship perspective, a proper relationship with leadership is closely linked to participating in the ongoing work of the apostles. As previously stated, the apostles Peter and Paul are exemplary leaders (1 Clem. 5), both of whom remained faithful to the end, even when they faced persecution due to envy (ζῆλος, 1 Clem. 5:4–5). They were adequately tested and remained loyal, and submission to the leadership of the ἐπισκόπους καὶ διακόνους is now linked to the endurance of the apostles. The author presents submission to the ἐπισκόπους καὶ διακόνους as an essential characteristic for group members.

Third, the author of 1 Clement understands the emerging leadership office as *scriptural*, and thus nothing new, οὐ καινῶς (42:5). The author asserts that the existence of the office of the ἐπίσκοπος is also discussed in Scripture, referencing the LXX version of Isa 60:17; "I will give your rulers in peace, and your guardians in righteousness" (καὶ δώσω τοὺς ἄρχοντάς σου ἐν εἰρήνῃ καὶ τοὺς ἐπισκόπους σου ἐν δικαιοσύνῃ).[108] A possible objection to the identity proposed by the author might be that if we are indeed God's chosen people, why do we not utilise the priestly office outlined in the Scriptures? The response from 1 Clement is that the office of the ἐπίσκοπος and the διάκονος is indeed ancient, as attested by Isaiah. Furthermore, just as the law-giving is associated with Moses, "blessed, faithful servant in the whole house" 43:1 (ὁ μακάριος πιστὸς θεράπων ἐν ὅλῳ τῷ οἴκῳ), the appointment of leaders in the congregation is associated with "those in Christ, entrusted by God for this work" (οἱ ἐν Χριστῷ πιστευθέντες παρὰ θεοῦ ἔργον τοιοῦτο, 43:1). Faith and faithfulness are already

---

[106] BDAG, s.v. δοκιμάζω

[107] Following the translation of Ehrman 2003a, 109.

[108] Following BDAG, s.v. ἐπίσκοπος. It is worth noting that 1 Clement has an alternate reading of Isa 60:17, since it reads καταστήσω τοὺς ἐπισκόπους αὐτῶν ἐν δικαιοσύνῃ καὶ τοὺς διακόνους αὐτῶν ἐν πίστει.

mentioned in 1:2 of the letter and are here associated with Moses, the apostles, and the desired prototypical life of the Corinthians. Faith, as important as it is for the theology of the early Christ movement, is also at work in the construction of the leadership office. Thus, the message conveyed by the author is that faithful servants, such as Moses and the apostles who appointed the leaders of the congregation, are to be equally trusted. The scriptural evidence for the offices, along with the theologically significant association of πίστις with the apostolic appointers and Moses the lawgiver, provides a foundation for the necessity of submitting to the appointed leadership.

Fourth, 1 Clement suggests that the episcopal ministry is the will of God, and an *antidote for schismatic behaviour*. Already Moses suffered from envy (ζῆλος) regarding the leadership of the Israelites (43:2), and God provided miraculous signs for the people to understand the "electedness" of the Aaronite tribe. The author asserts a divine sanction (43:5–6, Num 17) for the emerging offices, both in Num and in 1 Clement, as a means to prevent discord. Thus, in 43:1, the role of the ἐπίσκοπος is likened to the emergence of the priesthood in the Pentateuch. The text implies that the schism in the congregation of Corinth is connected to the emergence and authority of an office within the community, akin to the situation involving Moses and the Israelites. In light of this, in the subsequent verses of 1 Clement 43, the author reiterates Numbers 17, focusing on the competition over the priesthood. The divine intervention in Numbers 17 is also relevant to the episcopal office in the congregation in Corinth, ensuring that there is no strife or schism in Israel or within the congregation of Corinth. The apostles, who were aware of the conflict regarding the emerging office (ἔρις ἔσται ἐπὶ τοῦ ὀνόματος τῆς ἐπισκοπῆς), are compared to Moses, who is said to have had foreknowledge (προῄδει) of a solution for the strife in Israel concerning the priesthood. The apostles' foreknowledge likewise indicated a solution to the potential dangers for the ingroup identity, as the appointed men were to be succeeded by others. These men were tested and installed in the office after the deaths of the original office holders (διαδέξωνται ἕτεροι δεδοκιμασμένοι ἄνδρες τὴν λειτουργίαν αὐτῶν, 44:2). The need to avoid disorder in Israel, the people of God, implies that the congregation in Corinth must also avoid disorder, as they are now the people of God. The way to act in accordance with this desired peace is to reinstate and submit to the leaders appointed by the apostles.

The picture presented by the author of 1 Clement is that the leadership structure from which the deposed leaders emerged was integral to the group's identity. Continuing with the schismatic behaviour that had occurred in Corinth would be impossible while still adhering to the prototypicality exhorted by the author, prompting the readers to address the mistakes they made.

7.4 Conclusion

From this analysis, three main conclusions can be drawn. The first pertains to the prototypicality of the officials among the followers of Jesus. The second pertains to the formation of a Jesus follower identity through the office in 1 Clement. The third pertains to the implications for the parting of the ways.

7.4.1 Prototypical Leaders in First Clement

We have explored how the episcopal office connects with certain ingroup values that are prototypical behaviours for followers of Jesus. Jewish Scriptures and traditions of Jesus support these prototypes, according to 1 Clement. This is analogous to the use of examples often found in Hellenistic tradition: the sources from Jewish Scriptures and gospel tradition create a new παράδειγμα to follow, aligned with the identity in Christ. Even if it is not explicitly stated, the impression given by 1 Clement is that being connected to God means being in harmony with the congregation of Jesus followers. The Jewish Scriptures support the prototype of a Jesus follower, and by making this claim, the author subtly dismisses Jewish identity as a valid option for members. The prototypical member is portrayed as virtuous and steadfast in faith, self-controlled and gentle, hospitable, insightful, well-versed in gospel tradition or Scripture, impartial, subordinate to leaders, humble, and generous. Young individuals are to be temperate and honourable, while women are to be blameless, honourable, holy, capable household managers, well-charactered, sensible, and submissive. The traits concerning submission to leaders, humility, and understanding one's proper place in the group, were particularly emphasised in the first three chapters of the letter. All these traits were expected to be displayed. They are thoroughly linked to Scripture passages and gospel traditions. Moreover, the leaders of the congregation are represented as exemplary in their prototypicality, thus serving as models to follow, whereas the factionists in the congregation are portrayed as the opposite, especially framed as ζῆλος towards the leaders. Furthermore, the removed leaders, characterised by humility, are associated with both ancient and contemporary leaders who suffered for ingroup values, which grants them the reputable standing of exemplary characters in Jewish Scriptures and recent events. The mobilisation process initiated by the author of 1 Clement calls upon the congregation to re-engage with group prototypes by re-establishing the old leaders. Given that the leadership office of ἐπίσκοπος and διάκονος is closely linked to heroes of faith and scriptural history, submission to the episcopal office is deemed the sole possible path to live according to ingroup values.

Throughout the letter, the deposed leaders illustrate examples of ingroup values. To reclaim the lost esteemed status described in the first two chapters, the Corinthians must take action to reinstall the leaders, which would resolve the dire situation in which the Corinthian congregation has placed itself.

7.4.2 The Episcopal Office, Entrepreneurship, and Impresarioship

As presented in 1 Clement, the episcopal office exemplifies the author's prowess as an identity entrepreneur, designed to mobilise the group to act in ways aligned with the prototypical blueprint. For the author of 1 Clement, the ancient nature and provenance of the episcopal office, as attested by Scripture, suggest that living in submission to the leaders means living a life intimately connected to the ancient heroes of faith and the apostles. Throughout 1 Clement, the message regarding the leadership structure is that it is exigent, apostolic, scriptural, and serves as an antidote to schisms. Consequently, the author advocates for the reinstatement of old leaders and, with them, the return to the old prototypicality, as affirmed by the Scriptures.

The author additionally assumes the role of an identity impresario. God's word (within which, according to 1 Clement, one finds the episcopal office) is imperative to observe, as failing to do so equals destruction and death. Since the ἐπίσκοπος is associated with the apostolic ministry, it is also linked to the apostles and to Jesus's long-term work. This office is scriptural and thus serves as a sign of ingroup values, meticulously outlined throughout the letter. As observed, the episcopal office is closely tied to the ideal of orderliness, functioning as a remedy for schisms. The establishment of the office aligns with Moses's (and ultimately God's) foreknowledge concerning the schisms threatening the community. The office therefore signifies what it means to be a follower of Jesus: the ingroup identity is embedded within the episcopal structure. Submission to the ἐπίσκοπος is a clear demonstration of identity impresarioship, fostering an ingroup culture where the ideals of the Scriptures and the priestly office (formerly associated with a Jewish identity) are fully transferred into the episcopal office. Thus, alternative options (such as a Jewish identity, for example) are neither recommended nor feasible; instead, access to God is granted if members lead lives free of factions, submitting to their leaders.

7.4.3 The Episcopal Office and the Parting of the Ways Debate in First Clement

This provides crucial insights into the relationship between Christ groups and Jewish synagogues. First, the prototype presented by 1 Clement is a Christian one. The ideal member is no longer a Jew but is instead depicted as someone living according to the ingroup prototype. This ingroup prototype gains essential information about ingroup ideals from Jewish Scriptures, which are no longer understood to offer insight into Jewish identity. Moreover, to live in accordance with this ingroup prototype is to align oneself with the appointed leaders, in this case, the episcopal office. This office is a fundamental and inevitable aspect of what it means to be a follower of Jesus.

We can thus observe the emergence of a structure in 1 Clement that is closely linked to an identity as a follower of Jesus, distinct from a Jewish identity (the latter is dismissed as unimportant and outmoded), which provides significant theological incentives for adherence to the structure. Essentially, the discourse regarding exigency and apostolicity, grounded in scriptural ideals, leaves a reader who accepts the reasoning in 1 Clement with no alternative but to closely associate oneself with the burgeoning episcopal office and abandon other identities.

8. The ἐπίσκοπος in the Pastoral Letters from an SIT Perspective

In this chapter, I will provide an analysis of the ἐπίσκοπος in the Pastoral epistles from an SIT perspective, particularly 1 Tim 3:1–7 and Titus 1:5–9. These passages explicitly discuss the expectations placed on the ἐπίσκοπος.

The Pastoral epistles are distinctive in this study, as they address the prototypicality of the ἐπίσκοπος directly. While other texts compel us to draw implicit conclusions, the Pastorals are unambiguous. However, the ἐπίσκοπος is characterised only in terms of prototypicality. Aside from the expectation that the ἐπίσκοπος must be able to teach, no further descriptions of the role are provided. Nevertheless, this role is recognised as significant for the identity construction of the group. Considering the narrative of the Pastoral letters, a pattern analogous to other second-century texts can be identified. Here, the work of Paul is succeeded by the congregational order discernible in the Pastorals. Thus, the ἐπίσκοπος is, as we shall see, perceived as a continuation of the work of Paul and, in the longer term, of Jesus. The ἐπίσκοπος becomes emblematic of the identity of Christ followers. Consequently, dimensions of prototypical leadership and identity impresarioship are present in the Pastorals.

In the first section of this chapter, I will situate the text group in terms of authorship and date. Second, I will discuss the narrative of the letters, in which the author, "Paul," establishes a congregational order through Timothy and Titus. In this order, the ἐπίσκοπος has a key role. Consequently, the structure incorporating the ἐπίσκοπος embeds Christian identity within itself. The author here functions as an identity impresario. Third, I will analyse the ἐπίσκοπος as a prototypical leader. The ethical expectations placed on the ἐπίσκοπος will be examined and related to other existing group norms. The ideals from the Pastoral Epistles will be compared with other lists of Greco-Roman ideals of the period. Then I will contrast the ideals from the Pastorals with existing ideals from Jewish groups of the same time. A significant portion of this chapter focuses on comparing the expectations of the ἐπίσκοπος (the ideal member of the Christ group) with those of ideal members of other groups. According to SIT theory, the prototypicality of a group is constructed to display the maximum contrast to outgroups (see chapter 2 above). Therefore, analysing the differences between the Pastorals and other existing lists of group norms should provide us with valuable insights into how the ideal member of the Christ group differed from those in other groups. This comparison yields a unique set of expectations for the leader figure within the Christ groups, differentiating it from both contemporary Jewish ideals and Hellenistic ones. Thus, the ἐπίσκοπος represents what is distinctly Christian within the Christ groups. Last, the results will be summarised and connected to the parting of the ways.

8.1 Authorship and Date of the Pastoral Epistles

It is noteworthy that the Pastoral Epistles could be regarded as a unity. "[T]he PE were opened and read as a collection in the second century, and perhaps even in the first (regardless of whether the letters had also an individual pre-existence)."[1] The original order of the Pastorals should be understood as Titus, followed by 1 Timothy and concluding with 2 Timothy. This arrangement explains the lengthy salutation in Titus 1.[2] This would also fit well into a pattern of understanding the Pastorals as a spiritual testament of Paul, in which 2 Tim 4 concludes Paul's testament and presents Paul as a type of leader to follow.[3] Some scholars view spiritual testaments as a genre.[4] The concept of a spiritual testament would also lend weight to the instructions of the Pastorals to the followers.[5] Questions regarding genre and pseudepigraphal authorship are essential for our understanding of dating the Pastorals. These questions will be further explored in this section.

---

[1] Quinn 1990, 8.
[2] See McKnight 2023, 10, Quinn 1990, 7, and compare with Dunn 2000, 776–77, for a short compilation on different views only up to 2000.
[3] Quinn 1990, 8–9.
[4] See Quinn 1990, 9.
[5] Quinn 1990, 8.

8.1 Authorship and Date of the Pastoral Epistles

Since the days of F. E. D. Schmidt (1805) and F. Schleiermacher (1807), questions have been raised about whether Paul was indeed the author of the Pastorals.[6] The letters vary in style; while the other letters bearing Paul's name mainly are situational, the Pastorals offer *general* advice to their leaders, Timothy and Titus.[7] The letters appear to fit well with other literary features that signifies pseudepigrapha.[8] While differences in style might be attributed to the broader approach, or perhaps the use of a secretary,[9] we need to understand the choices of otherwise unusual words for Paul, terms that can be found predominantly in texts after the New Testament, or in the period between the Hebrew Bible and the New Testament.[10] Hanson, in a reading from the mid-twentieth century, also points out that Paul condemns rather than argues against heresies in these letters, referring to an already "existing body of teaching."[11] Similarly, in discussing the law with Timothy, a close companion in his mission, the complexity of the law's role in salvation, as Paul elaborates in Romans and Galatians, is simplified in 1 Timothy 1:7–10. It seems strange that a beloved companion of Paul, well-versed in his thinking, would receive such a one-dimensional rendition of these intricate matters. The letters are composed to be read aloud, given certain stylistic features, and their endings suggest that they were intended for a congregation to hear. The lack of a wish for good health for the close companions Timothy and Titus in the greetings indicates that the letters were not meant to be personal, either.[12] Hanson, already in the mid-twentieth century, succinctly proposed three solutions to the discrepancies between the

---

[6] Knight 1992, 45 (ePub), claims genuine Pauline authorship because of the face value of the text.

[7] Hanson 1966, 1.

[8] Donelson 2006, 54–55.

[9] Although this is an explanation that still has some difficulties attached to it. Wild in the beginning of the 1990's pointed to the unlikeliness that the same secretary (since the style in the pastoral letters seems to stem from the same author) should have joined Paul during the two winters that the timeline in the pastorals supposes, and thus write the letters both in Ephesus and Rome. See Wild 1990, 891–92.

[10] Hanson 1966, 2.

[11] Hanson 1966, 3.

[12] Collins 2002, 7.

other Pauline epistles, and the Pastorals:[13] (1) The letters are of Pauline origin, yet Paul was elderly and composed them with the assistance of a secretary. (2) These letters were penned by a prominent leader in the early church, possibly up to half a century after Paul's death, or (3) the Pastorals represent a blend of Pauline fragments and later writings.

The first solution, that the letters are genuinely Pauline in origin, but Paul was old and writing with the assistance of some kind of secretary, has its merits. This would explain the biographical information provided in the Pastorals and also account for the fact that until modern times, the Pauline authorship of the Pastorals was not questioned.[14] Several scholars such as William Mounce,[15] Donald Guthrie,[16] and Luke Timothy Johnson[17] hold to this perspective. The church fathers' use of the books in this manner, as for instance Irenaeus employs the Pastorals in the preface to *Haer.*, 1, would support this view.[18] A recent defence against the notion that the ethical discourse in the Pastorals, particularly in Titus in this instance, is entirely distinct from the genuine epistles has been put forward by Jermo van Nes.[19] While the argument is compelling regarding the similarities between the authentic letters and Titus, it is still not conclusive, as van Nes rightly points out. This merely demonstrates similarities in ethical concerns and a stylistic feature (enthymemes) within the different text groups.[20]

The early reception of the Pastorals is, of course, significant for this perspective. The use of the Pastorals in other texts, alongside the dating of additional New Testament and ancient Christian writings, holds great importance.[21] For

---

[13] Mounce, for example, also comments on the three possible ways of understanding the authorship of the Pastorals, Mounce 2000, cxviii–cxxix. Guthrie 1990, 24–32 also discuss these options.

[14] Hanson 1966, 4–5, for a more recent version of this, see also McKnight 2023, 3–4.

[15] Mounce 2000, cxxix.

[16] Guthrie 1990, 23–34.

[17] Johnson 2001, 98–99.

[18] See also Dunn 2000 and McKnight 2023, 5.

[19] Van Nes 2022.

[20] Van Nes 2022, 123.

[21] See Collins 2002, 1–2, for a dense but pedagogical overview.

instance, in his dating of 1 Clement and Polycarp, Scot McKnight takes an early stance: he views these texts as having been written "around the turn of the century into the second century CE."[22] McKnight also understands these texts as dependent on the Pastorals, suggesting that there is a *terminus ante quem* for the Pastorals around 90–100 CE. Michael Theobald and several others agree that Polycarp knew of the Pastorals.[23] Theobald, however, dates Polycarp's letter to the Philippians to about half a century later and is convinced that the author of 1 Clement did not know the Pastorals.[24] Therefore, a crucial question is whether or not the author of 1 Clement was aware of the Pastorals. One can note that the passages McKnight refers to, 1 Clem. 2:7, 60:4, and 61:2, are quite general in their formulations, and there are other ways to explain these similarities than that these letters depend on the Pastorals. Even if common thoughts are expressed about good deeds and the rulership of God throughout the ages, the texts are by no means a conclusive or exclusive product of literary dependence on 1 Tim 1:17, 2:7, and Titus 3:1. There is thus no conclusive evidence for the reception of the Pastorals until Polycarp *To the Philippians*.

The second solution suggested by Hanson is that the letters were written by a prominent leader in the early church, possibly up to half a century after Paul's death. Hanson favours this thesis but points out that it is difficult to argue that late legends could account for all the biographical notices of Paul in the Pastorals.[25] In many ways, variants of this hypothesis have remained the most successful solutions in accounting for the evidence.[26]

What kind of literature the Pastoral epistles represent is at the core of the discussion. Some modern commentators are certain that they must be understood as forgeries intended to deceive. Mounce, whom I believe understands the genre of pseudepigrapha too narrowly, writes that especially 2 Timothy "is so replete with personal allusions that either they are true, or the author *intends* to deceive."[27] I believe this perspective is too closely tied to a modern

---

[22] McKnight 2023, 5.
[23] Theobald 2016, 326.
[24] Theobald 2016, 330–31.
[25] Hanson 1966, 5–6.
[26] See also Dibelius and Conzelmann 1972, 1–5.
[27] Mounce 2000, cxii.

understanding. Instead, the genre aligns well with the works of several ancient historians, creating a continuation of the narratives of a deceased hero. Mounce also acknowledges that such versions did exist in the ancient world, even if he dismisses the notion that it was practised in Christ groups.[28] Raymond Collins understands the biblical tradition as one that is rather accepting of pseudepigraphical writings, of which the Pastorals are an example.[29] Michaela Veit-Engelmann distinguishes between the pseudepigraphic authors of 1 Timothy and those of 2 Timothy and Titus. She points out that, if her distinction is correct, this would place 1 Timothy in the same category as the Psalms being associated with King David. At the same time, the other two letters would be more problematic as they are more elaborate in their allusions to Paul.[30] On the other hand, she recognises that the early Christ groups acknowledged the Pastorals as Scriptures and finds, therefore, the letters to be interesting windows into the lives of second or third-generation Christians.[31] According to Veit-Engelmann, the reason for assuming different authors of the texts in the Pastorals would be that the language differences between 1 Timothy on the one hand and Titus and 2 Timothy on the other are measurable.[32] Several motifs, such as soteriology and ecclesiology, appear to differ between the letters.[33] Veit-Engelmann suggests that the author of 1 Timothy was aware of the earlier letters, 2 Timothy and Titus, and drew upon themes from these letters, but faced a different pastoral situation to address.[34] The thesis is, however, sensitive to that the differences in motifs and semantics between the texts in the Pastorals, which Veit-Engelmann points out, also can be found between 1 Thessalonians and Philippians.[35] While Veit-Engelmann's perspective has merit in discussing the language and themes in depth, the fact that differences can be found between texts

---

[28] Mounce 2000, cxxiv.
[29] Collins 2002, 7–9.
[30] Veit-Engelmann 2022, 24–26.
[31] Veit-Engelmann 2022, 25–26.
[32] Engelmann 2012, 107–17.
[33] Engelmann 2012, 118–76.
[34] Veit-Engelmann 2022, 21–24. See also Engelmann 2012.
[35] Van Nes and Koning 2017.

does not prove that they were written by different authors. The similarities among the Pastorals are, after all, greater than the differences.

Johnson observes that the phenomenon of pseudepigraphical writings was prevalent within Jewish circles but discusses whether it would have been acceptable in the second century to utilise the relatively recent life of Paul as a tool in discussions regarding current internal conflicts within Christ groups.[36] The suggestion made by Theobald that the Pastorals were added to the *Corpus Paulinum* as a guide to interpretation in the later stages seems plausible. In this manner, the author could tackle several perceived threats to the Pauline Christ groups and establish a framework for the reading.[37] Theobald works from the assumption that the author tried to make the readers assume that Paul actually wrote the letters. This implies that the detailed use of personal notes and a personal tone indicates a deliberate intent to make readers perceive the texts as older than they were.[38] This is a consequence of Theobald's thesis on the *Israel-Vergessenheit*, "Israel oblivion," in later generations of Christ followers. It assumes that the Pastorals are receptions of Romans that would inspire a new, less Jewish version of Christ followership.[39] As will become evident when we examine the Ignatian corpus, an SIT analysis suggests that the author of the Pastorals is engaged in identity entrepreneurship: a prototypical leader offers a novel understanding of the ingroup identity, which many followers are compelled to adhere to due to Paul's historical significance. This perspective will be further elaborated below.

The third solution is that the Pastorals are a combination of Pauline fragments and later writings. An ancient leader of the early church compiled these Pauline fragments to address the pastoral problems of the early congregations. Since the Pastorals show similarities with other texts from the early second century, many of the discrepancies in style, wording, and theological language can be explained by this mixed hypothesis, along with the biographical notes

---

[36] Johnson 2001, 83–84.
[37] Theobald 2022, 164–66.
[38] Theobald 2013, 327.
[39] Theobald 2013, 410–12.

concerning Paul.[40] This would also explain how the early church, around 200 CE, accepted the letters as Paul's writings.[41] A critique of this view is that it is merely a new version of the second suggestion mentioned above, which offers few substantial merits in this more elaborated version.[42]

One can note that an important reason for the scepticism regarding genuine Pauline authorship is the presence of an explicit ecclesial order, albeit not as evolved as that found in the Ignatian letters written a few decades later (see below).[43] In the genuine Pauline epistles, there is (as discussed in chapter 5 above) only one mention of διάκονος or ἐπίσκοπος in the plural, in Phil 1:1, but several other instances of leadership titles. In Acts and the Pastorals, which are later texts authored by individuals other than Paul, the leadership structures appear to have evolved towards διάκονος and/or ἐπίσκοπος. However, one should keep in mind that the early church came to regard the Pastorals as Pauline, and that these texts "show how the Pauline churches perceived and evaluated their great founding apostle and the heritage he left with them."[44] It seems that the Pastorals, in their purpose, seek to uphold and legitimise the ecclesial authority structure.[45] The structure appears to be a means of preventing heresies from taking root in the communities of faith in Jesus Christ. For instance, Quinn summarises the data collected from the Pastoral epistles thus: "[The Pastorals] aim at providing continuity in the apostolic and ecclesial mission of bringing *all* persons, ... to faith in and worship of Jesus."[46] The evolving leadership structures addressed in the Pastorals aim to secure the missional work of the Pauline congregations. To some extent, this ideal will be further developed by the Ignatian corpus but is most prominently highlighted in Irenaeus's *Against Heresies*, book three. This viewpoint is not articulated in the authentic Pauline epistles.

---

[40] This seems to be what James Dunn calls "living tradition," Dunn 2000, 779–80. See also McKnight 2023, 3–4.

[41] Dunn 2000, 780. Mounce criticises this third view heavily since in his view it "answers none of the problems and introduces a new set of issues," Mounce 2000, cxxiii.

[42] Mounce 2000, cxxxiii; Dibelius and Conzelmann 1972, 5.

[43] Dunn 2000, 779; Dibelius and Conzelmann 1972, 5–7.

[44] Dunn 2000, 781.

[45] Wild 1990, 892; Dibelius and Conzelmann 1972, 5–7.

[46] Quinn 1990, 21.

Another reason to question the genuine authorship of Paul is the *Israel-Vergessenheit*, mentioned above.[47] Theobald, who coined the term, recognises that in later New Testament texts, the authors appear to forget, or at least be indifferent to, the role of Israel in salvation history. Paul's struggle with the history of Israel and Israel's role in the Hebrew Bible is entirely absent, particularly when we compare Rom 9–11 to, for instance, the Pastorals.[48] This is even more astonishing, as the Pastorals appear to follow a pattern from Romans. Clearly, the author of the Pastorals had Romans (in a shorter version, according to Theobald) in mind when writing.[49] The theological themes of Romans resurface constantly throughout the Pastorals, while leaving out the main themes of Rom 9–11.[50]

A further reason to suggest a later dating of the Pastorals is the challenge of situating the composition of the Pastorals within the context of historical events in Paul's life. The description in Acts that Paul was free from his initial imprisonment suggests the idea that he subsequently embarked on further missionary journeys, including to Spain.[51] The actual evidence for this is lacking, and even if the idea of subsequent travels by Paul has been presented in different versions, it relies heavily on conjecture.[52] Acts, the genuine epistles, and the Pastorals contain different versions of Paul's itinerary.[53]

After considering this discussion, I assume that the Pastoral Epistles should be regarded as pseudepigrapha, authored by an early second-century Christian group leader. This interpretation best accounts for the sources and their relationship. The letters must be placed earlier than Polycarp's *To the Philippians*, due to literary dependence, but not necessarily earlier than 1 Clement. The perspective on a growing episcopal office is, as far as the data allows, less developed than in Ignatius. Furthermore, following Theobald, the oblivion of Israel suggests that relatively few Jews would have been members of the group being

---

[47] For a fuller argument, see Theobald 2013, 317.
[48] See also Theobald 2016.
[49] Theobald 2013, 369.
[50] See table in Theobald 2013, 370.
[51] Theobald 2013, 319.
[52] Theobald 2013, 322.
[53] Theobald 2013, 320–23.

addressed. This leads me to posit a date around 120–125 CE. We now turn to an SIT analysis of the Pastoral's view of the ἐπίσκοπος.

8.2 Identity Impresarioship and Entrepreneurship in the Congregational Order

As discussed above regarding the dating of the letter, the author of the Pastoral epistles suggests an ingroup identity aligned with Paul and his mission. This construction of identity represents an act of identity impresarioship and entrepreneurship.

Regarding impresarioship, the author links the ἐπίσκοπος with Paul the apostle, a central figure in the Christ groups, whose mission in the north-eastern quadrant of the Mediterranean world opened Christ groups to non-Jews as well. The mission of Paul is understood as the continuing mission of Jesus Christ (1 Tim 1:1) and is thus a significant structure for ingroup identity. The message of the Pastorals (for example Tim 1:1, 2 Tim 1:6–13, Titus 1:5–9) is that the mission of Paul is still possible to participate in when members lead their lives according to the guidelines found in the Pastorals. These SIT features in the Pastorals are evident in the following ways.

In relation to entrepreneurship, a leader's ability to modify ingroup prototypicality, the ethos of Paul the apostle is utilised when the author advocates for a specific kind of Christian identity. The prototypical Paul, who paid the ultimate price for the ingroup values, thus emerges as the most representative member imaginable, opting for a congregational order. The author expects that members align their lives with the ideals presented as representative of the congregational order. Other ways of being a Christian, as warned against by the author in 1 Tim 1:3–7, are consequently not aligned with Paul's expressed will. Here, alternative visions of ingroup identity are excluded.

8.2.1 The Mission of Timothy and Titus – Identity Impresarioship

In 1 Tim 1:3 and Titus 1:5, the author recapitulates the mission statements of Timothy and Titus. Titus should "appoint elders in every city" (καταστήσης κατὰ πόλιν πρεσβυτέρους), while Timothy should prevent false teachings in Ephesus. The method for achieving this is reflected in the congregational order proposed by the author. The inception of this order then generates essential impulses for group members. This authority of Paul is said to have been passed on to Timothy (and likely Titus), and from Timothy (and likely Titus) to whomever they choose, through the laying on of hands (διὰ τῆς ἐπιθέσεως τῶν χειρῶν μου).[54] The recapitulative narratives, such as 1 Tim 1:12–17, situate the congregational order within the grand narrative of Paul's mission and his experience of mercy. Paul's commands, the appointment of elders, and the emphasis on preventing false teachings suggest that participation in these structures will safeguard the members from falling short of God's redemptive actions. Therefore, it is essential for everyone who wishes to partake in the mercy of which Paul speaks to also be a member of the group. Furthermore, other ways of being Christian are seen as dangerous, particularly when linked to the empty talk and ancient myths in 1 Tim 1:4–6. The ingroup identity is portrayed as being closely tied to the order proposed by the author. Thus, the author acts as an identity impresario, embedding significant ingroup traits (the continuation of the apostolic ministry) into the leadership structure.

8.2.2 The Teaching ἐπίσκοπος – Identity Entrepreneurship

Throughout the Pastoral Epistles, there is a notable emphasis on correct teaching. Timothy and Titus are instructed to teach sound doctrine.[55] It appears that the content of this sound teaching encompasses, in part, traditions regarding Christ and his death and resurrection, as well as the meaning of baptism and the outpouring of the Spirit.[56] Further, there are exhortations concerning congregational order: an ordered congregational life,[57] leadership succession,[58] and liturgy/worship (1 Tim 2:8). As becomes abundantly clear, the πρεσβύτερος and the ἐπίσκοπος are associated with a continuing role of teaching, taken over from

---

[54] 2 Tim 1:6; 1 Tim 5:22; Titus 1:5.

[55] See for example 1 Tim 1:5; 3:16; 4:6; 4:11; 4:13; 4:16; 5:1; 5:7; 5:17; 6:2; 6:17–18; 2 Tim 2:15–19; 3:10; 3:14–17; 4:2–5; Titus 1:12; 2:1; 2:6–8; 2:15; 3:1; 3:8.

[56] 1 Tim 2:5–7; 3:14–16; Titus 2:14; 3:4–8, and so forth.

[57] 1 Tim 2:9–15; 3:1–13; 5:3–16.

[58] 1 Tim 4:13–14 suggests that the authority conferred upon leaders was not related to their age but to the laying on of hands. See also 1 Tim 5:22; 2 Tim 1:6.

Paul.[59] The titles appear as interchangeable in the Pastorals, a point noted in the extensive research history of Christian offices discussed in chapter 3 above. The potential difference between the πρεσβύτερος and the ἐπίσκοπος as teachers is hard to extract from the texts and would be a field of interesting further analysis if possible. In 1 Tim 3:2 and Titus 1:9, when the responsibilities for the ἐπίσκοπος are spelled out, good teaching skills are understood as necessary. The Pastorals' author provides, however, a repeated and coherent vision for the role of the ἐπίσκοπος that include teaching duties.

It appears, in any case, that the author has a relatively clear view of what teaching should be taught in the congregations, a view that becomes evident in the context of the general emphasis on teaching within the Pastorals: the traditions aligned with the author's recapitulation throughout the letters.

The inherent teaching aspect of the role of the ἐπίσκοπος, however, is worth noting, particularly so when applying an SIT perspective on the Pastorals. Similarly, from a parting of the ways perspective, it implies that local leaders, deemed prototypical, are given a mandate to continuously envision and reenact the ingroup identity in the life of the congregation. The author grants the ἐπίσκοπος, as a form of safeguard for the tradition (Titus 1:9), the authority to renegotiate ingroup identity, provided he is aligned with "sound teaching" and leads a prototypical life. The clear ideals posited for the ἐπίσκοπος signal the author's expectation for the ἐπίσκοπος to unite words and actions. Since the content of the teaching is oblivious to Israel and a salient Jewish identity, the course suggested by the author directs the groups of the Pastorals on a heading where the rift from a Jewish identity is constantly widening.[60] This is particularly true, as the view of ὁ νόμος in 1 Timothy 1:8–11 is predominantly regarded as significant when it is understood in conjunction with the sound teachings defined by the author.[61]

In the author's vision, the ἐπίσκοπος effectively serves as an entrepreneur of identity, as he is endowed with the authority to alter the prototypicality (and perhaps therefore also the identity) of the Christ group addressed by the

---

[59] 1 Tim 3:2, 5:17; Titus 1:5.
[60] Theobald 2016, 61–115.
[61] Cf. Mounce 2000, 33; Theobald 2016, 82; Johnson 2001, 167–68.

author. This holds, provided the ἐπίσκοπος embodies the prototypical traits expected of him. These traits, which portray ingroup prototypicality, also distinguish the group from others. We now turn to this uniquely Christian prototypicality.

8.3 Prototypicality in the Pastorals

A significant aspect of SIT, as I summarised in chapter 2, is that effective group leaders excel at embodying the ideals of the group. This ability is essential for the leader to cultivate followership within the group. The more a group leader personifies the group norms, the more likely they are to achieve success in terms of followers. In the Pastoral Epistles, we find clear illustrations of ethical standards in two instances, 1 Tim 3:1–7 and Titus 1:5–9 that correspond with the role of the ἐπίσκοπος.

1 Tim 3:1–7	Titus 1:5–9
πιστὸς ὁ λόγος. Εἴ τις ἐπισκοπῆς ὀρέγεται, καλοῦ ἔργου ἐπιθυμεῖ. δεῖ οὖν τὸν ἐπίσκοπον ἀνεπίλημπτον εἶναι, μιᾶς γυναικὸς ἄνδρα, νηφάλιον σώφρονα κόσμιον φιλόξενον διδακτικόν, μὴ πάροινον μὴ πλήκτην, ἀλλὰ ἐπιεικῆ ἄμαχον ἀφιλάργυρον, τοῦ ἰδίου οἴκου καλῶς προϊστάμενον, τέκνα ἔχοντα ἐν ὑποταγῇ, μετὰ πάσης σεμνότητος (εἰ δέ τις τοῦ ἰδίου οἴκου προστῆναι οὐκ οἶδεν, πῶς ἐκκλησίας θεοῦ ἐπιμελήσεται;), μὴ νεόφυτον, ἵνα μὴ τυφωθεὶς εἰς κρίμα ἐμπέσῃ τοῦ διαβόλου. δεῖ δὲ καὶ μαρτυρίαν καλὴν ἔχειν ἀπὸ τῶν ἔξωθεν, ἵνα μὴ εἰς ὀνειδισμὸν ἐμπέσῃ καὶ παγίδα τοῦ διαβόλου.	Τούτου χάριν ἀπέλιπόν σε ἐν Κρήτῃ ἵνα τὰ λείποντα ἐπιδιορθώσῃ, καὶ καταστήσῃς κατὰ πόλιν πρεσβυτέρους, ὡς ἐγώ σοι διεταξάμην, εἴ τίς ἐστιν ἀνέγκλητος, μιᾶς γυναικὸς ἀνήρ, τέκνα ἔχων πιστά, μὴ ἐν κατηγορίᾳ ἀσωτίας ἢ ἀνυπότακτα. δεῖ γὰρ τὸν ἐπίσκοπον ἀνέγκλητον εἶναι ὡς θεοῦ οἰκονόμον, μὴ αὐθάδη, μὴ ὀργίλον, μὴ πάροινον, μὴ πλήκτην, μὴ αἰσχροκερδῆ, ἀλλὰ φιλόξενον, φιλάγαθον, σώφρονα, δίκαιον, ὅσιον, ἐγκρατῆ, ἀντεχόμενον τοῦ κατὰ τὴν διδαχὴν πιστοῦ λόγου, ἵνα δυνατὸς ᾖ καὶ παρακαλεῖν ἐν τῇ διδασκαλίᾳ τῇ ὑγιαινούσῃ καὶ τοὺς ἀντιλέγοντας ἐλέγχειν.
The saying is sure: whoever aspires to the office of bishop desires a noble task. Now a bishop must be above reproach, married only once, temperate, self-controlled, respectable, hospitable, an apt teacher, not a drunkard, not violent but gentle, not quarrelsome, and not a lover of money. He must manage his	I left you behind in Crete for this reason, so that you should put in order what remained to be done and should appoint elders in every town, as I directed you: someone who is blameless, married only once, whose children are believers, not accused of debauchery and not rebellious. For a bishop, as God's

own household well, keeping his children submissive and respectful in every way, for if someone does not know how to manage his own household, how can he take care of God's church? He must not be a recent convert, or he may be puffed up with conceit and fall into the condemnation of the devil. Moreover, he must be well thought of by outsiders, so that he may not fall into disgrace and the snare of the devil. (NRSV)

steward, must be blameless; he must not be arrogant or quick-tempered or addicted to wine or violent or greedy for gain, but he must be hospitable, a lover of goodness, self-controlled, upright, devout, and restrained, holding tightly to the trustworthy word of the teaching, so that he may be able both to exhort with sound instruction and to refute those who contradict it. (NRSV)

Table 8.3. *Prototypical traits for an ἐπίσκοπος in the Pastoral Epistles.*

In addition to the ability to teach, addressed differently in the two texts (διδακτικόν in 1 Timothy, ἀντεχόμενον τοῦ κατὰ τὴν διδαχὴν πιστοῦ λόγου, ἵνα δυνατὸς ᾖ καὶ παρακαλεῖν ἐν τῇ διδασκαλίᾳ τῇ ὑγιαινούσῃ καὶ τοὺς ἀντιλέγοντας ἐλέγχειν in Titus), the lists fundamentally reflect the need for the ἐπίσκοπος to adhere to the norms that *every member of a Christian group should follow*; to be ἀνεπίλημπτον, irreproachable,[62] is indeed a high standard, but is not particularly distinct from, for instance, the list of the fruits of the Spirit in Gal 5:22–24, or, for that matter, the teachings of the Sermon on the Mount.[63] Therefore, it is reasonable to assume that the virtue lists of the ἐπίσκοπος is essentially a prototypical follower of Jesus. This also explains why the list for the διάκονοι in 1 Tim 3:8–10 is not particularly different from the list of the ἐπίσκοπος. It merely indicates a requirement for the group leaders to embody the Christ-group norms. But where exactly do these ideals originate? What is the unique aspect of the Christ-group norms? Could there possibly be other groups adhering to similar ideals? As we shall see, several scholars identify a Hellenistic moral vision in these ethical lists. This is not, in itself, anything new, even if it has been perceived as such: in 1932, Burton Scott Easton noted that the lists of virtues as a literary form are absent from the tradition of the Hebrew Bible; "Hebrew authors generally prefer to depict the goodness of a man by concrete instances

---

[62] BDAG, s.v. ἀνεπίλημπτον.
[63] Cf. Matt 5:48.

rather than by cataloguing his benevolent qualities."[64] He further notes that "just about half of the terms in the lists above [New Testament virtue lists such as Gal 5:22–24 and the lists in the Pastoral letters] are practically absent from the Biblical vocabulary of Hellenistic Judaism."[65] This would imply a unique feature of the Christ groups in comparison to prominent Jewish groups. On the other hand, several cardinal virtues are present in 4 Maccabees and the Wisdom of Solomon (see below). Thus, the ethical standards found in the Pastorals have counterparts in relatively contemporary Hellenistic Judaism, even if the precise structure of a virtue list is not identical to that in the Pastorals.

The presence of lists in the Hellenistic world that describe similar virtues suggests that the moral expectations of the Christ-group leaders align with those of other groups in the Hellenistic world. Therefore, this implies that the ideal member of a Christ-following group is not vastly different from their Hellenistic counterparts. The prevailing view on the virtue lists in the Pastoral Epistles is that they reflect a literary form that endorses common Hellenistic morals ground.[66] Much of the content is already familiar from several other ancient authors. Most recently, Theobald notes that the philosopher Celsus believes the Christians have simply misunderstood Plato and dismisses them as old news ethically.[67] Essentially, the ethical lists in the Pastorals are receptions of the Stoic cardinal virtues.[68] According to Theobald, this is a result of an emerging need from the Christian ἐκκλησία to demonstrate its decency to outsiders. While the first generation focused on discussing ethics within its own walls, subsequent early generations displayed an increasing concern for the relationship with outsiders. This, according to Theobald, can be traced in the lists of episcopal traits presented in this chapter discusses.[69] The desired qualities for the ἐπίσκοπος begin within the inner circle of the household. This implies that the ἐπίσκοπος functions as a *paterfamilias*, who also had semi-official

---

[64] Easton 1932, 10.

[65] Easton 1932, 10.

[66] See Dibelius and Conzelmann 1972, 50–51; Towner 2006, 352 (ePub version); Mounce 2000, 160–67.

[67] Theobald 2022, 176–77.

[68] Theobald 2022, 175.

[69] Theobald 2022, 168–75.

and official roles in various spheres of ancient Greco-Roman society. Consequently, this ethical focus of the inner circle expands to encompass the broader Greco-Roman society during the second century.[70] There would thus be incitements for the Christ movement to develop a Hellenized moral code.

Further, turning to the moral vision of Hellenistic authors contemporary to the Pastorals, there are examples of Hellenistic virtue lists that in both lexicographic as well as general content show striking similarities to the lists in the Pastoral epistles. Such lists seem to have been a Hellenistic way of describing virtue.[71] However, there are also some virtue lists from Jewish groups roughly contemporary to the Pastoral Epistles that bear similarities to the characteristics of the ideal Christ-group member in the Pastoral Epistles. Is it possible, then, to demonstrate that the Pastorals' ideals possess any distinctive features for Christ followers?

In the following, I will compare the lists from the Pastoral Epistles with existing lists from various schools of thought that were roughly contemporary with the Pastoral Epistles. As can be observed, the Pastoral Epistles reflect ideals from both Jewish and Hellenistic traditions, *while also containing some distinctive features for Christian groups*. These distinctive features demonstrate that the emerging episcopal structure offered a unique ideal that was indeed distinct from the surrounding world. I will analyse several points where ethical ideals become prominent in the culture contemporary with the Pastorals: the Stoic cardinal virtues (including their reception by Plutarch and Diogenes Laertius), Onosander's expectations of a στρατηγός, the ideal individual according to the Jewish writings Wisdom of Solomon and 4 Maccabees, and lastly, the ideals presented by 1QS from the Qumran library. Following this, some conclusions regarding the ideals in the Pastoral epistles can be drawn, relating to the ethical standards of the Christ-group prototypicality.

---

[70] Theobald 2022, 173–75.
[71] Dibelius and Conzelmann 1972, 50–51.

8.3.1 Stoic Versions of Hellenistic Cardinal Virtue and the Pastorals

Plutarch (ca 46–120 CE) offers one interpretation of the Stoic cardinal virtues, presented as a list, which allows us to examine the Stoic prototypicality in relation to the Christ-group prototypicality.

ἐπιφέρει κατὰ λέξιν ἡ δ' ἰσχὺς αὕτη καὶ τὸ κράτος, ὅταν μὲν ἐν τοῖς φανεῖσιν ἐμμενετέοις ἐγγένηται, ἐγκράτειά ἐστιν, ὅταν δ' ἐν τοῖς ὑπομενετέοις, ἀνδρεία· περὶ τὰς ἀξίας δὲ δικαιοσύνη περὶ δὲ τὰς αἱρέσεις καὶ ἐκκλίσεις σωφροσύνη.

> Then he continues in these exact words: 'This strength and might, when it arises in the sphere where persistence is manifestly called for, is control; in the sphere where endurance is called for, courage; concerning what is merited, justice; concerning choices and avoidances, moderation.' Plutarch *Stoic. Rep.* 1034 d–e.[72]

In Stoic philosophy, there was a continuous debate regarding the reception of Platonic and Socratic virtue. The virtues transmitted by Plato, which were received and refined through Stoic discourse, have served as a set of moral standards since the fourth century BCE. When comparing different accounts of the cardinal virtues, it is evident that there were varying understandings of which four virtues were identified.[73] The main debate centred on whether one should understand σοφία or φρόνησις as the source of all other virtues, as some Stoic philosophers, including Plutarch (as previously quoted) and Aristo of Chios,

---

[72] Translation by Schofield 2013, 17–18.

[73] For an excellent review on this matter, see Schofield 2013, 12–22. In Cicero, *De Officiis*, a lengthier definition of each virtue follows: *Formam quidem ipsam, Marce fili, et tamquam faciem honesti vides, "quae si oculis cerneretur, mirabiles amores," ut ait Plato, "excitaret sapientiae." Sed omne, quod est honestum, id quattuor partium oritur ex aliqua: aut enim in perspicientia veri sollertiaque versatur aut in hominum societate tuenda tribuendoque suum cuique et rerum contractarum fide aut in animi excelsi atque invicti magnitudine ac robore aut in omnium, quae fiunt quaeque dicuntur, ordine et modo, in quo inest modestia et temperantia.* "You see here, Marcus, my son, the very form and as it were the face of Moral Goodness; 'and if,' as Plato says, 'it could be seen with the physical eye, it would awaken a marvellous love of wisdom.' But all that is morally right rises from some one of four sources: it is concerned either (1) with the full perception and intelligent development of the true; or (2) with the conservation of organized society, with rendering to every man his due, and with the faithful discharge of obligations assumed ; or (3) with the greatness and strength of a noble and invincible spirit; or (4) with the orderliness and moderation of everything that is said and done, wherein consist temperance and self-control." Cicero, *De Officiis* 1.15, translation Miller 1913, 16–17. . .

argued, or if one should not.⁷⁴ In the course of examining φρόνησις within a debate regarding Stoic philosophy, Plutarch observes that Zeno's successor Cleanthes (ca. 330–230 BCE) opts for ἐγκράτεια ("self-control") instead of φρόνησιν.⁷⁵ Malcolm Schofield suggests that there appear to have been various receptions of the virtues, and the form employed by Plutarch when discussing Cleanthes reflects the reception of Antisthenes Xenophon.⁷⁶ This becomes clear as Plutarch holds a general understanding of virtue as "strength."⁷⁷ Titus employs three of the four cardinal virtues, whereas 1 Timothy includes only one of Plutarch's virtues; the vocabulary of Titus lacks ἀνδρεῖος from the viewpoint of Stoic virtue. It remains unclear why one list of virtues from the same author, pertaining to the same role, diverges from the other in relation to Stoic virtue. The most common reception of the four virtues, which follows Plutarch and Diogenes Laertius's *Lives of Eminent Philosophers*, book seven, is to name them as follows: φρόνησις, ἀνδρεία, δικαιοσύνη, and σωφροσύνη. They are commonly translated as wisdom, courage, justice, and moderation.⁷⁸ The lists for the prototypical ἐπίσκοπος in the Pastoral Epistles were clearly influenced by these four cardinal virtues that Stoic thinkers utilised as moral principles for guidance.⁷⁹ The account from Diogenes reads as follows:

> Τῶν δ' ἀρετῶν τὰς μὲν πρώτας, τὰς δὲ ταύταις ὑποτεταγμένας. πρώτας μὲν τάσδε, φρόνησιν, ἀνδρείαν, δικαιοσύνην, σωφροσύνην ....
>
> Some virtues are primary, some subordinate to those. The primary are these: intelligence, courage, justice, and moderation.⁸⁰

The intention behind the lists in the Pastorals is clearly to present an ideal for leadership within the Christ group that embodies the group's values. The appropriate individual to become an ἐπίσκοπος was to no small extent also

---

⁷⁴ Schofield 2013, 12–13.
⁷⁵ Cf BDAG, s. v. ἐγκράτεια
⁷⁶ Schofield 2013, 18–19.
⁷⁷ Schofield 2013, 18–19, White 2020, 232, provides a translation of Diogenes Laertius, *Lives* 6:11 ("Socratic strength" Σωκρατικῆς ἰσχύος).
⁷⁸ Schofield 2013, 12.
⁷⁹ Towner 2006, 312 (ePub).
⁸⁰ Diogenes Laertius, *Lives* 7:92, trans. White 2020, 294.

virtuous according to widely accepted Stoic ideals.[81] This is likely related to the need for a good reputation among outsiders.

It is worth noting that Diogenes Laertius wrote somewhat later than the Pastoral epistles – between 190 and 230 CE.[82] He is, however, citing Stoic philosophers and thereby providing a window into earlier Stoic sources. Diogenes is generally understood to be important source material, with a reasonable provenance.[83] In the sections of our interest from Book Seven, he discusses the practices and teachings of Zenon and other Stoic authors. Of course, the connection we can discern between the Pastoral Epistles and Diogenes is that they share similar ideals, but not a common source.

From the lengthy account in Diogenes, several comparable points can be drawn between the virtue lists of the Pastorals and the views of the Stoics.[84] In the areas concerning family, wine consumption, manners, and relationships with the divine, there is clearly a common ideal reflected in both the Pastorals and Diogenes. The list in Titus 1, more prominently than that in 1 Tim 3, echoes the ideals of the Stoic authors. The necessity to lead a quiet family life and to exhibit piety, as well as moderation in wine consumption and behaviour, is encouraged in all three texts. The texts present an ideal for prominent men as wise, temperate, just, somewhat family-oriented, and pious. Titus, both in this context and in its relationship to Plutarch, is the text from the Pastoral Epistles most closely aligned with Diogenes.

While these parallels exist, there are also some notable differences. For instance, Diogenes argues that a person in slavery is, by definition, living in a form of foolishness. This notion has no equivalent in the Pastoral Epistles.

---

[81] As noted by Mounce 2000, 160.

[82] For a detailed discussion on the date, see White 2020, 2–8.

[83] As seen in Sellars 2006, 191–94, Diogenes's accounts have had a prominent role as a source concerning Stoicism. Sellars comments, "Diogenes' account of the Stoics draws upon an earlier source whom he names: Diocles of Magnesia. Diocles has been dated to the first century BCE, although this date may well be as uncertain as the date for Diogenes." 24.

[84] Cf. Bernard 1899, 57.

> μόνον τ' ἐλεύθερον, τοὺς δὲ φαύλους δούλους· εἶναι γὰρ τὴν ἐλευθερίαν ἐξουσίαν αὐτοπραγίας, τὴν δὲ δουλείαν στέρησιν αὐτοπραγίας. εἶναι δὲ καὶ ἄλλην δουλείαν τὴν ἐν ὑποτάξει καὶ τρίτην τὴν ἐν κτήσει τε καὶ ὑποτάξει, ᾗ ἀντιτίθεται ἡ δεσποτεία, φαύλη οὖσα καὶ αὕτη.

> Only he is free, and the foolish are slaves; for freedom is being entitled to act on your own, and slavery is being deprived of acting on your own. There is also another kind of slavery based on subordination, and a third based on ownership and subordination, and opposite to mastery, which is also something foolish. (7:121–122)

First Timothy 6:1–2, which is not part of the letter's virtue list but is related to the topic of behaviour within a congregation, discusses the role of slaves briefly. In this context, slaves and masters are regarded as family members within the household of God, with the slaves, rather than the masters, being the ones addressed as accountable for their own actions. Conversely, the slaves are urged to act in accordance with their status and in submission to their masters. The author of the Pastorals seems, as Theobald points out, to reject any form of rebellious behaviour, ensuring that the testimony remains acceptable to outsiders.[85] Regarding the ἐπίσκοπος, nothing is said explicitly about slavery. However, the requirement for the ἐπίσκοπος to manage his own household (1 Tim 3:4) may also likely pertain to slave ownership.

One other topic that explicitly differentiates a σοφός, according to Diogenes, from the ἐπίσκοπος of the Pastorals, is the need for public approval:

> ἄτυφόν τ' εἶναι τὸν σοφόν· ἴσως γὰρ ἔχειν πρός τε τὸ ἔνδοξον καὶ τὸ ἄδοξον.

> The wise man also has no presumption, for he is indifferent to public approval and disapproval (*Lives* 7:117)

The Stoic ideal of indifference is considerably more apparent in the records of Diogenes, whereas the Pastorals place a fair amount of emphasis on the approval of outsiders.

In conclusion, Titus and 1 Timothy use different names for the virtues. The formulations in Titus are closer to those of Diogenes and Plutarch. The virtue lists in the Pastorals demonstrate a general alignment with a Stoic ideal, as seen in the important works of Diogenes and Plutarch, and there are various points where the ideals from these sources overlap with those in the Pastorals. The

---

[85] Theobald 2022, 172.

Stoic texts we have briefly examined suggest that the Pastorals represent Christian receptions of the Stoic cardinal virtues, reflecting an interest likely held by the Christ groups to be acceptable to outsiders. While several aspects, apart from the cardinal virtues, are similar to the Stoic sources (such as the relationship to family, wine, manners, and the divine), there are also notable differences (specifically regarding views on slavery and public approval). This indicates that many ideals are comparable, and that Diogenes and the author of the Pastoral letters appear to have somewhat similar (though not identical) reference points regarding virtue. Conversely, the author of the Pastorals did not anticipate a purely Stoic morality, unlike a version of Stoic ideals as conveyed through Diogenes. The divergence between the two sets of virtue lists for the ἐπίσκοπος suggests that the ideals in the Christ groups were also broader than those of the Stoics' wise man. Additionally, the author maintains a different perspective on slavery (as later mentioned in 1 Tim 6) and public approval. The Christ groups reflected in the Pastorals held ideals that were not entirely the same as those of the Stoics, despite a significant overlap. Instead, they aimed to establish a morality that demonstrated their acceptability to outsiders (in alignment with Theobald), while also being distinct enough to ensure the group's prototypicality would stand out in contrast to other groups.

8.3.2 Onosander

After this review of Stoic virtues, we now turn to another list that provides an ideal for a professional στρατήγος (military general). This list is provided by the first-century Stoic philosopher Onosander, whose main surviving work was the book Στρατηγικός, dedicated to the general Quintus Veranius. The book is interesting in this context, as it is the only extant list serving as a point of reference between a Hellenistic professional leader and a (semi-)professional Christ-group leader. Several commentators have noted the resemblance between the lists in 1 Timothy and Titus, on the one hand, and Onosander's list of expectations for a military general on the other.[86] Compared to the texts from 1 Timothy and Titus, there are several reference points:

---

[86] First noted by Dibelius 1912, 100.

Φημὶ τοίνυν αἱρεῖσθαι τὸν στρατηγὸν οὐ κατὰ γένη κρίνοντας, ὥσπερ τοὺς ἱερέας, οὐδὲ κατ' οὐσίας, ὡς τοὺς γυμνασιάρχους, ἀλλὰ σώφρονα, ἐγκρατῆ, νήπτην, λιτόν, διάπονον, νοερόν, ἀφιλάργυρον, μήτε νέον μήτε πρεσβύτερον, ἂν τύχῃ καὶ πατέρα παίδων, ἱκανὸν λέγειν, ἔνδοξον.

I believe, then, that we must choose a general, not because of noble birth as priests are chosen, nor because of wealth as the superintendents of the gymnasia, but because he is temperate, self-restrained, vigilant, frugal, hardened to labour, alert, free from avarice, neither too young nor too old, indeed a father of children if possible, a ready speaker, and a man with a good reputation.[87]

We can observe that ἀφιλάργυρον appears in 1 Timothy and Onosander, while Titus employs a negation of αἰσχροκερδῆ ("greediness"). The theme of self-restraint is present in all texts (ἐγκρατῆ, νηφάλιον σώφρον), along with various positive traits related to ethical integrity (1 Timothy: μὴ πάροινον μὴ πλήκτην, ἀλλὰ ἐπιεικῆ ἄμαχον ἀφιλάργυρον; Titus: φιλόξενον, φιλάγαθον, σώφρονα, δίκαιον, ὅσιον, ἐγκρατῆ; Onosander: νήπτην, λιτόν, διάπονον, νοερόν). Notably, 1 Timothy and Titus stress that the ἐπίσκοπος must not be violent (πλήκτης). While the military general may not have engaged in violence himself, it was certainly a part of his role to at least direct or threaten such actions. The idea that a leader should be a competent teacher or speaker is reflected in each text. Both themes relating to having a family and gaining respect from outsiders are evident across all texts. One can observe that in 1 Timothy, both the need to be κόσμιον ("well behaved, respectable") and the assertion that the leader must have a good reputation among outsiders (δεῖ δὲ καὶ μαρτυρίαν καλὴν ἔχειν ἀπὸ τῶν ἔξωθεν, ἵνα μὴ εἰς ὀνειδισμὸν ἐμπέσῃ καὶ παγίδα τοῦ διαβόλου) imply that the author of 1 Timothy was more concerned with how the leader was perceived by outsiders than Onosander, who seems content to expect that the στρατηγός should be ἔνδοξος. Additionally, something is mentioned regarding age or, even better, maturity; the idea in Onosander that the general should be neither too young nor too old, μήτε νέον μήτε πρεσβύτερον, finds a counterpart in the notion that the ἐπίσκοπος ought not to be too recent in his faith; μὴ νεόφυτον, ἵνα μὴ τυφωθεὶς εἰς κρίμα ἐμπέσῃ τοῦ διαβόλου. The distinction between the texts is that in 1 Timothy and Titus, the expectation for the ἐπίσκοπος is to be μιᾶς

---

[87] Conzelmann and Dibelius 1972, 158.

γυναικὸς ἄνδρα. Themes regarding sexual behaviour recur frequently in the NT and Christ-group texts, in ways that, for example, Onosander lacks.

In conclusion, several themes are present across all texts. The similarities highlight commonalities in the moral expectations of leadership, indicating that embodying group ideals (prototypicality) also entails reflecting the ideals of the surrounding community, especially when compared to the expectations of a professional military general. The texts from Titus and 1 Timothy, however, stand out in the realms of marital relations and their explicitly cautious stance towards violence, presenting a somewhat deviant portrayal of the prototypical Christ-group member. These minor differences suggest that the Christ groups depicted in the texts endeavoured to balance a specific ingroup prototypicality that contrasted with outsiders. The topics of marital and sexual relations, along with violence, would not be particularly provocative for Hellenistic outsiders, even if they might seem a bit strange.

8.3.3 Wisdom of Solomon and 4 Maccabees

Following this exposition of virtue lists and wise man or leader ideals from the non-Jewish world, we now turn to comparable virtue lists from notably Jewish texts. Such lists, as previously mentioned, are absent from the Hebrew Bible. However, there are a few examples in the LXX: 4 Macc 1:6, 18; 2:21–23; 5:22–24; 15:10 and Wis 8:7, which demonstrate a clear influence from Stoic as well as general Hellenistic philosophical moral teachings, where the virtue of the wise mind is commended.[88] The primary distinction between the Hellenistic Jewish texts and the non-Jewish texts lies in the Jewish texts' understanding that σοφός/σοφία originates from the word of God. As we shall see, this specific speculation about wisdom is not explicitly pronounced in 1QS. The virtues in the Wisdom of Solomon and 4 Maccabees arise from keeping the commandments of the Torah. Thus, faithfulness to the ideals of a specific ingroup is central for the authors of 4 Maccabees and the Wisdom of Solomon, just as it is for the author of the Pastoral Epistles, albeit with a partially different set of ideals. The most discernible difference from the Pastoral Epistles is that the authors of 4 Maccabees and the Wisdom of Solomon adhere to different ideals considered

---

[88] Towner 2006, 312 (ePub).

essential for faithfulness, which will be demonstrated below. Central to 4 Maccabees and the Wisdom of Solomon is the commitment to being a faithful keeper of the Torah, thereby attaining wisdom.

The writings of 4 Maccabees and the Wisdom of Solomon are generally regarded as late and originating from a Hellenized Jewish context. Regarding the date of 4 Maccabees, DeSilva remarks soberly,

> Modern scholars agree that 4 Maccabees was composed sometime between the turn of the era and the early second century CE. For a work that is attached to no known author, connected with no known location, tied to no particular occasion, and devoid of references to contemporary events, one might look in vain for greater specificity than that.[89]

Despite this lack of author and circumstances, many scholars hold that the text was composed in Alexandria, perhaps at the turn of the era. The Wisdom of Solomon is also linked to Alexandria, composed between 24 BCE and 41 CE, that is "during or between the reigns of Augustus and Caligula [...] probably before the letter issued by Claudius in A.D. 41."[90]

A brief examination of texts from these books reveals a significant interest in the philosophical cardinal virtues. The instances of 4 Macc 1:6, 18; 2:21–23; 5:22–24; and 15:10 all discuss aspects of wisdom, viewed through the lens of the cardinal virtues φρόνησις (or σοφία), ἀνδρεία, δικαιοσύνη, and σωφροσύνη. Most instances, namely 1:6; 2:21–23; 5:22–24; and 15:10, lack φρόνησις/σοφία, likely because it was regarded as the fountainhead of virtues and was closely associated with the Torah. In the Wisdom of Solomon, all the cardinal virtues are present:

> καὶ εἰ δικαιοσύνην ἀγαπᾷ τις, οἱ πόνοι ταύτης εἰσὶν ἀρεταί· σωφροσύνην γὰρ καὶ φρόνησιν ἐκδιδάσκει, δικαιοσύνην καὶ ἀνδρείαν, ὧν χρησιμώτερον οὐδέν ἐστιν ἐν βίῳ ἀνθρώποις.

> And if anyone loves righteousness, her labors are virtues, for she teaches self-control and prudence, justice and courage; nothing in life is more profitable for mortals than these. (Wisdom of Solomon 8:7; NRSV)

These cardinal virtues clearly resonate with the Stoic ideals, which are also present in the works of Plutarch and Diogenes Laertius. Furthermore, as DeSilva points out concerning 4 Maccabees, the "author's definition of 'wisdom'

---

[89] From DeSilva 2006, XIV.
[90] Glicksman 2011, 14–24.

(σοφία) is taken directly from 'the Greco-Roman Dictionary of Philosophy'."[91] The descriptions of the wise man fit not only into a Stoic pattern but also within a general Hellenistic philosophical framework. In 4 Maccabees, the connection between the instruction from the Law (ἡ τοῦ νόμου παιδεία) and wisdom is equivalent (4 Macc 1:17). The beginning of the entire book serves as an exordium in which the author asserts a philosophical goal intertwined with piety.[92] The author of 4 Maccabees is, from an SIT perspective, providing prototypical leader figures through the legendary material of the seven Maccabean brothers.[93] Consequently, 4 Maccabees showcases prototypes to emulate while constructing a vision of what it means to be faithful to the Torah (identity entrepreneurship) through the narrative of the seven brothers who did not waver in their willingness to suffer for the ideals of their group (prototypical behaviour, costly displays; see chapter 2 above). In this manner, the Maccabean brothers embodied both Hellenistic wisdom ideals and faithfulness to the Torah simultaneously. Thus, the moral of 4 Maccabees is that wisdom arises from understanding the Law, which leads to a life of wisdom that is comparable to, or even superior to, the lives that Hellenistic philosophical schools aspired to. Being guided by the Law results in a life of virtue akin to Hellenistic ideals, and a devout life represents a pathway to virtue that is preferable to betraying one's commitment to the Torah. The aim of the descriptions of a wise life in 4 Maccabees could be characterised as a Jewish philosophical school.[94]

A similar idea is evident in Wis 8:7–8, which refers to the four cardinal virtues and also describes what constitutes a wise man, according to Sir 39:1–5.[95] As can be seen in the section from 38:31, the wise man is distinguished from manual labourers, and the opportunity to be wise arises from eager study ἐν

---

[91] Cf. DeSilva 2006, 85.

[92] φιλοσοφώτατο(ν) λόγον ἐπιδ[ε]ίκνυσθαι μέλλων, εἰ αὐτοδέσποτός ἐστιν τῶν παθῶ(ν) ὁ εὐσεβὴς λογισμός, συμβουλεύσαιμ' ἄ(ν) ὑμῖν ὀρθῶς ὅπως προσέχητε προθύμως τῇ φιλοσοφίᾳ. ("Since I am about to demonstrate a most philosophical statement – that pious reason is absolute master of the passions – I would rightly counsel you that you should pay close attention to this philosophical inquiry"). Ed. and trans. DeSilva 2006, 2–3.

[93] DeSilva 2006, xxviii–xxix.

[94] DeSilva 2006, 85.

[95] Hayman 2003, 37.

νόμῳ ὑψίστου and from the prophets (Sir 39:1). In Sirach, a slightly different conception of the wise man can be discerned – the four cardinal virtues are not explicitly mentioned. Instead, Sirach appears to suggest that the wise man operates within the administration of rulers (Sir 39:3–4). This ideal is also found in other Hebrew Bible texts, such as Prov 1. The portrayal in Wisdom of Solomon represents a more Hellenised version of the wise man than that presented in Sirach. Wisdom of Solomon depicts a wise man in terms similar to those of the Greek philosophical schools. Thus, from an SIT perspective, the wise man embodies the virtues of Greek philosophy as well as those of the Torah; a wise man according to Wisdom of Solomon is recognisable as wise through his actions (in which the Greek cardinal virtues are identifiable), and the wisdom of which the wise man partakes is a personified radiance of God (illustrated as God's feminine counterpart).[96] The wise man is presenting the ideal of the Hellenized Jewish communities, to be able to be a part of the surrounding communities, and at the same time be understood as faithful to the ancestral faith.

To conclude: The relationship between the ideal wise man as depicted in the Wisdom of Solomon and 4 Maccabees, and the ἐπίσκοπος of the Pastorals, is fundamentally rooted in the shared Hellenistic wisdom ideal. This ideal manifests in both the Pastorals (to a lesser extent) and in the Wisdom of Solomon and 4 Maccabees (to a greater extent). The author of the Pastorals never explicitly discusses wisdom as a theological source, particularly not as wisdom that partakes in the λόγος. Instead, the author condemns overly vivid speculation arising from Jewish thought (1 Tim 1:3–5) and piety linked to Torah observance (1 Tim 1:8–11). The similarities identified (as shown above) between the Hellenistic ideal and the Wisdom of Solomon/4 Maccabees, on one hand, and the Pastoral epistles, on the other, indicate a shared cultural sphere. While Wisdom of Solomon and 4 Maccabees assert that piety and adherence to the Torah lead to philosophical virtue, the author of the Pastorals expects the ἐπίσκοπος to be a noticeably pious individual, yet without any reference to the Torah. Instead, the author of the Pastoral epistles suggests an identity that differs slightly from both the wise man of the philosophers and the pious wise man of the Wisdom of Solomon and 4 Maccabees. According to the author of the Pastorals, Torah

---

[96] Hayman 2003, 36–37.

observance is not something in which a prototypical member of the Christian group should engage (1 Tim 1:8). This will be further discussed below. Nevertheless, the clearly discernible points of reference between 4 Maccabees, the Wisdom of Solomon, and the Pastoral Epistles demonstrate that the authors were positioned within a cultural milieu that shared common ideals regarding the traits of an individual possessing integrity, namely, a Hellenistic cultural milieu. The source of virtue is what most distinctly separates the groups (adhering to the Torah or living as a member of a Christ group).

8.3.4 The Community Rule and Ideals in the Qumran Community

A version of the virtue lists originates from the Qumran community, which will be the final text I examine as parallel. While the Hellenised Christ group and the Jewish writings of the Wisdom of Solomon and 4 Maccabees exhibit some similarities in their versions of prototypicality, the interpretation offered by the Qumran community is markedly different, as we shall see. In the Community Rule from Cave 1 (1QS), IV, 2–8, there exists an actual list detailing the virtues of those who walk in the spirit of light:

> 2 ...ואלה דרכיהן בתבל להאיר בלבב איש ולישר לפניו כול דרכי צדק אמת ולפחד לבבו
> במשפטי 3 אל ורוח ענוה וא'רך אפים ורוב רחמים וטוב עולמים ושכל ובינה וחכמה גבורה
> מאמנה בכול 4 מעשי אל ונשענת ברוב חסדו ורוח דעת בכול מחשבת מעשה וקנאת משפטי
> צדק ומחשבת 5 קודש ביצר חסדים על כול הני אמת וטהרת כבוד מתעב כול גלול נדה
> והצנע לכת 6 בערמה כול וחבא לאמת לבני רזי דעת ... אלה סודי רוח אמת לבני תבל ופקודת
> כול הולכי בה למרפא 7 ורוב שלום באורך ימים ופרות זרע עם כול ברכות עד ושמחת
> עולמים בחיי נצח וכליל כבוד 8 עם מדת הדר באור עולמים ...

> These are their [those of the spirit of light] paths in the world: to enlighten the heart of man, straighten out in front of him all the paths of true justice, establish in his heart respect for the precepts of God; it is a spirit of meekness, of patience, generous compassion, eternal goodness, intelligence, understanding, potent wisdom which trusts in all the deeds of God and depends on his abundant mercy; a spirit of knowledge in all the plans of action, of enthusiasm for the decrees of justice, of holy plans with firm purpose, of generous compassion with all the sons of truth, of magnificent purity which detests all unclean idols, of careful behaviour in wisdom concerning everything, of concealment concerning the truth of the mysteries of knowledge. Blank These are the foundations of the spirit of the sons of truth (in) the world. And the reward for all those who walk in it will be for healing, plentiful peace in a long life, fruitful offspring with all everlasting

blessings, eternal enjoyment with endless life, and a crown of glory with majestic raiment in eternal light.⁹⁷

The version from Cave 1 in Qumran (1QS) is the only version of the Community Rule that includes the first four columns.⁹⁸ The fourth column, from 4b, has, however, a parallel in 4Q257, column 5.⁹⁹ These first columns appear to have undergone different stages in their compositional history, with the version in 1QS being the most recent form.¹⁰⁰ In short bullet points, the ideal (prototypical) sons of light are described.¹⁰¹

At first glance, there appears to be some overlap in themes regarding the Hellenistic ideals we have observed in the various versions above. However, on a deeper level, few direct connections to any Hellenised ideals can be identified. In IV, 3, several positive characteristics of a person following the Spirit of Light are noted. While it is intriguing that the term חכמת גבורה ("potent wisdom" according to Martínez) is employed, since strength is also linked to wisdom (in the virtue of ἐγκράτεια, as mentioned above), the similarities do not extend much further.¹⁰² The view of wisdom as strength only acknowledges that wisdom was seen to require conversion into practice; the word חכמה is commonly referred to as "skill in technical matters," and shows no signs of being borrowed from Hellenistic ideals.¹⁰³ As for ארך, "patience, foreberance, composure, calmness,"¹⁰⁴ this could be regarded as a synonym for ἐγκράτεια. Therefore, the concept of wisdom and the ideal of a wise person appear to carry similar connotations across various spheres and periods of antiquity, despite the absence of direct correspondence or translation.

---

[97] Martínez and Tigchelaar 1999, 76–77.
[98] Hempel 2020, 28, see also 99–101.
[99] Hempel 2020, 105.
[100] Hempel 2020, 101–2.
[101] Hempel 2020, 116.
[102] Cf. Diogenes Laertius 6:11 (White 2020, 232).
[103] HALOT, s.v. חכמה. The other meanings listed are "experience, shrewdness," "wordly wisdom," "the pious wisdom of Israel," "God's wisdom," "wisdom personified"-
[104] HALOT, s.v. ארך.

On the other hand, the concept of ענוה, meaning "humility," frequently translated with cognates to ταπεινοφροσύνη in the LXX,[105] is neither significant nor even present in the concepts of the Hellenistic ideal wise man.[106] The word בערמת in 4, 6 (translated with "moderation" by Martínez) carries connotations of shrewdness and cleverness.[107] In the two instances listed where it is used in the Hebrew Bible, 1 Sam 23:22 and Prov 15:5, the LXX reads πανουργεύσηται and πανουργότερος, where πανουργία most commonly translates into English as cunning, craftiness, trickery.[108] This is something slightly different from being wise; according to BDAG, the word πανοῦργος never carries positive connotations in New Testament material but can do so in Aristotle and also the mentioned instance in the LXX version of Proverbs.[109] Hempel translates בערמת "with prudence,"[110] but never connects it to any other ideal than the Qumran community's dualistic worldview.[111] In other words, this ideal of wisdom stems from a source different from any Hellenised or Hellenised Jewish philosophy.

What is striking about this list from the Qumran movement, which seems to have had the study of the Pentateuchal law and the prophets at its core, is that the virtues presented in 1QS IV are nearly as focused on wisdom and insight as they are on moral behaviour. Understanding the meaning of the Torah is as important as acting morally:

---

[105] Zeph 2:3, Proverbs 18:12
[106] HALOT, s.v. ענוה.
[107] Cf. HALOT, s.v. ערום, "cunning," "clever."
[108] BDAG, s.v. πανουργία.
[109] BDAG, s.v. πανοῦργος.
[110] Hempel 2020, 105.
[111] Hempel 2020, 117.

Virtues of the mind	Virtues of ethical behaviour
Intelligence	A spirit of meekness
Understanding	Patience
Potent wisdom that trusts in all the deeds of God and depends on his abundant mercy	Generous compassion
A spirit of knowledge in all the plans of action	Eternal goodness
Holy plans with firm purpose	Generous compassion with all the sons of truth
Prudence in respect of the truth concerning the mysteries of knowledge	Magnificent purity which detests all unclean idols
	Unpretentious behaviour with moderation in everything

Table 8.3.4. *Overview of the virtues of the mind and behavioural virtues in 1QS IV, 2–6.*[112]

This Jewish group, which provides us with a list of virtues, is primarily focused on the ability to understand and interpret the Torah correctly. Contrary to the common moral ground of the Hellenistic period, the virtue list in 1QS promotes a specific aim focused on achieving a correct understanding and appropriate behaviour regarding the Pentateuchal law. 1QS regards correct hermeneutic practice as equally crucial as proper behaviour.

Last, in this section, if we compare the list of virtues in 1QS with those in the Pastorals, we find the following: The lists in the Pastorals include several mundane concerns such as hospitality, family relationships, and money that contrast with the list of intellectual concerns found in 1QS. Furthermore, the outsiders in this section of 1QS possess an opposing spirit to that of the ingroup within the Qumran community. Thus, maintaining a good reputation among outsiders is entirely irrelevant for 1QS. However, the lists share ideals concerning goodness, patience/self-control, zeal for the ingroup's teachings, and moderation/unpretentious behaviour.

In conclusion, the list of 1QS IV, 2–6 shares some connotations with the Hellenised world regarding what it meant to be wise, particularly in terms of self-restraint. While the ideal ἐπίσκοπος shares certain traits with the ideal Children of Light, especially concerning moderation and zeal for ingroup teaching,

---

[112] Transl. Martínez and Tigchelaar 1999.

each group demonstrates distinctly exclusive ideals. The Qumran community values a member with good intelligence and understanding of the truth, whereas the communities receiving the Pastorals had more mundane concerns for the ideal member; issues of everyday life, such as family life, were of paramount importance.

8.4 Conclusion: The ἐπίσκοπος in the Pastorals

There are two concluding topics I will address in this section. The first concerns the prototypical behaviour expected of group members as analysed in this chapter. The second relates to how these varying prototypicalities offer insights into the parting of the ways between Christ groups and salient Jewish groups. Alternatively, how the ἐπίσκοπος becomes a bearer of a specific ingroup identity and prototypicality, leaving little room for alternate identities.

8.4.1 Prototypical Behaviour in the Texts Compared

As we have seen in this first section of this chapter, the prototypical member of the Christ group, as reflected in expectations regarding the ἐπίσκοπος, demonstrates that the Christ group has some unique features as well as some certain similarities with the surrounding culture. The similarities are evident in the necessity for the ἐπίσκοπος to exhibit self-restraint (to possess ἐγκράτεια) and moderation (σωφροσύνη). These two characteristics are common to virtually all other lists of groups that have been studied (a version of this can also be perceived in 1QS) and are two of the four Stoic cardinal virtues (as debated in Plutarch).

Since the Wisdom of Solomon and 4 Maccabees present an ideal of a wise man that largely aligns with Hellenistic ideals, a significant overlap exists between the Pastorals and the virtue lists found in these texts. However, the organising framework for a wise man, according to the Wisdom of Solomon and 4 Maccabees, is wisdom as God's consort and as an emanation of God's λογός. Thus, the Wisdom of Solomon and 4 Maccabees provide a clear source of virtue that is closely linked to the observance of the Torah. This is a feature entirely absent in the Pastoral epistles. Rather, 1 Tim 1:8 reflects a hesitant approach to employing the Torah at all for full members of the group.

The prototypical member of the Qumran community was regarded as someone who could accurately grasp and contemplate the Torah and the group's teachings. The list of the Sons of Light primarily concentrates on intellectual faculties, in contrast to the more mundane concerns of the Pastorals.

Aside from some of the Stoic cardinal virtues, the ordinary aspects of the virtue lists in the Pastorals are shared with Onosander's expectations of the ideal (prototypical) στρατηγός. The explicit expectations in Onosander (to be a proficient speaker, to be of mature age, to maintain a good reputation, and to be a father) all have counterparts in the Pastorals. The distinction between the Pastorals and Onosander lies in the former's hesitance towards violence and the expectation to be μιᾶς γυναικὸς ἄνδρα.

This indicates that the prototypical ἐπίσκοπος, according to the Pastorals, should embody philosophical cardinal virtues while also being attentive to the ordinary aspects of life. The ἐπίσκοπος is thus not primarily envisioned as a wise man or philosopher in the Stoic sense, who would pay little attention to the minutiae of everyday life. Furthermore, the ἐπίσκοπος is not expected to contemplate the Torah, but is rather perceived as a socially well-integrated individual with primary concerns in family matters and the daily affairs of the congregation. The emphasis within the Pastorals on gaining outsider approval for the ἐπίσκοπος suggests that relationships with other social circles were becoming increasingly significant. An effective ἐπίσκοπος was not only capable of governing his household and the congregation but could also manage the expectations of the surrounding society. The ideal portrayed in the Pastorals presents a well-established man, akin to the *paterfamilias*, easily identifiable as part of a Greco-Roman city. The ideals concerning the Torah and Wisdom, or the contemplation of the Torah that offers significant insight for the ideal member, are absent in the Pastorals' prototypical member, the ἐπίσκοπος. The prototypical member of the Christ group is thus somewhat distinct from both the philosophical schools of its time and the Jewish communities depicted in 4 Maccabees and the Wisdom of Solomon on one side, and 1QS on the other.

8.4.2 The ἐπίσκοπος in the Pastoral Epistles and the Parting of the Ways

As we have observed in this chapter, the author of the Pastoral epistles engages in various forms of identity-shaping rhetoric. Partly, the author embeds ingroup identity within the congregational order, acting as an identity impresario, while also conveying prototypical behaviour for the ingroup that significantly differs from the ideals of surrounding groups.

Concerning impresarioship, Paul the Apostle's ethos underpins the teachings on how the ingroup should be organised. The ἐπίσκοπος safeguards the teachings of the group and is entrusted with the authority to reenact ingroup identity, provided he exemplifies prototypical behaviour in accordance with sound teaching. The group's structure aligns with Paul's mission, facilitated by his laying hands upon Timothy (and Titus). Being part of the group means being associated with God's saving acts through Christ. The outgroups, particularly those displaying salient Jewish behaviours, are viewed with scepticism.

Regarding prototypical behaviour, the ἐπίσκοπος is tied to ingroup ideals that notably lack elements important for groups with a pronounced Jewish identity. This is especially evident in their perspective on the Torah. While the author of the Pastorals suggests a group identity reminiscent of a Hellenistic *paterfamilias* – similar to the views discussed by Onosander and several Stoic writers – the groups with a strong Jewish identity posit that the Torah is the wellspring of wisdom. Therefore, a positive view of the Torah is crucial for understanding the integration of these Jewish groups within Hellenistic society. Conversely, this perspective is absent in the Christ groups, whose teachings predominate in the Pastorals.

In both prototypicality and impresarioship, the Pastorals' view of the Torah implies an identity in which the practice of Jewish halakah is unachievable, as the Torah is accepted only through the lens of "sound teaching." In practice, membership in the group affords little space for differing views on halakah. The group identity portrayed by the Pastoral epistles, where the ἐπίσκοπος is a prominent leader embodying prototypical traits, markedly differs from the identity illustrated by Ben Sira or the earlier Qumran group.

This leads to the conclusion that the author's incorporation of Christian identity into the ἐπίσκοπος leaves no room for a distinct Jewish identity characterised by Torah piety. As the episcopal order is emphasised, the activities associated with Torah observance are minimised. Where the ἐπίσκοπος embodies Christian identity, a specific relationship to teaching is maintained. These teachings regard Torah observance with the scepticism evident in 1 Tim 1:3–11. The ἐπίσκοπος renders closer relationships with Torah-observant groups impossible. This, of course, profoundly impacts how the ingroup of the Pastorals perceives a Jewish identity. As 1 Tim 1:3–11 suggests, observing Torah is frowned upon. The Torah is utilised solely as a negative instrument, directed against the lawless (ἄνομος), rather than in a positive sense as a vital activity for ingroup identity. Consequently, membership in the group entails that the Torah assumes a minimal and negative role, perceived as worthless by ingroup members. Thus, to be a prototypical member of the group addressed by the Pastorals, along with its emerging episcopal structure, effectively means renouncing salient Torah-keeping activities.

9. The ἐπίσκοπος as Prototypical Christ Believer in Ignatius of Antioch

In the early writings of Christ groups, officeholders are increasingly portrayed as examples to follow, that is, as prototypical believers embodying prominent group traits. Within this prototypical leadership, the tensions between the ἐκκλησία and the synagogue are growing: the prototype represented by the leaders of the ἐκκλησία significantly diverges from a prominent, Torah-observing Jewish identity. Additionally, as we shall see, the author of the Ignatian corpus employs the prototypicality of the purported sender, Ignatius, to propose new interpretations of what it means to be a follower of Christ for the Christ-group members in Asia Minor in the latter half of the second century CE. The author also integrates the identity of Christ followers within the emerging episcopal structure. All this suggests that the tension between an old Jewish identity and a new Christian identity is palpable in the Ignatian letters, to which we now turn.

9.1 On The Provenance and Date of the Ignatian Letters

To contextualise the letters, I will provide a comprehensive overview of the debate surrounding the date and authorship of the Ignatian letters. This will also place the present work within the field of Ignatian research. I will demonstrate why I consider the Ignatian corpus of the middle recension to be late (second half of the second century CE) and inauthentic.

9.1.1 The Debate

Three different versions of the Ignatian letters exist – the long, the middle, and the short recension. The long recension consists of thirteen letters (twelve attributed to Ignatius as the author, and one addressed to him). As a whole, it has not been regarded as authentic in modern times. The middle recension comprises seven letters, while the short recension contains three letters in a briefer form derived from a Syriac tradition. For a considerable time, there was a consensus regarding the authenticity of the middle recension, but this has been significantly challenged, particularly during the latter part of the 2010s. However, the first signs of this shift emerged during the second half of the twentieth century. This now-disputed scholarly consensus primarily stemmed from the works of Joseph Lightfoot and Theodor Zahn in the latter part of the nineteenth century.[1] In his important commentary from 1985, William Schoedel observed that the consensus view remains upheld some hundred years later. He summarised the debate up to that point as follows.

> Yet the conclusion of our commentary is that there is nothing in the middle recension of Ignatius clearly anachronistic and that the cumulative weight of arguments against its authenticity is insufficient to dislodge it from its place in the history of the early church.[2]

The debate regarding the provenance and date has, however, been ignited by the contributions of several scholars from both German and Anglo-Saxon research. One of the primary reasons for questioning the provenance of the letters is the advanced perspective on offices in the early Christian era groups.[3] What later came to be known as the monarchical episcopacy could hardly have emerged in the early second century. It has been argued by several scholars, both previously by, for example, Ferdinand Baur,[4] and in recent times by, for example, Ferdinand Prostmeier,[5] that the letters of Ignatius were not really written by Ignatius on his way to be martyred in Rome. Instead, the texts were written later in the second century, roughly between 160 and 180 CE. In the late twentieth century, Josep Rius-Camps and Robert Joly argued that some of

---

[1] Lightfoot 1868; Zahn 1873.
[2] Schoedel 1985, 7.
[3] Eurell 2022, 188.
[4] See Baur 1838.
[5] See Prostmeier 2018.

the letters (Rius-Camps) or all (Joly) were forgeries.[6] The view of Baur and Joly that the middle recension was written by a different hand than Ignatius around 160–180 CE has, however, most recently been supported by, among others, Reinhard Hübner, Thomas Lechner, Michael Theobald, and above-mentioned Prostmeier (see note 3). Markus Vinzent, based on a thorough text-critical comparison, maintains the same opinion.[7] His work on the recensions of the Ignatian corpus represents a significant contribution to the debate. Vizient also suggests that the shortest recension, which included Ign. *Rom.*, Ign. *Eph.*, and Ign. *Pol.*, was the only one known to several ancient Christian authors, such as Origen.[8] As recently as 2022, John-Christian Eurell proposed that Romans ought to be regarded as the only authentic letter.[9]

Most arguments for or against an authentic body of letters hinge on four factors, the first of which is the previously mentioned perspective on the episcopal structure. Jonathon Lookadoo aptly summarises the other three.

> Key pieces of evidence include the trustworthiness of the Ignatian date given by Eusebius, the way in which the descriptions of Ignatius in Pol. *Phil.* 9.1; 13.2 relate to one another, and Ignatius's place alongside the Second Sophistic.[10]

A more detailed account of these points will follow below. Before that, it is worth mentioning that this partly represents a progression in topic from the earlier debate in the twentieth century, which revolved around theological concepts deemed to be too early, allusions to relatively late writings, the view of the mono-episcopate, and so forth. The scholarly view of date and authorship remains ambiguous, but for different reasons compared to those of the late twentieth century. Lookadoo, once again referencing the anthology edited by Bauer and von Möllendorff (2018), points out that "a significant number of Ignatian researchers views the Ignatian letters as pseudepigraphic compositions and

---

[6] Rius-Camps 1980 and Joly 1979. Ign. *Rom.*; Ign. *Magn.*; Ign. *Trall.*; and Ign. *Eph.* are to be considered actual writings from Ignatius's own hand according to Rius-Camps.

[7] Vinzent 2019, 362–63.

[8] Vinzent 2019 282.

[9] Eurell 2022.

[10] Lookadoo 2020, 105.

dates them to the end of the second century."[11] The tides have turned in some scholarship towards a later dating. Lookadoo, however, emphasises that a later dating of the Ignatian letters does not necessitate viewing the letters as pseudepigrapha, which I will return to below. He also highlights the differing perspectives on dating and authenticity in different research traditions. In the German-speaking research community, it has been more common to regard the Ignatian letters as pseudepigrapha.[12] In anglophone research, however, there has been a tendency to defend the letters' authenticity.

To summarise the various perspectives, three viewpoints can be identified:

1. An early date and genuine Ignatian letters. At the early stage of the current debate (late twentieth century and forward) this view has been defended by Andreas Lindemann,[13] Georg Schöllgen,[14] Mark Edwards,[15] Hermann Josef Vogt,[16] and Allen Brent.[17] In later years, Piepenbrink[18] and von Möllendorff[19] have also defended their authenticity.
2. A later date but an authentic author (perhaps redacted) is a view held by Paul Foster,[20] Timothy Barnes,[21] and Alistair Stewart.[22]
3. A third perspective is that the Ignatian letters are pseudepigrapha and ought to be dated to the latter half or possibly the final quarter of the second century. The proponents of this view are Reinhard Hübner[23] (who argued based on Robert Joly's work from 1979),[24] Thomas

---

[11] Lookadoo 2020, 94.
[12] Lookadoo 2020, 94.
[13] Lindemann 1997.
[14] Schöllgen 1998.
[15] Edwards 1998.
[16] Vogt 1999.
[17] Brent 2006 and 2007.
[18] Piepenbrink 2018.
[19] Von Möllendorff, 2018.
[20] Foster 2007.
[21] Barnes 2008.
[22] Stewart 2013 and 2014.
[23] Hübner 1997.
[24] Joly 1979.

Lechner,[25] Walter Schmithals,[26] Otto Zwierlein,[27] and Michael Theobald,[28] and Markus Vinzent.[29]

As mentioned previously, there are four primary topics to consider regarding the date and authenticity of the Ignatian corpus.[30] These are the trustworthiness of Eusebius's dating regarding the Ignatian events, the relationship between the mentions of Ignatius in the letter of Polycarp chapters 9 and 13, the relationship of Ignatius to the Second Sophists, and, of course, the ever-lingering question of the episcopal structure.[31] In the following sections, I shall provide a brief summary of each topic.

9.1.2 The Dating of Eusebius

The earliest ancient source to discuss the date of Ignatius's death and to quote from the Ignatian letters is Eusebius (*Eccl. hist* 3.36.2.).[32] He (and much later John Malalas) suggests a date for the death of Ignatius during Trajan's reign. However, there are several problematic aspects of Eusebius's account. Lechner notes that the primary reason for an early dating is the chronology provided by

---

[25] Lechner 1999.
[26] Schmithals 2009.
[27] Zwierlein 2010; 2011; 2013; and 2014.
[28] Theobald 2016.
[29] Vinzent 1999. Vinzent also suggests, several years later, that the short recension (after ca. 150 CE) should be understood as earlier than the middle recension, Vinzent 2019, 363–64. Vinzent's thorough review of the recensions and their reception and redaction calls upon a new perspective on the Ignatian letters, in which the older taxonomy of three recensions is updated.
[30] It is interesting to note that a question that would not shed light on the provenance question is that of genre. Since the letters, in some instances, show similarities to the Pastoral Letters, which are commonly perceived as deutero-Pauline, some insights from that debate would apply. However, no such thing has appeared in the discussion. The similarities should, however, be interesting to compare in a later work.
[31] A part of the debate has also been how Lucian of Samosata's satirical work *De Morte Peregrine*, dated around 180 CE helps us understand the reception of Ignatius, and thus the date of the letters. While some like Lechner 1999, 66–67, find it hard to use Lucian's work, it carries some value that will be discussed at the end of this part of the chapter.
[32] Irenaeus, around 180 CE, briefly quotes Ign. *Eph.* before Eusebius. This will be discussed further in this chapter.

Eusebius.³³ Eusebius also provides some information and references to the literary works attributed to Ignatius.³⁴ The date of Ignatius's martyrdom is not explicitly stated, so one must triangulate this information from other references in Eusebius. Ignatius is reported to have become "well known" simultaneously with Polycarp's appointment as ἐπίσκοπος. His reputation also coincided with that of Papias of Hierapolis. Ignatius was already designated as ἐπίσκοπος by the time he gained recognition. Eusebius is clearly not addressing his appointment as ἐπίσκοπος of Antioch, but rather the timing of his fame. This occurs, according to Eusebius, "at that time" (γε μὴν κατὰ τούτους), which refers to the period of Polycarp's appointment as ἐπίσκοπος of Smyrna, happening concurrently with Justus's succession to the episcopal throne of Jerusalem (*Eccl. hist.* 3.35). This also seems to coincide with the period when Everastus was appointed ἐπίσκοπος in Rome, which allegedly occurred in the third year of Trajan's reign (101 CE, *Eccl. hist.* 3.34.). These data points have been called into question, even among those who assert that the Ignatian letters were authored by the historical figure Ignatius.³⁵ Most scholars advocating for an early date, however, reference a date between 107 and 110.³⁶ Eusebius writes his History approximately two hundred years after the events he describes, and his sources are not entirely clear. Consequently, his statements regarding Ignatius are somewhat ambiguous, which raises the reasonable possibility that the death of Ignatius, along with the letters attributed to him, may date from a later time than Eusebius indicates.

9.1.3 Chapter 9 and 13 in the Letter of Polycarp

The second part of the debate pertains to the Letter of Polycarp to the Philippians. The crux of the question concerns whether chapter 13 is an interpolation. Several peculiarities arise: in chapter 9, Ignatius is mentioned for the first time outside the Ignatian corpus, in a manner that suggests he has died a martyr's

---

[33] Lechner 1999, 4.
[34] Eurell 2022, 189.
[35] Foster 2007, 87; Stewart 2014, 239–40.
[36] Brent 2006; Lindemann 1997; Schöllgen 1998, for example.

death (9:2).³⁷ However, in chapter 13, he is mentioned once more, as though he is alive and composing letters. Furthermore, the finest Greek manuscripts omit chapter 13. Certainly, if one regards the letter corpus of Ignatius as authentic, one interprets chapter 13 as an original composition by Polycarp, as it addresses Ignatius's whereabouts and letter-writing.³⁸ The author of chapter 13 states that "we have forwarded to you the letters of Ignatius that he sent to us, just as you directed us to do."³⁹ This peculiarity could suggest (a) a peculiar use of language by Polycarp in which his formulations of Ignatius are at best unclear since he appears to be dead in chapter 9 but alive in chapter 13; it could suggest (b) that Pol. *Phil.* is, in fact, a compilation of letters and that the chapters had a different order in the correspondence; or it could suggest (c) that chapter 13 is an interpolation by another hand than Polycarp.⁴⁰ The missing chapter 13 in the Greek manuscripts speaks in favour of this last hypothesis.

The ambiguities surrounding Ignatius's whereabouts in Pol. *Phil.* 9 and 13 were, for Robert Joly, an essential argument against the authenticity of the Ignatian corpus.⁴¹ Thus, the case for the Letter to Polycarp is equally significant for Reinhard Hübner's study, which follows Joly's lead. Even in later evaluations of the authenticity of the Ignatian corpus, the letter of Polycarp remains crucial: Michael Theobald regards the letter, in his view written in the 140s, as an inspiration for a forger.⁴² Chapter 13 of Pol. *Phil.* is therefore seen as the outcome of this forgery.⁴³ In Theobald's work, the primary focus is the Pastoral Epistles, which he believes, as mentioned above, were written sometime between 125 and 150. According to his interpretation of the Ignatian letters, they reference the Pastorals, thus establishing a *terminus ante quem* for the Ignatian corpus.⁴⁴ In contrast to this view, Eurell understands Pol. *Phil.* as authentic. He

---

[37] After 9:2, all nine of the surviving Greek manuscripts break off. Chapter 13 is only preserved in Greek by the quotations of Eusebius. Ehrman 2003a, 329–30.

[38] Cf Lookadoo, 2020, 95. See also Lindenman 1997, 193; Schöllgen 1998, 24–25.

[39] Pol. *Phil.* 13.2. Trans. Ehrman 2003a, 351.

[40] Ehrman 2003a, 327–29.

[41] Lookadoo 2020, 90.

[42] Theobald 2016, 323.

[43] Lookadoo 2020, 93.

[44] Lookadoo 2020, 93.

dates it very early, perhaps from the 90s, as the close relationship between Irenaeus and Polycarp, along with Irenaeus's mention of letter-writing, supports the authenticity of Pol. *Phil*.[45] One can thus note that scholars regarding the Ignatian letters as inauthentic also tend to understand chapter 13 of the Pol *Phil* as such also, Eurell being one exception.[46]

9.1.4 The Second Sophists and Ignatius

The contextual understanding of the Ignatian content has been a hotly debated issue. The overarching question, however, is methodological: to what extent are comparisons to other texts valid as a means of dating a text? This question becomes particularly acute in the discussion of the Second Sophists. This ideological movement has been understood as the backdrop against which the Ignatian correspondence should be read. The Second Sophistic movement was a prominent cultural and intellectual movement of the first and second centuries CE.[47] Aelius Aristides (117–187 CE), Dio Chrysostom (40–120 CE), and Philostratus (ca. 170–240 CE) are examples of authors associated with the movement. The ideology was formulated as a claim that the Greek city states in Asia Minor "formed a common Hellenistic culture, characterised by its contemporary mystery religions, its common history, and autonomous political institutions that were the city-state."[48] Within this framework, the external imperial Rome was integrated into the system and perceived as divine and transcendent.[49] The imperial cult became a means through which the Second Sophists could find the external force of Rome acceptable; it possibly even facilitated peace among the city-states from an ideological standpoint, as they competed against each other to secure honorary positions related to the imperial cult.[50]

Allen Brent has argued for a specific kind of typology through which cultic theology associated with the Second Sophist movement was expressed in Asia Minor. In this typology, specific roles were performed by cultic personnel as

---

[45] Eurell 2022, 196–200.
[46] Eurell 2022, 199.
[47] Brent 2006, 1.
[48] Brent 2006, 1.
[49] Brent 2006, 2–4.
[50] Brent 2006, 3.

they participated in public processions.⁵¹ The priests demonstrated the power of their deity publicly through these processions. Brent contends that it is against this backdrop that we must understand the Ignatian letters, as they appear to share several key concepts.⁵² According to Brent, the emerging ἐκκλησία was a counterculture to the imperial cult: "A group, deprived of status and significance by the wider culture, sets up its own contra-culture that mirrors and reverses the values of the former, granting the status and significance to its members that the former has denied them."⁵³ Thus, the Ignatian letters should be read as a revision of the imperial cult, specifically, the Second Sophistic reception of the same. The evidence for a typology of Second Sophists in the Ignatian corpus is found in pagan cultic ideals regarding how the gods and goddesses were perceived to behave and become present through their priests and priestesses, as recorded on several steles and in written sources.⁵⁴ Brent discusses, in several instances, the relationship between the "Greco-Roman religious and political culture of Asia Minor"⁵⁵ and the Ignatian discourse from the late first century and during the second century.⁵⁶ He uses this imperial ideology as a backdrop for Ignatius's views, which should also explain the silence of other theologians from the Christ groups. Ignatius's views are too indebted to the imperial cult to be comfortable for the broader network of the emerging Christ groups.⁵⁷ The views of later figures such as Irenaeus or Hegesippus, who believed that the ἐπίσκοπος was in succession to the apostles, are absent from Ignatius's view of the emerging order of the congregation, according to Brent's Second Sophistic theory. Instead, the offices are essentially regarded as a reflection of the heavenly drama through the liturgy.⁵⁸ Later views, such as Irenaeus's, that the ἐπίσκοπος is the sole inheritor of apostolic authority, are lacking in Ignatius, according to Brent. Brent paints an intriguing picture in which

---

⁵¹ Brent 2006, 41–42.
⁵² Brent 2006, 42–66.
⁵³ Brent 1999, xxi.
⁵⁴ Brent 2006, 43–66.
⁵⁵ Brent 2006, 23.
⁵⁶ See also, apart from his other publications, Brent 1998.
⁵⁷ Brent 2006, 20.
⁵⁸ Brent 2006, 26.

the wording in Ign. *Magn.* 6 mirrors a liturgical situation with the ἐπίσκοπος presiding in the midst as God (προκαθημένου τοῦ ἐπισκόπου εἰς τόπον θεοῦ),[59] surrounded in a horseshoe-shaped formation by the presbytery and διάκονοι.[60] This liturgical situation, in turn, mirrors the depiction of heavenly worship in Rev 7:12. Therefore, Brent argues that the Ignatian letters present a liturgical vision grounded in the typology of the Second Sophists.

> For Ignatius, therefore, the significance of ministerial office is that the three kinds of office holders, bishop, priests and deacons, create the Church by reflecting, in the corporate, liturgical life of the community, the ongoing drama of redemption.[61]

Even though these are intriguing ideas, they contain a methodological flaw: they offer no fixed point for dating the Ignatian corpus. It is by no means impossible that the texts could be constructed later than the texts from the Second Sophists. Lechner argues against Allen Brent's use of the Second Sophist as a general political theology in the first and second centuries CE.[62] He points to the methodological issue in Brent's use of the concept of a specific Ignatian version of the typology of the Second Sophists.[63] Particularly, Brent is using merely a tiny portion of the Ignatian letters (for example Ign. *Eph.* 9:2) as grounds for claiming that the entire letter corpus constitutes a single Ignatian version of Second Sophistic typology, which the initial recipients were understood to be capable of comprehending.[64] The original readers' lack of access to

---

[59] "[W]hen the ἐπίσκοπος preside in God's place."

[60] Brent 1999, 217–18. The wording of the horse-shoe shaped table is described through genitive clauses connected to the unity under the ἐπίσκοπος: ἀξιοπλόκου πνευματικοῦ στεφάνου τοῦ πρεσβυτερίου ὑμῶν

[61] Brent 2006, 27.

[62] Lechner 2020.

[63] Lechner, 2020, 37, Brent 2006, 5–17.

[64] Lechner 2020, 41. One can note that Brent is by no means alone to use rather small portions of the Ignatian corpus as evidence for a highly specified understanding. Eurell (2022, 194) comments that small amounts of text several times have been the basis for sweeping conclusions regarding the precise situation of the Ignatian correspondence: "The problem with the proposals of Hübner, Lechner, and Vinzent is that they are very specific despite being built on details in small portions of the corpus. Their studies are valuable to situate the theological milieu of Pseudo-Ignatius in general but do not substantiate their very specific conclusions."

every letter in the corpus, if genuine, makes it difficult to assume that these readers could have understood Ignatius's language as a reflection of Second Sophistic discourse. In Lechner's view, a specific feature of the language of the Ignatian letters would only further suggest that the corpus should be considered a single document, and thus of a later date than suggested by Brent.

Thus, the question of methodology remains significant in the debate. There is a risk of drawing overly broad conclusions from limited sources and only certain aspects of the Ignatian correspondence.

9.1.5 A Fully Developed Mono-Episcopate in Early Second Century?

During the debate on the Ignatian letters, a question of great importance has been the extent to which the idea of a mono-episcopate could have developed in the early second century. This question relates to the degree of other theological notions in Ignatius, such as χριστιανισμός and καθολικὴ ἐκκλησία.[65] The debate bears similarities to that concerning the Second Sophists, as we only have access to the historical context through a collection of texts and inscriptions that require continual thorough interpretation. Therefore, we cannot attain exhaustive knowledge of the actual development. Ignatius is among the earliest authors of the emerging Christian era, following the New Testament, who offers a theologised vision of the role of the ἐπίσκοπος. As chapter 4 above shows, the notion of ἐπίσκοπος is not entirely new in the second century. However, the role is not particularly utilised theologically until the Ignatian letters, where it is outlined in a manner that other early Christian texts appear to overlook. After the Reformation began, the primacy of the Roman papacy was questioned; consequently, reformed theologians argued that the lengthy recension (which was debated until James Ussher discovered the middle recension in 1644 in a Latin translation) had been interpolated and possibly entirely forged.[66] The establishment of the middle recension, which, through the work of Lightfoot and Zahn, came to be regarded as genuine, upheld the idea that Ignatius's letters could indeed be seen by almost everyone as early sources of the episcopal order. However, as previously mentioned, Joly, in 1979, seriously

---

[65] Isacson 2004, 14; Vinzent 2019, 365.
[66] Vinzent 2019, 368; Schoedel 1985, 2.

challenged the consensus of genuineness for the first time since the discovery of the middle recension.[67] The thesis of Joly once again exhibits the methodological problem inherent in the debate. There is scant external evidence fixed in time, which complicates the postulation of an early or late mono-episcopate, or "catholicisation." Although Joly's challenge initially failed to gain traction, the works of Hübner and Lechner have continued to develop lines emerging from Joly's research. The ongoing debate surrounding the development of the episcopacy in the early second century was further advanced by Theobald in 2016, who, from the perspective presented in the Pastoral Letters regarding episcopacy, enriches our understanding of episcopal views in the Ignatian letters.[68] The important perspective in his reading of the Ignatian letters lies in his explicit connection between the Pastorals and the Ignatian corpus. According to Theobald, the concept of "Vergessenheit" ("oblivion") is key to understanding the Pastoral letters.[69] This oblivion focuses on the Jewish perspective regarding faith in Jesus. The phase of the early congregations reflected in the Pastorals is not the period when direct polemics were aimed at the Jewish background. Instead, the strategy during this phase was silence; to forget it.[70] However, as the traditions of the Christ groups evolve, the emerging role of the ἐπίσκοπος reflects the group's need to explicitly address the question of outgroups. The newly established office of the ἐπίσκοπος is defining the characteristics of both in- and outgroups. Theobald's view, therefore, is that the Ignatian letters are later forgeries, modelled on the template of Pauline letters. In the Ignatian letters, the outgroups are addressed more thoroughly, through the skills of a legendary office-holder from Syria. Thus, the letters operate from an evolved episcopacy. According to Theobald, since the Ignatian letters exhibit traces of the Pastorals, as does Polycarp's letter to the Philippians, and since the Pol. *Phil.* is dated in the second quarter of the second century,[71] the Ignatian letters, depending on both the Pastorals and Pol. *Phil.*, should be dated around

---

[67] See Schoedel 1985, 6–7; Isacson 2004, 13–14.
[68] Theobald 2016.
[69] Theobald 2016, 114.
[70] See also Lechner 2020, 57.
[71] Theobald 2016, 328–30.

160 or 170.⁷² Thus, there is no genuine situational discourse in the letters; only "ignatianized" Pauline templates.⁷³ Theobald places the Ignatian letters in a trajectory reaching back to the Pastoral corpus, consolidating the mono-episcopate's developmental stages.⁷⁴ Thus, the claim that the mono-episcopate represents the new pastoral modus operandi for the early church is connected to the Pastorals and the Letter of Polycarp (regardless of whether it is an interpolated version). Despite the absence of conclusive evidence, the pattern identified by Theobald is substantial enough to warrant further investigation.

To summarise the chapter thus far: the debate on the authenticity of the middle recension has been reignited, particularly over the past decade. This debate has taken different forms in the German-speaking world compared to the English-speaking one. Many scholars from the German-speaking community regard the Ignatian letters as inauthentic, while English-speaking scholars, to a greater extent, still uphold the authenticity of the Ignatian letters, despite several expressing doubts about the early dating of the corpus. The struggle over the date and authenticity has revolved around four areas of research: the reliability of Eusebius's dating, the relation between the mentions of Ignatius in the letter of Pol. *Phil.* 9 and 13, Ignatius's relationship to the Second Sophists and other second-century texts, and the extent of development in the episcopal structure and other theological concepts following the second century.

9.1.6 The Ignatian Corpus in the Present Work

The time now has come to review the topic of this book in light of the aforementioned debate. This work will continue from the perspective of Theobald, as the trajectory of the emerging episcopate appears intrinsically linked to the developing self-identification of Christian congregations as Christians, that is, in the sense of non-Jews and other outgroups. Although the thesis of this work does not fully depend on an early or late dating of the Ignatian corpus, the trajectory of Theobald noted above is of considerable interest, as it illustrates the theological development of a significant concept for group identity known

---

⁷² Theobald 2016, 371.
⁷³ Lechner 2020, 60–61.
⁷⁴ Theobald 2016, 63.

from the New Testament. The theoretical scope of SIT can provide further insights into the development of Christian identity, linked to the emerging episcopal structure.

Based on this discussion, I assume that the Ignatian corpus is late, perhaps with the exception of Ign. *Rom.* To be specific, the corpus was created after 160 CE but sometime before 180 CE. Irenaeus quotes Ign. *Rom.* in *Haer.* 5.28.4. and perhaps alludes to other letters of Ignatius in 4.33.5. Furthermore, I assume that the letter of Polycarp *To the Philippians* was written 150–156 , given its knowledge of the Pastoral Epistles, which I assume were written between 120–125.[75] This also implies that the Ignatian corpus is pseudepigraphic. These views are not uncontested. Therefore, I will allocate some space to support my arguments. As mentioned in the first section of this chapter, there are, of course, several positions one can take on the date of the Ignatian corpus. Although the prevailing tendency in the research history has been to postpone the date and, as I discussed above, question the authenticity, there is no evidence conclusively ruling out an early dating.[76] However, certain factors render a later date more likely.

The Absent Ignatius

First, silence surrounds Ignatian texts until approximately the late 170s CE. Following this period, several ancient authors refer or allude to him. Before we examine the Christian writers, it is essential to address the relationship between Ignatius and Lucian of Samosata. Lucian penned *De Morti Peregrini*, a satire concerning Peregrinus, a form of prophet and cult leader who dispatched

---

[75] One can see how Irenaeus is suggesting that those claiming that Christ was only imaginary are to be judged. The closeness in topic to Ign. *Trall.* 9–11; Ign. *Smyr.* 2–3; and Ign. *Magn.* suggests that Irenaeus also knew these letters. It does not rule out that Irenaeus might have also considered other texts.

[76] It is important to remember that since the main idea of this work is related to Group identity development, an early dating would not counter the findings of the episcopal office's effect on Christian identity from an SIT perspective. It would, however, have effects on our understanding of the separation between Christ groups and synagogues, since the effects this book traces regarding the ἐπίσκοπος as a prototype, entrepreneur, and impresario of identity, would then have to be placed somewhat earlier.

letters to notable figures cities.[77] The text is widely accepted to date from around 180 CE.[78] The terminology used to refer to Jesus's followers as "Christians" is interesting in itself.[79] However, it seems that Lucian was aware of the letters of Ignatius.[80] Especially *Peregr.* 41 discusses the sending of letters to notable cities. This raises the crucial question of the direction of literary dependence (assuming there is a literary dependence). Vinzent understood the short recension as originally composed around 150 CE. He suggests that the mocking portrayal of a Christian martyr by Lucian prompted other Christian writers to respond in Ignatius's name, thereby producing the letters found in the additional letters of the middle recension. This would have been much easier to imagine due to the comment in Ign. *Rom.* (which Vinzent assumes is originally by Ignatius) 4:1, that Ignatius would write to "all the congregations" (γράφω πάσαις ταῖς ἐκκλεσίαις), and the later addition of Pol. *Phil.* 13.[81] This dissertation will not provide new evidence in these matters, and the suggestion by Vinzent is somewhat speculative, of course. However, it appears that around 180 CE, several texts began to quote or allude to Ignatius. If Lucian refers to Ignatius around 180, the texts must be somewhat earlier. Until around 180 CE, silence regarding Ignatius was considerable. After that, a sudden outburst of scribal activity can be attested in the various texts referring to Ignatius that were written.

Furthermore, when we examine ancient Christian authors, we discover that Irenaeus quotes Ign. *Rom.* between 177 and 180 CE. In this quotation, however, Ignatius is not mentioned by name. The earliest reference to Ignatius by name – excluding the mention in passing in Pol. *Phil.* 9 and the reference through a probable interpolation in chapter 13 – is quite late. The combination of Ignatius's name and authorship of letters is absent for a long time. Irenaeus

---

[77] Bremmer 2017, 67–70, notes how Lucian employs several synonyms for group leadership to describe Peregrinus's role as the most prominent in the Christ group of which he allegedly became a leader. It is certainly interesting that Lucian understands the leaders to have written texts, and to have taught from holy books.

[78] Bremmer 2018, 76.

[79] Bremmer 2017, 66.

[80] Bremmer 2017, 72. See also Waldner 2006, 118.

[81] Vinzent 2019, 364.

cites only Ignatius's self-description as the wheat of God from Ign. *Rom.* 4:1.[82] In Irenaeus's use of Ignatius, it is rather Ignatius's use of wheat as a metaphor that is found interesting, rather than Ignatius as a person: the quotation is anonymously presented as stemming from "a man of ours" – τις τῶν ἡμετέρων. Also, around the late 170s CE, Athenagoras *Legatio,* 11, and also, perhaps, Theophilus of Antioch *Ad Autolycum* 2.12 reference Ign. *Eph.* 19 and (in Theophilus's case, perhaps Ign. *Trall.* 6 should also be considered).[83] Additionally, a case from Eusebius may perhaps originate from around this time.[84] Origen, during the first half of the third century, quotes Ignatian letters on three occasions; on one of these, he may provide biographical information, to which I will soon return. Other ancient authors at the beginning of the third century increasingly utilise the texts of Ignatius. However, it is only Eusebius, writing around the first quarter of the fourth century, who provides detailed information about Ignatius. This peculiar silence – given that the manuscript tradition of Pol. *Phil.* 13 suggests it is a later interpolation – is one of the data that leads Lechner to assume a later date for the corpus: the Ignatian text has no reception history until the quotations and allusions circa 180.[85]

Furthermore, Irenaeus quotes only Ign. *Rom.* What about the other letters? The citation clarifies that Irenaeus was quite familiar with Ign. *Rom.*, which suggests that more texts from the corpus (at least Ign. *Smyrn.* and Ign. *Trall.*) could underpin his general reasoning concerning docetism in *Haer.* 4.33.5.[86]

---

[82] σῖτός εἰμι θεοῦ καὶ δι' ὀδόντων θηρίων ἀλήθομαι, ἵνα καθαρὸς ἄρτος εὑρεθῶ τοῦ Χριστοῦ. ("I am the wheat of God and am ground by the teeth of wild animals, so that I may be found to be the pure bread of Christ").

[83] Vinzent 2019, 287.

[84] A rendition of a letter from the churches in Vienne and Gaul is recorded in Eusebius's *Eccl. Hist.* 5.1, which has been argued to stem from this time, seems to suggest a knowledge of Ign. *Eph.* and Ign. *Pol.*, Vinzent 2019, 287, n. 67.

[85] Lechner 1999, 3, 306.

[86] On a sidenote, it is worth mentioning the case Eurell has made for Ign. *Rom.* as the sole early and authentic Ignatian letter Eurell 2022, 191–96. The discussion and evidence, however, needs to be further investigated before anything conclusive can be said. The letters to the Magnesians, Trallians, Philadelphians, and Smyrnaeans, appear to be more similar to one another, and less similar to the letter to the Romans. Thus, these letters seem to have been shaped by another template than Ign. *Rom.*

The question of whether Christ suffered in the flesh is also addressed in Ign. *Trall.* 10 and Ign. *Smyr.* 2–5, and perhaps Irenaeus is even alluding to Ign. *Eph.* 7. Since Ign. *Rom.* is the only letter *quoted* by Irenaeus, and significantly later by Origen (who most importantly quotes Ign. *Eph.* 19:1 in *In Lucam Homiliae VI*, which will be further discussed shortly),[87] Eurell suggests that the Ign. *Rom.* is the template on which the other letters are produced.[88] The main impulse and suggestion regarding Ign. *Rom.* is a vital contribution to the discussion. However, since the letters addressed to the congregations of Asia Minor are more conventional, the idea proposed by Eurell is perhaps even more likely to succeed if one begins with, for example, Ign. *Eph.* as a template.[89] The interesting special case in Ign. *Rom.* does not alter the preconditions for this thesis; it remains true that the first quotations and the discussion of the contents of the letters originate from around 177 CE. This makes Ign. *Rom.* perhaps the most important letter to examine closely in future research projects.[90]

The anonymity of Ignatius in the first centuries following his death is peculiar. Lechner highlights the improbability that a martyr of the great renown traditionally attributed to him, was not even mentioned by name by Irenaeus.[91] This peculiarity suggests that Irenaeus did not associate the wheat metaphor in Ign. *Rom.* 4 with the name of Ignatius. Similarly, there have been suggestions that Origen's designation (*Hom. Luc.* VI) of Ignatius as the third ἐπίσκοπος of Antioch is an interpolation.[92] While this remains uncertain, the reference to

---

[87] Vinzent perceives tendencies suggesting that Origen was aware of the short or middle recension: Vinzent 2019, 360–61.

[88] Eurell 2022, 195–96.

[89] This book does not contain the space to discuss the topic of a template, but one could of course argue that epistolary conventions is enough of an explanation.

[90] Ign. *Rom.* is also significant, since it belongs to a certain manuscript tradition. The manuscript from Florence, published by Isaac Voss in 1646, did not contain Ign. *Rom.*, which has instead in several important cases been transmitted separated from the other six letters. In one important finding by James Cureton (1845), only Ign. *Rom.*, Ign. *Eph.*, and Ign. *Pol.* are included. Uninterpolated versions of Ign. *Rom.* are well established without the other six letters, which makes it suitable to discuss a separate manuscript tradition concerning this letter, Ehrman 2003a, 211–14.

[91] Lechner 1999, 69.

[92] Lechner 1999, 72–73.

Ignatius as the third ἐπίσκοπος does not provide substantial proof. Lechner suggests that this indicates merely that Origen had access to a list of officeholders in Antioch that did not include chronological information.[93] The other references to the Ignatian letters in Origen (*De Oratione* 20, *Commentary on the Song of Songs*, prologue) do not provide any biographical information.

The arguments regarding the late dating that Lechner suggests have been discussed and contested in several publications.[94] Counterarguments have primarily proposed an alternative backdrop or context; however, they do not significantly challenge Lechner's perspective. Piepenbrink (and also Isacson),[95] for instance, works from the situational aspect of every letter.[96] The strength of this perspective lies in the fact that one does not have to rely on a reconstruction of the development of the offices but can instead depend on merely exegetical tools. Piepenbrink herself rightly highlights the problematic features of such development-reconstructions.[97] The outcome of Piepenbrink's analysis of the Ignatian corpus indicates that Ignatius's authority as a charismatic martyr *in spe*, rather than his office, is the primary factor contributing to his ethos; thus, Ignatius exemplifies a prototypical leader in SIT terms.[98] Lookadoo presents a case for an earlier date along similar lines, raising the valid objection that Lechner (and Hübner) consistently presupposes that Ignatius exhibits literary dependence on sources like Noetus of Smyrna. However, there may be alternative explanations, such as a shared source for both Noetus and Ignatius, like Paul's letter to the Romans.[99] He also points out that Emperor Trajan was suppressing and hindering voluntary associations from meeting. However, Ignatius, in his letters, shows no awareness of such suppression, which, in Lookadoo's view, suggests that the letters were written before Trajan implemented this

---

[93] Lechner 1999, 73.
[94] For a pedagogic review, see Lookadoo 2020, 99–101.
[95] Isacson (2004) emphasises that every letter should be understood on its own terms, which is why he also attempts to reconstruct the rhetorical situation of each letter.
[96] Piepenbrink 2018.
[97] Piepenbrink 2018, 131–33.
[98] Piepenbrink 2018, 145.
[99] Lookadoo 2018a, 19.

policy in the early 110s.[100] This perspective also aligns with Eusebius's dating of Ignatius. Consequently, Lookadoo situates Ignatius's corpus early, posing the rhetorical question of whether it is "possible to be any more specific than a date sometime in the first half of the second century?"[101]

While these objections to the Lechner-Theobald perspective are worth noting, they cannot refute the late date hypothesis. The notes on charismatic authority and literary dependence are significant observations. Still, they do not carry enough weight to counter the realities of Ignatius's absence until Irenaeus and the sudden emergence of intertextual connections around 180 CE. Regarding Trajan, one might also argue that Ignatius's eagerness for the congregation to meet applies equally during the reign of Marcus Aurelius, within the timeframe of Lechner's proposal.

Polycarp's Letter to the Philippians and Its Implications

Second, we have the question of Pol. *Phil*. Scholars who delay the date of the Ignatian corpus as a whole tend also to defer the date of Pol. *Phil*. As we have seen, Theobald, in his analysis of the leadership discourse of the early church, dates the letter to the second quarter of the second century, based on several of the above factors.[102] A brief recapitulation may still be beneficial. Three factors merit mention. First, Polycarp was familiar with the Pastoral Letters, which Theobald dates between 120 and 150 CE.[103] The second factor is the proposed death of Polycarp in 156, along with the schism in the Roman congregation(s) resulting from Marcion's teaching in 144.[104] This renders it virtually impossible for Pol. *Phil*. to be composed prior to 144. The third factor pertains to the interpolations in 1:1a and chapter 13. Lechner, in agreement with Theobald, considers the references to Ignatius and his letters (chapters 9 and 13 in Pol. *Phil*.) to be later interpolations.[105] I am not certain that the mention in chapter 9 needs to be an interpolation, but given the textual traditions of the letter,

---

[100] Lookadoo 2018a, 22.
[101] Lookadoo 2018a, 21.
[102] Lechner 2020, 62–63.
[103] Theobald 2016, 331.
[104] Lechner 2020, 63.
[105] Lechner 2020, 63–64; Theobald 2016, 316.

chapter 13 is probably not original. Since Pol. *Phil.* is also aware of the Pastoral Letters, it must have been written after the Pastorals, likely between 150 and 156 CE.[106]

The Theological and Cultural Backcloth of the Second Century

The third question, mentioned on several occasions previously, concerns which cultural background is the most reasonable to assume for the Ignatian correspondence. Lechner demonstrated that the context of the Second Sophistic is problematic.[107] His earlier works rather suggest that the cultural context is essentially so-called Valentinianism.[108] According to Lechner's view in his early work (1999), two features of the Ignatian corpus are especially noteworthy when considering the cultural milieu in which it exists: (a) The rule of faith, *Glaubensformel,*[109] of Ign. *Eph.* 18:2 and (b) the Star hymn in the context of Ign. *Eph.* 18–20:1.[110]

A. In the *Glaubensformel*, Jesus is recognised as God, born of the virgin Mary, from the seed of David, "and from the Holy Spirit" (πνεύματος δὲ ἁγίου). Here, Jesus baptism is emphasized, so that he might clenase the water "through his suffering" (τῷ πάθει). According to Lechner, these formulations explicitly address Valentinian beliefs, such as the notion that the Redeemer is divided into two entities: one from the earth and one from the Pleroma. It also tackles the Valentinian avoidance of recognising Mary as the physical mother of the Redeemer, and posits that the Redeemer only attained the title after his baptism.[111] Lechner also contends that the *Glaubensformel* evident in the *Acts of Paul* (ca. 190) originates from Ignatius and an even earlier context in Asia Minor. The author of the Ignatian letters utilises and adapts this tradition from its

---

[106] Lechner 1999, 64, also suggests this date. According to Lechner, the interpolation in the letter of Polycarp was done by the author of the Ignatian letters between 165 and 175 CE (Lechner 1999, 64).

[107] Lechner 2020, 22–26.

[108] Lechner 1999, 306; 2020, 55–65.

[109] Lechner 1999, 150–218.

[110] Lechner 1999, 297.

[111] Lechner 1999, 218–19.

initial form in Asia Minor. These modifications are embraced by the *Acts of Paul*, which demonstrates a progression of thought through Ignatius.[112]

B. According to Lechner, the Star hymn of Ign. *Eph.* 18 is a "polemical commentary" on the Valentinian myth, which reinterprets the myth of "a spiritual redeemer" so that the differences between the Aeon and the redeemer become clear.[113] Lechner finds chapter 74 of the text *Excerpta ex Theodoto* as the most reasonable text with which to compare the Star hymn and puts it in its immediate and ideological contexts.[114] Lookadoo rightly points out that in "order to challenge Lechner's interpretation of the passage and corresponding late date of the letters, one must put forth another reading [of Ign. *Eph.* 19] that makes sense not only of the historical background but also of the theological and rhetorical contexts of Ephesians."[115] While Lookadoo points to the difficulties in referencing concepts as final evidence for when the Ignatian corpus was written, he also provides one additional cultural backdrop that Lechner hardly takes into account. When pointing to the messianic expectations, explicit in the labelling of Jesus as Son of David in Ign. *Eph.* 18:2 (ἐκ σπέρματος μὲν Δαυίδ), Lookadoo makes use of another *religionsgesichtliche Faktor*, Jesus the Messiah.[116] Political ideology, along with several other Jewish theological strands, makes use of Num 24:17, which describes a messianic figure modelled as a rising star. However, as Lookadoo mentions, this merely demonstrates that the Star hymn can be fitted into various theological patterns and does not refute the overall point regarding the dating of Ignatius, according to Lechner. It does, however, highlight the difficulties in dating the Ignatian corpus, which employs language that is not uncommon among various theological factions of the Christ groups during the first and second centuries CE. A robust dating of the letters must consider more than merely reflecting the supposed context of the correspondence. The points made by Lookadoo also underscore the absence of Jewish motifs in our understanding of the Ignatian corpus.

---

[112] Lechner 1999, 219.
[113] Lechner 1999, 297.
[114] Lechner 1999, 275–80.
[115] Lookadoo 2018b, 699.
[116] Lookadoo 2018b, 701.

However, the context in which the Ignatian corpus is emerging, in Lechner's view, corresponds to the clash between the Ignatian group (referred to in the corpus as ἡ καθολικὴ ἐκκλησία, Ign. *Smyrn.* 7:2) and the Valentinian group. This perspective is somewhat refined by Theobald, who shares a similar understanding of the dating and authenticity of the corpus as well as Lechner.[117] In summary, Theobald argues that the Ignatian letters rely on the Pastoral Letters.[118] This means that the Pastorals provide the natural context for understanding the Ignatian corpus.[119] Theobald interprets the Pastoral Letters as an example of the reception of Paul's letter Romans. One prominent theme in Romans is notably absent in the Pastoral Epistles: the role of Israel, which is primarily discussed in chapters 9–11. Thus, the term from Theobald's title, *Israel-Vergessenheit*, is a way of describing a subject most important in the Roman discourse.[120] The Pastoral Letters also reflect a period in Asia Minor prior to Marcion's emergence on the theological stage.

According to Theobald, a theme perceivable in the Ignatian corpus is the character Ignatius's mimicking of Paul's life.[121] The themes and travels of Paul are reflected in the Ignatian letters.[122] The backdrop of the Ignatian letters is best imagined as a painting that combines elements of Paul's life and theology as understood by the author of the letters, alongside the doctrinal disputes among various Christ groups of differing factions.

To summarise, I conclude that the dating of the Ignatian letters falls between 160 and 175 CE. This conclusion is based on the works of Lechner and Theobald. Crucial points for my understanding include the absence of Ignatius during the second century, the implications of Polycarp's letter to the Philippians, and the theological and cultural context that best aligns with the aftermath of Valentinian influence in Rome. The first clearly identifiable reference to an Ignatian text appears in Irenaeus between 177 and 180. The Pastoral

---

[117] Lechner 2020, 64–65.
[118] Theobald 2016, 61–115.
[119] Theobald 2016, 258.
[120] Theobald 2016, 114, 353–60.
[121] Theobald 2016, 291.
[122] Theobald 2016, 291.

Letters suggest a leadership pattern that is also discernible (but extended) in the Ignatian corpus.

The Author of the Corpus

As noted in passing, I take the author of the Ignatian corpus to be an anonymous leader of the Christ groups in the latter part of the second century. This option is the only viable one, as I perceive the texts not to be written by the martyred ἐπίσκοπος of Syria. According to Lechner, the interpolations in Pol. *Phil.* are the works of the same author who wrote the Ignatian corpus.[123] The author of the Ignatian letters took one of the actual martyrs mentioned in Polycarp's letter to the Philippians and wrote theological treatises in his name, formatted as letters. If Lechner's interpretation is correct, one must assume that Ignatius died early in the second century; therefore, he did not write any letters concerning theological debates in the mid-100s. It is difficult to gather any external evidence about the author. The writer of Polycarp's letter mentions Ignatius even without interpolations but does not demonstrate any awareness of letters written by him.[124] The author of the letters is identified within the group referred to in Ign. *Smyrn.* 7:2 as ἡ καθολικὴ ἐκκλησία. We do not know if the individual was an ἐπίσκοπος, but he appears to be well-versed in theological issues and crucial traditions for the ἐκκλησία, particularly those that we today recognise as the New Testament. It is noteworthy that the anonymous author seems to hold a positive view of the Hebrew Bible in theory, even though he does not quote them extensively. He appears to be aware of temple discourse, as well as of gentile cult traditions in Ephesus.[125] The author seems to have liturgical and charismatic experience.[126] The author's aim, importantly, seems to be to promote ἡ καθολικὴ ἐκκλησία through reinforcement of the ἐπίσκοπος and *qui cum eo sunt*. For the sake of convenience, I will label the author Ignatius in the following analysis.

---

[123] Lechner 1999, 62.
[124] Lechner 1999, 64.
[125] Legarth 1992, 346.
[126] See for example Ign. *Eph.* 4, Ign. *Phld.* 7.

Given the internal evidence and the impossibility of establishing clear external evidence, this is as far as I deem it safe to go: the Ignatian corpus in the middle recension, first quoted by Irenaeus between 177 and 180 CE, was written around 160–175 CE by an anonymous author, most likely from Asia Minor. To push the date earlier becomes too speculative, which is why this dissertation will proceed from the conclusions defined above.

Excursus: The Martyrdom of Polycarp and the Episcopate

Before we turn to the actual SIT analysis of the Ignatian letters, a short excursus needs to address the Martyrdom of Polycarp, because Polycarp is an important character in Ignatian research, and the text we have access to actually mentions the title ἐπίσκοπος. In the latest LCL edition of the Greek text the word ἐπίσκοπος is mentioned three times, in the title of the work; in 16:2; and in 23:2 (the ending of the Moscow manuscript from the thirteenth century).[127]

The events reported by the text about Polycarp's martyrdom occurred between 150 and 156 CE, if we follow Eusebius, Pseudo-Pionius and internal evidence such as 9:3 where Polycarp says that he has served Christ for 86 years. Also, if Montanism is addressed in Mart. Pol 4, the text cannot be earlier than the late 160s CE.[128] According to the traditional understanding, the text should have been written quite soon after the reported events.[129] As is the case with the Ignatian correspondence, the Martyrdom of Polycarp is also hotly debated in terms of date and integrity.[130] While several scholars understand it as the beginning of martyr accounts from the mid-second century, others like Candida Moss argue that the text in its present form most likely stems from early third century.[131] Moss's argumentation takes into account several of the peculiarities of the text: the problematic legal procedure, the inconsistencies in the account of the Roman officials in Mart. Pol. 21, and the scriptural intertexts that compare Polycarp with the Passion narratives in the gospels.[132] While Moss's

---

[127] Ehrman 2003a, 363.
[128] Moss 2010, 545.
[129] Ehrman 2003, 361–62.
[130] Moss 2010, 539–41.
[131] Moss 2010, 540.
[132] Moss 2010, 548–57.

argumentation is careful, it cannot fully prove that the text as a whole is a third-century product. But Éric Rebillard extends the argument in his claim that the text might be seen as a way of conveying authority for a certain Pionius, who might be the character in Mart. Pol 22:3. Pionius associates himself with Polycarp, and thus borrows Polycarp's authority.[133] This reason for the composition of the text, or gathering of traditions, suggests a much later date than the mid-century events

The Martyrdom of Polycarp is transmitted to us from primarily two accounts: Pseudo-Pionius (see Mart. Pol. 21–22) and Eusebius's *Ecclesiastical History*. Eusebius's version is the shorter one, in which several of the "parallels between the death of Polycarp and the passion narratives" that arguably have been interpolated at a later state later are absent.[134] There has been a debate whether Mart. Pol. 1–19 has been redacted or not. Some think the core would have been an original eye-witness account, to which the redactor(s) added several layers.[135] The theory was championed by Hans Freiherr von Campenhausen in the mid-twentieth century. While von Campenhausen's treatment has been criticised, it has also gained a certain traction. The aim of the interpolations appears to have been to parallel the death of Polycarp with the death of Christ.[136] The exemplarity of Polycarp has thus been at the fore in the discussion.

On balance, it is more probable that the text was composed (or rather compiled) in the early third than in the late second century. The composition is probably a product of several redactors (Mart. Pol 21–23). Could some of the redacted material nevertheless provide a window into late second-century views on episcopal leadership? Before one can answer that question, one needs to address to what extent the instances that mention ἐπίσκοπος comes from the second century at all. As several scholars have noted, the title ("Martyrdom of the holy Polycarp, ἐπίσκοπος of Smyrna") stems from a much later time in the transmission history. Eusebius's quotation lacks the title, and it appears to be a

---

[133] Rebillard 2021, 13–14.
[134] Dehandschutter 1993; Moss 2010, 541.
[135] Von Campenhausen 1957, 8.
[136] Von Campenhausen 1957, 9–16, esp. p. 13.

subscript to the text rather than a rubric. Thus, the title provides little information for our understanding of the episcopal function in the second century.

Further, the alternative ending of the Moscow manuscript in which Polycarp is labelled an ἐπίσκοπος, appears to be late, too.[137] The reading in the manuscript is unique: the single manuscript we have for this reading comes from the thirteenth century and all other manuscripts follow the shorter reading, without any mention of an ἐπίσκοπος. The Moscow manuscript appears to be closer to Eusebius's text, which is a later version of the account.[138] When we analyse the content, the impression is that it must stem from the third century. It discusses Polycarp's relation to Irenaeus, who had been a "disciple of Polycarp" (μαθητῇ γεγονότι τοῦ ἁγίου Πολυκάρπου, 23:2), Polycarp's stance on Marcionism (23:3), wondrous reports on the martyrdom of Polycarp (23:4), and the immediate tradition history of the text, according to the author/redactor of the Moscow manuscript (23:5). The internal evidence thus suggests that Irenaeus had been dead for some time when the traditions were compiled (23:1; 5), which brings the mention in passing of ἐπίσκοπος in chapter 23:2 well into a period after our timeframe (κατὰ τὸν καιρὸν τοῦ μαρτυρίου τοῦ ἐπισκόπου Πολυκάρπου).

This means that the only mention of ἐπίσκοπος in the text that is relevant to consider is 16:2. The text reads Πολύκαρπος, ἐν τοῖς καθ'ἡμᾶς χρόνοις διδάσκαλος ἀποστολικὸς καὶ προφητικὸς γενόμενος ἐπίσκοπός τε τῆς ἐν Σμύρνῃ καθολικῆς ἐκκλησίας ("Polycarp, who in our time was an apostolic teacher and prophet and ἐπίσκοπος for the universal congregation in Smyrna"). As is clear from a comparison between Eusebius's *Eccl. Hist* 4 and Mart. Pol. 16:2, the texts differ on several minor points.[139] From this does not automatically follow, that the labelling of Polycarp as διδάσκαλος ἀποστολικὸς καὶ προφητικὸς γενόμενος ἐπίσκοπός τε τῆς ἐν Σμύρνῃ καθολικῆς ἐκκλησίας would be an interpolation in an original *urtext*. It does, however, remind us of the uncertainties in the original text, even in chapter 16. Also, the narrative voice that shifts the tone in a

---

[137] See Rebillard 2021, 37–43 for the function of the colophon as a cue for understanding how to read the text. This would place the Martyrdom of Polycarp firmly in the early third century.
[138] Ehrman 2003a, 362–63.
[139] See Ehrman 2003a, 388–91.

conclusive manner in 16:2 would suggest that the titles added to Polycarp are not original but from a later time. On balance, one can note the discussion in Irenaeus's *Haer.* 3.3, where the apostolicity of the episcopal order is emphasised. This text is from the late second century (see chapter 10 below) and discusses the episcopal order as a safeguard against heresies. It is therefore hard to say whether 16:2 belongs to an early stratum of the text or not, mirroring the situation in the late second century. If, for the sake of argument we assume this to be the case, what could be said about 16:2 when we apply the SIT categories?

Prototypicality and Impresarioship in Mart. Pol. 16:2

When we analyse the portrayal of Polycarp in the text that we have access to, it becomes abundantly clear that Polycarp is set forth as an example to emulate. He is the prototypical Christ-group leader who not only is pious (Mart. Pol. 7–8) but also steadfast (chapter 9–10), prophetic, apostolic (16:2), and wonder-working (16:1). Polycarp signals costly displays in his willingness to rather die than revoke his faith.[140] He is antithetical to the character Quintus in chapter 4, who not only revoked his own faith, but also convinced others to do so (Mart. Pol. 4). The prototypicality of his leadership is perhaps the most obvious aspect of the text.

This prototypical character is then associated with the role Polycarp had in the Smyrnean Catholic church (Σμύρνη καθολικῆς ἐκκλησία). He is said to be an apostolic and prophetic teacher and an ἐπίσκοπος. The titles of the ancient leaders, who are labelled teachers, apostles, and prophets, appear to be synonymous with the episcopal title given to Polycarp. The text is thus a small example of impresarioship: the ancient heroes of faith are associated with Polycarp through his title. The structure that the readers probably would recognise from their own time is also present in the martyrdom of Polycarp. Irenaeus's description of the apostolic character of the episcopate appears to be not too far away (see chapter 10 below). In a similar way, Irenaeus associates the episcopal leadership with the apostles through apostolic succession in *Haer.* 3.1–3. This idea of succession is also present in Mart. Pol. 23:2 (the ending of the Moscow manuscript), where the refutation of heresies and succession of teachings are

---

[140] Henrich 2009, 247.

intertwined. The picture that emerges from an SIT perspective is thus rather close to the perspectives on episcopal structures in *Against Heresies*. If 16:2 is part of a stratum from the second century, then it brings no new information about the understanding of the episcopal leadership in Christ-group texts associated with an apostolic succession, but rather attests to the view of Irenaeus.

9.2 An SIT Analysis of the Ignatian Letters

Following this rather lengthy introduction to the debate surrounding the Ignatian letters, we shall now proceed to a SIT analysis of the Ignatian corpus. As we have seen thus far in the book, several features that convey social identity have been adopted by Christ groups in the role of the ἐπίσκοπος. In the Christ-group texts we have examined so far, the episcopal figure has embodied Christ-group prototypicality. Additionally, we have encountered examples of how this character has been endowed with the authority to teach, which provides ample opportunities to serve as an identity entrepreneur – altering ingroup prototypicality. We have also observed that the episcopal structure, to varying degrees, has been understood to embed Christ-group identity; this serves as an example of identity impresarioship. We will now explore how the leadership in the Ignatian letters conveys Christ-group identity, and how this positions the ingroup against alternative group identities, such as a prominent Jewish one. In the following second part of this chapter, I will first examine in depth the Christ-group prototypicality of the Ignatian letters. Subsequently, I will demonstrate how the Ignatian letters assert that the episcopal structure is essential for ingroup prototypicality, thus embedding the Christian identity within this structure. The author thereby serves as an identity impresario.

9.2.1 Christian Prototypicality in Ignatius of Antioch

First, it is essential to acknowledge the ethos of Ignatius, which is vital for the effectiveness of the arguments throughout the letters. Ignatius indeed exemplifies characteristics reminiscent of Paul. He is mentioned in Pol. *Phil.* 9 as an example of a martyr. As discussed in the first part of the chapter, I do not question the authenticity of Pol. *Phil.* 9. In this section, Ignatius is depicted as a hero of the faith in Jesus, who does not shy away from enduring pain and suffering for Christ, thereby embodying the norms of his group. Just as Paul writes letters to different congregations in Asia Minor, so too does Ignatius. In Pol. *Phil.* 9, Ignatius is mentioned alongside Zosimus and Rufus, eventually including Paul. They are portrayed as being together with Jesus after having suffered alongside him (καὶ ὅτι εἰς τὸν ὀφειλόμενον αὐτοῖς τόπον εἰσὶ παρὰ τῷ κυρίῳ, ᾧ καὶ συνέπαθον). This brief chapter highlights the prototypical nature of Ignatius, Zosimus, Rufus, and Paul. As noted in chapter 2 above, prototypicality signifies the leader's ability to embody the ideals of their group; the better a leader manages to represent these ideals, the more followership they are likely to attract. Even though the letters of Ignatius are likely inauthentic in terms of authorship and date, they still serve as genuine examples of how a prototypical leader of a second-century Christ group encourages followers to adhere to group norms and illustrates how exclusive ingroup prototypicality was constructed for the Christ movement during the late second century. Ignatius himself, along with the characters depicted in the letters, represents different versions of exemplary members.

Throughout the seven letters of Ignatius in the middle recension, the language regarding ingroup norms is quite evident. The overwhelming majority of the 98 chapters in total contain language that suggests boundaries and expectations regarding the behaviour of group members. Comparison to outgroups is, as we have observed in chapter two above, a significant feature of human group dynamics.[141] Most of the rules do not address moral behaviour in a general sense (i.e., "right" and "wrong") but rather to how to correctly interact with ingroup members and leaders, as well as how to distinguish between ingroup and outgroup members. For this reason, an inevitable overlap between the SIT categories becomes apparent when discussing prototypicality, as the embedding of ingroup identity (identity impresarioship) is also presented as norms to adhere to. One must consider the taxonomy to be somewhat heuristic; even so, it aids in understanding the shape and nuances of the constant exhortations in the Ignatian letters. For clarity, this first section, which analyses prototypicality, will discuss ideals concerning ethics and dogmas in two subsections. Both these subsections broadly relate to individual behaviour and

---

[141] See above, and Tajfel 1981, 258.

belief. In the second section below, the author as identity impresario – namely, the embedding of ingroup identity within the structure and rites of the group – will be analysed. This focus arises since these norms essentially concentrate on the structure of the group rather than the individual behaviour.

How should a new member grasp what it means to be a follower of Jesus Christ? How do ingroup norms become apparent? While reading through the Ignatian letters, two types of norms emerge (both of which will be covered in the first section below on prototypicality): norms concerning ethical behaviour derived from Christ-group traditions and the Hebrew Bible, as well as group norms related to gatherings and dogma, that is, how the member(s) should interact with the ἐπίσκοπος. The connection to the ἐπίσκοπος is a prominent aspect of the Ignatian letters from the middle recension.

Norms Regarding Ethical Behaviour Stemming from Hebrew Bible and Christ-Group Traditions

First, there exist moral codes that define a general sense of right and wrong. This appears primarily as an abstract of Christ-group writings and gospel traditions, encompassing both the synoptic traditions and John's Gospel. Additionally, some references to the Hebrew Bible are discernible. Several instances also highlight ethical teachings that originated from what became the New Testament.[142]

A few of these instances are particularly noteworthy. In Ign. *Eph.* 10, the use of gospel traditions is discernible. Schoedel remarks that "apparently we have a commonplace of early Christian preaching before us."[143] He identifies various links to early traditions regarding Jesus (Matt 5:39–42, Luke 6:27–28). In other words, a particular moral discourse concerning appropriate ethical behaviour, attitudes towards outsiders, and responses to persecution is traceable in the Ignatian letters.

---

[142] In Ign. *Eph.*, chapters 5; 8; 10–11; 14–16 contain NT ethical teachings. Ign. *Magn.*: chapters 1 and 7. Ign. *Trall.*, chapters 8 and 12. Ign. *Rom.* chapters 2–5; 7. Ign. *Phld.*, chapters 3 and 7. Ign. *Smyrn.* chapters 6 and 11. Ign. *Pol.*, chapter 6.

[143] Schoedel 1985, 69.

Consistency between words and actions is crucial for the author. In Ign. *Eph.* 14:2, the author echoes Matt 12:33, stating, "the tree is known by its fruit." Believers are expected to ensure that their faith and behaviour are in harmony. Chapter 15 highlights the behaviour of the ἐπίσκοπος Onesimus as exemplary. In chapter 6 of the letter, Ignatius mentions criticism directed at Onesimus, who is described as being silent (σιγῶντα) and depicted as a man of few words. There are grounds to suggest that the reference in chapter 15 also alludes to the quiet ἐπίσκοπος Onesimus, as noted in chapter 6. Consequently, the passage in chapter 15 also addresses the prototypicality of Onesimus:

> Ἄμεινόν ἐστιν σιωπᾶν καὶ εἶναι, ἢ λαλοῦντα μὴ εἶναι. καλὸν τὸ διδάσκειν, ἐὰν ὁ λέγων ποιῇ. εἷς οὖν διδάσκαλος, ὃς εἶπεν, καὶ ἐγένετο· καὶ ἃ σιγῶν δὲ πεποίηκεν, ἄξια τοῦ πατρός ἐστιν.
>
> It is better to be silent and to be, than to speak and not be. It is good to teach, if the one who speaks also acts. Now there is one teacher who spoke, and it happened, and what he has done while remaining silent is worthy of the Father.

In this instance, the actions of the silent Onesimus are regarded not as flaws but as exemplary behaviour. Schoedel writes that "empty talk characterises the false teachers."[144] This perspective continually resurfaces not only in Ign. *Eph.*, but indeed throughout the letter corpus. The consistency between words and actions in harmony with the ideals of the ἐκκλησία is a sign of the similarity between Jesus and Onesimus. The formulation should thus be understood primarily as discussing the significance of harmony between words and deeds, continuing the theme from chapter 14.[145] The phrase καὶ ἃ σιγῶν δὲ πεποίηκεν, ἄξια τοῦ πατρός ἐστιν[146] is therefore not only referring to the teacher who spoke and it happened (Jesus) but also to Onesimus – while he was silent, he acted in ways worthy of the Father. Verse 15:2 also emphasises that Onesimus's silence is just as valuable as his teaching – words and deeds signify the same thing in reality.[147] The references to Psalm 33 will be examined below.

---

[144] Schoedel 1985, 77.

[145] See, however, also Kelhoffer 2023, 197–99 for a reading of the passage using Hellenistic musical theory.

[146] "And what he has done while being silent is worthy of the Father."

[147] Schoedel 1985, 76–78.

For the author of the Ignatian letters, it is of utmost importance that Ignatius followed through, suffered, and died. Costly displays signify credibility, as discussed above in chapter 2. The ultimate test was whether Ignatius merely spoke of martyrdom or was indeed martyred. The general use of language in Ign. *Rom.* 3:2, 4:2, and 5:1 suggests that Ignatius is measured by the same standards as everyone elsewhere, reflecting the Gospel tradition's emphasis on harmony between words and deeds; "so that I will not only call myself a Christian but also be found as one," – ἵνα μὴ μόνον λέγωμαι Χριστιανός, ἀλλὰ καὶ εὑρεθῶ, Ign. *Rom.* 3:2. The character of the purported author is thereby assessed by the consistency between his words and actions.

Moreover, various New Testament traditions related to moral behaviour are evident throughout the letters, chiefly from the Pauline and deutero-Pauline letters. In Ign. *Smyrn.* 11:3 (τέλειοι ὄντες τέλεια καὶ φρονεῖτε – "Being perfect, also think perfect things"), the author echoes Philippians 3:15: Ὅσοι οὖν τέλειοι, τοῦτο φρονῶμεν ("let those of us then who are mature be of the same mind," NRSV). Both the (post-)Pauline tradition in Ephesians 6:12 (τὰς ἀρχάς, πρὸς τὰς ἐξουσίας, πρὸς τοὺς κοσμοκράτορας τοῦ σκότους τούτου – "against the rulers, against the authorities, against the cosmic powers of this present darkness," NRSV), and for example, Ign. *Magn.* 1:2 (ἄρχοντος τοῦ αἰῶνος τούτου – "the ruler of this age") echo the idea that the enemies of the congregation are not humans but spiritual forces. This, of course, provides the group with ethical impulses concerning members of outgroups. The author emphasises ingroup traditions over scriptural sources, while not discarding the Scriptures.

In Ign. *Phld.* 7, the moral exhortation in spiritual preaching, apart from the sayings commending the ἐπίσκοπος and unity with him, concludes with the almost laconic μιμηταὶ γίνεσθε Ἰησοῦ Χριστοῦ, ὡς καὶ αὐτὸς τοῦ πατρὸς αὐτοῦ. ("be Jesus Christ's imitators, as he is of his Father"). In the next chapter of the letter, Ignatius continues the discussion by emphasising that the Gospel tradition holds greater significance than the Hebrew prophets: ἐμοὶ δὲ ἀρχεῖά ἐστιν Ἰησοῦς Χριστός, τὰ ἄθικτα ἀρχεῖα, ὁ σταυρὸς αὐτοῦ καὶ ὁ θάνατος καὶ ἡ ἀνάστασις αὐτοῦ ("for me, Jesus Christ is the original document; the inviolable original documents are his cross and death and his resurrection"). Ignatius's most prominent theological and ethical source is the gospel tradition.

It is interesting, on the same note, that explicit references to the Hebrew Bible/LXX are scarce. In contrast to 1 Clement, where the LXX/Hebrew Bible serves as the primary source for exhortations and as a model for an ethical life, this role is instead assumed by gospel and Christ-group traditions. There are a few instances in which the Hebrew Bible is alluded to, such as Isaiah 66:18 in Ign. *Magn.* 10 and Proverbs 18:17 in Ign. *Magn.* 12. In Ign. *Trall.* 8:2, a direct quotation from the LXX translation of Isa 52:5 is found, and Ign. *Eph.* 15:1 may allude to Psalms 33:9, even if, as I argue above, a reference to Jesus is the most prominent allusion here. One can thus observe that Ignatius's use of Scripture is double-edged: he is keen not to discard the Hebrew Bible/LXX, but rather uses it as a foreshadowing of the gospel. This becomes abundantly clear in Ign. *Magn.* 10:3, with its reference to Isa 66:18. The author states that χριστιανισμός is the entity to which people who believe in God from every tongue are gathered (εἰς ὃν πᾶσα γλῶσσα πιστεύσασα εἰς θεὸν συνήχθη). Here, God's promise to gather people of every tongue in Jerusalem is reinterpreted to mean that God will gather people of every tongue to χριστιανισμός. This dovetails with the author's description of faith in Christ as superseding the old temple, as shown in Ign. *Phld.* 9.

In summary, the ethical teachings of the Christ group, as reflected in the Ignatian letters, are primarily drawn from the Gospels and the Pauline epistles. Being a member of the ingroup entails adherence to specific ethical standards found in these sources. Other avenues for ethical guidance, such as the LXX/Hebrew Bible, are, if not entirely absent, at least quite limited and scarce.[148] The LXX/Hebrew Bible is interpreted through the lens of Christ-group theology and is utilised as a proof text for the unique position of the ingroup before God. The aggregate of the ethical teachings offers a pattern of life that congregants are expected to follow. Failing to adhere to ethical standards is linked to a failure to engage in communal life. Ignatius, who demonstrated costly displays in his martyrdom, serves as an example of behaviour that is commended, as his aim is to live a life consistent with ingroup values.

---

[148] Prov. 3:34 is echoed in Ign. *Eph.* 5:3 (which is also found in Jas 4:6), Ps 33:9 is echoed Ign. *Eph.* 15:1, but as discussed above, the reference to a teacher on this occasion suggests that Jesus primarily was in the scope of the author.

As mentioned in the SIT introduction in chapter 2, self-categorisation is one of the most important aspects of becoming a member of a group.[149] In the Ignatian letters, the author provides an authoritative basis for members to connect with the apostolic traditions regarding Jesus. The Hebrew Bible, as interpreted by the Christ group, can also offer teaching when aligned with the views of the Christ group. The message conveyed to members by the author is clear: anyone who has identified as a member of the congregation and seeks to understand the expected behaviour will find that the handed-down tradition offers vital information. The letters suggest that the contents of the gospel traditions were widely known among the Christ groups whom Ignatius addressed. Therefore, when commending these norms, Ignatius must comply with them himself. Since members that "identify more strongly with a group ... pay more attention to information that seems most informative about the group prototype and thus to what and who is more prototypical,"[150] it is essential for anyone in leadership to demonstrate adherence to group norms. The letters also emphasise that the norms of the Christ group, as presented, are embodied by Ignatius, making him a prototypical role model to emulate.

Group Behaviour Relating to Gatherings and Dogmas

The next set of explicit regulations for the Christian groups in the Ignatian letters comprises codes that address group behaviour, including the imperative to abstain from heresies. Such behaviour is generally considered unethical, but these codes regulate how members should perceive their own membership and how they should relate to one another. Additionally, they govern how dogmas and participation in worship ought to be enacted by the members. Both dogmas and involvement in worship relate to how the member enacts structural aspects of the group membership. There are several overlaps between this category and the next, as the regulation of group behaviour largely hinges on the members' relationship with their ἐπίσκοπος. In all letters, except Ign. *Rom.* and

---

[149] Hogg, van Knippenberg, and Rast 2012, 262.
[150] Hogg, van Knippenberg, and Rast 2012, 264.

Ign. *Pol.*, dogmatic group norms are prominent features of the text.[151] In Ign. *Rom.* and Ign. *Pol.*, these norms are mentioned less frequently but are not absent.

Ign. *Eph.* 18 presents dogmatic norms regarding the reception of New Testament traditions about the identity of Jesus as the Messiah.[152] To be part of the congregation is to believe that Jesus is intimately connected to the Father (ἐν σαρκὶ γενόμενος θεός), that He truly was born (not merely in appearance) of the Virgin Mary (7:2; 18:2), originates from the seed of David but also from the Holy Spirit (ἐκ σπέρματος μὲν Δαυίδ, πνεύματος δὲ ἁγίου, 18:2), was baptised, suffered, died, and rose again.[153] Being a part of the ἐκκλησία thus requires a set of beliefs in Jesus, alongside the traditions and developing theology surrounding him. To reject these theological claims is to be "anointed with the odour of the teaching of the ruler of this age" (ἀλείφεσθε δυσωδίαν τῆς διδασκαλίας τοῦ ἄρχοντος τοῦ αἰῶνος τούτου, Ign. *Eph.* 17:1).

The notion that the end times are imminent exists, but is not prominent, in the Ignatian letters. Nevertheless, Christ followers should adapt their lives to align with God's patience, which emerges in Ign. *Eph.* 11.

Regarding private life, there are norms to follow, drawing from New Testament exhortations about purity. Ignatius, in Ign. *Eph.* 16, appears to echo Pauline formulations once more, this time referencing 1 Cor 6:9. In this passage, Paul addresses forbidden sexual behaviours, which are also mentioned in Ign. *Eph.* 16. However, the argument advances further, which is the reason this section is discussed here, rather than in relation to the New Testament ethical traditions mentioned above. Rather than merely prohibiting the illicit sexual act of adultery (οἰκοφθόρος), Ignatius argues that it is even more grievous to corrupt the household of God by undermining the congregation through false teaching. Therefore, heresy is, by comparison, even worse than adultery.[154]

---

[151] Exhortations to adhere to gathering norms and dogmas for Christ-group members are found in Ign. *Eph.* 6; 9; 13; 16–18. In Ign. *Magn.* 7–11; 13. In Ign. *Trall.* 6–7; 9–11. In Ign. *Rom.* 5; 7. In Ign. *Phld.*, 2–6; 8–9. In Ign. *Smyrn.* 1–5; 7–8; 10. In Ign. *Pol.*, chapter 6.

[152] The ideas present in these chapters can also be found in Ign. *Magn.* 11; Ign. *Trall.* 9; Ign. *Smyrn.* 1 and 3. Parallels can also be found in Ign. *Rom.* 5 and 7.

[153] See Ign. *Smyrn.* 3.

[154] Schoedel 1985, 79.

Hence, the norm urged by Ignatius is that heresy should be avoided even more fervently than deadly adultery.

However, the requirements extend beyond mere intellectual beliefs. Frequency and behaviour related to gatherings often intersect. Ign. *Eph.* 13 exemplifies how frequent gatherings are valued in their own right, while Ign. *Magn.* 7 illustrates how these gatherings should be properly conducted, particularly with the presence of the ἐπίσκοπος. Thus, not only do the Ignatian letters encourage their recipients to engage in frequent gatherings, but they also outline a context in which an officer is expected to proclaim group beliefs and perform ritual acts that reflect the core beliefs of the ἐκκλησία (Ign. *Magn.* 6, Ign. *Trall.* 8, Ign. *Phld.* 4).

In Ign. *Smyrn.*, the author elaborates on the dogmas for the ἐκκλησία, distinct from the dogmatic statements of the offices. Ignatius provides a thorough account of Christological matters in chapters 1–3 and contends that Jesus should not merely have appeared to suffer (οὐχ ὥσπερ ἄπιστοί τινες λέγουσιν, τὸ δοκεῖν αὐτὸν πεπονθέναι "not like some unbelievers say, that he only appeared to have suffered," Ign. *Smyrn.* 2). Instead, he emphasises that Jesus Christ both died and was resurrected "in the flesh": ἀληθῶς ἐπὶ Ποντίου Πιλάτου καὶ Ἡρώδου τετράρχου καθηλωμένον ὑπὲρ ἡμῶν ἐν σαρκί ("truly, during the time of Pontius Pilate and the tetrarch Herod, he was nailed for us in the flesh"; Ign. *Smyrn.* 1:2), μετὰ δὲ τὴν ἀνάστασιν συνέφαγεν αὐτοῖς καὶ συνέπιεν ὡς σαρκικός, καίπερ πνευματικῶς ἡνωμένος τῷ πατρί ("and after his resurrection he ate and drank together with them as a material being, although he was spiritually united with the Father"; Ign. *Smyrn.* 3:3). This is incredibly important for the author, as it is linked to the martyrdom of Ignatius (4:1): why would Ignatius be willing to suffer in his flesh if Christ merely appeared to have done so? In other words, the prototypical understanding of group dogmas is that they hold greater significance than life itself. Ignatius (as the alleged author of the letter), bearing the weight of a martyr-to-be, portrays himself as prepared to die for the sake of Jesus Christ and the group dogmas concerning him, since Jesus physically triumphed over death. To be part of the ingroup, then, is to follow the prototypical example set by Ignatius.

But how do dogmas and gatherings relate to SIT? The emphasis on meeting together regularly in an ingroup, defined by a common narrative connected to specific norms, is crucial for self-definition. A general principle applies here: Fellowships where members regularly convene are more successful in shifting deviant members' beliefs toward the dominant viewpoint. Two longstanding yet comprehensive studies indicate that group identity is strengthened when members meet regularly.[155] While this may seem obvious, it illustrates that beliefs and social life are closely interconnected.[156] When members of an ἐκκλησία met for worship, they did so in a context where a specific set of norms was expected. The likelihood of adhering to these norms becomes highly probable when members meet regularly (especially if the participants, unlike in the two modern studies, were intrinsically motivated to comply with group norms). The spiritual formation of members requires fairly frequent gatherings, and the prototypical behaviour encouraged by Ignatius would, therefore, be instrumental in shaping members' behaviour and beliefs.

9.2.2 Identity Impresarioship in the Ignatian Letters

Finally, we now address the codes governing the believer's relationship with the ἐπίσκοπος. This constitutes a central theme in the Ignatian correspondence. It serves as the most significant exhortation throughout the corpus.[157] As will be

---

[155] The Bennington study has been analysed in two essential works: Newcomb 1961 and Newcomb, Koenig, Flacks, and Warwick 1967. Also, Siegel and Siegel 1957, performed a similar study that showed similar results. To briefly summarise the Bennington study, it serves as a valuable example of how frequency in fellowship alters political beliefs. The change occurred through something as simple as housing. This study measured the political preferences of students from conservative homes during their education at the liberal Bennington College, in Bennington, Vermont. The study demonstrated that students shifted from a Republican to a Democratic view of politics during their education. This shift became increasingly evident each year after the students arrived at Bennington College, particularly among those in their senior year. Notably, students housed in environments where liberal political views were predominant (such as dormitories rather than sorority houses) were more likely to lean to the left on the political spectrum.

[156] Brown and Pherson 2020, 52–53.

[157] Chapters where exhortations to Christ-group members on a correct way to interact with the ἐπίσκοπος are recorded: Ign. *Eph.*, chapters 1–6 and 20; Ign. *Magn.*, chapters 3–4; 6–7; 13; 15; Ign. *Trall.*, chapters 2–3 and 12; Ign. *Rom.* 2–3, Ign. *Phld.*, Introduction, 1; 3–4; 7; Ign. *Smyrn.* 8–9; Ign. *Pol.*, chapter 6, while chapters 1–5 and 7 describes how the ἐπίσκοπος should interact with the congregants.

abundantly clear, the author assumes the role of an identity impresario when discussing the ἐπίσκοπος. Christian identity, as opposed to various suggestions of what that identity could entail, is intimately intertwined with the episcopal structure advocated by the author. The author embeds Christian identity within the group's structure and its associated rituals. The author's impresarioship regarding the ἐπίσκοπος can be categorised into three distinct subcategories: subjection to the ἐπίσκοπος, unity with the ἐπίσκοπος, and taking the ἐπίσκοπος as a role model.

Subjection to the ἐπίσκοπος

Throughout the letters, the theme of subjection under the ἐπίσκοπος recurs. With the exception of Romans (which is a special case, see below), subjection to the ἐπίσκοπος is mentioned and emphasised in every letter. Most often, the term ὑποταγή is used, which is defined as "the state of submissiveness, subjection, subordination."[158] Other cognates are also found to a lesser degree. In Ign. *Eph.* 2, the first example of this concept in the corpus, Ignatius claims that the best way to give glory to Jesus Christ is to subject oneself (ὑποταγή) to the ἐπίσκοπος Onesimus. In this act of submission, the congregation will be made holy (ἡγιωμένοι) and complete (κατηρτισμένοι). This call to submission is further emphasised using πρέπον οὖν ἐστιν, which translates to "for it is fitting." Ignatius reminds the congregation of the proper actions of Christ believers, what they owe in giving honour. The right way of acting, that which is fitting, is to submit to the ἐπίσκοπος. This is closely related to the saving act of Christ. In Ign. *Magn.* 13:2 the author writes:

ὑποτάγητε τῷ ἐπισκόπῳ καὶ ἀλλήλοις, ὡς Ἰησοῦς Χριστὸς τῷ πατρὶ κατὰ σάρκα καὶ οἱ ἀπόστολοι τῷ Χριστῷ καὶ τῷ πατρί, ἵνα ἕνωσις ᾖ σαρκική τε καὶ πνευματική

---

[158] BDAG s.v. ὑποταγέ. One can note that the most common word is ὑποταγέ, used in Ign. *Eph.*; Ign. *Magn.*; Ign. *Trall.*; Ign. *Phld.*; and Ign. *Pol.* However, in Ign. *Smyrn.*, "everyone should follow the ἐπίσκοπος as Jesus Christ followed the Father" (πάντες τῷ ἐπισκόπῳ ἀκολουθεῖτε, ὡς Ἰησοῦς Χριστὸς τῷ Πατρί), the concept of followership is used. BDAG. s.v. ἀκολουθέω defines the word thus: "2. to follow or accompany someone who takes the lead ... 3. to follow someone as a disciple ... 4. gener. to comply with, follow, obey."

> Submit to the ἐπίσκοπος and each other, as Jesus Christ, according to the flesh, submitted to the Father and as the apostles were submitted to Christ and to the Father and to the Spirit, so that there may be unity in flesh as well as in spirit.

When submitting to "the ἐπίσκοπος and each other," the ingroup members also mirror the actions of prototypical examples such as Christ and the apostles. According to the author, there is truly no other way to be a member of the group than to submit to the ἐπίσκοπος.

At the beginning of the Ign. *Magn.*, Ignatius presents the ἐπίσκοπος Damas, the πρεσβύτεροι Bassus and Apollonius, and the διάκονος Zotion as examples. Damas is described as "your ἐπίσκοπος worthy of God" (ἀξιοθέου ὑμῶν ἐπισκόπου). Bassus and Apollonius are described as ἀξίων, worthy, while Zotion is closely linked with Ignatius himself as a fellow slave/servant: τοῦ συνδούλου μου διακόνου. The immediate benefit of labelling the leaders that Ignatius allegedly met is to demonstrate how they embody the expectations of leadership within a Christian group (he endorses their prototypicality), and how their rank (which reflects the divine reality, according to Ign. *Magn.* 7) warrants a certain level of respect. The leaders of the Magnesian group also serve as examples to emulate; Zotion exemplifies his role by submitting to Damas on one hand and to Bassus and Apollonius on the other. Ignatius even likens Zotion's submission to the submission under the grace of God and the law of Christ (ὑποτάσσεται τῷ ἐπισκόπῳ ὡς χάριτι θεοῦ καὶ τῷ πρεσβυτερίῳ ὡς νόμῳ Ἰησοῦ Χριστοῦ). Even had the leaders been unknown as individuals, their roles as exemplary leaders would likely have been easily recognised. Thus, the author's endorsement of these leaders offered a general pattern to follow.

In Ign. *Magn.* 4, correct ethical behaviour through submission to the ἐπίσκοπος is suggested to the Magnesians as closely tied to their identity as followers of Christ. Just as Zotion in Ign. *Magn.* 2 properly submitted himself to the ἐπίσκοπος, so should a true Christian submit him- or herself. The distinction between being called a Christian and being a Christian lies in submission to the ἐπίσκοπος, even if the ἐπίσκοπος appears to be too young for his office. It is difficult to imagine a clearer way of expressing how the author connects Christian identity with the role of the ἐπίσκοπος, thereby acting as an identity impresario. This relates to the author associating the congregation with the ἐπίσκοπος in the same way as the Father has a close relationship with Jesus (Ign.

Magn. 7). In chapter 6, the ἐπίσκοπος is certainly portrayed as a prototype of Christ: he should preside in the place that belongs to God (προκαθημένου τοῦ ἐπισκόπου εἰς τόπον θεοῦ). Some manuscripts also read τύπον instead of τόπον, that is, as a representation of Christ. The other leadership roles are also perceived as prototypical: "the presbyters in the place of the council of the apostles, and the deacons, who are most dear to me and who have been entrusted with the ministry of Jesus Christ" (καὶ τῶν πρεσβυτέρων εἰς τόπον συνεδρίου τῶν ἀποστόλων, καὶ τῶν διακόνων τῶν ἐμοὶ γλυκυτάτων πεπιστευμένων διακονίαν Ἰησοῦ Χριστοῦ). In other words, these leadership roles are as essential for the congregation as the Father is to Jesus. The patterns embedded in the esteemed leaders are reflections of a celestial reality.

Furthermore, in private matters, members of Christ groups should maintain a close relationship with the bishop, as the author suggests. In Ign. *Pol.* the consent (μετὰ γνώμης τοῦ ἐπισκόπου) of the ἐπίσκοπος is essential if a couple within the group wishes to marry. Polycarp is also urged to determine which widows should receive financial support and which slaves could be bought free with collective funds (Ign. *Pol.* 4–5). According to the author, being a Christian entails engaging with every level of life within the episcopal structure.

In summary, a genuine way of living as a believer in Christ is to submit to the ἐπίσκοπος. By doing so, Christ-followers reflect a supernatural reality as outlined by the author. The ingroup identity, as those saved by Christ, is embedded in the structure to which every member is expected to subject themselves.

Unity with the ἐπίσκοπος.

Closely related to the first point of impresarioship is the unity within the congregation, where members, as stated in Ign. *Eph.* 3:2, should run together (συντρέχητε) with the ἐπίσκοπος. The ἐπίσκοπος is depicted as sharing the mind of Christ. Not only in Ephesus but to the ends of the world (τὰ πέρατα), the appointed (ὁρισθέντες) ἐπίσκοποι share in the mind of Christ.

Furthermore, the need for unity with the ἐπίσκοπος would prevent members from celebrating the eucharist or gathering for worship on the Sabbath. Since the ἐπίσκοπος was crucial for self-definition, his absence would be problematic. It would also establish a boundary against those who advocated for gatherings on Sabbaths rather than on "the Lord's Day." In Ign. *Magn.* 9, the author warns against celebrating the Eucharist on the Sabbath. To be a member of the congregation is to gain new hope, καινότητα ἐλπίδος, and thus, living according to the old ways equates to not being disciples of Jesus Christ (μαθηταὶ Ἰησοῦ Χριστοῦ). Life in Christ demands a life in unity with the ἐπίσκοπος.

The two distinct types of argumentation derived from theological ideas that Ignatius employs in Ign. *Magn.* 7 – the analogy from Christology and the analogy from sacrificial theology – urge the congregants towards unity. If God and Christ are united, why do you not live in harmony? If there is a singular sacrificial action performed by Christ, it is essential to align with that action, as the author suggests. This utilisation of examples encourages the congregants to pursue a unified path.

Taking the ἐπίσκοπος as a Role Model/ Respecting the ἐπίσκοπος

The final aspect of impresarioship is double-edged and is really a mixture between prototypicality and impresarioship. From the connection between the episcopal structure and the heavenly realities that we have observed above, it does not necessarily follow that the individual ἐπίσκοπος should be seen as a model to emulate. As noted in Herm. Sim. 9.27 (104), non-exemplary leaders were not unthinkable. One could, therefore, argue that the ἐπίσκοπος as a role model is not a matter of impresarioship (the embedding of ingroup identity in a structure or ritual) but rather of prototypicality (the exemplary character of the individual leader). However, as one reads through the Ignatian letters, no instances of non-exemplary ἐπίσκοποι are found. The ἐπίσκοπος is consistently portrayed as a local role model to follow. The closest example of a non-prototypical ἐπίσκοπος appears to be the alleged self-descriptions of Ignatius at certain points (see for example Ign. *Smyrn.* 11). This becomes especially salient when there are opportunities to escape from suffering. Suffering serves as a hallmark of a prototypical leader. The depiction of Ignatius, however, is never explicitly non-exemplary; rather, it reflects the author's way of addressing the potential for escaping from suffering. It is thus reasonable to assume that the author of the letters understands true ἐπίσκοποι, who are steadfast in suffering, as local examples to emulate. Thus, two aspects of SIT leadership occur simultaneously: The ingroup prototypicality is embodied in the local leader, and the ingroup identity is embedded in the structure they uphold.

In *Ign. Eph.* 1, the ἐπίσκοπος Onesimus is described as τῷ ἐν ἀγάπῃ ἀδιηγήτῳ, ὑμῶν δὲ ἐν σαρκὶ ἐπισκόπῳ, "who is abiding in an inexpressible love and is your ἐπίσκοπος in the flesh" (Ign. *Eph.* 1.3). Ignatius praises Jesus Christ, as the congregation deserves a bishop like Onesimus ("for blessed is the one who has given you grace to be worthy to have gained such an ἐπίσκοπος" – εὐλογητὸς γὰρ ὁ χαρισάμενος ὑμῖν ἀξίοις οὖσι τοιοῦτον ἐπίσκοπον κεκτῆσθαι). Onesimus is presented as an example, closely linked with Jesus.

The letter to the Trallians outlines a similar pattern. The ἐπίσκοπος Polybios is presented as an example to follow: "whose own way of life is an instruction and whose humbleness is power. I understand him as respected also by the godless" (οὗ αὐτὸ τὸ κατάστημα μεγάλη μαθητεία, ἡ δὲ πραότης αὐτοῦ δύναμις· ὃν λογίζομαι καὶ τοὺς ἀθέους ἐντρέπεσθαι Ign. *Trall.* 3:2). All the values esteemed by the group, with which the Trallian congregants are expected to identify, are found in Polybios. The author of the Ignatian letters also emphasises that Ignatius, as ἐπίσκοπος, is genuinely someone who acts in accordance with group values. For instance, in Ign. *Trall.* 12:3, Ignatius perceives his trial and death as a test to endure. If his testimony is to hold value, it must remain steadfast in death.

A similar situation arises in the letter to the Philadelphians. Already in 1:2, the author commends the unnamed ἐπίσκοπος as a model. This unnamed ἐπίσκοπος serves as a figure to imitate.

> συνευρύθμισται γὰρ ταῖς ἐντολαῖς ὡς χορδαῖς κιθάρα. διὸ μακαρίζει μου ἡ ψυχὴ τὴν εἰς θεὸν αὐτοῦ γνώμην, ἐπιγνοὺς ἐνάρετον καὶ τέλειον οὖσαν, τὸ ἀκίνητον αὐτοῦ καὶ τὸ ἀόργητον αὐτοῦ ἐν πάσῃ ἐπιεικείᾳ θεοῦ ζῶντος.

> For he is in harmony with the commandments like the harp to the strings. Therefore my soul blesses his mind that knows God, in that it knows to be virtuous and perfect: his character is unwavering and wrath-free in all graciousness, which comes from the living God.

Once again, as seen in the letter to the Ephesians, the pattern of life conveys the strongest message, rather than the words of the unnamed ἐπίσκοπος. Accordingly, the author offers readers a prototypical example, which is presented as familiar to the recipients, making it possible to imitate. Therefore, the ἐπίσκοπος who exhibits such behaviours is deserving of imitation.

9.2 An SIT Analysis of the Ignatian Letters

The letter to the Romans is a special case. Ignatius writes primarily to prevent prominent members of the Roman congregation from intervening on his behalf; his eyes are fixed on his martyrdom, as that will allow him to attain God (θεοῦ ἐπιτυχεῖν, Ign. *Rom.* 1:2; 2:1; 4:1; and so forth). Instead of urging the Roman congregation with advice on how to live according to group norms, Ignatius paints a self-portrait of a humble follower of Christ who wishes to "attain God" through martyrdom. In this way, Ignatius presents himself (an ἐπίσκοπος) as an example, a prototype, rather than rhetorically urging adherence to group norms. Initially, Ignatius seems hesitant to position himself as an example. However, he is clearly portraying himself as someone prepared to suffer for the faith, which, despite his modest language, grants him the authority to speak as he endures pain for the unique ingroup identity. He does what Philip Esler describes as "manifesting what it means to be a member of the ingroup and in representing it in ways that differentiate it from outgroups."[159] Therefore, in several instances, Ignatius is depicted as a prototypical hero for the ingroup values. In Ign. *Rom.* 2, Ignatius, being a most prominent figure, desires martyrdom. As described above in chapter 2, Ignatius is signalling costly displays in his readiness to suffer for ingroup values. As a martyr, he becomes an example to follow: "I do not want you to please people, but to please God, which you also do" (Οὐ γὰρ θέλω ὑμᾶς ἀνθρωπαρεσκῆσαι, ἀλλὰ θεῷ ἀρέσαι, ὥσπερ καὶ ἀρέσκετε). This is elaborated in the chapter.

> πλέον δέ μοι μὴ παράσχησθε τοῦ σπονδισθῆναι θεῷ, ὡς ἔτι θυσιαστήριον ἕτοιμόν ἐστιν, ἵνα ἐν ἀγάπῃ χορὸς γενόμενοι ᾄσητε τῷ πατρὶ ἐν Ἰησοῦ Χριστῷ, ὅτι τὸν ἐπίσκοπον Συρίας κατηξίωσεν ὁ θεὸς εὑρεθῆναι εἰς δύσιν ἀπὸ ἀνατολῆς μεταπεμψάμενος.
>
> But make nothing more happen than that I become a libation to God as it still is an altar ready, so that I become a chorus in love, which you may sing to the Father in Jesus Christ. For God has deemed the Syrian ἐπίσκοπος worthy to be found at the setting sun, after that he sent him from where it rises. (Ign. *Rom.* 2:2)

For Ignatius, the phrase "God deemed the ἐπίσκοπος of Syria worthy" (τὸν ἐπίσκοπον Συρίας κατηξίωσεν ὁ θεὸς εὑρεθῆναι) signifies being martyred for one's faith in Jesus Christ. This is regarded as the ultimate honour. As demonstrated by the example of the silent ἐπίσκοπος of the Ephesian congregation, the matter

---

[159] Esler 2021, 42.

at stake is primarily a question of confession through actions, not merely empty words. Schoedel comments:

> Here is another indication that for Ignatius silence (however singularly defined in this context) is a matter of letting deeds speak for themselves [...] Rather he was contrasting an authentic and inauthentic witness to God. The silence of the Roman Christians will permit Ignatius to prove the profession of his faith by laying down his life. This (silent) deed will authenticate his claim to be a Christian and transform that claim from an empty sound to a meaningful word.[160]

This consistent alignment between words and actions is also evident in Ign. Rom. 3. In verse 2, Ignatius writes,

> μόνον μοι δύναμιν αἰτεῖσθε ἔσωθέν τε καὶ ἔξωθεν, ἵνα μὴ μόνον λέγω, ἀλλὰ καὶ θέλω, ἵνα μὴ μόνον λέγωμαι Χριστιανός, ἀλλὰ καὶ εὑρεθῶ. ἐὰν γὰρ εὑρεθῶ, καὶ λέγεσθαι δύναμαι καὶ τότε πιστὸς εἶναι, ὅταν κόσμῳ μὴ φαίνωμαι.

> Pray for me, only that I have power both on the inside and outside, that I not only speak but also have the willingness, that I not only should call myself Christian but also be found as one. For if I would be found [as a Christian], I can also be said to have power to be faithful, when I no longer am visible in the world.

The portrait of Ignatius seeks to exemplify faithfulness towards Jesus Christ even in trial and death. Ignatius's request to the leaders of the Roman congregation is for their support in his efforts to remain consistent. The reference in the previous chapter, where it states that Ignatius will be a "word of God" (ἐγὼ λόγος θεοῦ) if the Roman congregation does not intervene on his behalf, raises a question regarding the testimony of Ignatius. Consequently, it becomes a matter of his prototypicality. The author appears to believe that Ignatius's example will enhance the trustworthiness of the mission of the congregations.

Identity Impresarioship in the Ignatian Letters – Concluding Remarks

As we have seen, the identity impresarioship in Ignatius pertains to three sometimes overlapping areas: subordination to the ἐπίσκοπος, unity with the ἐπίσκοπος, and respecting the ἐπίσκοπος as a role model.

The examples of identity impresarioship provided by the Ignatian letters are closely connected to unity with and subordination to the ἐπίσκοπος. Since, as

---

[160] Schoedel 1985, 170.

demonstrated in, for instance, Ign. *Eph.* 3:2 and Ign. *Magn.* 7, the ἐπίσκοπος is as intimately connected to his followers or subjects as God the Father is to Jesus, the implications indicate that it is of utmost importance to maintain a proper relationship with him. The unity that Christ shares with the Father translates into social behaviour, with group members living in unity with the ἐπίσκοπος. It is crucial to remember that the theological concepts and the ingroup norms perceived as prototypical must also convey why adhering to the prototype is significant.

> The organization of social action – meetings, parades, celebrations, memorials, and more besides – should, in miniature and in the here and now, stand in anticipation of the world to come. So, as well as articulating a vision, the skills of leadership extend to putting on a show of that vision. This means that successful leaders need to be impresarios as well as artists of identity.[161]

The concept of unity is, in a theological sense, crucial for the group. The group should not only comply with the emerging episcopacy but also regard it as important, as it is a structure that mirrors the ingroup narrative. The structure, as described by the author of the Ignatian letters, suggests that the members are aligned with the nature of God and gain access to it through congregational gatherings. Consequently, the structure produces theological incentives for group stability, which is characteristic of the social identity perspective leadership: "Leadership ... is about getting followers to want to follow rather than about forcing them to do so."[162] Thus, subjection and unity with the ἐπίσκοπος represent a proper relationship with God. Moreover, the congregants assume the role of Jesus if the ἐπίσκοπος embodies the role of God the Father. By gathering together, the congregation actively participates in a significant idea that expresses a distinct group identity: that Jesus is profoundly connected to the Father.

Concerning the ἐπίσκοπος as a role model deserving of respect, it is evident that the ethical guidelines reflected in existing New Testament traditions not only required heroes from other parts of the empire, such as martyrs like Ignatius, but also necessitated a local role model who could embody the group's

---

[161] Haslam, Reicher, and Platow 2011, 179.
[162] Haslam, Reicher, and Platow 2011, 166.

norms in a prototypical manner. We have limited knowledge of how the process of installing leaders occurred. The only instance in the Ignatian letters that indirectly discusses how someone was installed is in Ign. *Phld*. 1, where the anonymous ἐπίσκοπος is said to *not* have obtained (κεκτῆσθαι[163]) his ministry by himself. Instead, it is influenced by the love of God and Jesus Christ. This does not offer any significant clarity regarding how leaders emerged, but on a general level, successful leadership relies on their ability to embody the group norms.[164] The author chooses to consistently portray local ἐπίσκοποι as prototypical in their behaviour, which suggests that the structure into which the letters invest authority does not contradict individual prototypicality among the ἐπίσκοποι but rather expects it. Aside from what has been previously stated about prototypicality in this chapter, effective group leadership (such as embodying how to follow Jesus Christ and rightly participate in the ἐκκλησία τοῦ θεοῦ) "facilitates the development of a sense of shared social identity."[165] This is nearly impossible if the group norms do not apply to the leader. The leader's ability to earn respect from followers depends on their capacity to adhere to group norms. Michael Hogg concludes, "Within a salient group, ... people who are perceived to occupy the most prototypical position are perceived to best embody the behaviours to which other, less prototypical members are conforming."[166] The more pronounced the group identity is, the more crucial it becomes to be prototypical, whether established as a leader (as in the cases described in the letters of Ignatius) or emerging as one.[167] In the letters of Ignatius, we observe that an interconnection is anticipated: the ἐπίσκοποι should exemplify prototypical behaviour while their role within the structure reflects Jesus's relationship with the Father, thus serving as an embodiment (example of impresarioship) of a Christian group identity.

---

[163] BADG, s.v. κτάομαι, def. 3, "Possess".

[164] One can note the descriptions of the requirements of the ἐπίσκοπος in the Pastoral Letters (1 Tim 3:2–7, Titus 1:7–9.) These descriptions are of course also norms for ordinary members of a congregation.

[165] Haslam and Reicher 2007, 140.

[166] Hogg 2001, 189.

[167] Hogg 2001, 190.

9.3 Conclusion: The ἐπίσκοπος in Ignatius, Christian Identity, and the Parting of the Ways

To summarise this section, we have identified existing group norms for Christ followers in the Ignatian letters. These norms pertain to ethical behaviour, dogmas, gatherings, and the congregants' relationship with their ἐπίσκοπος. This illustrates how the author of the Ignatian letters constructs prominent group norms (i.e., prototypical behaviour) expected of members and embeds these significant group norms within the episcopal structure (identity impresarioship).

The ethical behaviour expected from members of the groups is informed by normative New Testament traditions, including gospel traditions and Pauline as well as deutero-Pauline traditions. These traditions serve as a significant source for prototypical behaviour. The Hebrew Bible/LXX serves as a foundation for ethical considerations only when viewed through one's own theological narrative. Consequently, little space remains for a prominent Jewish identity in describing a prototypical member.

The norms concerning dogmas and gatherings are both intellectual and practical. On one hand, there is a set of concepts and dogmas essential for understanding the nature of Jesus Christ and his relationship with the Father. According to the author of the Ignatian letters, these dogmas are worth dying for. On the other hand, these dogmas are accompanied by behaviours that incorporate them into the everyday lives of believers: gathering in unity reflects the dogmatic statements. The episcopal structure serves as a means for the author to be an Identity Impresario, connecting members with a meaningful framework that embodies the theological reality described by ingroup rhetoric. The congregation and its ἐπίσκοπος provide an earthly representation of the supernatural reality articulated in the dogmas, particularly when gatherings are conducted correctly (that is, in submission to the ἐπίσκοπος). Consequently, the structure proposed by the Ignatian letters serves as a vehicle for the social identity of a specific Christian group.

To further investigate the embedding mechanisms in the episcopal structure of the Ignatian letters, the examples of impresarioship are threefold: the members are expected to live in unity with the ἐπίσκοπος, be subjected to the ἐπίσκοπος, and take the ἐπίσκοπος as a role model for their behaviour as group members. Unity with and subjection to the ἐπίσκοπος are once again examples of embedded social identity: the ἐπίσκοπος becomes a symbol of the theological self-understanding of the Christ groups. This influences the view on which day would be appropriate for communal worship. The correct day excludes prominent Jewish identity, for which the Sabbath would naturally be chosen for worship gatherings. The ἐπίσκοπος as a role model provides indications of how group prototypicality is embodied in the office holders of the Christ groups. While the Ignatian letters disregard the process of installing new leaders, they do expect the installed ἐπίσκοπος to exemplify prototypicality according to ethical norms. Thus, Ignatius is also portrayed as someone striving to reflect Christ in his martyrdom. It is important to note that Ignatius, as the implied sender, remains a powerful example to follow, even if the letters are later forgeries. After all, he is depicted as being on his way to Rome to die for the beliefs of the Christ groups.

How does all this help us better understand the role of the ἐπίσκοπος in relation to the parting of the ways? As we have seen, in the Ignatian letters of the middle recension, the ἐπίσκοπος embodies a specific Christian prototypicality and simultaneously reflects the embedding of Christian identity within the leadership structure.

The constructed prototypicality signifies the ideals present in the writings of the Christ group and in the Hebrew Bible as interpreted by them. Within these ideals, there is no room for a prominent Jewish identity. The "ancient records" referenced in Ign. *Phld.* 9 are regarded as less significant than the gospel of Jesus Christ. This implies that observance of the Torah, including purity and other halakic issues, does not align with ingroup values. This notion is further confirmed by the rejection of any Sabbath observance mentioned in Ign. *Magn.* 9. Instead, the values reinforced by the gospels or other writings of the Christ group are deemed the only acceptable ones. Additionally, the author's perspective (who is purportedly the ἐπίσκοπος from Syria demonstrating costly displays) on a correct interpretation of the Hebrew Bible, as noted in Ign. *Magn.* 10:3, suggests that χριστιανισμός has supplanted Jewish identity as the people of God. Throughout the letters, the ἐπίσκοποι are depicted as exemplary members of the Christ group, embodying ingroup values through their harmonious actions and words. Consequently, the ἐπίσκοπος of the congregation serves as a local role model for Christ-group members.

In terms of impresarioship, the ἐπίσκοπος and the associated leadership structure are portrayed as earthly representations of the celestial realm. The author of the Ignatian letters, who utilises the ethos of the costly displays of a martyred ἐπίσκοπος, acts as an identity impresario who links the group's vision to a concrete structure (the presiding ἐπίσκοπος) and specific actions (worship and Eucharist on the correct day, in the presence of the ἐπίσκοπος) within these frameworks. The ἐπίσκοπος presides over the worship gatherings as a representative of God, surrounded by πρεσβύτεροι and διάκονοι fulfilling the roles of Christ and the apostles. Consequently, the Christ group's view of God and Christ as intimately and uniquely connected is reflected in the episcopal order (Ign. *Trall*. 7; Ign. *Smyrn*. 8, and so forth). Within the ἐπίσκοπος, the central narrative of the Christ group is embodied during the worship gathering. Those wishing to become members can only do so to the extent that they accept the practices associated with the episcopal structure. This renders the presence of, and submission to, the ἐπίσκοπος a natural way for each member to lead a distinctly Christian life. The ἐπίσκοπος, who exemplifies the values of the Christ group, is essential for every gathering (Ign. *Smyrn*. 8). Thus, the ἐπίσκοπος becomes the local authority ensuring that alternative group identities, such as docetist (Ign. *Trall*.; Ign. *Smyr*.) or Judaizing (Ign. *Phld*.; Ign. *Magn*.), find no space within the congregations. The presence of Christ in the Eucharist (Ign. *Phld*. 4), the necessity to worship on Sundays rather than Saturdays (Ign. *Magn*. 9), and the theological understanding of the episcopal structure as an expression of the Christ-group narrative all reflect a stereotyping of behaviour and belief tied to the ἐπίσκοπος. According to SIT, such stereotyping of behaviour is expected in any group. Therefore, we can conclude that as long as the ἐπίσκοπος was emphasised as a representation of Christ-group theology, any form of group identity that did not accept this view of the ἐπίσκοπος would be excluded. Thus, no room was left for a prominent Jewish identity within the episcopal Christ groups. The ἐπίσκοπος in the Ignatian letters widened the rift between Christ groups and Jewish groups.

10. The ἐπίσκοπος and Christian Identity in Irenaeus's *Against Heresies*, Book Three

As we have seen throughout this study, the term ἐπίσκοπος encompasses a variety of leadership models. From 60 to 180 CE, the precise meaning of this role appears to develop gradually. The reference in Philippians 1 invites speculation, and as we noted, this speculation can lead scholars to assume various interpretations, ranging from an economic responsibility or a role akin to that of an ἀρχισυνάγωγος on one hand, to spiritual leadership on the other. Although evidence is scarce in the early part of this period, reflections on the role of the ἐπίσκοπος in the Didache, 1 Clement, the Pastoral letters, and the Ignatian correspondence indicate that the emerging episcopal structure gradually solidifies into a foundation for the Christian tradition by the end of the second century. This is achieved through the expected prototypicality of office holders, who embody a distinct Christian ideal, and through the incorporation of Christian identity within these structures, as articulated by second-century Christian authors who were architects of identity. By the late second century, Irenaeus offers insights into the episcopal office as it had developed up to that point. He perceives the role of the ἐπίσκοπος as a continuation of the apostles' office. In this chapter, as a concluding piece of evidence, I will analyse the episcopal office from an SIT perspective in Irenaeus's *Against Heresies*, book three. Irenaeus is well-known for his departure from Jewish beliefs (for example, 4.5.4). As we shall see in the concluding section, his perspective on the episcopal office aligns with his broader views on the Jews.

10.1 Date and Authorship of *Against Heresies*

No serious case has been made for any other author of *Against Heresies*. than Irenaeus. The questions concerning the opus relate more to its composition and place of origin. There are also certain questions regarding the life of Irenaeus. As can be seen in the research history pertaining to Irenaeus, it is notoriously difficult to discern both his exact place and time of birth.[1] Several suggestions have been made regarding the birth year, covering the period between 98 and 147 CE.[2] Osborn concludes, and Chipparini concurs, that a probable date lies between 120 and 130 CE: "The early estimates ignore the late development of his writing. The late estimates probably make him too young for episcopacy in 177, when he succeeded the ninety-year-old Pothinus."[3] Regarding the birthplace, suggestions have been made based on Irenaeus's name and the social composition of Lyon that Irenaeus originated from Gaul, or perhaps had Celtic ancestry.[4] A different, earlier suggestion in modern scholarship has identified Syria as a potential location for his birth.[5] Other ideas have also been proposed. Given his significant influences from Polycarp in the royal court of Smyrna, a birth in Asia Minor is perhaps more plausible.[6] Although the exact location remains uncertain, we can gain some insight into his whereabouts during his lifetime. Aside from his own account of having met Polycarp in Smyrna at what we must presume was a relatively young age, he is closely associated with the congregations in Lyon and Vienne. He became ἐπίσκοπος when Pothinus, his predecessor as ἐπίσκοπος, died while imprisoned during a persecution in Lyon and Vienne around the year 177. This left Irenaeus as the new

---

[1] There has also been a heated debate on Irenaeus's skills as an author and theologian. The point here is rather that Irenaeus seems to have been well respected in the proto-catholic tradition and he argues for a proto-catholic development. The role of tradition is indeed the focal point for Irenaeus, and the warrant for that tradition is the episcopal office as successors of the apostles. See Osborn's dense research history regarding the qualities of Irenaeus, Osborn 2001, 9–12.

[2] Chipparini 2014, 97, n. 5; Osborn 2001, 2.

[3] Osborn 2001, 2.

[4] Osborn 2001, 2–3.

[5] Harvey 1857, cliv.

[6] The passage cited in Grant 1997, 3, certainly seems to suggest a certain alienation in his experience of living "among the Celts."

ἐπίσκοπος in Lyon.⁷ About this time, Gallican confessors recommended Irenaeus to Eleutherius of Rome, as he went to mediate the relationship between the Montanist sect and the congregations associated with Rome in Gaul.⁸ Irenaeus then returned to Lyon, where he resided for several years as the leader of the congregation(s) before journeying to Rome once more. Around 190 CE, Irenaeus went to meet Victor of Rome to mediate between the Roman congregations and the Quartodeciman group from Asia Minor.⁹ Aside from these events, the scarce sources do not cover much more: Jerome's commentary on Isaiah, chapter 64, suggests that Irenaeus died a martyr's death in 202 or 203 (which may possibly be a later interpolation).¹⁰ Later traditions such as those by Gregory of Tours (538–594 CE) also suggest that Irenaeus died as a martyr. Although these accounts are considerably later than the events they describe, it is reasonable to conclude that Irenaeus died in the early third century, even if we cannot ascertain the precise date, possibly as a martyr.

It is commonly believed that *Against Heresies* was written in Lyon, prior to Irenaeus's trip to Rome in 190, even though he gathered the material much earlier. Considering his interest in Valentinianism, it is reasonable that he conceived some of his ideas in Rome.¹¹ The original shape and date of this main work have, however, been contested. Typically, the year 180 CE is cited as the date of composition, and perhaps the subsequent decade also comes into consideration.¹² The oldest fragment of the work, found in Egypt, is dated before the end of the second century, and is thus a *terminus ante quem* for the work.¹³ One can, however, note that there are reasons to suppose that *Against Heresies* has existed in various versions, as the preface to book one seems to necessitate a different structure from the preface to the next book two.¹⁴ The traditional

---

⁷ Osborn 2001, 3–4.
⁸ McGuckin 2017, 48.
⁹ McGuckin 2017, 48–49. See also Grant 1997, 6–7; Osborn 2001, 5.
¹⁰ Osborn 2001, 2.
¹¹ See however Chiapparini 2014, 3–4 for a closer discussion.
¹² Chipparini 2014, 2. See also Osborn 2001, 1.
¹³ Grant 1997, 5.
¹⁴ Chiapparini 2014, 2–3.

dating around 180 is still largely uncontested and will serve as the vantage point for this chapter, as no other credible dating has been presented recently.

10.2 The Content

As can be seen when referring to *Against Heresies,* the original Greek text survived only in fragments. A complete Latin translation exists from 380 CE, which, however, aligns well with the remaining earlier Greek fragments. This leads us to conclude that some parts of the original formulations are no longer retrievable, even though the later Latin translation suggests a faithful representation of the Greek fragments still extant.[15] While it is not the aim to analyse the entire opus here, the overarching theme of the work is worth noting. The primary idea is to refute heresies, particularly what is identified as Valentinianism. One important aspect of Irenaeus's strategy is his connection of a particular teaching to an arch-heretic, "a single figure of dubious character," through theological genealogies.[16] Irenaeus uses Simon Magus (a character found in Acts 8; however, Irenaeus mentions nothing of Simon's repentance as described there) as that dubious figure. Simon Magus is connected to all heresies through a genealogical approach, in which Irenaeus associates the content of a thought he deems heretical back to Simon Magus (*Haer.* 1.23.1). Consequently, a stream of heresies follows from Simon Magus, most of which embody some hidden or esoteric teaching ("gnostic"[17] teaching) at their core, passed down from heretic to heretic.[18]

This method of refuting heresies as originating from a single source has a proto-orthodox counterpart in the genealogy of apostolic teaching in book

---

[15] Osborn 2001, 1.

[16] Marjanen, 2008, 204.

[17] As Marjanen 2008, 204–5, points out, "Gnosticism" is a proto-orthodox umbrella term for various movements with various doctrines and understandings. The term "gnostic" or "Gnosticism" is thus a way to mount criticism on movements as dubious (from a character like Simon Magus), and stemming from the same source, but yet diverging (that is, non-coherent) in practices and doctrine. The findings of texts in Nag Hammadi have made the older, typological approach harder to uphold, given the diversity of the movements, see further Marjanen 2008, 205–7, 216–17.

[18] Marjanen 2008, 205.

three of *Against Heresies*. The apostolic teachings derive from Jesus Christ and ultimately from God, passed down from one ἐπίσκοπος to the next in apostolic succession. Consequently, the episcopal order and structure serve as the antidote to heresy, as it preserves the apostolic tradition through faithful leaders. This prompts me to focus on book three in the current analysis.

Throughout book three, Irenaeus advocates for the apostolic faith, tradition, and succession. By the end of the second century, there was not yet a fixed canon, which makes Irenaeus's insistence on four canonical gospels (*Haer.* 3.1.1; 3.11.8) and a clearly discernible relationship between the gospels and the apostles even more significant.[19] The emphasis on apostolic tradition as a tool against what Irenaeus perceived as heresies may also reflect an impulse to elevate Christian texts (such as the Gospel traditions) above the Jewish texts of the LXX/Hebrew Bible.[20] The apostolic tradition is regarded as crucial to the identity of Christians in the significant work of Irenaeus. This becomes even clearer when we consider that maintaining the tradition in practice must have entailed preaching and teaching the tradition.[21]

Book three, chapters 1–3, in which Irenaeus discusses the tradition from the apostles and apostolic succession, is fragmented, and some sections, such as 3.3.1, are extant only in Latin translation. Nevertheless, the train of thought in this source links true faith to the apostles, and the connection to the apostles is through the *episcopi*[22] in the congregation (*ecclesiis*).

> *Traditionem itaque Apostolorum in toto mundo manifestatam, in omni Ecclesia adest perspicere omnibus qui vera velint videre, et habemus annummerare eos qui ab Apostolis instituti sunt Episcopi in ecclesiis, et successiones eorum usque ad nos, qui nihil tale docuerunt, neque cognoverunt, quale ab his deliratur.*[23]

Thus the tradition of the apostles, manifest in the whole world, is present in every church to be perceived by all who wish to see the truth. We can enumerate those who

---

[19] Holmes 2008, 418.

[20] Cf. Young 2008, 850.

[21] McGuckin 2017, 986.

[22] I understand the words *episcopus* in Latin and ἐπίσκοπος in Greek to be essentially equivalent, and will thus use ἐπίσκοπος in the following, for a consistent usage throughout the study.

[23] Text from Harvey 1857, 8.

were appointed by the apostles as bishops in the churches as their successors even to our time, men who taught or knew nothing of the sort that they madly imagine.[24]

Importantly, the officers who received the tradition did not pass on any additional secrets, such as some form of (for lack of better terms) "gnostic" teaching – how could those entrusted with the responsibilities for the congregations remain unaware of this?

> *Etenim si recondita mysteria scissent Apostoli, quae seorsim et latenter ab reliquis perfectos docebant, his vel maxime traderent ea quibus etiam ipsas ecclesias commitebant.*[25]

> If however the apostles had known secret mysteries that they would have taught secretly to the "perfect," unknown to the others, they would certainly have transmitted them especially to those to whom they entrusted the churches.[26]

In 3:2, Irenaeus presents crucial claims about the apostolic succession in Rome being the most prominent example of such succession, and that faith was passed on to members of other congregations by an ἐπίσκοπος.[27] Irenaeus holds regarding the Roman congregation that it "is necessary for every church – that is, the believers from everywhere – to agree with this church, in which the tradition from the apostles has always been preserved by those who are from everywhere, because of its more excellent origin."[28]

Following this, the next section of chapter 3 (3.2–4) provides a list of names, beginning with Linus. The transfer of authority is described as the passing on of a λειτουργία, which means an office or ministry: "They committed into the hands of Linus the ministry/office of supervision" (Λίνῳ τὴν τῆς ἐπισκοπῆς λειτουργίαν ἐνεχείρισαν). Consequently, the apostles Paul and Peter are closely associated to the office of the ἐπίσκοπος. The Linus mentioned in 2 Tim 4:21 is immediately connected to this Linus in Rome, indicating that this tradition and the deutero-Pauline tradition are seamlessly integrated. Clement, the third

---

[24] Translation, Robert Grant, found in Grant 1997, 94.

[25] Harvey 1857, 9.

[26] Grant 1997, 94.

[27] The phrase in Latin: *per succecssiones Episcoporum.*

[28] Grant 1997, 94. Latin original: *ad hanc enim ecclesiam propter potentiorem principalitatem necesse est omnem convenire ecclesiam, hoc est, eos qui sunt undique, conservata est ae quae est ab Apostolis traditio.* Harvey 1857, 9.

ἐπίσκοπος of the Roman congregation, is reported to have seen and met the apostles, and "had the apostolic preaching in his ears and the tradition before his eyes" (3.3.3).[29] In the preface to the book, it becomes apparent that the *Sitz im Leben* for *Against Heresies.* involved the refutation of the Valentinian teachings,[30] which are accused of being significantly younger.

The case for the proto-Catholic faith put forward by Irenaeus is fivefold: it is conveyed by the apostles; it is traceable through the episcopal order; the episcopal order signifies the continuation of the apostolic order; it is transmitted openly; and the Roman congregation holds particular significance in doctrinal matters due to its founders. The role of the ἐπίσκοπος is thus to serve as a guarantee for the tradition and a continuation of the apostolic function within the congregation. This prompts us to conduct an SIT analysis of the episcopal order as presented in *Against Heresies*. However, before proceeding, we must provide some additional background regarding Irenaeus's perspective on Jewish group identity.

10.3 *Against Heresies* and the Jews

As is well known, Irenaeus is harsh in his condemnation of the Jews. This is especially prominent in book four, which discusses the Jewish background to Christian beliefs in some depth. In book four, the Jews are, for example, called "Christ-killers." While still refuting Valentinian heresies, this book portrays apostolic Christians as a middle ground between heretics and Jews who follow an obsolete path. The Christians, who express their faith in Christ correctly through episcopal congregations, are the true inheritors of Abraham (4.5.3–5). This perspective is articulated on several occasions: In 4.2, Irenaeus distinguishes between Jews who have come to Christ and those who have not. Those who have not are connected to the scribes and Pharisees, receiving doom sayings such as Jer 4:22 (4.2.7). But Irenaeus does not stop there. Jerusalem was regarded as a valid city of God only as long as Christ and the apostles could bear

---

[29] Grant 1997, 94, καὶ ἔτι ἔναυλον τὸ κήρυγμα τῶν Ἀποστόλων καὶ τὴν παράδοσιν πρὸ ὀφθαλμῶν ἔχων, Harvey 1857, 10.

[30] This is the main reason why the text known as 1 Clement is used (and perhaps a bit stretched, Grant 1997, 6).

fruit there (4.4.1), and thus it was to be abandoned when the apostles left. The Jews' guardianship of God's word ceased with John the Baptist (4.4.2). This is also conveyed as paths that diverge: leaving behind the Jewish identity and stepping into a new identity is prominent in *Haer.* 4.5, in which figures like Abraham and Isaac are portrayed as forerunners of belief in Christ. Indeed, the apostles are understood to have left their old ways and embarked on a new path (4.5.4). To be part of the Jewish group is thus to miss the mark, according to Irenaeus, who goes on to call the Jews "Christ-killers" and compares them to Cain (4.18.3). His condemnation of the Jewish people asserts that the correct way to offer sacrifices to God can be found in Irenaeus's ingroup, the episcopal congregation, through their sincere offering of the Eucharist (4.18.4). The Jews, on the other hand, have, according to Irenaeus, blood on their hands, are insincere in their sacrifices, and are categorised alongside the heretics, who fail to offer proper sacrifices. Thus, both Jews and heretics fall short in their efforts to attain proper faith. The apostolic faith, preserved through the episcopal order, is the only viable option for Irenaeus.

The view of the Jews in *Against Heresies.* is that Jewish identity is obsolete, and only those who, like the apostles, have abandoned their ancestral faith have acquired a right way of life. This perspective on Jewish life can now be compared with the provenance of the apostolic faith that Irenaeus presents.

10.4 An SIT Perspective on the ἐπίσκοπος in Irenaeus

A few important components help us understand what the ἐπίσκοπος signifies in *Against Heresies*. The first is the question of authority invested in the office, which is closely associated with the prototypicality of the apostles and the earlier episcopal leaders. Secondly, there is the embedding of identity into the episcopal office as provided by Irenaeus. The office acts as a warrant for true faith, calling upon readers and members to adhere to the episcopal order. Thus, Irenaeus is also performing identity impresarioship. Impresarioship, as we recall from chapter 2, refers to a leader's ability to embed ingroup identity within structures or rituals. The rhetorical construct of a structure that encapsulates salient group beliefs serves as an example of this. According to Irenaeus, what is proper and right is to associate oneself not with Valentinian orders but with the ancient and true order of the ἐπίσκοπος. Therefore, Irenaeus functions as an identity impresario by favouring the episcopal order. Engaging in the episcopal order in the ways advocated by Irenaeus means participating in a structure that expresses salient group ideals. Thirdly, the office is linked to teaching the tradition, making episcopal leaders potential entrepreneurs of identity. This means, as we recall from chapter 2, that the prototypical leader possesses the authority to alter ingroup ideals and redefine ingroup prototypicality, often through rhetorical means. In Irenaeus' work, the Roman congregation is given priority as the arbiter of the correct tradition to follow.

10.4.1 Prototypicality

Irenaeus's description of the episcopal order emphasises the importance of ideal faith and lifestyle. While this may not be the most prominent feature of the episcopal leader, it undergirds the structure of the argument. The safeguarding of tradition is closely tied to the moral character of the leader. In 3.2, it is noted that the apostles are labelled μακάριοι. Although this does not necessarily reflect a prototypical behaviour, Matt 5:1–11 employs the term in various contexts, serving as a label for those who will inherit the earth or see God, for instance. Irenaeus had probably access to some version of Jesus tradition.[31] The word μακάριοι in Matt 5–7 describes a condition resulting from receiving the kingdom of God. As we read in 3.1, perfection is expected from the successors: "For they wanted those whom they left as successors, and to whom they transmitted their own position of teaching, to be perfect and blameless ... in every respect. If these men acted rightly, it would be a great benefit, while if they failed it would be the greatest calamity."[32] This reflects the high standards expected of the ἐπίσκοπος in the Pastoral Epistles. The anticipated ingroup values are similarly mirrored to some extent in the examples or actions of the

---

[31] For example, relatively soon in Book 3 (3.8.1 and 3.9.3), the beginning of Matthew is explicitly discussed and explained. In 3.1.1, Matthew is said to have been contemporary with Peter and Paul during the founding of the congregation in Rome. These few examples suffice to show that Matthew and his writings appear to have been well known to the intended readers of Irenaeus.

[32] Grant 1997, 94. The Latin reads: *Valde enim perfectos et irreprehensibiles in omnibus eos volebant esse, quos et successores relinquebant, suum ipsorum locum magisterii tradentes: quibus emendate agentibus fieret magna utilitas, lapsis summa calamitas.* Harvey 1857, 9.

subsequent men labelled ἐπίσκοπος. Clement acts as an agent for distributing peace and renewal of faith (εἰς εἰρήνην συμβιβάζουσα αὐτοὺς, καὶ ἀνανεοῦσα τὴν πίστιν αὐτῶν, 3.3.2) through his correspondence to Corinth. Telesphorus is noted as an ἐπίσκοπος who "achieved martyrdom most gloriously" ὃς καὶ ἐνδόξως ἐμαρτύρησεν.[33]

To summarise the prototypical behaviour expected of the succeeding ἐπίσκοπος, the expectations are essentially as high as those placed on the apostles, who were labelled as μακάριοι. The spiritual provenance of the traditions perhaps does not depend on the prototypical lives of the men designated as ἐπίσκοπος, but it is at least verified by the prototypicality of the earlier apostles and ἐπίσκοποι. The authority invested in the office is also matched by the lifestyle of the list of successors, according to Irenaeus's understanding. However, the main point of apostolic succession is not the exemplary leaders within the ranks, but rather the identity-forming warrant these leaders provide for the tradition. Therefore, we now turn to the embedding of group identity (which makes Irenaeus an identity impresario) that is created by the idea of succession from the apostles.

10.4.2 Identity Embedment

As we observed above in the second chapter, identity impresarioship discusses how ingroup structures embed the group's self-perception within rituals or frameworks, where significant ingroup traits are closely connected to a specific structure or ritual. Questions one might pose to detect how a text suggests new structures include the following: What new structures are described as meaningful embodiments of ingroup identity? Who is permitted to participate in these structures? How do these structures embody the ingroup's self-perception? The embedding process essentially authorises the form of the group in relation to its self-identity. This signifies that the self-definition of the group and its structures are intrinsically linked. It is indeed through the structure that self-identity is meaningfully expressed.

What Irenaeus is doing when he explicitly ties the function of the office and the shape of the congregation to the apostolic tradition is associate group

---

[33] Harvey 1857, 11; Grant 1997, 94.

10.4 An SIT Perspective on the ἐπίσκοπος in Irenaeus

members with the apostles. The apostles, obviously, are linked to Jesus and the saving acts of God. Thus, being a member of the episcopal congregation grants access to the saving acts of God, whereas the opposite places one in grave danger. In Irenaeus's rhetoric in *Against Heresies.*, book two, to deviate from the apostolic tradition means aligning oneself with the Valentinian group. The portrayal of the episcopal camp as the true inheritors of the apostolic tradition is evident throughout Irenaeus's description of the office in book 3, chapters 1–3. The progression of thought is as follows: First, he refutes the idea that a better means of gaining access to the salvific actions of Jesus could be found elsewhere, in a secret tradition.

> *Nec enim fas est dicere, quoniam ante prædicaverunt quam perfectam haberent agnitationem; sicut quidam audent dicere, gloriantes emendatores se esse Apostolorum. Postea enim quam surrexit Dominus noster a mortuis, et induti sunt supervenientes Spiritus sancti virtutem ex alto, de omnibus adimpleti sunt, et habuerunt perfectam agnitationem; exieruntin fines terræ, ea quæ a Deo nobis bona evangelizantes, et cœlestem pacem homnibus annuntiantes, qui quidem et omnes partier et singuli eorum habentes Evangelium Dei.*[34]

> It is not right to say that they preached before they had perfect knowledge, as some venture to say, boasting that they are correctors of the apostles. For after our Lord arose from the dead and they were clad with power from on high [...] by the coming of the Holy Spirit [...], they were filled concerning everything and had perfect knowledge. They went forth to the ends of the earth, proclaiming the news of the good gifts to us from God and announcing heavenly peace to men [...]. Collectively and individually they had the Gospel of God.[35]

Then Irenaeus continues to state that the episcopal office is a continuation of the apostles' work. The apostles, through the gospel writings, passed down the preaching linked to the powerful actions of God.[36] The ἐπίσκοπος, as the

---

[34] Harvey 1857, 2.

[35] Grant 1997, 93.

[36] Grant 1997, 93: "Thus Matthew published among the Hebrews a gospel written in their language, at the time when Peter and Paul were preaching at Rome and founding the church there. After their death Mark, the disciple and interpreter of Peter, himself delivered to us in writing what had been announced by Peter. Luke, the follower of Paul, put down in a book the Gospel preached by him. Later John the Lord's disciple, who reclined on his bosom (John 13:23;

guardian of the tradition handed down, thus renders the tradition accessible "for all who wish to see the truth" (*omnibus qui vera velint videre*),[37] 3.1. The list of episcopal officers that, according to Irenaeus, is traceable in, for example, Rome, serves as a warrant for the provenance of the tradition, and thus for the alignment of what is said in the congregations with the apostolic preaching. This stands in contrast to a Valentinian message, which seems to assert a secret knowledge into which only a select few are initiated. Consequently, the episcopal structure of the ingroup is crucial for the group's self-identification as being associated with the work of the apostles and, ultimately, with Jesus Christ. To align with the episcopal structure is to align with God. The pattern found in the Ignatian corpus is also present here. The ἐπίσκοπος is thus not only prototypical, providing an embodiment of the ingroup identity but also ensures an ingroup identity that is consistent with the saving acts of God. McGuckin is likely correct, even if the data is insufficient to consider it proven, when he traces the tension between loosely defined teachers in "gnostic" communities, who preached hidden teachings concealed unless prospective members are initiated, and the ἐπίσκοπος who teaches apostolic tradition. Thus, according to McGuckin, no other teacher but the tradition-keeping ἐπίσκοπος was permitted to lead the congregation, which may have sparked a tension between learned laymen and the ἐπίσκοπος.[38] This alignment between Irenaeus's contemporaries, who were part of the Christian ingroup, and the saving acts of God becomes abundantly clear in 3.2, where the ingroup is linked to the founding of the Roman congregation by Peter and Paul. The actions of Peter and Paul are passed down through a line of worthy (prototypical) leaders up until the day Irenaeus writes. A similar pattern can be observed in Irenaeus's view of

---

21:20), himself published the Gospel while staying at Ephesus in Asia." Harvey, 1857, 3–6: Ὁ μὲν δὴ Ματθαῖος ἐν τοῖς Ἑβραίοις τῇ ἰδίᾳ διαλέκτῳ αὐτῶν, καὶ γραφὴν ἐξήνεγκεν εὐαγγελίου, τοῦ Πέτρου καὶ τοῦ Παύλου ἐν Ῥώμῃ εὐαγγελιζομένων, καὶ θεμελιούντων τὴν ἐκκλησίαν. Μετὰ δὲ τὴν τούτων ἔξοδον, Μάρκος ὁ μαθητὴς καὶ ἑρμηνευτὴς Πέτρου, καὶ αὐτὸς τὰ ὑπὸ Πέτρου κηρυσσόμενα ἐγγράφως ἡμῖν παραδέδωκε. Καὶ Λουκᾶς δὲ ὁ ἀκόλουθος Παύλου, τὸ ὑπ' ἐκείνου κηρυσσόμενον εὐαγγέλιον ἐν βιβλίῳ κατέθετο. Ἔπειτα Ἰωάννης ὁ μαθητὴς τοῦ Κυρίου, ὁ καὶ ἐπὶ τὸ στῆθος αὐτοῦ ἀναπεσών, καὶ αὐτὸς ἐξέδωκε τὸ εὐαγγέλιον, ἐν Ἐφέσῳ τῆς Ἀσίας διατρίβων.

[37] Harvey 1857, 8.
[38] McGuckin 2017, 987.

the congregation of Ephesus, founded by Paul (3.4), and the long-time abode of John the apostle: the association with apostolic authority is significant in the defence against other teachings. However, the Roman congregation is a fitting place to commence this emphasis on apostolic succession, as the connection with Peter and Paul seems to be already held in high regard. Thus, apostolic succession in Rome became an argument for the distinguished position of the Roman congregation among those in the Mediterranean region.[39] One can always discuss the power dynamics within the Roman congregation, given Irenaeus's reliance on maintaining good relations with the congregation for his mission. However, this falls outside the aims of this dissertation, although, as we shall see, the prominence of the Roman congregation is of some interest. In any case, Irenaeus's work suggests a theological necessity for a hierarchical structure within the group. In Irenaeus's thought, this hierarchical structure becomes intimately associated with ingroup prototypicality and thus identity.

In 3.3, after recounting the episcopal succession order for Rome, Irenaeus concludes, "This [episcopal succession] is a complete proof that the life-giving faith is one and the same, preserved and transmitted in truth in the church from the apostles up till now."[40] This summarises the identity-shaping quality of the episcopal order in Irenaeus's thought. Irenaeus serves as an impresario of group identity when he describes how apostolic teaching is accessible through apostolic succession. Anyone who wishes to associate themselves with the apostolic teachings must align themselves with the episcopal congregation. The episcopal congregation provides an apt means for leading a life in accordance with members' self-designation as "Christians."

---

[39] Harvey 1857, 9, translation Grant 1997, 94: *Ad hanc enim ecclesiam propter potentiorem principalitatem necesse est omnem convenire Ecclesiam, hoc est, eos qui sunt undique fideles, in qua semper ab his, qui sunt undique, conservata est ea quæ est ab Apostolis traditio*, "For it is necessary for every church—that is, the believers from everywhere—to agree with this church, in which the tradition from the apostles has always been preserved by those who are from everywhere, because of its more excellent origin."

[40] Grant 1997, 95. Greek text, from Harvey 1857, 11–12: Τῇ αὐτῇ τάξει καὶ τῇ αὐτῇ διδαχῇ ἥ τε ἀπὸ τῶν ἀποστόλων ἐν τῇ ἐκκλησίᾳ παράδοσις καὶ τὸ τῆς ἀληθείας κήρυγμα κατήντηκεν εἰς ἡμᾶς.

10.4.3 Identity Entrepreneurship

Before turning to what this means for the relationship between the Christ groups and the synagogue, one important SIT feature remains to be analysed – even if it only has secondary implications for the relationship with Jewish groups. As we recall from chapter 2 above, a prototypical member of a group is afforded space to both expand upon and re-negotiate the group identity, which is the prototypical image of a group member. This feature is known as identity entrepreneurship. The expansion and preaching of the apostolic tradition are, of course, intended to provide guidance on a proper way of expressing the group identity. Furthermore, it can be re-negotiated through prototypical members as an adaptation to novel situations. While it is uncertain to what extent Irenaeus, in reference to his own prototypicality, re-negotiates the identity of the group, it is clear that he employs the apostolic tradition for such a negotiation. Peter and Paul are perhaps the most prototypical Christians there are. Since these historically significant group members are the founders of the Roman congregation, they provide a slightly new perspective on what group identity entails: the Roman congregation stands as the most prominent interpreter of what constitutes Christian faith. In his portrayal of the apostles, Irenaeus claims that they were intentional in their transmission of the tradition, and that this intentionality necessitates a form of the Jesus movement in which the Roman congregation is dominant, effectively sidelining other modes of gathering. This novel approach to formulating ingroup identity begins in 3.3.1 with the notion that nothing has been concealed in the apostolic tradition. Instead, it has been transmitted and presented openly by the apostolically authorised episcopal order. This establishes a solid foundation for the belief that the apostolic tradition ought to be preached and taught openly. It is the tradition, predominantly found in authorised gospel writings, that serves as the basis for spiritual guidance, and no esoteric tradition may supplant it.[41] At this point, the concept

---

[41] *Haer.* 3.1.1 decribes Irenaeus's claims regarding the apostolic tradition (Grant 1997, 93, also quoted above): "Thus Matthew published among the Hebrews a gospel written in their language, at the time when Peter and Paul were preaching at Rome and founding the church there. After their death Mark, the disciple and interpreter of Peter, himself delivered to us in writing

of the prominence of the Roman congregation follows. Irenaeus here asserts that the Roman congregation is the "greatest, most ancient [congregation], and known to all, founded and set up by the two most glorious apostles Peter and Paul at Rome" (3.2).[42] Its antiquity, fame, and provenance contribute to its dominance. Therefore, it is essential to avoid gatherings that either lack apostolic tradition or defy its prominent position: "we shall put to shame all who in any way, through infatuation or vainglory or blindness and a wicked doctrine, gather together wrongly."[43] The emphasis on the Roman episcopal see thus distinguishes Irenaeus, albeit slightly, from Ignatius, for example, who seems to believe that the ἐπίσκοπος in general is the safeguard of tradition. The subtly altered ingroup identity proposed by Irenaeus places the Roman episcopal see at the top of the hierarchical pyramid.

10.5 Conclusion

At the end of the second century, the episcopal office becomes closely associated with Christian self-identity, at least in Irenaeus's thoughts, as evidenced in *Against Heresies*. The emphasis on apostolic teachings, coupled with the

---

what had been announced by Peter. Luke, the follower of Paul, put down in a book the Gospel preached by him. Later John the Lord's disciple, who reclined on his bosom (John 13:23; 21:20), himself published the Gospel while staying at Ephesus in Asia." Harvey 1857, 3–6: Ὁ μὲν δὴ Ματθαῖος ἐν τοῖς Ἑβραίοις τῇ ἰδίᾳ διαλέκτῳ αὐτῶν, καὶ γραφὴν ἐξήνεγκεν εὐαγγελίου, τοῦ Πέτρου καὶ τοῦ Παύλου ἐν Ῥώμῃ εὐαγγελιζομένων, καὶ θεμελιούντων τὴν ἐκκλησίαν. Μετὰ δὲ τὴν τούτων ἔξοδον, Μάρκος ὁ μαθητὴς καὶ ἑρμηνευτὴς Πέτρου, καὶ αὐτὸς τὰ ὑπὸ Πέτρου κηρυσσόμενα ἐγγράφως ἡμῖν παραδέδωκε. Καὶ Λουκᾶς δὲ ὁ ἀκόλουθος Παύλου, τὸ ὑπ' ἐκείνου κηρυσσόμενον εὐαγγέλιον ἐν βιβλίῳ κατέθετο. Ἔπειτα Ἰωάννης ὁ μαθητὴς τοῦ Κυρίου, ὁ καὶ ἐπὶ τὸ στῆθος αὐτοῦ ἀναπεσών, καὶ αὐτὸς ἐξέδωκε τὸ εὐαγγέλιον, ἐν Ἐφέσῳ τῆς Ἀσίας διατρίβων. Further, 3.3.1 claims "Thus the tradition of the apostles, manifest in the whole world, is present in every church to be perceived by all who wish to see the truth," Grant 1997, 94. *Traditionem itaque Apostolorum in toto mundo manifestatam, in omnia Ecclesia adest perspicere omnibus qui vera velient videre*, Harvey 1857, 8.

[42] Grant 1997, 94; Harvey 1857, 9: *Sed quoniam valde longum est, in hoc tali volumine omnium ecclesarum enumarare successiones, maximæ, et antiquissimæ, et omnibus cogitæ, a gloriosissimis duobus Apostolis Petro et Paulo Romæ fundatæ et constitutæ ecclesiæ.*

[43] Grant 1997, 94; Harvey 1857, 9: *confundimus omnes eos, qui quoquo modo vel per sibiplacentiam malam, vel vanam gloriam, vel per cæcitatem et malam sententiam, præterquam oportet colligunt.*

notion that the ἐπίσκοπος is a successor of the apostles and thus a guarantor of apostolic tradition, as well as the focus on the prominence of the Roman episcopal see, helps to construct an ingroup identity in which the episcopal order is deemed crucial and non-optional for Christian self-definition. This becomes clearer when considering the ingroup prototypicality in which the ἐπίσκοπος is expected to resemble the apostles. The elevated standards establish an ethical example closely tied to the gospel tradition, as well as the ideals found in the Pastoral epistles. Although it is not explicitly stated what the consequences would be if the ἐπίσκοπος failed to meet the moral expectations, it would likely lead to "calamity." In Irenaeus's view, leadership still embodies ethical behaviour that is somewhat related to the Jesus tradition, and more explicitly to the apostles.

Furthermore, Irenaeus's impresarioship embeds Christian identity within the episcopal structure. Irenaeus argues that Christian faith must derive from apostolic teachings. These teachings are said to have been conveyed openly. Apostolic faith is therefore not esoteric. The Valentinian controversy, which serves as the backdrop for *Against Heresies,* leads Irenaeus to conclude that an esoteric teaching like the Valentinian doctrine is an antithesis to apostolic faith. This becomes evident through Irenaeus's genealogical approach. On the one hand, he traces the adversaries back to the dubious Simon Magus; on the other hand, he identifies the ingroup with the blessed and prototypical apostles. Thus, apostolic teaching is deeply rooted in the provenance of said teachings, which can be traced through episcopal succession. Given the connection between the ecclesial structure suggested by Irenaeus and apostolic provenance, the only way to be a Christian is to belong to the episcopal congregation. The content of the gospels, passed down through history by one faithful ἐπίσκοπος after another, defines Christian faith; therefore, to oppose the ἐπίσκοπος is to oppose the work of the apostles. Moreover, the self-definition of Christians is only achievable through apostolic teaching and not to the same extent as a reception of the LXX/Hebrew Bible. Irenaeus considers teaching about Moses, as conveyed through Clement, to be correct, provided it is taken as a counterargument against Valentinianism and does not present particularly positive views on Jewish identity. The episcopal office is not, as seen in 1 Clement, explicitly viewed as a priestly role that supplants the obsolete Levitical priesthood;

however, it still conveys an unequivocally Christian identity as the role of tradition keeper. The connection between office and apostolic teaching ties Christian identity to the apostles. It excludes any other form of identity (explicitly Valentinian, but also other self-identifications such as a Jewish identity).

This suggests that, according to Irenaeus's understanding, Christian identity is wholly invested in the episcopal office. The prototypical Christian leader, an ἐπίσκοπος, embodies and safeguards the apostolic teachings. The relative openness to Jewish halakah found in the early second century in the Didache, such as the prototypical life reflecting Jewish ideals in the Two Ways tractate in the Didache, which was embodied by the ἐπίσκοπος in Didache 15, is no longer present. This becomes abundantly clear when considering book four of *Against Heresies.* and its viewpoint. Here, the abandonment of the ancestral faith and the joining of the apostolic Christian groups are regarded as equivalent in Irenaeus's expressed views. For Irenaeus, this is as natural as the rejection of Valentinian beliefs. Indeed, apostolic Christian groups are seen as the heirs of Abraham. Therefore, the proper belief entails the rejection of both Jewish and Valentinian beliefs, alongside the affirmation of apostolic succession. By the end of the second century, the episcopal office actively preserves an exclusively Christian identity.

Part III

Conclusions

11. The Emerging Episcopal Office and the Parting of the Ways

Leadership and leadership structures convey group identity. Several examples of this can be found, both in early Christ groups and in later, fully developed Christianity. This book has primarily focused on how the emerging episcopal office influenced the identity formation of Christ groups, and how this new identity affected the relationship to the synagogue. While multiple books have been written about the parting of the ways and the emergence of the episcopal order in early Christ groups, none, to my knowledge, has conducted an analysis of how this emerging episcopal order communicated a distinct Christian identity for ingroup members. Moreover, while several books have explored social scientific perspectives on the parting of the ways, none, to my knowledge, has applied social identity theory categories to the emerging structures and ideals of Christ groups.

The purpose of this study, as stated in chapter 1, has been to gain a better understanding of how the emerging episcopal structure influenced perspectives on being a follower of Jesus in the first and second centuries. Consequently, the objective has been to examine how an evolving episcopal office impacted relationships with alternative identities within the Christ movement. The connection that is most easily traced is between the developing Christian identity and an alternative Jewish identity.

The method I have employed involves applying categories from social identity theory (SIT) to ancient texts. These categories originate from leadership research within SIT. To quickly refresh our memories from chapter 2, a key category that has been applied is prototypicality. Prototypicality refers to the set of norms that define the ideal group member, closely linked to research on how group membership influences personal identity. When we categorise someone, including ourselves, into a group, we cognitively apply a set of attributes associated with that group to the individual identified as a group member. Extensive research on group identity indicates that prototypical leaders – those who successfully embody these ideals – are more effective in their leadership roles and gain greater group compliance than non-prototypical leaders. If an individual endures hardships for the sake of group ideals, characterised as costly displays, their perceived credibility will increase further. Examples from this book include the construction of Ignatius, who is portrayed not only as charismatically experienced and well-versed in Scripture but also as willing, even eager, to suffer for ingroup ideals.

Identity entrepreneurship refers to the prototypical leaders who embody ingroup ideals and are given the opportunity to renegotiate these ideals, thereby altering the ingroup's prototypicality, often through rhetorical means. Impresarioship denotes a leader's ability to embed ingroup identity within structures or rituals, for instance. Furthermore, identity advancement signifies the leader's capacity to champion ingroup ideals among outsiders. This culminates in the following categories:

	Prototypicality	Entrepreneurship	Impresarioship	Advancement
Function	Embodiment of the ideal of the group	Redefinition of the ingroup prototypicality	Embedment of ingroup identity in structures and rituals and so forth	Advancement of ingroup interests, not least among outsiders.
Catch Phrase	"Being one of us"	"Crafting a sense of us"	"Doing it for us"	"Doing it for us"

Table 11.1. *SIT leadership categories summarised.*

This table serves as a summary of the categories that are explained in more detail in chapter 2 above. The aforementioned purposes were transformed into a set of research questions. These questions aim to demonstrate how the emerging leadership office influenced the self-perception of the Christ groups, as evidenced by the source material discussed throughout this book. First, *how did the emergence of the ἐπίσκοπος as Christ-group leader affect Christian group identity?* Second, *which theological ideas were transferred into social patterns through the theology of the episcopal office during the first and second centuries (which is what the sub-category impresarioship is about)?* Third, this leads up to the most significant question: *How did the emergence of the ἐπίσκοπος alter the relation between Christ groups and the Jewish synagogue in terms of social identity in the first and second centuries (which is related to the sub-category of identity entrepreneurship)?*

Throughout this book, I have examined several ancient texts, ranging from around 60 CE (Philippians) to approximately 180 CE (Irenaeus, *Against Heresies*) analysing them with the assistance of tools from SIT. Here, institutional patterns (such as episcopal structure) and ideals of membership (prototypicality) have been scrutinised. The next section includes a brief summary of the findings from each text before I conclude my observations in section 11.2 below.

11.1 Summary

In this book, I have reviewed all the texts I could find regarding the role of the ἐπίσκοπος during the first and second centuries. I have applied an SIT perspective to these texts, aiming to explore how the leadership structure influenced the relationship with other groups. This stems from the insistence in the SIT framework that effective leaders both embody, embed, and, at times, alter the self-perception of the ingroup's identity.

Before we summarise the SIT analysis, it is worth remembering where this analysis is situated in the research history of the parting of the ways. As we observed in chapter 3, the institutional perspective, as a sub-category of the sociological perspective in the parting of the ways debate, has been significantly developed recently. This development results from the research community's growing interest in voluntary associations. As a backdrop to this study, we must understand how the Christ-group members and synagogues were intertwined. As mentioned in chapter 3, I posit that the Christ groups that invested increasing authority and identity in the emerging episcopal structure were communities growing outside of the diaspora synagogue. The context for this assumption is that first- and second-century diaspora synagogues could encompass various groups. It is reasonable to suggest that associational synagogues formed around different common identities, such as occupational and locational identities. In the diaspora, non-Jewish members of Jewish groups may have existed, with the God of Israel as their patron deity, especially if group identity was centred around occupation. Furthermore, the textual evidence reviewed in this book implies that exclusively non-Jewish Christ-worshipping groups existed in the beginning of the second century.[1] These non-ethnic followers of Jesus developed anti-Jewish rhetoric, while the so-called Jewish believers in Christ faded away, as they found themselves trapped between, on the one hand, non-Jewish Jesus-following groups and, on the other, a gradually growing Rabbinic movement that advocated for a different Jewish identity. Non-Jewish Jesus-follower groups and Rabbinic synagogues never truly belonged together and, therefore, cannot part.[2] This is not to say, as we saw, that Jesus followers were thrown out of all synagogues at once, in a synchronized action.[3] Rather, it is a question of who belonged to what association; non-Jewish Jesus-followers in diaspora contexts seem to have formed their own groups quite early. Within these groups, boundaries against Jewish followers of Jesus observing a Jewish halakah were drawn.

As we saw in chapter 4 above, there has been a scholarly debate concerning the synonymity of ἐπίσκοποι and πρεσβύτεροι in the earliest Christian groups. This debate led to a consensus that the titles were used interchangeably in several texts. It also addressed whether the model from which Christ-group leadership was derived came from a Jewish template or Greco-Roman influences. The findings from the study of voluntary associations and diaspora synagogues suggest that the binary view is most certainly incorrect. Rather, the data support a view of mixed membership in many cases, based on occupation or neighbourhood. Thus, the organisational form might have differed significantly. As noted, the discussion on whether the episcopal functionary was, in fact, a financial officer draws attention to the fact that many early Christ-group texts testify to a financial dimension of the ἐπίσκοπος. Conversely, there are also multiple texts that describe the ἐπίσκοπος as embodying more than just a financial officer. At the same time, Burtchaell's suggestion that the ἐπίσκοπος truly

---

[1] Following Runesson 2022, 256–57.
[2] Runesson 2021, 51–52.
[3] Cirafesi 2023, 693–96.

conveyed continuity with the synagogue has been shown to be overly speculative. Nevertheless, he was correct in his impulse to understand structures as embedding group identity. While I believe Burtchaell's perspective to be flawed, it is evident in the sources I have consulted that the authors embedded group identity within the structures and connected these structures with certain Christ-group ideals.

I am sceptical of the ideas presented throughout the research history that suggest that the impulses for the ἐπίσκοπος as a leader of Christ groups must stem either from a Greco-Roman context or from an exclusively Jewish diaspora synagogue context. Rather, the mixed form of organisational patterns and the diverse audiences in diaspora synagogues suggested in recent research on synagogues and voluntary associations imply that the impulses for the ἐπίσκοπος were likely manifold. The binary interpretations in modern church history that position the ἐπίσκοπος as a leadership pattern either derived from a Jewish context or from a Greco-Roman one have been somewhat misguided. Conversely, the findings in this book indicate that while the office had predecessors traceable in various voluntary associations (including Jewish ones), the ἐπίσκοπος became a defining character in the Christ-group identity, as can be traced throughout the material. A rudimentary observation reveals an interesting connection between texts that emphasise the role of the ἐπίσκοπος (such as Irenaeus, Ignatius, 1 Clement, and to some extent the Pastoral Letters) and an increasing suspicion of a salient Jewish identity among members of a Christ group. The more elaboration on the role of the ἐπίσκοπος, the more sceptical the text becomes toward alternate Christian identities. This pattern is not unambiguous. The Didache, which mentions the ἐπίσκοπος once in chapter 15, clearly recommends a prominent Jewish identity, both in terms of prototypicality and impresarioship, by endorsing certain halakic patterns for individual group members. The trend in the material, however, is that the more pronounced the episcopal role, the greater the scepticism towards a salient Jewish identity. The identity-shaping features of the ἐπίσκοπος become clearer when categories from SIT leadership studies are applied to the texts.

11.1.1 Prototypicality

The first research question – *how did the emergence of the ἐπίσκοπος as the leader of Christ's group affect Christian group identity?* – is partially answered by the way a Christian prototype becomes detectable in the ἐπίσκοπος. Prototypical leadership within groups involves the embodiment of salient ingroup values. An SIT perspective aids in understanding how a leader who successfully embodies ingroup values is more likely to succeed. A member perceived as prototypical will be more adept at gaining followership among group members. This tendency is particularly pronounced because the categorisation process that humans employ to make sense of others leads us to (a) accentuate differences between categorised entities and (b) smooth over differences within the groups we categorise. Thus, prototypicality represents an assemblage of traits that members consider to be crucial within the ingroup. Furthermore, prototypicality captures certain dimensions of what followers interpret as charismatic leadership. An additional aspect is that a group member willing to endure hardships for ingroup values, showcasing what are termed "costly displays," is regarded by fellow members as a credible leader. Consequently, this member will attract followership. Assuming that the human mind operates much in the same manner today as it did in the first and second centuries CE, one must surmise that the behaviours expected from leaders mirrored those expected from every member, and vice versa.

Throughout this book, I have collected how Christ-group authors rhetorically describe expectations for members and group leaders, such as the ideal ἐπίσκοπος in the Pastoral Letters. One can note that leadership in the Christ groups seems to always be related to an expected prototypical behaviour. Identity advancement – that is, the advancement of ingroup interests, not least among outsiders – is the only category that does not necessarily demand that the leader is prototypical. Identity advancement means that the promotion of ingroup interests serves as a viable means of exercising leadership, even if the leader is un-prototypical in his or her behaviour. Considering the patron system so common in the Greco-Roman world, it would be reasonable to assume patronage as a prevalent feature of leadership, but this is absent in the ideals presented by the sources. The only exception that might be found is that the ἐπίσκοπος should be hospitable, as noted in Hermas, the Pastoral Epistles, and the Didache. This hospitality does not, however, imply that the ἐπίσκοπος must primarily be understood as a patron. The need for hospitality could pertain to other requirements of the group. The leader in all the texts, from Philippians to Irenaeus, is de facto expected to behave according to a set of norms applicable to all members, irrespective of social standing or sex. The ability to lead lives according to group norms is generally regarded as more crucial for the ἐπίσκοπος than for other members of the group. However, the norms for the ἐπίσκοπος in the Pastorals do not significantly differ from those for any other group member. That is to say, any group member should genuinely lead his or her life according to the norms for the ἐπίσκοπος pronounced in the Pastorals. This suggests that the patron dimension of an ἐπίσκοπος would be less significant than the capacity for the ἐπίσκοπος to lead an exemplary life.

Ingroup norms are central to considerations regarding when group leaders should be appointed. However, these ingroup norms develop and become slightly altered depending on which group is being addressed. It appears that the prototypical behaviour stems from Jesus as a prototype and his teachings, which is to be expected in all groups to some extent. Nonetheless, some differences can be observed.

The first group of texts analysed comprises the New Testament texts that contain brief mentions of the ἐπίσκοπος, as well as the Shepherd of Hermas, in the few instances where the term is employed by him. These texts date from approximately 60 to 140 CE. None of these texts discusses expectations or provides theological descriptions of the ἐπίσκοπος in any definitive way. The texts originate from various areas within the north-eastern quadrant of the Mediterranean area but are not necessarily more closely related. Nonetheless, all the texts are found within the sphere of the Christ groups and, in most cases, in what eventually became the New Testament canon (with the exception of Hermas).

It is important to note that in Acts and 1 Peter, there appears to be a conflation or a significant degree of synonymity between the ἐπίσκοπος and the πρεσβύτερος. The relationship is such that the elders exercise oversight over the members. The πρεσβύτερος exercises ἐπισκοπή. Therefore, I assume that the overlap is so substantial that what applies to the πρεσβύτερος in these two texts also applies to the ἐπίσκοπος. This aligns with the traditional understanding in the historical research on the development of a Christian office.

In Philippians, the evidence for the role of the ἐπίσκοπος is rather scant, as we have seen. The brief mention in one verse at the beginning of the letter of an ἐπίσκοπος requires us to rely heavily on conjecture, based on the SIT framework. The findings within this letter do not provide much insight into the office at the time Paul wrote. However, given the SIT framework and the fact that Paul addresses the ἐπίσκοποι explicitly, it is reasonable to assume that what Paul expects from any member is expected even more from the leaders. The ideals presented are theologically motivated, reflecting a perception of Christ as a humble, exemplary human. Consequently, the leaders would be expected to adhere to the ideals regarding humility, just as Paul himself did according to the text. Leadership, according to SIT, must be performed exemplarily to be effective. The leadership exercised by the anonymous leaders of the Christ group in Philippi was expected to be prototypical leadership, in alignment with Paul's example and teaching.

In Acts, the most significant SIT feature concerning episcopal leadership is not prototypicality, but the theological motivation for emerging episcopal leadership. This later aspect will be summarised below, under identity impresarioship. However, this theological motivation relies heavily on the author's description of the exemplarity of Peter and Paul throughout Acts as prototypical followers of Christ. The leadership structure is important for identity since it is initiated by the prototypical heroes of the faith, Peter and Paul. The complete example set by these leaders (essentially the entire plotline of Acts) is not analysed in this current work, but virtues such as boldness and perseverance are significant. Even if the ἐπίσκοπος is not explicitly bound to prototypical leadership, the role modelling of Peter and Paul is at the heart of the emerging office. As successors of these exemplary leaders, the ἐπίσκοπος has a particular role to fulfil in terms of prototypical living.

Prototypical leaders hold significant importance in 1 Peter, as Christ serves as the model for behaviour that guides the community. There exists a strong level of identification between the exemplarity of Christ and that of the πρεσβύτεροι in the letter. The expected behaviour for πρεσβύτεροι pertains to financial realities, inner motivation, and investment in the ingroup's life; these factors are articulated in such a way that the leader should act from inner motivation rather than from greed. The leader is also expected to be prepared to suffer for ingroup ideals. By doing so, while also maintaining humility (in accordance with the ideal presented in 1 Peter 4), the πρεσβύτεροι embody Christ-like qualities.

Prototypicality is almost exclusively the primary focus of leadership in Hermas. As the author of the book does not appear to be an officeholder himself, but rather a prophetic, charismatic figure aiming to discuss a social tension within the Christian community in Rome, he does not explicitly address the offices as constitutive for the ἐκκλησία. The foundational nature of apostles and prophets found in Ephesians 2:20 is not immediately expressed in Hermas. Instead, the leaders are foundational not from their title, but from their example. What matters in Hermas, then, is that leadership should not be exercised in a manner that allows leaders to unrighteously gain from their ministry. Thus, from an SIT perspective, leadership is not exercised as impresarioship (as in that the structure itself carries identity-shaping features), but through exemplarity/prototypicality. The failure to adhere to Christ-group norms as a leader and thereby robbing "widows and orphans" of their livelihood is described as a major sin that would necessitate repentance, Shepherd 9.26 (103). Therefore, the prototypicality of the leaders is emphasised when the ἐπίσκοπος is discussed.

As observed in these largely earlier texts from the sources, there are few explicit descriptions of the type of prototypicality that the ἐπίσκοπος should embody. Instead, through context, conjectures, or significant examples such as Christ, Peter, and Paul, one may conclude that humility, courage, generosity, a willingness to suffer for the sake of the group, and a refusal to gain financially from the position are the few concrete indicators of ingroup prototypicality. These traits are too general to allow for a definitive conclusion about a genuinely Christian prototype. However, it is worth noting that episcopal leaders are expected to lead lives that reflect and suffer for the ideals of the ingroup, as exemplified by Christ, Paul, and Peter. In the more extensive sources, we find considerably more precise descriptions of a Christian prototype.

The Didache, although it does not extensively discuss the role of the ἐπίσκοπος, provides crucial insights into what that role meant for the identity formation of the Didachist community. I assume the text to be a composite, which was probably redacted to its current form in Syria, circa 100–110 CE, and it does not fit neatly into the Early Catholicisation Schema, which has been a significant part of the debate surrounding the Didache. A straightforward transition from charismatic to Catholic leadership is not what the text supports. Instead, it describes a situation where different forms of leadership existed in parallel. This arrangement included itinerant prophets, teachers, and local leaders. Didache 15 appears to be an attempt in the composite text to harmonise the authority between prophets and teachers (itinerants), and ἐπίσκοποι and διάκονοι (local leaders). I proceed from the assumption that the text suggests a certain prototypicality is expected from the leaders, alongside discussions regarding their right to monetary compensation for their ministry. This implies that the leaders within the Didachist community were not patrons, that is, identity promoters. Rather, the expectations placed upon the leaders throughout the Didache indicate they derived their authority primarily from their prototypicality. The baptismal teaching described in chapters 1–6 represents an ideal with which the entire community is expected to align their lives. I also understand the ἐπίσκοπος to have performed overlapping duties with the itinerants, both in ritual matters and in teaching. Thus, the ἐπίσκοπος was also a teacher within the group, needing to convey the ideals found in Did. 1–6. These chapters suggest that the Didache endorsed a Jewish ethical ideal that can be seen in many neighbouring groups, as evidenced by the Two Ways tractate. It is reasonable to assume that non-Jews who converted to Christ were also included in the Didachist group, which bore a closer resemblance to other Jewish groups, such as the Pharisaic group (which was likely the group that the Didachist referred to as hypocrites in chapter 8). Simultaneously, the Didachist group derived its prototypicality from a unique combination of sources: Within the Didachist group, the *sectio evangelica* is combined with a predominantly Jewish Two Ways tractate, in which a Jewish perspective on non-Jews (characterised as practitioners of repulsive actions) is salient. Therefore, the in-group is understood as competing with alternative ideals, such as a Pharisaic ideal.

As we have seen, the Two Ways tractate originated from the second table of the Decalogue and defined itself against non-Jewish behaviour, which was deemed repulsive by many Jewish groups. Didache 6 suggested that non-Jews should adopt some aspects of Torah observance, in line with the Apostolic Decree in Acts 15. The members are also expected to live humble, quiet lives, guided by the ideals found in the tractate. The *sectio evangelica*, on the other hand, reflects a tradition of Jesus that likely distinguished the group from other Jewish groups due to their belief in Jesus as the Messiah. The Didachist group defined itself not only against non-Jews but also against other Jewish groups. The prototypical behaviour that set the group apart from these other Jewish groups was further emphasised when the group's teachers instructed that they should pray and fast not like the Pharisees, but as followers of Christ, presumably from their own halakah. Here, we begin to enter the realm of identity formation. It suffices to say that certain behaviours also possess an embedding quality.

Since the Didache throughout the text calls for leaders to have been tested and approved, the leaders in the Didache must be prototypical and embody a specific kind of ingroup ideal. This ideal is neither entirely rabbinic nor wholly non-Jewish, but rather idealises the unique kinds of Christ-believing Jews and non-Jews in Christ. It is somewhat more likely that leaders such as an ἐπίσκοπος would have been ethnically Jewish, given the expectation to undertake the "full yoke of the Lord" in chapter 8. A full yoke would most likely pertain to a halakic lifestyle. This, however, relies on conjecture.

In 1 Clement, which I date between 110 and 120 CE, we observed how the episcopal role is linked to certain ingroup values, representing a prototypical behaviour for Jesus followers, as opposed to an obsolete Jewish identity that is not even considered to be a viable option throughout the text. These ingroup prototypes are supported by and found within Jewish Scriptures and traditions about Jesus. As we examined, this has a counterpart frequently encountered in Hellenistic tradition: a Christian παράδειγμα to emulate, aligned with the identity in Christ and shaped by Scripture and Jesus traditions, is a Christian variation of the school example from Greco-Roman rhetoric traditions. The implicit picture conveyed in 1 Clement suggests that being connected to God entails being in harmony with the congregation of Jesus followers. This new kind of identity eschews a prominent Jewish identity (where, for example, halakic practices would be a significant part of one's lifestyle) and treats it as obsolete in practice. Ironically, Jewish Scriptures are employed to support a prototype of the Jesus follower that calls for the diminishment of a Jewish identity for the ingroup. The precise definition found in the examples is that the prototypical member is virtuous, steadfast in faith, self-controlled and gentle, hospitable, insightful, and well-versed in gospel tradition or Scripture, impartial, and submissive to leaders, as well as humble and generous. Young members must be temperate and honourable; women should be blameless, honourable, holy, capable managers of the household, well-charactered, sensible, and submissive. The qualities related to submission to leaders, humility, and understanding one's appropriate role within the group are emphasised in the first three chapters of the letter. It is reasonable to assume that these traits arise from a conflict in which leaders were overthrown by a faction of younger members. However, the encouraged traits apply to all members and are closely associated with Scripture passages and gospel traditions. Furthermore, the deposed leaders of the congregation are portrayed as exemplary and thus deserving of followership among the congregants. The factionists in the congregation are in stark contrast with this description, particularly as they exhibit envy, ζῆλος, towards the leaders. The leaders, in their humility, are linked to both ancient and recent figures who suffered for ingroup values, demonstrating costly displays through an applied SIT framework. The exemplary characters of the disposed leaders connect them with the heroes of Jewish Scriptures and contemporary events. As discussed in the chapter on 1 Clement, the author mobilises the readers into social actions for prototypicality. The author's call to mobilise offers the congregation the opportunity to engage with the ingroup prototypes, the exemplary state of scriptural heroes, by reinstating the former leaders. The leadership roles ἐπίσκοπος and διάκονος are closely tied to heroes of the faith and scriptural history, establishing that submission to the episcopal officer(s) is the sole means of adhering to ingroup values. Thus, for the Corinthians, according to the author of 1 Clement, the only viable path to follow Jesus involves re-associating with the prototypical leaders, leaving no space for alternative identities. This establishes a critical impetus for the relationship between Christ groups and the synagogue. The prototype articulated and interpreted through the ἐπίσκοπος in 1 Clement represents a Christian model. According to Scripture, the ideal member is no longer a Jew but is instead depicted as one living according to the ingroup prototype, in submission to the ἐπίσκοπος. This ingroup prototype derives essential insights regarding ingroup ideals from Jewish Scriptures, which are now no longer perceived as sources of information on Jewish identity. The notion of a life devoid of Christ belief, associated with a diaspora synagogue, has become untenable for the members, as the Scriptures are proclaimed to elucidate a life in Christ. To interpret the Scriptures correctly is to embrace faith in Christ, according to the author.

When we turn to the Pastoral Letters, we find a well-defined ideal that differs slightly from other groups. The prototypical member of the Christ group, as reflected in expectations for the ἐπίσκοπος, demonstrates that the Christ group shares some similarities with the surrounding culture while possessing some unique features. The similarities are evident in the necessity for the ἐπίσκοπος to be self-restrained (to have ἐγκράτεια) and temperate (to have σωφροσύνη). These two traits align with all the other lists of group ideals that have been examined. Additionally, these traits are two of the four Stoic cardinal virtues noted in Plutarch's reception. The Wisdom of Solomon and 4 Maccabees present an ideal of a wise man that is very similar to a Greco-Roman wise man, showing a significant overlap between the Pastoral epistles and the virtue lists of the wise man found in these texts. However, the Wisdom of Solomon and 4 Maccabees depict wisdom as God's consort and as an emanation of God's λόγος. This wisdom is achieved when someone pays proper attention to the Torah. Thus, the Wisdom of Solomon and 4 Maccabees provide a wellspring for virtue that is tied to the observance of the Torah, which has no counterpart in the Pastoral Epistles. The ideal for the ἐπίσκοπος in the Pastoral epistles significantly differs from the Jewish groups behind 4 Maccabees and the Wisdom of Solomon, owing to the view of Torah observance as the source of virtue found in 4 Maccabees and the Wisdom of Solomon. The lists in the Pastorals omit any explicit reasoning for virtue, while the other texts understand contemplation of the Torah in various ways as the root of wisdom.

Aside from some philosophical virtues, the common traits of the virtue lists in the Pastoral Epistles are shared by Onosander's expectations of the στρατηγός. The expectations found in Onosander – that the στρατηγός should be a good speaker, of mature age, have a good reputation, and be a family man – have counterparts in the Pastorals. The difference between the Pastoral Epistles and Onosander lies in the hesitation about violence and the expectation of being μιᾶς γυναικὸς ἄνδρα in the Pastorals. This indicates that the prototypical ἐπίσκοπος, according to the Pastoral Epistles, should embody philosophical and cardinal virtues while also remaining faithful in his everyday life. The ἐπίσκοπος is not primarily a Stoic wise man or a philosopher, nor is he in constant contemplation of the Torah, but rather a socially well-integrated individual with primary concerns regarding family matters and the everyday business of the congregation. Thus, the ideal presented by the Pastorals depicts a socially established man, akin to the *paterfamilias*, easily recognisable as part of Greco-Roman society. The ἐπίσκοπος does not engage in contemplation of the Torah; rather, as 1 Tim1:7–11 suggests, the author of the Pastorals holds a notably different view of the Torah's purpose. There, it is evident that ὁ νόμος is not for the righteous (ὅτι δικαίῳ νόμος οὐ κεῖται), but instead intended for all sinners and the lawless. From this perspective, a pious way of living is not linked to a life of Torah observance, which seems to be completely absent from the author's considerations. In contrast with, for instance, the Didache, which exhorts members of the ingroup (presumably ethnical non-Jews) to bear as much of the yoke of the Lord as possible (ὃ δύνῃ, τοῦτο ποίει), the passage in 1 Tim 1:8–11 appears to suggest a disinterest in Torah piety for ingroup members.

In the Ignatian letters, the prototypical behaviour of ingroup members is intertwined with the role of the ἐπίσκοπος in ways that make it difficult to distinguish neatly between the findings on ingroup prototypicality and identity impresarioship in various forms. However, a few things can be said regarding prototypicality per se in the corpus. The ideals expected of ingroup members by the author relate to ethical behaviour, dogmas, gatherings, and the congregants' relationship with their ἐπίσκοπος. This illustrates how the author of the Ignatian letters constructs salient group norms (that is, prototypical behaviour) expected from members and embeds these norms within the episcopal structure. The ethical behaviour anticipated from group members is informed by normative gospel traditions, as well as Pauline and deutero-Pauline and other New Testament traditions. These traditions and the instructions derived from them offer a crucial and non-optional source for prototypical behaviour. Although these norms are not the most prominent feature of the letters' purpose, the essence of the letters centres on how the author presents the ideals within the episcopal structure. Nonetheless, some practical normativity is provided regarding how members should lead their lives. The author pays particular attention to the relationship between members' everyday lives and their relationship to the polity of the ingroup. Therefore, as we observed in the chapter on Ignatius, norms concerning the relationship between the ἐπίσκοπος and the congregation are significant in the depiction that can be extrapolated from the letters regarding the prototypical member.

The ἐπίσκοπος, taken as a role model, exemplifies how group prototypicality is embodied in the office holders of the Christ groups, much like any other group, according to the SIT framework. While the Ignatian letters do not describe the process of appointing new leaders, they do expect the installed ἐπίσκοπος to be prototypical according to ethical norms. These norms reflect Christ's teachings and example at their core. Thus, Ignatius is also depicted as someone striving to embody Christ in his martyrdom. It is important to note that Ignatius, as the implied sender – regardless of whether the letters were later written by an unknown author – serves as a powerful example to follow. After all, he is portrayed as being on his way to Rome to die for the beliefs of the Christ groups. Both Ignatius's journey to Rome to die for ingroup ideals and the resident ἐπίσκοποι in the congregations serve as role models, providing examples to emulate. From this perspective, it is intriguing that the ideals presented are not primarily a matter of a specific ethical standpoint, such as in the Two Ways tractate in the Didache community or even the ideal ἐπίσκοπος in the Pastoral Epistles. Rather, the author's central interest lies in how members should relate to their ἐπίσκοπος and the broader polity of the Christ groups. While some version of ethics often recurs throughout the corpus, this ethical behaviour may not be the novelty in the Ignatian letters; instead, it is the embedding of these ideals into the structure of the groups. This will be addressed in its appropriate place in the next section concerning identity impresarioship.

Before we turn to the impresario section, however, a few words must be said regarding the treatment of episcopal leaders in Irenaeus's *Against Heresies*, book three. Here, leaders are also expected to lead lives in alignment with ingroup ideals. It is noteworthy that this ideal is not explicitly described in relation to the ἐπίσκοποι. Rather, Irenaeus seems to assume some kind of assemblage of ingroup ideals when he describes the episcopal leaders. The closest we come to an explicit ideal is that Irenaeus, by implication, expects the ἐπίσκοπος to act like the apostles and in accordance with apostolic ideals. These standards provide an ethical example that is closely connected to gospel tradition, as well as to the ideals from the Pastoral Epistles. Even if it is not explicitly stated what the consequences would be if the ἐπίσκοπος failed to live up to the moral expectations, it would generally result in "calamity." Leadership, according to Irenaeus, remains a matter of embodying ethical behaviour somewhat related to the Jesus tradition, and more explicitly to the apostles.

We have seen throughout these second-century Christ-group writings that the emerging episcopal office is connected to ideal behaviour. Although the sources differ slightly in their ideals, from Philippians to Irenaeus, some elements are evident. These elements address the first research question to a large extent.

First, leadership within the Christ group is not dissimilar to that in most other groups. The individual who embodies the group's ideals gains followership. The ideals expected of Christ-group members, which leaders are also meant to adhere to, may differ somewhat between various groups (most notably between the ideals of the Didache community and those of the Pastorals' community), yet they are often not incompatible. The prototypical dimension of the expected leadership, as an example for other members to follow, recurs consistently. Furthermore, the necessity for leaders to be tested so that they lead lives reflective of these expectations is present throughout the texts. Even if we seldom encounter specific examples of the election process, the high ideals evident in all texts suggest an implicit or explicit review of potential leaders' lives before they can be instated. The notion that the group leaders of the Didache, and possibly other groups, would have served as patrons of society and thus identity advancers is conceivable, as wealthier members could have covered group expenses to some extent. It is also plausible that the ἐπίσκοποι could have assumed this role to a certain degree. However, this identity advancement would not have come at the expense of prototypical behaviour from the leaders. On the contrary, all texts presuppose prototypicality among the ἐπίσκοποι. Since we do not have access to the actual lives of these groups, we remain unaware to what extent the prototypical ideals were upheld. What we do know is that the ideals expressed throughout all texts assert that ἐπίσκοποι are leaders who embody the group's ideals.

Second, one can note the tension among some of the groups covered by the texts examined in this study, particularly concerning the ideal presented (prototypicality). The clearest example relates to the use of the Torah among different groups. The group associated with the Didache, as well as the groups behind the other texts, differ in their understanding of halakah. In the Didache group, the ideals expected of the ἐπίσκοποι are closely tied to a distinct Christ-follower halakah, which pertains to fasting, purity, and prayer. This halakah is evident in the Didache, in the exhortations to fast and pray on specific occasions and in certain ways, and to embrace the "full yoke of the Lord" (Didache 8). These ideals are similar to those of other Jewish groups but also incorporate group-specific principles, presumably primarily related to the *sectio evangelica* of the Two Ways tractate. The halakah of the Didache sets forth ideals that establish boundaries towards non-Jews (who practised sorcery and various forms of sexual immorality according to the Didachist) as well as towards other Jewish factions. It is reasonable to assume that non-Jews who converted to Christ were also included in the Didachist's group, which appeared more akin to other Jewish groups such as the Pharisees. In the other texts, there is no indication of any interest in halakic concerns. The group that explicitly stands in stark contrast to the Didachist's group in this regard would be the recipients of the Pastoral Epistles. In these letters, the perspective on the Torah is that it serves primarily as a call to repentance for wrongdoers and transgressors of divine law rather than as a pathway to life embodied in a specific halakah. Consequently, the views of the Torah are monumentally different. The ideal member in the Pastorals, as described in the ἐπίσκοπος, bears a closer resemblance to the Greco-Roman *paterfamilias*, depicted as a well-integrated, wise, and sober member of society. Hence, the ideals that leaders are expected to embody are specific to each group.

Third, the ideals were not only ethical but also contained discussions on how to behave generally within the group. 1 Clement, the Ignatian correspondence, and to some extent Irenaeus, discuss how members of the Christ groups should behave towards their ἐπίσκοπος. While this foreshadows the identity impresario section, subjection to and respect for the ἐπίσκοπος is emphasised. A correct way to lead one's life, which showcases a member's prototypicality, is their ability to submit to leadership. When this is done successfully, members align with the saving actions of God that are manifest through the ἐπίσκοπος. The theological understanding of the emerging office calls members to a behaviour aligned with ingroup narrative. The correct and respectful attitude towards the ἐπίσκοπος is thus deemed necessary for members wishing to partake in the mission of God. First Clement serves as a prime example of this. It is a situational letter wherein a faction within the Christ group has removed its leaders. In this letter, the evidence for correct behaviour is drawn from scriptural proof texts that connect correct behaviour to ancient heroes of the faith. The Ignatian letters also had a situational context, likely related to the author's preference for the episcopal leadership model, which was theologically motivated. Irenaeus wrote explicitly to refute heresies, with the episcopal order serving as an antidote. Thus, an important cause existed for this behaviour – the behaviour of submission to the ἐπίσκοπος – was essential for the group's survival. Prototypical behaviour according to this model suggests that Christian identity is closely intertwined with this leadership model.

The general tendency throughout the material covered is that the group identity conveyed by these authors suggests a uniquely "Christian" prototypicality. The behaviour expected from ingroup members aligns members with a certain identity associated with self-definition as followers of Christ. While there are natural overlaps with outgroups, due to the fact that the Christ groups were situated as a movement among other movements in antiquity, different Christ groups come with slightly varying ideals. The Didachist's group appears to be more attentive to outgroups with similar attitudes towards the Torah than the group(s) behind the Pastoral Epistles, for example. Thus, the material demonstrates that the greater advocacy for episcopal order shown by the authors corresponds with less advocacy for ingroup halakah.

11.1.2 Identity Impresarioship

Following these conclusions regarding an emerging Christian prototype as reflected in the ἐπίσκοποι of early Christian writings, we now shift our focus to how ingroup identity is embedded within the episcopal office, serving as examples of identity impresarioship. This relates to the second research question: *Which theological ideas were transferred into social patterns through the theology of the episcopal office during the first and second centuries?* Here follows a recapitulation of the previous chapters.

As we observed at the prototypical level in Philippians, Paul does not invest any specific theological meaning or alter ingroup identity through the addressed ἐπίσκοποι in Philippians. We can conclude that the ἐπίσκοποι in Philippians were likely related to prototypical behaviour, but the data in the letter do not permit a more extensive analysis than that.

In Acts, however, the author imbues the emerging episcopal structure with theological significance. Luke serves as an identity impresario in his portrayal of the role of the πρεσβύτεροι who exercise oversight in Acts. To summarise the impresario findings of Acts, the office of the apostles, most strikingly represented by Peter, continues the mission of Jesus: participating in the Christ groups equates to engaging in the mission of the apostles, and thus the mission of Jesus. The commissioning of Matthias as a new apostle, the number twelve associated with the apostles, Peter's prototypicality, along with the developing leadership that continues the mission of Jesus, suggests that the emerging identity of the Christ groups is closely tied to the successors of the apostles. The message conveyed to the readers regarding Christian identity is that engaging in the Christ groups (which becomes evident through the successors of the apostles accessible via the episcopal structure) equates to participating in the mission of the apostles, and consequently, the mission of Jesus. The identity of the Christ group is intimately linked to the ongoing office of the apostles. By the association with proof texts from the LXX, this identity is also reflected in the ἐπίσκοπος. The leaders in Acts 20 are, furthermore, the successors of Paul the apostle, who will protect the congregation against false leaders and teachings that may lead the group astray. The remedy for an ingroup member is to remain close to the πρεσβύτερος/ἐπίσκοπος. This leadership structure thus becomes an expression of identity impresarioship, in which the readers can find a safe haven for their faith by entrusting themselves to the care of the leadership structure. While this leadership structure is presented in a rudimentary form, this aspect aligns with the views of Ignatius and Irenaeus later in the second century.

When we turn to 1 Peter, the embedding process is associated with the metaphor where God is portrayed as a shepherd. The role of the πρεσβύτεροι and the ἐπισκοπή exercised through them is compared to the shepherding theme prominent in the Hebrew Bible. On several occasions and in key passages in the Hebrew Bible, God is described as acting like a shepherd towards his people. Thus, when the πρεσβύτεροι fulfil their leadership duties correctly, they are linked to the salvific acts of God throughout the Hebrew Bible. To submit oneself to the ministry of the πρεσβύτεροι, then, is to submit to the works of God and Christ. The author of 1 Peter illustrates an example of identity impresarioship in which the salvific acts of God are associated with the episcopal ministry performed by the πρεσβύτεροι. To participate in the ministry of the leaders is to partake in the salvific actions of God through Jesus Christ. The identity-shaping aspects of the πρεσβύτεροι and their ἐπισκοπή are salient in the author's description of the emerging leadership structure. Since the author also connects ἐπισκοπή with Jesus Christ, the unique Christ-group theology, in which God's and Christ's saving actions are inseparable, suggests that Christ-group identity is embedded and re-actualised through the leadership ministry. The Christological perspective is unavoidable for members who accept the leadership structure.

It is interesting that, although the commonplace building metaphor is used in Hermas, and although οἱ ἀπόστολοι καὶ ἐπίσκοποι καὶ διδάσκαλοι καὶ διάκονοι are mentioned first and with honour in the explanation of the vision, it is not explicitly stated that they are the foundation, as the apostles and prophets are said to function in Eph 2:20 (ἐποικοδομηθέντες ἐπὶ τῷ θεμελίῳ τῶν ἀποστόλων καὶ προφητῶν). Rather, as noted above, the exemplarity of the leaders is the core interest in Hermas. If the leaders, however, successfully manage to embody the ideals of the Christ group, they are foundational for the Christ groups according to Hermas. Thus, impresarioship regarding the leaders is expressed by Hermas insofar as the leaders are prototypical. This can be summarised in an echo of the above conclusion: It is not the title that carries meaning in Hermas, but the exemplarity/prototypicality of a given leader's life.

In the Didache, the ἐπίσκοπος is one of the leadership categories regulated in the text. Probably, chapter 15 is an attempt to harmonise the roles of itinerants and local leaders, in which the same authority is invested as in the itinerants according to the Didachist. But how was identity invested and expressed through the ἐπίσκοπος? From conjecture, we can assume that the ἐπίσκοπος held some kind of liturgical office in the Didachist's community. Furthermore, baptism and eucharist rituals, likely officiated by the ἐπίσκοπος in the absence of a prophet, served to constitute group identity rather than, for instance, circumcision or ethnicity. The community appears to have included non-Jews in Christ as members of the congregation. Given the *sectio evangelica* and subsequent messianic views on Jesus from Nazareth, a group with a Christ-follower halakah for both Jews and non-Jews is perhaps the best description of the group. However, the rituals performed by the group suggest a unique identity that took several common Jewish themes for granted. At the same time, the group also distinguished itself from (proto)-Rabbinic groups. Baptism, for instance, shows a concern present among later Rabbinic scholars regarding the quality of purifying water, while the ritual was given a new meaning through initiation into the Father, Son, and Holy Spirit. In these rituals, the role of the ἐπίσκοπος is not elaborated upon, as mentioned. Instead, the ἐπίσκοπος is one of four functionaries. The characterisation of the local offices as performing the duties of the itinerants in the local community (chapter 15:1) suggests that, in practice, the ἐπίσκοπος was teaching (that is, constructing the local identity), performing identity-shaping rituals, and acting as a role model (embodying Christ's identity in ethical matters). Furthermore, the ἐπίσκοπος was associated with a priestly office (through the prophets and teachers) and could thus receive tithes. This identity links the entire community with a new temple and confers holiness upon the whole group. This represents a kind of impresarioship by the Didachist, as one's own identity is tied to the Jerusalem cult, with all its associated holiness. Consequently, this imparts a priestly quality to the entire community and signifies a significant role for the whole group. Regardless of what previous identities may have implied, the new identity in Christ, accessed through baptism and renewed in Eucharistic meals, connects the members with a temple office. The rudimentary episcopal structure therefore embeds the Christ-group identity within itself, even if the ἐπίσκοπος was not the sole functionary, as several leadership roles existed alongside one another. However, in the longer term, prophets appear to have become increasingly less common; in the groups addressed by the Ignatian letters and 1 Clement, they are absent as a function. The role of the teacher can be found within the office of the ἐπίσκοπος in later texts, such as 1 Clement, the Pastoral Epistles, and the

Ignatian letters. At this stage, the ἐπίσκοπος is a functionary within the emerging Christ group, but not the only one. Conversely, the ἐπίσκοπος seems to have fundamentally performed the same tasks as those described in other significant early Jesus-group texts and served as a representative of a Christ identity that is distinct from the identity of the outgroups. The construction of a Christian identity, which delineates itself from both Jewish identity and other group identities, is detectable, although not uniquely, in the role of the ἐπίσκοπος in the Didache.

The episcopal office as depicted in 1 Clement exemplifies the author's skill in embedding identity and entrepreneurship, aimed at mobilising the group to act in accord with the prototypical blueprint. For the author of 1 Clement, the antiquity and provenance of the episcopal office, as affirmed by Scripture, suggests a new kind of lifestyle: to live in submission to the leaders is to live a life intimately connected to the ancient heroes of faith and the apostles. Throughout 1 Clement, the leadership structure is portrayed as exigent, apostolic, scriptural, and an antidote to schisms. According to the author, God's word, wherein one finds the episcopal office, is crucial to observe, for failure to heed God's word is tantamount to destruction and death. The current trajectory of the addressees leads to a misguided identity, prompting the author to strongly recommend an alternative path. This new path aligns one's identity with the scriptural heroes of faith. Since the ἐπίσκοπος is linked to the apostolic ministry, the office is ultimately associated with the apostles and with the work of Jesus over time. Being scriptural, the office signifies ingroup values, thoroughly articulated throughout the letter, associated with the ideals embodied by its office holders. The episcopal office is also closely tied to the ideal of orderliness, serving as an antidote for schisms. The establishment of this office parallels God's foreknowledge concerning the schisms threatening the community and thus signifies divine providence for God's elect. The ἐπίσκοπος represents what it means to be a follower of Jesus. An alternative form of the congregation is difficult to envisage, given the scriptural evidence the author presents. This implies that subjection to the ἐπίσκοπος provides a theological structure for the ingroup, where the ideals of Scripture, along with the priestly office – once associated with a Jewish identity – are fully integrated into the episcopal office. This exemplifies the impresarioship conducted by the author. Other identity options are discouraged. Instead, access to God is granted if members lead faction-free lives submitted to their leaders. Correct adherence to the leadership structure serves as a guarantee for an acceptable life for followers of Christ. Thus, we perceive the emergence of a structure in 1 Clement that is intimately linked to an identity as a follower of Jesus, distinct from a Jewish identity (the Jewish identity is rendered silent and dismissed as unimportant and outdated) that offers compelling theological incentives for faithfulness to the structure. Fundamentally, the discourse surrounding exigency and apostolicity, grounded in scriptural ideals, leaves readers who accept the reasoning of 1 Clement with no choice but to closely associate themselves with the emerging episcopal office.

The author of the Pastoral Letters suggests an ingroup identity aligned with Paul and his mission. This construction of identity reflects an act of identity and impresarioship. The author connects the ἐπίσκοπος with Paul the apostle, a central hero of the Christ group, whose mission in the north-eastern quadrant of the Mediterranean world opened Christ groups to non-Jews as well. The mission of Paul remains accessible to those who lead their lives according to the guidelines in the Pastorals.

As we have seen, the theology of the Christ groups is linked to structures for leadership and worship throughout the Ignatian letters. On one hand, there is a set of theological propositions, similar to those of other Christ groups, that the author constantly emphasises. These propositions are essential for members to identify with and concern the nature of Jesus Christ and his relationship to the Father. Furthermore, according to the author, these theological propositions are worth dying for. On the other hand, these dogmas are complemented by behaviour that embeds them into the everyday lives of believers. A concrete example is the unity of the congregation, which reflects the dogmatic statements of Christ's unity with his Father. The episcopal structure serves as a means for the author to be an identity impresario, connecting members with a meaningful framework that embodies the theological reality described in the ingroup narrative. The congregation and its ἐπίσκοπος provide an earthly representation of the supernatural reality depicted in the ingroup narrative. When worship is performed correctly (that is, overseen by the ἐπίσκοπος), the group reflects heavenly realities. The structure suggested by the Ignatian letters acts as a vehicle for the social identity of a distinctly Christian group, in which ingroup-specific theological propositions, deemed worth dying for according to the author, are realised on earth. The space allocated for a Jewish identity that rejects the relationship between Christ and the Father as addressed in the Ignatian letters is non-existent. The author's insistence that proper worship is conducted in tandem with the ἐπίσκοπος, and that the ingroup identity is embodied in the suggested structure, effectively renders the ἐπίσκοπος a guarantee for the group's theology. As previously noted, the author dismisses the notions that "he (Christ) only appeared to suffer" (τὸ δοκεῖν πεπονθέναι αὐτόν, Ign.*Trall.* 10) and that ingroup members should "Judaize" (ἰουδαΐζειν, Ign. Magn. 10:3), instead favouring the episcopal structure as a representation of authentic Christian faith.

By the end of the second century, specifically around 180 CE, the episcopal office becomes increasingly tied to Christian self-identity. This can be traced in Irenaeus's *Against Heresies.* as evidenced by his emphasis on apostolic teachings, the notion that the *episcopus*/ἐπίσκοπος is a successor to the apostles, and the prominence of the Roman episcopal see. All these elements construct an ingroup identity in which the episcopal order becomes vital and non-negotiable for defining what it means to be Christian. Indeed, the episcopal order represents the only viable path in light of the various heresies that threaten to undermine this ingroup identity. In this manner, Irenaeus acts as an impresario for Christian faith, as this identity is deeply embedded within a structured leadership. Furthermore, Irenaeus's role highlights that Christian faith must stem from apostolic teachings, which stand in stark contrast to hidden, esoteric doctrines. This distinction is clarified through Irenaeus's genealogical approach. The adversaries trace their lineage to the dubious Simon Magus, while the ingroup traces its roots back to the apostles and, consequently, the salvific acts of Jesus Christ. In book three of *Against Heresies*, Christian faith is profoundly invested in the authenticity of apostolic teachings, which must, therefore, be traceable. This requirement is safeguarded by episcopal succession, suggesting that the only teachings the Christ groups could accept would be those assured by this apostolic lineage. The content of the handed-down tradition defines Christian faith, and teachings that oppose the gospel tradition must be excluded. Furthermore, the self-definition of Christians is informed by apostolic teaching, rather than being equivalent to a reception of the LXX/Hebrew Bible (at least explicitly). The apostolic teachings, warranted by the ἐπίσκοπος, provide the lens through which Jewish Scriptures are understood. Irenaeus regards a teaching about Moses, as relayed through Clement, as valid, provided the teaching serves as a counter-argument against Valentinianism and does not offer particularly positive views on a Jewish identity. The positive perspective on Moses could indeed be seen as an invitation to an identity more receptive to Jewish ideals regarding the law. However, this is not the case, as Moses is, in practice, merely secondary to the handed-down apostolic material, validated by succession. This becomes abundantly clear in book four of *Against Heresies*, where Irenaeus claims that the apostles abandoned their ancestral Jewish identity and embraced a new Christian identity when they began to follow Jesus. Additionally, the episcopal office is not, as seen in 1 Clement, explicitly regarded as a priestly role that replaces the obsolete Levitical priesthood; nonetheless, it conveys an unmistakably Christian identity as a tradition keeper. Therefore, the connection between office and apostolic teaching ties Christian identity to the apostles and excludes any alternative identities (explicitly Valentinian, but also other self-conceptions such as a Jewish identity, explicitly discussed in book four). According to Irenaeus, this implies that Christian identity is wholly invested in the episcopal office. The prototypical *episcopus*/ἐπίσκοπος embodies and safeguards the apostolic teachings. The openness to a certain degree of Jewish halakah found in the early second century within the Didache is absent by the close of the second century. During this period, a leadership pattern that ties Christian identity to itself and leaves no space for alternative identities has developed in the Christ groups in the north-eastern quadrant of the Mediterranean world.

11.1.3 Identity Entrepreneurship

The concept of entrepreneurship is defined as the leader's ability to create, develop, and maintain a coherent picture of identity and group norms (prototypicality). The identity of the group is constructed through prototypicality and the active development of identity – the narrative of the group – in which the leader plays an active and significant role. The prototypical leader, as an identity entrepreneur, can redefine ingroup identity when granted the authority to lead. In this book, I have utilised the definitions and taxonomy of Steffens et al. (2014) that suggest that identity entrepreneurship primarily involves the rhetorical construction of an ingroup identity. This relates to the third research question: *How did the emergence of the ἐπίσκοπος alter the relation between Christ groups and the Jewish synagogue in terms of Social Identity in the first and second centuries?* We now review the findings pertaining to entrepreneurship in the previous chapters.

A few words can be said regarding this in Acts. Luke is an entrepreneur and embedder of identity, as he suggests that following Christ is apostolic by nature, and that this apostolicity is present in the subsequent officers after the apostles. This theme can, of course, be further developed and discussed in other aspects of Acts, but in this book, it suffices to focus on the aspect of the emerging offices in the Christ group. What is important is that the embedding of ingroup identity (impresarioship) within the episcopal structure alters the ingroup prototypicality into a version where the followership of Jesus must include a defined structure.

This is similar to the situation in 1 Clement: to live according to the suggested ingroup prototype presented by the author is to align oneself with the deposed leaders, the episcopal functionaries. The episcopal structure is an unavoidable framework for Jesus followers to engage with. The author of 1 Clement transforms the identity from the factionists' version into one that is endorsed by Scriptural heroes and the martyrs' steadfastness. The author acts as an identity entrepreneur who proposes a new identity in light of the new leaders. This new identity leaves no room for a prominent Jewish identity.

In the Pastoral Epistles, the ethos of Paul the Apostle is utilised as the author argues for a specific type of Christian identity. The prototypical Paul, who sacrificed everything for the values of the ingroup, advocates for a congregational order. Timothy and Titus are sent to further the mission of the Apostle, and when they appoint episcopal leaders in "every city," the episcopal office becomes a re-enactment of Paul's purpose through the local episcopal leaders. Therefore, the appropriate way to lead a life in accordance with Paul's guidelines is to partake in the congregational order preferred by the Pastorals. Other expressions of Christ followership, such as those the author cautions against in 1 Tim 1:3–7, do not align with Paul's articulated will. Furthermore, the expectation that the ἐπίσκοπος should teach according to the content outlined in the Pastoral Epistles is significant from the perspective of an impresario. He is entrusted with the mandate to envision and continuously re-enact ingroup identity within the life of the congregation; the author grants the πρεσβύτερος/ἐπίσκοπος the authority to renegotiate ingroup identity, provided they adhere to "sound teaching" and lead exemplary lives. Since the teaching content, as reflected in the Pastoral Epistles, overlooks Israel and a prominent Jewish identity, the direction advised by the author propels the groups of the Pastorals towards a widening rift from Jewish identity. The teaching provided by the ἐπίσκοπος is intended to re-establish ingroup values and teachings within the local congregation.

In the Ignatian letters, the author engages in an alteration of prototypicality through the ethos of Ignatius. The letters present Ignatius as prototypical, in fact on his way to die for ingroup values. This also establishes an ethos for the suggested alteration of ingroup beliefs. The portrayal of Ignatius as a letter writer on his way to martyrdom reminds the addressees of the apostle Paul. His suggestions for leadership models, essential for a Christian identity, must carry some weight due to his willingness to suffer for the ingroup narrative. These suggestions leave little room for any other kind of Christian identity than one submitted to an episcopal structure. An identity as docetist or as someone who Judaizes is deemed invalid, according to the author. Therefore, the ἐπίσκοπος is the warrant for Christian faith.

11.2 Conclusions

So where do these conclusions lead us in relation to the Parting of the Ways paradigm? As we have seen throughout this book, the debate over how Christ groups and synagogues became separate entities, eventually evolving into Christianity and Judaism, has gained a sociological dimension in recent years. The explanatory models that began with theological statements have opened the door to perspectives from the social sciences and new methodologies. This book situates itself within this paradigm by providing insights from social identity theory about how group identity is shaped, altered, and embedded within structures.

In the SIT paradigm that I have applied to Christ-group texts predominantly from the second century, leadership roles have been of particular interest as shapers of identity. Through the leader's ability to be a prototypical member, an ingroup ideal becomes apparent. This is especially true, as a prototypical member also displays maximum contrast in relation to outgroups. Prototypical members exhibit the unique characteristics of the ingroup that distinguish it from outgroups. In Christ-group texts, substantial effort is devoted to describing ideal human behaviour. As discussed on multiple occasions, SIT leadership research finds the prototypical leader to be the most effective. The prototypical leader is also afforded some latitude by the group to reshape group identity, acting as identity entrepreneurs. Furthermore, the leader can become an impresario of identity by embedding ingroup identity within a structure or a ritual. Members can be mobilised to take action in accordance with the group vision. As we have observed throughout this book, the self-definition as a Christian or Christ follower has counterparts in the visions and structures presented by the authors of the Christ groups.

The authors of predominantly second-century texts within the Christ group have, on various occasions and in differing contexts, discussed leadership patterns emerging within the developing and maturing Christ movement. These patterns took on theological significance, thereby shaping identity. In this book, we have examined examples of how one such leadership pattern was imbued with theological importance to the extent that it became essential for the groups that adopted it. This is evident at multiple levels within the SIT paradigm. A certain level of ingroup prototypicality is apparent across all the texts, although it varies slightly among different groups. In instances where this is articulated most explicitly, as in the Pastoral Epistles, the ingroup prototypicality shows little interest in Torah observance, instead favouring ideals that align more closely with Stoic moral principles. This prototypicality is anticipated and attributed to the ἐπίσκοπος; yet, the SIT paradigm suggests that the demands on leaders are the same as those on members. Here, one can observe the tension between the prototypical ἐπίσκοπος depicted in the Pastoral Epistles and that of the Didache: within the Didachist community, there is a notable interest in Torah observance and halakic concerns. Given that the ἐπίσκοπος was expected to have been tested by the community, it is reasonable to assume that he embodied these ideals prior to his appointment. Apart from the Didache, one may observe that the ideals associated with the ἐπίσκοπος allow little room for a pronounced Jewish identity. As we noted in 1 Clement, the ἐπίσκοπος is linked to ideals of sanctity and orderliness and is contrasted with a Jewish identity deemed obsolete, as no halakic features are expected from members. The Ignatian letters portray the relationship and subservience to the ἐπίσκοπος as a crucial characteristic for ingroup members, owing to the theological depiction of the episcopal structure as a reflection of heavenly realities, where Christ is closely associated with the Father. Consequently, the author of the Ignatian letters explicitly allows no space for a Jewish identity. The prototypical ἐπίσκοπος in Irenaeus may potentially be reconciled with a Jewish identity, as Irenaeus connects the ἐπίσκοπος with the apostles. As apostles born Jews, it would have been plausible to assume some degree of positivity towards a Jewish identity in Irenaeus's perspective. However, this is not evident. Rather, Irenaeus states in book four of *Against Heresies* that the ancestral faith must be abandoned by Jewish members of the congregations. The ethical dimensions implicitly associated with the apostles suggest a certain assemblage of ethical ideals within the Christ group, in which the "Jewishness" of the apostles is absent. The role of the ἐπίσκοπος is not explicitly defined by prototypical traits in Irenaeus.

The diminishing space for a distinct Jewish identity becomes increasingly pressing within the contextual features of second-century Christ-group authors. As discussed and analysed across all the texts, the ἐπίσκοπος serves as a guarantee of apostolic faith, a reflection of the heavenly realm, a priest in a new temple, and an embodiment of Christ-group ideals. Leaders of the Christ-follower group, acting as impresarios of identity, defined the structure in which they gathered – a structure devoid of halakic concerns, yet one where members could access God's life-giving powers. Moreover, the leadership structure is characterised as a new temple, suggesting that the old temple is by implication obsolete. From an SIT perspective, the ἐπίσκοπος and the structure envisioned around him are emblematic of Christian identity, rendering a distinct Jewish identity (or any other identity) unattainable for members. Consequently, the emphasis on the ἐπίσκοπος leads Christ groups to exclude Jewish identity. The establishment of the episcopal office heightened tensions for Jewish Christ groups and followers, and exhorted an ideal where salient Jewish traits were excluded. According to the sources we have access, to observe halakic rules became impossible for the members of Christ groups, where the ἐπίσκοπος was presiding.

This dissertation began with a short, general overview of how the episcopal office was understood in early modern times. Catholics, Protestants, and Anglicans had different understandings of the value of the episcopal order. Furthermore, during critical times in Western church history, for example, the Reformation and the formation of Methodism, questions of polity became crucial for the self-definition of different churches and movements. The flip side of the coin is that leadership forms also became grounds for separation processes, since the episcopal order was understood as either a spiritless continuation of the apostolic mission or as originally intended by Jesus. The polity of churches conveyed a specific identity. Church orders, the mere existence of bishops, the understanding of the papal role – they all carried consequences for the self-definition of a given church. Given the SIT perspective applied to ancient texts throughout this book, this self-defining aspect of leadership comes as no surprise for us.

We can observe that the situation in the second century CE, along with that of the Methodist "founding fathers", was comparable, since the leadership question in the Methodist movement also was a significant feature in the parting of the ways between the Anglican and Methodist churches. The episcopacy conveys ingroup identity. The embedding of identity within a social structure can cause groups with different prototypicality to drift apart. This study examined how the episcopal structure widened the rift between the Christ group and the synagogue. The ἐπίσκοπος is crucial to understanding the parting of the ways.

Bibliography

Ancient Sources

The Ancient Synagogue From Its Origins to 200 C.E.: A Source Book. Edited and translated by Anders Runesson, Donald D. Binder, and Birger Olsson. AGJU 72. Leiden: Brill, 2008.

The Apostolic Fathers. Edited and translated by Bart D Ehrman. 2 vols. LCL 24–25. Cambridge, MA: Harvard University Press, 2003.

Die apostolischen Väter: Neubearbeitung der Funkschen Ausgabe, Didache, Barnabas, Klemens I und II, Ignatius, Polycarp, Papias, Quadratus, Diognetbrief, 3rd ed. Edited and translated by Karl Bihlmeyer. SAQ 1. Tübingen: Mohr, 1970.

Associations in the Greco-Roman World: A Sourcebook. Edited and translated by Richard S. Ascough, Philip A. Harland, and John S. Kloppenborg. Berlin: DeGruyter, 2013.

Barnabas and the Didache: A Translation and Commentary. The Apostolic Fathers, vol. 3. Edited and translated by Robert A. Kraft. New York: Thomas Nelson and Son, 1965.

Cicero. *De Officiis*. Translated by Walter Miller. LCL 30. Cambridge, MA: Harvard University Press, 1913.

Clementis Romani Ad Corinthos quæ dicuntur epistulæ: textum ad fidem codicum et Alexandrini et Constantinoploitani nuper inventi. Edited by Oscar de Gebhardt and Adolf von Harnack. Leipzig: Hinrich, 1876.

The Dead Sea Scrolls Translated: The Qumran Texts in English. Edited and translated by Florentino García Martínez. 2nd ed. Leiden: Brill, 1996.

The Dead Sea Scrolls Study Edition. Edited by Florentino García Martínez and Eibert J. C. Tigchelaar. Leiden: Brill, 1999.

Diogenes Laertius. *Lives of Eminent Philosophers: An Edited Translation*. Edited and translated by Stephen White. Cambridge: Cambridge University Press, 2020.

Donateurs et fondateurs dans les synagogues juives. Edited and translated by Baruch Lifshitz. Paris: Gabalda, 1967.

Epiphanius of Salamis. *Panarion: The Panarion of Epiphanius of Salamis*. Translated by Frank Williams. Leiden: Brill, 2009.

Greco-Roman Associations: Texts, Translations, and Commentary. Edited and translated by Richard S. Ascough and John S. Kloppenborg. BZNW 181. Berlin: DeGruyter, 2011.

Greco-Roman Associations: Texts, Translations, and Commentary II. North Coast of the Black Sea, Asia Minor. Edited and translated by Philip A. Harland. BZNW 204. Berlin: DeGruyter, 2014.

Inscriptions de Délos: décrets postérieurs a 166AV. J.-C. (NOS 1497;–1524); dédicaces postérieurs a 166 AV. J.-C. (NOS 1525–2219). Edited by Pierre Rouessel and Marcel Launey. Paris: Librarire Ancienne Honoré Champion, 1937.

Ireneaus. *Adversus Haereses*. Edited by W. Wigan Harvey. Cambridge: Typis Academicis, 1857.
Irenaeus of Lyons. Edited and translated by Robert A. Grant. London: Routledge, 1997.
Jewish Inscriptions of Western Europe (JIWE). 2 vols. Edited and translated by David Noy. Cambridge: Cambridge University Press, 1993–1995.
The Muratorian Fragment: Text, Translation, Commentary. Edited and translated by Clare K. Rothschild. STAC 132. Tübingen: Mohr Siebeck, 2022.
Novum Testamentum Graece. Edited by Eberhard Nestle, Kurt Aland and Barbara Aland. 28th ed. Stuttgart: Deutsche Bibelgesellschaft, 2012.
The Oxford Annotated Mishnah: A New Translation of the Mishnah with Introduction and Notes. 2 vols. Edited and translated by Shaye Cohen, Robert Goldenberg, and Hayim Lapin. Oxford: Oxford University Press, 2022–2023.
Septuaginta: Editio Altera. Edited by Alfred Rahlfs and Robert Hanhart. Stuttgart: Deutsche Bibelgesellschaft, 2006.
The Shepherd of Hermas: A New Translation and Commentary. Translated by Caroline P. Buie and Michael J. Svigel. Eugene, OR: Cascade Books, 2023.
Die Urfassungen der Martyria Polycarpi et Pionii und das Corpus Polycarpianum. 2 vols. Edited and translated by Otto Zwierlein. UALG 116. Berlin: De Gruyter, 2014.

Modern Sources

The Second Book of Discipline. With Introduction and Commentary. Edited by James Kirk. Renfrew: Robert MacLehose & Company, 1980.
Baptism, Eucharist, and Ministry. World Council of Churches: Faith and Order, Paper No. 111. Geneva: World Council of Churches, 1982.

Literature

Achtemeier, Paul J. 1996. *1 Peter: A Commentary*. Hermeneia. Minneapolis: Fortress Press.
Alexander, Philip S. 1999. "'The Parting of the Ways' from the Perspective of Rabbinic Judaism." Pages 1–26 in *Jews and Christians: The Parting of the Ways A.D. 70–135*. Edited by James D G Dunn. Grand Rapids: Eerdmans.
Allport, Floyd H. 1962. "A Structuronomic Conception of Behavior: Individual and Collective." *JASPs* 64:3–30.
Armstrong, Karl L. 2021. *Dating Acts in Its Jewish and Greco-Roman Contexts*. London: T&T Clark.
Arnold, Gottfried. 1732. *Die erste Liebe: Das ist: Wahre Abbildung der ersten Christen nach ihrem lebendigen Glauben und heiligen Leben, aus der ältesten und bewährtesten Kirchen-Scribenten eigenen Zeugnissen, Exempeln und Reden, nach der Wahrheit der ersten einigen christlichen Religion, allen Liebhabern der historischen Wahrheit, und sonderlich der Antiquität, als in einer nützlichen Kirche-Historie, treulich und unparteyisch entworfen, worinnen zugleich des Hn. William Cave erstes Christenthum: nach Nothdurft erläutert wird. In der dritten Ausfertigung mit einer nöthigen Verantwortung, wie auch vollständigen Summarien und Registern vermehret*. Leipzig: Samuel Benjamin Walthern.
Ascough, Richard S. 2015a. "What Are They Now Saying about Christ Groups and Associations?" *CBR* 2:207–44.

—. 2015b. "Paul, Synagogues, and Associations: Reframing the Question of Models for Pauline Christ Groups," *JJMJS* 2:27–52.
Ascough, Richard S, Philip A. Harland, and John S. Kloppenborg, eds. 2013. *Associations in the Greco-Roman World: A Sourcebook.* Berlin: DeGruyter.
Ascough, Richard S., and John S. Kloppenborg. 2011. *Greco-Roman Associations: Texts, Translations, and Commentary.* BZNW 181. Berlin: DeGruyter.
Audet, Jean-Paul. 1952. "Affinités littéraires et doctrinales du 'Manuel de discipline.'" *RB* 59:219–38.
—. 1958. *La Didachè : Instructions des apôtres.* Paris: Gabalda.
Baker, Coleman A. 2011. *Identity, Memory and Narrative in Early Christianity: Peter, Paul, and Recategorization in the Book of Acts.* Euguene, OR: Pickwick Publications.
Bakke, Odd M. 2001. *Concord and Peace: A Rhetorical Analysis of 1 Clement.* WUNT 143. Tübingen: Mohr Siebeck.
Baldovin, John F. 2016. Review of *The Original Bishops: Office and Order in the First Christian Communities. CH* 85:365–67.
Barclay, John M. G. 2011. *Pauline Churches and Diaspora Jews.* WUNT 275. Tübingen: Mohr Siebeck.
—. 2015. *Paul and the Gift.* Grand Rapids, MI: Eerdmans.
Barnes, Timothy D. 2008. "The Date of Ignatius." *ExpTim* 120:119–30
Batovici, Dan. 2017. "*The Shepherd* of Hermas in Recent Scholarship on the Canon: A Review Article." *ASEs* 34:89–105.
Baur, Ferdinand C. 1835. *Die sogenannten Pastoralbriefe des Apostels Paulus aufs neue kritisch untersucht.* Stuttgart and Tübingen: J. G. Cotta.
—. 1838. *Ueber den Ursprung des Episcopats in der christlichen Kirche. Prüfung der neuestens von Hrn. Dr. Rothe aufgestellten Ansicht.* Tübingen: Ludwig Friedrich.
Belleville, Linda L. 2021. *Philippians: A New Covenant Commentary.* Eugene, OR: Cascade Books.
Bernard, John Henry. 1899. *The Pastoral Epistles: With Introduction and Notes.* Cambridge: Cambridge University Press.
Beyer, Hermann. 1964. ἐπίσκοπος Pages 609–10 in *TDNT*, volume II. Edited by Gerhard Kittel and Gerhard Friedrich. 1964–1976. Translated by Geoffrey Bromiley. 10 volumes. Grand Rapids: Eerdmans.
Bihlmeyer, Karl. 1970. *Die apostolischen Väter: Neubearbeitung der Funkschen Ausgabe, Didache, Barnabas, Klemens I und II, Ignatius, Polycarp, Papias, Quadratus, Diognetbrief.* 3rd ed. SAQ 1. Tübingen: Mohr.
Binder, Donald B. *Into the Temple Courts: The Place of the Synagogues in the Second Temple Period.* Atlanta: Society of Biblical Literature.
Bobertz, Charles A. 1992. "The Development of Episcopal Order." Pages 183–311 in *Eusebius, Christianity, and Judaism.* Edited by Harold. Attridge and Gohei Hata. Detroit: Wayne State University Press.
Bockmuehl, Markus. 1997. *A Commentary on the Epistle to the Philippians.* London: A & C Black.
Bourdieu, Pierre. 1991. "Genesis and Structure of the Religious Field". Pages 1–44 in *Comparative Social Research: A Research Annual.* Edited by Craig Calhoun. London: JAI Press.

Bornkamm, Günther. 1968. Πρέσβυς. Pages 651–83 in *TDNT*, vol. VI. Edited by Gerhard Kittel and Gerhard Friedrich. Translation: Geoffrey Bromiley. Grand Rapids: Eerdmans.

Boyarin, Daniel. 2003. "Semantic differences; or 'Judaism'/'Christianity'," Pages 65–87 in *The Ways that Never Parted*. Edited by Anette Yoshiko Reed and Adam H. Becker. Tübingen: Mohr Siebeck.

Bradshaw, Paul F. 2000. "Hippolytus Revisited: The Identity of the So-Called 'Apostolic Tradition'." *Lit(E)* 16:6–11.

—. 2002. *The Search for the Origins of Christian Worship*. Oxford: Oxford University Press.

Bradshaw, Paul F, Maxwell E. Johnson and L. Edward Philips. 2002. *The Apostolic Tradition: A Commentary*. Hermeneia. Minneapolis: Fortress Press.

Bremmer, Jan N. 2017. *Magic, and Martyrs in Early Christianity*. WUNT 379. Tübingen: Mohr Siebeck.

—. 2018. "Peregrinus and Marcion." Pages 75–86 in *Marcion of Sinope as Religious Entrepreneur*. Edited by Markus Vinzent. StPatr vol. 99. Leuven: Peeters.

—. 2021. "Ioudaismos, Christianismos and the Parting of the Ways." Pages 57–88 in *Jews and Christians: Parting Ways in the First Two Centuries CE? Reflections on the Gains and Losses of a Model*. Edited by Jens Schröter, Benjamin Edsall, and Joseph Verheyden. Berlin: DeGruyter.

Brent, Allen. 1995. *Hippolytus and the Roman Church in the Third Century: Communities in Tension before the Emergence of a Monarch-Bishop*. VCSup 3. Leiden: Brill.

—. 1998. "Ignatius of Antioch and the Imperial Cult." *VC* 52:30–58.

—. 1999. *The Imperial Cult and the Development of Church Order: Concepts and Images of Authority in Paganism and Early Christianity Before the Age of Cyprian*. Leiden: Brill.

—. 2006. *Ignatius of Antioch and the Second Sophistic: A Study of an Early Christian Transformation of Pagan Culture*. STAC 36. Tübingen: Mohr Siebeck.

—. 2007. *Ignatius of Antioch: A Martyr Bishop and the Origin of Episcopacy*. London: T&T Clark.

Breytenbach, Cilliers. 2013. "The Historical Example in 1 Clement." *ZAC* 18:22–33.

Brown, Jeannine K. 2022. *Philippians: An Introduction and Commentary*. TNTC 11. Downers Grove, IL: IVP Academic.

Brown, Raymond E. 1980. "Episkope and Episkopos: The New Testament Evidence." *TS* 4:322–38.

Brown, Rupert and Sam Pherson. 2020. *Group Processes: Dynamics in and between Groups*. 3rd ed. Hoboken, NJ: John Wiley & Sons Inc.

Bruce, Fredrick F. 1988. *The Book of Acts*. NICNT, Grand Rapids: Eerdmans,

—. 1989. *Philippians*. NIBCNT. Peabody: Hendrickson Publishing.

Buie, Caroline P. 2022. "Hermas's Purpose: Ecclesiology in the *Shepherd of Hermas*." *CTR* 20:3–22.

Burtchaell, James T. 1991. *From Synagogue to Church*. Cambridge: Cambridge University Press.

Campell, R. Alastair. 1994. *The Elders: Seniority within the Earliest Christianity*. Edinburgh: T&T Clark.

—. 2005. Review of *The Elder and the Overseer: One Office in the Early Church* by Benjamin Merkle. *EvQ*:281–83.

Campbell, Donald T. 1958. "Common Fate, Similarity and Other Indices of the Status of Aggregates as Social Entities." *Behav. Sci.* 3:14–25.

Campenhausen, Hans von. 1957. *Bearbeitungen und Interpolationen des Polykarpmartyriums*. Heidelberg: Carl Winter Universitetsverlag.
—. 1969. *Ecclesiastical Authority and Spiritual Power in the Church of the First Three Centuries*. Translation J. A. Baker, London: A&C Black.
Carleton Paget, James. 2017. "1 Clement, Judaism and the Jews." *EC* 8:218–50.
—. 2018. "Jewish Revolts and Jewish-Christian Relations." Pages 276–306 in *Jews and Christians in the First and Second Centuries: The Interbellum 70–132 CE*. Edited by Joshua Schwartz and Peter Tomson. Leiden: Brill.
Catto, Stehpen. 2007. *Reconstructing the First-Century Synagogue: A Critical Analysis of Current Research*. London: T&T Clark.
Chipparini, Giuilano. 2013. "Irenaeus and the Gnostic Valentinus: Orthodoxy and Heresy in the Church of Rome around the Middle of the Second Century." *ZAC* 18:95–119.
Cinnirella, Marco. 1998. "Exploring Temporal Aspects of Social Identity: The Concept of Possible Social Identities." *EJSP* 28:227–48.
Cirafesi, Wally V. 2023. "Rethinking John and "the Synagogue" in Light of Expulsion from Public Assemblies in Antiquity," *JBL* 142:682–87.
Cohen, Shaye J.D. 2018. "The Ways that Parted: Jews, Christians, and Jewish-Christians, ca 100–150 CE." Pages 307–339 in *Jews and Christians in the First and Second Centuries: The Interbellum 70–132 CE*. Edited by Joshua Schwartz and Peter Tomson. Leiden: Brill.
Cohen, Shaye J.D., and Hayim Lapin. 2022. "Introduction." Pages 1–11 in *The Oxford Annotated Mishnah: A New Translation of the Mishnah with Introduction and Notes*. Vol. 1. Edited by Shaye Cohen, Robert Goldenberg, and Hayim Lapin. Oxford: Oxford University Press.
Collins, Raymond F. 2002. *1 & II Timothy and Titus: A Commentary*. NTL. Louisville: Westminster John Knox Press.
Conzelmann, Hans. 1987. *A Commentary on the Acts of the Apostles*. Translated by James Limburg, Thomas Kraabel, and Donald Juel. Hermenia. Philadelphia: Fortress Press.
Conzelmann, Hans and Martin Dibelius. 1972. *A Commentary on the Pastoral Epistles*. Translated by Philip Buttolph and Adela Yarbro. Hermeneia. Philadelphia: Fortress Press.
Danker, Frederick William, ed. 2000. *A Greek-English Lexicon of the New Testament and Other Early Christian Literature*. 3rd ed. Chicago: The University of Chicago Press.
Davids, Peter. 1982. *The Epistle of James*. NIGTC. Grand Rapids: Eerdmans. Kindle Version.
—. 1990. *The First Epistle of Peter*. NICNT. Grand Rapids: Eerdmans. Kindle version.
Dehandschutter, Boudewijn. 1993. "The Martyrium Polycarpi: A Century of Research." *ANRW* 27.1:485–522.
Delafosse, Henri. 1928. "La lettre de Clement Romain aux Corinthiens." *RHR* 97:53–89.
DeSilva, David A. 2006. *4 Maccabees: Introduction and Commentary on the Greek Text in Codex Sinaiticus*. Leiden: Brill.
Dibelius, Martin. 1912. *An die Kolosser, Epheser, an Philemon*. HNT 12. 3rd ed. Tübingen: Mohr.
Donelson, Lewis R. 1986. *Pseudepigraphy and Ethical Argument in the Pastoral Epistles*. HUT 22. Tübingen: Mohr Siebeck.
Draper, Jonathan A. 1996. "Christian Self-Definition against the Hypocrites in Didache VIII." Pages 223–44 in *The Didache in Modern Research*. AGJU 37. Edited by Jonathan Draper. Leiden: Brill.

—. 2005. "Do the Didache and Matthew Reflect an "Irrevocable Parting of the Ways" with Judaism?," Pages 217–41 in *Matthew and the Didache: Two Documents from the Same Jewish-Christian Milieu?* Edited by Huub van de Sandt. Assen: Van Gorcum.

—. 2007. "The Didache." Pages 13–20 in *The Writings of the Apostolic Fathers*. Edited by Paul Foster. London: T&T Clark.

—. 2008, "Apostles, Teachers, and Evangelists: Stability and Movement of Functionaries in Matthew, James and the Didache." Pages 139–76 in *Matthew, James, and the Didache: Three Related Documents in Their Jewish and Christian Setting*. Edited by Huub van de Sandt and Jürgen Zangenberg. Atlanta: Society of Biblical Literature.

—. 2010. "The Didache." Pages 7–24 in *The Apostolic Fathers: An Introduction*. Edited by Wilhelm Pratscher. Waco: Baylor University Press.

Dunn, James D.G. 2000. "The First and Second Letters to Timothy and the Letter to Titus." Pages 773–880 in *NIB* vol 11. Edited by Leander Keck. Nashville: Abingdon Press

Dunn, James D.G., ed. 1999. *Jews and Christians: The Parting of the Ways A.D. 70–135*. Grand Rapids: Eerdmans.

Easton, Burton S. 1932. "New Testament Ethical Lists." *JBL* 51:1–12.

Edwards, Mark J. 1998. "Ignatius and the Second Century: An Answer to R. Hübner." *ZAC* 2:214–26.

Ehrman, Bart D. 2003a–b. *The Apostolic Fathers*. 2 vols. LCL 24–25. Cambridge, MA: Harvard University Press, 2003.

—. 2003c. *Lost Christianities: The Battle for Scripture and the Faiths We Never Knew*. New York: Oxford University Press.

Elliott, John H. 2003. "Elders as Honored Household Heads and Not Holders of "Office" in Earliest Christianity." *BTB*:77–82.

Engelmann, Micahela. 2012. *Unzertrennliche Drillinge? Motivsemantische Untersuchungen zum literarischen Verhältnis der Pastoralbriefe*. BZNW 192. Berlin: DeGruyter.

Engvall Siegel, Alberta and Sidney Siegel. 1957. "Reference Groups, Membership Groups and Attitude Change." *JASPs* 55:360–64.

Eriksson, Larsolov. 1982. *Filipperbrevet*. KNT 11. Stockholm: EFS-Förlaget.

Esler, Philip. 2003. *Conflict and Identity in Romans: The Social Setting of Paul's Letter*. Minneapolis: Fortress Press.

—. 2022. *2 Corinthians: A Social Identity Commentary*: London: T&T Clark.

Eurell, John-Christian. 2022a. Ignatius, Polycarp, and Their Reception in the Second Century." *EC* 13:188–204.

—. 2022b. "The *Hypomnemata* of Hegesippus." *SJT* 75:148–57.

—. 2025. "Dating Acts in Its Jewish and Greco-Roman Contexts, by Karl Armstrong." *SEÅ* 89:155–59.

Fee, Gordon D. 1995. *Paul's Letter to the Philippians*. NICNT. Grand Rapids: Eerdmans.

Finlan, Stephen. 2015. "Identity in the Didache Community." Pages 17–33 in *The Didache: A Missing Piece of the Puzzle in Early Christianity*. Edited by Jonathan Draper and Clayton Jefford. Atlanta: SBL Press.

Fitzmyer, Joseph A. 1998. *The Acts of the Apostles: A New Translation with Introduction and Commentary*. AB. New York: Doubleday.

Foster, Paul. 2007. "The Epistles of Ignatius of Antioch." Pages 81–107 in *The Writings of the Apostolic Fathers*. Edited by Paul Foster. London: T&T Clark.

Frankfurter, David. 2003. "Beyond 'Jewish Christianity': Continuing Religious Sub-Cultures of the Second and Third Centuries and Their Documents." Pages 131–44 in *The Ways that Never Parted*. Edited by Anette Yoshiko Reed and Adam H. Becker. Tübingen: Mohr Siebeck

Fredriksen, Paula. 2003. "What Parting of the Ways?" Pages 35–64 in *The Ways that Never Parted*. Edited by Anette Yoshiko Reed and Adam H. Becker. Tübingen: Mohr Siebeck.

Frey, Jörg. 2013. "Die Juden im Johannesevangelium und die Frage nach der Trennung der Wege zwischen der johanneischen Gemeinde und der Synagoge," Pages 339–77 in *Die Herrlichkeit des Gekreuzigten. Studien zu den Johanneischen Schriften I* Edited by Juliane Schlegel. Tübingen: Mohr Siebeck.

Gabrielson, Timothy A. 2020. "An Early Reader of James? Ethical Parallels between the Epistle and 2 Enoch." *JSNT* 43:226–47.

Garrow, Alan. 2004. *The Gospel of Matthew's Dependence on the Didache*. London and New York: T&T Clark.

Gebhardt, Oscar de, and Adolf von Harnack. 1876. *Clementis Romani Ad Corinthos quæ dicuntur epistulæ: textum ad fidem codicum et Alexandrini et Constantinopolitani nuper inventi*. Leipzig: Hinrich.

Gillihan, Yonder M. 2012. *Civic Ideology, Organization, and Law in the Rule Scrolls: A Comparative Study of the Covenanters' Sect and Contemporary Voluntary Associations in Political Context*. STDJ 97. Leiden: Brill.

Glicksman, Andrew T. 2011. *Wisdom of Solomon 10: A Jewish Hellenistic Reinterpretation of Early Israelite History through Sapiential Lenses*. DCLS 9. Berlin: DeGruyter.

Goodman, Martin. 2003. "Modeling the 'Parting of the Ways'." Pages 119–30 in *The Ways that Never Parted*. Edited by Anette Yoshiko Reed and Adam H. Becker. Tübingen: Mohr Siebeck.

Gregory, Andrew F. 2002. "Disturbing Trajectories: 1 Clement, the Shepherd of Hermas and the Development of Early Christianity." Pages 142–66 in *Rome in the Bible and the Early Church*. Edited by Oakes, Peter. Grand Rapids: Baker Academic.

Grundeken, Mark. 2015. *Community Building in the Shepherd of Hermas: A Critical Study of Some Key Aspects*. VCSup 131. Leiden: Brill.

Guthrie, Donald. 1990. *The Pastoral Epistles*. 2nd ed. TNTC 14. Downers Grove, IL: IVP Academic.

Haar Romeny, Bas ter. 2005. "Hypotheses on the Development of Judaism and Christianity in Syria in the Period after 70 C.E." Pages 13–33 in *Matthew and the Didache*. Edited by Huub van de Sandt. Assen: Van Gorcum.

Hagner, Donald A. 1973. *The Use of the New Testament in Clement of Rome*. NovTSup 34. Leiden: Brill.

Hanson, Anthony T. 1966. *The Pastoral Epistles*. NCBC. Cambridge: Cambridge University Press.

Hanson, Richard. 1978. "Amt in Alte Kirche." Pages 533–52 in *TRE* III. Edited by Gerhard Krause and Gerhard Müller. Berlin: de Gruyter.

Harland, Philip A. 2000. "Honouring the Emperor or Assailing the Beast: Participation in Civic Life Among Associations (Jewish, Christian and Other) in Asia Minor and the Apocalypse of John." *JSNT* 77:99–121.

—. 2003. *Associations, Synagogues, and Congregations: Claiming a Place in Ancient Mediterranean Society*. Minneapolis: Fortress Press.

—. 2014. *Greco-Roman Associations: Texts, Translations, and Commentary II. North Coast of the Black Sea, Asia Minor.* BZNW 204.Berlin: DeGruyter.

Harnack, Adolf von. 1883. "Analecten von A. Harnack," in *Die Gesellschaftsverfassung der christlichen Kirchen im Altertum.* Edwin Hatch. Translation by Adolf von Harnack. Giessen: J. Ricker.

—. 1884. *Die Lehre der Zwölf Apostel: Untersuchungen zur ältesten Geschichte der Kirchenverfassung und des Kirkenrechts.* Leipzig: J. C. Hinrichs.

—. 1886. *Die Apostellehre und die jüdischen beiden Wege.* Leipzig: J. C. Hinrichs.

—. 1902. *Die Mission und Ausbreitung des Christentums in den ersten drei Jahrhunderten.* Leipzig: J. C. Hinrich.

—. 1911. *The Date of the Acts and of the Synoptic Gospels.* Translation by J. R. Wilkinson. CTL 33. New York: Putnam.

Harvey, W. Wigan, ed. 1857. *Sancti Irenaei episcopi Lugdunensis libros quinque adversus haereses: textu Graeco in locis nonnullis locupletato, versione Latina cum codicibus Claromontano ac Arundeliano denuo collata, praemissa de placitis gnosticorum prolusione, fragmenta necnon Graece, Syriace, Armeniace, commentatione perpetua et indicibus variis.* Cambridge: Typis Academicis.

Haslam, S. Alexander and Stephen D. Reicher. 2007. "Identity entrepreneurship and the consequences of identity failure: The dynamics of leadership in the BBC Prison Study." *Soc. Psych. Q* 70:125–37.

Haslam, S Alexander, Stephen D. Reicher, and Michael J. Platow. 2011. *The New Psychology of Leadership: Identity, Influence, and Power.* New York: Psychology Press.

Hatch, Edwin. 1881. *The Organization of the Early Christian Churches: Eight Lectures Delivered Before the University of Oxford, in the Year 1880.* London: Longmans, Green, and Co.

—. 1883. *Die Gesellschaftsverfassung der christlichen Kirchen im Altertum.* Translation by Adolf von Harnack. Giessen: J. Ricker.

Hawthorne, Gerald F. 1983. *Philippians.* WBC 43. Waco: Word.

Hawthorne, Gerald F. and Ralph P. Martin. 2015. *Philippians.* Rev. ed. WBC 43. Grand Rapids: Zondervan.

Hayman, A. Peter. 2003. *Wisdom of Solomon.* Eerdmans Commentary on the Bible. Grand Rapids, MI: Eerdmans.

Heemstra, Marius. 2010. *The Fiscus Judaicus and the Parting of the Ways.* WUNT II/277 Tübingen: Mohr Siebeck.

Henrich, Joseph. 2009. "The Evolution of Costly Displays, Cooperation and Religion: Credibility Enhancing Displays and Their Implications for Cultural Evolution." *Evol. Hum. Behav.* 30:244–60.

Hempel, Charlotte. 2020. *The Community Rules from Qumran: A Commentary.* TSAJ 183. Tübingen: Mohr Siebeck.

Hendriksen, William. 1962. *Philippians.* Edinburgh: The Banner of Truth Trust.

Herron, Thomas J. 1989. "The Most Probable Date of the First Epistle of Clement to the Corinthians." Pages 106–21 in *Second century, Tertullian to Nicaea in the West, Clement of Alexandria and Origen, Athanasius: The Papers Presented to the Tenth International Conference on Patristic Studies Held in Oxford 1987.* StPatr. 21. Edited by Elizabeth Livingstone. Leuven: Peeters.

Hogg, Michael A. 2001. "A Social Identity Theory of Leadership." *PSPR* 5:184–200.

Hogg, Michael A., Daan van Knippenberg and David E. Rast. 2012. "The Social Identity Theory of Leadership: Theoretical Origins, Research Findings, and Conceptual Developments." *ERSP* 23:258–304.

Holloway, Paul A. 1998. "The Apocryphal *Epistle to the Laodiceans* and the Partitioning of Philippians." *HTR* 91:321–25.

—. 2008. "*Alius Paulus*: Paul's Promise to Send Timothy at Philippians at Philippians 2.19-24." *NTS* 54:542–56.

—. 2009. *Coping with Prejudice: 1 Peter in a Social-Psychological Perspective*. WUNT 244. Tübingen: Mohr Siebeck.

—. 2017. *Philippians: A Commentary*. Hermeneia. Minneapolis: Fortress Press.

Holmberg, Bengt. 1990. *Sociology and the New Testament: An Appraisal*. Minneapolis: Fortress Press.

—. 2008. "Understanding the First Hundred Years of Christian Identity." Pages 1–32 in *Exploring Early Christian Identity*. Edited by Holmberg, Bengt. WUNT 226. Tübingen: Mohr Siebeck.

Holmes, Michael W. 2008. "The Biblical Canon." Pages 406–26 in *The Oxford Handbook of Early Christian Studies*. Edited by Susan Ashbrook Harvey and David Hunter. Oxford: Oxford University Press.

Holmstrand, Jonas. 1997. *Makers of Meaning in Paul*. ConBNT 28. Lund: Gleerups.

Hørning Jensen, Morten. 2019. Review of *The Role of the Synagoge in the Aims of Jesus* by Jordan J. Ryan. *JETS* 62:167–70.

Hübner, Reinhard M. 1997. "Thesen zur Echtheit und Datierung der sieben Briefe des Ignatius von Antiochien." *ZAC* 1:44–72.

Isacson, Mikael. 2004. *To Each Their Own Letter. Structure, Themes, and Rhetorical Strategies in the Letters of Ignatius of Antioch*. ConBNT 42. Stockholm: Almqvisk & Wiksell.

Jefford, Clayton N. 1989. *The Sayings of Jesus in the Teaching of the Twelve Apostles*. Leiden: Brill.

Jeremias, Joachim. 1962. *Jerusalem zur Zeit Jesu: eine kulturgeschichtliche Untersuchung zur neutestamentlichen Zeitgeschichte*. Göttingen: Vanderhoeck & Ruprecht.

—. 1981. *Die Briefe an Thimotheus und Titus*. 12th ed. Göttingen: Vanderhoeck & Ruprecht.

Jetten, Jolanda, Aarti Iyer, Paul Hutchison, and Matthew J. Hornsey. 2011. "Debating Deviance: Responding to Those who Fall from Grace." Pages 117–34 in *Rebels in Groups: Dissent, Deviance, Difference and Defiance*. Edited by Jolanda Jetten and Matthew Hornsey. Oxford: Wiley-Blackwell.

Jobes, Karen H. 2022. *1 Peter*. BECNT. Grand Rapids: Baker Academic.

Johnson, Luke Timothy. 1995. *The Letter of James: A New Translation with Introduction and Commentary*. AB 37A. New York: Doubleday.

—. 2001. *The First and Second Letters to Timothy: A New Translation with Introduction and Commentary*. AB 35A. New York: Doubleday.

Joly, Robert. 1979. *Le dossier d'Ignace d'Antioche*. Brussels: Éditions de l'Universite de Bruxelles.

Kazen, Thomas and Rikard Roitto. 2023. *Revenge, Compensation, and Forgiveness in the Ancient World: A Comparative Study of Interpersonal Infringement and Moral Repair*. WUNT 515. Tübingen: Mohr Siebeck.

Keener, Craig S. 2000. "Family and Household." Pages 353–68 in *DNTB*. Edited by Craig Evans and Stanley Porter. Downers Grove, IL: InterVarsity Press.

Kelhoffer, James A. 2023. "Passing the Audition: Mode and Harmony in Ignatius of Antioch's Chorus (Eph. 4.2; Rom. 2.2)." Pages 175–201 in *Why We Sing: Music, Word, and Liturgy in Early Christianity: Essays in Honour of Anders Ekenberg's 75th Birthday*. Edited by Carl-Johan Berglund, Barbara Crostini, and James Kelhoffer. VCSup 177. Leiden: Brill.

Khomych, Taras. 2015. "From Glorious Past to Miserable Present." Pages 51–60 in *Early Christian Communities between Ideal and Reality*. Edited by Mark Grundeken and Joseph Verheyden. WUNT 342. Tübingen: Mohr Siebeck.

King, Peter. 1691. *An Enquiry into the Constitution, Discipline, Unity and Worship of the Primitive Church*. London: J. Wyat and R. Robinson.

Kirk, James. 1980. *The Second Book of Discipline. With Introduction and Commentary*. Renfrew: Robert MacLehose & Company.

Kirk, Kenneth E. 1946. "The Apostolic Ministry." Pages 1–52 in *Essays on the History and the Doctrine of the Episcopacy*. Edited by Kenneth Kirk. London: Hodder and Stoughton.

Kittel, Gerhard and Gerhard Friedrich. 1964–1976. *Theological Dictionary of the New Testament*. Translated by Geoffrey. Bromiley. 10 volumes. Grand Rapids: Eerdmans.

Knight George W. 1992. *The Pastoral Epistles: A Commentary on the Greek Text*. NIGTC. Grand Rapids: Eerdmans, ePub version.

Kloppenborg, John S. 2005. Review of *"The Gospel of Matthew's Dependence on the Didache"* by Alan Garrow. *Bib* 86:438–41.

—. 2015. "Pneumatic Democracy and the Conflict in 1 Clement." Pages 61–81 in *Early Christian Communities between Ideal and Reality*. Edited by Joseph Verheyden and Mark Grundeken. WUNT 342. Tübingen: Mohr Siebeck.

—. 2019. *Christ's Associations: Connecting and Belonging in the Ancient City* New Haven: Yale University Press.

Knopf, Rudolf. 1905, *Das nachapostolische Zeitalter: Geschichte der christlichen Gemeinden vom Beginn der Flavierdynastie bis zum Ende Hadrians*. Tübingen: Verlag von J C B Mohr (Paul Siebeck).

—. 1920. *Die Lehre der zwölf Apostel; die zwei Clemensbriefe*. Tübingen: Mohr.

Koch, Dietrich-Alex. 2010. "Die Entwicklung der Ämter in frühchristlichen Gemeinden Kleinasiens." Pages 166–206 in *Neutestamentliche Ämtermodelle im Kontext*. Edited by Thomas Schmeller, Martin Ebner and Rudolf Hoppe. Freiburg: Herder.

Koehler, Ludwig, and Walter Baumgartner. 1994–1999. *The Hebrew and Aramaic Lexicon of the Old Testament*. 5 vols. Leiden: Brill.

Koester, Helmut. 1957. *Synoptische Überlieferung bei den apostolischen Vätern*. TU 65. Berlin: Akademie-Verlag.

—. 2007. "The Apostolic Fathers and The Struggle for Christian Identity." Pages 1–12 in *The Writings of the Apostolic Fathers*. Edited by Paul Foster. London: T&T Clark.

Kooten, George H van. 2010. "Ancestral, Oracular and Prophetic Authority: 'Scriptural Authority' according to Paul and Philo." Pages 267–308 in *Authoritative Scriptures in Ancient Judaism: Proceedings of the Symposium at the Qumran Institute Groningen*. Edited by Mladen Popović. Suppl. J. Study Jud. 141. Leiden: Brill.

Kraft, Heinrich. 1975. "Die Anfänge des geistliches Amtes." *TLZ* 100:81–98.

Kraft, Robert A. 1965. *Barnabas and the Didache*. The Apostolic Fathers, vol. 3. New York: Thomas Nelson and Son.

Kraus, Samuel. 1922. *Synagogale Altertümer*. Berlin: Verlag Benjamin Harz.

Kujanpää, Katja. 2020. "Scriptural Authority and Scriptural Argumentation in 1 Clement," *NTS* 66:125–43.
—. 2021. "Paul and the Author of 1 Clement as Entrepreneurs of Identity in Corinthian Crises of Leadership." *JSNT* 44:1–22.
Küng, Hans. 1967. *The Church*. Translated by Ray and Rosaleen Ockenden. New York: Sheed & Ward.
Lampe, Peter. 1987. *Die stadtrömischen Christen in den ersten beiden Jahrhunderten*. WUNT 18. Tübingen: Mohr Siebeck.
—. 2003. *From Paul to Valentinus: Christians at Rome in the First Two Centuries*. Translated by Michael Steinhauser. Minneapolis: Fortress.
Langford, Thomas A. 1983. *Practical Divinity: Theology in the Wesleyan Tradition*. Nashville: Abingdon Press.
Lechner, Thomas. 1999. *Ignatius adversus Valentinianos? Chronologische und theologiegeschichtliche Studien zu den Briefen des Ignatius von Antiochien*. VCSup, 47. Leiden: Brill.
—. 2020. "Ignatios von Antiochia und die Zweite Sophistik: Kritische Anmerkungen zu den Thesen von Allen Brent." Pages 19–68 in *Die Briefe des Ignatios von Antiochia: Motive, Strategie, Kontexten*. Edited by Thomas Johann Bauer and Peter von Möllendorff. Berlin: DeGruyter.
Legarth, Peter V. 1992. *Guds tempel: Tempelsymbolisme og Kristologi hos Ignatius af Antiokia*. Menighedsfakultetets videnskabelige serie 3. Århus: Kolon.
Leipoldt, Johannes. 1903. *Schenute von Atripe und die Entstehung des nationalagyptischen Christentums*. TU 25.Leipzig: Hinrichs.
Levine, Amy-Jill and Marc Zvi Brettler, eds. 2017. *The Jewish Annotated New Testament*. 2nd ed. New York: Oxford University Press.
Levine, Lee I. 2005. *The Ancient Synagogue: The First Thousand Years*. 2nd ed. New Haven: Yale University Press.
—. 2011. "Synagogue Art and the Rabbis in Late Antiquity," *JAJ* 2:79–114.
Lieu, Judith M. 2015. *Marcion and the Making of a Heretic: God and Scripture in the Second Century*. Cambridge: Cambridge University Press.
—. 2016. *Neither Jew nor Christian? Constructing Early Christianity*. 2nd ed. London: Bloomsbury T&T Clark.
Lifshitz, Baruch. 1967. *Donateurs et fondateurs dans les synagogues juives*. Paris: Gabalda.
Lightfoot, Joseph B. 1868. "Two Neglected Facts Bearing on the Ignatian Controversy." *JP* I:47–55.
—. 1881. *St. Paul's Epistle to the Philippians*. London: MacMillan.
—. 1890. *The Apostolic Fathers, vol 1*. London: MacMillan.
Lightstone, Jack N. 2008. "The Early Rabbinic Refashioning of Biblical Heilsgeschichte, The Fashioning of the Rabbinic Canon of Scriptures, and the Formation of the Early Rabbinic Movement." Pages 317–35 in *The Reception and Interpretation of the Bible in Late Antiquity: Proceedings of the Montréal Colloquium in Honour of Charles Kannengiesser, 11–13 October 2006*. Edited by Lorenzo DiTomasso and Lucian Turcescu. Leiden: Brill.
Lim, Sung Uk. 2015. "Pseudo-Clementines" *LBD*. Bellingham: Lexham Press.
Lindemann, Andreas. 1997. "Antwort auf die 'Thesen zur Echtheit und Datierung der sieben Briefe des Ignatius von Antiochien.'" *ZAC* 1:185–94.
—. 2010. "The First Epistle of Clement." Pages 47–69 in *The Apostolic Fathers: An Introduction*. Edited by Pratscher, Wilhelm. Waco, TX: Baylor University Press.

Linton, Olof. 1932. *Das Problem der Urkirche in der neueren Forschung: Eine kritische Darstellung*. Uppsala: Almqvist & Wiksell.

List, Nicholas. 2024. "An Earlier *terminus ante quem* for the Epistle of James? The Influence of James on Clement of Alexandria's Transmission of 1 Clement 17." *CBQ* 86:572–86.

Lona, Horacio. 1998. *Der erste Clemensbrief: Übersetzt und erklärt*. Göttingen: Vandenhoeck & Ruprecht.

Lookadoo, Jonathon. 2018a. *The High Priest and the Temple: Metaphorical Depictions of Jesus in the Letters of Ignatius of Antioch*. WUNT 473. Tübingen: Mohr Siebeck.

—. 2018b. "A Note on the Use of Αἰών in the Letters of Ignatius of Antioch." *ETL* 94:693–703.

—. 2020. "The Date and Authenticity of the Ignatian Letters: An Outline of Recent Discussions." *CBR* 19:88–114.

Lösch, Stefan. 1937. *Der Brief des Clemens Romanus*. Milano: FS P.Ubaldi, Pubblicazioni della Universitet cattolica del Sacro Cuore, ser.V 16.

Lührmann, Dieter. 1980. "Neutestamentliche Haustafeln und Antike Ökonomie." *NTS* 27:83–97.

Manstead Antony S. R. and Miles Hewstone. 1995. *The Blackwell Encyclopedia of Social Psychology*. Malden: Blackwell Publishers Ltd.

Markschies, Christoph J. 2021. "From 'Wide and Narrow Way' to 'The Ways that Never Parted'?" Pages 11–32 in *Jews and Christians: Parting Ways in the First Two Centuries CE? Reflections on the Gains and Losses of a Model*. Edited by Jens Schröter Benjamin Edsall, and Joseph Verheyden. Berlin: DeGruyter.

Marjanen, Antti. 2008. "Gnosticism." Pages 203–20 in *The Oxford Handbook of Early Christian Studies*. Edited by Susan Ashbrook Harvey and David Hunter. Oxford: Oxford University Press.

Martin, Ralph P. 1959. *Philippians: An Introduction and Commentary*. London: The Tyndale Press.

—. 1988. *James*. WBC 48. Grand Rapids, MI: Zondervan Academic.

Mason, Steve. 2003. *Josephus and the New Testament*. 2nd ed. Peabody, MA: Hendrickson Publishing.

—. 2007. "Jews, Judaeans, Judaizing, Judaism: Problems of Categorization in Ancient History." *JSJ* 38:457–512.

Massaux, Edouard. 1950. *Influence de l'Evévangile de saint Matthieu sur la littérature chrétienne avant saint Irénée*. Louvain: Publications Universitaires de Louvain.

Matthews, Shelly. 2010. *Perfect Martyr: The Stoning of Stephen and the Construction of Christian Identity*. Oxford: Oxford University Press.

Matthews, Steve H. 2022. "Rhetorical Criticism for Expository Preaching: An Analysis of 1 Peter 2:4-10." *AJBT*:55–75.

McGuckin, John Anthony. 2017. *The Path of Christianity: The First Thousand Years*. Downers Grove, IL: IVP Academic.

McKnight, Scot. 2023. *The Pastoral Epistles*. NCBC. Cambridge: Cambridge University Press.

Meier, John P. 1983. "Antioch." Pages 12–86 in *Antioch and Rome: New Testament Cradles of Catholic Christianity*. Edited by Brown, Raymond and John Meier. New York: Paulist Press.

Merkle, Benjamin L. 2003. *The Elder and the Overseer: One Office in the Early Church*. Frankfurt: Peter Lang.

Merrill, Elmer Truesdell. 1924. *Essays in Early Christian History*. London: Macmillan.

Michaelis, Wilhelm. 1953. *Das Ältestenamt der christlichen Gemeinde in Lichte der Heiligen Schrift*. Bern: Berchtold Haller Verlag.

Michaels, J. Ramsey. 1988. *1 Peter*. WBC 49. Grand Rapids: Zondervan.

Moraff, Jason F. 2020. "Recent Trends in the Study of Jews and Judaism in Luke-Acts." *CBR* 19:64–87.

Moss, Candida R. 2010. "On the Dating of Polycarp: Rethinking the Place of the Martyrdom of Polycarp in the History of Christianity." *EC*:539–74.

Mounce, William D. 2000. *Pastoral Epistles*. WBC 46. Grand Rapids: Zondervan Academic.

Möllendorff, Peter von. 2018. "Sonne über Smyrna: Überlegungen zur Konstruktion von Kirche und Raum in den Briefen des Ignatios von Antiochia." Pages 153–67 in *Die Briefe des Ignatius von Antiochia: Motive, Strategien, Kontexte*. Edited by Thomas Johann Bauer and Peter von Möllendorff. Berlin: DeGruyter.

Muddiman, John. 2005. "The Church in Ephesians, 2 Clement, and the Shepherd of Hermas." Pages 107–22 in *Trajectories through the New Testament and the Apostolic Fathers*. Edited by Andrew Gregory and Christopher Tuckett. Oxford: Oxford University Press.

Nanos, Mark D., and Magnus Zetterholm, eds. 2015. *Paul within Judaism: Restoring the First-Century Context of the Apostle*. Minneapolis: Fortress.

Nes, Jermo van. 2022. "Moral Language and Ethical Argument in Titus: A Reassessment of the Pseudonymity Hypothesis." Pages 103–24 in *"Ready for every Good Work (Titus: 3:1)": Implicit Ethics in the Letter to Titus*. Edited by Ruben Zimmermann and Dogara Ishaya Manomi. WUNT 484. Tübingen: Mohr Siebeck.

Nes, Jermo van, and Harro Koning. 2017. "Motif-Semantic Differences in Paul? A Question to Advocates of the Pastorals' Plural Authorship in Dialogue with Michaela Engelmann." *TynBul* 68:73–94.

Newcomb, Theodore M. 1961. *The Acquaintance Process*. New York: Holt, Rinehart and Winston.

Newcomb, Theodore M., Kathryn E. Koenig, Richard Flacks, and Donald P. Warwick. 1967. *Persistence and Change: Bennington College and Its Students After 25 Years*. New York: Wiley.

Niederwimmer, Kurt. 1998. *A Commentary on the Didache*. Hermeneia. Minneapolis: Fortress Press.

Nongbri, Brent. 2013. *Before Religion: A History of a Modern Concept*. New Haven: Yale University Press.

Noy, David. 1993–1995. *Jewish Inscriptions of Western Europe (JIWE)*. 2 vols. Cambridge: Cambridge University Press.

O'Brien, Peter T. 1991. *The Epistle to the Philippians: A Commentary on the Greek Text*. NIGTC. Grand Rapids: Eerdmans.

Ok, Janette H. 2021. *Constructing Ethnic Identity in 1 Peter: Who You Are No Longer*. London: T&T Clark.

Olsson, Birger. 1982. *Första Petrusbrevet*. Kommentar till Nya Testamentet 17. Stockholm: EFS-förlaget.

Osborn, Eric. 2001. *Irenaeus of Lyons*. Cambridge: Cambridge University Press.

Osiek, Carolyn. 1999. *Shepherd of Hermas: A Commentary*. Hermeneia. Minneapolis: Fortress Press.
Pervo, Richard I. 2006. *Dating Acts: Between the Evangelists and the Apologists*. Santa Rosa, CA: Polebridge Press.
—. 2009a. *Acts: A Commentary*. Hermeneia. Minneapolis: Fortress Press.
—. 2009b. "Acts in the Suburbs of the Apologists." Pages 29–46 in *Contemporary Studies in Acts*. Edited by Thomas Phillips. Macon, GA: Mercer University Press.
Peterlin, Davorin. 1995. *Paul's Letter to the Philippians in Light of Disunity in the Church*, NovTSup. Leiden: Brill.
Piepenbrink, Karen. 2018. "Zur Perzeption des kirchlichen Amtes durch einen 'Märtyrerbischof': Die Perspektive des Ignatios und ihre historische Kontextualisierung." Pages 131–52 in *Die Briefe des Ignatius von Antiochia: Motive, Strategien, Kontexte*. Edited by Thomas Johann Bauer and Peter von Möllendorff. Berlin: DeGruyter.
Platow, Michael J., and Daan van Knippenberg. 2001. "A Social Identity Analysis of Leadership Endorsement: The Effects of Leader Ingroup Prototypicality and Distributive Intergroup Fairness." *PSPB* 27:1508–19.
Powell, Douglas. 1981. "Clemens von Rom." Pages 113–20 in *TRE* VIII. Edited by Gerhard Krause and Gerhard Müller. Berlin: de Gruyter.
Prostmeier, Ferdinand R. 2018 "Cui bono?" Pages 169–99 in *Die Briefe des Ignatios von Antiochia: Motive, Strategien, Kontexte*. Edited by Thomas Johan Bauer and Peter von Möllendorff. Berlin: DeGruyter.
Quinn, Jerome D. 1990. *The Letter to Titus: A New Translation with Notes and Commentary and an Introduction to Titus, I and II Timothy, the Pastoral Epistles*. AB vol 35. New York: Doubleday.
Rackham, Richard B. 1899. "The Acts of the Apostles II. A Plea for an Early Date," *JTS* 1:76–87.
Rajak, Tessa, and David Noy. 1993. "*Archisynagogoi*: Office, Title and Social Status in the Greco-Jewish Synagogue." *JRS* 83:75–83.
Rebillard, Éric. 2021. *The Early Martyr Narratives: Neither Authentic Accounts nor Forgeries*. Philadelphia: University of Pennsylvania Press.
Reicher, Steve, and Nick Hopkins. 2001. *Self and Nation: Categorization, Contestation and Mobilization*. London: Sage Publications.
Reuman, John. 2008. *Philippians: A New Translation and Commentary*. AB 33. New Haven: Yale University Press.
Rius-Camps, Josep. 1980. *Four Authentic Letters of Ignatius the Martyr: A Critical Study on the Anomalies Contained in the Textus Receptus*. Rome: Pontificium Institutum Orientalium Studiorum
Robinson, Thomas A. 2009. *Ignatius of Antioch and the Parting of the Ways*. Peabody, MA: Hendricksons.
Rohte, Richard. 1837. *Die Anfänge der christlichen Kirche und ihrer Verfassung: Ein geschichtlicher Versuch*. Wittenberg: Zimmermann.
Ritschl, Albrecht. 1847. *Die Entstehung der altkatholischen Kirche: Eine kirchen- und dogmengeschichtliche Monographie*. 2nd ed. Bonn: Adolph Marcus.
Roitto, Rikard. 2020. *Behaving as a Christ-Believer: A Cognitive Perspective on Identity and Behaviour Norms in Ephesians*. Itero 5. Stockholm: Enskilda Högskolan.

Rordorf, Willy, and André Tuilier. 1978. *La Doctrine des Douze Apôtres (Didachè)*. Paris: Les Éditions du Cerf.
Rosell Nebreda, Sergio. 2011. *Christ Identity: A Social-Scientific Reading of Philippians 2.5–11*. FRLANT 240. Göttingen: Vandenhoeck & Ruprecht.
Rothschild, Clare K. 2022. *The Muratorian Fragment: Text, Translation, Commentary*. STAC 132. Tübingen: Mohr Siebeck.
Runesson, Anders. 2001. *The Origins of the Synagogue*. ConBNT 37. Stockholm: Almqvist & Wiksell International.
—. 2008. "Inventing Christian Identity: Paul, Ignatius, and Theodosius I." Pages 59–92 in *Exploring Early Christian Identity*. Edited by Bengt Holmberg. WUNT 226. Tübingen: Mohr Siebeck.
—. 2010. "Synagogue." *Oxford Bibliographies in Biblical Studies*. Edited by Christopher R. Matthews. Oxford: Oxford University Press. DOI: 10.1093/obo/9780195393361-0119
—. 2015a. "The Question of Terminology: The Architecture of Contemporary Discussions on Paul." Pages 53–78 in *Paul Within Judaism: Restoring the First-Century Context to the Apostle*. Mark Nanos and Magnus Zetterholm, eds. Minneapolis: Fortress Press.
—. 2015b, "Placing Paul: Institutional Structures and Theological Strategy in the World of the Early Christ-believers," *SEÅ* 80:43–44
—. 2021. "What Never Belonged Together Cannot Part." Pages 33–56 in *Jews and Christians – Parting Ways in the First Two Centuries CE? Reflections on the Gains and Losses of a Model*. Edited by Jens Schröter, Benjamin Edsall, and Joseph Verheyden. Berlin: DeGruyter.
—. 2022. *Judaism for Gentiles: Reading Paul beyond the Parting of the Ways Paradigm*. WUNT 494. Tübingen: Mohr Siebeck.
Runesson, Anders, Donald D. Binder and Birger Olsson. 2008. *The Ancient Synagogue From Its Origins to 200 C.E.: A Source Book*. AGJU 72. Leiden: Brill.
Runesson, Anna. 2011. *Exegesis in the Making: Post-Colonialism and New Testament Studies*. Leiden: Brill.
Ryan, Jordan J. 2017. *The Role of the Synagogue in the Aims of Jesus*. Minneapolis: Fortress Press.
Sabatier, Auguste. 1904. *The Religions of Authority and the Religion of the Spirit*. Translated by Louise Seymour Houghton. London: Williams & Norgate.
Saller, Richard P. 1982. *Personal Patronage under the Early Empire*. Cambridge: Cambridge University Press.
Sanday, William. 1887. "The Origin of the Christian Ministry," *The Expositor* 3:322–43.
Sandt, Huub van de. "Doctrina Apostolorum." *Brill Encyclopedia of Early Christianity Online*. Edited by David Hunter, Paul van Geest and Bert Jan Lietaert Peerbolte. https://referenceworks.brill.com/display/entries/EECO/SIM-00000959.xml?rskey=OIlObe&result=1
—, ed. 2005. *Matthew and the Didache: Two Documents from the Same Jewish-Christian Milieu?* Assen: Van Gorcum.
Sandt, Huub van de, and David Flusser. 2002. *The Didache: Its Jewish Sources and Its Place in Early Judaism and Christianity*. Assen: Royal Van Gorcum.
Sandt, Huub van de, and Jürgen Zangenberg, eds. 2008. *Matthew, James, and the Didache: Three Related Documents in Their Jewish and Christian Setting*. Atlanta: Society of Biblical Literature.

Schaff, Philip. 1886. *The Oldest Church Manual, Called the Teaching of the Twelve Apostles.* New York: Funk and Wagnalls.

Schellenberg, Ryan S. 2015. "The First Pauline Chronologist? Paul's Itinerary in the Letters and in Acts." *JBL* 134:193–213.

Schenk, Wolfgang. 1984. *Die Philipperbriefe des Paulus: Kommentar.* Stuttgart: Kohlhammer.

Schermann, Theodor. 1914. *Die allgemeine Kirchenordnung, frühchristliche Liturgien und kirchliche Überlieferung. Erster Teil: Die allgemeine Kirchenordnung des zweiten Jahrhunderts.* SGKA 3.1. Paderborn: F. Schöningh.

Schmithals, Walther. 2009. "Zu Ignatius von Antiochien." *ZAC* 13:181–203.

Schoedel, William R. 1985. *Ignatius of Antioch: A Commentary on the Letters of Ignatius of Antioch.* Hermeneia. Philadelphia: Fortress Press.

Schofield, Malcolm. 2013. "Cardinal virtues: A contested Socratic inheritance." Pages 11–28 in *Plato and the Stoics.* Edited by Alex Long. Cambridge: Cambridge University Press.

Schreckenberg, Heinz. 1993. *Die christlichen Adversus-Judaeos-Texte und ihr literarisches und historisches Umfeld (13.-20. Jh.).* Frankfurt am Main: Peter Lang.

Schröter, Jens, Benjamin A. Edsall, and Joseph Verheyden. 2021. "Introduction." Pages 1–11 in *Jews and Christians: Parting Ways in the First Two Centuries CE? Reflections on the Gains and Losses of a Model.* Edited by Jens Schröter, Benjamin Edsall, and Joseph Verheyden. Berlin: DeGruyter.

Schüssler Fiorenza, Elisabeth. 1994. *In Memory of Her: A Feminist Theological Reconstruction of Christian Origins.* 2nd ed. London: SCM Press.

Schöllgen, Georg. 1986. "Monepiskopat und monarchischer Episkopat: Eine Bemerkung zur Terminologie." *ZNW* 77:146–51.

—. 1998, "Die Ignatianen als pseudepigraphisches Briefcorpus: Anmerkung zu den Thesen von Reinhard M. Hübner." *ZAC* 2:16–25.

Schwartz, Seth. 2010. *Were the Jews a Mediterranean Society? Reciprocity and Solidarity in Ancient Judaism.* Princeton: Princeton University Press.

Sellars, John. 2006. *Stoicism.* London: Routledge.

Sellew, Philip. 1994. "*Laodiceans* and the Philippians Fragment Hypothesis." *HTR* 87:17–28.

Sherif, Carolyn W., and Muzafer Sherif. 1969. *Social Psychology.* New York: Harper and Row.

Skarsaune, Oskar. 2018. "Ethnic Discourse in Early Christianity." Pages 250–64 in *The Christian Second Century.* Edited by James Carleton Paget and Judith Lieu. Cambridge: Cambridge University Press.

Slee, Michelle. 2003. *The Church in Antioch in the First Century CE: Communion and Conflict.* JSNTSup 244. London: Sheffield Academic Press

Smith, Mitzi J. 2011. *The Literary Construction of the Other in the Acts of the Apostles: Charismatics, the Jews, and Women.* Eugene, OR: Pickwick Publications.

Smith, Morton. 1996. "Terminological Booby Traps and Real Problems in Second Temple Judaeo-Christian Studies." Pages 93–103 in *Studies in the Cult of Yahweh.* Edited by Shaye Cohen. New York: Brill.

Snyder, Glenn E. 2013. *Acts of Paul: The Formation of a Pauline Corpus.* WUNT 352, Tübingen: Mohr Siebeck.

Sohm, Rudolph. 1909. *Wesen und Ursprung des Katholizismus.* Darmstadt: Wissenschaftliche Buchgesellschaft.

—. 1923. *Kirchenrecht. Erster Band: Die geschichtlichen Grundlagen.* 2nd ed. München and Leipzig: Verlag von Duncker & Humblot.

—. 1958. *Outlines of Church History*. Trans. James Luther Adams. Boston: Beacon Hill.
Steffens, Niklas K., S. Alexander Haslam, Stephen D. Reicher, Michael J. Platow, Katrien Fransen, Jie Yang, Michelle K. Ryan, Jolanda Jetten, Kim Peters, and Filip Boen. 2014. "Leadership as social identity management: Introducing the Identity Leadership Inventory (ILI) to assess and validate a four-dimensional model." *Leadersh. Q* 25:1001–24.
Stempel, Hermann-Adolf. 1980. "Der Lehrer in der 'Lehre der Zwölf Apostel'." *VC* 34:209–17.
Stewart, Alistair. 2013. *Ignatius of Antioch*. Popular Patristics Series 49. Yonkers, NY: St. Vladimir's Seminary Press.
—. 2014. *The Original Bishops: Office and Order in the First Christian Communities*. Grand Rapids: Baker Academic.
Streeter, Burnett Hillman. 1928. *The Primitive Church: Studied with Special Reference to the Origins of the Christian Ministry*. London: MacMillan.
Tajfel, Henri. 1981. *Human Groups and Social Categories: Studies in Social Psychology*. *Cambridge*: Cambridge University Press.
Tajfel, Henri, and John C. Turner. 1979. "An Integrative Theory of Intergroup Conflict." Pages 33–47 in *The Social Psychology of Intergroup Relations*. Edited by William Austin and Stephen Worchel. Monterey, CA: Brooks/Cole.
Tajfel, Henri, Michael Billig, Robert P. Bundy and Claude Flament. 1971. "Social Categorization and Intergroup Behaviour." *EJSP* 1:149–78.
Thaarup, Jørgen. 1999. *The Ministry as Bishop and Leader within the United Methodist Church: A Revised Study Report for Use in the Baltic and Eurasia*. Copenhagen: The United Methodist Church, The Northern Europe Central Conference Committee on Episcopacy.
Theissen, Gerd. 1999. *The Religion of the Earliest Churches: Creating a Symbolic World*. Translated by John Bowden. Minneapolis: Fortress Press.
Theobald, Michael. 2013. "Israel- und Jerusalem-Vergessenheit im Corpus Pastorale? Zur Rezeption des Römerbriefs im Titus- sowie im 1. und 2. Timotheusbrief." Pages 317–412 in *Ancient Perspectives on Paul*. Edited by Tobias Nicklas, Andreas Merkt, and Joseph Verheyden. Göttingen: Vanderhoeck & Ruprecht.
—. 2016. *Israel-Vergessenheit in den Pastoralbriefen: Ein neuer Vorschlag zu ihrer historisch-theologischen Verortung im 2. Jahrhundert n. Chr. unter besonderer Berücksichtigung der Ignatius-Briefe*. SBS 229. Stuttgart: Katolisches Bibelwerke.
—. 2022. "Internal Ethos or Ethos before the Public Forum? Titus and His Construct of the Opponents." Pages 163–88 in *"Ready for Every Good Work" (Titus 3:1) Implicit Ethics in the Letter to Titus*. Edited by Ruben Zimmermann and Dogara Ishaya Manomi. WUNT 484. Tübingen: Mohr Siebeck.
Thiering, Barbara. 1981. "Mebaqqer and Episkopos in the Light of the Temple Scroll." *JBL* 100:59–74.
Torjesen, Karen Jo. 2008. "Clergy and Laity." Pages 389–405 in *The Oxford Handbook of Early Christian Studies*. Edited by Susan Ashbrook Harvey and David Hunter. Oxford: Oxford University Press.
Towner, Philip H. 2006. *The Letters to Timothy and Titus*. NICNT. Grand Rapids: Eerdmans, ePub version.

Turner, John C. 1982. "Towards a Cognitive Redefinition of the Social Group." Pages 15–40 in *Social Identity and Intergroup Relations*. Edited by Henri Tajfel. Cambridge: Cambridge University Press.

Tyson, Joseph B. 2006. *Marcion and Luke-Acts: A Defining Struggle*. Columbia: University of South Carolina Press.

Unnik, Willem C. van. 2004. "Studies on the So-Called First Epistle of Clement: The Literary Genre." Pages 115–81, in *Encounters with Hellenism, Studies on the First Letter of Clement*. Edited by Cilliers Breytenbach and Lawrence Welborn. Leiden: Brill.

Vranic, Vasilije. 2012. "επισκοπος and πρεσβυτερος in the Pastoral Epistles: The Governing Structure of the Early Christian Communities?" *CSt* 9:25–34.

Veit-Engelman, Michaela. 2022. *Die Briefe an Timotheus und Titus*. Göttingen: Vanderhoeck & Ruprecht.

Verheyden, Joseph. 2015. "Israels Fate in the Apostolic Fathers: The Case of 1 Clement and the Epistle of Barnabas." Pages 237–62 in *Q in Context I: The Separation between the Just and the Unjust in Early Judaism and in the Sayings Source*. Edited by Markus Tiwald. Bonn: Bonn University Press.

Vinzent, Markus. 1999 "'Ich bin kein körperloses Geistwesen': Zum Verhältnis von κήρυγμα Πέτρου, 'Doctrina Petri', διδασκαλία Πέτρου und IgnSm 3." Pages 241–86 in *Der Paradox Eine: Antignostischer Monarchianismus im zweiten Jahrhundert*. Edited by Reinhard Hübner. VCSup 50. Leiden: Brill.

—. 2019. *Writing the History of Early Christianity: From Reception to Retrospection*. Cambridge: Cambridge University Press.

Vogt, Hermann Josef. 1999. "Bemerkungen zur Echtheit der Ignatiusbriefe." *ZAC* 3:50–63.

Vokes, Frederick E. 1938. *The Riddle of the Didache: Fact or Fiction, Heresy or Catholicism?* London: Society for Promoting Christian Knowledge.

Waldner, Katharina. 2006. "Ignatius' Reise von Antiochia nach Rom: Zentralität und lokale Vernetzung im christlichen Diskurs des 2. Jahrhunderts." Pages 95–121 in *Zentralität und Religion*. Edited by Hubert Cancik, Alfred Schäfer, and Wolfgang Spickermann. STAC 39. Tübingen: Mohr Siebeck.

Weber, Max. 1968. *Economy and Society: An Outline of Interpretive Sociology*. Translation by Ephraim Fischoff et al. Edited by Guenther Roth and Claus Wittich. 3 volumes. New York: Bedminster.

—. 1976. *Wirtschaft und Gesellschaft: Grundriss der verstehenden Soziologie*. 5th ed. Tübingen: Mohr.

Weizsäcker, Karl Heinrich von. 1892. *Das apostolische Zeitalter der christlichen Kirche*. Freiburg im Breisgau: Mohr.

—. 1894–95. *The Apostolic Age of the Christian Church*. 2 vols. Translation by James Millar. London and Edinburgh: Williams & Norgate.

Welborn, Laurence L. 1984. "On the Date of 1 Clement." *BR* 29:35–54.

—. 2020. "Retrospect on a Challenge to the Consensus on the Date of 1 Clement." *BR* 65:95–103.

Wendel, Susan. 2011. *Scriptural Interpretation and Community Self-Definition in Luke-Acts and the Writings of Justin Martyr*. NovTSup 139. Leiden: Brill.

Wengst, Klaus. 1984. *Didache (Apostellehre). Barnabasbrief. Zweiter Klemensbrief. Schrift an Diognet*. Darmstadt: Wissenschaftliche Buchgesellschaft.

Weren, Wim J. C. 2008. "The Ideal Community According to Matthew, James, and the Didache." Pages 177–200 in *Matthew, James, and the Didache: Three Related Documents in Their Jewish and Christian Setting*. Edited by Huub van de Sandt and Jürgen Zangenberg. Atlanta: Society of Biblical Literature.

White, Stephen, ed and trans. 2020. *Lives of Eminent Philosophers: An Edited Translation*. Cambridge: Cambridge University Press.

Wild, Robert. 1990. "The Pastoral Letters." Pages 891–902 in *The New Jerome Biblical Commentary*. Edited by Raymond Brown, Joseph Fitzmyer, and Roland Murphy. Englewood Cliffs, NJ: Prentice Hall.

Wilhite, Shawn J. 2019. "Thirty-Five Years Later: A Summary of Didache Scholarship Since 1983." *CBR* 17:266–305.

Williams, J. Dennis. 2002. "From Presiding Elder to District Superintendent: The Development of an Office in Episcopal Methodism from 1792 to 1908." *MethH* 40:255–65.

Williams, Frank. 2009. *The Panarion of Epiphanius of Salamis*. Leiden: Brill.

Witherington, Ben. 1998. *The Acts of the Apostles: A Socio-Rhetorical Commentary*. Grand Rapids, MI: Eerdmans. Kindle version.

—. 2011. *Philippians: A Socio-Rhetorical Commentary*. Grand Rapids, MI: Eerdmans.

World Council of Churches. 1982. *Baptism, Eucharist, and Ministry*. Faith and Order, Paper No. 111. Geneva: World Council of Churches.

Yoshiko Reed, Anette and Adam H. Becker, eds. 2003. *The Ways that Never Parted*. Tübingen: Mohr Siebeck.

Young, Frances M. 1994. "On Episkopos and Presbyteros." *JTS* 45:142–48.

—. 2008. "Interpretation of Scripture." Pages 845–64 in *The Oxford Handbook of Early Christian Studies*. Edited by Susan Ashbrook Harvey and David Hunter. Oxford: Oxford University Press.

Young, Franklin W. 1948. "The Relation of I Clement to the Epistle of James." *JBL* 67:339–45.

Zahn, Theodor. 1873. *Ignatius von Antiochien*. Gotha: Friedrich Andreas Perthes.

Zamfir, Korinna. 2012. "Once More About the Origins and Background of the New Testament Episkopos." *Sacra Scripta* 10:202–22.

Zangenberg, Jürgen K. 2008. "Reconstructing the Social and Religious Milieu of the Didache: Observations and Possible Results." Pages 1–8 in *Matthew, James, and the Didache: Three Related Documents in Their Jewish and Christian Setting*. Edited by Huub van de Sandt and Jürgen Zangenberg. Atlanta: Society of Biblical Literature.

Zetterholm, Magnus. 2003. *The Formation of Christianity in Antioch: A Social-Scientific Approach to the Separation between Judaism and Christianity*. London: Routledge.

Zoccali, Cristopher. 2017. *Reading Philippians after Supersessionism: Jews, Gentiles, and Covenant Identity*. Eugene, OR: Cascade Books.

Zwierlein, Otto. 2010. *Petrus in Rom: Die literarischen Zeugnisse mit einer kritischen Edition der Martyrien des Petrus und Paulus auf neuer handschriftlicher Grundlage*. 2nd ed. UALG 96. Berlin: W. de Gruyter.

—. 2011. "Petrus in Rom? Die literarischen Zeugnisse." Pages 444–67 *in Petrus und Paulus in Rom: Eine interdisziplinäre Debatte*. Edited by Stefan Heid. Freiburg: Herder.

—. 2013. *Petrus und Paulus in Jerusalem und Rom: Vom Neuen Testament zu den apokryphen Apostelakten*. UALG 109. Berlin: De Gruyter.

—. 2014. *Die Urfassungen der Martyria Polycarpi et Pionii und das Corpus Polycarpianum.* 2 vols. UALG 116. Berlin: De Gruyter.

Index of Ancient Literature

Hebrew Bible

Genesis
49   *174*

Exodus
20   *209*
20:13–17   *208*

Leviticus
14: 5–9   *230*

Numbers
4:16   *121*
11:16   *130*
17   *266*
31:14   *123*

Deuteronomy
19:11–13   *130*
32:15   *255*

Joshua
23–24   *174*

First Samuel
4:3   *130*
8:4   *130*
12   *174*
15:30   *130*

1 Kings
21:8   *130*

4 Kingdoms (LXX)
11:6   *123*

Second Chronicles
24:12   *123*
24:17   *123*

Ezra
10:7–17   *130*

Nehemiah
2:16   *130*
4:8   *130*
11:9   *123*
14:22   *123*

Job
20:29   *161*

Psalms
1   *208*
22   *263*
23   *161*
33   *335*
33:9   *337*
34   *258*
36:11   *200*
100   *161*
108:8   *164, 171*
119:29–30   *208*

Proverbs
2:13   *208*
4:18–19   *208*
7:24   *210*

11:20	*208*
12:28	*208*
18:12	*299*
18:17	*337*

Isaiah
40:11	*161*
52:5	*337*
53	*160, 263*
60:17	*123*
66:18	*337*

Jeremiah
4:22	*361*
13:17	*161*
21:8	*208*

Ezekiel
34:11	*123*
34:23–24	*161*

Daniel
6:9	*229*
6:11	*229*

Zephaniah
2:3	*299*

Deutero-Canonical Books

1 Maccabees
1:51	*123*

2 Maccabees
	79
2:21	*77*

4 Maccabees
1:6	*293–294*
1:17	*295*
1:18	*293–294*
2:21–23	*293–294*
5:22–24	*293–294*
15:10	*293–294*

Sirach
38:31	*295*
39:1	*296*
39:1–5	*295*
39:3–4	*296*
51:26	*213*

Wisdom of Solomon
1:6	*161*
8:7	*293*
8:7–8	*295*

Pseudepigrapha

Assumption of Moses
174

1 Enoch
94:1–5	*201*

4 Ezra
10:25–54	*179*

Testament of Asher
1:2–9	*201*

Testament of the Twelve Patriarchs
174, 210

Ancient Jewish Writings

Josephus
C. Ap
2.175	*91*

A.J.
16.43	*91*
19.343–50	*168*
20.97–98	*168*
20.97–102	*168*
20.169–72	*168*

B.J.
2.261–63	*168*
2.285–92	*102*
2.292	*91*

Philo
Leg.
3.43 — *161*
156 — *91*
Mut.
39 — *161*
216 — *161*
Prob.
80–83 — *91*
Somn.
1.91 — *161*

Qumran
1QpHab
I, 3 — *203*

1QS
III, 18–IV:26 — *201, 208*
IV, 2–6 — *297, 300*
IV, 3 — *298*
V, 3 — *172*
VI, 16 — *172*

4Q257
V — *298*

New Testament
Matthew
5–7 — *52, 200, 363*
5:5 — *200*
5:5–11 — *363*
5:11–12 — *195*
5:39–42 — *334*
5:48 — *284*
6:9–13 — *229*
7:15–20 — *196*
10 — *193*
10:1 — *195*
10:9 — *225*
10:9–15 — *225*
10:10 — *162*
10:18–20 — *195*
11:29 — *213*
12:33 — *335*
18:20 — *211*
23:39 — *196*
28:19 — *230*

Mark
7:8 — *130*

Luke
1:2 — *166*
4:20 — *99*
6:27–28 — *334*
19:44 — *33*
21 — *168*
24:44 — *173*

John
7:1 — *78*
9:22 — *77, 95, 96*
10:14 — *162*
13–17 — *174*
13:23 — *365, 369*
21:20 — *369*
Acts
13:3 — *172*
20 — *130*
20:17–18 — *128*

Acts
1 — *171*
1:16 — *173*
1:20 — *33, 171*
5:36 — *168*
5:36–37 — *168*
6:1–2 — *111*
7 — *121, 169*
8 — *358*
12:21–23 — *168*
13:3 — *172*
14:23 — *152*
15 — *29, 57, 77, 207, 213–15, 232, 385*
15:10 — *214*

15:20	213	Philippians	
15:21	213	1	154, 170, 355
15:29	*91*	1:1	122, *123*, 148, 150–51,
18:1–17	185		154, 158, 278
20	122, 129–30, 161, 169,	1:1–2	111
	173–74, 183, 393	1:12–26	154
20:17	151, 165	2:5–11	154
20:17–18	128	3	150
20:17–36	160, 174	3:1	*149*
20:17–38	*167*	3:2	*149*, 150, 185
20:28	152	3:2–11	155
21:38	168	3:7	155
28	174	3:15	336
		4:3	242
Romans			
9:10–13	251	Colossians	
12:13	181	4:14	166
16	136		
		1 Thessalonians	
1 Corinthians		5	170
6:9	339		
7:10	253	1 Timothy	
9	162	1:1	280
9:3–14	162	1:3	280
10:1–13	*252*	1:4–6	281
12:28	97	1:5	*281*
		1:8	301
Galatians		1:12–17	281
1–3	29	1:17	275
1:13–14	79	2:5–7	*281*
2	77	2:7	275
2:11–14	227	2:9–15	*281*
5	170	3:2	181, 282
5:1	214	3:1–7	57, 271, 283
5:22	154	3:1–15	*281*
5:22–23	52	3:2–7	*350*
5:22–24	284–85	3:14–16	*281*
		3:16	*281*
Ephesians		4:6	*281*
2:20	179, 383, 394	4:11	*281*
4:11	162	4:13	*281*
4:11–16	*180*	4:13–14	*281*
6:12	336	4:14	111
		4:16	*281*

5:1	*281*	1 Peter	
5:3–16	*281*	1:1	157–58
5:7	*281*	1:18–21	156
5:17	*281, 282*	2:4–6	*159*
5:22	*281*	2:12	33
6:2	*281*	2:20–21	160
6:17–18	*281*	2:23	160
		2:23–25	163
2 Timothy		2:25	156, 160
1:6	*281*	2:26	160
1:6–13	280	4	158, 164, 383
2:15–19	*281*	4:9	181
3:1–4:8	*174*	4:12	158
3:10	*281*	4:17	158
3:14–17	*281*	5	159, 163
4:2–5	*281*	5:1	157
		5:2	32, 156, 159, 160–61
Titus		5:2–3	159
1	28, 36, 130, 272, 289	5:12	157
1:5	280, *282*	5:13	158
1:5–7	111		
1:5–8	128, 283	2 Peter	
1:5–10	57	3:1	156
1:7	134		
1:7–9	*350*	Revelation	
1:8	181	1:1	253
1:9	282	7:2	314
1:12	*281*		
2:1	*281*	**Early Christian Literature**	
2:6–8	*281*	1 Clement	
2:14	*281*	1–2	249–50, 252, 255
2:15	*281*	1	235
3:1	275, *281*	1:1	237–39, 240, *240*
3:4–8	*281*	1:1–3:1	246
3:8	*281*	1:2–2:1	247, 266
		1:2	257
Hebrews		2:2	249
13:2	181	2:7	275
		2:8	*249*
James		3–28	246
2:25	238	3–39	255
4:6	*337*	3–41	235
		3:1	255
		4	*246*

4–5	245	42:5	265
5	240, 265	43	266
5–6	237	43–44	235
5:4	237	43:1	265
5:4–5	265	43:2	266
5:5	237	43:5–6	266
6	237	44	235, 264
10–46	241	45:2	252
11	235	47	235, 239
11:2	246	50:3	33
12	235, 238	51	235
12:7	156	54	235
13	245, 257	60:4	275
13:1	253	61:2	275
15	262		
15–17	263	2 Clement	177
15:5	262		
15:7	263	Ambrosiaster	
16	252–53, 257, 262–63	*Commentary on Ephesians*	
16:1	262–63	4.11	111
16:2	253	*Commentary on 1 Timothy*	
16:3–14	263	3.10	111
16:16	263		
17	234	Apostolic Church Order	
17:1	253		201
18	235		
19–28	257	Apostolic Constitutions	
19:1–2	257	1–6	109
21:6	257		
22	258	Athenagoras	
22:1	252	*Legatio*	
23:3	246	11	320
24	258		
25:1	258	Cyprian of Carthage	
26	258	*Epist.*	
30:8	246	3	111
31:2	251	63.14	111
32:2	251, 252		
36:6–12	246	Didache	
39	246	1–3	202
40:2–5	121	1–6	187, 198, 206, 211,
41:3	264		215, 223, 232, 384
42	235	1–10	196
42–44	235	1:1	207

1:1–14	203	15:1	122, 198, 216, 219, 220, 226
1:1–6:3	200, 204, *206*		
1:3	206	15:2	218
1:3–2:1	190, 199–200		
1:5–6	221, 223	Didascalia Apostolorum *109*, 201	
2	203, 206, 209	2.27.1–2	*122*
2–6	200, 227		
2:1	206–7	Doctrina Apostolorum	
2:2	209		201
2:2–7	207		
3:4	209	Epiphanius of Salamais	
4	202	*Pan.*	
4:2–14	207	27.6	109
5	202, 206, 209	30.18.2	*101*
5:1	212		
5:1–2	207	Eusebius of Caesarea	
5:2	212	*Hist. Eccl.*	
6	213, 232	3.34	310
6:1	200	3.35	310
6:1–3	207	3.36.2	309
6:2	212, 227	3.39	*135*
6:3	213	4	330
7	229, 230	5.1	*320*
7–15	193		
7:1	211, 215, 227, 229, 230	Gospel of Thomas *119*	
7:2	229	Gregory the Great	
8:2	229	*Pastoral Rule*	
8:3	229	1.10	*112*
9–10	229		
9:1	229	Gregory of Nazianzus	
9:5	*196*	*Orat.*	
10:7	*196*, 229	2	*112*
11	224		
11–13	193	Ignatius of Antioch	
11–15	218	*To the Ephesians*	
11:1	*196*, 211, 227	1	346
11:7–11	195	1–6	*341*
11:7–12	*196*	1:3	346
11:9	229	2	342
11:10	196	3:2	344, 349
14:1	218	4	327
15	36, 187, 193, 216	5	*334*
		5:3	*337*

6	*339*	\multicolumn{2}{l}{*To the Trallians*}
7	321	2–3	*341*
8	*334*	3	*135*
9	*339*	3:2	346
9:2	314	6	320
10	334	6–7	*339*
10–11	*334*	7	353
11	*339*	8	*334*, 340
13	*339*, 340	8:2	337
14–16	*334*	9	*339*
14:2	335	9–11	*318*, *339*
15:1	337	10	321
16	*339*	12	*334*, *341*
16–18	*339*	12:3	346
17:1	*339*		
18	325, *339*	\multicolumn{2}{l}{*To the Romans*}
18–20:1	324	1:2	347
18:2	324–25	2	347
19	320, 325	2–5	*334*
20	*341*	2:1	347
		2:2	347
\multicolumn{2}{l}{*To the Magnesians*}	3:2	336, 348
1	*334*	4:1	319–20, 347
1:2	336	4:2	336
2	342	5	*339*
3–4	*341*	5:1	336
4	342	7	*334*, *339*
6	314, 340	9:1	32
6–7	*341*		
6:1	23	\multicolumn{2}{l}{*To the Philadelphians*}
7	*334*, 340, 342, 344–45, 349	Introd.	*341*
		1	350
7–11	*339*	1:2	346
7:6	110	2–6	*339*
9	77, 344, 350, 353	3	*334*
10	337, 398	3–4	*341*
10:3	251, 337, 350, 398	4	340, 353
11	*339*	7	327, *334*, 336, *341*
12	337	8	29
13	*339*, *341*	8–9	*339*
13:2	342	9	337, 350
15	*341*		

To the Smyrnaeans

1	*339*
1–3	*340*
1–5	*339*
1:2	*340*
2	*340*
2–3	*318*
2–5	*321*
3	*339*
3:3	*340*
4:1	*340*
6	*334*
7	*182–83*
7–8	*339*
7:2	*326–27*
8	*353*
8–9	*341*
8:2	*65*
10	*339*
11	*334, 345*
11:3	*336*

To Polycarp

1–5	*341*
4	*122*
4–5	*344*
6	*334, 339, 341*
7	*341*

Irenaeus of Lyon
Haer.

Preface	*274*
1.23.1	*358*
3.1	*366*
3.1.1	*166, 359*
3.1–3	*331, 365*
3.2	*366, 369*
3.2–4	*360*
3.3	*331, 367*
3.3.1	*359, 368*
3.3.1–3	*109*
3.3.2	*364*
3.3.3.	*23, 361*
3.4	*367*
3.8.1	*363*
3.9.3	*363*
3.10.1	*166*
3.11.8	*359*
4.2	*361*
4.2.7	*361*
4.5	*362*
4.5.3–5	*361*
4.5.4	*355*
4.9.2.	*156*
4.21.21–23	*251*
4.33.5	*320*
5.28.4	*318*

Jerome
Epist.

52.6	*121*
146	*111*

John Chrysostom
Hom. Phil. *111*
Sac. *112*

Justyn Martyr
1 Apol.

67	*121*

Dial.

137.2	*101*

Life of Saturnius

8.1–3	*101*

Life of Shenute *201*

Martyrdom of Polycarp

1–19	*329*
4	*328, 331*
7	*331*
16:2	*31, 330–31*
21	*328*
21–23	*329*
22:3	*329*
23:2	*331*

Index of Ancient Literature

Origen
De Oratione
20   322
Commentary on the Song of Songs
Prologue   322

Polycarp
To the Philippians
1.1   323
4   *121*
9   310–312, 317, 319, 323, 332–33
9.1   307
13   310–312, 317, 319–20, 323
13.2   307

Ps.-Clement
Ad Virgines   *191*

The Shepherd of Hermas
Visions
1.1 (1)   176
1.3 (3)   180
2.4.2 (8.2)   242
2.4.3 (8.3)   240
3.1.6 (9.6)   178
3.1.9 (9.9)   178
3.2 (10)   179
3.2.2 (10.2)   178
3.2.6 (10.6)   178
3.2.7–9 (10.7–9)   178
3.3.3 (11.3)   178
3.4 (12)   178
3.5–3.8 (13–16)   *179*
3.5.1 (13.1)   176, 178, 243
3.5.5 (13.5)   178, 179

Similitudes
9.17.4 (94.4)   180
9.26 (103)   182
9.26.2 (103.2)   181
9.27 (104)   *121*, 345
9.27.2 (104.2)   176, 180

Theodore of Mopsuestia
Commentary on 1 Timothy
3   *111*

Theophilus of Antioch
Ad Autolycum
2.12   320

Rabbinic Literature

b. Ta'an
12a   228

m. Avot
1   203
3.5   213

m. Ber.
2:2   213
4:1   229
7:1   229

m. Meg.
1.2   228
3   228
3.6   228

m. Mik.
1:1–8   23

m. Ned
5:5   93

m. Quid.
4.1   70

m. Sanh.
10:1   70

m. Shabb.   99

m. Sotah.   100
7:8   *100*

m. Ta'an		Diogenes Laertius	
2.1	*228*	*Lives*	
4.2	*228*	6.11	*288–89, 298*
		7.92	*288*
m. Yoma	*100*	7.117	*290*
7:1	*100*	7.121	*290*

t. Ber.		Hesiod	
6:3	*229*	*Op.*	
		287–89	*201*

t. Meg.		Life of Alexander Severus	
3	*100*	28.7	*101*
3:21	*99*		

t. Sanh.		Lucian of Samosata	
13:4	*70*	*Peregr.*	*191*
		41	*319*

t. Sukkah		Onosander	
4:6	*99*	*De Imperatoris Officio*	
		1	*222, 292–93, 302–3,*

Greco-Roman Literature

Cicero
De Officiis
1.15   *287*

Plutarch
Stoic. Rep.
1034 d–e   *287–88, 387*

Dio Chrysostom
2 Tars.
1.4.   *122*
Sec.
2.2   *122*
Tumult.
6.14   *122*
Ven.
26.2–4   *122*

Strabo
Geogr.
14.2.5   *122*
The Theodosian Code
16.8.4   *101*

Xenophon
Mem.
2.1.21–34   *201*

Index of Modern Authors

Achtemeier, Paul J. *157, 158,* 160, *161–63*
Alexander, Philip S. *67, 70, 126*
Allport, Floyd H. 40
Armstrong, Karl L. *167,* 168–70
Arnold, Gottfried 117–18
Ascough, Richard S. 84–86, *91, 94, 221–23*
Audet, Jean-Paul *199,* 208, *210*

Baker, Coleman A. *167–70,* 171, 173, *174*
Bakke, Odd M. *236, 240, 247*
Baldovin, John F. *136*
Barclay, John M. G. *39,* 47, *221*
Barnes, Timothy D. 308
Batovici, Dan 176
Baur, Ferdinand Christian 80, 127, 306
Becker, Adam H. 73, *74*
Belleville, Linda L. 149
Bernard, John Henry. *289*
Bihlmeyer, Karl *192*
Binder, Donald D. 88, *89,* 91, *93, 103*
Bobertz, Charles A. 121
Bockmuehl, Markus 151–52
Bourdieu, Pierre 107, 110, 118–19
Bornkamm, Günther 129–131, 134
Boyarin, Daniel 76–77, 81
Bradshaw, Paul F. *97,* 98, 110, *120,* 135
Bremmer, Jan N. *74, 79, 319*
Brent, Allen *136,* 308, *310,* 312–15
Brettler, Marc Zvi 213
Breytenbach, Cilliers *235–36,* 253–54, 256

Brown, Jeannine K. 153
Brown, Raymond E. *123*
Brown, Rupert *40–42, 44–46, 51, 341*
Bruce, Fredrick F. *153, 168, 170*
Buie, Caroline P. *176–77, 179–80, 182*
Burtchaell, James T. 23–24, 87–88, 103–5, *113–14,* 115–16, *117–18,* 121, 124–26, 138, 140, *378–79*

Campell, R. Alastair 34, 128–29, 131–34. 139
Campbell, Donald T. *41.*
Campenhausen, Hans von *121, 133,* 151, 329
Carleton Paget, James *74, 251–52*
Catto, Stehpen *88,* 89
Chipparini, Giuilano *356, 357*
Cinnirella, Marco *226, 261*
Cirafesi, Wally V. *90, 95, 99, 378*
Cohen, Shaye J.D. *68,* 71, *79, 95*
Collins, Raymond F. *273–74,* 276
Conzelmann, Hans *165–68, 170, 172, 174, 222, 275, 278, 285–86, 292*

Davids, Peter *157–58, 161–62*
Dehandschutter, Boudewijn *329*
Delafosse, Henri 239
DeSilva, David A. 294, *295*
Dibelius, Martin *211, 222, 275, 278, 285–86, 291–92*
Donelson, Lewis R. *273*
Draper, Jonathan A. *189–91,* 192, *193,* 194–95, *196,* 197–98, *199–200,* 202, *205, 209, 214,* 219–21, *228*

Dunn, James D.G. 69–70, 76, 80–81, 272, 274, 278

Easton, Burton S. 284, 285
Edsall, Benjamin 67, 76
Edwards, Mark J. 308
Ehrman, Bart D. 81, 176–77, 178, 180–81, 189–91, 200, 216, 219, 235, 237, 239, 240, 246, 248, 256, 265, 311, 321, 328, 330
Elliott, John H. 34
Engelmann, Micahela, see Veit-Engelmann, Michaela
Engvall Siegel, Alberta 341
Eriksson, Larsolov 152
Esler, Philip 46–48, 50, 51–52, 55, 60–61, 76, 215, 220, 228, 261, 347
Eurell, John-Christian 110, 159, 168, 306, 307, 310, 311–12, 314, 320, 321

Fee, Gordon D. 153
Finlan, Stephen 193, 199–200, 205–6, 228–29, 231
Fitzmyer, Joseph A. 165, 167, 170
Flacks, Richard 341
Flusser, David 189–191, 192, 199–200, 202, 208, 209
Foster, Paul 308, 310
Frankfurter, David 76
Fredriksen, Paula 73, 74, 75, 83
Frey, Jörg 74

Gabrielson, Timothy A. 238
Garrow, Alan 202
Gebhardt, Oscar de 237
Gillihan, Yonder M. 84, 85
Glicksman, Andrew T. 294
Goodman, Martin 68, 69, 74–75
Grant, Robert M. 356–357, 360–61, 363–65, 367–69
Gregory, Andrew F. 239, 240
Grundeken, Mark 177–79
Guthrie, Donald 274

Haar Romeny, Bas ter 191
Hagner, Donald A. 252
Hanson, Anthony T. 273, 275
Hanson, Richard 239
Harland, Philip A. 83, 84, 86, 92
Harnack, Adolf von 97–98, 114, 117, 124, 126, 128, 138–39, 167, 193, 194–95, 213, 237
Harvey, W. Wigan 356, 359–61, 363–67, 369
Haslam, S. Alexander 40, 44, 48, 49, 55–56, 58–59, 226, 230, 236, 245, 259, 261, 349–50
Hatch, Edwin 90, 97, 114, 120–22, 124, 127, 128, 138–39, 182
Hawthorne, Gerald F. 127, 152, 153–55
Hayman, A. Peter 295–96
Heemstra, Marius 67, 74
Henrich, Joseph 52–53, 331
Hempel, Charlotte 298, 299
Herron, Thomas J. 238
Hewstone, Miles 44
Hogg, Michael A. 43, 50, 55, 56, 247, 338, 350
Holloway, Paul A. 148, 149, 150, 153, 157
Holmberg, Bengt 39, 66–67, 82, 97
Holmes, Michael W. 359
Holmstrand, Jonas 149
Hopkins, Nick 261
Horning Jensen, Morten 93
Hübner, Reinhard M. 307–8, 311, 314, 316, 322

Isacson, Mikael 315–16, 322

Jefford, Clayton N. 191, 214
Jeremias, Joachim 120, 123, 129, 133
Jetten, Jolanda 61
Jobes, Karen H. 156–58
Johnson, Luke Timothy 238, 274, 277, 282.
Johnson, Maxwell E. 110
Joly, Robert 306–8, 311, 315–16

Index of Modern Authors

Kazen, Thomas 202
Keener, Craig S. 211
Kelhoffer, James A. 335
Khomych, Taras 246, 264
King, Peter 25
Kirk, James 117
Kirk, Kenneth E. 127
Knight George W. 127, 273
Kloppenborg, John S. 83, 84, 85, 94, 202, 221–22
Knippenberg, Daan van 43, 50, 55, 56, 247, 338
Knopf, Rudolf 213, 237
Koch, Dietrich-Alex 108
Koester, Helmut 199–200
Koenig, Katryn E. 341
Koning, Harro 276
Kooten, George H van 252
Kraft, Heinrich 194
Kraft, Robert A. 190, 202
Kraus, Samuel 88
Kujanpää, Katja 49, 226, 241–42, 245, 246, 248, 251–54, 258, 261, 262
Küng, Hans 23, 24

Lampe, Peter 136, 176, 177, 179, 242, 243
Langford, Thomas A. 27
Lapin, Hayim 95
Lechner, Thomas 307, 309–10, 314–16, 317, 320–27
Legarth, Peter V. 327
Leipoldt, Johannes 201
Levine, Amy-Jill 213
Levine, Lee I. 88–91, 92–93, 96, 98–101, 102, 104, 126
Lieu, Judith M. 71, 72, 74, 75, 79, 81, 82, 169
Lifshitz, Baruch 99
Lightfoot, Joseph B. 69, 80, 113, 114, 117, 127–28, 132, 174, 237, 242, 243, 306, 315
Lightstone, Jack N. 95
Lim, Sung Uk 243

Lindemann, Andreas 237, 241–42, 308, 310
Linton, Olof 115, 127
List, Nicholas 238
Lona, Horacio 236–37, 239, 241, 242, 250–51, 264
Lookadoo, Jonathon 307, 308, 311, 322–23, 325
Lösch, Stefan 243
Lührmann, Dieter 211

Manstead Antony S. R. 44
Markschies, Christoph J. 74
Marjanen, Antti 358
Martin, Ralph P. 149, 150–52, 153–55, 238
Mason, Steve 77–79, 166, 168, 169
Massaux, Edouard 200
Matthews, Shelly 165, 169
Matthews, Steve H. 159
McGuckin, John Anthony 109–11, 112, 357, 359, 366
McKnight, Scot 272, 274, 275, 278
Meier, John P. 190
Merkle, Benjamin L. 127–28
Merrill, Elmer Truesdell 238–39
Michaelis, Wilhelm 128
Michaels, J. Ramsey 156, 157–59, 160, 161–63
Moraff, Jason F. 165, 171
Moss, Candida R. 328, 329
Mounce, William D. 112, 127, 274–76. 278, 282, 285, 289
Möllendorff, Peter von 307–8
Muddiman, John 177, 179–180

Nanos, Mark D. 68
Nes, Jermo van 274,.276
Newcomb, Theodore M. 341
Niederwimmer, Kurt 187–90, 192, 195, 199–202, 204–6, 208–9, 210, 211–12, 213, 214, 218, 219, 220–21, 223, 225, 227–28, 230
Nongbri, Brent 81

Noy, David 99, 100–101, *102*

O'Brien, Peter T. 152
Ok, Janette H. 157
Olsson, Birger 88, *89*, 91, *103*, 157–58, 160
Osborn, Eric 356, *357–58*
Osiek, Carolyn *178*, 179, *181–82*

Pervo, Richard I. *167*, 168–69
Peterlin, Davorin. 148–50, *154*
Pherson, Sam 40–42, 44–46, *51*, *341*
Philips, L. Edward 110
Piepenbrink, Karen 308, 322
Platow, Michael J. 40, 44, , *48*, 49, 55–56, 58–59, *230*, *245*, *259*, *261*, *349*
Powell, Douglas *238*
Prostmeier, Ferdinand R. 306–7

Quinn, Jerome D. 272, 278

Rackham, Richard B. *167*
Rajak, Tessa 100–101, *102*
Rast, David E. *43*, 50, 55, *56*, *247*, *338*
Rebillard, Éric 329, *330*
Reicher, Stephen D. 40, 44, 48, 49, 55–56, 58–59, 226, 230, 245, 259, 261, 349–50
Reuman, John 152
Rius-Camps, Josep 306–7
Robinson, Thomas A. 71–73
Rohte, Richard *128*
Ritschl, Albrecht *128*
Roitto, Rikard 51, *52*, *201*
Rordorf, Willy *187*, 214
Rosell Nebreda, Sergio 27, *42–43*, 44
Rothschild, Clare K. *166*
Runesson, Anders 76, 78, *79–81*, 83, 87–89, 90–91, *92–93*, 94–96, *103–4*, *125–26*, *139*, *378*
Runesson, Anna *81*
Ryan, Jordan J. *91*, *93*

Sabatier, Auguste *118*
Saller, Richard P. *221*

Sanday, William *118*
Sandt, Huub van de *189–91*, 192, *199–201*, 202, 208, *209*
Schaff, Philip *213*
Schenk, Wolfgang 148
Schermann, Theodor *201*
Schellenberg, Ryan S. 167, *168*
Schmithals, Walther 309
Schoedel, William R. 306, *315–16*, 334–35, *339*, 348
Schofield, Malcolm *287*, 288
Schreckenberg, Heinz 252
Schröter, Jens *66*, *76*
Schüssler Fiorenza, Elisabeth 133
Schöllgen, Georg 116, 308, *310–11*
Schwarz, Seth *221*
Sellars, John *289*
Sellew, Philip *149*, 150
Siegel, Sidney *341*
Svigel, Michael J. 177, *179–80*, 182
Sherif, Carolyn W. *41*
Sherif, Muzafer *41*
Skarsaune, Oskar 252
Slee, Michelle *190*, *201*, 227–29
Smith, Mitzi J. 170
Smith, Morton *81*
Snyder, Glenn E. 169
Sohm, Rudolph 85, *118*, 132–34
Steffens, Niklas K. *48*, 49, *50*, *57–61*, *62*, *261*, 400
Stempel, Hermann-Adolf 194, *202*
Stewart, Alistair 25, *113*, 115–16, *117*, 121–22, *123*, 124, 127, *128–29*, 136–40, 153, 182, 308, 310
Streeter, Burnett Hillman 115

Tajfel, Henri 40–42, *44–45*, 47, *51*, *333*
Thaarup, Jørgen *25*
Theobald, Michael 275, 277, 279, *282*, 285, *286*, 290–91, 307, *309*, 311, 316–17, 323, 326
Thiering, Barbara 123
Theissen, Gerd *97*
Torjesen, Karen Jo *110*, 116, *118–19*

Towner, Philip H. *285, 288,* 293
Turner, John C. 41, 43–44, 47
Tyson, Joseph B. 169

Unnik, Willem C. van *240, 253*

Vranic, Vasilije 126, *134*
Veit-Engelman, Michaela *120,* 276
Verheyden, Joseph *66, 76,* 251, *252*
Vinzent, Markus 307, 309, *314–15,* 319, *320–21*
Vogt, Hermann Josef 308
Vokes, Frederick E. 200

Waldner, Katharina *319*
Warwick, Donald P. 341
Weber, Max 117, 119, 193–95, 198
Weizsäcker, Karl Heinrich von *118*
Welborn, Laurence L. 233–39, *240, 243*
Wendel, Susan *165,* 169, *170*

Wengst, Klaus *192, 200*
Weren, Wim J. C. *222,* 227–28
Wild, Robert *273,* 278
Wilhite, Shawn J. *191–92*
Williams, J. Dennis *26*
Williams, Frank *101*
Witherington, Ben 152, 155, *165, 167, 170, 172, 174*

Yoshiko Reed, Anette 73, *74*
Young, Frances M. *34,* 134–36, 139, *359*
Young, Franklin W. *238*

Zahn, Theodor 306, 315
Zamfir, Korinna *121,* 122–24
Zangenberg, Jürgen *188, 190, 192,* 197, *216,* 229–30
Zetterholm, Magnus *68, 190*
Zoccali, Cristopher 155
Zwierlein, Otto 309

Index of Subjects

abortion 207, 209
Abraham 251, 255–57, 361, 362, 371
adultery 207, 209, 210, 212, 339, 340
Ambrosiaster 111
Anglican 23, 25, 27, 28, 38, 87, 113, 117, 404
anti-Jewish 87, 95, 102, 378
apostasy, apostates 180, 255
apostle 29, 31, 37, 56, 65, 97, 98, 113, 114, 135, 145, 147, 152, 154–56, 159, 164, 165, 172–75, 178, 179, 181–85, 187, 193–95, 218, 225–27, 235, 236, 259, 260, 265–68, 278, 280, 303, 313, 331, 343, 344, 353, 355, 356, 359–71, 383, 390, 393, 394, 396–401, 403
apostolic, apostolicity 23, 24, 31, 32, 36–38, 69, 108–10, 112, 113, 115, 117, 127, 129, 145, 147, 152, 165, 171, 173, 183, 189, 201, 223, 232, 261, 264, 266, 268, 269, 278, 281, 313, 330–32, 338, 358–62, 364–71, 385, 390, 396–400, 403, 404
appoint, appointment 24, 25, 33, 34, 87, 107, 108, 110, 134, 135, 152, 165, 172, 217, 223–25, 239, 264–67, 269, 280, 281, 283, 310, 344, 360, 381, 389, 400, 403
appropriation 165, 251
archisynagogos 102, 126
association (voluntary) 30, 35, 80, 83–97, 105, 108, 114, 120, 121, 123, 128, 134, 135, 138–40, 160, 161, 198, 210, 213, 216, 223, 231, 260, 266, 322, 367, 377–79, 393
astrology 80.

Athenagoras 320

baptism 24, 51, 52, 77, 170, 187, 191, 196, 201, 202–3, 207–9, 212, 213, 215, 218, 224, 227, 230, 232, 233, 281, 324, 339, 384, 395
behaviour 26, 27, 36, 37, 41–44, 48, 50–57, 61, 65, 147, 162, 164, 175, 179–84, 187, 188, 193, 196, 199, 201, 202, 209–11, 215–18, 223–25, 227, 228, 232, 233, 235, 236, 245–49, 255, 257–59, 261, 263, 264, 266, 267, 289, 290, 292, 293, 295, 297, 299–301, 303, 313, 333–38, 340, 341, 343, 349–53, 363, 364, 370, 380–82, 384, 385, 388–93, 397, 402
belief 30, 38, 56, 58, 67, 70, 77, 78, 80, 97, 147, 171, 184, 232, 250, 324, 334, 339–41, 352, 353, 355, 361, 362, 368, 371, 385, 387, 389, 401
bishop 23, 25–27, 87, 98, 109–14, 116, 117, 148, 283, 314, 344, 346, 360, 404
blasphemy 209
blessing 99, 204, 205, 247, 251, 252, 265, 298, 346, 370
body, bodies 85, 116, 128–31, 134, 180, 235, 273, 307

cardinal virtues 285–88, 291, 294–96, 301, 302, 387, 388
categorisation 42, 43, 49, 50, 59, 342, 362, 375, 380
catholicisation 36, 188, 193–96, 198, 231, 316, 384

catholicity 117
Catholics 23, 24, 38, 113, 117, 118, 133, 134, 193, 331, 384, 404
celibacy 52
charisma 23, 35, 98, 107, 114, 116–20, 132–34, 136, 137, 170, 182, 187, 193–95, 198, 202, 219, 220, 224, 225, 322, 323, 327, 376, 380, 383, 384
Christ groups 29, 65, 87, 180, 284, 331, 332, 378, 402
Christianismos 77–79
Christianity 38, 63, 66–70, 72–79, 81, 82, 85, 91, 98, 119, 140, 375, 401
Christ-killers 361, 362
Christology 67–69, 253, 340, 345, 394
church orders 109–10, 112–13, 115, 120, 189, 192, 201, 218, 225, 404
circumcision 29, 395
citizenship 152
Cleanthes 288
clergy 25, 110, 112, 113, 116–19, 133, 195
collegia, *see also* association 97
congregation 23, 24, 30, 36, 37, 80, 93, 98, 100, 103, 107, 111, 114, 116, 118, 120, 121, 123, 125, 126, 128, 129, 135–38, 147, 152–54, 157, 160, 164, 165, 174–83, 195–97, 207, 211, 212, 214, 223, 225, 230, 235, 236, 239, 241, 242, 244–49, 255–59, 262–68, 273, 277, 278, 282, 290, 302, 313, 316, 317, 319, 321, 323, 330, 333, 336–39, 341–51, 353, 356, 357, 359–70, 385, 386, 388, 389, 393, 395–97, 401, 403
congregationalist 23, 24, 113, 117–19, 124, 137, 271, 280, 281, 303, 349, 400
connectivity 84
cult 77, 80, 85, 86, 90, 93, 96, 112, 121, 233, 312, 313, 318, 327, 395
cunningness 299
Cyprian of Carthage 111, 112

deacon 98, 110–12, 114, 148, 153, 178, 314, 344

decalogue 187, 207–9, 212, 215, 232, 384
deliberative rhetoric 236, 253, 254
depersonalisation 42, 44, 50
deuteronomistic history 201, 255
Deutero-Pauline 309, 336, 351, 360, 388
Dio Chrysostom 122, 254, 312
Diocles of Magnesia 289
Diogenes Laertius 286, 288–91, 294, 298
disciples 214, 330, 342, 345, 365, 368, 369
divination 215
Domitian's persecution 74, 237–40

Ebionites 101
ecclesiology 177, 179, 276
ecumenical 113, 117, 129
elders 26, 101, 103, 104, 120, 124–27, 129, 130, 132, 134, 135, 139, 151, 157, 161–63, 165, 174, 175, 248, 255, 257, 280, 281, 283, 381
election 61, 98, 131, 172, 219, 221, 225, 266, 243, 256, 390, 396
Eleutherius of Rome 357.
Elijah 248, 255
embodiment 50, 52, 54, 55, 59, 62, 97, 151, 160, 164, 173, 174, 178, 182, 184, 187, 188, 199, 212, 215–17, 223, 244, 245, 247, 260, 261, 263, 283, 284, 288, 293, 295, 296, 302–5, 332, 333, 338, 343, 345, 349–53, 355, 358, 364, 366, 370, 371, 376–78, 380, 383, 385, 388–91, 394–99, 403
Epiphanius of Salamis 101
eschatology 179, 205, 206
esoterism 358, 368, 370, 398
Essenes 103, 123, 125, 138.
ethnic, ethnicity 30, 66, 78, 79, 86, 93, 94, 96, 138, 192, 202, 214, 221, 228, 385, 388, 395
ethos 32, 259, 260, 280, 303, 322, 332, 353, 400, 401
etic/emic 66, 73, 76–78, 80, 86, 98.

eucharist 24, 58, 111, 133, 196, 197, 224, 230, 232, 344, 345, 353, 362, 395
exemplarity 52, 112, 185, 329, 382, 383, 394
exordium 258, 295

fairness 41, 206
family-orientation 289
federation 127, 136, 137, 139
Fiscus judaicus 68, 74
followership 49, 51, 60, 215, 217, 219, 220, 277, 283, 333, 342, 380, 386, 390, 400
forgery 166, 275, 306, 311, 315, 316, 352

Galilee 92, 93, 157, 158
Gaul 320, 356, 357
gentile Christians 33, 170, 187, 204, 205, 209, 226, 227
gerousiarch 102
Glaubensformel 324
Gnosticism 37, 358, 360, 366
gospel 89, 101, 154, 166, 172, 190, 191, 196, 199, 200, 202–4, 209, 215, 225, 229, 247, 257, 258, 265, 267, 268, 328, 334, 336–38, 351, 352, 359, 365, 366, 368–70, 386, 388, 390, 398
Göteborg/Gothenburg 46
governance 77, 113, 117, 118, 129–32, 134, 152, 302, 338, 341
grace 27, 118, 257, 263, 343, 346
Greco-Roman 30, 32, 35, 57, 83, 90, 92–94, 107, 113, 119–24, 127–29, 131, 134, 135, 137, 138, 141, 171, 221, 271, 286, 295, 302, 313, 378–80, 385, 387, 388, 391
Gregory of Nazianzus 112
gymnasia 222, 292

halakah, halakic 29, 65, 66, 79, 95, 96, 206, 207, 212–15, 228, 233, 303, 352, 371, 378, 379, 385, 391, 392, 395, 399, 402–4
Haustafel 207, 211, 212

Hegesippus 109, 237, 240, 313
Hellenism 77, 86, 88, 98, 123, 139, 201–3, 208, 211, 215, 218, 235, 240, 242–44, 250, 253–55, 267, 272, 284–87, 291, 293–301, 303, 312, 335, 385
heresy 182, 339, 340, 358, 359
hermeneutics 39, 81, 300
Hesiod 201
hierarchy 34, 88, 107, 110, 116–20, 137, 151, 153, 160, 367, 369
Hippolytus of Rome 109
honour 33, 60, 100, 102, 103, 105, 118, 129–31, 134, 162, 179, 197, 218, 220, 221, 223, 224, 248, 249, 267, 342, 347, 386, 394
hospitality 181, 225, 247, 256, 267, 283, 284, 300, 380, 381, 386
household 35, 93, 127, 134–36, 139, 152, 211, 267, 284, 285, 290, 302, 339, 386
humbleness 164, 166, 184, 199, 200, 206, 210, 212, 215, 217, 222, 225, 226, 232, 248, 257, 260, 262, 263, 267, 346, 347, 382, 385, 386

identification 26, 27, 38, 42–44, 50, 165, 284, 338, 346, 382, 397
identity advancement 35, 49, 60–62, 151, 217–20, 222, 224, 231, 376, 380, 390
identity artistry 49, 59, 349
identity embedment 36, 57–59, 62, 97, 105, 110, 147, 151, 163, 171, 173–75, 182–85, 188, 194, 211, 216, 228, 229, 231–33, 235, 236, 260, 261, 269, 271, 281, 303, 332–34, 342, 344, 345, 351, 352, 362, 364, 370, 376, 377, 379, 385, 388, 389, 392–98, 400–402, 404
identity engineering 58, 59
identity entrepreneurship 27, 31, 35–37, 48, 49, 54–59, 61, 62, 141, 151, 165, 173, 175, 184, 226, 232, 233, 236, 246, 261–63, 268, 277, 280–82,

295, 318, 332, 363, 368, 376, 377, 396, 399, 400, 402
identity impresarioship 27, 31, 35–37, 49, 57–62, 95, 97, 110, 141, 147, 151, 162–65, 171–73, 175, 180, 182–84, 188, 193, 211, 216, 219, 226, 228, 229, 231–33, 235, 236, 260, 261, 263, 265, 268, 269, 271, 280, 281, 303, 318, 331–34, 341–45, 348–51, 353, 362–64, 367, 370, 376, 377, 379, 382, 383, 388, 389, 391–98, 400–403
Ignatius of Antioch 28, 31, 37, 53, 56, 57, 65, 69, 71, 72, 75, 79, 108, 118, 122, 141, 146, 175, 182, 183, 240, 241, 251, 279, 305–7, 309–15, 317–27, 332, 333, 335–43, 345–52, 369, 376, 379, 389, 393, 401
ingroup (incl. in contrast to out-groups) 27, 36, 41–45, 49–62, 66, 68, 70, 72, 79, 87, 97, 105, 108, 145, 147, 151, 155, 161–65, 170, 171, 173–75, 178, 180, 182–85, 187, 196, 199, 201, 203, 206, 211, 212, 216–19, 223, 224, 226, 228–31, 233, 235, 244, 258, 260, 261, 263, 266–69, 277, 280–83, 293, 300, 301, 303, 304, 332–34, 336, 337, 340, 343–45, 347, 349, 351, 352, 362–64, 366–70, 375–77, 380–89, 392, 393, 396–404
ingroup favouritism 41
institution 30, 35, 38, 65, 67, 76, 82, 83, 89–98, 103, 105, 107, 139–41, 172, 228, 312, 377
institutionalisation 83, 96, 97, 103, 133
intelligence 287, 288, 297, 300, 301
intergroup relations 28, 39, 42–45, 50, 62, 73, 97, 376
Irenaeus 23, 27, 31, 37, 109, 145, 146, 156, 166, 175, 178, 183, 237, 251, 274, 278, 309, 312, 313, 318–21, 323, 326, 328, 330–32, 355–71, 377, 379, 381, 389–93, 398, 399, 403
Israel 78, 89, 94, 96, 129, 163, 172, 228, 235, 251, 252, 255, 257, 260, 264, 266, 277, 279, 282, 298, 326, 378, 401
Israel-Vergessenheit, *or* Israel oblivion 277, 279, 282, 316, 326
itinerants 23, 98, 114, 187, 188, 190, 191, 193–99, 202, 211, 216–20, 223–25, 228, 231–33, 384, 394, 395

Jacob 235, 251, 252, 255, 256
Jerusalem 33, 69, 77, 78, 88, 93, 131, 158, 167, 168, 174, 198, 233, 310, 337, 361, 395
Jesus 23, 24, 27, 29, 30, 33, 36, 38, 58, 65–68, 70, 71, 73, 74, 77–80, 82, 83, 90, 93–97, 99, 104, 116, 123, 124, 130–33, 148, 154, 157–63, 165, 167, 170, 172, 173, 175, 183–85, 187–91, 193, 196, 198–200, 202, 203, 205, 206, 211, 213, 215, 228–30, 232, 233, 235–40, 244, 245, 248, 250–57, 261–63, 265, 267, 269, 271, 278, 280, 284, 316, 324, 325, 332–40, 342–52, 359, 363, 365, 366, 368, 370, 375, 378, 381, 385, 386, 390, 393–400, 404
Jew, Jewish 23, 28–32, 35–38, 46, 57, 62, 65–71, 74–80, 83, 86–96, 98, 101–5, 113, 114, 118–20, 123, 125–41, 147, 152, 155, 156, 159, 165, 169–72, 185, 187, 188, 191, 199–203, 205, 206, 208–12, 214, 215, 218, 221, 224, 227–29, 232, 233, 242–44, 248, 250–55, 261, 267–69, 272, 277, 279, 282, 285, 286, 293–97, 299–305, 316, 325, 332, 351–53, 355, 359, 361, 362, 368, 370, 371, 375, 377–79, 384–87, 391, 395–401, 403, 404
John Malalas 309
Josephus 90, 91, 102, 166, 168–70
Judah 251
Judaism 38, 63, 66, 68–76, 78, 80–82, 96, 104, 105, 169–71, 192, 203, 227, 285, 401
judaize 28, 72, 79, 353, 398, 401

Index of Subjects

Judea, Judeans 77, 78, 89, 92, 93, 171
jurisdiction 117, 118

laying on of hands, *see also ordination*
  117, 172, 281, 303
leadership 24–30, 34, 35, 37, 40, 41,
  48–51, 53–56, 58–62, 67, 71, 83, 86,
  87, 91, 92, 97–100, 103, 105–9, 112,
  114–19, 123, 125, 128, 129, 132, 134,
  136, 137, 139–41, 145, 147, 148, 151,
  152, 154–56, 158, 160–65, 171, 173–
  75, 179, 180, 183–85, 187, 189, 190,
  193, 194, 197, 199, 211, 216, 217, 219–
  21, 226, 231, 232, 235, 236, 240, 241,
  244, 245, 247, 248, 258–68, 271,
  278, 281, 288, 293, 305, 319, 323,
  327, 329, 331, 332, 338, 343–45, 349,
  350, 352, 353, 355, 370, 375–80, 382–
  84, 386, 390–99, 401–4
legalism 118, 119, 132, 134, 137, 138
Levites, Levitical 121, 251, 260, 370, 399
liturgy, liturgical 88, 91, 95, 99–102,
  104, 121–23, 128, 188, 190, 196, 198,
  216, 219, 229, 264, 281, 313, 314, 327,
  395
Luke 33, 99, 131, 164, 166–70, 172–75,
  184, 202, 238, 274, 334, 365, 369, ---
  -393, 400
Luke-Acts 165–71

Maccabees 79, 285, 286, 293–97, 301,
  302, 387
magic 80, 170, 193, 207, 209
Marcion, Marcionite 79, 168, 169, 239,
  241, 323, 326, 330, 407, 414, 421
marriage 213, 283, 344
martyrdom, martyrs 31, 52, 56, 57, 69,
  71, 101, 165, 167, 169, 237, 306, 310,
  319, 321, 322, 327–32, 336, 337, 340,
  347, 349, 352, 353, 357, 364, 389,
  400, 401
Matthew 189–91, 193–96, 200, 202,
  205, 211, 214, 215, 363, 365, 368
meekness 166, 297, 300

messiah, messianic 29, 66, 68, 70, 77,
  94, 95, 185, 187, 232, 263, 325, 339,
  385, 395
methodism 25–28, 38, 87, 113, 404
ministry 24, 36, 65, 68, 98, 112, 116, 122,
  132, 151, 164, 181, 183, 190, 193, 194,
  198, 216–20, 224, 232, 259, 264,
  266, 268, 281, 344, 350, 360, 383,
  384, 394, 396
Mishna 96, 100, 101, 130, 230.
mission 26, 29, 97, 147, 152, 157, 158,
  163, 165, 172–75, 182–85, 211, 273,
  278, 280, 281, 303, 348, 367, 392,
  393, 397, 400, 404
mobilisation 55, 60, 62, 261–63, 268,
  386, 396, 402
moderation 287–89, 299–301
monarch-bishop, mono-episcopate
  111, 115, 116, 118, 133, 140, 198, 306,
  307, 315–17
morality 202, 206, 218, 229, 291
Moscow manuscript 328, 330, 331
mutual authorization 250, 252

narrative 55, 75, 147, 170, 171, 175, 184,
  226, 258, 261–63, 271, 276, 281, 295,
  328–30, 340, 349, 351, 353, 392, 397,
  399, 401
non-Jew 28, 29, 35, 67, 68, 87, 90, 94–
  96, 134, 138, 139, 155, 158, 159, 171,
  192, 201, 203, 206, 207, 209, 213–15,
  227, 232, 252, 280, 293, 317, 378,
  384, 385, 388, 391, 395, 397
norm, normative 37, 41–44, 48, 50–
  56, 60, 61, 70, 154, 162, 182, 183,
  224, 244, 246, 247, 271, 272, 283,
  284, 333, 334, 338–41, 347, 349–52,
  375, 381, 383, 388, 389, 399

office 23, 24, 26, 27, 29–35, 37, 38, 63,
  85, 94, 97, 99–102, 104–11, 113–20,
  122–24, 126, 127, 129, 131–34, 136–
  38, 140, 141, 145–48, 150, 152–55,
  161, 164, 171, 172, 174–76, 181–84,

194–99, 216, 219, 220, 222, 228, 231, 233, 236, 240, 251, 258–61, 264–69, 279, 282, 306, 313, 314, 316, 318, 322, 340, 343, 352, 355, 356, 360, 362–65, 369–71, 375–77, 379, 382, 383, 389, 390, 392, 393, 395–400, 403, 404
Onesimus 335, 342, 346
Onosander 222, 223, 286, 291–93, 302, 303, 387
ordination, *see also laying on of hands* 25, 112, 242
orgeōnes, see also association 221
overseer 32, 99, 127, 128, 152, 153, 161, 163, 171–75, 178, 183, 184

paganism, pagan 170, 201, 313, 407
Palestine 96, 191
Palladius 101
participation 30, 40, 41, 57, 58, 60, 68, 69, 84, 92, 94, 173, 230, 231, 265, 280, 281, 313, 338, 341, 349, 350, 363, 364, 393, 394
particularism 69, 70
parting of the ways 28–30, 35, 40, 62, 65–67, 69–76, 80–83, 86, 98, 105, 137–39, 146, 165, 267, 269, 272, 282, 301, 303, 351, 352, 375, 377, 401, 404
patron, patronage 60, 66, 86, 94, 100, 138, 197, 198, 219–24, 231, 378, 380, 381, 384, 390
pederasty 207, 209
Pentateuch 130, 266, 299, 300
Peregrinus 318, 319, 407
Pharisees, pharisaic 69, 101, 169, 170, 192, 195, 226, 228, 229, 232, 233, 361, 384, 385, 391
Philo 90, 91, 161
Philotheos 114, 188
Pliny the Younger 158
Plutarch 166, 254, 286–90, 294, 301, 387
polity 23–25, 27, 38, 84, 117, 151, 169, 175, 180, 389, 404
Pothinus 356

praying 91, 99, 178, 204, 205, 224, 228, 229, 232, 348, 385, 391
preaching 27, 111, 117, 154, 172, 211, 334, 336, 359, 361, 365, 366, 368, 369
presbyterate 98, 102, 103, 111, 115, 125, 127, 128, 130–36, 138, 139, 164, 248, 259, 344
Presbyterian 113
pride 101, 155, 248, 256, 262, 263
priesthood 77, 112, 196–98, 220, 231, 233, 251, 265, 266, 269, 370, 395, 396, 399
proselytes 201, 202, 227
Protestant 23, 24, 107, 113, 115–19, 127, 132, 133, 137, 404
proto-catholic 116, 133, 138, 356, 361
proto-episcopal 180
proto-orthodox 27, 75, 358
prototypicality 26–28, 30–32, 35–38, 42, 43, 48–57, 59, 60, 62, 140, 147, 151, 153–56, 160–65, 170, 171, 173–75, 178–85, 187–89, 193, 196, 198–200, 202, 203, 205, 207, 211, 212, 215–20, 223–28, 232, 233, 235, 236, 240, 244–47, 249, 250, 252, 255–64, 266–69, 271, 272, 277, 280, 282–84, 286–88, 291, 293, 295, 297, 298, 301–5, 318, 322, 331–35, 338, 340, 341, 343–52, 355, 362–64, 366–68, 370, 371, 375–77, 379–94, 396, 399–404
pseudepigrapha 149, 174, 272, 273, 275–77, 279, 307, 308, 318
Pseudo-Ignatius 314
pseudonymity 156, 157
purity, purification 112, 178, 179, 230, 247, 249, 297, 300, 320, 339, 352, 391

Quakers 117
Quintus Veranius 291, 331

Index of Subjects

rabbinic Judaism 69–71, 76, 95, 96, 99–101, 105, 126, 203, 213, 228, 229, 232, 378, 385, 395
Reformation, reformers 23, 24, 26, 38, 112, 113, 315, 404
repentance 179, 256–59, 264, 358, 383, 391
rhetoric 32, 45, 48, 49, 53–57, 59, 62, 81, 82, 87, 95, 141, 155, 157, 158, 226, 232, 236, 238, 250, 253–56, 258, 262, 263, 303, 322, 323, 325, 347, 351, 362, 363, 365, 376, 378, 380, 385, 400
routinisation of charisma 107, 114, 118, 119, 137, 193–95

sabbath 344, 345, 352
sacrifice 52, 77, 121, 255, 260, 345, 362, 400
salient behaviour or traits 43, 48, 57, 62, 65, 93, 96, 117, 147, 170, 171, 181, 183, 184, 220, 244, 247, 282, 301, 303, 304, 345, 350, 362, 363, 379, 380, 384, 388, 394, 404
salvation 58, 155, 161, 164, 249, 262, 273, 279, 365, 394, 398
schism 244, 249, 255, 264, 266–69, 323, 396
Scripture 29, 36, 66, 91, 104, 113, 125, 164, 170, 172, 173, 176, 190, 201, 232, 236, 242–45, 248–56, 258–61, 265, 267–69, 276, 336, 337, 376, 385–87, 396, 399
Second Sophistic movement 307, 309, 312–15, 317, 324
self-categorisation, SCT 41, 43, 44, 58, 97, 246, 259, 338
shepherding 32, 104, 125, 156, 161–65, 174, 180, 393, 394
shrewdness 298, 299
Smyrna 310, 322, 329, 330, 356, 416
socialisation 192
sociology 34, 39, 73–75, 83, 85, 107, 117, 118, 377, 401
sorcery 207, 209, 218, 227, 391

soul 161, 176, 257, 346
stele 66, 102, 121, 313
stereotyped behaviour 43, 51, 52, 353
Stoicism 37, 57, 211, 285–91, 293–95, 301–3, 387, 388, 402
submission 164, 214, 248, 254, 262, 265–69, 290, 342–44, 351, 353, 386, 391, 392, 394, 396, 397, 401
superintendent 25, 26, 222, 292
supersessionism 251
synagogue 23, 29–31, 35–39, 66, 67, 71, 72, 80, 83, 86–105, 108, 114, 115, 120, 124–29, 131, 132, 134–41, 185, 221, 236, 243, 269, 305, 318, 368, 375, 377–79, 386, 387, 400, 401, 404
synod, synodal 109, 112, 113, 117
synoptic gospels 205, 334

taxation 68, 74, 102
teachers 23, 65, 98, 101, 114, 122, 133, 136, 174, 178, 180, 181, 188, 190, 193, 197, 198, 210, 211, 216–18, 220, 223, 224, 226, 228, 231–33, 282, 283, 292, 330, 331, 335, 337, 366, 384, 385, 395
temperance 222, 248, 267, 283, 287, 289, 292, 386, 387
Theodosian Code 101
Torah-observance 79, 159, 227, 304, 305
typology 312–14, 358

Valentinianism 324–26, 357, 358, 361, 362, 365, 366, 370, 371, 399
violence, violent 165, 207, 283, 284, 292, 293, 302, 387
virtue 181, 201, 222, 246, 247, 249, 254, 267, 284–91, 293–302, 346, 382, 386–88

warrant 23, 109, 112, 121, 145–47, 174, 182, 317, 343, 356, 362, 364, 366, 401
wealth 181, 222, 223, 292
Wesley, John 25, 27, 38

wisdom 129, 201, 210, 213, 257–59, 285–88, 293–303, 387
witchcraft 207

yoke 207, 212–14, 228, 257, 263, 385, 388, 391

Dissertationes Theologicae Holmienses

1. Eurell, John-Christian. *Peter's Legacy in Early Christianity: The Appropriation and Use of Peter's Authority in the First Three Centuries.* DTH 1. Stockholm: Enskilda Högskolan Stockholm, 2021.
2. Mannerfelt, Frida. *Co-preaching: The Practice of Preaching in Digital Culture and Spaces.* DTH 2. Stockholm: Enskilda Högskolan Stockholm, 2023.
3. Appelfeldt, Joel. *Dopet som hantverk: Gudstjänstkreativitet och liturgisk taktik i Svenska kyrkan och Equmeniakyrkan.* DTH 3. Skellefteå: Artos Academic, 2023.
4. Gobena, Abate. *Sanctity and Environment in Ethiopian Hagiography: The Case of Gedle Gebre Menfes Qiddus.* DTH 4. Stockholm: Enskilda Högskolan Stockholm, 2023.
5. Lockneus, Elin. *Kyrkbänksteologi.* DTH 5. Skellefteå: Artos Academic, 2023.
6. Asserhed, Björn. *Gardens in the Wasteland: Christian Formation in Three Swedish Church Plants.* DTH 6. Stockholm: Enskilda Högskolan Stockholm, 2024.
7. Hallonsten, Simon. *Online Small Groups as Sites of Teaching: An Action Research Dissertation into Christian Religious Education in the Church of Sweden.* Stockholm: Enskilda Högskolan Stockholm, 2024.
8. Plantin, Lisa. *Birth Metaphors in the Book of Job: A Blending Theory Analysis.* DTH 8. Stockholm: Enskilda Högskolan Stockholm, 2024.
9. Nõmmik, Aldar. *Robes, Romans, and Rituals in First Corinthians: Paul and the Conflict over Head-Coverings.* DTH 9. Stockholm: Enskilda Högskolan Stockholm, 2025.
10. Toll, Torbjörn. *ACT Alliance and the Refugee Crisis: Ecclesiology and Tensions in Refugee Assistance.* DHT 10. Stockholm: Enskilda Högskolan Stockholm, 2025.

11. Landgren, Martin, *The Episcopate and the Parting of the Ways: A Social Identity Perspective on the Emergence of Christian Identity*. DTH 11. Stockholm: Enskilda Högskolan Stockholm, 2025.

www.ingramcontent.com/pod-product-compliance
Lightning Source LLC
Chambersburg PA
CBHW052049290426
44111CB00011B/1675